The Economics of Budget Deficits
Volume I

The International Library of Critical Writings in Economics

Series Editor: Mark Blaug

Professor Emeritus, University of London, UK
Professor Emeritus, University of Buckingham, UK
Visiting Professor, University of Amsterdam, The Netherlands
Visiting Professor, Erasmus University of Rotterdam, The Netherlands

This series is an essential reference source for students, researchers and lecturers in economics. It presents by theme a selection of the most important articles across the entire spectrum of economics. Each volume has been prepared by a leading specialist who has written an authoritative introduction to the literature included.

A full list of published and future titles in this series is printed at the end of this volume.

For a list of all Edward Elgar published titles visit our site on the World Wide Web at
http://www.e-elgar.co.uk

DEDICATION

We dedicate these volumes to those members of our respective families, as named below, who remain yet too young to be eligible to vote. Their future economic well-being will be immeasurably enhanced should the American people rein in the size of the federal government by passing a balanced budget and tax limitation amendment to the United States Constitution.

For Charles K. Rowley:
Elizabeth Mae Owens (aged five years and four months)
Daniel Andrew Pavlik (aged three years and six months)
Robert Atticus Owens (aged one year and eight months)
Benjamin Davies Pavlik (aged seventeen days)

For William F. Shughart II:
William Franklin Shughart III (aged fifteen years)
Frank Jefferson Shughart (aged thirteen years)

For Robert D. Tollison:
Zachariah Robert Tollison (aged ten years and four months)
Katie Jane Tollison (aged five years and two months)
Annabel Kleinfeldt (aged one year and one month)

The Economics of Budget Deficits
Volume I

Edited by

Charles K. Rowley

*Duncan Black Professor of Economics, George Mason University
and General Director, The Locke Institute, Fairfax, VA, USA*

William F. Shughart II

*Frederick A.P. Barnard Distinguished Professor of Economics
and Robert M. Hearin Chair, University of Mississippi, USA*

and

Robert D. Tollison

Robert M. Hearin Professor of Economics, University of Mississippi, USA

THE INTERNATIONAL LIBRARY OF CRITICAL WRITINGS IN ECONOMICS

An Elgar Reference Collection
Cheltenham, UK • Northampton, MA, USA

Published by
Edward Elgar Publishing Limited
Glensanda House
Montpellier Parade
Cheltenham
Glos GL50 lUA
UK

Edward Elgar Publishing, Inc.
136 West Street
Suite 202
Northampton
Massachusetts 01060
USA

A catalogue record for this book is available from the British Library

Library of Congress Cataloguing in Publication Data

The economics of budget deficits / edited by Charles K. Rowley ... [et al.].
    p. cm. — (The international library of critical writings in economics; 153) (An Elgar reference collection)
Includes bibliographical references and index.
1. Budget deficits. 2. Deficit financing. 3. Debts, Public. I. Rowley, Charles Kershaw. II. Series.

HJ2005.E27 2002
339.5'23—dc21

2002027148

ISBN 1 85898 798 9 (2 volume set)

Printed and bound in Great Britain by MPG Books Ltd, Bodmin, Cornwall

Contents

PART III   KEYNESIAN PUBLIC DEBT THEORY

PART IV   THE BURDEN OF DEBT RE-EXAMINED

Acknowledgements

The editors and publishers wish to thank the authors and the following publishers who have kindly given permission for the use of copyright material.

American Economic Association for articles: Mario I. Blejer and Adrienne Cheasty (1991), 'The Measurement of Fiscal Deficits: Analytical and Methodological Issues', *Journal of Economic Literature*, **XXIX** (4), December, 1644–78; Laurence J. Kotlikoff and Bernd Raffelhüschen (1999), 'Generational Accounting Around the Globe', *American Economic Review Papers and Proceedings*, **89** (2), May, 161–6; Alberto Alesina (2000), 'The Political Economy of the Budget Surplus in the United States', *Journal of Economic Perspectives*, **14** (3), Summer, 3–19.

Gary M. Anderson for his own excerpt: (1986), 'The US Federal Deficit and National Debt: A Political and Economic History', in James M. Buchanan, Charles K. Rowley and Robert D. Tollison (eds), *Deficits*, Chapter 2, 9–46.

Blackwell Publishing Ltd for articles: Franco Modigliani (1961), 'Long-Run Implications of Alternative Fiscal Policies and the Burden of the National Debt', *Economic Journal*, **LXXI**, December, 730–55; James Tobin (1965), 'The Burden of the Public Debt: A Review Article', *Journal of Finance*, **XX**, 679–82; James M. Buchanan (1966), 'The Icons of Public Debt', *Journal of Finance*, **XXI**, 544–6; James Tobin (1966), 'Reply', *Journal of Finance*, **XXI**, 547.

Cambridge University Press for excerpt: T.R. Malthus (1803/1992), 'Of Poor-Laws, continued', in Donald Winch (ed.), *An Essay on the Principle of Population; or A View of its past and present Effects on Human Happiness; With an Inquiry into our Prospects respecting the future Removal or Mitigation of the Evils which it occasions*, Book III, Chapter VII, 110–23.

Independent Institute for article: Jody W. Lipford (2001), 'How Transparent is the U.S. Budget?', *Independent Review: A Journal of Political Economy*, **V** (4), Spring, 575–91.

Liberty Fund, Inc. for excerpts: David Ricardo (1821/1951), 'Taxes on Other Commodities than Raw Produce', in Piero Sraffa (ed.) with M.H. Dobb, *The Works and Correspondence of David Ricardo, Volume I: On the Principles of Political Economy and Taxation*, Chapter XVII, 243–56; James M. Buchanan (1958), 'Concerning Future Generations', Chapter Four, and 'A Suggested Conceptual Revaluation of the National Debt', Appendix, in *Public Principles of Public Debt: A Defense and Restatement*, 31–47 and 196–215.

Macmillan Ltd for excerpt: John Maynard Keynes (1936/1973), 'The Marginal Propensity to Consume and the Multiplier', in *The Collected Writings of John Maynard Keynes: Volume VII, The General Theory of Employment Interest and Money*, Chapter 10, 113–31.

McGraw-Hill Companies for excerpts: Paul A. Samuelson (1948), 'Fiscal Policy and Full Employment without Inflation', in *Economics: An Introductory Analysis*, First Edition, Chapter 18, 409–43; Richard A. Musgrave (1959), 'Classical Theory of Public Debt', in *The Theory of Public Finance: A Study in Public Economy*, Chapter 23, 556–80; Paul A. Samuelson (1970), 'Fiscal Policy and Full Employment without Inflation', in *Economics*, Eighth Edition, Chapter 19, 330–53.

MIT Press Journals and the President and Fellows of Harvard College for article: Abba P. Lerner (1961), 'The Burden of Debt', *Review of Economics and Statistics*, **XLIII**, 139–41.

W.W. Norton and Company, Inc. for excerpt: Abba P. Lerner (1948), 'The Burden of the National Debt', in *Income, Employment, and Public Policy: Essays in Honor of Alvin H. Hansen*, Chapter II, 255–75.

Oxford University Press for excerpt and articles: Adam Smith (1776/1976), 'Of Publick Debts', in R.H. Campbell, A.S. Skinner and W.B. Todd (eds), *An Inquiry into the Nature and Causes of the Wealth of Nations*, Volume II, Book V, Chapter III, 907–47; J. E. Meade (1958), 'Is the National Debt a Burden?', *Oxford Economic Papers*, **10** (2), New Series, June, 163–83; J.E. Meade (1959), 'Is the National Debt a Burden? A Correction', *Oxford Economic Papers*, **11**, New Series, 109–10.

Social Research for article: Abba P. Lerner (1943), 'Functional Finance and the Federal Debt', *Social Research*, **10** (1), February, 38–51.

University of North Carolina Press for excerpt: James M. Buchanan (1964), 'Public Debt, Cost Theory, and the Fiscal Illusion', in James M. Ferguson (ed.), *Public Debt and Future Generations*, Chapter Six, 150–63.

University of Toronto Press for excerpt: John Stuart Mill (1848/1965), 'Of a National Debt', in J.M. Robson (ed.), *Principles of Political Economy with Some of Their Applications to Social Philosophy*, Book V, Chapter VII, 873–9.

Every effort has been made to trace all the copyright holders but if any have been inadvertently overlooked the publishers will be pleased to make the necessary arrangement at the first opportunity.

In addition the publishers wish to thank the Marshall Library of Economics, Cambridge University, the Library of the University of Warwick and the Library of Indiana University at Bloomington, USA for their assistance in obtaining these articles.

Introduction

I. The National Debt and Budgetary Performance in Historical Perspective

The Economics of Budget Deficits presents a literature relevant *de minimus* to all the Western democracies, including the United States – here defined not as a democracy, but as a constitutional republic. Nevertheless, this section will focus on the experience of the United States. This experience is broadly reflected, at least over the past 50 years, in the less politically fragmented countries of Western Europe, countries that, with the exception of the United Kingdom, have performed less well than the United States in confronting the underlying problem of budget deficits.

The national debt is measured as a stock at a point in time. It is the total of all outstanding government debt obligations held by the public. The national debt, thus measured, is the algebraic sum of all past budget deficits less debt repayments. Budget deficits and surpluses, in contrast, are measured as flow variables reflecting the excess of government spending over revenues, or the excess of government revenues over spending in a given year. The public (both domestic and foreign) holds the national debt in the form of outstanding government debt obligations, notably government bonds, treasury bills and similar debt instruments. The government uses current tax revenues to pay interest on these obligations unless it decides to default on its commitments.

Although the national debt is usually calculated as the aggregate obligations of the *central* government, this is misleading in a federal system like the United States where state and local governments also borrow significantly to finance budget deficits. Despite the fact that many states are constrained by constitutional or legislative rules to avoid or limit deficits, state and local debt levels amounted in 2001 to approximately 25 per cent of the total US national debt. These figures are relevant in assessing the overall pressure exerted by government on credit markets. Furthermore, unlike the federal debt, state and local debt cannot be liquidated by printing money.

Ignoring (for the moment) problems of measurement, the magnitudes of the national debt, deficits and surpluses are best placed into perspective by comparing them to gross domestic product. Such a measure indicates the percentage of annual output required to liquidate the debt at any point in time. Using this measuring-rod, and focusing exclusively on the obligations of the US *federal* government, the magnitude of debt obligations is seen to have fluctuated widely over time (Anderson, 1986; Alesina, 2000).

The period 1789 to 1830 was one of net budget surpluses whereby the national debt accumulated during the War of Independence was liquidated. From 1830 to 1860 the federal government balanced the budget taking one year with another, with the consequence that there was no national debt to speak about at the onset of the Civil War in 1861, despite the fact that the US had fought two costly wars during that interval (the War of 1812 and the Mexican War).

A significant volume of debt was compiled during the Civil War, but this was largely redeemed via an unbroken streak of budget surpluses throughout the period 1866 to 1893. At the turn of the century, the federal debt was only 6.7 per cent of GDP, a ratio that fell yet further to 2.9 per cent of GDP by 1915 prior to the entry of the US into the First World War. From 1917 the federal debt rose significantly, peaking at 26 per cent of GDP in 1919. There then followed another unbroken streak of budget surpluses from 1920 to 1929 when the debt to GDP ratio stood at 16.4 per cent.

From 1931 the federal budget shifted into an unbroken streak of budget deficits as a consequence, first, of the Great Depression and, second, of the participation of the United States in the Second World War. By 1946, the national debt stood at an all-time high of 122 per cent of GDP. Over the period 1947 to 1960, the budget fluctuated between surplus and deficit, albeit with an overall surplus of revenues over spending. Combined with the growth in GDP over that period, the ratio of the national debt to GDP declined from its peak of 122 per cent in 1946 to 58.4 in 1960, notwithstanding the participation of the United States in the Korean War.

To this point, the budgetary behavior of the United States federal government displays significant historical consistency. Deficits occur only during periods of recession, financial panics, and wars. These deficits largely are defrayed by budget surpluses during periods of peace and prosperity. From 1961, such consistency is no longer apparent although the national debt consequences of budget imbalance do not seriously manifest themselves until the beginning of the 1980s.

From 1961 to 1998, with only one year's exception in 1969, the federal budget moved into continuous deficit. In part because of rising GDP, and in part because of high rates of price inflation, the ratio of the national debt to GDP continued to decline until 1979 when it bottomed out at 32 per cent, despite OPEC-induced oil shocks in 1974 and 1979 and the participation of the United States in a military conflict in Vietnam during which US policy-makers pursued a guns *and* butter program of federal spending.

From 1981, however, a combination of higher fiscal deficits, declining inflation, and low rates of growth of GDP reversed this trend. The ratio of the national debt to GDP evidenced an unbroken streak of continuous increase until 1995 when it peaked at 68 per cent. The budget moved into surplus only in 1999 following several years of rapid economic growth, coupled with a significant decline in defense expenditures as a response to the end of the Cold War.

For reasons that we shall outline later in this essay, it would be extremely unwise to expect that the current phase of budget surpluses will be as long-lived as the Congressional Budget Office currently forecasts. Indeed, if account is taken of the implied contingent liabilities of the federal entitlements programs, the accounting surplus significantly misrepresents the parlous nature of the US budgetary situation.

In any event, the multi-decade era of deficit financing in the United States and the associated problem of the national debt is far from at an end. Indeed, the looming crisis of budget deficits in the United States must soon become apparent to all but the most myopic of actors in the political system.

II.   Measurement Issues in Fiscal Accounting

Despite the widely acknowledged economic importance of fiscal imbalances, there is no widespread consensus as to the appropriate method of measuring budgetary performance (Blejer and Cheasty, 1991). There are so many budget concepts, each with some presumptive claim to respectability, that one can choose one's budget concept more or less to fit one's case (Gramlich, 1989, p. 74). In this section, we briefly outline the method of budget measurement adopted by the US federal government and evaluate it in terms of the major criticisms that have been leveled against it.

The US federal budget, known as the *unified budget*, is essentially a cash budget. Fiscal deficits, as conventionally defined on this basis, measure the difference between total governmental cash outlays and total cash receipts with a number of exceptions. In defining cash outlays, the unified budget adds interest payments to non-debt-related expenditures, but excludes amortization payments on the outstanding stock of public debt. In defining cash receipts, the unified budget includes tax and non-tax revenue and grants but excludes proceeds from borrowing.

In this manner, fiscal deficits reflect the gap to be covered by *net* government borrowing, including direct borrowing from the central bank. Measured in this conventional way, the recorded deficit defines the public sector borrowing requirement and identifies the government's recourse to new financial resources net of repayment of previously incurred debt. Despite the many weaknesses of this measure, the unified budget does have an advantage in transparency over all alternative measures. From the perspective of public choice, this advantage is of decisive importance, as we shall explain later in this essay.

One criticism leveled against the unified budget concerns its relevance under conditions of price inflation (Eisner and Pieper, 1984; Eisner, 1986). This criticism focuses attention on the so-called *real* deficit, defined so as to correspond to real changes in the public debt.

In this view, the real value of the net federal debt is treated as the algebraic sum of three components: the nominal deficit exclusive of offsetting changes in financial assets and liabilities; changes in the nominal market value of existing financial assets and liabilities due to changes in nominal interest rates; and changes in the real values due to changes in the general level of prices. When the interest rate and price effects are subtracted from the federal budget deficit, the real deficit is identified. The real deficit corresponds to the change in the real value of net government debt, and this is not the same as the nominal deficit divided by a price deflator.

During periods of high and rising inflation, the real deficit typically lies well below the nominal deficit (and may even be a surplus) as higher prices serve as an inflation tax on the holders of the debt and as inflation-augmented interest rates further depress the market value of government securities. Many economists contend that the real deficit is the appropriate standard against which fiscal policy should be evaluated.

This is an unacceptable viewpoint. There are only three ways to finance government expenditures, namely taxes, borrowing, and inflation. Of these, unexpected inflation surely is the most insidious, taxing existing debt-holders by stealth without prior recourse to the ballot box, and without regard for the sanctity of the debt contract.

Public choice predicts that the inflation route will be utilized once the burden of the debt becomes troublesome to the political system. It will be most tempting when foreigners hold a significant proportion of the national debt. An accounting method that rewards politicians for reneging on debt repayment promises encourages irresponsible, if not deceitful, political behavior.

A second criticism leveled against the unified budget is its failure to distinguish between current and capital outlays in determining budget balance. Current spending refers to expenditures for services that are consumed within the budget period, whereas capital spending refers to expenditures for durable items that are expected to yield services over a longer time-horizon. By lumping the two together, the accounting procedures for the unified budget differ sharply from the standard procedures adopted by US corporations and by many state and local governments where separate budgets are maintained for current and capital outlays.

It is argued that such a separation of the budget would provide a more accurate picture of the federal government's financial status, always provided that corresponding depreciation charges were incorporated into the budget (Eisner, 1986). Eisner calculated that, if the federal government had used capital budgeting in 1985, such an adjustment would have reduced the conventionally measured budget deficit by one-third to one-half.

Certainly, the absence of capital budgeting encourages government to engage in political maneuvers designed artificially to depress the magnitude of the deficit. In particular, a favored strategy to reduce the deficit is the sale of publicly owned assets to the private sector. In essence, this simply represents the trading of one asset for another. In terms of the unified budget, however, such a trade serves to reduce the recorded deficit. Even though such sales typically improve economic performance, governments concerned to maintain an image of fiscal integrity do not necessarily implement them for that purpose.

In our view, any such transparency-related advantages of the capital budgeting approach are overwhelmed by problems of distinguishing between current and capital expenditures in the federal government accounts. Proponents of any new spending initiative would be tempted to claim it as an investment in order to protect it from the constraints of maintaining budget balance.

Such political mischief, by no means, would be limited to borderline distinctions. For example, in 1993, the Clinton administration's budgetary proposals identified all transfer programs, including the food stamp program, as investments, claiming that improved diets for the poor would enhance the latter's future productivity. Humbug such as this renders the distinction between capital and current spending entirely meaningless (Rosen, 1995, p. 462).

A third criticism leveled against the unified budget focuses on the neglected accounting implications of implicit obligations of the federal government. Government bonds are not the only method used by government to promise money in the future. Legislation also carries such promises. The most important such examples in the United States concern social security and Medicare legislation, both of which promise benefits to future retirees that must be paid out of future tax revenues. If such obligations are taken into consideration, the US national debt is approximately triple its recorded value. To take account of such future obligations, a number of scholars (e.g. Kotlikoff and Raffelhüschen, 1999) have argued the case for the implementation of intergenerational accounting procedures designed to identify the fiscal burden on future generations implicit in current policy initiatives.

Sympathetic though we are to this line of reform, on balance we reject arguments in favor of adjusting the unified budget to take explicit account of the present value of future obligations or of replacing the unified budget with generational accounting measures.

First, it is important to recognize that legislative promises are not the equivalent of the official debt. Explicit forms of debt represent legal commitments, whereas social security and

Medicare obligations cannot be legally binding in the absence of a constitutional amendment since no Congress can control the actions of its successor.

Second, any procedural change that complicates the calculation of budgetary performance plays into the hands of political actors for reasons of public choice that we outline in Section VIII of this essay. Even though the unified budget is flawed as a method of defining budgetary performance, and is clearly vulnerable to political manipulation (Lipford, 2001), it retains significant advantages of transparency by comparison with its more sophisticated alternatives.

III. Budget Imbalance from the Perspective of Classical Economics

The first task is to define 'classical economics', an expression originally coined by Karl Marx. Here (Coates, 1971, p. 3), it will be taken to refer to the corpus of economic analysis and policy recommendations produced by the following writers: Adam Smith (1723-90), Jeremy Bentham (1748-1832), Thomas Robert Malthus (1766-1834), David Ricardo (1772-1823), James Mill (1773-1836), Robert Torrens (1780-1864), John Ramsay McCulloch (1789-1864), Nassau William Senior (1790-1864), and John Stuart Mill (1806-73).

These scholars are usually regarded as comprising the genuine doctrinal 'classical school'. Despite their frequent and sometimes significant differences of opinion, there is a discernible, coherent doctrine evident in their economic writings, combined with a consistent approach to economic policy that was a direct outcome of a commonly shared and comprehensive liberal (in the Whig sense) philosophy.

They were united in their support of a limited 'night-watchman' state in which the government was responsible for maintaining the rule of law, protecting private property rights and defending citizens from foreign interventions. Otherwise, they generally favored private over public orderings of economic activity as being both more productive and more favorable to the maintenance of individual freedom. Their focus was more on the determinants of the dynamic process of economic growth than on attaining some static concept of economic efficiency.

The classical economists did not advocate *laissez-faire*, if that expression is taken to mean an essentially negative conception of the economic and social role of government. Without question, they were suspicious of government activity, believing it to be frequently partisan, corrupt, and inefficient. Yet, they admitted several exceptions (notably in the case of commodities now classified as public goods) to the general rule that government should not intervene directly beyond its 'night-watchman' responsibilities.

The case in favor of reducing the economic role of the state was not advanced as an end in itself; rather, it was predicated on the higher goals of increasing the freedom of the individual and of improving the overall wealth of the nation. As a counterpart to this proposed reduction in the role of the state, the classical economists recognized the importance of the evolution of a variety of extra-legal constraints, of a cultural and moral nature, essential for the effective organization of what Adam Smith termed 'the commercial society' (Rowley, 1987a, p. 58).

From the viewpoint of public finance, the philosophical predilections of the classical economists against fiscal policy intervention were reinforced by economic doctrine. For

Smith, Ricardo, and Mill – three of the four classical economists whose writings are reproduced in the present volumes – the economy was viewed as self-equilibrating, susceptible certainly to the downturns of business cycles, but fully capable of self-correcting to full employment equilibrium without the assistance of government.

Depressions could not be permanent because supply creates its own demand through automatic price and interest rate adjustments. This proposition is known as 'Say's Equality' (or 'Say's Law') and asserts that an excess supply of goods or an excess demand for money tends to be self-correcting:

> If demand proves insufficient to sell all goods at cost-covering prices, including the going rate of profit, prices must fall. The purchasing power of nominal cash holdings will rise and everyone will find himself holding excess real balances; there is at such times an excess demand for money. In the effort to reduce the level of individual cash holdings, the demand for commodities increases until the excess supply in commodity markets is eliminated. A zero excess demand for money is an equilibrium condition because prices, along with the rate of interest, will continue to fall as long as there is an excess demand for cash. (Blaug, 1997, p. 149)

Only Malthus expressed doubts on this issue, envisioning in 1820 the possibility of over-saving in violation of Say's Law. Such doubts, as we shall see, conditioned Malthus to raise a lone, dissenting classical voice against the otherwise dominant view that there was no role for deficit financing as an effective means of countering temporary downturns in the level of overall economic activity.

In order to outline the broad parameters of classical doctrine on issues of the national debt and budget deficits, this section briefly reviews and compares the contributions of the three most important contributors, namely Adam Smith, Thomas Robert Malthus, and David Ricardo. The views of these scholars, later reflected also in the writings of John Stuart Mill, would become the focus of a bitter and sustained intellectual attack from the disciples of John Maynard Keynes as they forged their case for the use of deficit financing as a public policy response to downturns in the business cycle.

Adam Smith possessed the most acute insight into the nature of the economic process of all the classical economists, and the greatest wisdom concerning the role of the state in a commercial society, even though he was perhaps less analytically competent than, say, David Ricardo (Blaug, 1997, p. 62). Smith's views on the debt and on budget deficits undoubtedly established the foundation of the classical doctrine.

Smith's (1776/1976) views on the national debt were a clear and direct product of his anti-mercantilist philosophy. He viewed the apparatus of the state, as it existed in late-eighteenth-century Western Europe, as grossly inefficient from the standpoint of wealth creation and grossly restrictive of individual liberties. The state, through taxation and deficit financing, transferred savings from merchants and industrialists and wasted such funds on often unjustified, or at least overextended, wars and in riotous living, thus diverting resources away from capital goods toward consumption.

Where industry or commerce financed budget deficits by the purchase of government securities, profligate governments thereby deprived a capital-poor society of revenues that otherwise would have been productively invested. Taxes instead of loans admittedly would involve a similar diversion of resources; however, they would induce a negative reaction sufficient to restrain the spending propensities of government: 'When a nation is already overburdened with taxes, nothing but the necessities of a new war, nothing but either the animosity of national vengeance, or the anxiety for national security, can induce the people to submit, with tolerable patience, to a new tax' (Smith, 1776/1976, p. 921).

Smith recognized that governments, for the most part, are obliged to finance wars through budget deficits. Even if taxes were to be raised at the onset of war, the proceeds would not be reaped in time to finance the war effort. In such an exigency, 'government can have no other resource but in borrowing' (Smith, 1776/1976, p. 909). Unfortunately, the return of peace seldom resulted in the liquidation of the accumulated national debt, even when sinking funds were established, as Smith chronicled by reference to British experience from 1689 to 1776: 'During the most profound peace, various events occur which require an extraordinary expence, and government finds it always more convenient to defray this expence by misapplying the sinking fund than by imposing a new tax' (1776/1976, p. 920).

Smith directly confronted, and rejected on two grounds, the apology, prevalent among statist thinkers in the late eighteenth century, that the public debt bears no burden: 'In the payment of the interest of the publick debt, it has been said, it is the right hand which pays the left ... This apology is founded altogether in the sophistry of the mercantile system' (1776/1976, pp. 926–7).

First, as Smith chronicled in the case of Britain, part of the British national debt was held by the Dutch, as well as by other foreign nations, in which case clearly 'we do not owe it to ourselves'. Second, even with respect to the internal debt, public debt does more than induce the annual transfer of interest from taxpayers to bondholders. It involves a reallocation of resources from productive to unproductive agents:

> To transfer from the owners of those two great sources of revenue, land and capital stock, from the persons immediately interested in the good condition of every particular portion of land, and in the good management of every particular portion of capital stock, to another set of persons (the creditors of the publick, who have no such particular interest) the greater part of the revenue arising from either, must, in the long run, occasion both the neglect of land, and the waste or removal of capital stock. (1776/1976, p. 928)

Finally, in a comment full of insight, Smith noted that the purchaser of a government bond underwent no sacrifice at the time of purchase, when the debt was created, but rather made money by lending to the government:

> By lending money to government, they do not even for a moment diminish their ability to carry on their trade and manufactures. On the contrary, they commonly augment it ... The merchant or monied man makes money by lending money to government, and instead of diminishing, increases his trading capital. He generally considers it a favour, therefore, when the administration admits him to share in the first subscription for a new loan. (1776/1976, pp. 910–12)

In thus recognizing the mutuality of advantage in voluntary exchange, Smith signaled an approach to public debt analysis that would be attacked by the Keynesians, only to be resuscitated in the 1950s, against the weight of professional economic opinion. In essence, there is no burden of debt at the time of its creation. The entire burden of the debt burden falls on future generations. As usual, the maestro was absolutely correct in this important early political-economic insight.

The sole dissenter among the classical economists on the implications of the public debt was Thomas Robert Malthus (1798/1951; 1803/1992). Malthus was less convinced than were other classical economists about the self-adjusting characteristics of the market economy. His defense of the existing debt carries an uncanny Keynesian ring. Those who live on the interest from the public debt, like statesmen, soldiers, and sailors, 'contribute powerfully to distribution and demand ... [T]hey ensure that effective consumption which is necessary to give the proper stimulus to production ...' (Malthus, 1798/1951, p. 409).

The debt, once created, therefore, is not a great evil. Since even the greatest powers of production are comparatively useless without effective consumption, 'it would be the height of rashness to determine, under all circumstances, that the sudden diminution of the national debt and the removal of taxation must necessarily tend to increase the national wealth, and provide employment for the labouring classes' (Malthus, 1798/1951, p. 411).

Malthus hesitated to press this logic to its ultimate conclusion. There were perceived offsetting disadvantages associated with a sizable national debt. The taxation required to meet interest payments itself might exert harmful influences. Taxpayers might so resent such interest commitments as to become insecure. The existence of debt defined in nominal terms aggravated the evils arising from changes in the value of money.

These disadvantages properly must be weighed against the advantage of supporting a body of unproductive consumers who encouraged wealth creation by maintaining a balance between production and consumption. Malthus, in particular, was opposed to systems of wealth transfer in support of the poor, whether financed by debt or taxes. Such policies encouraged countervailing population growth and thus were unproductive.

The classical economist whose views on the debt and on deficit financing are most widely cited at the present time undoubtedly is David Ricardo. Writing at the end of the Napoleonic Wars, Ricardo (1821/1951) generally shared Smith's antipathy to financing debt created by budget deficits. By 1816, Great Britain's public debt stood at £500 million, approximately double its magnitude at the beginning of the century. Ricardo castigated this debt as 'one of the most terrible scourges which was ever invented to afflict a nation' (1820/1951, p. 197).

Ricardo, like Smith before him, emphasized that the primary economic cost of the debt lay in the loss of original capital, as represented in the resources withdrawn from the productive capital of the nation:

> When, for the expenses of a year's war, twenty millions are raised by means of a loan, it is the twenty millions which are withdrawn from the productive capital of the nation. The million per annum which is raised by taxes to pay the interest of this loan, is merely transferred from those who pay it to those who receive it, from the contributor to the tax, to the national creditor. The real expense is the twenty millions, and not the interest which must be paid for it. (1821/1951, p. 244)

Once the debt had been accumulated, Ricardo was more sanguine than Smith with respect to who should bear the burden of financing it. The effects of the annual transfer from taxpayers to debt-holders must depend on how these groups respectively would employ the relevant resources:

> It is not, then, by the payment of the interest on the national debt, that a country is distressed, nor is it by the exoneration from payment that it can be relieved. It is only by saving from income, and retrenching in expenditure, that the national capital can be increased; and neither the income would be increased, nor the expenditure diminished by the annihilation of the national debt. (1821/1951, p. 246)

According to Ricardo, future tax payments are fully capitalized by the rational citizen. In this sense, Ricardo departs from the view of Adam Smith. A choice of debt rather than of tax financing of public expenditures does not shift the real cost of government expenditure forward in time: 'The argument of charging posterity with the interest of our debt, or of relieving them from a portion of such interest, is often used by otherwise well-informed people, but we confess to see no weight in it' (1820/1951, p. 187).

Ricardo outlined the equivalence between taxation and debt in the following example:

> A man who has 10,000*l.*, paying him an income of 500*l.*, out of which he has to pay 100*l.* per annum towards the interest of the debt, is really worth only 8000*l.*, and would be equally rich, whether he continued to pay 100*l.* per annum, or at once, and for only once, sacrificed 2000*l.* (1817/1951, p. 248)

This statement cannot be taken to imply that Ricardo argued in favor of the equivalence between debt and taxes, in point of fact. Ricardo clearly recognized that individuals do not behave with perfect foresight like hypothetical transactors:

> But the people who pay taxes never so estimate them, and therefore, do not manage their private affairs accordingly. We are too apt to think that the war is burdensome only in proportion to what we are at the moment called to pay for it in taxes, without reflecting on the probable duration of such taxes. It would be difficult to convince a man possessed of 20,000*l.*, or any other sum, that a perpetual payment of 50*l.* per annum is equally burdensome with a single tax of 1000*l.* (1820/1951, p. 186)

Finally, Ricardo (1821/1951) anticipated the public choice revolution, recognizing that the existence of a large national debt created political incentives for those confronting the tax burden to shift that burden on to others:

> A country which has accumulated a large debt, is placed in a most artificial situation ... it becomes in the interest of every contributor to withdraw his shoulder from the burthen, and to shift this payment from himself to another; and the temptation to remove himself and his capital to another country, where he will be exempted from such burthens, becomes at last irresistible, and overcomes the natural reluctance which every man feels to quit the place of his birth, and the scene of his early associations. (1821/1951, p. 248)

It is clear from these various quotations that the 'Ricardian equivalence theorem' between debt and taxes – as it came to be called in the mid-1970s – demonstrates a complete misreading of Ricardo's stated views on this important issue.

IV. Budget Imbalance from the Perspective of Keynes and the Keynesians

Prior to the publication of *The General Theory of Employment, Interest and Money* in 1936 by John Maynard Keynes, Say's Law permeated all macroeconomic thinking. The idea that the competitive process continuously drove the economy back toward a steady state of full employment whenever it fell below the full-capacity utilization of the capital stock remained virtually unchallenged as doctrine inherited from the classical economists.

Even the evolution of the quantity theory of money into its Wicksellian form had left monetary economists focused on the determination of prices rather than the national income. The key flexible price that equilibrated saving and investment plans was still seen to be the rate of interest (Blaug, 1997, p. 641). Confronted in the early 1930s by the Great Depression, orthodox classical economists offered little in the way of remedies other than those of balancing the budget and deflating the economy in order to drive down real wages.

The Austrian economists (Hayek, 1931; Robbins, 1934) alternatively argued that the economy should be allowed simply to run its course in order to cleanse the way for a healthy boom – i.e. one fueled not by loose money, as had been the case during the 1920s, but by economic fundamentals. Since more than one-fourth of 'the potential labor force was unemployed throughout the Western World, throughout the early 1930s, such arguments inevitably were widely viewed as the counsel of despair.

By 1936, the scene was set for an alternative economic theory capable of justifying the deficit financing of government expenditures as a tool for attacking downturns in the business cycle. In the United States, Germany, and the Scandinavian countries (though to a much lesser extent in the United Kingdom) governments had already adopted such policies, generating huge budget deficits without encountering any serious opposition from their respective economics professions (Blaug, 1997, p. 644).

The classical notion of competitive markets for commodities and labor had already been displaced by socialistic policy interventions in all Western countries under the influence of Fabian socialist dogma (Mises, 1948/1960). The minimal state no longer existed as a real-world institutional reality. In such circumstances, classical economists could no longer rely on Say's Law to correct an economic depression, since the competitive market conditions underpinning Say's Law had been aborted by government (Mises, 1947/1960).

In 1936, Keynes produced a rationalization for activist fiscal policy measures, setting out his own theory against the backcloth of a very simplified version of classical economic doctrine. Keynes argued that the classical theory of employment depended on two postulates, namely that the wage rate is equal to the marginal product of labor, and that the utility of the wage to the worker equals the marginal disutility of employment. Keynes (1936) accepted the former postulate but denied the latter, because the latter implied the impossibility of involuntary unemployment evident everywhere in 1936.

The central message of *The General Theory* is that economies are not supply-driven, that Say's Law does not hold, and that an equilibrium level of income and output need not correspond to a situation of full employment. Indeed, in the absence of appropriate intervention by government, Keynes argued that the economy was likely to find itself locked into a low-level employment equilibrium trap. There was no spontaneous, self-adjusting mechanism that would necessarily return an under-performing economy to full-employment equilibrium.

Keynes justified this theory on the basis of a number of novel propositions. He argued that consumption was primarily a function of income and not of the rate of interest; that autonomous injections into aggregate demand were accentuated by a multiplier greater than unity that was the reciprocal of the marginal propensity to save; that this multiplier applied equally to government and to private investment expenditures; that the interest rate elasticity of investment was very low; that the interest rate elasticity of the demand for money was very high and indeed was infinite at some minimum rate of interest; and that the investment function was unstable, governed by 'animal spirits'.

In such circumstances, monetary policy might be incapable of lifting a severely recessed economy to full employment through the interest rate mechanism alone, in the absence of some fiscal stimulus. For these reasons, Keynes placed considerable emphasis on public works as the principal engine for employment expansion, even though he was concerned that such outlays might be countermanded in part by a partial crowding out of private investment:

> If, for example, a government employs 100,000 additional men on public works, and if the multiplier ... is 4, it is not safe to assume that aggregate employment will increase by 400,000. For the new policy may have adverse reactions on investment in other directions. (Keynes, 1936, p. 119)

Keynes argued further that the multiplier might lose power well before a situation of full employment had been achieved and that public works were best suited to conditions of severe unemployment:

> It is also obvious ... that the employment of a given number of men on public works will ... have a much larger effect on aggregate employment at a time when there is severe unemployment, than it will have later on when full employment is approached. ... Thus public works even of doubtful utility may pay for themselves over and over again at a time of severe unemployment. (1936, p. 127)

So convinced was Keynes of the 'free lunch' characteristics of public works programs that he evidenced support for injecting demand into an under-employed economy through entirely wasteful programs of public expenditure:

> [T]he above reasoning shows how 'wasteful' loan expenditure may nevertheless enrich the community on balance. Pyramid-building, earthquakes, even wars may serve to increase wealth, if the education of our statesmen on the principles of the classical economics stands in the way of anything better. (1936, pp. 128–9)

Although *The General Theory* explicitly supports public works programs and the expansion of public investment, it does not direct attention to the implications of such interventions for budget balance. Implicitly, budgetary deficits must have been in the author's mind, since the concept of the balanced budget multiplier was unheard of in 1936. In calling for expanded public works programs, therefore, Keynes must have intended the raiding of the Sinking Fund and the new issuance of debt. The concept of levering up the scale of a balanced budget would have been viewed as policy-neutral until the balanced budget theorem was fully developed and evaluated.

Keynes himself strongly supported deficit financing throughout the early 1930s in his polemical writings. In *The General Theory* itself, he openly derided, as philistine, the balanced budget ethic of William Ewart Gladstone:

> Petty's 'entertainments', magnificent shews, triumphal arches etc. gave place to the penny-wisdom of Gladstonian finance and to a state system which 'could not afford' hospitals, open spaces, noble buildings, even the preservation of its ancient monuments, far less the splendours of music and the drama, all of which were consigned to the private charity or magnanimity of improvident individuals. (1936, p. 362)

In *The General Theory*, Keynes challenged both the fiscal austerity of the classical economics doctrine and the strict standards of Victorian household budget morality in a reasoned assault on the balanced budget principle (Rowley, 1987b, p. 149). This challenge was seized upon by several of his immediate disciples, most notably by Abba Lerner (1943) and Paul Samuelson (1948), who enthusiastically embraced the doctrine of 'functional finance' implicit in *The General Theory*. Lerner (1943) outlined the new doctrine in its most uncompromising form:

> The central idea is that government fiscal policy, its spending and taxing, its borrowing and repayment of loans, its issue of new money and its withdrawal of money, shall all be undertaken with an eye only to the *results* of these actions on the economy and not to any established traditional doctrine about what is sound or unsound. ... The principle of judging fiscal measures by the way they work or function in the economy we may call *Functional Finance*. (Lerner, 1943, p. 39; emphasis in original)

Lerner (1943) set out three 'laws' of functional finance that should determine the fiscal and monetary policies of any government. First, government should so adjust its spending and taxing as to maintain aggregate demand at a level that will buy full-employment output at current prices. In this exercise, budget balance or imbalance is irrelevant. Second, government should borrow money or repay debt, thereby changing the proportions in which the public holds its wealth in money and in bonds, only as a means of influencing the rate of interest. Government should never borrow merely to finance a deficit, a purpose better served by printing money. Third, as a derivative of the first two laws, government should print or destroy money in such a volume as to reconcile the objectives of functional finance.

Keynes initially denounced Lerner's doctrine as 'humbug' and publicly shamed Lerner 'in language so intemperate that he later felt moved to retract his words publicly and to substitute for them the highest admiration' (Scitovsky, 1984, p. 1561). Evsey Domar and Richard Musgrave have also chronicled their initial rage when first confronted with the functional finance doctrine (Colander, 1984).

Once Keynes announced support, however, his disciples quickly fell into line. When Paul Samuelson unreservedly embraced the doctrine of functional finance in the first edition of his textbook, *Economics: An Introductory Analysis* (1948), the expanding economics profession in the postwar Western economies moved decisively behind the doctrine, thereby squaring economic theory with the observed behavior of national governments.

Keynesian scholars, for the most part, focused on the behavior of economies suffering from under-employment equilibrium. For this reason, the 'hydraulic' Keynesian model, developed by John Hicks (1937) and extended by Alvin Hansen (1953), was explicated in real terms without any reference to potential problems of inflation.

The now infamous 'inverse-L' theory of aggregate supply supposed that economies could be expanded right up to the level of full employment without any impact upon the general price level. The governments of Western countries flirted with this notion, and financed budget deficits through the printing-press, only to confront rising inflationary pressures.

By the late 1950s, however dimly, even such committed Keynesians as Don Patinkin (1965) began to recognize that they might be crucifying Western economies on the 'Keynesian Cross'. Gradually, Keynesian economics was modified, not without a good degree of internal dissension, by the Keynesians themselves into a compromise between the classical model and the Keynesian model that became known as the 'neoclassical synthesis'.

This compromise combined (i) the Keynesian theory of aggregate demand with (ii) the classical economics theory of aggregate supply, and with (iii) the 'Phillips curve' theory of how prices adjust in situations in which aggregate demand exceeds aggregate supply to provide a macroeconomic model capable of incorporating the inflationary as well as the real effects of fiscal and monetary policy.

The shift from Keynesian to neoclassical modeling of the macroeconomy led economists to become more circumspect about budget deficits, whether funded by debt or through the printing-press. In particular, they became more convinced that significant swings in aggregate demand must be avoided if the twin evils of unemployment and inflation were to be mitigated. The early sanguinity of Lerner (1943) and Samuelson (1948) with respect to the beneficial implications of budget deficits no longer dominated economic thinking.

Nevertheless, comforted by their beliefs, first, that the Phillips curve trade-off between unemployment and the rate of price inflation was stable and, second, that fiscal policy was more potent than monetary policy, such leading neo-Keynesians as Samuelson and Solow (1960) remained strong advocates of unbalancing the budget in order to balance the economy. By the mid-1960s, this intellectual complacency began to erode as the predictions of the neoclassical synthesis began to be falsified and as a monetarist counter-revolution began to challenge the hegemony of neoclassical economics (Parkin, 1984).

V. Budget Imbalance from the Perspective of Monetarism

The quantity theory of money was an important component of classical economics, defining the causal relationship between the supply of money and the price level. The behavioral version took the form $MV_y = P_y$, where M denotes the exogenously determined nominal money supply, Vy denotes the income velocity of circulation of money, P denotes the price level, and y denotes the level of real income. According to classical economics as it was understood immediately prior to *The General Theory*, the direction of causation must run from M to P. That is because y is determined largely, though not in the short run exclusively, outside the system, and V_y is relatively, though not in the short run, completely stable (Blaug, 1997, pp. 614–18).

In the long run, with a stable V_y, P varies in exact proportion to changes in M. The adjustment process implicit in this equilibrium relationship was recognized as involving two distinct transmission mechanisms from M to P, namely the 'direct' and the 'indirect'. Each mechanism reinforces the impact of the other.

The direct mechanism relies on any disequilibrium between actual and desired real money balances to induce spending that eventually generates a change in prices proportionate to the initial injection of money. The indirect mechanism relies on the reduction in interest rates induced by any increase in the money supply to stimulate private investment and, thus, to exert an upward pressure on prices until the equilibrium real rate of interest is restored.

In the long run, therefore, classical economics viewed money as neutral. That was not necessarily the case in the short run, however. Through an increase in income velocity, an increase in the money supply in the short run was viewed as exerting an expansionary impact on real output, as well as on prices during the recessionary phase of the business cycle. Every classical economist, except David Ricardo and James Mill, accepted the non-neutrality of money in the short run as so defined (Blaug, 1997, p. 616).

In *The General Theory*, Keynes categorically rejected the quantity theory as outlined above. In an under-employed economy, changes in spending were viewed as impacting on employment and output rather than on prices. Keynes, therefore, reversed the assumptions of the quantity theory, treating prices as fixed and output as flexible (Friedman, 1970; Blaug, 1997, p. 626).

Keynes and the Keynesians incorrectly caricatured the quantity theory as claiming that the income velocity of circulation of money was a constant. They categorically rejected that notion, asserting instead that V_y was flexible, and moved generally in the opposite direction to changes in the money supply. Thus, V_y served as a cushion, minimizing the impact of any change in the supply of money on the level of nominal income.

On this basis, money was viewed as playing little role in the economy with respect either to real or to nominal variables. Given that 'you cannot push on a string', the case for using fiscal policy as a stabilization instrument, with budget deficits financed either by debt or by printing money, was significantly enhanced.

The monetarist counter-revolution, initiated by Milton Friedman in 1956, and implemented over the period 1956 to 1970, together with a growing body of evidence that falsified Keynesian predictions, combined to erode confidence throughout the economics profession, government, and the general public in the validity of the Keynesian model in general, and of fiscal policy as an instrument of economic stabilization in particular (Rowley, 1987b, pp. 160–62).

Ironically, Keynes provided the initial insight that culminated in the monetarist revival. By distinguishing in *The General Theory* between the transactions demand, the precautionary demand, and the speculative demand for money, he shifted attention from the role of money as a medium of exchange to its function as a store of value, pursuing an idea earlier expounded by John Hicks (1935).

In 1956, Friedman extended this insight to its logical conclusion by outlining 'a precise and complete specification of the relevant constraints and opportunity cost variables entering a household's money demand function' (Blaug, 1997, p. 627). Friedman hypothesized as a testable proposition that the demand for money (k), thus defined as a function of a limited number of empirically specifiable variables, was stable.

On the basis of this claim, Friedman and his colleagues proceeded, through a sequence of empirical studies and a massive historical survey (Friedman and Schwartz, 1963), to launch a monetarist counter-revolution. This research program convincingly established the long-run proportional relationship between the quantity of money and prices and, despite evidence of growing instability in the demand for money function during the 1970s, a significant short-run causal relationship between changes in the quantity of money and changes in the level of nominal income (Friedman, 1971).

The monetarist challenge to the neoclassical synthesis went well beyond reestablishing the case that 'money matters'. Evidence was presented to the effect that the interest rate elasticity of private investment is much higher than the Keynesians had allowed, that absolute liquidity preference is not evident in the demand for money function, that the multiplier with respect to government expenditures, if it exists at all, is radically smaller than had been argued, and that the Great Depression was caused by monetary factors and not by a collapse of the private investment function.

Most devastating of all for the neoclassical synthesis was Friedman's powerful attack on the notion that there exists a stable Phillips curve trade-off between the rate of price inflation and the level of employment. In his 1967 address to the American Economic Association – 'easily the most influential paper on macroeconomics published in the post-war era' (Blaug, 1997, p. 678) – Friedman (1968) rejected the original Phillips curve theory on the ground that it focused attention on nominal rather than real labor market variables.

Central to Friedman's argument is the concept of the 'natural rate of unemployment' defined as that level of voluntary unemployment that clears the labor market and produces a real wage consistent with multi-market equilibrium. According to Friedman, the long-run Phillips curve is vertical at this rate and provides no trade-off between the rate of price inflation and the level of unemployment.

The short-run Phillips curve, reformulated by Friedman in 'expectations-augmented' form, is stable only when unemployment holds at the natural rate. Should government intervene to drive unemployment below the natural rate, the short-run Phillips curve will shift upwards, offering a more adverse trade-off between the rate of price inflation and the level of unemployment. Only by running the economy at a rate of unemployment in excess of the natural rate in order to rid the economy of inflation expectations can government restore the original short-run Phillips curve. In such circumstances, governments deploy inflation-inducing fiscal policy at their peril.

Finally, the shift from fixed to floating exchange rates during the early 1970s by increasingly open economies, in an environment characterized by increasingly high capital mobility, raised the specter that expansionary fiscal policies could exert little or no impact on the level of aggregate demand. According to the Mundell–Fleming model (Fleming, 1962; Mundell, 1968), the LM curve is vertical in exchange rate and real output space under conditions of floating exchange rates. This implies that the position of the aggregate demand curve in exchange rate and real output space is determined entirely in the money market.

Should government expenditure increase at a given price level under such conditions, shifting the IS curve to the right, the exchange rate appreciates to nullify any effects of the shift, and there is no output effect. In such circumstances, there is no point in resorting to fiscal expansion as a solution to an economic recession.

The theoretical analysis and empirical testing central to the monetarist counter-revolution undoubtedly forced the neoclassical synthesis into a state of crisis during the 1970s and significantly eroded the confidence of economists concerning the effectiveness of expansionary fiscal policy in alleviating economic recessions. The *coup de grâce*, however, was applied by unfolding economic events both in the United States and in Great Britain.

In 1966, for example, the United States manifested a tight monetary policy and an expansionary fiscal policy. The Keynesians predicted rapid economic expansion throughout 1967; the monetarists predicted a decline in the rate of growth of economic activity. The monetarists proved to be correct. In 1968 fiscal policy was tightened and the money supply became more expansionary. The Keynesians predicted an economic downturn; the monetarists predicted an inflationary boom. Once again, the monetarists proved to be correct.

In Britain, the Labour government effected a major redistribution of income in 1974 from capitalists to workers. According to Keynesian economic theory, this should have depressed the saving ratio and increased consumption expenditures. Between 1974 and 1976, consumer spending declined from 92 to 87 per cent of household disposable income.

Most devastating of all for the credibility of the neoclassical synthesis was the empirical death during the mid-1970s of the treasured Phillips curve trade-off. As Western economies entered into an extended period of 'stagflation', and as empirical studies evidenced Phillips curves with positive slopes, economists began to migrate from the Keynesian first to the monetarist and then to the new classical camp. Economists, in many cases, were preceded in this flight by leading Western socialist politicians (for example, in 1976, by Britain's Prime Minister James Callaghan) who had no intention of crucifying their careers on some misguided 'Keynesian Cross'.

VI.   Budget Imbalance from the Perspective of Rational Expectations

John Muth (1961) first developed the theory of rational expectations. He did so with respect to the behavior of security and commodity markets. In justifying the 'random walk' hypothesis, Muth argued that speculators make instantaneous use of all economically relevant information when predicting the path of future prices. In this sense, their expectations are rational.

From the viewpoint of an economics profession still dominated by Keynesian macroeconomic thinking, his contribution was a decade premature. It waited in the wings until research on the microeconomic foundations of macroeconomics, and most notably Friedman's (1968) reformulation of the Phillips curve, had paved the way for its effective deployment. In 1972, Robert Lucas pioneered the use of rational expectations in macroeconomic theory within a framework that is now known as the 'New Classical School'. Thomas Sargent (1973) quickly consolidated on Lucas's original insight.

Lucas and Sargent modeled the economy as one in which all agents are rational expected-utility maximizers, and in which all markets clear instantaneously, yielding an equilibrium price vector at which excess demand is eliminated (Blaug, 1997, pp. 684–5). In essence, they justified a stochastic version of the long-ignored Say's Law.

Since economic agents access the same information as policy-makers, they respond to systematic policy initiatives by neutralizing them. Of course, mistakes are possible since foresight is not perfect in a world where the economy is always vulnerable to unpredictable, random shocks. Random error alone causes an economy to deviate from general equilibrium and full employment.

The early pioneers of the new classical economics recognized that random forecasting errors could not fully explain the more or less regular sequence of business cycles that characterized all Western economies. They explained such business cycles in terms of the Lucas (1972) 'islands model' in which agents experienced initial signal extraction problems in distinguishing between nominal and real price changes when confronted with unexpected changes in the nominal money supply.

Under such circumstances, money is non-neutral in the short run, although agents learn quickly, and neutralize any systematic attempt by government to exploit such a signal extraction problem. According to this theory, fiscal policy, whether in the form of an upward adjustment in a balanced budget or of a shift to budget deficits, exerts no impact on the equilibrium level of output and employment, only on the level of prices. Of course, changes in the level and composition of public expenditures, of taxes, or of both, may influence the level of equilibrium real output through microeconomic 'supply-side' effects.

If the new classical economic theory poses seemingly intractable problems for Keynesian fiscal policy, its implications for econometric policy evaluation are equally devastating. In 1976, Lucas addressed problems in relying on the estimated structural equations of econometric models of the macroeconomy to evaluate the impact of specific government interventions: '[G]iven that the structural equations consist of optimal decision rules of economic agents, and that optimal decision rules vary systematically with changes in the structure of series relevant to the decision-maker, it follows that any change in policy will systematically alter the structure of econometric models' (Lucas, 1976, p. 46).

Suppose, therefore, that the new classical economics conditions do not fully hold. Suppose further that fiscal policy conceivably may have some potential impact on the real economy. The Lucas 'critique' suggests that policy-makers would be extremely unwise to rely on estimated macroeconomic models to determine an appropriate fiscal response to a perceived economic recession.

The monetary misperception explanation of business cycles is difficult to test since expectations cannot be directly observed, and since they are not formulated in the Lucas (1972) model in full conformity with fully informed rational expectations. Such testing as was carried out, at best, gave lukewarm support for the theory, with later tests involving the advanced economies of the United States and Western Europe more adverse to the theory than earlier tests. As a consequence, papers by Kydland and Prescott (1982, 1990), King and Plosser (1984), and Prescott (1986) shifted the attention of the new classical economics away from the monetary misperceptions theory to the real business cycle theory of business fluctuations.

Real business cycle theory replaced monetary demand-side shocks with non-monetary supply-side shocks in the form of random changes in technology, emphasizing real forces as the causes of business cycles. In essence, there is no difference between trend and cycle in this analysis; the trend is cyclical (Blaug, 1997, p. 686). The long-run Phillips curve is vertical and there is no short-run Phillips curve. Money is always neutral and the economy is always fully employed. Different levels of observed employment are explained in terms of changes in the intertemporal rates of substitution between income and leisure.

Real business cycle theory leaves no macroeconomic role for fiscal policy. Since the supply of money only determines the price level, if inflation is perceived to impose net social costs, the theory strongly favors the introduction of non-discretionary monetary rules designed to stabilize the price level. Should the 1930s levels of unemployment ever recur, real business cycle theory indeed would be viewed as a counsel of despair.

Real business cycle theory has signally failed to impress policy-makers anywhere in the world. Both governments and the general public continue to place considerable confidence in the role of monetary policy as a relevant instrument for macroeconomic stabilization as the relationship between Federal Reserve Board monetary interventions and stock market reactions in the United States clearly indicate. Moreover, the high rates of observed unemployment throughout continental Western Europe over the period 1980 to 2000 are not as readily rationalized by reference to adverse economic institutions in the eyes either of the public at large or of the growing body of New Keynesian economists as it is by the new classical economists themselves.

The Keynesian and neoclassical models of the macroeconomy were hit hard by the rational expectations revolution. The microeconomic foundations developed in the late 1960s to incorporate flexible wage–price relationships into the Keynesian model proved to be incompatible with the rational expectations assumption. There is no Keynesian role in economies in which only unanticipated demand or supply shocks have any real impact and where stabilization policy is anticipated, counterbalanced and, therefore, rendered ineffective.

However, many Keynesians refused to quit the field of battle and slowly began to regroup behind a New Keynesian standard that incorporates the rational expectations assumption but rejects the full information, full market-clearing assumptions of new classical economics. From this perspective, the New Keynesian models purport to reestablish micro foundations for the basic Keynesian tenet that demand as well as supply shocks are capable of inducing persistent slumps and that monetary policy (and to a lesser extent, fiscal policy) is an effective instrument for stabilizing the macroeconomy (Phelps, 1990, p. 52; Blaug, 1997, p. 687).

The New Keynesians initially focused attention on alleged rigidities in nominal wage rates resulting from the infrequent and staggered adjustment of wage contracts and wage commitments (Phelps and Taylor, 1977; Fischer, 1977; Taylor, 1979; Blanchard, 1983). Suppose that such nominal rigidities are incorporated into a rational expectations model characterized by the neutrality of money and steady-state equilibrium unemployment. A credibly pre-announced increase in the money supply would not instantaneously induce a proportional increase in the average nominal wage. The monetary intervention, thus, would not be effectively neutralized.

An evident weakness of this New Keynesian theory is the question as to why agents allow such nominal rigidities to continue once they experience noticeable reductions in real wage rates. Although there are costs to wage renegotiation, rational agents would surely increase the frequency of wage negotiations, or require built-in wage flexibility in their wage contracts, as they become increasingly exposed to monetary manipulation. It is difficult to explain substantial fluctuations in real output in terms of such predictably small nominal rigidities as staggered wage contracts provide.

In recognition of the limited power of rigid nominal wages to induce major recessions, the New Keynesians switched attention to alleged rigidities in nominal prices, arguing that 'menu costs' constrain profit-maximizing firms from adjusting prices to market-clearing levels in response to economic shocks (Akerlof and Yellen, 1985; Mankiw, 1985). In such circumstances, demand shocks may result in an under-employment equilibrium, and monetary intervention may exert a stabilizing role.

Once again, the New Keynesians were forced to acknowledge that price rigidities resulting from menu costs are likely to be small. They have gone to great lengths to argue that small nominal rigidities may give rise to large real rigidities. Their arguments are less than convincing (Phelps, 1990, p. 63).

The New Keynesian rational expectations models of fluctuations so far examined imply that when prices are flexible, in the absence of supply-side shocks, the economy has a unique equilibrium. Fluctuations arise only in models with nominal wage or price stickiness. Since the nominal stickiness models are less than convincing, stalwart New Keynesians recently have shifted their focus to developing models of market failure. Problems of imperfect competition, incomplete markets, and asymmetric information purportedly are abundant in the advanced economies. Models intertwining such market failure assumptions with nominal wage and price rigidities are capable of providing 'explanations' of business cycles. Such models provide a limited scope for fiscal as well as for monetary interventions in the macroeconomy.

Even the most Keynesian of rational expectations economists, however, necessarily has had to retreat from the functional finance doctrine advanced by Abba Lerner (1943). Budget deficits are advocated as a meaningful policy response to economic recessions only by unreconstructed Keynesians. Of course, that does not mean that economists or politicians have abandoned all support for budget deficits. Those who carry a mercantilist torch for the growth of public expenditure, whether for reasons of private or of public choice, predictably react benignly to deficit financing, even when the functional finance justification is weak or non-existent.

VII. The Evolving Debate over the Burden of the Debt

The classical economists all agreed that debt imposed some kind of a burden on future generations, even when all of the debt was internally held. As we have noted, they differed somewhat concerning the precise nature of this burden. This consensus disappeared, however, in the wake of the Keynesian revolution. Despite significant adjustments in economic thinking in the wake of the Keynesian episode, consensus concerning the burden of the debt has not re-emerged. This section reviews the evolution of the debate on the burden of the debt.

The most categorical denouncement of classical doctrine on the debt burden issue emanated from Keynes's foremost disciple, Abba Lerner (1948). Lerner acknowledged that external borrowing does impose a burden on future generations whose consumption must be curtailed when the debt repayment comes due. There is no equivalent burden in the case of internal debt:

> Very few economists need to be reminded that if our children or grandchildren repay some of the national debt these payments will be made *to* our children or grandchildren and to nobody else. Taking them together they will be no more impoverished by making the repayments than they will be enriched by receiving them. (Lerner, 1948, p. 256; emphasis in original)

Lerner (1948) recognized, in arguing that 'we owe it to ourselves', that the creation of debt is likely to involve income redistribution. The benefits from interest payments on the national debt are unlikely to accrue to every individual in society in exactly the same degree as the harm inflicted on him by the additional taxes required to service the debt. However, such redistribution 'can be ignored because we have no more reason for supposing that the new distribution is worse than the old one as for assuming the opposite' (Lerner, 1948, p. 261).

Lerner (1948) also recognized that any additional taxes required to service the debt theoretically might reduce the net yield from private investment and render socially useful investments unprofitable. However, as a committed Keynesian, he argued that such outcomes would be unlikely. Increases in government spending would occur during periods of inadequate aggregate demand and would not require additional taxation. In such circumstances, an increase in the national debt actually makes bondholders better off and will increase consumption (presumably through the Pigou effect).

Lerner (1948) ignored completely the possibility that deficit financed government expenditure might crowd out private investment. No doubt, this judgment was based on Keynesian notions that government spending during a period of recession was a free lunch, and on the notion that the interest rate elasticity of private investment was low if not zero. In any event, he felt able to conclude his essay by urging that 'the kinds of evil most popularly ascribed to national debt are wholly imaginary' (Lerner, 1948, p. 275).

Lerner's views, even in 1948, were not fully shared by Paul Samuelson, then well on his way to becoming the leading Keynesian among American scholars. Certainly, Samuelson endorsed Lerner's view that internal debt imposes no direct burden on future generations: 'Can it be truthfully said that "internal borrowing shifts the war burden to future generations while taxing places it on the present generation?" A thousand times no!' (Samuelson, 1948, p. 427).

Nevertheless, Samuelson was aware of the possibility that private investment might be deterred by the taxes required to finance interest on the debt. Even if each individual's taxes exactly matched the debt interest that he received, a deadweight loss would still occur as taxes distorted the relationship between work and leisure and adversely affected willingness to venture capital on risky enterprises. In 1948, Samuelson followed Lerner in making no reference to the possibility that increased government expenditure might crowd out private investment.

Thus, the first wave of Keynesian economists viewed a growing public debt as offering an unambiguous net benefit to society. Deficit spending increased national income directly both through the multiplier effect and through the wealth effects experienced by bondholders. Any adverse effects from taxes imposed to service or to amortize the debt were viewed as a small price to pay for the large benefits derived through stabilization policies.

By the late 1950s, the shift in focus from problems of recession to problems of inflation eroded much of the original Keynesian complacency about an increasing national debt, as essays by James Meade (1958), Richard Musgrave (1959), and Franco Modigliani (1961) clearly indicate. Meade's contribution admirably summarizes this phase in the debate over the burden of the debt.

James Meade (1958) focused attention on the harmful rather than the beneficial effects of a domestic debt, arguing that 'quite apart from any distributional effects, a domestic debt may have far-reaching effects upon incentives to work, to save, and to take risks' (Meade, 1958, p. 163). Meade explicitly predicated his critique on the inflationary environment of the late 1950s.

Meade's analysis retained the Keynesian focus on macroeconomic aggregates. A large internal debt, he argued, eroded incentives to counter inflation through tightening monetary policy since high interest rates increased the cost of servicing the debt: 'A deadweight debt may have been a blessing in the 1930s, but it is a curse in the 1950s' (Meade, 1958, p. 169). The disappearance of the deadweight debt would have 'a revolutionary effect in the capital and money markets through changes in the amount and structure of capital assets available to be held by the banks and the rest of the private sector of the economy' (1958, p. 172).

These and other similar arguments imply a widespread recognition within the Keynesian community that public debt imposes a burden on future generations, largely because it reduces incentives to engage in private capital formation and encourages inflationary monetary policies. Lerner himself remained an unreconstructed old Keynesian on these matters, as the following passage indicates:

> There is no shift of resources or of burdens between different points in time. It is possible for a *part* of the economy (the Lowells) to shift *its* burden into the future only as long as *another part* of the

present economy (the Thomases) is ready to take it over for the intervening period. It is not possible for *the whole* of the present generation to shift a burden into the future because there are no Thomases left to play the magician's assistant in the illusion. (Lerner, 1961, p. 140; emphasis in original)

Lerner's (1961) last stand failed to stem the flow of Keynesian thinking back toward the classical economics position. In 1970, Samuelson reflected this shift of perspective, recognizing explicitly that 'the main way that one generation can put a burden on a later generation is by using up currently the nation's stock of capital goods, or by failing to add the usual investment increment to the stock of capital' (Samuelson, 1970, p. 341).

Ironically, as early as 1974, Barro's rational expectations revisionism would reintroduce to freshman economics classes in the United States the unqualified doctrine that public debt imposes no burden on future generations. No longer, however, would this doctrine be associated with the Keynesian revolution.

During the terminal phase of the Keynesian episode, the perspective on the burden of the debt shifted perceptibly in favor of the classical position that future generations would be burdened with the consequences of reduced private capital formation. Nowhere within the Keynesian camp was there any recognition of the insight of Adam Smith, concerning mutuality of exchange, which placed the entire burden of the debt on future generations. James M. Buchanan (1958/1999, 1964, 1976), working essentially outside the Keynesian research program, was primarily responsible for restoring this important insight.

In 1958, Buchanan directly confronted the conventional Keynesian perspective with this alternative insight. Starting with the classical notion of full employment, and assuming that the debt is created for real purposes, and thus draws resources entirely from private capital formation, Buchanan focused on the economic conditions of the United States in the late 1950s. Within this framework, he convincingly argued that the issuing of new debt imposes no burden on the current generation:

> The mere shifting of resources from private to public employment does not carry with it any implication of sacrifice or payment. If the shift takes place through the voluntary actions of private people, it is meaningless to speak of any sacrifice having taken place. An elemental recognition of the mutuality of advantage from trade is sufficient to show this. If an individual freely chooses to purchase a government bond, he is presumably moving to a preferred position on his utility surface by so doing. He has improved, not worsened, his lot by the transaction. This must be true for each bond purchaser, the only individual who actually gives up a current command over economic resources. (Buchanan, 1958/1999, p. 28)

Even within this individualistic framework, Buchanan (1958/1999) recognized one exception to this general rule, reflective of an insight by David Ricardo. Suppose that the creation of the debt, with its corresponding obligation to meet the service charges from future tax revenues, should cause individual taxpayers to write down the present value of their future income streams. Under such circumstances, the current generation indeed will bear the burden of new debt. Here, Buchanan clearly anticipated the so-called 'Ricardian equivalence theorem'.

It is noteworthy that the Keynesians explicitly rejected this Ricardian justification of the Lerner hypothesis. Samuelson (1948) is categorical in this respect: 'Every citizen who owns government bonds includes them when drawing up his periodic balance sheet, along with his other assets. But he is a very rare man indeed if he also includes as a present liability the amount of *future* taxes which he may have to pay to finance government interest payments or debt retirement. He does not even have a way of estimating his share of these taxes' (Samuelson, 1948, p. 428).

Buchanan (1958/1999) was also skeptical of the tax-offsetting hypothesis. Where an individual owns no capital assets other than his own body, Buchanan noted that he had no opportunity to capitalize the future tax burden involved in interest charges. Where an individual owned capital assets but had no interest in the welfare of his heirs, capitalization of the burden would not occur. Finally, where individuals did not perceive the tax implications of new debt issuance, the Ricardian equivalence theorem would not hold:

> The primary burden of the debt, in the only sense in which this concept is meaningful, must rest with future generations at least in large part. These are the individuals who suffer the consequences of wasteful government expenditure and who reap the benefits of useful government expenditure. All other parties to the debt transactions are acting in accordance with ordinary economic motivations. (Buchanan, 1958/1999, p. 37)

Buchanan analyzed the public debt problem from the perspective of individual actors who collectively choose, through a democratic polity, both the level of government expenditures and the method of financing such expenditures. To understand this decision process, Buchanan (1969) focused attention on the subjective nature of the opportunity cost considerations relevant to the making of fiscal choices.

In this perspective, choice-influencing cost consists of each individual's own evaluation, in utility space, of the sacrifice made in selecting some course of action. Subjective cost is imbued with the following important characteristics:

1. It must be borne exclusively by those who choose; it cannot be shifted to others who do not make the choice.
2. It is subjective, existing in the mind of each individual chooser, and nowhere else.
3. It is an *ex ante* concept, based on anticipations and not on retrospective calculation.
4. Only the individual who is confronted with the choice can measure the choice-influencing cost.
5. It is dated at the moment of choice and no other point in time.

Quite distinct from choice-influencing cost are the consequences that flow from the choices that are made. Buchanan (1969) designated such consequences as choice-influenced cost. Choice-influenced cost does not reflect an evaluation of sacrificed alternatives, since such alternatives are in the past. Thus, it does not represent opportunity cost. It is a future burden that emanates from current decisions (Rowley, 1987a, pp. 62–4).

Choice-influenced cost may be experienced both by individuals who were party to the original choice and by individuals who were not. The burden of the debt experienced by future generations evidently is of this kind. At the moment of choice, rational individuals would not endorse a fiscal outcome unless the anticipated benefits outweigh their respective choice-influencing costs. Their ability to reduce such choice-influencing costs by deficit financing designed to push choice-influenced costs on to future generations undoubtedly biases fiscal decisions in favor of increased government expenditures (see Section VIII).

The first wave of Keynesian economists, under the influence of Abba Lerner, argued forcefully that an increasing public debt increased net wealth and that this increase provided a welcome stimulus to real output through the Pigou effect. By 1965, Keynesian enthusiasm for this notion had waned, not least because the economy had moved to near full-employment equilibrium.

In 1965, Tobin challenged the 'asymmetric illusion' implicit in the net wealth argument: 'Society fools itself into consuming more, thinking that possession of government paper provides for its future. Why don't those who will have to pay taxes to service the debt – or even those who will be squeezed out of consumers goods markets when the holders of government paper spend it – consider themselves poorer and save more accordingly?' (Tobin, 1965, p. 681).

Predictably, the rational expectations revolution generated a more fundamental attack on the notion that fiscal illusion plays any role in influencing economic behavior. In 1974, Robert Barro presented a rational expectations model in which government bonds do not constitute net wealth, and in which changes in the relative amounts of tax and debt finance for a given amount of public expenditure exert no impact on aggregate demand, interest rates, or capital formation.

Barro (1974) noted that government bonds should be perceived as net wealth only if their value exceeds the capitalized value of the implied stream of future tax liabilities. His model assumes that individuals confront finite lives, but that current generations are connected to future generations by a chain of private bequests. As the public debt increases, all members of the current generation increase their saving rates so as to compensate future generations, through larger bequests, for the implied increase in future tax liabilities. In this manner, changes in future tax liabilities are fully capitalized through intergenerational transfers. The bequest motive thus serves to neutralize the impact of any change in the fiscal stance of government.

If Barro (1974) is correct, then Buchanan's concern that debt financing burdens the future generations more or less evaporates. Individuals confronting a budget financing choice fully account for relevant future burdens in their subjective evaluations of choice-influencing cost. All relevant costs are capitalized in the choice calculus at that time. Subsequent choice-influenced burdens, albeit evaluated in different utility space, are fully anticipated and ameliorated. Fundamentally, the decision-makers impose the choice-influenced costs upon themselves.

As the papers included in Volume II, Part I clearly demonstrate, more than an unbroken sequence of intergenerational linkages is required for the equivalence between debt and taxes to hold. Is public expenditure in the initial period invariant as between the two financing instruments? Barro (1974) set aside this discussion by assuming that it is invariant. Must public debt once issued be amortized and/or serviced, or can it be defaulted? Barro (1974) ignores the default option.

Are capital markets perfect in the sense that individuals can borrow or lend at the same rate as the government? Barro (1974) acknowledged that governments may borrow on more favorable terms than private individuals, but he discounts the significance of such a discrepancy. Are all taxes levied lump sum? Barro (1974) advanced this unrealistic assumption in order to neutralize the deadweight costs of non lump-sum taxes.

Tobin (1980) critiqued Barro's intergenerational linkage assumption, suggesting that it would not hold in the case of (a) childless members of the generation living when the public debt was issued, (b) those who are indifferent or hostile to the well-being of their children, (c) those who perceive that their descendants will be better off than they are, and (d) households that are constrained by considerations of liquidity from transferring wealth inter-temporarily. If these conditions do hold, then net wealth effects might well exert an impact on real economic variables.

Barro (1974) was unaware of the prior scholarship of David Ricardo on the debt versus taxes issue. He was taken to task for his omission by Buchanan (1976, p. 337), who noted that Ricardo (1821/1951) had originally argued in favor of the view that public debt issue is equivalent to taxation. In this essay, Buchanan introduced the term 'Ricardian equivalence theorem' into the lexicon of economics. In so doing, he failed to acknowledge the full complexity of the Ricardian position. Ricardian equivalence has become a widely accepted doctrine of public finance, despite the fact that Ricardo introduced the concept only *in point of economy* and rejected it *in point of fact* (see O'Driscoll, 1977, p. 208). In reality (as we established in Section II), Ricardo should be remembered for his 'non-equivalence theorem'.

Brennan and Buchanan (1980) turned to microeconomic foundations to critique Barro's (1974) equivalence theorem. Focusing on the changes in individual behavior that would be induced by the issuance of public debt when the full tax implications are perceived, they note that individuals would be tempted to reduce their current tax burdens by shifting income intertemporally. Such behavior would impair capital formation.

Even if future tax obligations should be fully anticipated, individual taxpayers would confront a prisoner's dilemma situation in effecting their choices between taxes and public debt issues:

> [I]t is rational for the individual to adjust to the alternatives that he privately confronts, and to do so independently of the actions of other persons, even if he recognizes the nature of the interdependence. If instead of this privately-rational behavior, an individual tries to behave as he would prefer that all persons behave ... he would become vulnerable to 'exploitation' by others in the sense that his relative share in the aggregate fiscal liability would be increased. (Brennan and Buchanan, 1980, p. 11)

Brennan and Buchanan (1980), therefore, concluded that debt issue would systematically discourage saving and capital accumulation relative to the tax financing of the same volume of public expenditures.

Ultimately, of course, the models of Barro, Feldstein (1976), and Brennan and Buchanan are simply testable hypotheses and not economic 'laws'. They are only as valid as the evidence determines. It turns out that the empirical evidence weighs heavily against the Barro equivalence theorem (see, e.g., Evans, 1993; Stanley, 1998). In such circumstances, the already suspect auxiliary assumptions on which Barro (1974) rests his model are rendered intellectually indefensible, even if the rational expectations postulate should be retained.

In our judgment, the great debate on the burden of the public debt opened up by John Maynard Keynes in 1936 has been decisively resolved in favor of the classical doctrine that the burden of the public debt falls primarily on the shoulders of the future generations. This conclusion has significant implications for the behavior of political markets, with respect both to the size and to the rate of growth of public expenditures.

VIII.   The Perspective of Public Choice

Throughout the century and a half before the onset of the Great Depression, governments both in the United States and Great Britain created budget deficits only in response to the exigencies of war and of recession (Buchanan, Rowley and Tollison, 1987). Even such periodic deficits were regarded with suspicion and concern. In years of peace and economic boom, budget surpluses were common, and were used to retire debt accumulated during the years of war and recession.

Following the major disruptions of the Great Depression and of the Second World War, the early postwar United States governments reestablished the pre-1930s norm. Between 1947 and 1960, US budgets recorded seven years of surplus and seven years of deficit, with budget deficits, once again, corresponding roughly with periods of war and recession. Yet, beneath the surface, everything was not the same. During this early postwar period, significant constraint adjustments occurred. These adjustments would prove to be public choice harbingers of a 40-year period of continuous federal budget deficits in the United States.

The first constraint adjustment was the weakening of the gold exchange standard. The establishment of the Federal Reserve System in 1913 had weakened the standard by encouraging the growth of fiat money in excess of gold reserves. President Roosevelt had further weakened the standard in 1933 by repudiating the commitment of the federal government to exchange privately held fiat money for gold. The fixed exchange rate system established at Bretton Woods at the end of the Second World War only loosely reestablished the pre-1930s linkage between the dollar and gold. The Bretton Woods system itself was finally swept away during the early 1970s as economic recovery in Europe coupled with a loose US monetary policy systematically eased the US dollar from a position of shortage into a position of surplus.

The gold standard had played a significant role, during its heyday, in constraining profligate fiscal policies. By prohibiting discretionary recourse by governments to their respective printing-presses, the inflation tax was all but eliminated as a source of financing government expenditure or of amortizing the public debt. In consequence, politicians confronted a direct choice between debt creation and taxation as methods of financing growth in public expenditures. Neither option was especially palatable politically during the gold standard era.

The second constraint adjustment was the erosion of Victorian moral principles against burdening future generations with high levels of public debt. These principles were epitomized in the Gladstone balanced budget ethic that had dominated British politics throughout the late nineteenth century. By 1918, in the wake of the First World War, relativist philosophy invaded the absolute values of late Victorian society and began to weaken the thrift motive.

By 1960, as intergenerational linkages finally broke down throughout the Western democracies, with the collapse of the extended family and with rising rates of divorce and illegitimacy, concern for the debt burdens imposed on future generations sharply diminished. Self-interested politicians responded predictably to this avenue of opportunity for budget profligacy. For, after all, 'the future generations do not vote!'.

The third constraint adjustment during the early postwar period came with the growing acceptance within government of Keynesian macroeconomic ideas. The 'paradox of thrift' provided intellectual justification for politicians to abandon the prudential policies of the Victorian era. The concept of the 'burden-less debt' consigned classical economic fears of deficit financing to 40 years of policy irrelevance.

The Keynesian 'constructivist rationalists' came to believe that they could fine-tune the budget to eliminate the business cycle and that an omniscient and benevolent government would efficiently implement their budgetary proposals. In 1960 the era of 'Keynesian Camelot' began. By 1963, when the brief era of Camelot was foreclosed by a rifle shot in Dallas, economists of all brands had lost influence with government. The forces of public choice overwhelmed élitist Keynesian fine-tuning advice, swept aside all remaining institutional constraints, and introduced a permanent deficit bias into the budget deliberations of the Western democracies (Buchanan and Wagner, 1977).

The public choice approach outlined in this essay is that developed, for the most part, by the Virginia School. It provides the groundwork for a theory of political market failure that counterbalances the theory of private market failure advanced in the early postwar period as the 'new' welfare economics (Rowley, 2000).

In this perspective, rational individuals access political markets for purposes of expected utility maximization. For the most part, political markets are viewed as brokering wealth transfers at some net cost to society as a whole. Rarely are they accessed directly to rectify market failures, and even then, unintended social costs tend to accompany such welfare-improving interventions.

Although all agents pursue the goal of expected wealth maximization, the Virginia model does not view political market equilibrium as sharing the efficiency characteristics depicted by general equilibrium theory in competitive private market situations. Important differences in the auxiliary conditions of the public choice model preclude such efficiency outcomes in the case of competitive political markets.

First, although politicians are viewed primarily as brokers rather than as purveyors of policy, they are not analyzed exclusively as price-takers in political markets. There is a role for policy, discretion, ideology, or shirking as it is variously categorized. Second, although political markets are modeled for the most part as competitive, the prices at which individual agents agree to transact are not necessarily market clearing; nor do they necessarily reflect full information, even though all agents are assumed to engage in optimal search.

In particular, expected utility-maximizing voters may choose to remain rationally ignorant with respect to the policies of competing political parties because their individual votes are perceived to lack influence over political outcomes. A number of important consequences follow from this insight.

First, expected vote-maximizing politicians, contrary to the assertion of Anthony Downs (1957), may enjoy sufficient policy discretion as to evade the dictates of median preference voters, even when the conditions of Downs otherwise hold. Second, with the political clout of the median voters thus reduced, political market opportunities open up for effective interest groups to distort political outcomes away from the median (Olson, 1965). Such interest groups purchase the support of politicians who utilize the monies so received to finance their reelection campaigns.

Third, because interest groups operate most effectively in opaque political environments, they focus on in-kind rather than on money transfer mechanisms, thereby imposing high deadweight (Marshallian) costs upon society. Fourth, because their lobbying outlays are rarely in the form of costless transfer to politicians, interest groups impose high rent-seeking (Tullock) costs on society (Tullock, 1967), typically in return for securing non-wealth-enhancing transfers from other members of society to their own members.

The concepts of 'demand' and 'supply' in this stylized model require a somewhat special interpretation (Rowley, Shughart and Tollison, 1987). 'Demand' consists of willingness to pay, whether in the currency of money transfers or of votes, by well-organized special interests, in return for wealth transfers carrying a positive net present value only to the groups concerned.

Such rent seeking is not limited to the ultimate beneficiaries of programs of wealth redistribution. The latter are joined by bureaucrats employed in the relevant departments of government, as well as by government-dependent private contractors whose budgets are enhanced by the wealth transfer programs. Indeed, the 'iron triangles' comprising the relevant congressional committee, interest group, and federal bureau form bulwarks that even the most enterprising of would-be deregulators find great difficulty in breaching.

'Supply' consists of the unwillingness or inability of those from whom wealth transfers are sought, at the margin, to protect themselves by countervailing offers of money transfer or votes to the brokering mechanism. 'Supply' of wealth transfers through the political process, for the most part, is coerced and does not constitute part of a voluntary transaction.

For the most part, too, producer groups tend to dominate consumer groups in lobbying through the political process (Olson, 1965). Wealth transfers, for this reason, tend to take the form of concentrated benefits and diffused costs, whether through the expenditure or the tax side of the budget. Future generations cannot engage in interest group lobbying. Herein lies the vulnerability of the political process to deficit financing once politicians are released from moral and institutional constraints.

Public choice thus fills the gap between economic theory and political reality in the élitist Keynesian model. It explains why politicians broker rising levels of government expenditure, why they prefer financing expenditure growth through debt rather than through taxes, why they are tempted to lower taxes even during periods of rising budget deficits, and, ultimately, why more or less continuous budget deficits are predictable counterparts to unconstrained democracy.

Of course, institutions matter, as we demonstrate in Parts II and III of Volume II. Constitutional rules and conservative institutions impact beneficially both on the size and the rate of growth of government spending and on the magnitude and duration of budget deficits. Unconstrained parliamentary democracies deliver differentially large levels of public spending and differentially large budget deficits in comparison with constitutional republics.

However, even in the constitutional republics, interest group pressures predictably overwhelm constitutional constraints and liberalize political institutions as a means of facilitating wealth transfers by breaking the balanced budget constraint. In recognizing this natural tendency, public choice restores to economic policy analysis a realism that was sacrificed by economists when they retreated from classical political economy into the narrow specialization of neoclassical economics.

The basic contributions to public choice, theoretical and empirical, are already available in comprehensive volumes in *The International Library of Critical Writings in Economics* (see e.g. Rowley, 1993, Volumes I–III; Tollison and Congleton, 1995). No attempt is made to reproduce any of these essays in this volume. Instead, Volume II, Part II, focuses attention on the impact on the public debt of such institutional features of political markets as fiscal illusion, project durability, time inconsistency, and term limits. For the most part, these institutional features are shown to exaggerate the underlying public choice bias in favor of deficit financing and to exacerbate the difficulty of moving to a balanced budget political equilibrium, even when voters are well-informed about the long-term consequences of alternative fiscal actions.

Browning (1975) developed a majority-voting model to analyze the determination of taxes and transfers in a system of 'pay-as-you-go' social insurance. By breaking down the electorate into a number of age cohorts, with incomes rising steadily over time in a growing economy, and with pensions following retirement depending only on the current social security tax rate, Browning shows, in the absence of fiscal illusion, that the young and the retired plausibly will coalesce as a majority, voting for tax rates in excess of optimal lifetime saving rates in a private system.

Majority voting predictably provides an excessively large social security system. Should voters suffer from fiscal illusion, failing to recognize that they bear the full incidence of the employers' contribution to the social security tax, the majority vote bias in favor of an excessively large social security system will be further exacerbated.

A sequence of essays (Persson and Svensson, 1989; Glazer, 1989; Alesina and Tabellini, 1990; Tabellini and Alesina, 1990) focus theoretical attention on predictable strategic behavior by governments designed to constrain the budgetary policies of their rivals once they are removed from office. In these models, strategic behavior is viewed as exaggerating the basic public choice bias in favor of persistent budget deficits. It also explains persistent deficit financing in the absence of rational voter ignorance and fiscal illusion where time-inconsistent preferences dominate political choices.

Persson and Svensson (1989) evaluate the likely behavior of a conservative government that recognizes that its liberal successor would prefer to increase public spending. Recognizing that the public spending decisions of its successor will be constrained by the level of public debt, the time-limited conservative administration may choose to incur budget deficits when otherwise they would be anathema to its supporters. This may explain, at least in part, why the Reagan administration tolerated a doubling of real debt per capita over a short eight-year period of term-limited government.

Alesina and Tabellini (1990) developed a general equilibrium model in which two ideologically motivated political parties randomly alternate in office and disagree not on the level of, but on the optimal composition of, public spending and/or on the optimal level of taxation of different constituencies. Once again, they show that strategic behavior on the part of both parties results in continuous deficit financing as the public debt becomes a choice variable in the political calculus. The equilibrium level of debt is larger, the larger the degree of polarization between alternating governments, and the less likely it is that the current government will be reelected.

In 1990, Tabellini and Alesina focus attention on the budgetary implications of the inability of current voters to pre-commit the political choices of future voters. This lack of commitment, when associated with an expected disagreement between current and future majorities, introduces another form of time inconsistency into the political system. Such time inconsistency predictably induces the current majority to choose a debt policy that would not be deemed optimal were pre-commitment feasible. For a large class of individual utility functions, deficit financing is the predictable political equilibrium.

We close our discussion of public choice and public debt with a sequence of empirical studies that do not falsify the various theories of strategic behavior outlined above. Besley and Case (1995) analyze the behavior of US governors over the period 1950 to 1986. They present evidence on the effect of term limits on state taxes and state expenditures, using data for the 48 continental US states. The evidence suggests that states led by governors who could not stand for reelection experienced greater increases in income taxes, sales taxes, and overall state per capita spending than states where term limits were not binding.

Crain and Tollison (1993) employed data for the US states over the period 1969 to 1989 to evaluate the importance of time inconsistency for policy outcomes. They determined that the greater the degree of political stability, the less is the volatility of the rate of growth of state budget imbalances, state revenues, and state expenditures as a share of state income. They concluded that frequent turnover of partisan political control leads to greater variability in state fiscal decisions.

Finally, Crain and Oakley (1995) developed an empirical model of strategic fiscal policy to analyze the substantial observed differences in the public capital stock across the US states. They detect a significant bias toward public capital projects in the absence of durability-enhancing institutions and stable political regimes. Their results strongly imply that the marginal productivity of public capital across political jurisdictions and over time depends on the interplay between existing institutional arrangements and the strategic use of expenditures on the infrastructure.

The principles of public choice outlined in this section suggest that it is naïve to model fiscal policy-makers as being guided by the goals of economic stabilization and efficient tax smoothing. Rational political actors optimize with respect to budgetary policy in terms of a political rather than an economic calculus. The political calculus, in the absence of effective constitutional constraints, systematically stimulates excessively large levels of public expenditure financed by excessively large volumes of public debt. Such outcomes are not to be blamed on the prejudice or bad judgment of particular politicians. They are more correctly to be viewed as the predictable outcomes of *politics without romance*.

IX. The Perspective of Constitutional Political Economy

Section VIII graphically outlined the vulnerability of unconstrained representative government to public choice pressures exerted against budget balance by special interests within a generalized environment of rational voter ignorance. Politicians, in search of personal wealth and future votes, are aware that public expenditure programs that provide concentrated benefits and dispersed costs are popular and that tax increases are unpopular among the more effective of their constituents. They respond to such incentives and costs by brokering budget deficits and by eliminating budget surpluses as expeditiously as possible.

The temptation for government to broker budget deficits is endemic in all democracies. Until the middle years of the twentieth century, this temptation was constrained by the prevailing social convention that budget deficits were immoral, by the classical economic doctrine that budget deficits placed unjustifiable burdens on the future generations, and by the institutional constraint imposed by the gold standard. By 1960, all such constraints had been swept aside, and politicians found themselves completely exposed to the powerful special interests that thrive on budget deficits.

Where Parliament is sovereign, there is little prospect of curtailing deficit bias, except through education. Since the public education lobby thrives on budget deficits, a serious problem of incentive-incompatibility exists, unless education is subject to private provision. In this section, therefore, we focus attention on the United States, a constitutional republic in which the people have access to constitutional constraints, should they elect to deploy them.

Specifically, by passing a balanced budget amendment (with or without a tax limitation clause) to the US Constitution, the US electorate could protect itself from the long-term economic harm inflicted by a rising burden of public debt. Indeed, had the founding fathers not taken for granted the concept of limited government, they might well have incorporated a balanced budget amendment into the original Constitution. As early as 1798, Thomas Jefferson regretted this original omission: 'I wish it were possible to obtain a single amendment to our Constitution. I would be willing to depend on that alone for the reduction of the administration of our government to the genuine principles of its Constitution. I mean an additional article, taking from the federal government the power of borrowing' (cited in Rabushka, 1982/1987, p. 213).

The founding fathers adopted two constitutional provisions and assumed a third that together restrained federal spending (Rabushka, 1982/1987, p. 216). One provision reserved powers to the states and to the people, unless expressly delegated to the federal government. The second provided for per capita distribution among the states of taxes on income. The third implicitly assumed that federal spending would not exceed federal revenues except in times of war and recession.

All three have been abrogated or eroded over the past two centuries, not least as a consequence of the Sixteenth Amendment (income tax) in 1913 and of expansive interpretations by the US Supreme Court concerning the reach of the Interstate Commerce Clause. A balanced budget amendment, therefore, would simply restore fiscal constraints originally provided by the founding fathers. Article V of the US Constitution provides two alternative routes for such greatly needed constitutional reform. Only the former of these two alternative routes has been successfully utilized in practice.

The first method requires the proposal of an amendment by two-thirds of each House of Congress, and ratification by the legislatures of three-fourths of the states. The second method requires the Congress to call a Convention for proposing an amendment, in response to an application by the legislatures of two-thirds of the states, and for the ratification, by the legislatures of three-fourths of the states, of any amendment emanating from that Convention.

Although the convention route has never been successful, this does not mean that it has been devoid of influence in shaping constitutional change. Congress has proposed amendments that ran counter to its immediate interest, in order to pre-empt the convention outcome. For example, Congress proposed the Bill of Rights (the first ten amendments) in 1789, despite the fact that these amendments limited its powers, only in response to convention petitions by Virginia and New York. Similarly, Congress proposed the Seventeenth Amendment, providing for the direct election of Senators, only to head off a convention petition from the states.

The convention threat predictably is relevant, if Congress is ever to propose a balanced budget amendment, since such an amendment would categorically diminish its fiscal authority. It is noteworthy that no Congress has yet mustered the necessary two-thirds majority in both Houses, despite the fact that some 70 per cent or more of the electorate has expressed consistent support for some such measure over the past quarter-century and beyond.

If a suitable constitutional moment should arise, the proponents of the balanced budget amendment should take counsel from public choice analysis in submitting a specific proposal to the ratification process. To be successful, they must base their proposal on a full understanding of the forces that lead to budget deficit bias. Just such insights have led Friedman (1978) and Rabushka (1982/1987) to advocate the inclusion of a tax limitation clause in any balanced budget amendment proposal.

Suppose that the federal government is required simply to balance the budget on an annual basis. Undoubtedly, the replacement of debt by taxes will rein in the tendency for government to spend excessively. It is unlikely, however, to eliminate excess spending in its entirety.

Bias remains because of the phenomenon of concentrated benefits and dispersed costs referred to above. Politicians secure electoral advantage by concentrating public expenditures on a small number of well-organized groups while dispersing the costs of such spending across the much larger and more diverse group of general taxpayers.

According to the logic of collective action (Olson, 1965), special interests systematically dominate general interests in the political process. In consequence, even well-informed taxpayers find it extremely difficult to counter the spending pressures that emanate from special interests. Herein lies the logic of attaching a tax limitation clause to any balanced budget amendment.

An effective balanced budget and tax limitation amendment to the United States Constitution might take the following general form. Congress would be required to plan to balance its budget every year by adopting a budget statement in which planned outlays do not exceed planned revenues, appropriately defined (see Section II of this essay). Congress would be free to amend this statement by a simple majority vote in each House, provided that the revised outlays do not exceed the revised receipts.

Congress would be empowered to plan for an excess of outlays over receipts for a particular budget year only when three-fifths of the entire membership of each House should deem it necessary.

Congress and the President would be required to oversee the budget process to ensure that actual outlays do not exceed planned outlays as set forth in the statement by Congress. All budget appropriations would remain subject to a potential presidential veto.

The tax limitation clause would limit the planned receipts of the federal government to some predetermined percentage of gross domestic product, for example, 19 per cent. Congress would be allowed to change this percentage in the upward direction only by a three-fifths majority of the full membership of each House and subject to a presidential veto. Changes in the downward direction would require a simple majority vote in both Houses, again subject to presidential veto.

The assertion that the US budget is now in surplus – an assertion belied by any reasonable accounting of the contingent liabilities of the federal government – does not weaken our support for imposing constitutional constraints on fiscal policy-making. Because using the 'surplus' for retiring the public debt rather than cutting taxes provides political cover for those interested in maintaining a high present value of government spending, we think that rules requiring budget balance and limiting tax increases are as important now as they would have been during the postwar deficit era.

As a first approximation, such rules should also mandate that budget surpluses be returned to the taxpayers and that decisions to 'spend' revenues in excess of current expenditures on debt retirement be subject to an affirmative congressional vote. Retiring debt, after all, transfers wealth from unwilling taxpayers to willing bondholders. While reducing the public debt does indeed reduce future tax liabilities, it also keeps the current tax burden high, and allows politicians to avoid reducing the size of government.

Skeptical readers may well respond to this proposal by asking how rational individuals, who cannot obtain sufficient support for its implementation through the ordinary political process, could possibly muster the required supra-majorities necessary for such a constitutional amendment. James Buchanan and Gordon Tullock jointly provided the answer to this important question in their seminal work on constitutional political economy, *The Calculus of Consent* (1962).

Constitutional rules, by their nature, they argued, are expected to be long-lived, since constitutional change is subject to highly inclusive rules of decision-making. The rational individual, confronting a constitutional choice, is inevitably uncertain of his particular interest at some unspecified future time. In such circumstances, he will selfishly tend to choose rules that maximize the expected utility of some random individual. Such far-sightedness in constitutional decision-making contrasts sharply with the more myopic, sectional-based approach of the rational individual in the ordinary business of politics.

In Volume II, Part III of these readings a wide range of leading contributions is presented that treat the problem of budget deficits from a constitutional perspective. Contributions range across the moral dimensions of the debate, the theoretical insights offered by constitutional political economy and the insights provided by cutting-edge empirical research that investigates the effects of actual fiscal rules and other institutional features on budgetary behavior.

Taken as a whole, these readings offer an optimistic framework for effectively eradicating the deficit bias from political markets through the mechanism of a balanced budget and tax limitation amendment to the United States Constitution. We understand the nature of the forces that produce the budget deficit bias. We comprehend the nature of the necessary constitutional solution.

What remains for effective action to be taken is the emergence of effective leadership to focus the attention of the people on a constitutional amendment that, more than any other single political intervention, would ensure that the twenty-first century would follow the twentieth as the second American century. Fortunately, effective leadership, with respect to constitutional change, is not restricted to politicians, of whatever party, whose vision is institutionally blurred by the omnipresent exigencies of politics as it is.

Acknowledgements

We owe an immeasurable debt to James M. Buchanan and Gordon Tullock, who jointly founded the Virginia School of Political Economy and thus provided us with a powerful lens through which to comprehend the nature of the public debt problem. Charles K. Rowley acknowledges the support provided by The Locke Institute and the James M. Buchanan Center for Political Economy in providing time and facilities for his work on this project. He is very grateful to his wife, Marjorie, for her continuing personal support and encouragement. William F. Shughart II acknowledges the research assistance provided by Michael Reksulak and Birsel Tavukcu and the summer financial support of the Robert M. Hearin Support Foundation. He is very grateful to his wife, Hilary, for keeping the home base warm. Robert D. Tollison acknowledges the summer financial support provided by the Robert M. Hearin Support Foundation. He is very grateful to his wife, Anna, for her continuing personal support and encouragement. The original impetus for this project was stimulated by a grant provided by the John M. Olin Foundation to the Center for Study of Public Choice at George Mason University.

Charles K. Rowley
William F. Shughart II
Robert D. Tollison

September 2002

References

Akerlof, G.A. and Yellen, J.L. (1985), 'A Near-Rational Model of the Business Cycle', *Quarterly Journal of Economics*, **100**, 823–38.

Alesina, A. (2000), 'The Political Economy of the Budget Surplus in the United States', *Journal of Economic Perspectives*, **14**, 3–19.*

Alesina, A. and Tabellini, G. (1990), 'A Positive Theory of Fiscal Deficits and Government Debt', *Review of Economic Studies*, **57**, 403–14.*

Anderson, G.M. (1986), 'The US Federal Deficit and National Debt: A Political and Economic History', in James M. Buchanan, Charles K. Rowley and Robert D. Tollison (eds), *Deficits*. Oxford: Basil Blackwell, pp. 9–46.*

Barro, R.J. (1974), 'Are Government Bonds Net Wealth?', *Journal of Political Economy*, **82**, 1095–117.*

Besley, T.J. and Case, A. (1995), 'Does Electoral Accountability Affect Economic Policy Choices? Evidence from Gubernatorial Term Limits', *Quarterly Journal of Economics*, **110**, 769–98.*

Blanchard, O.J. (1983), 'Price Asynchronization and Price Level Inertia', in R. Dorbusch and M. Simonsen (eds), *Inflation, Debt, and Indexation*. Cambridge, MA: MIT Press, pp. 3–25.

Blaug, M. (1997), *Economic Theory in Retrospect*, Fifth Edition. Cambridge: Cambridge University Press.

Blejer, M.L. and Cheasty, A. (1991), 'The Political Economy of the Budget Surplus in the United States', *Journal of Economic Literature*, **29**, 1644–78.*

Brennan, H.G. and Buchanan, J.M. (1980), 'The Logic of the Ricardian Equivalence Theorem', *Finanzarchiv*, **38**, 4–16.*

Browning, E.K. (1975), 'Why the Social Insurance Budget Is Too Large in a Democracy', *Economic Inquiry*, **13**, 373–88.*

Buchanan, J.M. (1958/1999), 'Concerning Future Generations', in H. Geoffrey Brennan, Hartmut Kliemt and Robert D. Tollison (eds), *Public Principles of Public Debt: A Defense and Restatement. The Collected Works of James M. Buchanan, Volume 2*. Indianapolis, IN: Liberty Fund, pp. 26–37.*

Buchanan, J.M. (1964), 'Public Debt, Cost Theory, and the Fiscal Illusion', in James M. Ferguson (ed.), *Public Debt and Future Generations*. Chapel Hill, NC: University of North Carolina press, pp. 150–63.*

Buchanan, J.M. (1969), *Cost and Choice*. Chicago: Markham Publishing Company.
Buchanan, J.M. (1976), 'Barro on the Ricardian Equivalence Theorem', *Journal of Political Economy*, **84**, 337–42.*
Buchanan, J.M., Rowley, C.K. and Tollison, R.D. (eds) (1987). *Deficits*, Oxford: Basil Blackwell.
Buchanan, J.M. and Tullock, G. (1962), *The Calculus of Consent: Logical Foundations of Constitutional Democracy*. Ann Arbor, MI: University of Michigan Press.
Buchanan, J.M. and Wagner, R.E. (1977), *Democracy in Deficit: The Political Legacy of Lord Keynes*. New York: Academic Press.
Coates, A.W. (1971), 'Editor's Introduction', in *The Classical Economists and Economic Policy*. London: Methuen & Co.
Colander, D. (1984), 'Was Keynes a Keynesian or a Lernerian?', *Journal of Economic Literature*, **22**, 1572–5.
Crain, W.M. and Oakley, L.K. (1995), 'The Politics of Infrastructure', *Journal of Law and Economics*, **38**, 1–17.*
Crain, W.M. and Tollison, R.D. (1993), 'Time Inconsistency and Fiscal Policy: Empirical Analysis of US States, 1969–89', *Journal of Public Economics*, **51**, 153–9.*
Downs, A. (1957), *An Economic Theory of Democracy*. New York: Harper and Row.
Eisner, R. (1986), *How Real is the Federal Deficit?* New York: The Free Press.
Eisner, R. and Pieper, P.J. (1984), 'A New View of the Federal Debt and Budget Deficits', *American Economic Review*, **74**, 11–29.
Evans, P. (1993), 'Consumers are Not Ricardian: Evidence from Nineteen Countries', *Economic Inquiry*, **31**, 534–48.*
Feldstein, M. (1976), 'Perceived Wealth in Bonds and Social Security: A Comment', *Journal of Political Economy*, **84** (2), 331–6.*
Fischer, S. (1977), 'Long-Term Contracts, Rational Expectations, and the Optimal Money-Supply Rule', *Journal of Political Economy*, **85**, 191–205.
Fleming, J.M. (1962), 'Domestic Financial Policies Under Fixed and Under Floating Exchange Rates', *International Monetary Fund Staff Papers*, **ix**, 369–80.
Friedman, M. (1968), 'The Role of Monetary Policy', *American Economic Review*, **58**, 1–17.
Friedman, M. (1970), 'A Theoretical Framework for Monetary Analysis', *Journal of Political Economy*, **78**, 193–238.
Friedman, M. (1971), 'A Monetary Theory of Nominal Income', *Journal of Political Economy*, **79**, 323–37.
Friedman, M. (1978), 'The Limitations of Tax Limitations', *Policy Review*, **5**, 7–14.*
Friedman, M. and Schwartz, A.J. (1963), *A Monetary History of the United States, 1867–1960*. Princeton, NJ: Princeton University Press.
Glazer, A. (1989), 'Politics and the Choice of Durability', *American Economic Review*, **79**, 1207–13.*
Gramlich, E.M. (1989), 'Budget Deficits and National Saving: Are Politicians Exogenous?', *Journal of Economic Perspectives*, **3**, 73–93.
Hansen, A. (1953), *A Guide to Keynes*. New York: McGraw-Hill.
Hayek, F.A. (1931), *Prices and Production*. New York: Augustus M. Kelley.
Hicks, J.R. (1935), 'A Suggestion for Simplifying the Theory of Money', *Economica*, **2**, 1–19.
Hicks, J.R. (1937), 'Mr Keynes and the Classics: A Suggested Interpretation', *Econometrica*, **5**, 147–59.
Keynes, J.M. (1936), 'The Marginal Propensity to Consume and the Multiplier', in *The General Theory of Employment, Interest and Money*, Book III, Chapter 10. New York: Harcourt, Brace and World, pp. 113–31.*
King, R.G. and Plosser, C.I. (1984), 'Money, Credit, and Prices in a Real Business Cycle', *American Economic Review*, **74**, 363–80.
Kotlikoff, L.J. and Raffelhüschen, B. (1999), 'Generational Accounting around the Globe', *American Economic Review Papers and Proceedings*, **89**, 161–6.*
Kydland, F.E. and Prescott, E.C. (1982), 'Time to Build and Aggregate Fluctuations', *Econometrica*, **50**, 1345–70.
Kydland, F.E. and Prescott, E.C. (1990), 'Business Cycles: Real Facts and a Monetary Myth', *Quarterly*

Review (Federal Reserve Bank of Minneapolis), **14**, 3-18.

Lerner, A.P. (1943), 'Functional Finance and the Federal Deficit', *Social Research*, **10**, 38-51.*

Lerner, A.P. (1948), 'The Burden of the National Debt', in Lloyd Metzler *et al.* (eds), *Income, Employment, and Public Policy: Essays in Honor of Alvin Hansen*. New York: Norton, pp. 255-75.*

Lerner, A.P. (1961), 'The Burden of Debt', *Review of Economics and Statistics*, **43**, 139-41.*

Lipford, J.W. (2001), 'How Transparent is the U.S. Budget?', *Independent Review*, **5**, 575-91.*

Lucas, R.E. (1972), 'Expectations and the Neutrality of Money', *Journal of Economic Theory*, **4**, 103-24.

Lucas, R.E. (1976), 'Econometric Policy Evaluation: A Critique', *Journal of Monetary Economics*, **1**, 19-46.

Malthus, T.R. (1798/1951), Principles of Political Economy, Considered with a View to their Practical Application, 2nd ed. New York: Augustus M. Kelly.

Malthus, T.R. (1803/1992), 'Of Poor-Laws continued', in *An Essay on the Principle of Population; or A View of its Past and Present Effects on Human Happiness; with an Inquiry into our Prospects Respecting the Future Removal or Mitigation of the Evils which it Occasions*, Book III, Chapter VII, Cambridge: Cambridge University Press, pp. 110-23.*

Mankiw, N.G. (1985), 'Small Menu Costs and Large Business Cycles: A Macroeconomic Model of Monopoly', *Quarterly Journal of Economics*, **100**, 529-37.

Meade, J.E. (1958), 'Is the National Debt a Burden?', *Oxford Economic Papers*, **10**, 163-83.*

Mill, J.S. (1848/1973), 'Of a National Debt', in Sir William Ashley (ed.), *Principles of Political Economy with Some of Their Applications to Social Philosophy*, Book V, Chapter VII. Clifton, NJ: Augustus M. Kelley, pp. 873-80.*

Mises, L. von (1947/1960), 'Lord Keynes and Say's Law', in Henry Hazlitt (ed.), *The Critics of Keynesian Economics*. Princeton, NJ: Van Nostrand, pp. 315-21.

Mises, L. von (1948/1960), 'Stones into Bread: The Keynesian Miracle', in Henry Hazlitt (ed.), *The Critics of Keynesian Economics*. Princeton, NJ: Van Nostrand, pp. 305-15.

Modigliani, F. (1961), 'Long-Run Implications of Alternative Fiscal Policies and the Burden of the National Debt', *Economic Journal*, **71**, 730-55.

Mundell, R.A. (1968), *International Economics*. New York: Macmillan.

Musgrave, R.A. (1959), 'Classical Theory of Debt', in *The Theory of Public Finance: A Study in Public Economy*, Chapter 23. New York: McGraw-Hill, pp. 556-80.*

Muth, J. (1961), 'Rational Expectations and the Theory of Price Movements', *Journal of the American Statistical Society*, **55**, 315-34.

O'Driscoll, G.P. Jr. (1977), 'The Ricardian Nonequivalence Theorem', *Journal of Political Economy*, **85**, 207-10.*

Olson, M. (1965), *The Logic of Collective Action: Public Goods and the Theory of Groups*. Cambridge, MA: Harvard University Press.

Parkin, M. (1984), *Macroeconomics*. Englewood Cliffs, NJ: Prentice-Hall, Inc.

Patinkin, D. (1965), *Money, Interest, and Prices*, Second Edition. New York: Harper & Row.

Persson, T. and Svensson, L.E.O. (1989), 'Why a Stubborn Conservative Would Run a Deficit Policy with Time-Inconsistent Preferences', *Quarterly Journal of Economics*, **104**, 325-45.*

Phelps, E.S. (1990), *Seven Schools of Macroeconomic Thought*. Oxford: Clarendon Press.

Phelps, E.S. and Taylor, J.B. (1977), 'Stabilizing Powers of Monetary Policy under Rational Expectations', *Journal of Political Economy*, **85**, 163-90.

Prescott, E.C. (1986), 'Theory Ahead of Business-Cycle Measurement', *Carnegie-Rochester Conference Series on Public Policy*, **25**, 11-44.

Rabushka, A. (1982/1987), 'A Compelling Case for a Constitutional Amendment to Balance the Budget and Limit Taxes', in Richard H. Fink and Jack C. High (eds), *A Nation in Debt: Economists Debate the Federal Budget Deficit*. Frederick, MD: University Publications of America, pp. 212-30.*

Ricardo, D. (1820/1951), 'Funding System, 1820', in Piero Sraffa (ed.) with M.H. Dobb, *Pamphlets and Papers, 1815-1823, The Works and Correspondence of David Ricardo*, Volume IV. Cambridge: Cambridge University Press, pp. 143-200.

Ricardo, D. (1821/1951), 'Taxes on Other Commodities than Raw Produce', in Piero Sraffa (ed.) with M.H. Dobb, *On the Principles of Political Economy and Taxation. The Works and Correspondence* *of David Ricardo*, Third Edition, Volume I, Chapter XVII. Cambridge: Cambridge University Press, pp. 243–56.*

Robbins, L. (1934), *The Great Depression*. London: Macmillan.

Rosen, H.S. (1995), *Public Finance*, Fourth Edition, Chapter 19. Boston, MA: Irwin.

Rowley, C.K. (1987a), 'Classical Political Economy and the Debt Issue', in James M. Buchanan, Charles K. Rowley and Robert D. Tollison (eds), *Deficits*. Oxford: Basil Blackwell, pp. 49–74.

Rowley, C.K. (1987b), 'The Legacy of Keynes: From the General Theory to Generalized Budget Deficits', in James M. Buchanan, Charles K. Rowley and Robert D. Tollison (eds), *Deficits*. Oxford: Basil Blackwell, pp. 143–72.

Rowley, C.K. (1993), *Readings in Public Choice Theory*, Volumes I–III. Aldershot: Edward Elgar Publishing.

Rowley, C.K. (2000), 'Budget Deficits and the Size of Government in the UK and US: A Public Choice Perspective on the Thatcher and Reagan Years', in K. Alec Chrystal and Rubert Pennant-Rea (eds), *Public Choice Analysis of Economic Policy*. London: Macmillan, and New York: St Martin's Press.*

Rowley, C.K., Shughart, W.F. II and Tollison, R.D. (1987), 'Interest Groups and Deficits', in James M. Buchanan, Charles K. Rowley and Robert D. Tollison (eds), *Deficits*. Oxford: Basil Blackwell, pp. 263–80.

Samuelson, P.A. (1948), 'Fiscal Policy and Full Employment without Inflation', in *Economics: An Introductory Analysis*, First Edition, Chapter 18. New York: McGraw-Hill, pp. 409–43.*

Samuelson, P.A. (1970), 'Fiscal Policy and Full Employment without Inflation', in *Economics*, Chapter 19, Eighth Edition. New York: McGraw-Hill, pp. 330–53.*

Samuelson, P.A. and Solow, R.M. (1960), 'Analytical Aspects of Anti-Inflation Policy', *American Economic Review*, **70**, 177–94.

Sargent, T. (1973), 'Rational Expectations, the Real Rate of Interest, and the Natural Rate of Unemployment', *Brookings Papers on Economic Activity*, Volume 2. Washington, DC: Brookings, pp. 429–72.

Scitovsky, T. (1984), 'Lerner's Contribution to Economics', *Journal of Economic Literature*, **22**, 1547–71.

Smith, A. (1776/1976), 'Of Publick Debts', in R.H. Campbell, A.S. Skinner and W.B. Todd (eds), *An Inquiry into the Nature and Causes of the Wealth of Nations. Glasgow Edition of the Works and Correspondence of Adam Smith*, Volume II, Book V, Chapter III. Oxford: Clarendon Press, pp. 907–47.*

Stanley, T.D. (1998), 'New Wine in Old Bottles: A Meta-Analysis of Ricardian Equivalence', *Southern Economic Journal*, **64**, 713–27.*

Tabellini, G. and Alesina, A. (1990), 'Voting on the Budget Deficit', *American Economic Review*, **80**, 37–49.*

Taylor, J.B. (1979), 'Estimation and Control of a Macroeconomic Model with Rational Expectations', *Econometrica*, **47**, 1267–86.

Tobin, J. (1965), 'The Burden of the Public Debt: A Review Article', *Journal of Finance*, **20**, 679–82.*

Tobin, J. (1980), *Asset Accumulation and Economic Activity*, Chicago: University Press.

Tollison, R.D. and Congleton, R.D. (1995), *The Economic Analysis of Rent Seeking*; Aldershot: Edward Elgar Publishing.

Tullock, G. (1967), 'The Welfare Costs of Tariffs, Monopolies and Theft', *Western Economic Journal*, **9**, 379–92.

* Indicates that the essay is included in *The Economics of Budget Deficits*.

Part I
The History and Measurement of Budget Deficits

Part I: An Overview

The essays in this introductory section place government fiscal policy in an appropriate historical perspective. They also identify myriad problems encountered in assessing the relationship between public expenditures and receipts.

Any determination that the public budget is or is not 'in the red' turns out to beg a host of questions concerning the proper treatment of such matters as the financing of capital projects that contribute to an economy's infrastructure and to the national defense, the future obligations accrued by social insurance and pension programs, the budgets of state-owned enterprises, the balance sheets of government loan programs, the values of publicly owned lands and mineral rights, and many other public sector activities, both off-budget and on. Because governments generally do not follow standard accounting practices and procedures utilized in the private sector, the magnitude of the net balance of the public budget (and even its algebraic sign) is a matter of considerable scholarly controversy. Because accounting conventions differ widely across nations, as do the sizes and scopes of those nations' respective public sectors, cross-country comparisons of fiscal stance turn out to be even more problematic.

Whether measured as the simple difference between current revenues and current outlays, or adjusted to include the present values of the public sector's most significant future obligations, it seems clear that the last 40 years of the twentieth century were a unique period in the history of public finance. Prior to 1961, budget balance, for the most part, was the norm throughout much of the industrialized world. Deficit spending typically was confined to periods of 'hard necessity' produced by wartime emergencies and severe economic contractions, and the debt accumulated during those episodes was quickly retired once such crises ended.

For reasons not yet fully understood, that pattern was broken in the post-1960 era. In the United States, for example, the federal budget moved into systematic deficit from 1961 (with one year of respite in 1969) until 1998. From 1970, the annual budget deficits assumed significant magnitudes. After 1980, the inflation tax was no longer sufficient to prevent major annual increases in the real value of the per capita federal debt.

The proximate cause of persistent US budget deficits was a massive growth in so-called entitlement programs, especially Medicare and Medicaid, established to help pay the health care bills of elderly and poor Americans. Such programs, which are open-ended in the sense of providing benefits to all individuals who meet defined eligibility criteria, ensured that spending would rise continuously with growth in the populations of qualified recipients, even in the absence of any increase in benefit levels or of any relaxation of eligibility requirements.

In 1974 changes in federal budgeting procedures designed to give greater weight to the preferences of congressional subcommittees – changes imposed by Congress on a Watergate-weakened executive branch – may also have played a role in shifting the balance in favor of deficit finance. But a fundamental question remains to be answered: why did government by red ink dominate the fiscal landscape throughout the period 1961 to 1998?

No doubt, the fault lies, in part, with John Maynard Keynes, who supplied a theoretical rationale for activist, counter-cyclical fiscal policies, judged not by their effects on budget balance, but by their effects on restoring balance to the national economy. However, if the fault lies with Keynes, why did it take so long for the Keynesian bias to become political reality? Might not the transmission mechanism have been Paul Samuelson's translation of Keynesian economics into a widely used undergraduate textbook that became the Bible of the economics establishment, at least in the United States?

In any case, deficits appear to have afflicted all governments in the modern period, democratic and despotic alike. Where autocracy takes the form of the roving rather than the stationary bandit (as in much of sub-Saharan Africa), it is entirely understandable that there will be little regard for the future. It is much more difficult, however, at least by reference to neoclassical economics, to explain such a high rate of time preference under conditions of representative democracy or constitutional republicanism.

The principles of public choice become relevant in sketching out a convincing explanation. In the public choice model, the vote motives of rationally self-interested politicians, who serve limited terms of office and who consequently have short time horizons, combine with rational voter ignorance to provide incentives for shifting the burden of financing government to future generations. A bias toward budget deficits is the logical outcome of an imbalance between the political benefits associated with increased spending in important electoral constituencies and the political costs of raising current taxes to finance those benefits.

Reinforced by budgetary institutions that regard public revenues as a common pool resource, and by budgetary processes that lack transparency, voters systematically overestimate the benefits (and underestimate the costs) of government – misperceptions that politicians exploit for their own gain. Even if such fiscal illusion does not fully explain such political bias, voters must overcome a daunting free-rider problem in order to constrain the deficit spending proclivities of their political representatives.

As a consequence of relatively high rates of per capita economic growth throughout the decade of the 1990s, the United States ostensibly entered into a period of anticipated federal budget surpluses at the dawning of the twenty-first century. Yet, any realistic accounting of the contingent liabilities of the US government suggests that this surplus is simply a current accounting mirage created by a temporarily favorable conjunction between current social security tax receipts and current benefit payments. Of course, the government can renege on its implied commitments to aging 'baby boomers' (and predictably will do so if the fiscal climate worsens). If future fiscal obligations are taken seriously, however, the US federal budget clearly remains in deficit in terms of present value calculations.

Yet even as this overview is being written, heated arguments are under way as legislation is being written with respect to the disposition of the federal fiscal 'surplus'. In the absence of widely endorsed rules or guidelines, the debate is fraught with the usual heavy dose of politicization of policy. Those who favor statist policies resist even modest, 'back-loaded' tax cuts and argue in favor of debt reduction as a way of maintaining a high present value of government spending. Those who favor anti-statist policies insist on tax cuts as a way of reducing the future size of government by starving it of revenue. This debate, pitting those who want to 'save social security first' against others contending that surpluses are evidence of a higher than warranted tax burden, some of which ought to be returned to the taxpayers, illustrates that the discussion of the appropriate size and scope of the public sector can be divorced neither from a discussion of the merits or demerits of budget balance nor from the methodology of its calculation.

Charles K. Rowley
William F. Shughart II
Robert D. Tollison

[1]

The US Federal Deficit and National Debt: a Political and Economic History

GARY M. ANDERSON

2.1 Introduction

The balancing of revenues and expenditures is rightly deemed to be of the essence of a budget. In this way only can the relationship between the two sides of the national accounts be established, and the effect of the action had, or proposed, upon the financial situation of the government be made known. (Willoughby 1927, p. 6)

Prior to the end of the Second World War there was no 'deficit problem'. The federal budget was normally in balance. While deficits frequently occurred, they were invariably the result of unforeseen revenue shortfalls occurring during depressions, recessions, or wartime emergency. Following the end of any of these circumstances, expenditures were rapidly brought into line with revenues. It rarely occurred to policymakers or academic economists to even consider peacetime deficits as a policy option. When writers and politicians discussed budgetary balance, they usually argued over what degree of *overbalance* was appropriate; peacetime budgets were ordinarily substantially in surplus. Surpluses were used to retire the national debt, and the speed of such retirement, and consequently the economic effects of surpluses, were a frequent cause of controversy. In fact, in the last quarter of the nineteenth century there arose what was widely perceived to be a 'surplus problem' – persistent high surpluses were criticized as representing irresponsible fiscal policy, and particularly as generating an excessive growth in government spending (curiously mirroring the concerns of modern critics of persistent *deficits*).

It is clear throughout the history of the United States that the concept of balanced budgets and steady reduction in the real debt had a stable majority constituency. This remained true even after the rise of persistent high deficits in the 1970s. The deficit problem did not emerge because balanced budgets lost favour with voters and taxpayers, but many deficits have been the unintended side effect of other developments concerning the composition of federal outlays and internal changes in the process of budgetary decisionmaking in Congress. The purpose of the present paper is to present the history of both the federal deficit and the national debt in the context of public and political opinion and action, and to demonstrate the high degree of consistency among these variables until quite recently.

With these intentions in mind, the present paper is divided into seven sections. Section 2.2 outlines the history of federal deficits and surpluses since 1789 and summarizes the history of the debt over the same period. Section 2.3 examines the rhetoric and reality of political policy regarding balanced budgets and the national debt from the founding of the United States to the election of Franklin Roosevelt. Secton 2.4 outlines and critically evaluates the notion of the 'fiscal revolution' in the USA following the election of Franklin Roosevelt, and assesses the significance of this development in explaining the emergence of the modern deficit problem. Section 2.5 considers the changing composition of federal outlays in the period following 1965 and the significance of these developments on the federal deficit and national debt. The final section concludes by summarizing the main argument.

2.2   A Simple History of Deficits and the Debt

The Federal government has actually operated under a budget in the strict sense since the passage of the Budget and Accounting Act on 10 June 1921. The act gave the President the authority to prepare and submit a budget to Congress each year. However, the idea of a federal budget was 'clearly in the minds of leading political and financial leaders as early as the revolutionary and formative periods' although unfortunately there was an 'absence of logical or systematic budget methods . . . throughout the nineteenth century' (Kimmel 1958, p. 2). Consequently, achieving a precise balance between revenues and expenditures in any given year was highly improbable, assuming that this was a policy goal.[1] But although the tools available to fiscal policymakers may have been cumbersome and imprecise compared with their modern analogues, the record which emerges is extremely consistent.

Between 1789 and 1799 there were five periods of surplus and four of deficit (1789–91 was a single 'fiscal year'). This early period was fiscally unsettled, as the new government began operations and gradually became organized, but even so there was a greater tendency towards surplus than towards deficit.[2]

US Federal Deficit and National Debt   **11**

Table 2.1 Federal surpluses on deficits as a percentage of total outlays, 1789–1899

1789–91: +3.51			
1792: −27.75	1819: +14.62	1846: +6.96	1873: +14.94
1793: +3.81	1820: −2.08	1847: −53.74	1874: +0.77
1794: −22.30	1821: −7.82	1848: −21.12	1875: +4.87
1795: −18.89	1822: +34.88	1849: −30.72	1876: +10.93
1796: +46.28	1823: +39.66	1850: +10.26	1877: +16.60
1797: +41.65	1824: −4.64	1851: +10.16	1878: +8.77
1798: +2.91	1825: +37.73	1852: +12.78	1879: +2.57
1799: −2.19	1826: +48.13	1853: +27.81	1880: +24.61
1800: +0.58	1827: +42.30	1854: +27.14	1881: +38.38
1801: +37.69	1828: +51.26	1855: +9.38	1882: +56.41
1802: +90.74	1829: +63.30	1856: +6.44	1883: +50.06
1803: +40.90	1830: +64.06	1857: +1.72	1884: +42.76
1804: +35.63	1831: +87.08	1858: −37.09	1885: +24.38
1805: +29.06	1832: +84.08	1859: −22.56	1886: +38.74
1806: +58.71	1833: +47.48	1860: −11.19	1887: +38.61
1807: +96.28	1834: +16.98	1861: −37.62	1888: +41.55
1808: +71.76	1835: +101.61	1862: −89.04	1889: +29.32
1809: −24.38	1836: +64.65	1863: −84.23	1890: +26.73
1810: +15.05	1837: −32.99	1864: −69.41	1891: +7.33
1811: +78.98	1838: −22.32	1865: −74.28	1892: +2.87
1812: −51.67	1839: +17.04	1866: +7.14	1893: +0.61
1813: −54.73	1840: −19.89	1867: +37.22	1894: −16.64
1814: −67.79	1841: −36.53	1868: +7.49	1895: −8.83
1815: −51.91	1842: −20.74	1869: +14.89	1896: −3.98
1816: +55.87	1843: −29.97	1870: +32.81	1897: −4.93
1817: +51.52	1844: +30.26	1871: +31.19	1898: −8.58
1818: +8.87	1845: +30.66	1872: +34.80	1899: −14.72

Source: Historical Statistics . . . , v.2; p.1104; and additional calculations.

The history of the federal deficit over the period 1800–1900 is easy to summarize because it is so uniform. Over that period there were revenue surpluses in 69 of the 101 years. Fifteen of the 32 years of deficit occurred during the four major wars fought by the United States during the period. The remaining 17 years of deficit occurred during years of depression or recession, or as the consequence of financial panics, in addition to the difficulties of precisely estimating either spending or revenues in the pre-budget period.[3] Table 2.1 shows federal deficits and surpluses for the period 1789–1900 as annual averages of the percentage of federal expenditures. The federal government was ordinarily in surplus during peacetime, and surplus was typically large in proportion to total spending. Large deficits (relative to total outlays) were run during each of the four major wars which occurred in this period (the War of 1812, the Mexican War, the Civil War, and the Spanish-American War), but these episodes were both preceded and succeeded by periods of significant surplus. In every case but one both the five-year period before and the five-year period following the war had shown a net surplus.[4] In every case the wartime deficits were followed by a large five-year net surplus. Following the Civil War, every year from 1866 to 1893 showed a surplus; surpluses over the period 1880–90 averaged about 37 per cent of expenditures per annum.

The record for the period 1901–30 is essentially more of the same. Between 1901 and 1916 there were 8 years of deficit, corresponding to the recessions of 1904, 1908, and 1912 (with the downturn of 1908 being especially severe).[5] However, these deficits were quite small as a percentage of total federal expenditures. Large deficits recurred during the First World War, consistent with previous American experience. Immediately following the war, surpluses returned – every year between 1920 and 1930 found the budget substantially in surplus.[6] The period 1931–46 produced an unbroken string of budget deficits. Those in the sub-period 1931–39 occurred during the Great Depression, and those in the sub-period 1940–46 occurred during (and in the military build-up preceding) the Second World War.

Following the traditional American pattern, there was a substantial budget surplus in the first year following demobilization after the Second World War. Eight of the 24 years between 1947 and 1970 showed surpluses, the remainder showed deficits. The average deficit for the 1946–70 period was 0.28 per cent of total spending. Post-war deficits also were generally quite small as a percentage of total spending; the average deficit for the period 1947–70 was only 5.35 per cent.

Since 1971 the federal deficit has begun to approach Depression levels as a percentage of total spending. The 1983 net budget deficit as a percentage of total spending (25.70 per cent) was the highest annual deficit since 1946, and it was significantly higher than two Depression era deficits (1931, 12.91 per cent; and 1938, 17.39 per cent). The record of federal surpluses and deficits since 1901 is summarized in table 2.2.

Table 2.2 shows the history of the US national debt from 1900–84 in the form of average annual debt. Between 1789 and 1811 the large debt which had accumulated as a result of the Revolutionary War was gradually retired. But by the end of the War of 1812, the debt had again increased from $45 million to over $127 million. Once again, a rigorous and steady programme of debt retirement reduced this figure, until in 1834 the federal debt was only $38,000.[7] In consequence of a string of budget deficits associated with the panic of 1837 and its aftermath, the debt increased to $15 million in 1846, rising to $63 million in 1846 as a result of the Mexican War.

The most radical war-related increase in the national debt occurred during the Civil War. The nominal average annual debt during 1861–5 was over 22 times that of 1856–60. The Civil War produced both exceptionally

US Federal Deficit and National Debt   13

Table 2.2 Federal surpluses on deficits as a percentage of total outlays, 1900–84

1900: +8.91	1922: +22.38	1944: −52.08	1966: −2.74
1901: +12.02	1923: +22.68	1945: −51.29	1967: −5.48
1902: +15.91	1924: +33.12	1946: −28.85	1968: −14.12
1903: +8.67	1925: +24.52	1947: +11.64	1969: +1.76
1904: −7.29	1926: +29.53	1948: +39.63	1970: −1.45
1905: −4.05	1927: +40.43	1949: +1.49	1971: −10.96
1906: +4.34	1928: +31.71	1950: −7.32	1972: −10.13
1907: +14.97	1929: +23.48	1951: +13.40	1973: −6.06
1908: −8.69	1930: +22.21	1952: −2.24	1974: −2.27
1909: −12.88	1931: −12.91	1953: −8.53	1975: −16.02
1910: −2.61	1932: −58.70	1954: −1.62	1976: −19.82
1911: +1.53	1933: −56.57	1955: −4.37	1977: −13.10
1912: +0.39	1934: −54.62	1956: +5.58	1978: −12.85
1913: −0.05	1935: −42.95	1957: +4.45	1979: −7.97
1914: −0.05	1936: −52.53	1958: −3.36	1980: −12.49
1915: −8.40	1937: −35.91	1959: −13.95	1981: −11.63
1916: +6.79	1938: −17.39	1960: +0.32	1982: −17.15
1917: −43.64	1939: −43.68	1961: −3.41	1983: −25.70
1918: −71.24	1940: −30.84	1962: −6.68	1984: −21.75
1919: −72.65	1941: −36.18	1963: −4.27	
1920: +4.58	1942: −58.65	1964: −4.99	
1921: +10.05	1943: −69.44	1965: −1.19	

Source: Historical Statistics . . . , v.2; p.1104; and additional calculations.

large deficits and an enormously expanded public debt.[8] But after reaching a high of $2.75 billion in 1866, the nominal debt was gradually but quite steadily reduced.[9]

From after the Civil War until the First World War, the federal debt generally fell both in nominal terms and as a percentage of GNP. From 1916 to 1919 it rose rapidly, again both in nominal and real terms. From 1919 to 1929 it again fell fairly consistently as a percentage of GNP, although the nominal debt was only slightly reduced at the end of the period. Still, as a percentage of GNP the federal debt fell by about 40 per cent over this period as the wartime debt was serviced and gradually retired.

The roller-coaster ride of the federal debt began in 1930, when gross debt as a percentage of GNP increased to 17.8 per cent. It proceeded to increase quite steadily over the course of the Great Depression until one year after the end of the Second World War, when it reached an incredible 134.2 per cent of GNP. Thereafter, debt as a proportion of GNP proceeded to drop consistently. In 1950, it fell to 96.9; 1960, 58.4; 1970, 39.5; and in 1980, 35.5. At the same time, the gross federal debt consistently rose in nominal terms, after falling from $241 billion in 1946 to $214 billion in 1949 (and following a blip in 1950, when it rose to $219 before falling to

Table 2.3 The federal debt, 1792–1984 (selected years)

	Total gross federal debt (billions)	Gross federal debt (% GNP)
1792	0.080	
1800	0.083	
1810	0.048	
1815	0.127	
1820	0.089	
1830	0.039	
1835	0.00038	
1840	0.005	
1850	0.063	
1860	0.064	
1865	2.677	
1870	2.436	
1880	2.090	
1890	1.122	8.5%
1900	1.263	6.7%
1910	1.146	3.2%
1915	1.191	2.9%
1920	24.299	26.5%
1929	16.931	16.4%
1930	16.185	17.8%
1940	50.639	53.4%
1945	260.123	119.9%
1950	256.853	97.9%
1955	274.366	72.1%
1960	290.862	58.4%
1965	323.154	49.0%
1970	382.603	39.5%
1975	544.131	36.8%
1976	631.866	38.5%
1977	709.138	38.1%
1978	780.425	37.3%
1979	83.751	35.4%
1980	914.317	35.5%
1981	1003.941	34.8%
1982	1146.987	37.7%
1983	1381.886	42.9%
1984	1576.748	44.0%

Source: Historical Statistics . . . , v.1, p. 224; and v.2, p.1104 for 1792 to 1939; and *Historical Tables . . .* , Table 1–1 for 1940–1984.

$214 billion in 1951). In 1952, the gross federal debt was $214 billion; by 1980 it had reached $914 billion. But despite this huge nominal increase, this figure reflects a *fall* of 40.9 per cent in relation to GNP.

Coincidentally, the downward trend in the federal debt as a percentage of GNP which had begun after the Second World War ceased in the same year that the nominal debt broke the $1 trillion mark, 1981. Since 1981 the gross federal debt as a percentage of GNP has risen rapidly, until it reached the highest level since 1968 in 1984. The history of the federal debt since 1792 is described in table 2.3.

2.3 Fiscal Discipline and the Politicians, 1789–1932

Have the publicly professed positions, rhetoric, and policy recommendations regarding balanced budgets and the national debt changed over the course of US history? Obviously, tracing the opinions and policy positions of all important federal government politicians for the past two centuries would be a daunting, if not impossible, task. In the present paper, I have chosen to approach the question using a convenient proxy: the publicly professed policy positions of Presidents of the United States.

Several reasons appear to justify this choice. The President is the only elected official who has been elected by a majority of voters across the nation as a whole. His policy commitments can be taken to reflect, albeit imperfectly, the expressed electoral preferences of a majority of Americans. The policy positions of Presidents on virtually all important issues are well documented and readily accessible. Questions involving the federal 'budget' (using that term loosely for reasons previously noted) and national debt have always been national rather than regional issues, while members of Congress have tended to specialize in more regional issues of concern to their constituencies. Other federal decisionmakers have rarely had the inclination or the occasion to articulate positions on questions of balanced budgets or the debt in any detail.

A few things need to be said about public opinion poll results before proceeding. Simply stated, public opinion polls since 1936 have consistently found that large majorities favour balanced budgets as a fundamental feature of federal policy. Polls during the Great Depression showed that reducing the (historically) large budget deficits of the period was a significant public concern (see Gallup 1972, vol. 1, p. 47). Balanced budgets continued to be a major public concern after the Second World War and during the 1950s, when the deficits that did occur were very small, both as a percentage of total federal outlays and as a percentage of GNP (see Gallup 1972, vol. 2, p. 1165). Concern over deficits and support for balanced budgets

16   *G. M. Anderson*

remained very strong during the seventies and continues to do so, according
to the most recent polling results available.[10]

Following the War of Independence, the new federal government faced
a large national debt due primarily to war-related expenses.[11] For the period
1789–97 interest payments on the debt actually accounted for more than
half of total federal expenditures (Kimmel 1958, p. 10). The administrations
of both George Washington (1789–97) and John Adams (1797–1801) were
strongly committed to prompt debt reduction and approximate balance
between revenues and expenditures (ibid., pp. 11–12). However, the debt
actually increased slightly over this period and the 'approximate balance'
was indeed approximate – deficits over the period exceeded surpluses by
about 36 per cent. However, government spending was exceedingly low in
real terms over this period as well.[12]

The tone of political rhetoric regarding both budget deficits and the
national debt was set by President Thomas Jefferson in the early nineteenth
century, and did not radically change for the remainder of the century.
Balanced budgets were considered a necessary mark of fiscal responsibility,
and public debt a burden, the discharge of which was of the highest priority.
Perhaps Jefferson's strongest public statement on the subject of the national
debt was in his second annual message, delivered on 15 December 1802,
in which he expressed satisfaction concerning the 'large and effectual
payments toward the discharge of our public debt and the emancipation of
our posterity from that mortal cancer' (quoted in Kimmel 1958, p. 14).[13]

The Presidents who followed Jefferson before the Civil War all favoured
a balanced peacetime budget and all were publicly committed to steadily
reducing and promptly eliminating the national debt. The stated rationale
for such a policy was threefold: first, the moral requirements of responsible
fiscal policy; second, the belief that reduction of the federal debt was a
requirement for maintaining a strong federal credit; and third, that reducing
the debt would make public revenues available for other purposes.[14]

These various Presidents expressed opinions that evidently had widespread support in Congress and among academics and the general public.
A general consensus existed to the effect that a low level of public expenditures was desirable, the federal budget should be balanced in peacetime,
and the federal debt ought to be speedily extinguished.[15]

The Civil War provided the major exception to both the rhetoric and
practice of balanced budgets and determined debt reduction during the
nineteenth century. As one author claims, '[the] Civil War revolutionized
the financial methods of the United States' (Kimmel 1958, p. 64). A national
banking system was established in February 1863, largely to afford a ready
outlet for the sale of government bonds. A tax of 10 per cent per annum
on the value of state bank notes was imposed, effectively establishing US
notes as monopoly medium of exchange. An income tax was imposed, tariffs

were increased, relatively large deficits were run and a large national debt was accumulated.[16]

The latter two developments were typical of US wartime fiscal practice during earlier wars (although the relative magnitudes of each were much greater as was the intensity and length of the war considerably greater). What *was* unprecedented was that the President of the United States was on public record as believing that neither deficits nor the national debt constituted a serious problem. In fact, Lincoln's attitude was reminiscent of the claims of twentieth-century New Dealers and Keynesians such as Rexford Tugwell and Abba Lerner. Toward the end of the war Lincoln declared:

Held, as it is, for the most part by our own people, the debt has become a substantial branch of national, though private, property. For obvious reasons the more nearly this property can be distributed along all the people the better. . . . The greater advantage of citizens being creditors as well as debtors with relation to the public debt is obvious. *Men readily perceive that they can not be much oppressed by a debt which they owe to themselves.* (Quoted in Kimmel 1958, p. 65; italics added)

Lincoln did not live to apply this novel fiscal philosophy to the national debt in peacetime conditions. His successor returned to the traditional view of the debt as an evil and a burden on the economy. He regarded both deficits and the debt as 'financial evils that necessarily followed a state of civil war' (ibid., p. 66). He suggested a 17-year plan to extinguish the debt, which he failed to persuade Congress to enact.[17]

Lincoln's successors, Grant (1864–77) and Arthur (1881–5), both favoured eventual elimination of the debt but were relatively more concerned with reducing the burden of taxes on the economy than reducing the debt.[18] Both emphasized that the growth of the economy tended to lighten the burden of the debt. Ironically, both Presidents expressed concern with the growth of budget *surpluses*, which they took as evidence of excessively high taxes. They claimed that large surpluses were likely to produce increased and excessive spending, neatly turning on its head the modern argument that increasing deficits cause government growth. (On Grant's views, see Kimmel 1958, p. 68; on Arthur's, see Howe 1934, p. 228.) Large surpluses were regarded as a cause of increasing expenditure. According to a biographer of President Arthur, 'The temptation to squander money was overwhelming; the Rivers and Harbors Act passed over Arthur's veto in 1882 demonstrated how strongly it lay upon Congress. Pensions, another politically ingratiating form of spending, absorbed increasing amounts although no general act was passed' (Howe 1934, p. 228).

Grover Cleveland (1885–8) took an even more extreme stand against continued surpluses in favour of revenue reductions. He maintained that a surplus involves 'a perversion of the relations between the people and their

18   *G. M. Anderson*

Government and a dangerous departure from the rules which limit the right of Federal Taxation', and referred to revenues in excess of legitimate expenditure needs as 'ruthless extortion' and 'a violation of the fundamental principles of a free government' (quoted in Kimmell 1958, p. 73). But despite Cleveland's vehement objections to large continuing surpluses, he consistently opposed major changes in the US system of high protective tariffs (which accounted for between 52 and 58 per cent of federal receipts during his administration).

Cleveland's view does not appear to have been shared by any economists of note, although some economic writers produced polemics along similar lines. In fact, the record of the growth of government spending over the period 1866–1900 suggests that the theory of surplus-driven government spending was entirely irrelevant, for the simple reason that *real* rates of government growth were actually negative: the average annual rate of nominal government spending growth following the Civil War was just under 1 per cent, while nominal GNP was growing at an average annual rate of 2 to 3 per cent (given the period of prolonged deflation following the Civil War, inflation-adjusted rates of both were higher than nominal rates).

In any event, the problem with the federal finances that caused the greatest concern in the last two decades of the nineteenth century was the problem of *surpluses*. There was a surplus over federal expenditures every year from 1866 to 1893. As a percentage of expenditures the surplus reached a high of 56.4 per cent in 1882.

On its face, this phenomenon would seem to have constituted a simple counter-example to the modern arguments which postulate a strong tendency for politicians to prefer deficit to tax finance, *ceteris paribus*, because of the short time-horizons and corresponding high political discount rates elected officials confront. In the last half of the nineteenth century, political decisionmakers at the federal level, facing no different constitutional constraints than those faced by modern politicians, failed to pursue deficit financing; it might seem that they actually *over*balanced the federal budget quite substantially.

However, the ordinary figures for levels of federal government expenditures over the period 1866–1900 fail to incorporate the cost of one major federal spending programme – the system of land grants of the public domain. Between 1866 and 1923 the federal government granted approximately 500 million acres of land to individuals, railroad companies, and state governments essentially at zero price (with about 275 million acres granted between 1866 and 1900). Another 70 million acres were sold at prices which were on average probably far below their actual market value. Over the same period that the federal government was acting with supposed excess zeal in balancing the budget by running huge apparent surpluses, it

US Federal Deficit and National Debt   19

was 'spending' and therefore liquidating a major portion of its fixed capital assets. In a recent paper, Anderson and Martin (1986) argue that if the conservatively estimated total capital value of land granted by the various federal transfer programmes (e.g. the Homestead Act, grants to railroads, etc.) over the period 1866–93 is subtracted from the total (cash) surpluses for the same period, the surpluses would be cancelled out. A less conservative estimate of the average value per acre of land granted, along with a plausible estimate of the capital value of land sold over the same period at below market prices, would produce a substantial net *deficit* when subtracted from the apparent surpluses over the same period. Hence, when all federal spending is brought 'on budget', the large apparent annual surpluses evaporate.

Nominal dollar cash surpluses generally declined during the Harrison administration (1889–93) due to a gradual decline in budget receipts, in turn mostly the result of a gradual tariff revenue reduction caused by the recession in the early 1890s.[19] However, the nineteenth century ended with six years in a row of budget deficits due mostly to a fall in tax receipts associated with the depression from 1894 to 1897.[20] But the federal government was substantially in surplus again by 1900.

The record during the first decade and a half of the twentieth century was consistent with that of the preceding century and in no way constituted a radical departure in the area of fiscal policy. Both presidents Theodore Roosevelt (1901–9) and William Howard Taft (1909–13) were significantly more sympathetic to the idea of a widening scope of governmental responsibility and were, relatively speaking, strong advocates of increasing levels of economic intervention by government. Both were on record as strongly favouring balanced budgets.[21] Roosevelt was highly critical of large surpluses, as most post-Civil War Presidents had been, although in his case it is not clear whether he took a large surplus to imply excessive tax collections (as had his predecessors) or inadequate spending levels.[22] However, there were significant deficits for years between 1901 and 1909. These apparently were the result of unanticipated revenue shortfalls resulting from the recession of 1903 and the financial panic of 1907 and were not intentional policy. In any event, they were not particularly large by modern standards, the largest equalling only 12.8 per cent of total outlays (in 1909).

When Taft took office in 1909, the government was still operating with a substantial deficit (essentially in the aftermath of the 1907 panic). Taft promptly announced that eliminating the deficit was a high priority of his administration. This has been interpreted by some historians as his rationalization for enacting an excise tax on corporations and proposing the income tax amendment.[23]

Woodrow Wilson (1913–21) favoured balanced peacetime budgets. Although some writers maintain that his attitude about the national debt

20   *G. M. Anderson*

was more 'modern' that his predecessors' (i.e. less stringent), his actions
do not suggest a significant difference from that of his predecessors.[24] After
the large increases in the national debt incurred during the First World
War, he favoured a careful, planned reduction of the debt and approved
the sinking-fund provision in the Victory Liberty Loan Act of 1919.[25]

If in fact Wilson did hold views on the proper role and scope of government and on the burden of the national debt that were more 'modern' than
his predecessors', his successors during the 1920s – Harding (1921–3) and
Coolidge (1923–9) – advocated as well as practised a traditional regime of
limited federal government and unambiguously defined fiscal responsibility
with balanced budgets. Harding frequently emphasized the need to balance
the budget, retire the debt, and keep the size and scope of government
small (Kimmel 1958, p. 89).

President Harding frequently expressed concern over the burden of
federal taxation and the 'menace of [federal] indebtedness'. His brief administration was followed by that of a successor who, if anything, held the same
view even more strongly. Coolidge could be described as something of a
firebrand in his staunch advocacy of debt reduction and smaller government.
As Kimmel (1958, p. 93) notes, '[a] balanced budget, rigid expenditure
control, and reduction of the federal debt constituted the three major planks
in the programme that the President and other high officials regarded as
essential'. Coolidge considered the national debt to be a most serious
problem, and like most post-Civil War Presidents he emphasized economic
rather than moral arguments. In a speech in 1927 about the debt, he
declared:

It is a menace to our credit. It is the greatest weakness in our line of national
defense. It is the largest obstacle in the path of our economic development. It
should be retired as fast as possible under a system of reasonable taxation. This
can be done only by continuing the policy of rigid government economy. ('Address
of President Coolidge before the Union League Club of Philadelphia', *New York
Times*, 18 November 1927, p. 4).

Coolidge consistently maintained that this goal, as well as simple fiscal
prudence, required a balanced budget each and every year.[26] However, he
was opposed to a policy of maximizing tax surpluses, as he felt that large
surpluses implied an excessive tax burden.[27]

The Hoover administration (1929–32) in some ways represented a sharp
break with the past record of fiscal theory and practice in the executive
branch. But Hoover's policy with respect to balancing the federal budget
was consistent with the positions expressed by every President since the
Civil War. What was remarkable about this consistency was the fact that it
remained the priority goal of administration policy through the dark and
early depths of the Great Depression. Debt reduction was also a persistent

concern of the administration. In fact, balancing the federal budget was the centrepiece of administration recovery policy. As Kimmel (1958, p. 152) explains:

A balanced budget was regarded as a prerequisite for a revival of business confidence. Federal borrowing was viewed as competitive with business and other private borrowing; interest rates were higher because of federal competition for loan funds. Normal capital flows, it was reasoned, could not be restored as long as the government continued to borrow large sums. The exigencies of the times required a balanced budget "not merely for maintaining unimpaired the credit of the Government, but also for reinvigorating the entire credit structure of the country" [quoting Secretary of the Treasury, Andrew Mellon].

Although rhetorically committed to balancing the federal budget, during his administration Hoover supported a variety of expenditure increases (see below). His administration promoted tax increases to reduce the deficit. During the 1932 election campaign Hoover began to call for a reduction in expenditures for the purpose of deficit reduction.[28] The federal deficit became a leading campaign issue, with the Democratic candidate Franklin Roosevelt attacking the fiscal irresponsibility of the Hoover administration for failing to balance the budget and for failing to reduce expenditures.[29] The 1932 election was not a duel between the defender of traditional fiscal conservatism versus a new-style fiscal revolutionary, but more a battle for the mantle of old-style fiscal responsibility.

Hoover's claim to a radical break with past Presidents lay in the substance of his philosophy of government action rather than his notion of fiscal responsibility. Hoover created the Reconstruction Finance Corporation in January 1932;[30] the Federal Farm Board in 1929;[31] the Federal Home Loan Bank System in mid-1932;[32] supported massive increases in Public Works spending by late 1929;[33] and engaged in an active campaign to keep industrial wage rates from falling (using the Office of the President to variously cajole and threaten industries to fall into line).[34] Generally speaking, Hoover was a determined advocate of a substantially increased federal government role in the economy, whose programmatic response to the Depression was in many ways similar to that of Roosevelt's later New Deal.

Two conclusions can confidently be drawn with respect to the consensus of opinion among leading politicians and the general public in the United States until 1933. First, balanced budgets – or, more precisely, a balance of expenditure with receipts (given that there was no actual federal budget prior to 1921) – were considered to be a necessary feature of ordinarily responsible fiscal management on the part of the federal government during peacetime. Deficits were considered to be a necessary evil during wartime, and occasionally resulted from unexpected revenue shortfalls associated with temporary recessions. The national debt was regarded as a burden

22   *G. M. Anderson*

resulting from wartime necessity, which should be steadily (however gradually) retired; annual surpluses were generally regarded as an appropriate
fiscal means for achieving this end.

Second, the appropriate size and scope of government was generally
thought to be fairly small and federal spending and involvement in the
economy regarded with prudent suspicion. In this respect, the consensus
is somewhat more difficult to identify, and had numerous exceptions. In
fact, the last President during this period appears to have favoured a
significant increase in government intervention, both as a response to the
Depression and on general principles.

Nevertheless, Franklin Roosevelt was elected in 1932 after a campaign
whose principal themes included pledges to limit government as well as an
attack on the fiscal irresponsibility of the Hoover administration for permitting budget deficits in peacetime for three years in a row.[35]

2.4   The Fiscal Revolution and Its Aftermath

Herbert Stein has argued that a revolution occurred in US economic policy
between the stock market crash of 1929 and the Kennedy tax cut of 1964.
This 'fiscal revolution in America' took the form of a gradual transition,
from the belief that balanced budgets were a necessity for prudent and
responsible internal governmental management to the radically different
commitment to use federal government spending and taxing authority to
stabilize the macroeconomy – to employ planned deficits to increase effective
demand in recessions and restore full employment, and planned surpluses
to reduce inflation when the economy had reached full employment (to
prevent it from 'overheating'). This replacement of traditional notions of
fiscal responsibility with the very different policy of discretionary compensatory fiscal policy in the political realm *was* ultimately the result of the
Keynesian revolution in the economics profession. The actual mechanism
for this shift in policy preferences was the gradual infiltration of the federal
government by younger, Keynesian-trained economists and the consequent
replacement of older advocates of the traditional views. It was not that
older, non-Keynesian economists merely retired, but that the younger
Keynesians were promoted by the Roosevelt administration.

Surprisingly, Stein does not explain why the administration was so taken
with the younger Keynesians, although the likely answer seems obvious.
The Keynesians provided a theoretical underpinning for the policies which
the administration had been pursuing anyway for other reasons since the
early 1930s. The large deficits characteristic of the federal budgets of the
period had essentially occurred as a distasteful by-product of administration

fiscal policy, and had not been consciously planned. Naturally, the proponents of an economic doctrine that provided theoretical reasons for employing deficit finance in a depression as an expression of enlightened public policy attracted the interest of the administration. However, this obvious source of attraction was not sufficient to propel the Keynesian economists to positions of more than marginal influence until the end of the decade.[36]

By 1939, however, the influx of the Keynesian school into Washington began to grow rapidly; this may not have reflected conscious policy on the part of the federal government, but may have been largely accidental. According to Stein (1969, p. 168):

> The growing predominance of Keynesians in the government then and later was not entirely due to conscious selection. The need for economists was rising, and a large proportion of all economists, especially of the younger ones who were available to come to Washington, thought in the way taught by the *General Theory*. Once it started, the movement was self-reinforcing. Members of the school tended to know, prefer, and recruit others.

In fact, according to Lebergott (1984, pp. 458–9) the belief that Keynesian fiscal policy was part and parcel of the New Deal was originally promulgated by the anti-Roosevelt Liberty League in the 1930s and later picked up by Roosevelt's Keynesian admirers after the Second World War. But as early as 1933 the administration boasted of its substantial revenue increases designed to restrain budget deficits, and pursued policies that increased the real effective Federal tax rate by *700 per cent* from 1932 to 1939. Lebergott's conclusion is that '[fiscal] policy in the 1930's was not an expansionary Keynesian device as some historians have it, but a fairly efficient system for keeping down expenditures and minimizing public debt' (ibid.).

Keynesian fiscal policy as a response to a depression had gained substantial support in the federal government by the outbreak of the Second World War, by which time it had become largely irrelevant. The large deficits during the war were merely a repetition of a pattern of wartime deficits common in American history, reflecting fiscal expediency rather than the intentional application of any abstract theory. Following the war, although policy discussion had an agenda which had been established by the Keynesians, two distinct views of the feasible and proper role of fiscal policy had emerged within that group. While there was a general consensus to the effect that the government must take responsibility for the maintenance of full employment (however defined) and that active fiscal policy should be a major instrument, the two views of proper Keynesian strategy reflected very different attitudes about balancing the budget. One view held that the government should employ fiscal policy as a precise instrument for maintaining full employment, and implied that manipulation of expenditures was the best means available. Balanced budgets were rejected as an appropriate goal of fiscal policy. The second view held that stabilization policy should emphasize the use of revenues as a tool, and argued that revenues provided a kind of automatic, built-in stabilizing force. Proponents of this view were less sanguine about the prospects for precise, detailed fine-tuning of the economy through the expenditure side. Their attitude about balanced budgets was also different. As Stein explains (1969, p. 194), these latter fiscal stabilizationists continued to use the idea of a balanced budget as a guide to fiscal policy, but insisted that this guide be sufficiently flexible so as to allow for effective discretionary fiscal policy. The former group took a more radical view that budget-balancing was a 'mere shibboleth' and had no legitimate justification.

To accurately simplify a complex set of events in the evolution of fiscal policy, the proponents of the second view came out on top after the Second World War. The idea of balancing the budget over the business cycle achieved a widespread consensus in both the economics profession and among professional policymakers in Washington.

By 1953, when the Eisenhower administration entered office, the revolution in fiscal policy was widespread and entrenched in the economics profession, but it remained unclear what difference it would make in the implementation of actual fiscal policy. In fact, the Eisenhower administration paid conspicuous attention to budget balancing across both terms of office. But Stein argues that the Eisenhower administration accepted the main tenets of compensatory fiscal policy, and the responsibility of the federal government for maintaining full employment: '[the] essential point was that the desirability of balancing the budget was not given by some eternal principle but depended on economic conditions which would vary' (1969, p. 283). This 'enlightened' twist to the traditional commitment to fiscal responsibility was favourably reviewed by a number of Keynesian economists, notably including J. K. Galbraith.[37]

The Eisenhower administration in fact sharply increased deficits during the recession of 1957–8 and earlier, more minor, downturns. In any event, President Eisenhower himself orchestrated the drive for a big (compensating) surplus in 1959–60, and succeeded in achieving a small surplus of $331 million (0.1 per cent of GNP) in 1960. Stein agrees with Richard Nixon's expressed opinion that this drive for a surplus contributed to the latter's defeat in the 1960 election – Nixon had requested an expansionary fiscal policy by the administration to promote his electoral prospects (1969, pp. 370–1).

Stein maintains that Kennedy came into office believing in balancing the budget: 'neither [his] platform nor . . . campaign speeches suggested that Eisenhower's fiscal policy had been too restrictive, in the sense of having too large surpluses, or that the Democrats would believe differently in that respect' (1969, p. 377). In 1961, Kennedy declared that a deficit would only be justified in a 'grave national emergency' or a 'serious recession' (ibid.). However, Kennedy appointed a number of prominent Democrat economists as close advisers, and these happened to be Keynesians. Advisers to the Kennedy administration on fiscal policy included Galbraith, (Seymour) Harris, Samuelson, and Tobin.

These advisers rejected balanced budgets as a proper goal of fiscal policy. Stein writes (1969, p. 381):

The Kennedy economists, like most American economists of 1960, believed that the chief economic problem of the country was to achieve and maintain high and rapidly rising total output. That is, the problem was full employment and economic growth. The keys to the management of that problem were fiscal policy and monetary policy, with fiscal policy being the senior partner in the combination. Full employment – or economic stabilization – and economic growth were the main objectives and guides of fiscal policy; budget-balancing was an irrelevancy.

Stein maintains that under the influence of this high-powered group of New Economists, Kennedy became an enthusiastic proponent of the use of compensatory fiscal policy on Keynesian grounds, although his conversion was not as complete as some of them would have liked. This influence was expressed in the tax cut of 1964, which was designed expressly as expansionary fiscal policy in a time of already existing deficits. Stein explains that the 1964 tax cut was a major fiscal policy watershed (1969, p. 454), because this signalled the replacement of budget balancing by compensatory fiscal policy at the federal level.

Stein's effort is an able attempt to trace the evolution of the influence of Keynesian New Economics on the policymaking decisions of political actors. His conclusion – that by 1964, budget balancing had been replaced by compensating finance as a major determinant of fiscal policy – is most certainly *literally* correct. The question remains, however, of how much difference this intellectual situation made in the actual conduct of fiscal affairs. For example, the vaunted 1964 tax cut helped to produce a deficit that was only 1 per cent of GNP. The deficit for the following year (1965) was even lower, 0.2 per cent of GNP – the lowest actual *deficit* in the post-war period until that time.

Stein's argument, that the rhetoric of balancing the budget within the Eisenhower administration was mostly honoured in the breach and was essentially a sop to the general public which had yet to understand the economics of compensatory fiscal policy, ignores the fact that the political rhetoric was quite consistent with the record of the deficit over the period. As table 2.4 shows, the average yearly deficit for the period 1951–5 was 0.67 per cent of total federal spending, and over the period 1956–60 it was

26   *G. M. Anderson*

Table 2.4 Net federal deficit surplus as a percentage of total spending, 1940–70

Year	Value	Average:	
1940	−30.84		
1941	−36.18		
1942	−58.35		
1943	−69.44		
1944	−52.08		
1945	−51.29		
1946	−28.85		
1947	+11.64		
1948	+39.63		
1949	+1.49		
1950	−7.32		
1951	+13.40		
1952	−2.24		
1953	−8.53		
1954	−1.62		
1955	−4.37		
1056	+5.58	Average:	
1957	+4.45	1940–1945:	−59.63
1958	−3.36	1946–1950:	+3.31
1959	−13.95	1951–1955:	−0.67
1960	+0.32	1956–1960:	−1.39
1961	−3.41	1961–1965:	−4.10
1962	−6.68	1966–1970:	−4.40
1963	−4.27		
1964	−4.99	1954–1960:	−1.85
1965	−1.19		
1966	−2.74		
1967	−5.48		
1968	−14.12		
1969	+1.76		
1970	−1.45		

Source: Historical Tables: Budget of the US Government Fiscal Year 1986 (Washington, DC: Office of Management and Budget) Table 1–2.

1.39 per cent. Admittedly, the former period includes the final two years of the Truman administration, but also the three years of the Korean War. The average annual deficit of the period 1954–60 (i.e. the Eisenhower administration after the Korean War) was only 1.85 per cent of total federal spending. This was well within the bounds of typical pre-Depression fiscal practice.

Furthermore, while the Kennedy administration may have been a watershed on the spread of Keynesian notions of fiscal policy to the realm of political decisionmaking, net deficits as a percentage of total outlays remained very low by the standards of the 1930s and 1940s, and were generally well within the range of the deficits of the 1950s. A major difference between the periods 1951–60 and 1961–70 was that the former yielded four annual surpluses, but the latter only one (in 1969). Still, the average annual deficit for 1961–70 was 4.25 per cent of total spending, even though the last six years in this period were during an undeclared, but nonetheless expensive, war.

The 'fiscal revolution' Stein so ably outlines appears to have affected political rhetoric more than actual fiscal policy. In 1955, the first full year following Korean War mobilization, federal outlays were 18 per cent of GNP; in 1965, the first year of limited involvement in the Vietnam War,

Table 2.5 Federal outlays and deficits surpluses as a percentage of the GNP, 1954–65

	Outlays as % of GNP	Change from previous year	Deficit as % of GNP
1954	19.5	−7.5	−0.3
1955	18.0	−7.6	−0.8
1956	17.2	−4.4	1.0
1957	17.6	2.3	0.8
1958	18.6	5.6	−0.6
1959	19.4	4.3	−2.7
1960	18.5	−4.6	0.1
1961	19.2	3.7	−0.7
1962	19.5	1.5	−1.3
1963	19.3	−1.0	−0.8
1964	19.2	−0.5	−1.0
1965	17.9	−6.7	−0.2

Source: Historical Tables: Budget of the US Government Fiscal Year 1986 (Washington, DC: Office of Management and Budget) Table 1–2, and additional calculations.

federal outlays were 17.9 per cent of GNP. Of course, as table 2.5 indicates, outlays as a percentage of GNP reached a high of 19.5 in 1962 and fluctuated considerably throughout, but the outcome of the 'fiscal revolution' does not appear to have been a relative increase in the size of the federal sector.

Our conclusion is that the Keynesian revolution was surely an important factor in the demise of balanced budgets and the rise of persistent, huge deficits, but that by itself is not a sufficient explanation. Peacetime budget deficits in the period after the Second World War (prior to 1970) were small, both as a percentage of total outlays and of GNP, and surpluses were common, if not as large as deficits in general. During the heyday of Keynesian influence in the executive branch and Congress (1961–9) both peacetime and *wartime* deficits were small, and the period actually ended with a small budget surplus. The employment of discretionary, compensatory fiscal policy for purposes of macroeconomic stabilization constituted a repudiation of the traditional doctrine of balanced budgets as a goal of prudent and responsible public finance, but replaced it with a variant which retained at least a family resemblance.[38] The new doctrine held that budgets should be brought into balance when full employment was achieved in order to prevent inflation, and deficits run during periods of less than full employment. But this strategy of a 'full employment deficit' merely relaxed the traditional budgetary norms in a supposedly precise manner in response to particular measurable economic conditions. However relaxed, these norms were not abandoned.

An argument has been advanced by Buchanan and others to the effect that the principal long-term effect of the Keynesian revolution was to gradually wear away the traditional constraint on deficit spending and introduce moral confusion about balanced budgets. It was not necessary for the New Economics to convince politicians and voters that deficits don't matter and that the debt was not a burden because 'we owe it to ourselves' – the transition from unambiguous opposition to deficits and public debt, to confusion with respect to what level of deficits represented a problem, and doubt about why balanced budgets made any difference, was sufficient. Once actual balanced administrative budgets were no longer considered an appropriate goal of public finance, no unambiguous and therefore effective constraint on deficit spending remained. If a deficit of 1 per cent of total expenditures was not too high, what about 10 per cent, or for that matter 50 per cent? When even Keynesian economists disagree over the appropriate level of deficit spending given macroeconomic conditions, how can politicians or the general public be expected to achieve a stable consensus which serves to guide fiscal policy in a meaningful way?

It is surely not to sell the argument short to point out that it fails to constitute in any sense a complete explanation of deficits in excess of 5 per cent of GNP during a peacetime economic expansion. Perhaps most obviously, there is little evidence that the general public – voters and taxpayers – have at any time during the past 40 years abandoned balanced budgets as a high priority. As we noted above, public opinion polls have failed to discern a significant dent in the overwhelming support amongst the voting public for balanced budgets.[39]

However, if other relevant constraints shifted significantly during the same period in which confusion increased about the validity of balanced budgets as an appropriate fiscal goal, the growth of huge, persistent deficits is easier to understand.

The rapid increase in spending via means tested programmes and entitlements was one such shift in constraints affecting political decisionmakers in Congress. This form of income transfer to individuals generated accelerating spending obligations for the federal government which were essentially automatic – i.e. obligations increased without the necessity of actual Congressional votes for such increases. Meanwhile, revenues did not increase automatically to cover these increasing obligations. Although the inflation tax in the form of 'bracket creep' did produce a relatively minor 'automatic' revenue increase, in general increasing taxes required politically costly votes in Congress. Under these circumstances, spending tended to grow at a faster rate than revenues, creating burgeoning deficits during the course of the 1970s. This and other related arguments based on changing structural constraints in Congress will be considered in more detail in section 2.6.

At the same time that federal budget deficits were generally trending upwards, another highly significant trend was emerging. This took the form of a most dramatic change which occurred in the level of transfer payments to individuals. In 1940, transfer payments constituted only 17.5 per cent of the total budget, and 1.7 per cent of GNP. But by 1980, the corresponding statistics were 47 and 10.8 percent, respectively. The growth of federal transfer payments is presented in Table 2.6.

It has sometimes been asserted that the federal budget has been changing its composition in very fundamental ways, most importantly in terms of a purported shift from capital investment to current consumption, particularly in the form of transfer payments. This appears in fact to have been the case. At the same time that transfer payments to individuals were increasing from 17.5 to 47 per cent of total spending, federal spending for physical capital investment was falling with equal rapidity as a proportion of total spending and GNP. In 1940, outlays for major physical capital investment constituted 34.8 per cent of federal spending. By 1984 this had fallen to only 12 per cent. Capital investment as a share of GNP also fell, from 3.5 per cent in 1940 to 2.8 per cent in 1984; such investment has fallen gradually but quite consistently from a post-Second World War high of 6.4 per cent in 1953.

Decomposing this record, national defence capital investment fell steadily from its post-Second World War high of 27.2 per cent of federal outlays in 1954 to a low of 5.1 per cent in 1978. This category includes not only military construction (bases, housing for military personnel, etc.) but all procurement of weapons and other equipment as well. At the same time as military capital investment fell by 81.5 per cent in terms of total outlays, national defence expenditures as a percentage of the total budget were also falling, but by a lesser extent. While national defense investment fell from 16.6 per cent in 1962 to 5.1 per cent in 1978, total national defence spending fell from 48.6 to 25.8 per cent of the total budget. In other words, capital investment as a component of national defence investment fell from

Table 2.6 Federal transfer payments, 1940–84 (selected years)

	As a % of budget outlays	As a % of GNP outlays
1940	17.5	1.7
1945	2.4	1.0
1950	32.1	5.2
1955	20.9	3.8
1960	26.2	4.9
1965	27.8	5.0
1967	27.2	5.5
1968	27.8	6.0
1969	31.1	6.3
1970	33.0	6.7
1971	38.2	7.8
1972	40.3	8.2
1973	42.5	8.3
1974	44.6	8.7
1975	46.2	10.4
1976	48.4	11.0
1977	48.0	10.5
1978	46.0	10.1
1979	46.2	9.9
1980	47.0	10.8
1981	47.7	11.2
1982	47.8	11.7
1983	48.9	12.3
1984	46.9	11.2

Source: Historical Tables: Budget of the US Government, Fiscal Year 1986 (Washington, DC: Office of Management and Budget 1985); Table 11–1.

34.1 to 19.7 per cent over this period. An increasingly large proportion of the defence budget has been allocated to wages of military personnel.[40]

Another dramatic change in federal spending behaviour since 1940 has been the rapid increase in 'uncontrollable' spending. This can be divided into three categories: interest on the federal debt, payments due for contracts and obligations entered upon in the past but payable in the present, and entitlement programmes. None of these categories of spending is literally 'uncontrollable', of course; they represent outlays which will occur unless the federal government takes positive action to limit or stop them. Interest on the national debt in future periods can be reduced by retiring part of

US Federal Deficit and National Debt   31

Table 2.7 Relatively uncontrollable spending as a percentage of total budget outlays, 1967–84

	Total relatively uncontrollable	Open-ended programmes (and fixed costs)	Open-ended programmes: payments for individuals
1967	57.0	33.3	25.5
1968	58.0	34.0	26.0
1969	61.1	38.1	29.1
1970	61.5	40.0	30.7
1971	63.0	43.5	35.0
1972	63.0	45.5	36.4
1973	66.9	50.0	38.3
1974	68.4	51.3	40.3
1975	66.9	50.8	42.0
1976	67.3	52.9	43.8
1977	67.2	52.9	43.5
1978	68.7	51.9	41.6
1979	68.6	51.6	41.6
1980	70.0	52.6	41.7
1981	70.2	54.2	42.4
1982	72.6	55.3	42.9
1983	73.4	57.5	43.8
1984	73.3	56.2	42.0

Source: Historical Tables: Budget of the United States Government, Fiscal Year 1986 (Washington, DC: Office of Management and Budget 1985); Table 8–1.

that debt in the present, and debt repudiation is always a possible, if improbable, policy option. Payments due can be manipulated in various ways (such as by altering the lead-times of weapons systems). Entitlement programmes can be eliminated, or their eligibility standards changed. But all of these forms of spending require positive political action to limit or stop rather than positive political action to increase.[41] Hence, 'uncontrollable' is a misnomer in that it only refers to that portion of the budget which is designed to increase in an automatic, exogenously determined, fashion. In the accurate phrase of one scholar, these programmes represent the portion of the budget on auto-pilot.

Table 2.7 shows the growth of relatively uncontrollable outlays over the period 1967–84. In 1967, 57 per cent of the federal budget was relatively uncontrollable. By 1984 this had risen to 73.3 per cent, an increase of 28.59 per cent. But most of this growth occurred in the realm of payments for individuals in open-ended programmes (e.g., social security, SSI, AFDC, etc.); this component grew from 25.5 per cent of total outlays in 1967 to

32   *G. M. Anderson*

42 per cent in 1984, an increase of 64.7 per cent. Payments for individuals in open-ended programmes in 1984 exceeded $357 billion.

Programmes such as social security, Medicare, and the various means tested entitlements (AFDC, etc.) should perhaps better be termed 'non-controlled' or 'automatic' than uncontrollable: while individuals become automatically eligible who belong to certain categories without specific Congressional action allocating funds to those particular individuals, the eligibility standards themselves are determined by Congress.[42] Further, benefit levels are determined ultimately by Congress, even if in many cases such levels are technically assigned by particular agencies.[43]

The salient feature of 'uncontrollable' open-ended transfer programmes is that there is a significant political cost differential between increased and decreased spending. No politician has to vote actively for increased spending, whereas decreased spending requires both a vote and likely open confrontation with a powerful and effectively organized beneficiary interest group. A member of Congress, for example, will confront a high political cost of voting against an automatic cost of living increase for social security recipients but a very low cost of failing to actively oppose the otherwise automatic increase. In addition, beneficiaries of deficit reduction are diffuse and unorganized, while beneficiaries of the cost-of-living-allowance increase are concentrated and highly organized, able to reward effectively supporters (both overt and implicit) as well as to punish opponents.

How can we determine any effect of the growth of uncontrollable spending for social programmes on the federal deficit since the 1960s? If we assume that the enormous growth in open-ended transfer programmes since 1967 had been restrained, and had remained at the 1967 level as a percentage of the total budget, *ceteris paribus*, what sort of reduction in the level of the federal deficit might have been expected? Table 2.8 reports the results of this exercise, by comparing federal deficits over the period 1967–84, with the net growth (expressed in nominal terms) of open-ended transfer programmes. By adding together the former and the latter, all but four of the net deficits over the period become net surpluses of substantial size. The most extreme case is 1982, where a net deficit of $127,940 million becomes a net surplus of $43,572 million. While this exercise is merely a counterfactual thought experiment, it illustrates the significance of the rise of the transfer state for the deficit problem during the past 17 years.

The main point here is simply one apparent proximate cause of the rapid growth in unplanned, peacetime budget deficits since 1970 has been the growth of transfer payment expenditures relative to tax receipts. The federal government has increasingly tended to finance transfer payments – a form of current consumption – by borrowing rather than taxing. This is not to imply that the growth in the deficit is the result of the growth in transfer payments *per se*. Transfer payments prior to 1970 had almost always been

US Federal Deficit and National Debt   33

Table 2.8   The net federal deficit: some relevant dimensions

	(1) Total, open- ended programmes and fixed costs	(2) Net growth in (1) nominal terms, per annum	(3) Net federal deficit	(4) [(2)+(3)]
1967	52,456			
1968	60,650	1,068	− 25,161	−24,092
1969	69,876	8,814	+ 3,242	+12,056
1970	78,311	13,108	− 2,837	+10,271
1971	91,449	21,437	− 23,033	− 1,596
1972	104,993	28,143	− 23,373	+ 4,770
1973	122,934	41,033	− 14,904	+26,129
1974	138,245	48,484	− 6,135	+42,349
1975	168,932	58,158	− 53,242	+ 4,916
1976	196,586	72,868	− 73,719	− 851
1977	216,357	80,203	− 53,644	+26,559
1978	238,070	85,323	− 58,982	+26,341
1979	259,929	92,133	− 40,161	+51,972
1980	310,672	114,047	− 73,808	+40,239
1981	367,795	141,745	− 78,936	+62,809
1982	414,949	171,512	−127,940	+43,572
1983	464,755	195,615	−207,764	−12,149
1984	478,756	195,057	−185,324	+ 9,733

Calculated from data provided in *Historical Tables: Budget of the United States Government, Fiscal Year 1986* (Washington, DC: Office of Management and Budget, 1985); Tables 1–1, and 11–1.

financed fully by tax revenues, and consequently had no effect on the level of the deficit.

2.5   What Happened?

The emergence of large and rapidly growing federal budget deficits after 1970, following 180 years of (approximately) balanced budgets except during periods of war or depression, is an obvious historical aberration. The long and consistent US history of fiscal responsibility at the national level has led some scholars to conclude that the current deficit problem is *only* a temporary aberration, a kind of blip in the fiscal record. To these writers, the natural US political tendency towards balanced budgets can be expected soon to reassert itself; recent deficits are the result of the peculiar and

34   *G. M. Anderson*

irresponsible policies of the Reagan administration which supposedly cut taxes excessively in 1981 with an unrealistic view to the consequences. Both the administration and its Congressional supporters will soon feel the wrath of the median voter at the ballot box, and the deficit problem will recede.

Many such plausible and *ad hoc* theories are conceivable, granting different political villains the lead role, and all suffer from the same basic flaw: they fail to explain why, in the previous long history of the federal government, similar aberrations did not occur. For about 180 years, there was some strong equilibrating tendency which consistently caused budgets in peacetime to return towards balance. But since 1970, real federal deficits have steadily trended upwards; the federal debt has doubled since 1980. The previously strong equilibrating forces may still exist, but they have at least been seriously weakened. This weakening needs to be explained.

Simply stated, such an explanation requires two components. It must explain why transfer payments to individuals rapidly accelerated over the past 20 years, and why tax revenues were not increased sufficiently to finance these increases.

What caused the rapid acceleration in transfers to individuals via the federal budget after 1967? This particular development cannot be blamed on the Keynesian revolution in any direct sense, because Keynesian fiscal theory did not recommend massive transfers of wealth *per se*. A more plausible explanation lies in the improved efficiency of Congress as a device for producing income transfers from about 1966 on into the 1970s.

Schick (1983) argues that Congress significantly increased its efficiency as a producer of redistributive transfers through a series of small, uncoordinated incremental changes in organization and rules. Prior to these institutional changes, in the 1950s Congress was organized in such a way that spending increases occurred in a controlled and limited manner, the growth in federal spending approximately keeping pace with the growth rate in GNP. The effective hegemony of the appropriations committees severely restricted the power of the authorizing committees on which most members of Congress sat. Authorizing committees were interested in particular programmes and hence the amount of funds going to programme operators and beneficiaries, whereas appropriations committees provided funds for agencies to spend on their own operations and did not act as agents for particular programme constituencies. This hegemony provided a constraint on the rate of growth of transfers by separating decisionmaking about the level of appropriations from those committees which were actively promoting programmes benefiting particular interest groups.

Gradually this functional separation began to break down. This process accelerated after about 1966. Various Congressional internal reforms caused Congress to become increasingly fragmented with less effective control over appropriations decisions. In addition to the shift from permanent to

US Federal Deficit and National Debt   35

temporary authorizations, a number of other reforms 'gave outsiders an additional channel of influence and made them less dependent on the Appropriations committees' (p. 267). This 'opening up of Congress' was achieved as a result of the gradual relaxation of seniority rules, the increase in both size and budget of the staffs of committees and individual members (enhancing effective access to Congress by lobbyists), the relatively inc-reasing power of subcommittees with monopoly jurisdictions over particular spending programmes, the breakdown in party discipline and the cor-responding authority of party leaders, and various reforms mandating that committees conduct their business in the open (greatly increasing the effectiveness of the monitoring of legislators' behaviour by special interest groups).

In consequence of these various changes in rules and the informal institutional environment, Congress became a more efficient mechanism for transferring income to organized groups of individuals. Traditional constraints on the process of generating increasing levels of income transfers were gradually relaxed, and the divisions of labour within Congress expanded, leading to significant gains from increased specialization. Of course, these particular efficiency gains refer only to the Congress as a producer of coercive wealth transfers. Output increased in the form of transfers to individuals. But by extension of Schick's argument, the same institutional changes and reforms which tended to increase the transfer output of Congress also relaxed controls on appropriations which had traditionally served to guard against large unplanned deficits.

Schepsle and Weingast (1985) have refined this general argument by focusing on the specific role of the proliferation and growth in importance of Congressional subcommittees. They maintain that in the 1950s and 1960s most of the important Congressional business originated in the 15 standing committees of the Senate and the 20 standing committees of the House; subcommittees were used but did not control the development of legislation. However, in the 1970s a number of internal Congressional reform measures (including the 1973 'Subcommittee Bill of Rights' passed by the House) substantially increased the autonomy and influence of sub-committees.

This seemingly subtle change had important effects because of the nature and composition of subcommittees as opposed to committees. Members of subcommittees typically are legislators from districts with constituents who have a strong economic interest in the issues in which the particular subcommittee specializes. They argue that the new system has increased the power of programme advocates, who assiduously protect both existing benefits and increasing future benefits to their constituents. The influence of subcommittees on protecting and extending programmes is easily overlooked because their strongest power is negative and need not be actively exercised in order to be effective – i.e. the capacity to block proposed cuts or changes in programmes in their jurisdiction. This subcommittee 'veto power' is a significant factor in determining the 'downward inflexibility' of levels of spending in transfer programmes (Schepsle and Weingast 1985, pp.114–15).

These authors claim that the trend toward decentralization in Congressional decisionmaking has tended to increase rates of growth in governmental spending and increase fiscal irresponsibility at the federal level. While these developments allegedly began 50 years ago, legislative events during the seventies greatly accelerated the effects of the trend. The legislative Reorganization Act (1970), the Subcommittee Bill of Rights (1973), and the Committee Reform Amendments (1974) all served simultaneously to weaken committees and strengthen subcommittees. Together with other developments (including importantly the reduction in the relative authority of the 'old power center', the Speaker of the House, party leaders, and committee chairmen), these developments significantly increased the efficiency with which senators and representatives can serve their geographic constituencies – or, expressed from a different perspective, substantially enhanced the ability of organized interest groups to procure income transfers via the legislative process. Once a programme or agency is in place, subcommittees are powerful enemies of any changes or reductions which organized groups of the members' constituents oppose. The end result of the expanded authority of subcommittees is the growth of so-called 'uncontrollable' spending.

While expenses associated with multi-year defence contracts are one subcategory of uncontrollable spending (as mentioned previously), weapons procurement still requires a formal vote by Congress to initiate. But in the case of social security and the assorted means tested benefit programmes of transfers to individuals, spending levels are determined endogenously; as the number of eligible individuals increases, this automatically requires outlays to increase. In general, the political process tends to be biased in favour of spending increases against tax reduction because spending can usually be readily targeted on concentrated and organized beneficiary groups while taxation is diffused. Effective, organized interest groups are more likely to achieve spending increases benefiting their members than selective tax reductions. The shifting institutional constraints within Congress have tended to exacerbate this phenomenon by improving the ability of organized interest groups of certain sorts to monitor and influence legislators. Interest groups are now more able to make stable and enforceable contracts with the small subgroup of legislators with a monopoly jurisdiction over their area of interest.

Another result of the relatively increased specialization within Congress is that the differential cost of opposing the growth in transfer programmes by comparison with other forms of spending has risen significantly.

This has an obvious potential relevance for growth of the federal deficit. Members of Congress who are provided with jurisdiction over individual income transfer programmes are political residual claimants with respect to growth in spending in those areas. At the same time, other members of Congress would tend to benefit from limiting that spending growth through the deficit reduction that was thereby provided. But reduction in the deficit (and the national debt) is a public good, and effective action designed to produce a lower deficit confronts a free-rider problem: all members of Congress would benefit from the restriction on the growth in (or actual reduction of) any particular transfer programme – with the exception of the minority of members who directly benefit from the programme's increase – regardless of whether or not they actively bore their share of the political costs. Under these circumstances it would be surprising if deficit reduction were *not* underprovided. This free-rider problem was minimized by the various institutional devices which Schepsle and Weingast explain were dissolved over the past two decades. The problem of the federal deficit grew as a result of an increasing efficiency of Congress as a producer of income transfers to individuals.

These structural models have some serious problems, not the least of which is the difficulty of empirical testing. But the structural approach offers a potentially powerful explanation of the recent development of large unplanned budget deficits, especially on the margin of the 'timing problem' (e.g., why we have deficits now but did not have them for most of American history). The overall approach is plausible and interesting, and seems to merit more rigorous investigation in the future.

There are basically two levels of argument concerning the economic costs of deficit spending. The first level involves the indirect costs of government deficits to the private sector, including the degree to which deficits cause inflation and increasing interest rates in capital markets (the 'crowding out effect'). The problem of whether the deficit 'matters' (i.e. generates significant indirect costs in terms of reduced economic efficiency) and if so, how much, has usually dominated the public controversy over deficit spending since the 1950s and has recently generated a considerable literature in the economics profession.[44] However, this controversy has largely neglected an additional 'cost' of deficits that was a principal concern among the classical economists – the effect of deficit spending in causing an increasing rate of growth in government expenditures.

According to the arguments developed by members of the public choice school (cf. Buchanan and Wagner 1977), political actors regard expenditures as a good and taxes as a bad, because the benefits derived from spending increase voter support on the margin while the costs resulting from taxing tend to decrease voter support. Hence the need to finance additional expenditures by means of increased taxes tends to minimize the political bias in favour of spending. But to the extent that political actors are able to engage in deficit financing of increased spending and avoid direct tax increases in the same period, voters/taxpayers falsely perceive the prices of those spending increases to be smaller than they really are (ibid., pp. 128–30). Naturally, at the end of the day the cows come home; *ceteris paribus*, the voting/taxpaying public will be forced to pay for the present period's spending increase with increased future period taxes, and deficit spending politicians will eventually bear the political cost of voter opposition to increasing taxes. But politicians in modern democracies tend to have limited tenure and therefore limited political time horizons; they generally have little initiative to avoid behaviour that will only create widespread voter opposition *after* they have left office (see Buchanan and Lee 1982).

In the case of growing deficits (both in nominal terms – as a percentage of total outlays – and as a percentage of GNP) in the United States since 1969, it is clear that their *proximate* cause has been the higher rate of growth of spending compared with tax revenues. Over the period 1970–82, when the federal budget deficit grew from $2.83 billion (0.3 per cent of GNP) to $127.9 billion (4.2 per cent of GNP), receipts grew from $192.8 billion (19.9 per cent GNP) to $617.7 billion (20.3 per cent of GNP). Although there were fluctuations along the way, the trend for receipts was generally upwards since 1969 (the last year of budget surplus).[46]

As we have seen, the spectacular growth in federal spending since the 1960s has largely been due to the rapid rise in transfer spending. A number of writers have tended to overlook this relative growth in transfers. For instance, Hughes (1977, p. 220) maintains that 'in 1950 [there] began an era of ceaseless increases in government expenditures, the "great Keynesian updraft," related to continuous large scale military and quasi-military expenditures, which have never ended'. But the real 'updraft' was neither military nor Keynesian. National defence as a percentage of total federal outlays declined from 52.2 per cent in 1960 to 22.7 per cent in 1980. Moreover, during the same period federal outlays for major physical capital devoted to national defence (which includes base construction and weapons procurement) fell from 18.6 per cent of total outlays to 6.9 per cent. An increasing proportion of the defence budget was allocated to wages (and retirement benefits) while a decreasing proportion was purchasing weapons and other defence capital.

2.6 Conclusion

Large budget deficits not directly related to war or depression are a very recent innovation in US history. Following the Second World War budget deficits under peacetime non-recessionary conditions began to become commonplace for the first time, but for most of the period since 1945 had remained in general very small as a percentage of total outlays, and regularly alternated with surpluses. The problem of persistent and increasing federal deficits has developed only since the end of the 1960s.

The Keynesian revolution has probably contributed to this development but did not directly cause it. The significant change that can be traced to the New Economics was the increasing acceptability of compensatory fiscal policy– involving relatively small, intentionally planned budget deficits ostensibly designed to produce full employment – by politicians and the general public. Keynesian theory also constituted an intellectual foundation for increasing economic intervention by government. But mainstream practitioners of the New Economics did not imply that deficits don't matter, and neither politicians nor the general public appears to have developed this belief since the Keynesian revolution. By introducing confusion in the public mind and the minds of politicians regarding the appropriate size of the budget deficit, Keynesian doctrine surely mitigated the effectiveness of one important constraint in the form of popular opinion which had long contributed to balanced budgets. It accomplished this by suggesting that the appropriate federal deficit was not simply zero under normal peacetime circumstances, but some number which varied according to circumstances and which was subject to varying estimates by different economists. This relative relaxation of traditional constraints probably contributed significantly to the haemorrhaging federal budget deficits of the 1970s but was not the direct cause.

Its direct cause appears to have been the rapid increase in relatively uncontrollable transfer spending to individuals since the late 1960s. This component of federal spending accounted for most of the growth in outlays as a percentage of GNP over the past 20 years. As the growth in spending for income transfers became increasingly automatic, individual politicians were able to evade responsibility for ballooning deficits, in the eyes of voters. Meanwhile, automatic spending increases became more difficult to oppose and, as a consequence of numerous institutional reforms in Congress, easier for beneficiary interest groups to identify and support. This growing downward (political) price rigidity has caused a significantly higher rate of growth in federal obligations than in federal revenues. In the absence of any general earmarking provision tying the growth of federal spending to the growth in federal revenues, this has created the record deficits of the 1980s. After nearly 35 years of fairly steady decline, the national debt as a percentage of GNP (the most useful way of defining the real debt) has begun a rapid growth which represents a dramatic change.

40   *G. M. Anderson*

Notes

All budget data for the period before 1970 is from US Census Bureau (1970, vol. 2) and all data for the period 1970–85 is from Office of Management and Budget (1986), unless otherwise noted.

1 In fact, in the post-Civil War era, the problem of significant underestimates of surpluses caused persistent concern. See Kimmel (1958, pp. 70–5).

2 Achieving a balance between expenditures and receipts on an annual basis was a major concern of the Founding Fathers, especially Alexander Hamilton. According to one historian, 'During Washington's two administrations the United States was governed practically by [Hamilton's] ideas, if not by his will' (Croly 1909, pp. 38–9).

3 According to Juglar (1893) there were seven significant financial panics in the nineteenth century, each lasting a year or more.

4 Only in the case of the Mexican War (1846–8) was there a net deficit for the preceding five-year period (resulting in this case from the economic slump associated with the panic of 1837).

5 The average monthly deficit for the three months centred on the initial trough of the 1908 recession was $10.9 million, the highest since 1879. See Firestone (1960, p. 162).

6 This reflected conscious policy on the part of both Congress and the executive branch. See section 2.4 below.

7 This reduction in the national debt was mostly the result of large public auction sales of elements of the public domain, proceeds from which were earmarked for debt payment (Gates 1984, p. 37).

8 In 1860 the (nominal) deficit was $7.066 million and the debt was $64.844 million. In 1865 the respective figures were $963.841 million and $2,677.929 million.

9 However, the period 1866–80 was also one of rapid deflation; in 1866 the Consumer Price Index was 167 (1860 = 100) and by 1880 it had fallen to 110. Hence, in real terms the debt was little changed. Nevertheless, government obligations had been contracted under *inflationary* conditions, and nominal debt reduction was evidence of conscientious fiscal policy.

10 Unfortunately, most of these polling results provide very little indication of the price the majority of the general public is willing to pay in order to secure balanced budgets. (According to the authors of one recent study, Americans favour a balanced budget amendment to the Constitution 'for a smorgasbord of reasons and at an unclear price' (Blinder and Holtz-Eakin 1984, p. 148)). While one Harris poll (January 1979) seems to indicate that a large majority favours spending cuts to achieve a balanced budget but is unable to agree on any specific pattern of cuts, a more recent Harris poll, conducted in February 1985, suggests that majority support exists in principle for a number of specific deficit cutting packages involving spending cuts and tax increases. For the 1979 poll results, see Congressional Budget Office (1982, p. 30); for the 1985 poll results, see Harris (1985).

11 In fact, the existence of the War-related debt problem is usually taken to have contributed significantly to the ultimate creation of a strong federal government

itself. According to one historian, '[until] 1787 the movement to strengthen the Union was almost wholly directed toward settling the debt upon Congress and giving Congress the right to collect taxes' (Anderson 1983, p. 13). See also Kimmel (1958, p.10), and Dorfman (1946, p. 433).

12 In 1791, total expenditures were about $3 million. By 1799, they had risen to about $9 million. Over the entire period, military spending and interest on the debt constituted around 80 per cent of expenditures. See Dewey (1939, p. 111).

13 Elsewhere, he explained the basis of his conviction that one generation had no right to bind the next: 'the earth belongs to the living generation'. He thought that this consideration applied to national debts, and that if it was nevertheless absolutely necessary for the government to enter into debt, those debts should be completely extinguished in around 20 years (ibid).

14 These positions were held by Presidents James Madison (1809–17), James Monroe (1817–25), John Quincy Adams (1825–9), and Andrew Jackson (1829–37). When the latter took office, the prevailing belief was that the federal debt would in fact soon be extinguished. Referring to the happy time after this goal was expected to be achieved, Jackson maintained in his first annual message to Congress that 'our population will be relieved from a considerable portion of its present burthens, and will find out not only new motives to practice affection, but additional means for the display of individual enterprise' (quoted in Kimmel (1958, p. 19)). For Madison's views, see ibid. (p. 18); for Adams's see Bolles (1883, p. 92); and for Jackson's, see ibid. (p. 134).

15 In fact, the public debt *was* entirely paid off in 1835, although the period of zero national debt lasted only a few months. See Myers (1970, p. 95).

16 On the National Banking Act, see Myers (1970, pp. 162–3); on the tax on state bank notes see Kimmel (1958, p. 64); on the income tax, large tariff increases, and Treasury borrowing see Myers (1970, pp. 157–60, 160, and 149–53, respectively).

17 Johnson's plan was apparently considered too stringent by Congress. See Noyes (1902, pp. 30–2).

18 Although Hayes (1877–81) was concerned that foreigners held too much of the national debt, his position on balanced budgets and the debt generally is unclear. See Eckenrode (1930, p. 44).

19 See Noyes (1902, pp. 204–5). Despite the recession and the rapid deflation of the early 1890s, tariff rates were not reduced.

20 According to Firestone (1960, pp. 28–9) this revenue reduction followed the sharp rise in tariffs passed under McKinley in 1890.

21 See Kimmel (1958, p. 84). In his inaugural address, Taft specifically called for the expansion of the scope of government.

22 Ibid. (pp. 83–9). Given Roosevelt's general policy orientation, the latter seems more likely.

23 Kimmel (1958, p. 86), for example, makes this argument.

24 Wilson's supposed 'modernity' is emphasized by Kimmel (1958, p. 86). According to Waltman (1985, p. 33), Wilson's major fiscal concern was 'that the books be balanced and borrowing held to an absolute minimum', and that he strongly favoured the finance of the pre-war military build-up by taxation rather than borrowing.

25 This provided that during each fiscal year there should be *placed* in the sinking fund a credit amounting to 2½ per cent of the aggregate amount of Liberty Bonds and Victory Notes outstanding on 1 July 1920, with the sinking fund allocated exclusively to debt service and repayment. See Kimmel (1958, p. 317, n. 8).

26 It should also be noted that the balanced budgets during both the Harding and Coolidge administrations were 'real' in the sense that they represented basically the full 'spending' activities of the federal government. Although land grant activity continued, it was at a rapidly diminishing level and the average value of land granted per acre was low for the simple reason that by 1920 most of the more valuable land had either been already granted or excluded from sale or grant (e.g., the National Park System).

27 For a revisionist account of Coolidge as a highly principled libertarian intellectual, see Johnson (1983, pp. 67–80).

28 On 10 September 1932, President Hoover called for a reduction in expenditures for the fiscal year 1934 of $500 million. In the fiscal year 1933, expenditures were only $4,623 million. See *New York Times*, 11 September 1932; p. 1.

29 A contemporary account of the 1932 Presidential campaign asserted: 'In recent weeks, it has been impossible to page a newspaper or twirl a radio without being assailed by dissertation, invective, and propaganda regarding federal expenditures, deficits, and taxes' (Haig 1932, p. 234). On Roosevelt's use of the deficit as a major campaign theme, see ibid. (pp. 236–7). Roosevelt referred to the deficit under Hoover as 'staggering . . . so great it makes us catch our breath' and declared that '[the] budget is not balanced and the whole job must be done over again in the next session of Congress'.

30 The Reconstruction Finance Corporation was designed to provide loans to business enterprises at subsidized interest rates. See Leuchtenburg (1967, pp. 98–100).

31 The Federal Farm Board was designed to implement a 'proto-New Deal farm policy of attempting to raise and support farm prices' (Rothbard 1972, p. 137).

32 Despite the title this programme provided subsidized capital to the building and loan industry, not homeowners directly. See ibid. (p. 134).

33 Hoover proposed a $600 million increase in public works spending by the end of 1929, prompting J.M. Clark to praise the President's 'industrial statesmanship' (Clark 1930, p. 15).

34 This effort and its effects in exacerbating the Depression are discussed in Smiley (1983).

35 As Stein (1969, p. 43) observes: 'Candidate Roosevelt had strongly denounced Hoover for failure to balance the budget, *and had promised to perform that feat himself if elected*' (italics added).

36 President Hoover was so concerned about balancing the federal budget while maintaining (historically) high levels of outlays for social programmes and public works that his administration strongly promoted significant tax increases in 1931, in the depths of the Great Depression – a policy which Stein describes as a 'desperate folly' (1969, p. 38). However, similar concerns were shared by Roosevelt; for example, in a fireside chat of 24 July 1933, Hoover's successor

reviewed the progress of his recovery programme to date, and boasted that his new administration was determined to balance the budget where his 'irresponsible' predecessor had failed (1969, p. 46).

37 As Galbraith testified before the Joint Economic Committee of Congress in 1955, '[the Administration] has shown considerable grace and ease in getting away from the cliches of a balanced budget and the unspeakable evils of deficit financing . . . [it] has shown a remarkable flexibility of mind in the speed with which it has moved away from these slogans' (quoted in Stein 1969, pp. 283–4).

38 This variant is 'balancing the budget over the business cycle', and represents the modern Keynesian orthodoxy. See Dornbusch and Fischer (1978).

39 Unfortunately, public opinion polls provide little basis for evaluating the degree to which balanced budgets may have shifted over time as a priority among voters. If balanced budgets had fallen from one of the top three issues in public concern to seventy-fifth, for example, this might be equivalent to an abandonment of balanced budgets as a real goal by the voting public. But the overwhelming popular support for as stringent a measure as a balanced budget amendment to the US Constitution – favoured by overwhelming majorities in public opinion polls (see Gallup 1981, vol. 3, p. 1587) – suggests that large deficits continue to be a leading concern of the general public.

40 This shift has been one result of the transition to a volunteer military force since 1973.

41 As Hemel (1981, p. 16) explains: 'programs are "uncontrollable" because they are automatically funded each year, rather than being reviewed relatively as part of the Congressional appropriations process. . . . Like ghosts of Christmases past, the generosity of Congress past has left legacies that will haunt us for years to come.'

42 Although social security is undeniably an 'uncontrollable' spending programme, some would object to its inclusion in the list of programmes driving the recent increase in federal spending affecting the size of federal deficits. Social security is technically financed separately out of a trust fund which has been substantially in surplus since 1981 and has been projected to remain so for the next several years at least. Current-period expenditures of the social security system are entirely financed out of current-period social security payroll tax collections. Therefore it might plausibly be argued that the growth in social security outlays has been strictly irrelevant to the growth of federal budget deficits since 1970.

The major flaw in this reasoning is that the aforementioned surpluses in the social security trust fund are routinely added to the gross federal deficit by the Office of Management and Budget in order to determine the 'net deficit', i.e. the deficit figures which are referred to in usual policy discussions. For example, in the 1986 fiscal budget, the net federal deficit for fiscal 1985 is projected as $222 billion. But the *gross* deficit – before the addition of the social security surplus – is projected as $272 billion. Moreover, for six of the 10 years between 1975 and 1985, the social security trust fund was substantially in deficit. This is the same period that saw the unprecedentedly rapid growth of peacetime net deficits from 3.6 per cent of GNP to 5.7 per cent (est.). Athough large annual surpluses in the social security trust fund are projected through 1990, there seems to be no valid reason for segregating social security spending from other

G. M. Anderson

transfers to individuals when analysing the growth of the federal deficit.

43 According to Hemel (1981, p. 17): 'rarely does a year go by when provisions of each of the major entitlement programs are not modified in one way or another [by Congress or the Executive Branch]'.

44 For example, Schick's argument relies heavily on a purported shift in power in Congress in which fiscal conservatives in key positions lost authority over the budgetary process, a hypothesis which seems ad hoc and extremely difficult to test. The Schepsle–Weingast work is not subject to this particular objection, but has another major problem: namely that the alleged shift in authority from full committees to subcommittees is not reflected in the available statistics. The total number of Congressional subcommittees grew from 109 in 1955–6 to 148 in 1967–8. But the numbers have fluctuated greatly since. In 1971–2, there were only 135. By 1975–6 this had increased to 168. The number fell until in 1983–4 (the period in which really large unplanned deficits developed) there were only 136 subcommittees (Ornstein et al. 1984, p. 109). Of course, this does not in itself necessarily constitute a falsification of their hypothesis, but at least suggests that a relevant empirical test would probably be very difficult.

45 The literature is immense. One of the more comprehensive recent collections of essays and technical papers is Cagan (1985).

46 In some respects the modern public choice theory of effects of deficits on the rate of growth of government spending was anticipated by the classical economists. Both Smith and Ricardo argued that deficit spending caused excessive government growth, and that this represented the major economic cost of deficits (on Ricardo, see Anderson and Tollison (1986); on Smith see Smith (1979, pp. 895–6)). This line of reasoning was largely neglected by later economic writers. Smith specifically argued that the frequency and intensity of government involvement in war was functionally related to the availability of borrowing as opposed to taxation to politicians. In other words, deficit spending tended to increase government spending *during wartime.*

This interesting theory is consistent with the history of budget deficits in the US since 1900. Before 1969, large deficits occurred primarily during war, with balanced federal budgets (or significant surpluses) the rule during peacetime. If we compare federal spending as a percentage of GNP one year prior to US involvement in each major war with the same figure for the second year following the conclusion of hostilities, we find dramatic growth; from 1.4 to 6.9 per cent (a growth of 397 per cent) for the First World War; from 9.0 to 16.8 per cent (a growth of 85 per cent) for the Second World War; and from 15.3 to 17.2 per cent (a growth of almost 12 per cent) for the Korean War. Deficits during war may have been a significant determinant of government growth in the US for most of this century at least.

References

Anderson, Gary M. and Martin, Dolores T. 1986: Leviathan as Landlord: Explaining Nineteenth Century Federal Land Policy, *Cato Journal* (forthcoming).

US Federal Deficit and National Debt 45

Anderson, Gary M. and Tollison, Robert D. 1986: Ricardo on the Public Debt: Principle Versus Practice, *History of Economics Society Bulletin* (forthcoming).

Anderson, William G. 1983: *The Price of Liberty: The Public Debt of the American Revolution.* Charlottesville, Va.: University Press of Virginia.

Bolles, Albert S. 1883: *The Financial History of the U.S. from 1789 to 1860.* New York: D. Appleton and Co.

Buchanan, James M. and Lee, Dwight R. 1982: Politics, Time, and the Laffer Curve, *Journal of Political Economy*, 40, 816–19.

Buchanan, James M. and Wagner, Richard E. 1977: *Democracy in Deficit.* New York: Academic Press.

Cagan, Phillip (ed.) 1985: *The Economy in Deficit.* Washington, D.C.: American Enterprise Institute.

Clark, John Maurice 1930: Public Works and Unemployment, *American Economic Review, Papers and Proceedings*, 30, 15–19.

Congressional Budget Office 1982: *Balancing the Federal Budget and Limiting Federal Spending: Constitutional and Statutary Approaches.* Washington, D.C.

Croly, Herbert 1909: *The Promise of American Life.* New York: G.P. Putnam's Sons.

Dewey, Davis R. 1939: *Financial History of the U.S.* New York: Longmans, Green and Co.

Dornbusch, Rudiger and Fischer, Stanley 1978: *Macroeconomics.* New York: McGraw-Hill.

Eckenrode, H.J. 1930: *Rutherford B. Hayes: Statesman of Reunion.* New York: F. Ungar.

Firestone, John M. 1960: *Federal Receipts and Expenditures during Business Cycles, 1879–1958*, Princeton, N.J.: Princeton University Press.

Gallup, George H. 1972, 1978, 1981: *The Gallup Poll of Public Opinion, 1935–1980.* Willington, Del.: Scholarly Resources, Inc.

Gates, Paul W. 1984: The Federal Lands – Why We Retained Them, in Brubaker, S. (ed.) *Rethinking the Federal Lands.* Washington, D.C.: Resources for the Future, Inc.

Haig, Robert M. 1932: The State of the Federal Finances, *The Yale Review*, 221, 234–51.

Harris, C. Lowell (ed.) 1985: *Control of Federal Spending: Proceedings of the Academy of Political Science*, vol. 35. New York: Academy of Political Science.

Hemel, Eric 1981: The Expensive Myth of 'Uncontrollable' Spending, *Journal of Contemporary Studies*, 4, 15–26.

Howe, George F. 1934: *Chester A. Arthur: A Quarter Century of Machine Politics.* New York: F. Ungar.

Hughes, Jonathan R.T. 1977: *The Governmental Habit.* New York: Basic Books.

Juglar, Clement 1893: *A Brief History of Panics.* New York: G.P. Putnam's Sons.

Kimmel, Lewis H. 1958: *Federal Budget and Fiscal Policy, 1789–1958.* Washington, D.C.: The Brookings Institution.

Lebergott, Stanley 1984: *The Americans: An Economic Record.* New York: W.W. Norton and Co.

Leuchtenburg, William E. 1967: The New Deal and the Analogue of War, in Braeman, J., Bremmer, R.H. and Walters, E. (eds), *Change and Continuity in Twentieth Century America.* New York: Harper and Row, pp. 81–143.

Myers, Margaret G. 1970: *A Financial History of the U.S.* New York: Colombia University Press.

Noyes, Alexander D. 1902: *Thirty Years of American Finance: 1865–1896.* New York: G.P. Putnam's Sons.

Office of Management and Budget 1986: *Historical Tables: Budget of the United States Government.* Washington, D.C.

Ornstein, Norman J., Mann, Thomas E., Malbin, Michael J., Schick, Allen and Bibby, John F. 1984: *Vital Statistics on Congress, 1984–1985.* Washington, D.C.: American Enterprise Institute for Public Policy Research.

Rothbard, Murray N. 1972: Herbert Hoover and the Myth of Laissez-Faire, in Radosh, Ronald and Rothbard, Murray, N. (eds), *A New History of Leviathan.* New York: E.P. Dutton, pp. 111–45.

Schick, Allen 1983: The Distributive Congress, in Schick, Allen (ed.), *Making Economic Policy in Congress.* Washington, D.C.: American Enterprise Institute, pp. 257–74.

Schepsle, Kenneth A. and Weingast, Barry R. 1985: Policy Consequences of Government by Congressional Subcommittees, in Harris, C. Lowell (ed.), *Control of Federal Spending.* Montpelier, Vt.: Capital City Press.

Smiley, Gene 1983: Federal Government Spending and Taxation and the Recovery from the Great Depression. Marquette University (unpublished).

Smith, Adam, 1979: *An Inquiry into the Nature and Causes of the Wealth of Nations.* Cambridge, Cambridge University Press.

Stein, Herbert 1969: *The Fiscal Revolution in America.* Chicago: University of Chicago Press.

Waltman, Jerold L. 1985: *Political Origins of the U.S. Income Tax.* Jackson, Miss.: University Press of Mississippi.

Willoughby, William F. 1927: *The National Budget System: with Suggestions for its Improvement.* Baltimore, Md.: Johns Hopkins.

US Census Bureau 1970: *Historical Statistics of the United Staes*, Vols 1 and 2. Washington D.C.: U.S. Department of Commerce.

2

Journal of Economic Perspectives—Volume 14, Number 3—Summer 2000—Pages 3–19

The Political Economy of the Budget Surplus in the United States

Alberto Alesina

I n 1998, the federal government of the United States reached a budget surplus for the first time in 30 years. Even though many commentators have described this event as a rare and major success, what is remarkable is not that the U.S. government has reached a surplus, but that this result is perceived as so "exceptional." In fact, given the strong expansion of the U.S. economy in the last eight years, and the "peace dividend" due to the end of the cold war, nobody should be overly surprised at the much improved fiscal balance. The reason why a surplus for the federal government appears so unusual is that American citizens, like those of many other industrial countries, have become accustomed to large and persistent deficits from the mid-1970s onward. In fact, many European countries, which have had much lower growth than the United States and higher interest rates, are still struggling with this legacy of accumulated debts.[1]

While current budget surpluses should be viewed as relatively normal, the large budget deficits of the 1980s were exceptional. According to the "tax-smoothing" theory, the budget balance should be used as a buffer to allow tax rates to be approximately constant at the level that keeps the budget in intertemporal balance.[2] Thus, temporary deficits are expected to occur during recessions and

---

[1] The "peace dividend" was proportionally much lower for European countries, since their defense spending was already much lower than in the United States during the cold war period.

[2] The theory is based on convex distortionary costs of taxation. An example of such a tax is a proportional income tax in a labor supply model where individuals choose between leisure and consumption. In a fully specified model, general equilibrium effects may lead to nonconstant tax rates, although they would still be less variable than fluctuations in spending (Barro, 1979; Lucas and Stokey, 1993).

■ *Alberto Alesina is Professor of Economics and Government, Harvard University, and Research Associate, National Bureau of Economic Research, both in Cambridge, Massachusetts. He is also Research Fellow, Center for Economic Policy Research, London, United Kingdom.*

periods of exceptionally high spending. Conversely, budget surpluses should be the norm during expansions, like the current one in the United States, and periods of temporarily low spending, like when a (cold or hot) war ends. These are also the empirical predictions of a traditional Keynesian model of fiscal policy. Therefore, the view that the current surpluses are exceptional and offer an opportunity for doing something extraordinary has to be vastly toned down.[3] The tax-smoothing theory, however, does not take into account the political economy of deficits and surpluses.[4] How to divide the common pool of fiscal revenues and how to allocate the tax burden are the critical political battlefields in every country. The academic literatures on the macroeconomic effects of fiscal policy often ignore redistributive issues. The only type of redistribution captured by standard (nonpolitical economy) macroeconomic models of fiscal policy capture is that which occurs across generations.[5]

If the conflict over how to allocate fiscal resources is taken into account, then the current debate over the surplus becomes hardly surprising. In many respects, this debate is similar to the one on the question of "Who should pay for the deficits?" In a period of deficits, the conflict is about which taxes should be raised and which spending programs cut; in a period of surpluses, it is the reverse. However, there is an interesting difference between the political economy of surpluses and deficits. In a situation of fiscal surplus, resources are available to compensate the temporary "losers" of reforms that benefit a majority. In many situations, the short-run costs of certain reforms which fall on a vocal minority of the population may be sufficient to defeat the reform politically. A temporary abundance of fiscal revenues may help circumvent these political blocks. In a period of deficits, instead, compensating the losers may be more difficult if additional increases in deficits are economically (or politically) costly.

In many OECD countries, including the United States, pension reforms are the critical fiscal issue of the next decade, with important implications for long-term fiscal balance. In the last three decades, the component of government spending that has fueled the growth of government in OECD countries has been transfers, as opposed to public consumption of goods and services. Among the transfer components, pensions are in many countries the type of spending that is most "out of balance" in an intertemporal sense, because of the aging population and generous benefits. Therefore, pension reforms have to be critical ingredients of long-term fiscal stabilization in many OECD countries. However, the fraction of the current generation that would see its social security benefits reduced, or its

---

[3] Talvi and Vegh (2000) support the tax-smoothing hypothesis empirically for G-7 countries. Evidence drawn on developing countries shows, instead, procyclicality of fiscal policy. On the same point, see also Gavin and Perotti (1997).

[4] For a review of the literature on the political economy of fiscal policy, which departs from the tax-smoothing model and enriches it with redistributive conflicts and political competition, see Alesina and Perotti (1995a).

[5] The pathbreaking papers on intergenerational redistribution and public debt are Diamond (1965) and Barro (1974).

contribution increased, often has enough political influence to block social security reforms, particularly those in which the main beneficiaries are future generations. Countries in fiscal stress are caught between a rock and a hard place. On the one hand, they need pension reforms to achieve long-run fiscal stability. On the other hand, they can hardly afford compensation schemes for the losers and can hardly finance transitional measures. A country in temporary surplus with a long-run problem of solvency of its Social Security system is in a more favorable position to overcome potential vetoes to pension reforms.

One can rephrase the same concept in a tax-smoothing framework: the current U.S. surpluses are accompanied by a realization that in the not-too-distant future, the Social Security system will either require more funding or a structural reform. Thus, without welfare and Social Security reform, future spending is expected to be higher than today. According to tax smoothing, taxes should be increased today, unless reforms are introduced to reduce future spending. The argument of this paper is, then, that the tax-smoothing theory suggests the current surplus should be used to retire debt and reduce the debt over GDP ratio. In addition, if one links the current surplus to the long-run solvency problems of the Social Security system, then the surplus allows for some richer policy alternatives to only retiring debt. However, the political battle over the surplus may lead to a flurry of uncoordinated tax cuts and spending increases, which might eliminate both the options of retiring debt or linking the surpluses to Social Security reform.

The next section of this paper reviews the current and past fiscal history of the United States, which led to the surpluses, and discusses projections for the future. I then discuss the various possible alternatives concerning the question of "what to do with the surplus."

The Budget in the United States: Yesterday, Today and Tomorrow

Figure 1 shows the debt/GNP ratio in the United States in the last 200 years.[6] The "tax-smoothing" hypothesis describes much of U.S. fiscal history very well. The debt/GNP ratio sharply increases during wars and declines after them. Also, as the Great Depression shows, the debt/GNP ratio increases when growth is low or negative: as a result of the Depression, the debt/GNP ratio in the interwar period did not decline as quickly as after World War II.

Figure 1 also highlights the precipitous downward trend of debt/GNP in the postwar period, from 122 percent of GNP in 1946 to 32 percent in 1979. This pattern is briefly interrupted only by recessions, especially the one after the first oil shock, and by the "local" military conflicts of Korea and Vietnam. The trend toward a declining debt/GNP ratio, which was consistent with the tax-smoothing hypothesis, is clearly reversed in the late 1970s and early 1980s. While the mediocre growth

---

[6] This is the only case in which, because of data availability, ratios of fiscal variables are expressed over GNP. Everywhere else in the paper they are expressed in terms of GDP.

Figure 1
U.S. Public Debt Since 1790

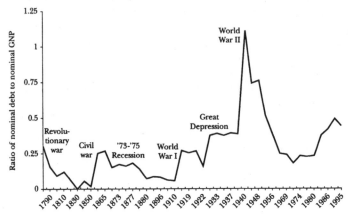

Source: Barro (1993)

performance in the period 1979-1982 contributes to the increase in deficits, the rest of the 1980s clearly show a radical departure from tax smoothing, as budget deficits accumulated in a period of peace and sustained growth. The debt/GDP ratio increased to 68 percent in 1995 (half held by the public): these are the levels of the debt/GDP ratio of the mid-1950s, only a few years after the end of World War II. One may argue that the 1980s were, in a sense, a period of "war"—namely, the final push to end the cold war. While this interpretation cannot be completely dismissed, it is, in my judgement, not enough to rationalize the budget outcomes of the 1980s. In summary, the fiscal policy of the 1980s was unsound from the point of view of tax smoothing.

The current budget surpluses have been the result of: 1) the exceptional performance of the American economy since 1991, a performance which has generated a surge of tax revenues; 2) low interest rates; and 3) a large reduction in defense spending as a share of GDP. In terms of discretionary policy, the Omnibus Budget Reconciliation Act of 1993 is the most important deficit reduction act of the decade, and it included a variety of tax increases and spending cuts.[7] As argued below, however, this act would have not eliminated the deficit without the exceptional performance of the economy and the "peace dividend."

Table 1 shows the pattern of various components of spending as a share of GDP. After the cuts in the early 1980s, GDP domestic discretionary spending has remained constant (as a share of GDP) from the late 1980s onward, while defense spending has fallen from 5.9 percent of GDP in 1988 to 3.2 percent in 1998, the

---

[7] See Auerbach (1994) for a much more detailed discussion of this policy package.

Table 1

Outlays as a share of GDP

Year	Discretionary Spending				Entitlements and Other Mandatory Spending					
	Defense	Domestic	International	Total	Medicaid	Medicare	Social Security	Other Retirement And Disability	Total[a]	Total Outlays
1988	5.9	3.2	0.3	9.4	0.6	1.7	4.4	1.1	10.2	21.5
1989	5.7	3.1	0.3	9.1	0.6	1.8	4.3	1.1	10.3	21.4
1990	5.3	3.2	0.3	8.8	0.7	1.9	4.3	1.1	11	22.1
1991	5.5	3.3	0.3	9.1	0.9	1.9	4.6	1.1	12	22.6
1992	4.9	3.5	0.3	8.7	1.1	2.1	4.6	1.1	11.7	22.5
1993	4.5	3.5	0.3	8.3	1.2	2.2	4.7	1.1	11.4	21.8
1994	4.1	3.5	0.3	7.9	1.2	2.3	4.6	1.1	11.4	21.3
1995	3.8	3.5	0.3	7.6	1.2	2.5	4.6	1.0	11.4	21.1
1996	3.5	3.3	0.2	7.1	1.2	2.5	4.6	1.0	11.4	20.7
1997	3.4	3.2	0.2	6.9	1.2	2.6	4.5	1.0	11.2	20.1
1998	3.2	3.2	0.2	6.6	1.3	2.5	4.5	1.0	11.2	19.6

Source: Congressional Budget Office (1999).

[a] Not reported are farm price support, deposit insurance, unemployment compensation and "others."

lowest level of the last 50 years. Given many localized conflicts requiring NATO intervention, today's defense spending may have reached a level that is, unfortunately, hard to reduce much further.[8] Discretionary domestic spending has instead remained constant as a share of GDP at around 3.2 percent despite various "budget deals" and "spending caps" imposed in the 1990s.

In the mandatory spending part of the budget, Medicare and Medicaid have almost doubled their share of GDP in ten years: these two programs combined were 2.3 percent of GDP in 1988 and are 3.8 in 1998. Reducing the growth of mandatory spending and entitlements is very difficult politically because these programs affect a large fraction of the population and any significant reduction of spending requires a change of entitlement rules. Even in the days of the so-called "Reagan revolution" and the welfare cuts often discussed at that time, only those programs with relatively specific beneficiaries were reduced, while broad-based programs were largely unaffected (see contributions in Alesina and Carliner, 1991).

On the revenue side, as shown in Table 2, an increase in the share of revenues as a share of GDP begins in 1994, partly as a result of the Omnibus Budget Reconciliation Act of 1993. As pointed out by Munnell (1998), the large surge in fiscal revenues has gone beyond what could be expected even with the strong economy of the 1990s. An interesting question is how much of the reduction in the debt/GDP ratio is due to the behavior of the economy (growth rates and interest

---

[8] In fact, the presidential candidate of the Republican Party, George W. Bush, is advocating a substantial increase in military spending.

Table 2
Revenues as a Share of GDP

Year	Individual Income Taxes	Corporate Income Taxes	Social Insurance Taxes	Excise Taxes	Total Revenues
1988	8.1	1.9	6.7	0.7	18.3
1989	8.3	1.9	6.7	0.6	18.5
1990	8.2	1.6	6.7	0.6	18.2
1991	8.0	1.7	6.8	0.7	18.0
1992	7.7	1.6	6.7	0.7	17.7
1993	7.9	1.8	6.6	0.7	17.8
1994	7.9	2.0	6.7	0.8	18.4
1995	8.2	2.2	6.7	0.8	18.8
1996	8.7	2.3	6.8	0.7	19.3
1997	9.3	2.3	6.8	0.7	19.8
1998	9.9	2.2	6.8	0.7	20.5

Source: Congressional Budget Office (1999).

rates) and how much of it is due to a discretionary fiscal adjustment. The difficulties in answering this question are several. First, the behavior of the economy may be influenced by fiscal policy; therefore, the effects of policy and the economy cannot be separated. Second, the baseline for a "normal" economy is controversial. Third, the methods of correcting for cyclical effects of various items of the budget varies with alternative hypotheses and procedures.

In any case, an intriguing (although rough) comparison is between the United States and countries of the euro area, many of which were going through fiscal adjustments in the 1990s. An interesting question is the following: What would have happened to the U.S. budget if the American economy had grown at the same rate as Euroland and had faced the same interest rates? One way of answering this question is to follow the procedure suggested by Auerbach (1994, p. 170, eq. 9). This expression shows how to calculate "the immediate, permanent reduction in the primary deficit . . . that if projections prove accurate, would be needed to bring the debt-GDP ratio at some date T in the future down to some initial level t." Using this formula, I calculated how much bigger the reduction of the primary deficit/GDP ratio in 1993 would have needed to be to achieve the 1998 level of the debt/GDP ratio, if the spread between the interest rates and the growth in the United States had been the same as that of an average of the current eleven members of the European Monetary Union.[9] The average spread between long-term real interest rates and the growth rate in the countries that joined the European monetary union was about 3 percent; the same spread in the U.S.

---

[9] These countries are Austria, Belgium, Finland, France, Germany, Ireland, Italy, Luxembourg, Netherlands, Portugal, and Spain.

economy was 1 percent.[10] I chose 1993 because this is a turning point when the debt/GDP ratio in the United States stopped growing, and this is the year of the Omnibus Budget Reconciliation Act of 1993.

The answer is that if the U.S. economy from 1994 to 1998 had performed like the economy of Europe, then the United States would have needed to have an additional permanent reduction in the deficit/GDP ratio of about 1.3 percentage point starting in 1993 to achieve the actual debt/GDP ratio that was reached in 1998. Europe was not doing too well economically in the 1990s, so this figure may be an upper bound, but it highlights how much the strong U.S. economy helped its fiscal improvement. As a matter of comparison, the primary deficit in the United States fell by about 1.2 percent in 1994, the year after OBRA, according to OECD data. Given the strong economy of 1994, a portion of this effect is due to the cyclical effect of GDP growth, beyond OBRA.

What about the future? For how long will surpluses accumulate? In a series of papers on fiscal adjustments in OECD economies, I have argued that fiscal adjustments which do not tackle the dynamic of entitlements are not long-lasting and tend to be reversed, simply because tax revenues cannot keep up with the growth of mandatory spending (Alesina and Perotti, 1995b, 1997; Alesina and Ardagna, 1997; see also Ardagna, 1999). Looking at the international evidence, one of the strongest indicators of whether a fiscal adjustment is long-lasting is the share of the deficit reduction obtained by stopping the growth of entitlements. In the same spirit, Auerbach (1994) argues that the Omnibus Reconciliation Act of 1993 did not provide a long-run fix for the budget, but only a short-term benefit which would disappear in the medium run.

The Congressional Budget Office (1999) has provided a very optimistic forecast on the accumulation of budget surpluses in the next decade.[11] The CBO predicted that surpluses will continue to increase in the next three years, reaching about 3 percent of GDP in 2009. As required by law, these forecasts are based upon a legal definition of unchanged legislation. However, from an economic point of view, these predictions vastly overestimate the surpluses. The CBO assumed that the spending caps imposed by the Deficit Control Act of 1997 will remain in place and will be fully implemented. Given the "emergency spending" in the Omnibus Consolidated Emergency Supplemental Appropriation Act of 1999 that added $21.4 billion of dollars to 1999 discretionary spending, the CBO predicted that until 2002, various cuts will compensate for this extra spending. This implies that discretionary spending will have to decline in *nominal terms* until 2002, falling from $575 billion in 1999 to $568 billion in 2002. After 2002, discretionary spending is expected to increase at the rate of inflation. These projections about spending lead

---

[10] To maintain comparability between United States and Europe I used OECD (*Economic Outlook*, June 1999) data for these calculations. More details are available from the author.

[11] The statistical work underlying this paper was performed in August 1999, and used the latest CBO forecasts available then.

to a predicted reduction of discretionary spending from 6.6 percent of GDP in 1999 to 5.0 percent in 2009.

It is virtually impossible that the current spending caps will be enforced in a decade of budget surpluses. First, it is hard to imagine that defense spending can continue to fall at the same rate of the 1990s. The "peace dividend" is pretty much a one-shot event associated with the collapse of the Soviet bloc, and as noted earlier in Table 1, defense spending as a share of GDP is about half of what it was in 1988. Therefore, the reduction of 1.6 percent of GDP in discretionary spending envisioned by the CBO would need to come largely from cuts in nondefense spending. If defense spending remains roughly constant as a share of GDP, the predicted cut in discretionary spending would require halving discretionary domestic spending as a share of GDP. This is very unlikely to happen. The additional $21.4 billion of discretionary spending in 1999 was "the highest level of emergency spending enacted in the 1990s, excluding spending for the Persian Gulf War" (CBO, 1999). Different readers may disagree about whether all the items of this bill were truly "emergencies." The point is that in a period of surplus and spending caps, the definition of an "emergency" will almost certainly become quite relaxed. To put it differently, the CBO projects into the future a legislation which has the nature of a single, unique legislation implemented in a period of fiscal adjustment. In addition, a one-shot "peace dividend" is projected into the future.

A more economically meaningful baseline of "unchanged policies" is one in which discretionary spending increases at the same rate of GDP. Under this much more reasonable assumption that discretionary spending will remain at the same share of GDP in the next decade, the size of the surplus in 2009 is roughly halved, from 3 percent of GDP to about 1.5 percent, even without taking into account that a slower reduction of the debt/GDP ratio implies a slower reduction of interest payments (for given interest rates). The CBO also assumes that tax revenue as a share of GDP will remain roughly constant. If even a fraction of the tax cuts discussed in Congress are passed, this baseline assumption is very optimistic.

The CBO assumptions about interest payments are, by implication, also quite optimistic. Interest spending is expected to fall from 2.3 percent of GDP in 1999 to 0.6 percent in 2003, as a result of low interest rates and the rapid reduction of the stock of debt. Given the large surpluses that the CBO predicts, the debt held by the public is predicted to fall sharply, reaching less than 10 percent of GDP in 2009. However, if surpluses accumulate less rapidly, the stock of debt will decline more slowly and interest payments will remain a higher fraction of GDP than what was predicted by the CBO. The CBO's predictions about interest rates appear reasonable, but since they are consistent with the hypothesis of a large drop in outstanding government debt which may not materialize, the interest rate projections are probably on the optimistic side.

In summary, under the realistic assumption that discretionary spending will not decrease much as a share of GDP, and that a small tax cut will be implemented in the next few years, the projected surpluses are less than half of the much-publicized forecasts of the CBO. In fact, even half of what the CBO predicts appears as a rather optimistic forecast. If one considers a time horizon beyond 10 years, the optimism about surpluses have to be toned down even more. As Auerbach (1994, 1997) forcefully pointed out, because of the effects of the aging generation of the "baby boomers" on Medicare, Medicaid and Social Security, the U.S. budget is, in the long run, in deficit, rather than in surplus; that is, in order to prevent the debt/GDP ratio from increasing in the next few decades, one would need an increase in the surplus well beyond the already optimistic predictions of the CBO. As pointed out in Table 1, the rapid growth of Medicare and Medicaid is already happening, and the growth of Social Security spending will appear as the "baby boomers" retire.

What To Do With the (Alleged) Surpluses?

First, I briefly discuss how economic theory would answer the question of what to do with the budget surpluses, and then I will analyze the politics surrounding it.

The Economics of Surpluses: Implications from Theory

Given the discussion of the previous section, the theorists' answer to the question of what to do with the surplus is simple: retire outstanding debt. Two arguments support this view: first, debt should be issued in recessions and retired in booms according to tax smoothing; second, current surpluses follow the excessive deficits of the 1980s. The argument for a temporary tax cut is weak, given the current state of the U.S. economy. More generally, the use of discretionary fiscal policy for fine-tuning is highly questionable, due to the "long and variable lags" argument. An argument for a permanent tax cut should ultimately rely on two grounds: Either spending is or is expected to be permanently lower; or economic growth is permanently higher, so lower tax rates will generate higher revenues.[12] I have serious doubts on both assumptions.

In any event, the point is that an argument in favor of a tax cut should be largely unrelated to the current temporary surplus. In fact, the effect of the future retirement of the baby boomers implies an expected *increase* in outlays for the government, at unchanged legislation. This effect calls for a permanent tax *increase*, rather than a tax cut. Obviously, legislation can change. Therefore, a different and interesting argument suggests using the surplus to finance tax reforms, particularly Social Security reforms. This issue is discussed below.

The criticisms directed to the proposals of using the surplus to cut taxes apply, in reverse, to proposals for spending hikes. Whether or not one favors more domestic spending, it is simply incoherent to argue that the current temporary surplus can support new spending programs, which, regardless of the intentions of the legislators, most often become permanent. Given the structure of the dynamic

---

[12] I do not even consider a Laffer curve argument, according to which lower tax rates would produce higher revenues automatically.

of spending discussed above, any proposal for more domestic discretionary spending requires a statement about how to finance it, either with higher taxes, or lower spending for entitlements, or more borrowing (that is, more taxes later) or a combination of the above.

The Politics of Surpluses

In many respects, the political economy of surpluses is similar to the political economy of deficits. In both cases, various lobbies, factions, pressure groups, and their representatives fight over the allocation of the costs of adjustment (in the case of deficits) or the benefits of the common pool of resources (in the case of surpluses). In different countries and at different points in time, political institutions are more or less capable of coordinating these pressures into a coherent and sound fiscal policy.[13]

The academic literature has pointed out that the fragmentation of a political system is an obstacle to the implementation of the appropriate fiscal decisions, particularly when various shocks require a swift fiscal response. In the most general sense, political fragmentation is a situation in which many political groups have a voice in fiscal decisions, and many have veto power.[14] The point is not that fragmentation necessarily creates budget deficits, but that fragmentation creates obstacles to policy changes, because it becomes more difficult to reach agreements about corrective fiscal measures. For example, the British political system is non-fragmented, since, by design, the same party controls the executive and legislative branches of government. Interestingly, despite Britain's less-than-stellar economic performance since World War II, the United Kingdom is not a country with a debt problem. At the end of World War II, the United Kingdom had a debt/GDP ratio of more than 250 percent. Currently it is around 60 percent, one of the lowest in Europe, and the United Kingdom was not one of the countries in danger of not making the fiscal criteria for joining the European Monetary Union, although it opted out. On the other extreme, countries with large and fragmented coalition governments have not managed to quickly adjust to the shocks of the '70s, and have accumulated very large debt. The best examples are Belgium and Italy, two countries with fragmented political systems, and whose debt/GDP ratios are currently well above 100 percent. These two countries were almost not admitted in the European Monetary Union because of their poor fiscal performance.

Divided government is the U.S. version of the coalition governments of parliamentary democracies. It is defined as any situation in which the same party does not hold the presidency, the House of Representatives, and the Senate. Several observers have attributed the deficit of the 1980s to a fiscal deadlock caused by divided government (for instance, McCubbins, 1991). However, it is far from clear that divided government in the federal government has created budget deficits.

---

[13] For a discussion of political models of fiscal adjustments, see Alesina, Perotti and Tavares (1998).
[14] For theoretical work on this point, see Alesina and Drazen (1991). For empirical work on a cross section of countries, see Roubini and Sachs (1989) and Perotti and Kontopoulos (1998).

Other periods of divided government at the federal level have not systematically produced deficits; in fact, the budget was balanced at the end of the 1990s in a period of divided government.

Evidence gathered concerning fragmentation and budgets at the state level has a different tone. States with divided governments have tended to delay the adjustment to negative fiscal shocks relative to states with unified governments (Poterba, 1994; Alt and Lowry, 1994). Even positive fiscal shocks—like unexpected higher tax revenues—have created fiscal deadlocks and delayed legislation in states with divided governments. This finding hints that the politics of deficits and surpluses are similar. In both cases, negative or positive fiscal shocks generate a similar political battle: Who should pay for the deficits in one case and who should benefit from the surpluses in the other?

An interesting question is whether in a situation of divided government, which is becoming more and more the rule rather than the exception in the United States, these battles over the budget are more or less likely to result in what Niskanen (1997) labeled "an incoherent mishmash of small spending increases and tiny tax cuts." Neither of the two American parties is immune from pork barrel politics. However, the balance provided by divided government may help avoid the most egregious deals to some extent. On the other hand, divided government may create an obstacle to the adoption of a coherent fiscal plan, if the latter is the result of a badly worked out compromise between conflicting plans of an administration and a Congress not held by the same party. In other words, relative to unified government, divided government offers more moderation and checks and balances, but also it creates the risk of fiscal confusion; in this case, a proliferation of uncoordinated bills leading to a waste of the temporary surplus without addressing the long-run fiscal deficits of the Social Security system.

The early stages of the discussion of what to do with the budget surplus show elements of both the positive and the negative aspects of divided government. Both parties have kept doors open to pork barrel politics. Debates in Congress often show examples of proposals for favors to various constituencies.[15] On the other hand, the extreme proposals on each side of the political spectrum will face opposition in one of the two branches of government, if the latter is divided. A Democratic president would veto the most extravagant tax cutting proposals from a Republican House. If a Democratic administration wanted to spend the surplus in domestic programs, a Republican House would object. This is precisely why American voters do not view divided government as an "accident," but a way of enforcing centrist policies.[16]

Beyond the standard battle over pork barrel favors, a few general themes about the use of the surplus have taken shape. Three kinds of general proposals have emerged.

---

[15] For humorous descriptions of some of the pork barrel proposals discussed in Congress, see several issues of *The Economist* magazine in July–August 1999.

[16] See Alesina and Rosenthal (1995) for an extensive theoretical and empirical discussion of this point.

1) Cut taxes across the board. Republicans in the House and the Senate have been pushing for major tax cuts, the biggest since those of the first Reagan administration. These cuts range from very broad-based ones, like proportional reduction of income tax rates, to more specific items of the tax code, like the inheritance tax. The philosophy underlying these proposals is that even through the first-best fiscal policy may call for retiring debt, current or future Democratic legislators and presidents are likely to spend the surplus in "wasteful" domestic programs, if surpluses continue to materialize.[17] Given this political constraint, the second-best policy for a fiscal conservative is to reduce fiscal revenues available to big spenders.

This idea cannot be easily dismissed, if one looks back at the 1980s. The Reagan plan of tax cuts and spending reductions—more of the former than the latter—gave rise to substantial deficits.[18] Once the deficits materialized, the Republicans both in the administration and in Congress held their ground against major tax increases. Many observers noted that, in the end, the deficits would have imposed a binding constraint on spending, an outcome at least non-disliked by many conservatives. A similar view briefly reemerged during the Dole presidential campaign of 1996.

From the point of view of someone who believes that government is too big, the policy of cutting taxes in order to "force" spending cuts in the future is reasonable, if not pushed to excess. Persson and Svensson (1989) and Alesina and Tabellini (1990) provide a model consistent with this implication. A "conservative" policymaker, opposed to the growth of domestic spending programs, may choose to abandon fiscal balance and let public debt accumulate. Future "liberal" governments will have to use a relatively large fraction of tax revenues to service the debt and they will be limited in the amount of tax revenues they can use for domestic spending. From the point of view of the conservative government, the cost of abandoning tax smoothing is more than compensated for by the constraint imposed on domestic spending. More generally, if one believes that institutional failures lead to an upward bias in spending levels, then a policy of tax cuts balances this distortion. One reason why spending might have an upward bias, for example, is related to the incentives of legislators to concentrate benefits of pork barrel projects in their districts, without internalizing the costs of taxation, which are spread across multiple districts.[19]

The Reagan deficits of the 1980s certainly contributed to a subsequent reductions of the size of government, measured as noninterest spending over GDP. If the Clinton administration did not face a deficit problem, spending caps probably would have not been imposed and it is quite likely that discretionary spending

---

[17] See Talvi and Vegh (2000) for a model that characterizes the effect of fiscal policies when surpluses automatically fuel spending.

[18] For a discussion of the reasons why the deficits increased in the early 1980s, see the contributions by Poterba, Stockman and Shultze in Feldstein (1994a).

[19] See Alesina and Perotti (1995a) for a survey and Milesi Ferretti, Perotti and Rostagno (2000) for some recent empirical evidence on spending biases in different institutional systems.

would not have remained constant. If a relatively large fraction of fiscal revenues had not been needed to service the debt accumulated in the 1980s, there would have been more room for spending in the 1990s. In other words, the argument that "if fiscal resources are available, they are spent" implies, logically, that the only way of enforcing spending cuts is to lower taxes. This is the "Starve the Leviathan" policy.

The Achilles' heel of these proposals is that, realistically, the only way to cut spending significantly in the long run is to do something about Social Security. Republican advocates of major tax cuts are typically not in the front line amongst the advocates of cuts of Social Security benefits.

The current proposals of the Clinton administration do not show a tendency to large increases in discretionary spending, but favor repaying the debt. However, conservatives argue that after a display of "moderation" in an election year, the true spirit of the big-spending Democrats will resurface. The idea of restraint of spending in election years is exactly the opposite prediction of the traditional "political business cycle" of Nordhaus (1975). This observation simply shows that Nordhaus's model offers only a partial view of the political process. In fact, the Democratic party, sensitive to accusations of lack of fiscal restraint, is moving toward the political middle of the road on fiscal issues.[20] Republicans argue that this moderation will not last long after the election.

2) Use the surplus to finance more discretionary domestic spending. This proposal, although not explicitly advocated by the Clinton administration and even less by Congress, has some support; see for instance, Reich (1999), Eisner (1998) and Baker (1998). These authors, amongst others, favor the use of surpluses to finance public investments in education, infrastructure, and so on.

Given the budget arithmetic discussed above, the view that many resources are available to increase domestic spending without raising taxes is simply incorrect. In fact, the argument for using current (temporary) surpluses to finance permanent spending hikes has the same flaws of the argument for permanent tax cuts. It may very well be true that current level of spending in education, infrastructure, poverty alleviation programs, and so on are too low. This does not mean that spending in these areas can be increased without either cutting some other forms of spending or increasing current taxes or future taxes (after issuing current debt). Advocates of more discretionary spending are not amongst those who favor cuts in entitlements, and almost nobody in the United States seems to favor higher taxes, at least openly.

Proponents of the "increase spending" argument may, in fact, be perfectly aware of the budget arithmetic, but they may have in mind the reverse of the "Starve the Leviathan" argument. They hope that once in place, new spending programs will create constituencies who favor them so that the fiscal resources necessary to finance them will be found, eventually.

3) Use the surplus to finance Social Security reforms. Any reform of the Social

---

[20] For models consistent with the view that parties display "moderation" in election years and then if elected, show their "true" nature, see Alesina and Rosenthal (1995, 2000).

Security system which moves it from a "pay as you go" system to a "fully funded" one implies transitional costs for the current generation. In Diamond's (1999, p. 4) words: "[S]ignificantly improving the financial value of Social Security for future generations would come at the costs of worsening the financial value of Social Security for current generations or would require that general revenues be devoted to Social Security." A hypothetical social planner would optimally trade off the costs for the current generation against the benefits for the infinite future, but in all political systems, the current generation has more voice than future, unborn generations. This essay is not the place to discuss alternative proposals for Social Security reform in any detail; the concern here is simply to sketch different implications for the budget surplus. Without such reforms, the costs of Social Security will begin to exceed payroll revenues by about 2013, and within a few years of 2032, the current trust fund would be bankrupt.

One side of the range of Social Security reform proposals would maintain the current "pay as you go" system and further increase the "advance funding" in anticipation of future solvency problems. This is largely the approach of the Clinton administration. Critics of this proposal argue that "there is a significant chance that some future Congress would use at least some of the funds to increase benefits or reduce taxes or possibly spend them for other purposes"(Diamond, 1999, p. 99). Note that this is the same logic underlying the "Starve the Leviathan" logic of tax cut proposals. In fact, on the Republican side, critics argue that President Clinton's proposal for "saving Social Security" is a ploy to collect more revenues and to avoid scaling down the size of government.[21]

One could pass legislation geared toward preventing the use of the Social Security trust fund for other purposes, but this kind of "binding" legislation can often be circumvented, at least up to a point. One example of this type of legislation would be a complete separation of the Social Security budget from the rest of the budget as advocated, for instance, by Munnell (1998). This step might avoid using the Social Security surplus for discretionary spending, but it would not avoid increasing Social Security benefits for current generations of voters at the expense of future generations.

An alternative type of proposal is to use the current surplus to finance the transition to a broader adoption of personal retirement accounts of the 401(k) type. Feldstein and Samwick (1997, 1999) and Feldstein (1999b) have put forward a specific proposal along this line. The idea is that individuals would receive a 2.3 percent tax cut on income up to the Social Security earning limit (currently around $68,000) on the condition that the tax cut is saved in a Personal Retirement Account (PRA). An individual who reaches retirement age can then withdraw payments from the PRA. Individuals' Social Security benefits would be replaced by 75 cents for every dollar of PRA withdrawal. Feldstein and Samwick (1999, p. 3) calculate that financing this scheme would cost about 0.9 percent of GDP in tax

---

[21] For a specific discussion and criticism of the Clinton administration's plan for Social Security, see Feldstein (1999a).

revenues, "less than the currently projected budget surpluses." Actually, with the more realistic projections about the surplus discussed earlier in this paper, the cost of this scheme may exhaust all the available surplus. As Feldstein (1997) noted, "[I]f the near term surpluses are too optimistic, the PRA tax credits could push the budget into deficits." In any case, even in the most optimistic scenario, a temporary tax increase will be needed at some point to finance the full transition to PRA accounts. From a tax-smoothing point of view, a temporary deficit incurred to help finance a future large increase in spending is appropriate, especially if the temporary deficits also serve the purpose of reducing future outlays.

Leaving aside a broader discussion of the pros and cons of how to structure individual retirement accounts, including the transaction costs of such accounts and how much freedom individuals would have to invest their money in different ways, this general type of reform would create a more solid commitment to use the surplus to "save Social Security" than simply increasing the trust fund. In addition, this kind of proposal may be politically palatable, since it combines an element of tax cut, favored by many Republicans, with an element of "using the surplus to save Social Security," an argument favored by the Clinton administration. A standard criticism of these proposals is that individuals may reduce other sources of savings if they receive this tax cut linked to forced savings. The reply of the proponents is that the savings rate of most recipients of this scheme is so low already that it is unlikely to offset the forced saving induced by the scheme. Also, they argue that the change in the time profile of disposable income may actually increase savings. Finally, different solutions to the Social Security problem, with or without individual accounts, have different distributive implications. The current surplus may help to "smooth" distributional flows during the transition.

What is Ahead?

Current budget surpluses have been achieved mainly thanks to a combination of an exceptionally strong economy, low interest rates, and large cuts in the defense budget as a share of GDP. The current surplus will create political pressure for tax cuts and spending increases, even though the expected growth of entitlements in the next few decades raises serious doubt on the long-run fiscal balance. Even in the most optimistic scenarios about how Congress and the president will coordinate these demands, the surpluses in the next decade are likely to be much smaller, probably less than half, than what is predicted by the CBO, with unchanged legislation. Almost certainly, pork barrel politics will dissipate part of the surplus in "favors" to various constituencies. What will happen to the rest of the surplus will depend on how the political game unfolds after the November 2000 election. Whoever is in office in the next decade will have to face the growth of Medicare, Medicaid and the effects of the baby boomers on Social Security. The current surpluses offer an opportunity to help in achieving a solid long-run balance of the government budget. Seizing this opportunity will require careful and prudent policies, not just a reliance on the miracles of the "new economy," which eventually, will look more and more like the old one, with its cycles and downturns.

■ *I thank Brad De Long, Peter Diamond, Martin Feldstein, Alan Krueger, James Poterba, Roberto Perotti, Bob Solow, and Timothy Taylor for very useful suggestions and Silvia Ardagna for excellent research assistance. This research is supported by a NSF grant to the NBER. I am very grateful to both organizations for their support.*

References

Alt, James and Robert Lowry. 1994. "Divided Government, Fiscal Institutions and Budget Deficits: Evidence from the States." *American Political Science Review.* 88:4, pp. 811–24.

Alesina, Alberto and Guido Tabellini. 1990. "A Positive Theory of Fiscal Deficits and Government Debt." *Review of Economic Studies.* 57:3, pp. 403–14.

Alesina, Alberto and Howard Rosenthal. 1995. *Partisan Politics, Divided Government and the Economy.* Cambridge: Cambridge University Press.

Alesina, Alberto and Howard Rosenthal. 2000. "Polarized Platforms and Moderated Policies with Checks and Balances." *Journal of Public Economics.* January, 75:1, pp. 1–20.

Alesina, Alberto and Roberto Perotti. 1995a. "The Political Economy of Budget Deficits." *IMF Staff Papers.* March, pp. 1–31.

Alesina, Alberto and Roberto Perotti. 1995b. "Fiscal Expansions and Fiscal Adjustments in OECD Countries." *Economic Policy.* 21, pp. 205–40.

Alesina, Alberto and Roberto Perotti. 1997. Fiscal Adjustments in OECD Countries: Composition and Macroeconomic Effects. *IMF Staff Papers,* pp. 210–48.

Alesina, Alberto and Silvia Ardagna. 1997. "Tales of Fiscal Adjustments." *Economic Policy.* 27, pp. 487–546.

Alesina, Alberto and A. Drazen. 1991. "Why are Stabilizations Delayed?" *American Economic Review.* 82, pp. 1,170–1,188.

Alesina, Alberto and G. Carliner, eds. 1991. *Politics and Economics in the Eighties.* Chicago: University of Chicago Press.

Alesina, Alberto, Roberto Perotti and Jose Tavares. 1998. "The Political Economy of Budget Deficits." *Brookings Paper on Economic Activity,* 1, pp. 197–266.

Ardagna, Silvia 1999. "Fiscal Adjustments: Which Ones Work and Why." Boston College, Unpublished.

Auerbach, Alan J. 1994. "The US Fiscal Problem: Where We Are, How We Got Here, And Where We Are Going." *NBER Macroeconomic Annual.* W4709, pp. 141–75.

Auerbach, Alan J. 1997. "Quantifying the Current U.S. Fiscal Imbalance." *NBER Working Paper.* W6119.

Baker, David 1998. "The Great Surplus Debate: Invest it." *The American Spectator.* May–June, pp. 83–86.

Barro, Robert J. 1974. "Are Government Bonds Net Wealth?" *Journal of Political Economy.* 82:6, pp. 1,095–1,117.

Barro, Robert J. 1979. "On the Determination of Public Debt." *Journal of Political Economy.* 87:5, pp. 940–71.

Barro, Robert J. 1993. *Microeconomics.* Fourth Ed. New York: John Wiley.

Congressional Budget Office. 1999. "The Economic and Budget Outlook: Fiscal Years 2000–2009." Washington D.C.: GPO.

Diamond, Peter A. 1965. "National Debt in a Neoclassical Growth Model." *American Economic Review.* 55:5, pp. 1,126–1,150.

Diamond, Peter A. 1999. *Issues in Privatizing Social Security: Report of an Expert Panel of the National Academy of Social Insurance.* Cambridge: MIT Press.

The Economist. 1999. "Who's not for tax cuts." July 17, pp. 23–24.

The Economist. 1999. "The Tax-Cutters' Song." August 7, pp. 21–22.

Eisner, Robert. 1998. "The Great Surplus Debate: Understand It." *The American Spectator.* May–June, pp. 86–87.

Feldstein Martin, ed. 1994a. *American Economic Policy in the Eighties.* University of Chicago Press and NBER

Feldstein, Martin. 1994b. "Comments on Auerbach." *NBER Macroeconomic Annual,* pp. 175–81.

Feldstein, Martin. 1997. "Do Not Waste the Surplus." *Wall Street Journal.* November 17.

Feldstein, Martin and Andrew Samwick. 1997. "Potential Effects of Two Percent Personnel Retirement Accounts." *Tax Notes.* May, pp. 615–20.

Feldstein, Martin. 1998. "How to Save Social Security." *New York Times.* July 27.

Feldstein, Martin. 1999a. "Clinton's Social Security Sham." *Wall Street Journal.* February 1.

Feldstein, Martin. 1999b. "Protecting Retirement Income." *Testimony Before the Senate Finance Committee.* March 16.

Feldstein, Martin and Andrew Samwick. 1999. *Maintaining Social Security Benefits and Tax Rates through Personnel Retirement Accounts: An Update Based on the 1998 Social Security Trustees Report.* NBER Working paper (updated version available electronically at ⟨www.NBER.org⟩).

Gavin Michael and Roberto Perotti. 1997. "Fiscal Policy in Latin America." NBER Macroeconomic Annual, pp. 11–61.

Lucas Jr., Robert E. and Nancy L. Stokey. 1994. "Optimal Fiscal and Monetary Policy in an Economy Without Capital." *Monetary and Fiscal Policy.* Torsten Persson and Guido Tabellini, eds, pp. 347–88.

Milesi Ferretti, Gian Maria, Roberto Perotti and Massimo Rostagno. 2000. "Electoral Systems and Public Spending," unpublished.

McCubbins, Matthew. 1991. "Party Governance and US Budget Deficits: Divided Government and Fiscal Stalemate," in *Politics and Economics in the Eighties.* Alberto Alesina and Geoffrey Carliner, eds. Chicago: U. of Chicago Press.

Munnell, Alicia. 1998. "The Great Surplus Debate: Save It." *The American Spectator.* May–June, pp. 80–83.

Niskanen, William. 1997. "Use a Pending Budget Surplus Only for Major Fiscal Reforms." *Congressional Testimony to the House Budget Committee.*

Nordhaus, William D. 1975. "The Political Business Cycle." *Review of Economic Studies.* 42:2, pp. 169–90.

Perotti, Roberto and Yanor Kontpoulos. 1998. "Fragmented Fiscal Policy," unpublished.

Persson, Torsten and Lars Svensson. 1989. "What Stubborn Conservative Would Run a Deficit?" *Quarterly Journal of Economics.* 104, pp. 325–45.

Poterba, James. 1994. "State Responses to Fiscal Cases: "Natural Experiments for Studying the Effects of Budget Institutions." *Journal of Political Economy.* 102:4, pp. 799–821.

Reich, Robert. 1999. "The Other Surplus Option." *New York Times.* August 11.

Roubini, Novriel and Jeffrey Sachs. 1989. "Political and Economic Determinants of Budget Deficits in the Industrial Democracies." *European Economic Review.* 33, pp. 903–33.

Talvi, Ernesto and Carlos Vegh. 2000. "Tax Base Variability and Procyclieal Fiscal Policy." NBER Working Paper, 7499, January.

3

Journal of Economic Literature
Vol. XXIX (December 1991), pp. 1644–1678

The Measurement of Fiscal Deficits: Analytical and Methodological Issues

By MARIO I. BLEJER

and

ADRIENNE CHEASTY

International Monetary Fund

The authors are indebted to Jonathan Levin, Vito Tanzi, and colleagues at the International Monetary Fund for their valuable comments. The views expressed are the sole responsibility of the authors.

A budget deficit is like sin. To most of the public it is morally wrong, very difficult to avoid, but always easy to identify, and susceptible to considerable bias in measurement. (Robert Eisner 1984)

I. Introduction

IN PRACTICE, fiscal policies may be applied inappropriately because conventional measures of the fiscal deficit miscalculate the public sector's true budget constraint and give a misleading picture of the economy's fiscal stance. For diagnosing economic problems and finding appropriate fiscal policies to address them, the correct *measurement* of the public sector's net requirements is a vital prerequisite. But, to understand a country's fiscal stance, it may be necessary to view the budget from several angles. And, from one country to the next, the considerations that need recognition in budgetary analysis (for instance, level of development and openness) may vary widely. Hence, the search for the single perfect deficit measure may be futile.

This paper surveys the many alternative deficit measures that have been used to assess budgetary policy, together with their analytical and policy-motivated underpinnings. The differences in these alternative measures, all of which purport to measure *"the* fiscal deficit," have to be made explicit before meaningful cross-country comparisons can be made and useful general conclusions drawn about fiscal policy.

Although the measurement of fiscal policy may be important mainly because of its macroeconomic consequences, this survey does not focus on the impact of the fiscal balance on the rest of the economy (i.e., on the deficit as a fiscal indicator), but rather on the methodological aspects of measuring it. Fiscal deficit measures must be specified over three dimensions: (1) the deficit has to be defined for a public sector of a given coverage; (2) the coverage, or size, of the public sector, and its composition must be delineated; and (3) the time-horizon relevant for assessing the magnitude of the deficit must be identified.[1] Issues falling into these three measurement categories have generated a substantial literature, which, taken as a whole, represents a methodology for assessing the true scope of budgetary policy.

Basic definitional issues—often forgotten when using a conventional budget deficit measure—are addressed in Section II. Section III discusses different measures of the deficit that have been considered operationally applicable as policy tools in various circumstances. Section IV deals with the scope and coverage of the public sector that is relevant for economic analysis.[2] Section V is concerned with the intertemporal dimensions of public sector activities, and their reflection in the government "net worth" concept. Even within the confines of measurement issues, the survey has to be selective and, sometimes, draw arbitrary lines. Thus, because they have already been the subject of exhaustive surveys (or because they merit such treatment), some subjects have purposely been excluded from detailed coverage.[3] In particular, the survey con-

fines itself to calculable measures of the deficit, although, for some cases cited, calculation might prove quite cumbersome.

II. *The Conventional Public Sector Deficit*

The impact of fiscal policy can be assessed with respect to any time frame. Nevertheless, the deficit has tended to be viewed as a summary of government transactions during a single budget period—usually one year—without attention to their longer run implications. These short-run measures of the deficit are discussed first.

Such measures fall into two categories: variants of the "accounting," or conventional, deficits that country authorities refer to in their budgets (discussed in this section); and some refinements of these conventional deficits (covered in the next section). The latter are special purpose measures that attempt to isolate in the annual deficit the magnitudes relevant for assessment of the deficit's effects on specific endogenous macro-variables, such as domestic demand, inflation, or the balance of payments.

The conventional deficit is more restrictive than the budget balance envisaged in the *balanced budget laws* in many countries' Constitutions.[4] Typically, such laws require only a very broadly defined balancing—that financing for all budgeted expenditures be identified prior to enactment of the Budget. The tighter concept of budgetary balance embodied in the conventional deficit requires financing to come from the government's "ordinary income" rather than from borrowing, if the budget

---

[1] Although most of the issues discussed here apply to positive as well as negative imbalances in the public sector, this paper refers mainly to "deficits," in line with the terminology widely used in the literature. See, for example, Michael Boskin (1982, p. 296).

[2] Coverage of the public sector, however, is defined somewhat narrowly here. It is evident that *control* by the public sector can extend far beyond its direct use of resources, not only through its transfer policies but also through its regulatory powers. While transfers are discussed briefly (in Section III), coverage of the impact of government regulation on the allocation of resources is largely omitted, for purposes of conciseness rather than because of a conceptual disparity.

[3] Most importantly, measurement of the impact of social security on the deficit is discussed only as part of the general issue of the appropriate time horizon over which the deficit should be measured (Section V), and the substitutability between tax and debt financing (Ricardian equivalence) is omitted. Surveys of social security include Anthony Atkinson (1987) and Lawrence Thompson (1983; United States only) and Ricardian equivalence is discussed in Douglas

Bernheim (1987), Leonardo Leiderman and Mario Blejer (1988), and Robert Barro (1989).

[4] See, for instance, the discussion of the Italian Constitution in Antonio Martino (1989, p. 708 ff), and the description of Indonesian "balanced budget policy" in Anwar Nasution (1989, p. 3).

1646   *Journal of Economic Literature, Vol. XXIX (December 1991)*

is to be considered balanced. Most countries record (sometimes only for internal use) some variant of this deficit. Perhaps the variant most widely used is the public sector borrowing requirement (PSBR), which measures government's use of new financial resources, net of repayment of previously incurred debt.[5]

In the absence of standardized accounting rules for government, the conventional deficit is not well defined, and the deficits of different countries are not directly comparable. Two main areas of variance are:

1. the distinction between the items that determine the deficit—income and outlays, and the items that finance it (drawing "the line"); and
2. specification of the time at which the resource use is measured (the cash versus the accrual deficit).

---

[5] Vito Tanzi et al. (1988, p. 5) use a definition of the deficit as follows: "Fiscal deficits, as conventionally defined on a cash basis, measure the difference between total government cash outlays, including interest outlays but excluding amortization payments on the outstanding stock of public debt, and total cash receipts, including tax and nontax revenue and grants but excluding borrowing proceeds. In other words, not all outlays related to public debt servicing are included in the measure of the deficit: interest payments are added to non-debt-related expenditures but amortization payments are excluded. On the other hand, current revenues are recorded as government income while proceeds from borrowing are not. In this manner, fiscal deficits reflect the gap to be covered by *net* government borrowing, including direct borrowing from the central bank."

According to the World Bank (1988, p. 56), deficit-determining components are: "Expenditure includes wages of public employees, spending on goods and fixed capital formation, interest on debt, transfers and subsidies. Revenue includes taxes, user charges, interest on public assets, transfers, operating surpluses of public companies, and sales of public assets." It may be noted here that the U.S. unified budget balance is, in this sense, a conventional deficit. Expenditure included in the measure includes capital formation as well as current transactions, though no distinction is made between them. Thus the unified budget deficit, like conventional deficits elsewhere, is not a measure of government saving, but of government saving less government investment.

1. *The Line*

There are two criteria for distinguishing between revenue/expenditure on the one hand, and financing on the other: the "government debt criterion" and the "public policy criterion."

a. *The Government Debt Criterion.* Transactions are thought to affect the deficit, and are therefore classified above the line (i.e., as revenue or expenditure) if they do not create or extinguish a liability for the government; if they do, then these transactions are considered positive or negative financing. Thus, for instance, interest payments on government debt (an unrequited factor payment) are part of government expenditure, while the repayment of principal is recorded below the line.

The economic underpinning of this distinction is that, while a shift in the level of net public expenditure affects aggregate demand, the repayment of outstanding debt does not represent new income to asset-holders and therefore leaves demand pressures unchanged.

When the public debt criterion is used to determine the fiscal deficit, the deficit equals the difference between total public debt outstanding at the beginning and the end of the year. A central problem is that the criterion has always been applied narrowly, defined only over direct government debt and ignoring, inter alia, liabilities incurred by the receipt of social security taxes and other revenues tied to contingent claims (Section V.b.(3) below) and the liabilities being repaid via the inflation component of interest payments on government debt (Section III.6 below).

b. *The Public Policy Criterion.* Alternatively, transactions are deficit-determining and classified as revenue or expenditure instead of financing, when they further the goals of policy makers rather than simply forming part of public

Blejer and Cheasty: The Measurement of Fiscal Deficits   1647

sector liquidity management. Unlike liquidity management, public policy motivated transactions change the prices facing the rest of the economy compared to what they would be if markets were left undisturbed.

This criterion is also imperfect because, in practice, government does not approach financial markets on the same terms as other borrowers. Typically, government can borrow on more favorable terms, for instance, by imposing restrictions on the placement of public institutions' funds—such as the requirement that the social security system hold a certain portion of its reserves in the form of government bonds. Moreover, governments often have a policy agenda underlying their ranking of financing sources (the central bank, commercial banks, different private sector groups, foreign sources), which may make them depart from least-cost borrowing/pure liquidity management. In other words, even through its financial intermediation, government may tax, subsidize, or effectively regulate parts of the economy and, therefore, the public policy criterion provides only a blurred analytical distinction between what belongs above or below the line.

The two criteria for drawing the line generate the same classification of most transactions; however, they diverge for three types of transactions and this divergence has led, in practice, to important discrepancies in the size of the conventional deficit as estimated by policy makers in different countries. These are: (i) budgetary "net lending"; (ii) external grants; and (iii) debt service.

(i) *"Net lending"*. Unlike other budgetary outlays, government lending operations to the private sector involve liability management (overt and contractual), and hence, by the government debt criterion, should go below the line. However, a significant portion of budgetary

"lending" is composed of direct capital infusion and of government credit programs undertaken for policy purposes: namely, to supply funds to preferred sectors who would otherwise not have access to financial markets or who would have to pay steeper rates. Given its implicit subsidy element, and the higher than market probability that some of the loans will never be repaid, net lending cannot be defined as pure financial intermediation, and the public policy criterion, then, would classify net lending as part of government expenditure—above the line.[6] As illustrated in Table 1 by the case of Venezuela (where the government allocates its petroleum revenues through domestic and external lending programs), the difference in classification can turn a deficit into a large surplus.[7]

From an analytical viewpoint, neither treatment is completely correct. Unless budgetary loans are uncollectable from the start (which would imply an outright transfer), they contain both pure loan and pure grant components; only the latter should be considered as a public policy element and included as part of the deficit.[8] Moreover, the subsidy (grant) component is usually spread over the entire lifetime of the loan, going beyond

---

[6] The two main international sources of budget statistics—the International Monetary Fund and the United Nations—differ in their treatment of net lending, the former showing it above the line, for policy reasons, and the latter classifying it as financing. See World Bank (1988, p. 45) for a description of the United Nations' System of National Accounts (SNA; 1968) and IMF's Government Finance Statistics (GFS; 1986) systems of budgetary data.

[7] The scale of government's direct lending is extremely large, even in highly developed, market-oriented economies. For example, the United States Federal Government's outstanding stock of direct loans at the end of 1987 was $234 billion, equivalent to 5 percent of GDP (United States 1988).

[8] As discussed in the context of central bank activities (Section IV.3), the economic cost of preferential credit is the amount that would have to be paid to a private bank to induce it to undertake the lending, i.e., the expected discounted future loss arising from the loan adjusted for risk.

TABLE 1

VENEZUELA: CONSOLIDATED CENTRAL GOVERNMENT[1]
(IN BILLIONS OF BOLIVARES)

	1985	1986
Balance excl. net lending	32	4
Balance incl. net lending	24	−9

Source: IMF. *Government Finance Statistics Yearbook,* 1988.

[1] In this and following tables a minus sign indicates a deficit.

TABLE 2

THE GAMBIA: CONSOLIDATED CENTRAL GOVERNMENT
(IN PERCENT OF GDP)

	1981	1982
Deficit incl. grants	−12	−7
Deficit excl. grants	−17	−17

Source: IMF. *Government Finance Statistics Yearbook,* 1988.

the budgetary year in which the loan is extended.[9]

(ii) *External grants.* Since grant aid from abroad represents financing without liability, the government debt criterion would include it with other government revenues. However, by the public policy criterion, grants are added to other foreign financing—below the line—on the argument that no government policy decision can elicit these grants, and, therefore, that the current expenditure that they finance could not take place if the grants are not forthcoming (Raja Chelliah 1973, p. 749).[10] Grants are discretionary financing by donors and can vary significantly from year to year. Their inclusion as regular revenue has been said to give an inappropriate confidence in their permanence, though they may have to be replaced by government borrowing at

[9] Michael Wattleworth (1988) examines in detail the role of credit subsidies in government lending and presents a technique to measure the financial cost to the government of these subsidies under certainty. See also Barry Bosworth et al. (1987) for extensive references on the budgetary dimension of U.S. Federal credit activity and United States, Congressional Budget Office (1989, 1990) for credit budget reform proposals.
[10] Indeed, grants are often explicitly earmarked for certain expenditures. Another case for treating external grants as financing is that, unlike tax revenues, they represent no reduction in aggregate demand but add net resources to the economy, and widen the "domestic deficit" (Section III.3).

any time. Particularly in developing countries where domestic incomes are very low, the classification of grants below the line can widen the deficit by more than 5 percentage points of GDP (Table 2).

(iii) *Debt service.* In some countries, it may be argued that present levels of public debt are not sustainable, and that amortized debt may not be voluntarily reinvested in new government bonds. In such cases, replacement financing for amortization could require a policy effort on the part of government akin to that of generating extra tax revenue. Under this scenario, the public policy criterion would suggest the inclusion of amortization above the line, and the resulting deficit would correspond to the government's *gross borrowing requirement,* rather than to its net increase in liabilities.

Such differences in classification as described above can substantially affect the measured deficit. Typically, classifications have evolved apolitically, and countries have maintained one consistent treatment of government transactions over time. However, it is clear that much scope exists for distorting the picture through judicious reclassification. Laurence Kotlikoff (1988, 1989) makes this point, showing how the government, by relabeling its transactions (as taxes/borrowing, in various combinations with expenditure/amortization), can shift operations from above to below the line (and vice versa) but, essentially, carry out the same policy while choosing to report either a balanced budget, a deficit, or a surplus. If governments do not maintain what might be termed "ethics in accounting standards," the fiscal deficit ceases to convey useful information.

2. The Cash and Accrual Deficits

The other main conceptual variation among conventional deficit measures is the choice between cash and accrual accounting. At one end of the spectrum is the *completely cash deficit*, where only government outlays for which cash has been disbursed during the 365-day period, and only actual cash revenues received, are included in the budget balance. At the other end is the *completely accrual deficit*, which attempts to capture the actual net resource preemption of government—the consequences of its policy decisions—during the fiscal year, regardless of whether or not transactions have actually been paid for. Thus—an important example—depreciation of fixed capital is included as an outlay in the accrual deficit, but does not show up in the cash deficit. A deficit calculated on the basis of the *system of national accounts* (SNA) would be an accrual measure; the *public sector borrowing requirement* (PSBR) is measured on a cash basis.[11]

In practice, countries' deficit measures lie somewhere in between the complete cash and complete accrual measures. Even in countries which use a PSBR (cash) deficit concept, interest payments are usually measured as they accrue, rather than when actually paid. On the other hand, revenues are almost always measured on a cash or quasi-cash basis

because *tax liabilities* may be disputed and some percentage will never be collected. Finally, the accounting treatment of *expenditures* can make a significant difference to the measured deficit. The administrative procedures for executing government expenditures are complex, and take place in several stages from the time the government decides to undertake the outlay to the time the supplier considers himself paid. The size of the deficit can depend on the particular step at which expenditure is recorded as having taken place (International Monetary Fund 1986, p. 87).[12] Comparison of deficits across countries with different recording practices, particularly during any fiscal year, can be misleading, as most expenditure commitments are made towards the beginning of the year, and most payments are made towards the end.

The economic analysis of accrual basis deficits is complicated by the institutional tendency to apply accrual accounting to the *budget document* rather than to the *fiscal year*. In other words, countries often prolong beyond 365 days the period over which transactions authorized in a given budget document may be carried out. (The extension is known as a "complementary period.") Thus, in any fiscal year, transactions that change the measured deficit of the previous year can continue to take place alongside transactions determining the current year's deficit. In such cases, the temporal common denominator for analyzing the

---

[11] See Mark Wasserman (1976, p. 39) for a detailed, albeit dated, comparison of SNA and cash budgetary accounting in several OECD countries.

[12] The sequence of expenditure execution differs according to the budgetary tradition of the country (British, French, United States, Hispano-American, etc.). The U.S. budget records expenditure at the "checks issued" stage (International Monetary Fund 1986, p. 89)—considered a quasi-cash measure; the French budget measures expenditure at the time the government decides to undertake it (*"engagement"*)—a quasi-accrual measure. Jack Diamond and Christian Schiller (1988) discuss the British and French systems.

TABLE 3

BURKINA FASO: CONSOLIDATED CENTRAL GOVERNMENT[1]
(IN BILLIONS OF CFA FRANCS)

	1982	1983	1984
Reported cash balance less:	-6.2	0.5	-3.3
Deferred payment vouchers equals:	1.7	-1.3	1.1
True cash balance	-4.5	-0.8	-2.2

Source: IMF. *Government Finance Statistics Yearbook,* 1988.

[1] Burkina Faso is also a good example of a country where measured expenditures can be greatly affected by the existence of a complementary period. Expenditure from the 1985 budget during calendar year 1985 was CFAF 49 billion; total expenditure carried out in calendar year 1985 (including from past budgets) was CFAF 55 billion; and total expenditure from the 1985 budget (some of which took place in 1986) was CFAF 61 billion.

budget balance together with other macro-variables is lost.

A difficult problem in the measurement of the conventional deficit arises with attempts to reconcile the cash and accrual concepts. As noted by Diamond and Schiller (1988, pp. 32, 42–44), if delays in payment are unanticipated, they represent forced borrowing from suppliers, with the result that the cash measure of the borrowing requirement misrepresents the sources of credits to government. If the delays are anticipated, suppliers will inflate their prices to compensate, and the government will pay a premium for its purchases.

The total reconciliation item between the cash and accrual deficits is often defined as *arrears*, but, because of justifiable lags in the expenditure process, because arrears may be run up through extrabudgetary expenditures, and because the emergence of arrears is often hidden by offsetting tax reliefs to suppliers, the definition of arrears is more complicated than a resolution of timing differences in expenditure recording. The

existence of arrears that cannot be measured reduces the validity of the deficit as a measure of the government's budget constraint or of its impact on the economy.

Worse, countries with chronic liquidity crunches have developed formal procedures for *turning arrears into longer term debt instruments,* which boost actual holdings of government debt above its long-run sustainable rate, inasmuch as they are usually held involuntarily by suppliers. The issue of chits or bonds in recognition of government's debt to suppliers is recorded as a cash payment, and thus inflates the recorded cash measure of the deficit compared with actual cash disbursements by government (Table 3).[13]

In the rest of this survey, it will be assumed that the *conventional* deficit is well specified (following footnote 5), and the discussion of refinements to the conventional deficit will ignore the basic problem just discussed—that every budget speech refers to a different kind of deficit.

III. *Special-Purpose Deficit Measures*

Though the conventional deficit measure exists in competing versions, all versions have at least one characteristic in common: in calculating the budget balance, they include, with the same weight, all government transactions. However, policy makers have, from time to time, calculated alternative measures of the deficit, with the aim of highlighting the differential impact of various budgetary transactions (such as investment, import purchases, or debt service) on important macroeconomic variables (such as savings, the balance of payments, and inflation).

[13] These procedures are particularly prevalent in francophone African countries which have externally-imposed ceilings on bank credit, and thus customarily run up arrears as residual financing.

The main types of special-purpose deficit that have been fairly widely calculated are: 1. the current deficit; 2. the deficit measuring the contribution of different transactions to aggregate demand; 3. the domestic deficit, a variant of (2) important in open economies; 4. structural and cyclically adjusted deficits; 5. the primary deficit; and 6. the operational deficit.

1. *The Current Deficit: Government Saving and the Capital Budget*

The conventional deficit measures the difference between public investment and public saving. In order to isolate public (dis)saving, the *current deficit* calculation omits investment outlays and capital revenues such as asset sales; i.e., the current deficit is the difference between noncapital revenues and expenditures. The current deficit is of particular interest to economists because the lack of public sector capital budgeting appears to be a shortcoming compared with accounting procedures of private firms:

> If we maintained a separate and conceptually correct current and capital account system, the deficit on current account would be the true deficit, [. . . because] for capital items, any excess of expenditures over receipts on capital account does not change the net asset position of the government, since the new debt is matched by a new government asset. (Boskin 1982, p. 298).

Moreover, in the 1960s, it was commonly held that current expenditures should be fully financed by taxes, whereas, like a private firm, the government could legitimately finance its socially profitable investment by debt (David Conklin and Adil Sayeed 1983, p. 28). According to this view, the deficit on current account provided a measure of the extent the government strayed from "prudent management."

Though the current deficit is intuitively simple, its calculations have had several shortcomings. First, the measure is useful primarily when comparing the government with the other components of the national accounts, or assessing government's accounts according to the accounting norms of the private sector. However, detailed public sector accounts are usually first available on a financial basis, rather than on the accrual basis compatible with other sectoral and/or enterprise accounts.[14] Second, accounting concepts of investment are much narrower than the economist would like. For instance, most investment in human capital is considered a current outlay, despite its importance in explaining growth (Chelliah 1973, p. 749; Richard Goode 1984, p. 240). Third, the current/capital mix of any "investment" project can be dissected (or, indeed, politically manipulated) in an almost infinite number of ways, to give many different measures of government saving.

Despite these operational problems, interest in the current deficit concept as applied to developing countries has increased, as externally financed programs of structural adjustment have become more prevalent. This is so because structural adjustment programs tend to disequilibrate the conventional balance, through temporarily large injections of subsidized lending for capital expenditure, and large one-time budget revenues from privatization. There is, therefore, pressure on the conventional deficit to widen, with the paradoxical implication that the structural adjustment has left the country even further from sustainable medium-term growth. To provide a more appropriate benchmark for judging these programs, it is argued that a deficit that excludes their temporary

---

[14] Of the adjustments that must then be made, the treatment of depreciation is perhaps particularly important. See, for example, Boskin (1988, p. 79) and Boskin, Marc S. Robinson, and John M. Roberts (1985).

influences on the capital account will give a better measure of permanent adjustment efforts. The change in government saving, though clearly a rough proxy, has thus resurfaced as a summary gauge of the gains from structural adjustment (World Bank 1988).

When using the current deficit as this kind of measure, however, further problems arise. First, structural policies (such as tax reform) often involve *J*-curve effects (such as short-run revenue losses during the shift to the new tax system) which reduce government saving at the time of the adjustment program, though with the expectation of improving it in the medium term. Conversely, many structural reforms involve investments which imply heavy recurrent costs following completion, so that government saving may fall in the medium term. Finally, it may be difficult, if not illegitimate, to separate the disequilibria caused by a structural adjustment program from the "disequilibria" caused by other exogenous shocks or the business cycle. If so, a core deficit or a cyclically adjusted deficit (discussed in 4. below) might be a more precise measure of the extent of permanent adjustment.

2. *The Impact of Government on Aggregate Demand*

Since different elements of government expenditure and revenue generate different net increases to, and withdrawals from, demand, policy makers have sometimes ambitiously attempted to isolate in the deficit measure the government's contribution to aggregate demand. The most widely applied aggregate demand-based measures have focused on the separation of exhaustive expenditures (on goods and services) and transfers. If private and public propensities to consume differ, it becomes important to identify the ultimate user of budgetary resources. Tax-financed transfers such as pensions and unemployment

benefits merely redistribute purchasing power from one part of the private sector to another. In terms of their impact on aggregate demand they are akin to negative taxes rather than to government's expenditure on goods and services (Boskin 1982, pp. 296–97; Willem Buiter 1985, p. 14; Charles Bean and Buiter 1987, pp. 5–6).[15]

Policy makers have also recognized that the inclusion of transfers in government spending may further overestimate government's contribution to aggregate demand because there are lags in how quickly transfers can be spent. This problem has been most apparent in economies with several layers of government: a transfer from central to local government may not increase aggregate demand until the year after it was recorded in the budget of the central administration.

It should be noted that this type of analysis is peculiarly Keynesian. A more monetarist approach would argue that any impact of government on aggregate demand comes through the monetary financing of the deficit.[16]

3. *The Domestic Deficit*

Since trade and capital flows between the public sector and the external sector vary enormously from country to country, a given conventional deficit can encompass a large spectrum of contributions to the domestic economy. For instance, expenditure on domestic goods that is fully financed by foreign grants increases aggregate demand with no offsetting withdrawal. Government imports financed by domestic taxes reduce aggregate demand by the full extent of the

---

[15] This point can be generalized to the revenue side, where different taxes may represent different net withdrawals from private sector aggregate demand, depending on the base of the tax.

[16] However, see Buiter (1985, p. 76) for a hybrid measure of the impact of the deficit on aggregate demand, where the impact of financing is included through its potential for crowding out.

import bill—a case where government expenditure may have contractionary rather than expansionary effects. The overall deficit could well be zero in each of the two examples, though they each imply an opposite domestic impact. To isolate the effect of government on aggregate demand in an open economy, "domestic" and "foreign" deficits have been, in many cases, separately calculated.

The domestic deficit is measured by including in the calculation only those budgetary elements that directly affect the domestic economy. The foreign deficit—the impact of the budget on the balance of payments—can be measured by including only budget transactions directly connected to the external sector. (See, for instance, Jitendra Borpujari and Teresa Ter-Minassian 1973, p. 815; Chelliah 1973, p. 770.)[17]

When the public sector has sizeable trade or capital flows to and from the rest of the world, the overall deficit measure can be particularly misleading: for instance, devaluation may cause the budget deficit to widen if government imports or foreign debt service are large, suggesting an expansionary fiscal policy—though resources injected into the economy by government remain unchanged or may even fall.

Most calculations of the domestic deficit measure have been carried out for oil exporting countries with a nationalized petroleum industry. Unless the monetary impact of oil receipts is sterilized, their use to finance expenditure will be expansionary but the conventional measure of the budget deficit would not predict the expansion.[18] Similar unremarked expansions can occur

when foreign grants are large. Oil exporting country studies include David Morgan (1979: 12 major oil exporters); Richard Stillson (1979: Indonesia, Jordan, and Oman); George Mackenzie (1981: Kuwait, Nigeria, and Saudi Arabia); Nasution (1989: Indonesia); José Gil-Díaz (1988: Bolivia); and Reza Vaez-Zadeh (1989: Venezuela).[19]

4. Removing the Effects of Fluctuations in Economic Activity on the Budget

While the budget deficit affects aggregate demand, aggregate demand also affects the budget deficit. Inter alia, income tax revenues will usually be lower and benefit transfers higher when unemployment is high. In other words, the budget deficit is affected by the business cycle, and the impact of discretionary policy changes may differ depending on at which stage of the business cycle they are implemented. Since the 1940s, but mainly in the 1970s, deficits abstracting from the impact of the business cycle have been calculated. These measures have, in their heyday, been surveyed comprehensively (Alan Blinder and Robert Solow 1974, and Peter Heller et al. 1986).

There are two main classes of "permanent" or long-run deficits. The *full-employment deficit* (or structural balance) was derived in the belief that "a small surplus in that budget would ensure a high level of national saving while permitting built-in fiscal stabilizers to damp

---

[17] Since there are usually second-order effects of domestic transactions on the foreign deficit and vice versa, the measures are approximations of the concept.

[18] Inflation caused by unsterilized government oil revenues in the presence of conventionally measured budget equilibrium, or even surpluses, has been one channel of transmission of Dutch disease.

[19] Although Morgan shows that the domestic budget balance determines the direct effect of the government budget on money creation, strictly speaking, the relevant deficit measure, from the monetary point of view, is the liquidity budget balance—that share of government requirements that has to be financed by domestic credit. Hence, the liquidity balance differs from the domestic balance because it excludes domestic nonbank borrowing by government (which amounts merely to a rearrangement of private sector portfolios and not to money creation), while including central bank profits transferred to government and government interest payments to domestic banks.

1654   *Journal of Economic Literature, Vol. XXIX (December 1991)*

cyclical fluctuations" (Frank de Leeuw and Thomas Holloway 1983, p. 27).[20] Notwithstanding its virtues, following a rule of full-employment budget balance could still imply the expansion of the public debt—since, on average, economies operate below full employment, so that, on average, expenditure would exceed revenue. Therefore, the *cyclically adjusted or trend budget balance* was developed to provide a budget balance rule that would maintain a constant level of public liabilities. The *methods* of calculation of the two approaches have differed little:

> To construct a cyclically adjusted budget, the essential steps are (1) choosing a reference trend for GNP free from short-run fluctuations, (2) determining the responsiveness of each category of receipts and expenditures to short-run movements in GNP (e.g., cyclical tax elasticities), (3) applying these responses to gaps between trend GNP and actual GNP, and (4) adding the expenditures and receipts "gross-ups" from step 3 to the actual budget to obtain a cyclically adjusted budget. The first step, selecting a GNP reference trend, is the most important and controversial. Other things being equal, the higher the level of the reference trend, the smaller the cyclically adjusted deficit. (de Leeuw and Holloway 1985, p. 232).

The full employment deficit can then be defined as the cyclically adjusted balance when the GNP reference trend selected is potential output (Patrice Muller and Robert Price 1984, p. 1). The change in full employment balance from year to year measures the fiscal impulse, i.e., the effect of fiscal *policy* (as opposed to all budget items) in total aggregate demand.[21] Attempts to measure the fiscal

impulse have led to several intermediate estimates of budgetary stance that use potential output as a benchmark for measuring revenue or (usually) expenditure (Thomas Dernburg 1975, p. 829; Heller et al. 1986; and Muller and Price 1984).

The *cyclically adjusted or trend deficit*, in which "neutral" expenditures and revenues are not estimated as functions of potential output but instead as functions of "average output," has been estimated by Muller and Price (for the OECD), de Leeuw and Holloway, and Heller et al. (for the IMF). Trend deficit measures, however, factor in the effects of transitory shocks and hence are subject to the disadvantage that they may not be equivalent to the "underlying" or "permanent" deficit in the economy. Particularly in countries undertaking structural reforms, one-time disturbances could be equivalent to several percentage points of GDP. Tanzi (1982) has recognized this problem in his description of a variant of the trend deficit, the *core* deficit, which removes from the actual deficit not only cyclical influences but also one-time or transitory shocks ("such as temporary taxes, postponement of inevitable wage increases, building up of arrears, and so on"; p. 6). However, no systematic series of core deficit estimates exists.

Olivier Blanchard (1990) goes further, making the point that deficit measures far simpler than trend deficits exist that distinguish between induced and discretionary fiscal policies, and that index sustainability. Trend deficits require needless assumptions about "whether there are cycles around a stable trend, (. . .) whether the economy will return to lower unemployment and so on" (p. 6). Instead, "[i]nduced changes in fiscal policy can be defined as those changes which come from changes in inflation, interest rates and output growth over the previous year—or over the previous ten year average—values. How to choose the

---

[20] Moreover, Robert Eisner and Paul Pieper (1988, p. 33 ff) found that high-employment deficits (adjusted for changes in the real value of net debt) were appropriate instruments of Keynesian expansionary policy, in the sense that they "were positively associated with subsequent increases in real GNP and reductions in unemployment."

[21] In order to avoid price level effects, the full-employment balance is usually calculated as a ratio to income.

benchmark is still a relevant question, but not one which requires taking a stand on where the economy will or should return." Moreover, "[w]hat matters in terms of sustainability is where the country expects to be over the next three to ten years, not necessarily some mid-cycle point" (p. 7). Blanchard derives alternative easy-to-calculate measures, the simplest of which do not require forecasts.

5. *The Primary Deficit: Removing the Effects of Previous Deficits on the Budget*

Although the structurally adjusted deficit is sometimes presented as measuring the impact of discretionary government policy, it includes an important nondiscretionary variable, namely, interest payments on the stock of public debt—which is usually predetermined by the size of previous deficits. The *primary deficit* (or "noninterest deficit") attempts to measure the discretionary budgetary stance by excluding net interest payments from the budget (James Barth et al. 1989).[22] The primary deficit could also reflect the success of policies in moving the economy towards a sustainable growth path:

> The primary deficit measures how current actions improve or worsen the public sector's net indebtedness, and it is important for evaluating the sustainability of government deficits. Although fiscal deficits can be run indefinitely, the primary balance must eventually become positive to cover at least part of the interest on current debt. If public revenue and the economy as a whole grow faster than the real interest rate, then even the primary balance can remain in deficit. However, it is generally not possible in the long run to always grow faster than the interest rate. (World Bank 1988, p. 56).[23]

A comparison of the primary and conventional deficits in Table 4 illustrates the heavy burden of interest payments even in relatively stable economies, such as Spain, that have accumulated large public debts. Despite positive primary balances, conventional deficits remain.

6. *The Operational Deficit: Removing the Effects of Inflation from Interest Payments*

The interest bill is beyond the control of current fiscal policy, not only because it represents the cost of previous deficits, but also because monetary policy can affect interest rates and hence budgetary interest payments. In addition, fluctuations in inflation can significantly change the size of government nominal debt service.

Inflation affects the budget in many ways. Besides its distortionary effects on real revenues (Tanzi 1977),[24] and its effects on the real value of government assets and liabilities (dealt with in Section V), inflation, while reducing the real value of the outstanding stock of unindexed public debt, may compensate creditors for such erosion in their real assets through higher nominal interest rates. In other words, some of the government's interest payments on its debt are in reality part of the amortization of that debt. If the inflationary component of interest rates is not removed from the interest bill, the deficit will be overstated by the size of the amortization element included

---

meaningful balanced budget rule might require that interest payments, debt, and GNP grow continuously at similar rates, therefore remaining constant in relative terms (Eisner and Pieper 1985, and Eisner 1990).

[24] Different revenue and expenditure components can have very different inflation elasticities. This raises significant problems which have hindered the development of budgets-in-real-terms. A satisfactory method for arriving at a fully inflation-adjusted deficit remains to be derived.

[22] The primary deficit has usually been calculated by subtracting total interest payments from government expenditure. However, conceptually, only the *net* interest paid by government should be removed.

[23] It should be pointed out, however, that in a growing economy, debt generally grows. Thus, a

1656   *Journal of Economic Literature, Vol. XXIX (December 1991)*

TABLE 4

MEASURES OF THE FISCAL BALANCE UNDER ALTERNATIVE
TREATMENTS OF INTEREST PAYMENTS[1]
(IN PERCENTAGE OF GDP)

	Conventional	Operational	Primary
Argentina			
1983	−10.2	−10.2	−4.2
1985	−4.1	−4.1	−1.7
1987	−6.3	−5.6	−1.6
Brazil			
1981	−13.0	−6.2	−4.8
1985	−27.9	−4.3	−0.6
1988	−45.3	−4.0	1.6
Chile			
1983	−2.8	n.a.	1.0
1986	−1.9	−1.2	2.8
1988	3.6	3.8	8.0
Ghana			
1981	−6.4	5.5	−4.3
1985	−2.7	−0.4	−1.2
1987	−0.3	−0.4	1.2
Israel			
1985	−5.4	−1.6	10.0
1988	−4.9	−3.6	4.2
Kenya			
1982	−6.5	−3.2	−2.9
1986	−5.4	−0.8	−0.5
1987	−7.6	−6.3	−2.9
Mexico			
1981	−13.8	−10.8	−9.1
1985	−9.5	−1.0	3.3
1987	−15.9	2.0	5.0
Spain			
1982	−5.6	. . .	−4.6
1985	−6.7	. . .	−3.2
1987	−3.6	. . .	0.1

Sources: Argentina, Brazil, Chile, and Mexico: Tanzi
(1989); Israel: Bank of Israel; Ghana and Kenya: Thanos
Catsambas and Miria Pigato (1989); Spain: IMF staff estimates.
[1] Since data are obtained from different sources and
country definitions may vary, the magnitudes are not
comparable across countries.

as interest payments above the line,
rather than below.

The magnitude of the deficit overstatement varies with the size of domestic

debt outstanding and with its terms and
denomination.[25] Solely because of the
composition of their debt, countries with
identical inflation, debt/GDP ratios, and
ratios of tax revenues and noninterest expenditures to GDP may show very different conventional fiscal deficits. These
shortcomings of the conventional deficit
under inflation have been analyzed by,
among others, Thanos Catsambas (1988),
Alex Cukierman and Jorgen Mortensen
(1983), Eisner (1984), Eisner and Pieper
(1984), Francisco Gil Díaz (1986), Marcus
Miller (1982), and Tanzi, Blejer, and Mario Teijeiro (1988).

The most popular alternative suggested to alleviate the problem is the
operational deficit, which omits the
inflation-induced portion of interest
payments from the deficit calculation;
i.e., it is defined as the primary deficit
plus the real component of interest payments. In some countries which had high
inflation, such as Brazil and Mexico (Table 4), immense differences arise between conventional and operational deficits. Moreover, trends in the two
alternative measures can diverge markedly. In both Brazil and Mexico, the conventional deficit indicates rapidly growing imbalances during the 1980s,
whereas the operational deficit signals
some improvement in Brazil and a remarkable adjustment in Mexico.

In order to compare the merits of the
operational deficit with the conventional
measure, it is necessary to review its economic rationale. The operational deficit
excludes inflation-induced interest payments on the assumption that they are
similar to amortization payments in their

[25] It is simple to show that, with floating-interest
debt, the deficit/GDP ratio is a positive function of
inflation and of the initial debt/GDP ratio. The opposite is true with long-term fixed interest bonds. Tanzi
et al. (1988, Apendix 1), includes a formal discussion
of the effects of inflation on the conventional deficit
in the presence of different types of debt instruments.

effects on the economy—namely, that they do not represent new income to recipients, and are willingly reinvested in government bonds, at existing market conditions, and therefore they do not affect the level of aggregate demand in real terms. Real interest payments, on the other hand, can be consumed without reducing a bondholder's net wealth, and thus have an expansionary impact similar to any other type of expenditure. The relative usefulness of the two deficit measures reduces, thus, to the question of how inflation-induced interest payments are spent: are they used to buy new bonds or to finance consumption? In other words, does rising inflation erode the real demand for government bonds, or is the sustainability of the public debt invariant to inflation?

If inflation were to reduce the real demand for bonds, then, in an economy with accelerating inflation, inflation-induced interest payments would not be fully refinanceable under existing market conditions but would require either higher real interest rates or higher bond liquidity, thus increasing demand pressures. The operational deficit measure excluding the inflation component of interest payments would then underestimate the degree of fiscal imbalance.

There are also technical problems in the calculation of the operational deficit. For instance, the choice of the price index is not straightforward and there are presentational difficulties when interest rates are negative in real terms, in which case the conventional deficit measure would have to be adjusted downwards by a magnitude greater than actual interest payments. Furthermore, the operational deficit has a macroeconomic deficiency: by correcting the deficit for the impact of inflation on it, the ability to assess the impact of the deficit on inflation is lost. Despite these difficulties, the operational deficit provides useful infor-

mation to policy makers when the inflation rate is very high. In principle, it is a lower-bound estimate for the public sector deficit, relevant when full rollover of broadly defined amortization is realistic.

IV. *The Composition of the Public Sector*

The discussion so far has taken as understood the identity of government, which, indeed, is subject to a fairly broad, if imprecise, consensus:

> The government of a country consists of the public authorities and their instrumentalities, established through political processes, exercising a monopoly of compulsory powers within a territorial area . . . and engaged primarily in the provision of public services differing in character, cost elements, and source of finance from the activities of other sectors. (International Monetary Fund 1986, p. 7).

However, at the operational level, difficulties arise in defining the scope of government for purposes of measuring the fiscal deficit. Increasingly, governments perform operations usually associated with other sectors: there are public enterprises, public financial institutions, and public administrative/nonprofit agencies. Conversely, other sectors have taken on quasi-governmental functions.[26] Moreover, these divergences from traditional roles usually arise from country-specific circumstances, which render cross-country comparisons of the government deficit painful.

An associated difficulty arises in defining and quantifying "transactions," when government has the option not only of purchases and sales and income transfers, but also of regulation and price-setting, whose financial magnitudes may be impossible to measure.

This section discusses the fiscal content

---

[26] For instance, there may be a difference only of degree between the compulsory pension system of a government and a firm's pension scheme which is mandatory for all employees.

of the components of the broader public sector, which includes public enterprises, the central bank, and public financial institutions.

1. The Traditional Scope of Government

It is tempting to think of traditional government as a pyramid, from the apex of the central decision maker(s), through the central administration, down through the numerous regional, municipal, and local governments. However, the different parts of traditional government are distinguished through more dimensions than can be represented in a pyramid. Governments, even at the central level, include a plethora of public agencies that cannot easily be ranked "above" or "below" one another, such as investment boards, industrial development authorities, utility regulating bodies, space research laboratories, social security funds, etc. Only rarely are their powers neatly subordinated to an overseeing ministry.

The difficulty of constructing a generally applicable organizational structure for government is such that it may be impossible to derive an exhaustive list of entities that should be taken into account in arriving at an undisputable figure for the fiscal deficit. Nonetheless, there are some guidelines—completeness of coverage and of consolidation, and the recognition of nonfinancial governmental activities—that are important for determining the scope of government.

a. *Completeness of Coverage and the Consolidation.* Ideally, the more comprehensive the picture of the public sector—not defined by the names of so-called government institutions, but by the nature of the transactions they carry out—the easier the interpretation of fiscal actions, and the more evenly the government will be able to spread out the impact of policy measures it deems necessary. However, there may be a trade-off between prompt fiscal responses to

emerging policy problems and availability of information. Hence, the fiscal deficit for short run policy purposes must often be calculated for a reduced subset of government levels, or, alternatively, for a reduced array of government activities. Moreover, as discussed below, there are many agencies that fit only partially into a meaningful definition of government. In these cases, a correct measure of the impact of government should include only the *fiscal* activities of such agencies; when this is impossible, the inclusion or exclusion of the agency becomes a matter of discretion.

A further aspect is the complicated web of financial interrelationships between agencies and levels of government. An accurate calculation of the deficit would net out all intragovernmental transactions, although the size of the deficit will be invariant to such netting out. However, if intragovernmental flows are (incorrectly) included, the *size* of government could be grossly overstated. Moreover, despite the resilience of the deficit measure to the completeness in consolidation, problems arise through the omission of a flow in one direction but not in the other, affecting the deficit's size.

b. *Recognition of Nonfinancial Government Activity.* There is another dimension in the distinction between the public and the private sector: government may affect the allocation of resources by changing the prices facing the private sector and by regulation of private activity (Boskin, M. Robinson and Alan Huber 1987, p. 2). An example of regulation is the pollution control devices required on new cars, which raise car prices and are counted as part of the automobile industry's activity "although they are close substitutes for the government levying a tax and paying the automobile companies to install them" (Boskin, M. Robinson, and Huber 1987). The military draft also allows the government to provide services at below market rates.[27] An ideal measure of government impact on resource use would place monetary values on all of these nonfinancial actions and include them in the calculation of the deficit. However, although much work has been done on assessing the economic impact of regulation, tax expenditures, and market intervention, the broad discussion of the valuation of these government actions goes beyond the scope of this survey.

2. Public Production and Trade

A strict definition of government presupposes a restricted array of public sector economic activities, merely the provision of nonmarket goods and services and the redistribution of income. However, the concepts of public sector and government increasingly diverge the more involved in production and commerce publicly owned entities become. While the activities of public enterprises, marketing boards, and other publicly owned entities that produce or trade are to some extent motivated by profit, they have special characteristics, in many cases monopolistic, with prices and, sometimes, quantities being primarily the result of government policy. Clearly, the effects of these activities should be factored into a meaningful measure of the public sector balance. However, this poses a number of conceptual and methodological problems including the appropriate measurement of the fiscal component of public enterprises' activities.

There are two aspects specific to the assessment of the fiscal impact of public enterprises that have a bearing on the proper measurement of budgetary

balance.[28] First, the enterprises that comprise the public sector must be selected, and, second, that portion of their operations which has a fiscal impact must be identified.

The choice of entities for inclusion in the public sector depends on the distinctions between government and enterprises and between "public" and "private." In International Monetary Fund (1986), the criterion used to distinguish between general government and nonfinancial public enterprises is not legal or institutional, but rather the nature of the activities they perform. The distinction comes both from the nature of the goods and services they supply and the differing character of their revenues: taxes are compulsory levies while income from market sales is essentially voluntary. In general, when the unregulated market cannot be expected to generate the optimal provision of the good or service but some price mechanism could still be set in motion, public enterprises rather than government may be called upon to execute a desired intervention.

The operational distinction between "public" and "private," which determines the extent to which transactions by entities outside general government should be incorporated in measures of fiscal activity, is more difficult to pin down.[29] A common criterion is the simple ownership principle: any enterprise is considered "public," if direct and indirect government participation in its equity exceeds 50 percent. This legal concept is not really satisfactory because it does not assess the degree of government's actual control over the enter-

---

[27] Price controls, quantitative trade restrictions, and other forms of direct market intervention would also fall into this category.

[28] We do not focus here on the roles, structure, and performance of public enterprises which have been the subject of extensive studies (for example, Robert Floyd et al. 1984).

[29] A more common question in the literature deals with the analytical underpinning of the existence of publicly owned enterprises (for example, William Baumol 1984).

1660   *Journal of Economic Literature, Vol. XXIX (December 1991)*

prises' decisions, nor does it evaluate the weight of public policy objectives in entities' operations. A different approach is taken by Peter Stella (1989) who looks at the overall impact of enterprises on the public finances and on net worth transfers. The operations of many enterprises, privately as well as publicly owned, are supported by a variety of state guarantees, tax benefits, or other types of financial assistance. If these interplays of government financing and enterprise operations are such as to raise private sector net worth, these results are akin to government deficits in their effect on private perception of wealth and hence on consumption. In this sense, their operations could therefore be considered part of the public sector.

A unifying, though not very operational, criterion for classification comes from the "soft budget constraint" concept developed by János Kornai (1986). It defines "public" firms as being immune from bankruptcy and therefore unconcerned with covering costs.[30] Soft budget constraints, with their contingent claim on budgetary resources, are the proximate reason for linking some of the operations of public enterprises with those of the government for an accurate assessment of global fiscal impact.

One approach for analyzing the macroeconomic dimension of public firms is to evaluate the budgetary impact of their operations—through the flows between public enterprises and the government (Arigapudi Premchand 1983) and through the effects of public enterprises on the overall volume of government revenue, expenditure, and public investment (e.g., Venkata Ramanadham 1984, ch.

3). A second approach, perhaps more valid, is to consolidate the relevant part of public enterprises' operations with the rest of the government budget. Consolidation, however, raises a number of important methodological measurement issues (Stella 1989). The central question is how to define and measure enterprise revenue and expenditure in a way that is compatible with government's concepts. Clearly, enterprises' gross sales revenue is not comparable to tax revenue, nor should the purchase of inputs be added to current budgetary expenditure. It could be argued, however, that public enterprise prices contain implicit subsidies and taxes that will be reflected in profits and losses and that these profits and losses are the financial flows that should be consolidated since they closely correspond to budgetary inflows or outlays.[31] A problem with this approach arises when profits are not explicitly transferred to the Treasury or they are lower than potential competitive profits owing to hidden subsidies. If the enterprise is making losses, the subsidy element may remain obscured through the enterprise's ability to borrow from domestic and foreign sources other than the government.

Practically, consolidation is difficult because of the problem that the structure of government and enterprise budgets are very different:

> The government budget is usually subdivided into receipts, expenditure, and borrowing. The budgets of enterprises are mostly organized, like commercial budgets, on a dual basis, viz., revenue and capital. (Premchand 1983)

In addition, enterprise accounts are almost always on an accrual basis while cash accounts are the usual budgetary

---

[30] Hard budget constraints are defined not only by the threat of bankruptcy but also by the possibility of replacing management. In a private market, less than optimal performance could lead to a corporate takeover or a management change. This insecurity of tenure is usually lacking in public firms.

[31] Indeed, the International Monetary Fund (1986, p. 102) methodology postulates that "Taxes also include the profits transferred to government from fiscal monopolies . . . which reflect use of the government's taxing power to collect excise-like revenue."

standard.[32] Stella (1989) claims that this difference cannot be resolved simply by converting enterprise flows into cash accounts because, in assessing the impact of the public sector on the economy, it is indeed more correct to measure enterprise activities, like any other business activities, on an accrual basis since this gives a truer reflection of performance. When capital expenditure is important, the divergences between cash and accrual accounting can be significant.[33]

In sum, the issue of how to measure the gross flow of *government-like* activities of public entities remains unresolved. In the case of a marketing board, for example, one would not want to amalgamate the gross value of purchases with treasury outlays, nor would one want to combine the gross value of sales receipts with tax revenue. The policy element is only the subsidy or tax implicit, if any, and the quantitative measure of the subsidy is the difference between buying and selling prices as reflected in the operating position of the enterprise.

3. The Quasi-fiscal Operations of Central Banks

In many countries, the distinction between the responsibilities of the Treasury and the central bank has become blurred, with the latter performing "quasi-fiscal" activities not specifically connected with monetary policy. These activities are diverse: they include the management of explicit subsidies, debt service and transfers, the provision of preferential credit, the bailout of ailing industries, etc. It has frequently been argued that these quasi-fiscal operations are similar to other budgetary activities and should be included in a comprehensive measure of the public sector balance. Particularly important, analytically, is the central bank's implicit levy of taxes, either through the exchange rate system,[34] or through the imposition of unremunerated reserve requirements.

There are many difficulties in separating the central bank's monetary from its quasi-fiscal activities.[35] Moreover, differences in accounting practices (e.g., cash versus accrual) raise consolidation problems akin to those of nonfinancial public enterprises. David Robinson and Stella (1988) start from a benchmark case: they claim that central banks that have operating profits and transfer them fully to the Treasury[36] do not distort the conventionally measured deficit even if they perform quasi-fiscal activities, provided that these activities only affect the central bank's profit-and-loss accounts during the budget year in question. Deviations from this benchmark would require an adjustment.

The two most important deviations arise: (i) from quasi-fiscal activities that change the composition of the central bank's balance sheet (rather than the

---

[32] For a review of the standard accounting practices of public enterprises, see Arthur Gitajn (1984, ch. 4).

[33] On the treatment of depreciation, valuation adjustments, and the purchase and sales of assets, see Section V.

[34] Implicit exchange taxes are levied when exporters must surrender foreign proceeds at prices lower than some importers can buy it from the central bank. The opposite is also prevalent: central banks may subsidize certain sectors by selling foreign exchange at rates below the rate it pays to exporters.

[35] Michiel de Kock (1974) lists "monetary" activities, which include currency issue, banking regulation and supervision, the aggregate control of credit, the clearance of balances between banks, and custody of the government's reserves. However, clear distinctions may be difficult. For example, bond rediscounting, generally considered a monetary activity, will take on a quasi-fiscal dimension if performed at subsidized rates.

[36] "Full" transfer of profits refers to the surplus remaining after reasonable reserves provisions. Notice that the implicit taxes mentioned above (such as the unremunerated reserve requirements) would generally be picked up in the central bank's profits and thus, when transferred, in the consolidated accounts. However, they would understate the magnitude of compulsory levies imposed by the state.

profit-and-loss account); and (ii) when the central bank makes a loss which is covered by an equivalent reduction in its net worth.[37]

(i) A prominent quasi-fiscal activity which entails a change in the composition of the central bank's balance sheet is its lending to the private sector for public policy purposes. An important example is preferential sectoral lending, financed by high-powered money. Because these loans could be very similar to budgetary loans, there is an argument for their inclusion as a deficit-determining item analogous to government's net lending (Section II, above). However, the gross incorporation of all central bank lending to the private sector into the fiscal deficit would clearly be misleading because much of it (for instance, rediscounting, open-market operations, and sterilization) is done for pure monetary—and not fiscal—reasons, and should not increase the consolidated fiscal deficit. To preserve distinctions among types of central bank lending, the ideal solution would be to transfer quasi-fiscal lending from the central bank to government's accounts, with a counterbalancing change in net credit to government from the central bank.[38]

Central banks' balance sheets can also be affected by capital gains and losses from valuation changes—for instance, when the central bank is forced to take over private (or public enterprise) debt or to rescue troubled financial institutions. Another common source of valuation changes is the change in the value of the central bank's net foreign exchange holdings, which could arise from external parity fluctuations or from a devaluation that changes the domestic currency counterpart of net foreign assets, resulting in an accounting capital profit or loss.[39]

There is no clear view on how these valuation changes should be treated in relation to the fiscal stance.[40] Robinson and Stella distinguish between unrealized and realized gains. They claim that unrealized gains should be excluded from central bank profits because they attract no new resources—i.e., they are not revenue-enhancing—while the expenditure "financed" by them is a deficit-determining item similar to other expenditure financed by central bank credit. Should the gains become realized, Robinson and Stella (1988, p. 27) claim that:

> compared with the situation that would have obtained with no revaluation gain, purchasing power in the private economy is reduced by the amount of the valuation gain, and thus expenditure "financed" by realized gains is similar to expenditure financed from revenue. If the central bank's accountants took note of the capital gain . . . transfers to the government would increase, reducing the fiscal deficit.

---

[37] Net worth will fall, for instance, when the deficit is "financed" by a reduction in reserves or by printing money. There is, however, considerable doubt whether the collection of seigniorage by money creation (and through other sources of "inflation tax") should be considered a quasi-fiscal activity. These sources of revenue are, in some cases, the essence of the existence of the central bank (Roy Meyers 1985) and, in any event, it is difficult to quantify them in an operational definition of the fiscal deficit.

[38] The full incorporation of central bank lending to the fiscal deficit may be inappropriate for a reason that also applies to budgetary net lending. In theory, the economic cost of preferential lending should be equal to the expected discounted future loss arising from the loan, adjusted for risk. Lending should, therefore, increase the fiscal deficit only by this amount, that is, by the implicit "cost" of lending and not by the full volume of the loan. In any event, there should be consistency between budgetary and central bank lending.

[39] On the issue of gains and losses on foreign assets, see Eisner and Pieper (1990).

[40] Robert Mundell (1971, p. 92) discusses the monetary consequences of treating devaluation gains as a regular source of revenue. Recently, German and Swiss authors discussed the practical procedures for covering their central bank losses arising from the depreciation of the U.S. dollar (for example, Peter Goerres 1985). British authors also analyzed the subject in connection with the losses of central banks which held pounds sterling following devaluation of the pound (Peter Praet 1982).

TABLE 5
CENTRAL BANK DEFICITS[1]
(IN PERCENTAGE OF GDP)

	1984	1986
Argentina	−2.5	−1.6
Costa Rica	−4.3	−3.8
Ghana	−2.1	−0.6
Kenya	−3.8	−5.4
Philippines	−5.2	−2.8
Uruguay	−4.2	−4.0

Sources: Argentina, Julio Piekarz (1987); Costa Rica, Ana Rodríguez Aguilera (1987); Ghana and Kenya, Catsambas and Pigato (1989); Philippines, IMF staff estimates; Uruguay, Dionisio Onandi and Luis Viana (1987).
[1] Since the indicators are taken from different sources, they are based on various definitions of the concept of central bank losses and thus are not strictly comparable.

(ii) The second deviation from the initial benchmark arises when central banks make losses. Significant central bank deficits are frequent in developing countries, sometimes exceeding conventional fiscal deficits (Table 5). Reasons for these losses vary. Their most common causes are quasi-fiscal, such as the requirement on central banks to lend without interest or at very low interest rates for policy purposes. Operational losses also arise from the administration of a multiple exchange rate system (which may include an implicit subsidy to preferred buyers) and from currency devaluations when the central bank has net foreign exchange liabilities vis-à-vis the domestic sector.[41]

Whether or not central bank losses arise from quasi-fiscal activities, there is a case, based on symmetry of treatment, for their explicit inclusion in the public sector deficit. Although it is common practice to transfer central bank profits to government, thus reducing the fiscal

[41] For a discussion of sources and treatment of central bank loans, see Mario Teijeiro (1989). The case of losses connected to foreign exchange liabilities is analyzed by Neven Mates (1989).

deficit, current losses do not elicit a transfer from the government to the central bank, so the measured deficit does not rise. To prevent measurement biases, central bank losses should be included in the public sector balance by recording, for example, a budgetary transfer or a subsidy from the government, thus properly increasing the recorded fiscal deficit.

To summarize, ideally, government accounts should incorporate quasi-fiscal revenues and expenditures, leaving central bank accounts covering only monetary activities. A second-best solution would be, first, that central bank operational losses be consolidated into the fiscal deficit by the addition of a transfer from government to the central bank financed by credit from the central bank. Second, an estimate of the size of central bank quasi-fiscal activities falling outside the profit-and-loss account should be made, and then amalgamated into the adjusted fiscal deficit. Such a hybrid deficit would mix net worth with cash concepts, but would have value as a supplementary indicator showing the approximate impact of central bank quasi-fiscal activities on the overall public sector balance.

4. The Budgetary Dimension of the Public Financial Sector

Typically, public financial institutions are excluded from the coverage of the public sector and are consolidated with the private banking system. However, these institutions often engage in a multitude of activities (such as preferential credit allocations, subsidized interest rates, etc.) with a clear fiscal content. To the extent that such activities go beyond pure liquidity management which could have been carried out by private financial intermediaries, it is possible that the exclusion of resources provided by the public financial system from the measured public sector balance creates a misleading impression of the fiscal policy stance.

As in the case of nonfinancial enterprises, in order to differentiate between public and private financial institutions, it would be appropriate to consider the implications of their operations on the distribution of income and wealth. Using this approach, pure commercial banks in which the government owns a large, or even a majority stake, should not be considered "public" if their activities have nothing to do with public policy and if they fully finance their operations at prevailing market conditions. The relevant public sector would therefore include only those public institutions such as development banks, sectoral credit institutions, mortgage banks, building and loan associations, finance and investment companies, as well as insurance companies and pension funds, which mobilize all or part of their resources through the receipt of contractual premia but only invest in assets frequently selected on public policy considerations.

Why should some or all of the activities of these institutions be considered quasi-fiscal? The answer appears to be related to the nature of their operations on both sides of the capital market. Public financial institutions are, in many countries, perhaps the most common means of directing credit for policy purposes (World Bank 1989). Therefore, the same considerations that apply to direct budgetary net lending by the government and to quasi-fiscal lending by the central bank seem to apply here.

There is, however, an important difference. Unlike the government and the monetary authority, but like typical private financial institutions, many public ones act as intermediaries financing at least part of their long-term financial claims by selling long-term financial assets to the public. Nevertheless, public institutions clearly operate in the capital market under special conditions. They were created to provide services that, for whatever reason, other institutions had found not worthwhile or too risky to provide. Thus, public institutions are likely to be less profitable, and be more exposed to risk, than other financial institutions, and at a disadvantage in mobilizing voluntary resources from the financial markets. Their survival hence often depends on government guarantees (giving them an edge in the market) or on explicit government subsidies, monopoly power over market segments, preferential access to government-mobilized resources or other forms of preference or protection, including exclusive access to external loans. This being the case, the operations of these institutions would exert crowding-out pressures on financial markets similar to those arising from the financing of other government activities, and therefore should not be neglected when assessing the overall economic impact of the consolidated public sector.[42]

V. *The Intertemporal Budget Constraint of the Public Sector*

Recent developments in the analysis of net public resource use have changed the way the deficit is viewed, and the uses to which the deficit measure is being put. This change in perspective has generated awareness of a further set of deficiencies in traditional measures of the deficit, refocused attention toward balance-sheet-based deficit measures, and

[42] A discussion of the fiscal role and the rationale for the public sector financial institutions is provided by Oded Liviatan (1990). He also raises some methodological issues regarding consolidation. Since a large part of the financing for public financial intermediaries is provided by other parts of the public sector, in order to prevent double counting only the portion of their lending which is *directly* financed through the domestic capital market or from abroad should be taken into account.

opened up a long menu of methodological issues of government balance sheet measurement. These are the topics of this section.

1. Intertemporal Shortcomings of the Conventional Deficit

Developments in private sector consumer theory have been paralleled (albeit with a lag) by changes in our understanding of public sector behavior. It was always clear that the public sector (being less liquidity-constrained than any private individual) did not finance its expenditure completely out of current income. However, several recent world developments have highlighted the fact that the government, even if infinitely-lived, is constrained—like private consumers— by the size of its permanent income.

The debt crisis has shown that there are perceived limits on governments' ability to repay borrowing from future generations to finance present consumption and the U.S. social security debate has generated awareness of the implications for today of government commitments to spend or repay tomorrow. The conclusion that governments face an intertemporal budget constraint not unlike that of private agents cannot be avoided. It has also become clear that governments' consumption paths are determined by wealth as well as by income: privatization programs that seemed to improve the financial position of public sectors have shown that governments can dissave to finance consumption in any period. Finally, it is now recognized that governments' consumption paths can be importantly affected by price and valuation changes. This has been amply illustrated by the effect on governments' financial position of swings in the value of the dollar over the 1980s, the various Latin American hyperinflations, and the development of debt buyback schemes through which governments have prof-

ited by the fall in value of their debt. [43]

Some deficiencies in traditional measures of the deficit become particularly evident when government behavior is recast in an intertemporal rather than annual framework—and when attention is shifted from short-run demand management to the sustainability of the deficit. Deficiencies include the omission of valuation adjustments, the treatment of asset sales, and of the financial implications of entitlement programs and government guarantees. Specifically, the problems are as follows:

a. The conventional deficit includes no provision for *valuation changes* in government assets or liabilities, though these could conceivably change the sign of the budget balance in any fiscal year. One facet of this issue has already been discussed: adjustments to the deficit that separate amortization from interest payments on public debt in inflationary regimes are a partial recognition of the impact that prices can have on the nominal deficit. However, government's ability to pay can also be affected, in real terms, by inflation, devaluation, changes in the terms of trade or in relative prices, and capital gains or losses on the purchasing power implicit in government assets and liabilities, though none of these effects is captured by a summary of government transactions during a given fiscal period. [44]

b. Conventional deficit measures usually include receipts from *privatization*

---

[43] Comparisons with developments in consumer theory cannot be taken too far. Few attempts have been made to situate government behavior in an optimizing framework. Buiter (1983, p. 337, text discussion, and especially footnote 3), however, presages such an advance in his illustration of a case where a rule of government consumption to maintain a constant net worth would not be optimal.

[44] Since the government has little control over valuation changes, there are arguments for omitting them from deficit measures to be used for policy design.

TABLE 6

ARGENTINA: THE SALE OF THE TOKYO EMBASSY[1]
(IN PERCENTAGE OF GDP)

	1988	1989 (II)	1989 (IV)
Current revenue	17.6	13.0	18.2
Capital revenue[2]	0.9	3.8	0.3

Source: Centro de Estudios Macroeconomicos de Argentina, Buenos Aires (unpublished).
[1] GDP ratios for 1988 are quarterly averages for the full year; 1989 ratios are for the second and fourth quarters.
[2] Includes proceeds from asset sales.

and the sale of other assets as a revenue item. Structural programs or pressures to cut the flow deficit have resulted in the conversion into liquid assets of nonfinancial tangible and even intangible assets that were not previously considered. When assets such as land, embassies, or aircraft are sold, they provide immediate cash to alleviate the current year's financing burden. The amounts can be important—and help to overcome drastic temporary downturns in tax revenue (as in the case of Argentina during its recent hyperinflation; Table 6). However, the government is worse off by the replacement cost of the assets (arguably their realized market sale value; Raymond Goldsmith 1985, p. 92).

The nature of the problem asset sales pose for the deficit differs depending on whether the assets disposed of have previously been purchased by government through the budget or whether they have "always" formed part of the public patrimony (for instance, in the case of mineral rights). Treating as revenue the sales of previously purchased investment goods in computing the measured deficit is justified by the unorthodox treatment of capital expenditure in government accounts. Unlike private sector capital (and the treatment of public capital in the SNA) which is depreciated over its lifetime,

public capital is fully expensed in the fiscal year it is purchased.[45] This merging of the current and investment accounts, which makes consistent the inclusion of the full value of an asset sale as a revenue item, can be justified when looking at the annual financing needs of government (Stella 1989, pp. 19–22), but is misleading regarding the sustainability of the government's policy stance.

The inclusion of revenues from assets other than investment goods as an "improvement" in government's ability to pay is incorrect by any private sector accounting practice. When the government sells land or mineral rights, for example, it has merely changed the composition of its portfolio: it has the cash but it no longer has the asset. If it earned the market value of the asset, then it is no better or worse off than prior to the sale.[46]

c. The conventional deficit can be severely affected by "revenues" which create liabilities for the future or "expenditures" which represent the liquidation of past liabilities. On the revenue side, the traditional deficit often includes changes in the net position of *social insurance programs*. However, social insurance contributions supposedly confer entitlements on contributors and as such commit the government to higher future spending. Thus, social security contributions do not represent free-and-clear revenues, and their inclusion in the deficit

[45] "On both a gross and a net basis the NIPA [National Income and Product Accounts measure for the USA] measure was shown to understate the size of government saving mainly because NIPA treats capital outlays as a current rather than a capital account item" (Attiat Ott and Jang Yoo 1980, p. 195).
[46] This is strictly true only when the value of the asset to the private sector is the same as to the government (Ali Mansoor 1988). If efficiency is higher in the private sector, the gain from the sale of the asset will be greater than or equal to the loss of its income stream (depending on whether the government or the private sector captures the capitalized value of the efficiency improvement). In cases where the gain is nonzero, the inclusion of a revenue item (positive or negative) would be appropriate.

overstates government's ability to pay. On the other hand, because they are contingent claims (contingent not only on contributors' attaining old age, or ill health, but also on changes in government legislation), the magnitude of outlays they will eventually require is difficult to determine.[47]

Analogously, the conventional deficit can be dramatically inflated in any year by government's payment of previously *guaranteed debt*, or insurance contracts, such as exchange guarantees or bail-outs of underwritten entities (like insolvent public enterprises, or the U.S. savings and loan industry). In reality, such payments are stock adjustments—the sum of the accumulated risk costs borne by government over the life of the guarantee. Unlike the private sector, which mitigates the impact of bad debts by accumulating loan loss reserves as offsetting stocks, the government usually fails to make provision for expected defaults. Hence, the costs of risk bearing are not spread out over the life of the risk, but are charged only upon realization of the risk's downside.

The measurement problem in the conventional deficit is not just that meeting current entitlements or paying up for past guarantees boosts the deficit, but also that, at any time, the conventional deficit provides an over-optimistic indicator of government's long-run ability to pay, because it does not factor in the expected future cost of entitlements and contingent liabilities assumed by government. Moreover, the calculation of the expected cost of contingent claims is complicated by the possibility of moral hazard: even if the entitlements and guarantees are not funded or provisioned against, the assumption of liability by

government may change private sector behavior. Eisner (1990, p. 15) clearly rephrases the problem:

> It may be pointed out that loan guarantees or deposit insurance indirectly finance real spending just as they might if treasury expenditures were made up front. In a sense, the explicit and implicit deposit insurance or guarantees raised the budget deficit at the time the S&Ls made the loans that ultimately turned bad . . . the expenditures were made then. They then financed the now half-empty office buildings or homes worth only a fraction of their construction costs. Current government borrowing to finance the purchases of S&L assets only makes explicit an element of deficit or debt that was implicit earlier in the commitment of backing to S&L liabilities.

Christopher Towe (1989, p. 2) takes these problems one step further, recasting them in terms of their implications for budgetary control:

> since the issuance of such contingencies may not impact the current budget, while having severe cash-flow implications for the future, there may not exist sufficient controls, under conventional accounting constraints, to maintain the level of such contingent liabilities at a prudent level.

Clearly, appropriate accounting for contingent claims requires an intertemporal framework.

2. The Deficit and Government Solvency: Changes in Public Sector Net Worth

The so-called deficiencies described above have one thing in common: unless the valuation changes are realized or the risks eventuate, they do not affect the current year's borrowing requirement.[48] Moreover, while the consequences of these issues generate ample debate, their combined effect on aggregate demand in any single year would be well-nigh impossible to measure. Hence, it should

---

[47] The discussion here does not depend on whether programs are funded or unfunded; however, the size of net future government expenditures will obviously depend on future social security revenues.

[48] Although they may well have an impact on the government debt.

1668   *Journal of Economic Literature, Vol. XXIX (December 1991)*

be stressed that the main reason for tackling these difficulties is in order to refocus the deficit as a measure of the long-run sustainability of government policy—put dramatically: of the solvency of government.

According to Bean and Buiter (1987, p. 27):

> A government is solvent if its spending programme, its tax-transfer programme and its planned future use of seigniorage are consistent with its outstanding, initial financial and real assets and liabilities (in the sense that the present value of its spending programme is equal to its comprehensive net worth).

In other words, while a government can shift consumption between periods by saving and borrowing, it will be unable to consume more, over its lifetime, than its total income plus its initial endowment.[49] Under this definition, the "fiscal deficit" would be equivalent to the dissaving of government (reduction in its net worth) in any year.

Like the net worth of a firm, the net worth of government is specified in its balance sheet, and the overall fiscal deficit in any period is equal to the difference in balance sheets at the beginning and end of the period. The methodological and measurement difficulties which bedevil the specification of the government balance sheet—far more than the firm's—are discussed below.

a. *Existing Government Balance Sheets.* Government balance sheets have two bases, one with its roots in government financial statistics and the other inspired by national income accounting. *Financial* balance sheets based on the government's net financial asset position can be extrapolated from studies which reconcile annual flow deficits with changes in outstanding public debt. (For instance, Eisner 1986, p. 16.) The most important methodological issue for this type of balance sheet is the treatment of valuation changes in government assets and liabilities (Subsection b.(1), below).

Alternatively, government balance sheets on an *SNA basis* attempt to put the government on a par with the other sectors of the economy in the income and wealth accounts of the nation, with the purpose of determining the sectoral distribution of the components of wealth. Goldsmith (1985) presents the most comprehensive international collection of SNA-based government balance sheets. Here, measurement problems are more extensive, encompassing as well the valuation of government real and intangible assets (Subsection b.(2), below). Some of the difficulties are not conceptually different from measurement problems in other SNA sectors—for instance, the choice of deflators and price indices, the derivation of stocks from flows,[50] and the treatment of inventories. Only measurement issues of relevance or sizeable importance to the public sector are covered here. For a broader discussion see Goldsmith (1985).

Continual time series of SNA-based balance sheets almost never exist, and so (with the exception of the change in net worth series presented by Ott and Yoo 1980, pp. 190–91) there appear to have been no studies that compare the change in balance sheets from one year to the next with flow-based deficits. Moreover, while SNA-based balance sheets provide valuable first approximations of governments' permanent in-

---

[49] While governments are normally considered infinitely lived, the issue of solvency seems to imply a terminal point. Practically, however, the issue is irrelevant, in the sense that present value calculations at a positive discount rate assign a weight approaching zero to transactions in the distant future.

[50] For a brief comment on the perpetual inventory method and its shortcomings, see Goldsmith (1985, p. 333).

come, they include only a subset of assets and liabilities and thus may not be a good indicator of the sustainability of fiscal policy.

b. *An Ideal Government Balance Sheet.* Buiter (1983, especially p. 310); also Bean and Buiter (1987, p. 28ff); describes the ideal "comprehensive consolidated public sector balance sheet at current market or implicit prices." To capture the complete array of ways in which government can increase or run down its net worth in a global balance sheet, government assets should include: financial assets; real capital—including nonmarketable social overhead capital, equity (mainly in public enterprises—partly marketable); land and mineral assets (discovered and undiscovered—partly marketable); the present value of the future tax program (including social security contributions); and the imputed present value of seigniorage. Liabilities would include government debt (domestic and foreign, indexed or not); the stock of high-powered money; and the present value of social insurance and other entitlement programs (including guarantees). Government net worth is then the balancing item.

While Buiter's construct provides a clear conceptual framework defining government net worth, it is far from operational. Even at the conceptual level, the definitions of capitalized values of tax and spending programs are subject to enormous controversy. And the valuation of tangible assets presents special difficulties when it must be undertaken on the massive scale necessary to encompass complete public sector holdings. Moreover, since public assets are less frequently traded than private assets, their prices may be difficult to identify. Indeed, were public assets traded, their prices and those of their currently traded substitutes might be very different from private sector prices in a thinner market

(not augmented by government purchases and sales).[51]

Despite these problems, valuable work has been done on many items in the comprehensive balance sheet. In particular, Eisner and Pieper (1984), Eisner (1986), and Boskin, M. Robinson, and Huber (1987), present improved balance sheets containing many innovations which address the deficiencies in deficit measurement detailed above.[52] Specifically, as discussed below, efforts have been made: (1) to assess the magnitude of valuation changes in financial net assets, for a more accurate picture of government liquidity; (2a) to provide a more economically correct estimate of capital formation and the capital stock, by applying a more realistic depreciation scheme than the current system of annual expensing; (2b and 2c) to provide a more comprehensive picture of government's ability to pay by including in the balance sheet public land and mineral rights; and (3) to create a framework for assessing the eventual impact of contingent claims on the budget. However, the remaining element of the comprehensive balance sheet, the present value of the tax program (4), presents conceptual difficulties large enough to cast doubt on the interpretation of any measure of government net worth.

(1) *The Valuation of Financial Assets.* Budget deficits have been considered damaging, in an intertemporal sense, because they add to the public debt and thereby erode the sustainability of the government's expenditure path at current levels of tax revenue. However, as Eisner (1984, p. 140) points out:

> The "underlying reality . . . that every dollar of deficit . . . adds a dollar to debt" is simply

---

[51] See Eisner (1976) on establishing the prices of capital assets.

[52] Boskin's work forms part of a large on-going project to refine government accounts; Eisner (1988) has incorporated his work in a proposal for improved global national income accounts.

not true in a real sense if prices are not constant. And if interest rates fluctuate, the statement is not true even with reference to the market value of nominal debt.

In particular, positive inflation rates erode the real value of public debt, so that governments that are net debtors can have rising net worth while continuing to run deficits. Moreover, increasing interest rates erode the market value of previously issued fixed-interest debt; and, if debt is callable, the government can profit by any movement in the interest rate.

Thus, to arrive at the change in net worth attributable to changes in the values of (net) financial assets, the change in their nominal par value from one balance sheet to the next should be augmented by two adjustments—the difference between the real and nominal values of net financial holdings, and the difference between their face value and their market value at the time the net worth calculation is being made.

These adjustments have been more widely applied than any other balance sheet reconciliation item, because, even when economists were not concerned directly with net worth measures, they were troubled by the discrepancy between measures of net government spending and measures of changes in net government liabilities (Muller and Price 1984, p. 8; Eisner and Pieper 1984, p. 12). Adjusted series for public debt appear in Marcus Miller (1982); Eisner and Pieper (1984; recalculated in Boskin, M. Robinson, and Huber 1987); de Leeuw and Holloway (1985); and Eisner (1986). Eisner (1976) presents revaluation estimates for a range of government assets and liabilities.

Benjamin Russo (1987, p. 12), however, has objected to the par-to-market adjustment, on the grounds that (save if the government were to raise taxes in order to prepay its debt) the public debt

is always amortized at its face value; neither gains nor losses from shifts in market valuation over the life of the loans are ever realized.[53] Hence, he claims, such shifts, however large their effect may be in any year, are irrelevant to the consideration of the sustainability of the deficit.

(2) *The Valuation of Real Assets.* While some valuation problems are common to all assets, specific issues arise in the valuation of depreciable assets, land, and mineral rights.

(a) *Real Capital and Depreciation.* Because the capital stock is estimated by accumulating annual government capital formation,[54] it is sensitive to the form of depreciation assumed across vintages of capital, i.e., to the assumption of the rate of *net* investment by government. The impact of different depreciation schemes on estimates of the capital stock is discussed in Boskin, M. Robinson, and Roberts (1985). Of course, the validity of any depreciation scheme depends on how closely it approximates economic depreciation. Boskin et al. apply a geometric depreciation scheme with rates inferred where possible from the ratio of new to used asset prices, on the argument that "Equipment depreciates faster than straightline in the early years, and structures depreciate more slowly" (p. 16).[55] Goldsmith, Ott and Austin, Eisner, and the Bureau of Economic Analysis (United States 1982) use straightline depreciation in their calculations, while John Ken-

---

[53] Prepayment of debt may not be unusual. It occurs, for instance, in secondary foreign debt markets or when consols have been retired.

[54] "The two main ingredients [in the perpetual inventory method of estimating the capital stock in the government sector] are a retirement pattern to yield gross stock and a depreciation method which will reasonably estimate net stocks" (Ott and Thomas Austin 1980, p. 266).

[55] The *SNA* recommends excluding military asset expenditure from capital formation. However, Goldsmith (1985, p. 67) notes that statistics usually do not permit the exclusion.

drick (1976) uses double-declining depreciation.

(b) *Land.* Methods of land valuation have been of concern to policy makers since governments started to collect taxes, and a wide literature exists at the microeconomic level. The problem for the government balance sheet is one of aggregation: the information required for the micro-oriented techniques is too detailed to be applied to all public sector holdings. There are also pitfalls in making global inferences from partial data: for many reasons, public sector land (such as military land) may not be a close substitute for private land; and, as mentioned above, were all public land marketable, land prices might be very different from what they are at present.

In fact, as Boskin et al. (1985, pp. 931–32) point out, global estimates of the value of U.S. federal government land (in Goldsmith 1985, Grace Milgram 1973, Ott and Yoo 1980, Eisner and Pieper 1984, and Boskin et al. 1985) are each simply extrapolations (using different combinations of price indices, and adjustments for changes in total acreage and in land composition) of a 1946 estimate made by J. E. Reeve (quoted in Boskin et al. 1985). "These studies [. . .] demonstrate how successive refinements of basic data often hang by a very slender thread." (p. 931) "A new benchmark estimate for the value of federal land in a particular year is especially important" (p. 935).

As to the valuation of government land in other countries, Goldsmith (1985, p. 119) cites difficulties in valuing nonagricultural land, which is often consolidated with the value of the buildings erected on it (so that a proportional valuation factor must be assumed), and in assessing the share of forest on so-called agricultural land.

(c) *Mineral Rights.* The inclusion of mineral rights in the government balance sheet is arguably even more important than the inclusion of government land, because changes in the pace of their direct exploitation, sale, or lease are seen by governments as an important way of improving their short-term financial position, and are therefore a prime generator of the problem mentioned earlier, whereby the sale of an asset/exhaustible resource gives a misleadingly optimistic picture of government wealth accumulation, by not offsetting the revenue by the cost of the depletion of the asset.[56] It is also true, however, that the large fluctuations in oil prices observed over the last two decades could create much volatility in government net worth from year to year, if applied directly to valuing the stock of mineral rights—unhelpful volatility since only a small portion of stocks would be sold.

One way or other, as Boskin et al. (1985, p. 924) point out, no work was done prior to their pioneering study on the valuation of federal mineral rights; and we have seen no applicable study in other countries. Boskin et al. (1985) estimate expected unproven as well as proven gas and oil reserves—in the spirit of Buiter's forward-looking comprehensive public sector balance sheet.[57] The inclusion of undiscovered reserves is important for the correct interpretation of government revenues, because the lease of mineral rights typically begins with the sale of exploration rights to unproven

---

[56] "National balance sheets for about a dozen countries . . . are nearly worthless unless they include the value of subsoil assets, particularly oil and gas" (Goldsmith 1985, p. 69).

[57] The paper contains a valuable exposition of measurement techniques (comparing the present value method, the land price method, and the net price method of determining a base year value to anchor the perpetual inventory calculation). Capital gains (an important issue in the case of exhaustible resources) are included via the assumption that prices grow with the interest rate. Estimates of federal mineral rights are extended to state and local levels in Boskin, M. Robinson, and Huber (1987).

fields. The government earns revenue (bonuses) by exploiting firms' expectations about reserves, even if the fields prove to be dry; and, as before, the revenues are not free and clear but come from the government's having ceded an (expected) asset.

Two measurement complications make accounting for exhaustible resources more difficult than accounting for the government's capital stock. First, stocks of undiscovered reserves must be recalculated each time discoveries are made—and the relationship between proven and unproven reserves may not be linear. Second, the inclusion of an estimate for mineral rights *with* estimates of the value of land is problematic, because it is not clear to what extent the value of land already internalizes the value of the minerals underneath.[58] Ignoring these complications, Boskin's work (Table 7) gives an idea of the implications of changes in the value of real assets for the fiscal deficit.[59]

(3) *The Valuation of Entitlements, Contingent Claims, and Guarantees.* Particularly in the United States, the proper treatment of social security obligations in the fiscal accounts has generated much discussion (for instance, David Rosenbaum 1990). Towe (1989, p. 10ff) describes the main options, from the most restrictive method (the accumulated benefit cost approach) to that most comparable to net worth (the actuarial balance). While these accounting treatments have been developed mainly for social security programs, their application can be considered for much broader ranges of entitlement schemes and insurance programs.

TABLE 7

UNITED STATES: INFLUENCES ON FEDERAL NET WORTH
(IN BILLIONS OF CURRENT U.S. DOLLARS)

	1979	1980
1. NIPA balance[1]	−16.1	−61.3
2. Change in value of Federal land	+17.2	+36.9
3. Change in value of oil and gas rights	+93.8	+208.8
4. Augmented balance (lines 1 + 2 + 3)[2]	+94.9	+184.4

Sources: Line 1: United States (1989a, Table B-79); Lines 2 and 3: Boskin et al. (1985b).
[1] Federal Government receipts less expenditures on a National Income and Product Accounts basis.
[2] Line 4 is illustrative only; it has not been checked for inconsistencies in definition.

The accumulated benefit cost approach to valuing the net impact of an entitlement/insurance program is used in the private sector, where the expected liability of the program is defined only with respect to current participants, and according to current rules (see also Boskin et al. 1987, p. 44). This approach would narrowly restrict the consideration of contingencies (and therefore of government solvency) to the question of whether present participants will continue to pay their expected subscriptions/premia and become eligible (for example, by living long enough) to collect their expected benefits.

The somewhat less restrictive actuarial fairness approach to valuation defines the deficit or surplus in a contingency program as the difference between the (aggregated) expected present value of the payouts to each of a program's participants over the program's duration and the expected net present value of their payments, thus allowing consideration of expected changes in policy and participation. "Fairness" requires that over the lifetime of each participant, the program must be in balance.

---

[58] These complications are exacerbated in the case of reproducible natural resources such as forests and fisheries (Goldsmith 1985, p. 68).

[59] If net worth series are calculated over a longer period, it would be more appropriate to adjust Table 7 for general inflation.

Actuarial balance requires that expected (present value) payments to *all* present and future participants be equivalent to total expected contributions (adjusted for operating expenses and any relevant endowment or reserve). If the former exceeds the latter, the program has a negative net worth. Boskin et al. (1987) present estimates of the U.S. social security balance based on this criterion calculated over 75 years. However, they use these estimates to illustrate the extreme sensitivity of such present value calculations to assumptions about contingencies: "[M]oving all of the economic and demographic projections from intermediate to either optimistic or pessimistic [assumptions] results in a change which is larger than the privately held national debt" (p. 45).

The calculation of program deficits under any of the above criteria also requires an estimate of probabilities. Degrees of certainty in payments can vary widely between programs, and have been used as classification criteria—distinguishing between, for instance, pension schemes, where expected outcomes are smooth and predictable once the demographics have been identified, and deposit insurance to financial institutions, where the risks are highly correlated, leading with a small probability to extremely high payouts (Boskin et al. 1987, especially p. 15). Moreover, risks may be even higher than guarantees or premia paid would suggest, if political or other pressures force government to treat noninsured agents on a par with insured agents during a systemic crisis.[60] Boskin et al. derive backward-looking estimates of probabilities for defaults on loans from the Small Business Administration, but caution

that "In the case of an insurance program, . . . where the risks of default across borrowers are highly correlated and very rare, a model based on historical experience can be misleading" (p. 32).

The approaches described measure only the first-order present value of the contingency program. Thus, according to these criteria, all programs in which guarantees are issued without charge (often the case with exchange guarantees (Robinson and Stella 1988, p. 29) are deemed to be in deficit—though the government would not have issued them without the expectation of some social benefit (such as risk-spreading). The value of the social benefit might conceivably be estimated—in some cases, by comparing costs in a market without the guarantees (Wattleworth 1988, p. 58), and imputed to the government accounts, but it will usually be impossible to assess the impact of the social benefit on other elements of the government balance sheet.[61]

A final point made by Towe concerns the treatment of reserves sometimes set up to finance contingency programs. While these reserves would seem to represent an offset to any calculation of a deficit in the program, they will do so only when not held in the form of other government liabilities.

(4) *The Valuation of the Present Value of the Tax Program.* Eisner (1984, pp. 139–40) takes the view that changes in the value of contingent claims are likely to be met by changes in taxes (or other redistributory legislation), and

---

[60] Robinson and Stella (1988, p. 29) cite the case of debt rescheduling, where the public sector is often forced to assume the external transfer portion of private sector debt even when the debt has not been guaranteed by government.

[61] The difficulty in capturing the second-order effects of government policy on government's balance sheet is, of course, generalizable to any revenue or expenditure program whose impact is diffuse. This issue could become particularly relevant in budgeting for pollution control and environmental management, which might have important effects—though unpredictable and far in the future—on government real assets.

hence, that the inclusion of such claims in the deficit could give a misleading measure of the fiscal stance, out of line with the private sector's perception of its claims on government. But if Ricardian equivalence is broadly defined, this view could be generalized to *all* potential reductions in government net worth, and the present value of the tax program simply replaces net worth as the balancing item in the comprehensive balance sheet.

Even if Ricardian equivalence does not hold, the government's power to control its long-run net worth through altering tax and expenditure legislation[62] suggests that, even if government has a negative net worth given today's policy package, it is not insolvent in the private sector sense, but merely must adjust the tax program by the amount of its "permanent deficit"[63] in order to return to sustainability. The indeterminacy of the net worth measure inherent in the flexibility of the government's power to tax is the main philosophical problem with balance sheet or net worth concepts of the deficit. Given this indeterminacy, it is not clear that net worth measures can be constrained to be any less arbitrary than are flow measures.

In the limit, thus, government's control over resources encompasses all of private sector income and wealth as well. Obviously, the sustainability of government policy would then depend on its impact on the total wealth of the econ-

omy—in other words, on private agents' view of their net worth.[64]

Kotlikoff (1989, p. 2) recognizes this broadest of interrelationships in his proposal to substitute a "Fiscal Balance Rule" for present indicators of budget sustainability:

> [The Fiscal Balance Rule] says take in net present value from each new young generation an amount equal to the flow of government consumption less interest on the difference between (a) the value of the economy's capital stock and (b) the present value difference between the future consumption and labor earnings of existing older generations. . . . [O]ne can use existing data to check whether it is being obeyed and, therefore, whether future generations are likely to be treated better or worse than current generations.

In other words, if the present labor force pays for government consumption by taxes augmented by its interest earnings on the capital stock net of that part which finances dissaving by the old, government policy will not run down the economy's capital stock and future generations will be as wealthy as past generations. Under this criterion, the fiscal deficit would be defined as government consumption in excess of taxes plus interest.

c. *Shortcomings of Net Worth Concepts of the Deficit: A Tentative Conclusion.* The jury is still out on the superiority of net worth calculations of the deficit compared with traditional flow measures. On the one hand, it is clear that they correct for several blatant errors in treatment in currently accepted economic indicators. On the other hand, they fall between two stools. As discussed above, they are not broad enough to take into

---

[62] One good example is the large drop in U.S. social security obligations following legislation in 1982 (Eisner 1986, p. 37).

[63] The permanent deficit (defined by Bean and Buiter 1987, p. 31) is the real perpetuity equivalent of the difference between the present value of real government spending plans and of net worth. "Although ex ante permanent deficits will not actually materialize, let alone be permanent, they represent the *permanent adjustment* that must be made, relative to the ex ante inconsistent plans, to the flows of spending, tax receipts, or seigniorage revenue in order to achieve solvency."

[64] Moses Abramovitz (in private correspondence) puts the point succinctly: "The government's "total income" is not an exogenous datum. It is a function of economic growth, which itself is influenced by government budget policy both on the expenditure and revenue sides . . . and by politics. How large a portion of future income will politics permit the government to obtain—and from whom?"

account the indeterminacy created by the government's power to change the present value of tax and entitlement programs. However, they *are* very broad measures. All of the authors surveyed have stressed the huge movements in net worth that can be occasioned by valuation changes in assets such as land that the government has no immediate intention of liquidating. Hence, net worth measures could be dangerous if used for near-term fiscal policy.[65] Even in the long run, as Stella (1989, p. 21) points out:

> [A]n important, though seemingly ignored, point is that the appropriateness of using the net present value approach depends on the government ultimately realizing the capital gains. While this might be reasonable for financial assets, it is certainly not the case for all real assets. . . . A key factor upholding the validity of accrual accounting is the expectation that the income will eventually be realized. In cases where the income will never be realized, accrual accounting is not justified.

VI. *Final Remarks*

The fiscal balance has a central role in macroeconomic analysis, and countless econometric studies have been constructed around data on fiscal deficits. Yet, a seemingly straightforward concept such as "the overall government deficit" hides a minefield of ambiguities, questions of usage, and conflicting definitional issues. Ideally, these should be resolved before conclusions from budgetary statistics are drawn. Problems include the accounting and classification procedures for government operations, the feedback between the budget and macroeconomic developments, the coverage of "government," the manner in which nonbud-

---

[65] Net worth concepts of the deficit may not be a good measure of private agents' perception of the impact of government on their net worth, since valuation changes in government's real assets are included in government net worth measures, while the private sector (perhaps because of a different time horizon) may not consider these changes as a factor affecting it.

getary operations (such as regulation and implicit guarantees) should be accounted for, and the temporal dimension of government operations. These measurement issues have generated the large body of methodological literature that has been the subject of this survey.

Although the survey is to some extent taxonomic, several central messages emerge. These bear on the implications of deficit measurement for policy, for cross-country comparison and time series analysis, and on the futility of a search for "one" deficit measure.

In the first place, it is evident that the measurement of the deficit is not a minor issue but one that has significant policy implications. Indeed, depending on how it is measured, and over what period of time, the government deficit can signal different stances and therefore call for different fiscal policies. Similarly, the definition of the public sector and the type of operations included have important consequences for the design, implementation, and monitoring of a macroeconomic package.

Second, cross-country comparisons may be extremely deceptive if they do not adjust for country-specific economic characteristics and accounting conventions. Moreoever, even the analyses of time trends in a given country may require the constant upgrading of concepts in response to changing economic conditions.

Third, the sole reliance on pure flow concepts of fiscal accounting can be misleading and inadequate for fiscal analysis. Rather, the literature suggests that the standard flow measures should be supplemented, and in some circumstances replaced, by stock-change concepts such as changes in government financial and real assets, actual and contingent liabilities, and global measures of net worth. It should be stressed, however, that many of these stock-based measures are

no less arbitrary, and probably more difficult to quantify, than the flow concepts
they are attempting to replace. Moreover, conventional flow measures are not
to be discarded since they have a specific
use in gauging the *short-term* financial
impact of government imbalances. But
in order to generate *longer-run* measures
of true fiscal impact it is necessary to consider what determines the solvency of
the public sector, and perhaps even of
the nation.

REFERENCES

ATKINSON, ANTHONY B. "Income Maintenance and
Social Insurance," in *The handbook of public economics*. Vol. 1. Eds.: ALAN J. AUERBACH AND MAR-
TIN FELDSTEIN. Amsterdam: North-Holland; 1987,
pp. 779–908.

BARRO, ROBERT J. "The Ricardian Approach to Budget Deficits," *J. Econ. Perspectives*, Spring 1989,
3(2), pp. 37–54.

BARTH, JAMES R. ET AL. "Effects of Federal Budget
Deficits on Interest Rates and the Composition of
Domestic Output." Presented at the Conference
on Fiscal Policy. Washington, DC: The Urban Institute, 1989.

BAUMOL, WILLIAM J. "Toward a Theory of Public
Enterprise," *Atlantic Econ. J.*, Mar. 1984, *12*(1),
pp. 12–19.

BEAN, CHARLES R. AND BUITER, WILLEM H. *The plain
man's guide to fiscal and financial policy*. London:
Employment Institute, Oct. 1987.

BERNHEIM, B. DOUGLAS. "Ricardian Equivalence: An
Evaluation of Theory and Evidence," in *NBER
Macroeconomics Annual, 1987*. Ed.: STANLEY
FISCHER. Cambridge, MA and London: MIT Press,
1987, pp. 263–304.

BLANCHARD, OLIVIER J. *Suggestions for a new set
of fiscal indicators*. OECD Economics and Statistics Department, Working Papers, No. 79, Apr.
1990.

BLEJER, MARIO I. AND CHEASTY, ADRIENNE, eds. *How
to measure the fiscal deficit*. Washington, DC: International Monetary Fund, forthcoming.

BLEJER, MARIO I. AND CHU, KE-YOUNG. *Measurement
of fiscal impact: Methodological issues*. Washington, DC: International Monetary Fund, 1988, pp.
32–47.

BLINDER, ALAN S. AND SOLOW, ROBERT M. "Analytical Foundations of Fiscal Policy," in *The economics
of public finance*. Eds.: ALAN S. BLINDER ET AL.
Washington, DC: Brookings Institution, 1974, pp.
3–115.

BORPUJARI, JITENDRA G. AND TER-MINASSIAN, TERESA.
"The Weighted Budget Balance Approach to Fiscal
Analysis: A Methodology and Some Case Studies,"
Int. Monet. Fund Staff Pap., Nov. 1973, *20*(3),
pp. 801–31.

BOSKIN, MICHAEL J. "Federal Government Deficits:
Some Myths and Realities," *Amer. Econ. Rev.*,
May 1982, *72*(2), pp. 296–303.

————. "Concepts and Measures of Federal Deficits
and Debt and Their Impact on Economic Activity,"
in *The economics of public debt*. Eds.: KENNETH
J. ARROW AND MICHAEL J. BOSKIN. NY: St. Martin's
Press, 1988, pp. 77–112.

BOSKIN, MICHAEL J.; ROBINSON, MARC S. AND HU-
BER, ALAN M. "Government Saving, Capital
Formation and Wealth in the United States, 1947–
1985." NBER Working Paper No. 2352. Cambridge, MA: National Bureau of Economic Research, 1987.

BOSKIN, MICHAEL J.; ROBINSON, MARC S. AND ROB-
ERTS, JOHN M. "New Estimates of Federal Govern-
ment Tangible Capital and Net Investment."
NBER Working Paper No. 1774. Cambridge, MA:
National Bureau of Economic Research, 1985.

BOSKIN, MICHAEL J. ET AL. "New Estimates of the
Value of Federal Mineral Rights and Land," *Amer.
Econ. Rev.*, Dec. 1985, *75*(5), pp. 923–36.

BOSKIN, MICHAEL J. ET AL. "The Federal Budget and
Federal Insurance Programs," in *Modern develop-
ments in public finance: Essays in honor of Arnold
Harberger*. Ed.: MICHAEL J. BOSKIN. Oxford and
NY: Basil Blackwell, 1987, pp. 14–39.

BOSWORTH, BARRY P.; CARRON, ANDREW S. AND
RHYNE, ELISABETH H. *The economics of federal
credit programs*. Washington, DC: The Brookings
Institution, 1987.

BUITER, WILLEM. "Measurement of the Public Sector
Deficit and Its Implications for Policy Evaluation
and Design," *Int. Monet. Fund Staff Pap.*, June
1983, *30*(2), pp. 306–49.

————. "A Guide to Public Sector Debt and Deficits," *Economic Policy: A European Forum*, Nov.
1985, *1*(1), pp. 14–79.

CATSAMBAS, THANOS. "Budget Deficits, Inflation Accounting, and Macroeconomic Policy: A Skeptical
Note," *J. Public Policy*, Jan.-Mar. 1988, *8*(1), pp.
49–60.

CATSAMBAS, THANOS AND PIGATO, MIRIA. "The Consistency of Government Deficits with Macroeconomic Adjustment: An Application to Kenya and
Ghana." World Bank PPR Working Paper, No.
287, 1989.

CHELLIAH, RAJA J. "Significance of Alternative Concepts of Budget Deficit," *Int. Monet. Fund Staff
Pap.*, Nov. 1973, *20*(3), pp. 741–84.

CONKLIN, DAVID W. AND SAYEED, ADIL. "Overview
of the Deficit Debate," in *Deficits: How big and
how bad?* Eds.: DAVID W. CONKLIN AND THOMAS
J. COURCHENE. Toronto: Ontario Economic Council, 1983, pp. 12–54.

CUKIERMAN, ALEX AND MORTENSEN, JORGEN. "Monetary Assets and Inflation-Induced Distortions of the
National Accounts," Commission of the European
Communities, *Economic Papers*, June 1983, (15),
pp. 1–115.

DERNBURG, THOMAS. "Fiscal Analysis in the Federal
Republic of Germany: The Cyclically Neutral Budget," *Int. Monet. Fund Staff Pap.*, Nov. 1975,
22(3), pp. 825–57.

Blejer and Cheasty: The Measurement of Fiscal Deficits   1677

DIAMOND, JACK AND SCHILLER, CHRISTIAN. "Government Arrears in Fiscal Adjustment Programs," in BLEJER AND CHU 1988, pp. 32–47.

EISNER, ROBERT. "Capital Gains and Income: Real Changes in the Value of Capital in the United States, 1946–77," in *The measurement of capital*. Ed.: DAN USHER. Chicago: U. of Chicago Press, 1976.

——. "Which Budget Deficit? Some Issues of Measurement and Their Implications," *Amer. Econ. Rev.*, May 1984, 74(2), pp. 138–43.

——. *How real is the federal deficit?* NY: Free Press, 1986.

——. "Extended Accounts for National Income and Product," *J. Econ. Lit.*, Dec. 1988, 26(4), pp. 1611–84.

——. "That (Non) Problem, the Budget Deficit," *Wall Street Journal*, June 19, 1990, p. 15.

EISNER, ROBERT AND PIEPER, PAUL. "A New View of the Federal Debt and Budget Deficits," *Amer. Econ. Rev.*, Mar. 1984, 74(1), pp. 11–29.

——. "Measurement and Effects of Government Debt and Deficits," *Studies in Banking and Finance*, 1985, 2, pp. 115–48.

——. "Deficits, Monetary Policy and Real Economic Activity," in *The economics of public debt*. Eds.: KENNETH J. ARROW AND MICHAEL J. BOSKIN. NY: Macmillan, 1988, pp. 3–38.

——. "The World's Greatest Debtor Nation," *North Amer. Rev. Econ. Finance*, 1990, 1(1), pp. 9–32.

FLOYD, ROBERT H.; GRAY, CLIVE S. AND SHORT, R. P. *Public enterprise in mixed economies: Some macroeconomic aspects*. Washington, DC: International Monetary Fund, 1984.

GIL DÍAZ, FRANCISCO. "Government Budget Measurement under Inflation in LDCs," in *Public finance and public debt*. Proceedings of the 40th Congress of the International Institute of Public Finance. Ed.: BERNARD P. HERBER. Detroit, MI: Wayne State U. Press, 1986, pp. 123–52.

GIL-DÍAZ, JOSÉ. "La Medición del Resultado Global de la Política Fiscal en Bolivia." Manuscript, International Monetary Fund, Aug. 1988.

GITAJN, ARTHUR. *Creating and financing public enterprises*. Washington, DC: Government Finance Research Center, 1984.

GOERRES, PETER ANSELM. "Die Ausschuetung der Notenbankgewinne an den Bund—weder 'free lunch' noch unsittlicher Griff in die Ladenkasse," *Jahr. Nationalokon. Statist.*, 1985, 200(4), pp. 383–400.

GOLDSMITH, RAYMOND. *Comparative national balance sheets: A study of twenty countries, 1688–1978*. Chicago and London: U. of Chicago Press, 1985.

GOODE, RICHARD. *Government finance in developing countries*. Washington, DC: The Brookings Institution, 1984.

HELLER, PETER S.; HAAS, RICHARD D. AND MANSUR, AHSAN. "A Review of the Fiscal Impulse Measure." Occasional Paper No. 44. Washington, DC: International Monetary Fund, May 1986.

INTERNATIONAL MONETARY FUND. *A manual on government finance statistics*. Washington, DC: International Monetary Fund, 1986.

——. *Government finance statistics yearbook*. Washington, DC: International Monetary Fund, various issues.

KENDRICK, JOHN. *The formation and stocks of total capital*. NY: Columbia U. Press, 1976.

DE KOCK, MICHIEL HENDRICK. *Central banking*. London: Crosby Lockwood Staples, 1974.

KORNAI, JÁNOS. "The Soft Budget Constraint," *Kyklos*, 1986, 39(1), pp. 3–30.

KOTLIKOFF, LAURENCE J. "The Deficit Is Not a Well-Defined Measure of Fiscal Policy," *Science*, Aug. 1988, 241(486), pp. 791–95.

——. "From Deficit Delusion to the Fiscal Balance Rule: Looking for an Economically Meaningful Way to Assess Fiscal Policy." Working Paper WP/89/50, International Monetary Fund, Washington, DC, 1989.

DE LEEUW, FRANK AND HOLLOWAY, THOMAS M. "Cyclical Adjustment of the Federal Budget and Federal Debt," *Surv. Curr. Bus.*, Dec. 1983, 63(12), pp. 25–40.

——. "The Measurement and Significance of the Cyclically Adjusted Federal Budget and Debt," *J. Money, Credit, Banking*, May 1985, 17(5), pp. 232–42.

LEIDERMAN, LEONARDO AND BLEJER, MARIO I. "Modeling and Testing Ricardian Equivalence," *Int. Monet. Fund Staff Pap.*, Mar. 1988, 35(1), pp. 1–35.

LIVIATAN, ODED. "The Impact of Public Financial Institutions on the Fiscal Stance," in BLEJER AND CHEASTY, forthcoming.

MACKENZIE, GEORGE A. "The Role of Non-Oil Revenues in the Fiscal Policy of Oil Exporting Countries." Ms., International Monetary Fund, Jan. 1981.

MANSOOR, ALI M. "The Budgetary Impact of Privatization," in BLEJER AND CHU 1988, pp. 48–56.

MARTINO, ANTONIO. "Budget Deficits and Constitutional Constraints," *Cato J.*, Winter 1989, 8(3), pp. 695–711.

MATES, NEVEN. "Measurement of Government Budget Deficit, Losses of Central Banks, and the Impact of the Aggregate Deficit of the Public Sector on Inflation." Ms., Zagreb, July 1989.

MEYERS, ROY T. *The budgetary status of the federal reserve system*. U.S. Congressional Budget Office. Washington, DC: U.S. GPO, 1985.

MILGRAM, GRACE. "Estimates of the Value of Land in the United States Held by Various Sectors of the Economy, Annually, 1952 to 1968," in *Institutional investors and corporate stock—a background study*. Ed.: RAYMOND W. GOLDSMITH. NY: Columbia U. Press for the NBER, 1973, pp. 343–77.

MILLER, MARCUS. "Inflation—Adjusting the Public Sector Financial Deficit," in *The 1982 budget*. Ed.: JOHN KAY. Oxford: Basil Blackwell, 1982, pp. 48–74.

MORGAN, DAVID R. "Fiscal Policy in Oil Exporting Countries, 1972–78," *Int. Monet. Fund Staff Pap.*, Mar. 1979, 26(1), pp. 55–86.

MULLER, PATRICE AND PRICE, ROBERT W. R. "Structural Budget Deficits and Fiscal Stance," *OECD Economics and Statistics Department, Working Papers*, July 1984, (15).

MUNDELL, ROBERT. *Monetary theory.* Pacific Palisades, CA: Goodyear, 1971.

NASUTION, ANWAR. "Monetary and Banking Policy in Its Relationship to Economic Growth in Indonesia, 1965–89." Ms., International Monetary Fund, 1989.

ONANDI, DIONISIO AND VIANA, LUIS. "El Deficit Parafiscal: Un Analisis de la Experiencia Uruguaya." Paper presented at the Central Bank of Brazil, 1987.

OTT, ATTIAT F. AND AUSTIN, THOMAS D. "Capital Formation by Government," in *The government and capital formation.* Ed.: GEORGE M. VON FURSTENBERG. Cambridge, MA: Ballinger, 1980, pp. 265–318.

OTT, ATTIAT F. AND YOO, JANG H. "The Measurement of Government Saving," in *The government and capital formation.* Ed.: GEORGE M. VON FURSTENBERG. Cambridge, MA: Ballinger, 1980, pp. 177–263.

PIEKARZ, JULIO A. "El Deficit Cuasifiscal del Banco Central." Paper presented at the Central Bank of Brazil, 1987.

PRAET, PETER. "Rates of Return on EEC Central Banks' Foreign Reserve Holdings (1960–1981)," *Cahiers Economiques de Bruxelles*, 1st Trímestre 1982, (93), pp. 53–77.

PREMCHAND, ARIGAPUDI. "Government and Public Enterprise: The Budget Link," in *Government and public enterprise: Essays in honour of Professor V. V. Ramanadham.* Ed.: G. RAM REDDY. London: Frank Cass, 1983, pp. 24–47.

RAMANADHAM, VENKATA V. *The nature of public enterprise.* London and Sydney: Croom Helm, 1984.

ROBINSON, DAVID J. AND STELLA, PETER. "Amalgamating Central Bank and Fiscal Deficits," in BLEJER AND CHU 1988, pp. 20–31.

RODRÍGUEZ AGUILERA, ANA. "Actividades Cuasifiscales de la Autoridad Monetaria: La Experiencia de Costa Rica." Paper presented at the Central Bank of Brazil, 1987.

ROSENBAUM, DAVID E. "Scoring Political Points on Social Security Tax," *New York Times*, Jan. 15, 1990, p. A12.

RUSSO, BENJAMIN. "The Real Market Value of the Net Federal Debt: Interest Rate Effects, Money Illusion, and the Efficacy of Fiscal Policy." Unpublished, U. of North Carolina, 1987.

STELLA, PETER. "Toward Defining and Measuring the Fiscal Impact of Public Enterprises," in BLEJER AND CHEASTY, forthcoming.

STILLSON, RICHARD T. "Some Policy Implications of Foreign Capital Flows in Certain Developing Countries," in *Money and finance in economic growth and development.* Ed.: RONALD I. McKINNON. NY and Basel: Marcel Dekker, June 1979, pp. 227–50.

TANZI, VITO. "Inflation, Lags in Collection, and the Real Value of Tax Revenue," *Int. Monet. Fund Staff Pap.*, Mar. 1977, 24(1), pp. 154–67.

——. "Fiscal Disequilibrium in Developing Countries," *World Devel.*, Dec. 1982, 10(12), pp. 1069–82.

——. "Fiscal Policy and Economic Reconstruction in Latin America." Working Paper WP/89/94, International Monetary Fund, Washington, DC, Nov. 1989.

TANZI, VITO; BLEJER, MARIO I. AND TEIJEIRO, MARIO O. "The Effects of Inflation on the Measurement of Fiscal Deficits," in BLEJER AND CHU 1988, pp. 4–19.

TEIJEIRO, MARIO O. *Central bank losses: Origins, conceptual issues, and measurement problems.* Washington, DC: Economic Dept., World Bank, Oct. 1989.

THOMPSON, LAWRENCE H. "The Social Security Reform Debate," *J. Econ. Lit.*, Dec. 1983, 21(4), pp. 1425–67.

TOWE, CHRISTOPHER M. "Government Contingent Liabilities and the Measurement of Fiscal Impact," in BLEJER AND CHEASTY, forthcoming.

UNITED NATIONS. DEPARTMENT OF ECONOMIC AND SOCIAL AFFAIRS. STATISTICAL OFFICE. *A system of national accounts*, Series F, No. 2, Rev. 3. NY: United Nations, 1968.

U.S., CONGRESSIONAL BUDGET OFFICE. *Credit reform: Comparable budget costs for cash and credit.* Washington, DC: U.S. GPO, Dec. 1989.

——. *The Federal deficit: Does it measure the Government's effect on national saving?* Washington, DC: U.S. GPO, Mar. 1990.

U.S., DEPARTMENT OF COMMERCE, BUREAU OF ECONOMIC ANALYSIS. *Fixed reproducible tangible wealth in the United States, 1925–79.* Washington, DC: U.S. GPO, 1982.

U.S., EXECUTIVE OFFICE OF THE PRESIDENT, OFFICE OF MANAGEMENT AND BUDGET. *Budget of the United States government, fiscal year 1989.* Washington, DC: U.S. GPO, February 1988.

U.S., EXECUTIVE OFFICE OF THE PRESIDENT, COUNCIL OF ECONOMIC ADVISERS. *Economic report of the President.* Washington, DC: U.S. GPO, Jan. 1989.

VAEZ-ZADEH, REZA. "Oil Wealth and Economic Behavior: The Case of Venezuela, 1965–81," *Int. Monet. Fund Staff Pap.*, June 1989, 36(2), pp. 343–84.

WASSERMAN, MARK. "Public Sector Budget Balances," *OECD economic outlook: Occasional studies*, July 1976, pp. 37–51.

WATTLEWORTH, MICHAEL. "Credit Subsidies in Budgetary Lending: Computation, Effects, and Fiscal Implications," in BLEJER AND CHU 1988, pp. 57–70.

WORLD BANK. *World development report, 1988, 1989.* Washington, DC: The World Bank.

[4]

Generational Accounting Around the Globe

By Laurence J. Kotlikoff and Bernd Raffelhüschen*

Generational accounting is a relatively new method of long-term fiscal planning and analysis. It addresses the following closely related questions. First, how large a fiscal burden does current policy imply for future generations? Second, is fiscal policy sustainable without major additional sacrifices on the part of current or future generations or major cutbacks in government purchases? Third, what alternative policies would suffice to produce *generational balance,* a situation in which future generations face the same fiscal burden as do current generations when adjusted for growth (when measured as a proportion of their lifetime earnings)? Fourth, how would different methods of achieving such balance affect the remaining lifetime fiscal burdens, the *generational accounts,* of those now alive?

Developed less than a decade ago by Alan Auerbach et al. (1991) and Kotlikoff (1992), generational accounting has spread around the globe, from New Zealand to Norway. Much of this accounting is being done at the governmental or multilateral institutional level. The U.S. Federal Reserve, the U.S. Congressional Budget Office, the U.S. Office of Management and Budget, the Bank of Japan, the Bank of England, Her Majesty's Treasury (United Kingdom), the Bundesbank, the Norwegian Ministry of Finance, the Bank of Italy, the New Zealand Treasury, the European Com-

mission,[1] the International Monetary Fund, and the World Bank have been or are currently involved, either directly or indirectly, in generational accounting. Generational accounting has also drawn considerable interest from academic and government economists.[2]

This paper presents a selection of the latest generational-accounting results for the following 22 countries: Argentina, Australia, Austria, Belgium, Brazil, Canada, Denmark, Finland, France, Germany, Ireland, Italy, Japan, the Netherlands, New Zealand, Norway, Portugal, Spain, Sweden, Thailand, the United Kingdom, and the United States. Many of these findings are reported in Auerbach et al.'s (1999) edited volume comparing generational accounts around the world and Raffelhüschen's (1998) edited volume comparing generational accounts in the European Union.

I. What Is Generational Accounting?

Generational accounts are defined as the present value of *net taxes* (taxes paid minus transfer payments received) that individuals of different age cohorts are expected to pay, under current policy, over their remaining lifetimes. Adding up the generational accounts of all currently living generations gives the collective contribution of those now alive toward paying the government's bills.

---

† *Discussants:* Jan Walliser, Congressional Budget Office; Jagadeesh Gokhale, Federal Reserve Bank of Cleveland.

* Kotlikoff: Department of Economics, Boston University, 270 Bay State Road, Boston, MA 02215, and the National Bureau of Economic Research; Raffelhüschen: University of Freiburg and University of Bergen. This paper draws on Roberto Cardarelli et al. (1998), Raffelhüschen (1998), and Alan J. Auerbach et al. (1999).

[1] The European Commission has an ongoing project to do generational accounting for European Union member nations under the direction of Raffelhüschen (see Raffelhüschen, 1998).

[2] David Cutler (1993), Auerbach et al. (1994), Robert Haveman (1994), Congressional Budget Office (1995), Peter Diamond (1996), Willhelm H. Buiter (1997), Hans Fehr and Kotlikoff (1996–1997), Kotlikoff (1997), Daniel Shaviro (1997), Raffelhüschen (1998), and others have debated its merits.

The government's bills refers to the present value of its current and future purchases of goods and services plus its net debt (its financial liabilities minus its financial and real assets, including the value of its public-sector enterprises). Those bills left unpaid by current generations must be paid by future generations. This is the hard message of the *government's intertemporal budget constraint,* the basic building block of modern dynamic analyses of fiscal policy.

This budget constraint can be expressed in a simple equation: $A + B = C + D$, where D is the government's net debt, C is the sum of future government purchases, valued to the present, B is the sum of the generational accounts of those now alive, and A is the sum of the generational accounts of future generations, valued to the present. Given the size of the government's bills, $C + D$, the choice of who will pay is a zero-sum game; the smaller is B, the net payments of those now alive, the larger is A, the net payments of those yet to be born.

The comparison of the generational accounts of current newborns and the growth-adjusted accounts of future newborns provides a precise measure of generational imbalance. The accounts of these two sets of parties are directly comparable because they involve net taxes over entire lifetimes. If future generations face, on a growth-adjusted basis, higher generational accounts than do current newborns, current policy is not only generationally imbalanced, it is also unsustainable. The government cannot continue, over time, to collect the same net taxes (measured as a share of lifetime income) from future generations as it would collect, under current policy, from current newborns without violating the intertemporal budget constraint. The same is true if future generations face a smaller growth-adjusted lifetime net tax burden than do current newborns. However, in this case, generational balance and fiscal sustainability can be achieved by reducing the fiscal burden facing current generations, rather than the other way around.

The calculation of generational imbalance is an informative counterfactual, not a likely policy scenario, because it imposes all requisite fiscal adjustments on those born in the future.

But it delivers a clear message about the need for policy adjustments. Once such a need is established, interest naturally turns to alternative means of achieving generational balance that do not involve foisting all the adjustment on future generations.

II. Generational Accounting versus Deficit Accounting

A critical feature of generational accounting is that the size of the fiscal burden confronting future generations (the term A in $A + B = C + D$) is invariant to the government's fiscal labeling (how it describes its receipts and payments). The same, unfortunately, is not true of the government's official debt. As described in Kotlikoff (1992, 1993), from the perspective of neoclassical economic theory, neither the government's official debt nor its change over time (the deficit) is a well-defined economic concept. Rather these are accounting constructs whose values are entirely dependent on the choice of fiscal vocabulary and bear no intrinsic relationship to any aspect of fiscal policy, including generational policy. In terms of our equation $A + B = C + D$, different choices of fiscal labels alter B and D by equal absolute amounts, leaving C and A unchanged.

To see the vacuity of fiscal labels, consider just three out of the infinite set of alternative ways a government could label its taking $100 more, measured in present value, in net taxes from a citizen named Nigel. Nigel's remaining lifetime net-tax payments increase by $100; there is an additional net flow of $100 to the government from Nigel this year, and no additional net flows from Nigel to the government next year. The government could say this is:

(i) "a $100 tax levied this year on Nigel";
(ii) "an $800 loan made this year by Nigel to the government less a $700 transfer payment to Nigel, plus a tax levied next year on Nigel of $800(1 + r$), plus a repayment next year to Nigel of $800(1 + r$) in principle plus interest"; or
(iii) "A $5,000,000,000 tax paid this year by Nigel, less a $4,999,999,900 loan to Nigel this year by the government, plus a

$4,999,999,900(1 + r)$ transfer payment next year to Nigel, plus a repayment next year by Nigel of principle and interest of $4,999,999,900(1 + r)$."

(In the last two cases, r is the interest rate.) Compared to case (i)'s language, using the language in the other cases will generate an $800 larger deficit in case (ii), and a $4,999,999,900 smaller deficit in case (iii). Although the government's reported deficit is dramatically different depending on how it labels the additional $100 it gets this year from Nigel, Nigel's economic circumstances are unchanged. Regardless of which language the government uses, it is still getting $100 more in present value from Nigel in net taxes, and Nigel's own economic resources are, in each case, depressed by $100. Since Nigel's annual cash flows are the same, alternative choices of language have no impact on the degree to which he is liquidity-constrained in choosing how much to consume and save.[3]

Unfortunately, the ability to avoid hard policy decisions by manipulating the reported deficit has not escaped politicians around the world. In the United States in the 1980's this practice was christened "smoke and mirrors." It was exemplified by the government's decision first to put the social-security system off budget when it was running deficits, and then to put in on budget when it was running surpluses. In France and Belgium substituting words for deeds was used in selling the assets of state-owned companies to get enough revenue to fall below Maastricht's deficit limit while maintaining these companies' major liabilities, their unfunded pension plans. In Germany, the Bundesbank had to prevent the federal government from revaluing its gold stock to meet Maastricht's deficit limit. These and countless other examples are symptomatic of a much deeper problem, namely, that there are no economic fundamentals underlying the deficit, and its use is an utter charade.

III. Generational Imbalances Around the Globe

Table 1 shows four mutually exclusive ways the 22 countries listed above could achieve generational balance. The alternatives are cutting government purchases, cutting government transfer payments, increasing all taxes, and increasing income taxes (corporate as well as personal). Each of these policies is described in terms of the immediate and permanent percentage adjustment needed. The magnitudes of these alternative adjustments provide an indirect measure of countries' generational imbalances.

The four different policies are considered under two definitions of government purchases and transfer payments. Definition A treats education as a government purchase and not as a transfer payment. Definition B does the opposite. Because of space limitations, we focus on definition B.

According to the second column in the table, 13 of the 22 countries need to cut their noneducational government spending by over one-fifth if they want to rely solely on such cuts to achieve generational balance. This group includes the United States and Japan and the three most important members of the European Monetary Union: Germany, France, and Italy. Four of the 13 countries (Austria, Finland, Spain, and Sweden) need to cut their noneducation purchases by more than half, and two countries (Austria and Finland) need to cut this spending by more than two thirds!

Bear in mind that generational accounting is comprehensive with respect to including regional, state, local, and federal levels of government. Therefore, the cuts being considered here are equal proportionate cuts in government spending at all levels. In the United States, where a large proportion of government spending is done at the state and local level, achieving generational balance by just

---

[3] Moreover, the same set of economic incentives Nigel faces for saving or working are provided in all three cases. For example, suppose the government imposes an additional marginal tax rate of t on Nigel's current labor income in order to generate the additional $100 in revenue measured in present value. In case (i), this would be described as "a tax at rate t on this year's labor earnings." In case (ii), it would be described as "a marginal subsidy at rate $7t$ to this year's labor supply plus a marginal tax on this year's labor supply at rate $8t(1 + r)$ where the payment is due next year." In case (iii), it would be described as "a marginal tax of $50t$ plus a marginal subsidy at rate $49t$ to be paid next year." In each case, the net marginal income from Nigel's earning an additional dollar this year is reduced by t times one dollar.

TABLE 1—INTERNATIONAL COMPARISONS OF
GENERATIONAL ACCOUNTING: ALTERNATIVE WAYS
TO ACHIEVE GENERATIONAL BALANCE

Country	Cut in government purchases		Cut in government transfers	
	A	B	A	B
Argentina	24.6	29.1	16.8	11.0
Australia	8.8	10.2	12.1	9.1
Austria	56.8	76.4	25.0	20.5
Belgium	11.2	12.4	6.0	4.6
Brazil	23.8	26.2	21.3	17.9
Canada	0.0	0.1	0.0	0.1
Denmark	9.9	29.0	4.7	4.5
Finland	47.6	67.6	26.5	21.2
France	17.2	22.2	11.5	9.8
Germany	21.1	25.9	17.6	14.1
Ireland	−2.1	−4.3	−2.5	−4.4
Italy	37.0	49.1	18.0	13.3
Japan	26.0	29.5	28.6	25.3
Netherlands	21.0	28.7	21.4	22.3
New Zealand	−1.0	−1.6	−0.8	−0.6
Norway	11.5	9.9	9.4	8.1
Portugal	7.6	9.8	9.6	7.5
Spain	50.6	62.2	22.5	17.0
Sweden	37.6	50.5	22.6	18.9
Thailand	−38.1	−47.7	−185.1	−114.2
United Kingdom	6.6	9.7	9.6	9.5
United States	18.7	27.0	19.8	20.3

Country	Increase in all taxes		Increase in income tax	
	A	B	A	B
Argentina	10.7	8.4	97.1	75.7
Australia	5.1	4.8	8.5	8.1
Austria	20.1	18.4	60.7	55.6
Belgium	3.7	3.1	11.7	10.0
Brazil	12.4	11.7	78.9	74.0
Canada	0.0	0.1	0.0	0.2
Denmark	3.4	4.0	5.8	6.7
Finland	20.6	19.4	54.1	50.8
France	7.1	6.9	66.0	64.0
Germany	9.5	9.5	29.5	29.5
Ireland	−1.1	−2.1	−2.5	−4.8
Italy	12.4	10.5	33.3	28.2
Japan	15.5	15.5	53.6	53.6
Netherlands	8.5	8.9	14.9	15.6
New Zealand	−0.4	−0.4	−0.8	−0.8
Norway	7.4	6.3	11.3	9.7
Portugal	4.2	4.2	13.3	13.3
Spain	17.4	14.5	53.9	44.9
Sweden	16.1	15.6	42.9	41.9
Thailand	−25.0	−25.0	−81.7	−81.8
United Kingdom	2.6	2.7	9.4	9.5
United States	10.5	10.8	23.8	24.4

Notes: Table entries are percentage adjustments needed to achieve generational balance. In the columns labeled "A," education expenditure is treated as government consumption. In the columns labeled "B," education expenditure is treated as government transfers and distributed by age groups.
Sources: Raffelhüschen (1998), Kotlikoff and Willi Leibfritz (1999), and authors' calculations.

cutting federal spending would require that spending be roughly halved. Given U.S. fiscal nomenclature, this means "running" federal surpluses that are more than $300 billion larger than is currently the case.[4]

Not all countries suffer from generational imbalances. In Ireland, New Zealand, and Thailand, future generations face a smaller fiscal burden, measured on a growth-adjusted basis, than do current ones given the government's current spending projections. Hence, governments in those countries can spend more over time without unduly burdening generations yet to come. There are also several countries in the list, including Canada and the United Kingdom, with zero or moderate generational imbalances as measured by the spending adjustment needed to achieve perfect balance. What explains these tremendous cross-country differences? Fiscal policies and demographics differ dramatically across countries. The United States, for example, suffers from rampant federal health-care spending. Japan's health-care spending is growing less rapidly, but it is aging much more quickly. The United Kingdom has a policy of keeping most transfer payments fixed over time in real terms. Germany is dealing with the ongoing costs of reunification.

One alternative to cutting spending is cutting transfer payments. In Japan, education, health care, social-security benefits, unemployment benefits, disability benefits, and all other transfer payments would need to be immediately and permanently slashed by 25 percent. In the United States, the figure is 20 percent; in Brazil, it is 18 percent; in Germany, it is 14 percent; and in Italy it is 13 percent.

These and similar figures for other countries represent dramatic cuts and would be very unpopular. So too would tax increases. If Japan were to rely exclusively on across-the-board tax hikes, tax rates at all levels of government (regional, state, local, and federal) and of all types (value-added, payroll, corporate income,

[4] These figures come from Jagadeesh Gokhale et al. (1999), a joint study of the Federal Reserve Bank of Cleveland and The Congressional Budget Office (CBO). They incorporate the latest CBO projections of federal government spending and receipts and, therefore, of federal surpluses.

personal income, excise, sales, property, estate, and gift) would have to rise overnight by more than 15 percent. In Austria and Finland, they would have to rise by more than 18 percent. If these three countries relied solely on income-tax hikes, they would need to raise their income-tax rates by over 50 percent! In France and Argentina, where income-tax bases are relatively small, income-tax rates would have to rise by much larger percentages. The requisite income-tax hikes in the United States and Germany are roughly one-quarter. In contrast, Ireland could cut its income-tax rates by about 5 percent before it needed to worry about overburdening future generations.

The longer countries wait to act, the bigger the adjustment needs to be when action is finally taken. Consider the United Kingdom. It needs an immediate permanent 9.5-percent income-tax hike, if it wants to achieve generational balance through that channel. But if it waits five years, the requisite income-tax hike is 11.1 percent; it is 15.2 percent with a 15-year delay, and 21.0 percent with a 25-year delay.

IV. Conclusion

Generational accounting is being done in a large and growing number of countries around the world. Notwithstanding its shortcomings, generational accounting has four major advantages over deficit accounting: it is forward-looking; it is comprehensive; it poses and answers economic questions; and its answers are invariant to the economically arbitrary choice of fiscal vocabulary.

The findings reported here are shocking. An array of countries, including the United States, Germany, and Japan, have severe generational imbalances. This is true notwithstanding the fact that the United States is currently reporting an official surplus, Germany's reported deficit is within Maastricht limits, and Japan has the lowest reported ratio of net debt to GDP of any of the leading industrialized countries. The imbalances in these and the majority of the other 19 countries considered in this paper place future generations at grave risk. They also augur high future rates of inflation, since printing money is the easiest way politicians have of "meeting" government obligations. Such a policy, if conducted in Western Eu-

rope, would seriously jeopardize the nascent European Monetary Union. For Japan, which is currently in recession, the insistence of the international community that it dramatically loosen its fiscal policy is advice well worth ignoring. Japan, like most countries considered here, needs to get its long-run fiscal house in order, and right away. The longer Japan and the other countries wait, the more severe their generational problems will become.

REFERENCES

Auerbach, Alan J.; Gokhale, Jagadeesh and Kotlikoff, Laurence J. "Generational Accounts: A Meaningful Alternative to Deficit Accounting," in D. Bradford, ed., *Tax policy and the economy*, Vol. 5. Cambridge, MA: MIT Press, 1991, pp. 55–110.

_____. "Generational Accounting: A Meaningful Way To Assess Generational Policy." *Journal of Economic Perspectives*, Winter 1994, *8*(1), pp. 73–94.

Auerbach, Alan J.; Kotlikoff, Laurence J. and Leibfritz, Willi, eds. *Generational accounting around the world.* Chicago: University of Chicago Press, 1999 (forthcoming).

Buiter, Willhelm H. "Generational Accounts, Aggregate Saving and Intergenerational Distribution." *Economica*, November 1997, *64*(256), pp. 605–26.

Cardarelli, Roberto; Sefton, James and Kotlikoff, Laurence J. "Generational Accounting in the UK." Mimeo, National Institute for Economic and Social Research, London, U.K., 1998.

Congressional Budget Office. *Who pays and when: An assessment of generational accounting.* Washington, DC: U.S. Government Printing Office, November 1995.

Cutler, David. "Review of Generational Accounting: Knowing Who Pays, and When, for What We Spend." *National Tax Journal*, March 1993, *46*(1), pp. 61–76.

Diamond, Peter. "Generational Accounts and Generational Balance: An Assessment." *National Tax Journal*, December 1996, *49*(4), pp. 597–607.

Fehr, Hans and Kotlikoff, Laurence J. "Generational Accounting in General Equilibrium." *Finanzarchiv*, 1996–1997, *53*(4), pp. 1–27.

Gokhale, Jagadeesh; Page, Benjamin R. and Sturrock, John R. "Generational Accounts for the U.S.: An Update," in Alan J. Auerbach, Laurence J. Kotlikoff, and Willi Leibfritz, eds., *Generational accounting around the world*. Chicago: University of Chicago Press, 1999 (forthcoming).

Haveman, Robert. "Should Generational Accounts Replace Public Budgets and Deficits?" *Journal of Economic Perspectives*, Winter 1994, *8*(1), pp. 95–111.

Kotlikoff, Laurence J. *Generational accounting*. New York: Free Press, 1992.

———. "From Deficit Delusion to the Fiscal Balance Rule: Looking for a Sensible Way To Describe Fiscal Policy." *Journal of Economics*, Supplement 1993, *7*, pp. 17–41.

———. "Reply to Diamond's and Cutler's Reviews of Generational Accounting." *National Tax Journal*, June 1997, *50*(2), pp. 303–14.

Kotlikoff, Laurence J. and Leibfritz, Willi. "An International Comparison of Generational Accounts," in Alan J. Auerbach, Laurence J. Kotlikoff, and Willi Leibfritz, eds., *Generational accounting around the world*. Chicago: University of Chicago Press, 1999 (forthcoming).

Raffelhüschen, Bernd. "Aging, Fiscal Policy and Social Insurances: A European Perspective." Mimeo, Albert Ludwigs University of Freiburg, Germany, 1998.

Shaviro, Daniel. *Do deficits matter?* Chicago: University of Chicago Press, 1997.

[5]

How Transparent
Is the U.S. Budget?

✦

JODY W. LIPFORD

In recent years, the federal government has experienced its first budget surpluses since 1969 and its first consecutive years of budget surplus since 1956–57. Further, the Congressional Budget Office (CBO) is forecasting budget surpluses of at least $4.5 trillion over the coming decade.[1] After decades of deficits, the federal government seems to have put its "fiscal house in order." Nevertheless, gross U.S. federal debt totals more than $5.6 trillion, or approximately 60 percent of gross domestic product (GDP), a figure down from the 1996 peak of 67.3 percent of GDP, but significantly higher than the post–World War II low of 32.5 percent set in 1981 (see CEA 2000, tables B-76 and B-77).

This debt and the recurrent deficits that created it not only call into question the viability of estimated surpluses, but also underscore the need for explanations of the government's proclivity for debt finance. Alesina and Roubini with Cohen (1997, 230–40) provide summaries of some explanations, including hypotheses of fiscal illusion, debt as a constraint on future administrations, intergenerational transfers, partisan conflicts, rent seeking, and inadequate institutional constraints.[2]

One institutional constraint that may be inadequate is budgetary transparency, which I define as the ease with which the public can interpret spending and budgetary fig-

Jody W. Lipford is an Associate Professor in the Department of Economics and Business Administration at Presbyterian College, Clinton, South Carolina.

1. Actual forecasted surpluses depend on assumptions made about the growth of discretionary spending. If discretionary spending grows at the rate of inflation, the forecasted surplus is $4.561 trillion, but if discretionary spending is held to statutory caps through 2002 and grows at the rate of inflation thereafter, the forecasted surplus is $5.774 trillion. See *The Economic and Budget Outlook: An Update*, July 2000, at <www.cbo.gov>.

2. For complete treatments of the hypotheses of fiscal illusion and of debt as a constraint on future administrations, see Buchanan and Wagner 1977 and Persson and Svensson 1989, respectively.

The Independent Review, v.V, n.4, Spring 2001, ISSN 1086-1653, Copyright © 2001, pp. 575–591.

ures, measure current and future tax liabilities, and evaluate the benefits of government programs.[3] If the government can combine understated figures for spending, taxes, and deficits with overstated benefits of government programs, then deficits and debt are the natural outcomes as citizens express their desire for additional government benefits through the electoral process without full knowledge of the costs of these benefits.

To the converse, budgetary transparency may serve as a constraint on government spending and debt (Alesina and Perotti 1996), either alone or in conjunction with other restraints, such as balanced-budget rules (Buchanan and Wagner 1977), supermajority voting rules for higher debt limits and tax increases (Niskanen 1992), or spending targets (Schultze 1992).

In this article, I evaluate the transparency of U.S. budgetary practices of the past twenty years, focusing on the first parts of the transparency definition. The insights gained from this analysis help not only to evaluate past budgetary practices, but also to determine whether common budgetary practices are likely to reduce projected surpluses.

First, I review the theoretical case for budgetary transparency, the rationale for political opposition to budgetary transparency, and evidence on the effectiveness of budgetary transparency as a means of fiscal discipline. Then, I analyze criteria that make a budget more or less transparent. Finally, I evaluate U.S. budget practices against the transparency criteria elaborated in the preceding section, an evaluation that yields a mixed review of U.S. budgetary practices. In the conclusion, I reconsider the question of budgetary transparency during an era of fiscal surpluses.

Budgetary Transparency: Effects, Political Opposition, and Evidence

To any U.S. taxpayer, the need for budgetary transparency may seem self-evident. Complex tax codes, continually manipulated by "omnibus budget reconciliation bills," combine with multi-billion-dollar spending programs with immeasurable effects so that individual taxpayers find the budgetary process and its effects incomprehensible.

On a macroeconomic level, transparency should lead to smaller spending and deficits. Buchanan and Wagner argue forcefully that "complex and indirect payment structures create a fiscal illusion that will systematically produce higher levels of public outlay than those that would be observed under single-payment structures. Budgets will be related directly to the complexity and indirectness of the tax system"

---

3. The International Monetary Fund Code of Good Practices on Fiscal Transparency includes four principles: (1) clarity in government's role in the economy and responsibilities; (2) readily available budgetary information for the public; (3) open budget preparations, execution, and reporting; and (4) independent assurances of integrity. Because U.S. budgetary practices arguably meet most of these standards, I concentrate on the definition of transparency given in the text. For the complete IMF Code of Good Practices on Fiscal Transparency, see <www.imf.org>.

(1977, 129). Simply put, budgetary complexities drive a wedge between the actual cost of government programs and the perceived cost of those programs. Voters suffering from "fiscal illusion" will support higher levels of spending and deficits than they would if budgetary transparency yielded full disclosure. Further, government debt offers opportunities for citizens to avoid future tax liabilities, perhaps through death, tax shelters, or other means, and thereby to transfer wealth from other citizens.

Nevertheless, an assumption of "fooled" or "irrational" voters is unnecessary in concluding that budgets lacking transparency lessen fiscal discipline. Because information is a scarce resource, some degree of voter ignorance is quite rational.[4] It is certainly plausible that politicians have an informational advantage with regard to the benefits and costs of their proposals, regardless of how "rational" voters might be. In discussing rational opportunistic models of the business cycle, Alesina and Roubini with Cohen offer an example that elucidates this possibility: "in an election year the incumbent government [may raise] certain transfers, claiming that no new taxes will be needed because a high expected growth rate will automatically increase revenues. Such a claim is quite hard for the average voter to check" (1997, 31). Similarly, Miller argues that the American people are ignorant of the budget in part because of the "propensity of politicians to mislead and obfuscate the budget for their own purposes" (1994, 124). Whatever assumption one makes about rational expectations, the link between complex and obfuscated budgets and fiscal excesses is apparent.

Facing voters subject to fiscal illusion or simply confronted with incomplete information, politicians may have strong incentives to distort the perceived costs and benefits of government expansion. These incentives are consistent with Leviathan and rent-seeking theories of government. If the government is a revenue-maximizing Leviathan, as Brennan and Buchanan (1980) suggest, politicians will want to overestimate the benefits of government programs and underestimate the current and future taxes required to pay for those programs. Similarly, special-interest groups and the politicians who do their bidding benefit from complex budgets that hide the costs of and expand the size of government programs that serve parochial interests. Findings by Mixon and Wilkinson (1999) that campaign contributions to members of Congress rise with the value of government spending and with reductions in the deficit that may threaten interest-group benefits are consistent with the hypothesis that interest groups favor large budgets. Simply put, if larger government outlays yield politicians greater power or prestige, greater gains from rent-seeking interest groups, or more opportunities to invoke their concept of the "public good," nontransparent budgeting will be politically appealing.

Although quantification of budgetary institutions and their effects is problematic, the nascent empirical work indicates that budgetary institutions, including trans-

---

4. For detailed arguments about why voters are unlikely to be highly informed on political issues, see Boudreaux 1996, 121–24.

parency, are important determinants of fiscal discipline. Analyzing a sample of twenty Latin American countries, Alesina, Hausmann, Hommes, and Stein find that "on average, a country with budgetary institutions which contain constraints on the deficit, are more hierarchical and more transparent can be expected to have primary deficits 2.9 percentage points lower than a country with fewer constraints, and more collegial and less transparent budget procedures" (1996, 20–21). Additional empirical work shows that a separate "transparency index" is not a statistically significant determinant of a country's primary deficit, but its sign is negative and its index value suffers from measurement problems.[5]

The Means of Nontransparent Budgeting

Politicians possess many means of distorting perceptions of the actual cost of government. Charlotte Twight (1988, 1994) argues that politicians intentionally manipulate the transactions costs of voter monitoring and political action to increase the scope and size of government. Augmenting transactions costs to further political ends is especially attractive and easy when complex issues, such as public budgets, are under consideration. Obfuscating language that cloaks "tax increases as 'deficit reduction' measures," "complex and indirect forms of taxation," misrepresented estimates of budget deficits, overstated baselines, misleading claims of statutory effects on deficits, and strategic use of off-budget revenues and expenditures provide politicians with ample means of lowering the perceived cost of government (Twight 1994, 208–11). In a similar vein, Alesina and Cukierman (1990) model how politicians utilize ambiguity to take positions that diverge from those of their constituencies and to avoid accountability.

Like Twight, Alesina and Perotti (1996) outline several means by which politicians may make public budgets less transparent, thereby raising the transaction costs of monitoring fiscal conditions for a public subject to fiscal illusion or incomplete information:[6] (1) biased macroeconomic forecasts, (2) biased estimates of the effects of policy changes on budgetary outcomes, (3) strategic use of on- and off-budget expenditures and receipts, (4) manipulation of budgetary baselines, and (5) multiyear budgeting.

Because budget forecasts are predicated on assumptions of economic performance, overly optimistic assumptions about the economic conditions that generate tax revenues or dictate spending requirements can yield deficit and debt forecasts that are, in turn, overly optimistic. Similarly, overestimating the revenues generated by changes in fiscal policies or underestimating the expenditures required from changes in fiscal policies yields forecasts of deficits and debt with a downward bias.

---

5. For a summary of other empirical work on budgetary transparency, see Alesina and Roubini, with Cohen 1997, 240.

6. Light 1999 provides a similar analysis of the lack of transparency in counting the federal workforce.

The use of off-budget expenditures and receipts to expand the size of government has long been recognized. By shifting expenditures to off-budget categories and agencies, the size of on-budget spending shrinks. Similarly, using off-budget revenues to fund on-budget expenditures masks the true fiscal condition of general budgets. Bennett and DiLorenzo (1982) show how local governments responded to the "tax revolt" of the 1970s by establishing and expanding off-budget enterprises that financed additional spending with the issuance of revenue bonds, thereby offsetting reductions in on-budget expenditures but creating a "hidden tax liability."[7]

Manipulating budgetary baselines is another gimmick that makes budgets less transparent. When expenditures are calculated relative to a baseline, an artificial inflation of that baseline makes spending increases appear as spending cuts.

Finally, the use of multiyear budgeting affords politicians opportunities to misrepresent future fiscal conditions by delaying politically unpopular policies—tax increases and spending cuts—while claiming politically popular deficit reduction over the life of the multiyear budget. The "backloaded" tax increases and spending cuts may never materialize, but even if they do, the current administration or majority party may be out of power at that time.

An Analysis of U.S. Budgetary Transparency

In an effort to evaluate U.S. budgetary transparency, I examine U.S. budget practices relative to the five criteria just discussed. To begin, I consider economic and deficit forecasts. I follow with analyses of off-budget expenditures and receipts, baseline budgeting, and multiyear budget deals. And I conclude this section by examining important budgetary legislation since the Budget and Impoundment Control Act of 1974.

Evidence from Macroeconomic and Budget Forecasts

The U.S. budget process begins with the president's proposed budget, which is based on economic projections by the executive branch Office of Management and Budget (OMB). Congress, on the other hand, uses its own fiscal agency, the Congressional Budget Office (CBO), to forecast economic outcomes. To determine whether the economic forecasts on which budgets are proposed and evaluated are biased, I gathered data from presidential budgets and the CBO *Economic and Budget Outlooks* for each year since 1980. I then compared forecasts of real GDP growth, inflation, unemployment, and the interest rate on short-term Treasury bills with actual economic outcomes of these variables for five years into the future. If the administration or Congress biases its economic forecasts in favor of stronger economic growth, lower inflation, lower unemployment, and lower interest rates than actual economic conditions are likely to yield, budgets lack transparency.

---

7. In an interesting empirical analysis, Merrifield 1994 considers whether on- and off-budget expenditures are substitutes or complements. His findings are mixed, offering some support for each hypothesis.

Table 1. An Analysis of OMB and CBO Economic Forecasts, 1980–1999				
Variables under consideration: Real GDP Growth, Inflation Rate, Unemployment Rate, Three-Month Treasury Bill Rate				
Forecast Error = Forecasted Value – Actual Value. Positive values are overestimates. Negative values are underestimates.				
Null hypothesis: Mean Forecast Error = 0				

	Years Ahead			
Variable: Real GDP Growth	1	2	3	4	5
t-Statistic for OMB Forecast	−1.416	0.737	1.052	0.610	0.620
t-Statistic for CBO Forecast	−1.723	0.287	0.338	−0.358	−0.264

	Years Ahead			
Variable: Inflation Rate	1	2	3	4	5
t-Statistic for OMB Forecast	1.147	1.762	1.896	1.852	1.076
t-Statistic for CBO Forecast	1.291	2.803	3.769	3.187	3.160

	Years Ahead			
Variable: Unemployment Rate	1	2	3	4	5
t-Statistic for OMB Forecast	1.784	0.333	−0.235	−0.399	−0.773
t-Statistic for CBO Forecast	1.342	0.468	0.140	0.349	0.504

Variable: Three-Month Treasury Bill Rate	Years Ahead			
	1	2	3	4	5
t-Statistic for OMB Forecast	−0.873	−0.621	−0.468	−0.833	−1.382
t-Statistic for CBO Forecast	−0.214	0.601	1.299	1.371	1.456

Table 1 shows results of hypothesis tests that the mean forecast errors differ from zero. The evidence indicates that generally neither OMB nor CBO macroeconomic forecasts are biased in favor of overly optimistic forecasts. For real GDP growth, only forecast errors one year into the future approach significance at conventional levels, and these errors indicate underestimation of real GDP growth. For inflation forecasts, OMB mean forecast errors for two to four years into the future and CBO mean forecast errors for two to five years into the future are statistically significant; however, the t-statistics are all positive, indicating that forecasters repeatedly did not anticipate the significant drop in inflation rates over the past two decades. The OMB's one-year mean forecast error for the unemployment rate is weakly significant, but its positive value indicates forecasted unemployment rates were overestimated. Finally, forecast errors for short-term Treasury bill rates are never significant.

Turning to budget forecasts, which for the executive branch incorporate taxing and spending proposals, we find in table 2 that long-term forecasts (for four to five years in the future) significantly underestimated deficits. Although presidential budg-

Table 2. An Analysis of OMB and CBO Budget Forecasts, 1980–1999

Variable under consideration: budget balance as a percentage of GDP
Forecast Error = Forecasted Value – Actual Value. Positive values underestimate deficits or overestimate surpluses. Negative values overestimate deficits or underestimate surpluses.
Null hypothesis: Mean Forecast Error = 0

	Years Ahead				
	1	2	3	4	5
t-Statistic for OMB Forecast	–1.007	1.138	1.637	2.155	2.249
t-Statistic for CBO Forecast	–0.763	–0.193	0.095	0.292	0.293

Note: Calculations assume negative values for deficits and positive values for surpluses.

For example, ignoring division by GDP, a forecasted deficit of $100 and an actual deficit of $150 gives a positive forecast error of $50. Likewise, a forecasted surplus of $100 and an actual surplus of $50 gives a positive forecast error of $50. So positive forecast errors indicate overly optimistic forecasts, either from underestimated deficits or from overestimated surpluses.

Similarly, a forecasted deficit of $100 and an actual deficit of $50 gives a negative forecast error of $50. Likewise, a forecasted surplus of $100 and an actual surplus of $150 gives a negative forecast error of $50. So negative forecast errors indicate overly pessimistic forecasts, either from overestimated deficits or from underestimated surpluses.

ets (and CBO analyses) consider projections of greater than two years as extrapolations of trends rather than true forecasts, the bias toward smaller deficits indicates failure by the executive to acknowledge the country's long-term budget problems. On the other hand, the CBO forecasts have been highly accurate.[8]

Figure 1 shows OMB budget-forecast errors over the period of analysis. The evidence confirms that short-term forecasts are more accurate than long-term forecasts and that the largest forecast errors, when deficits were underestimated, occurred early in Reagan's first term, throughout Reagan's second term,[9] and into Bush's term. Estimates during Clinton's terms have been generally accurate or, if anything, unduly pessimistic about the budget's balance. Figure 2 shows CBO budget forecast errors and reveals a similar pattern, though the errors are generally smaller throughout.

---

8. To test the possibility that macroeconomic forecasts may be influenced by electoral or partisan pressures, I regressed all forecast errors against dummy variables for election years, presidential election years, years with a Republican president, and years in which Republicans controlled both houses of Congress. These results, which may be obtained from me on request, reveal conflicting signs, few significant variables, poor fit, and virtually no explanatory power, suggesting that electoral and partisan pressures do not systematically bias macroeconomic forecasts.

9. Muris 2000 shows that although macroeconomic and budget forecasts early in Reagan's first term were inaccurate, so too were private-sector forecasts. Neither set of forecasters anticipated the incipient recession.

582 ✦ Jody W. Lipford

Figure 1. OMB Forecast Errors for the Budget

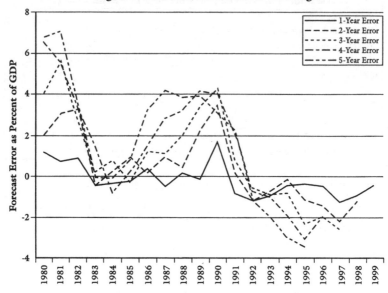

Figure 2. CBO Forecast Errors for the Budget

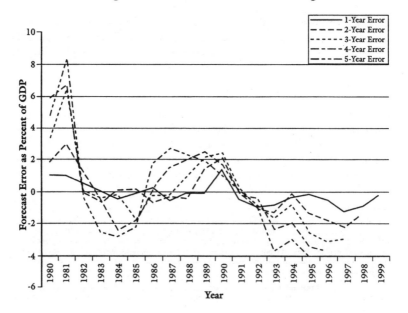

In sum, the evidence provided by macroeconomic and budgetary forecasts indicates that U.S. politicians do not generally diminish budgetary transparency by means of biased forecasts. Focusing on the budget balance, one sees that only long-term executive branch forecasts have had a statistically significant bias.

Evidence from Off-Budget Receipts

Since 1983, the off-budget balance of the U.S. budget has been positive. These off-budget surpluses, largely financed by Social Security receipts, have masked the size of on-budget deficits. As figure 3 shows, since the mid-1980s the on-budget balance has been consistently less than the total budget balance. Even in 1998, the year in which politicians rejoiced in the country's first fiscal surplus since 1969, the on-budget balance was in deficit by $30 billion. The total budget balance is projected to yield large surpluses in future years, but to the extent that those surpluses continue to result from off-budget Social Security surpluses that represent future expenditure obligations, the claim that the federal government has put its "fiscal house in order" must be called into question. The current use of funds meant to satisfy future obligations distorts the true fiscal condition of the government, making the budget less transparent than if on-budget receipts and expenditures were considered in isolation.

Figure 3. A Comparison of U.S. Total and On-Budget Balances

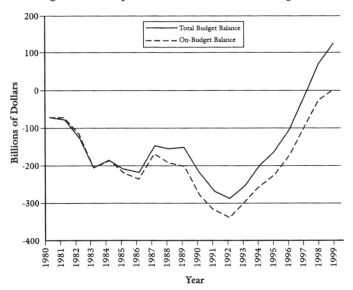

Evidence from Baseline Budgeting

The practice of baseline budgeting egregiously violates principles of budgetary transparency. The objective of baseline budgeting is ostensibly to provide estimates of how much it will cost the government to fund programs in the future, assuming no changes in policy. Yet, baseline budgeting serves political ends by obfuscating the budgetary process so that cuts in spending and deficits are claimed even though spending and deficits are rising.

Timothy Muris (1994, 57–67) provides detailed explanations of how baseline budgeting is used so that increases in spending and deficits can appear as cuts. The simplest method is to reduce spending below an inflated baseline projection so that a spending cut can be claimed while actual spending rises. But more subtle means abound. One is to count future tax and spending increases in the baselines so they do not appear as actual tax and spending hikes. Another is to extend taxes set to expire and then count those funds as "new" revenues to fund additional programs so that spending rises while tax collections are unchanged.

Because comparisons of actual spending with baselines in a given year are more difficult to understand and interpret than comparisons of actual spending in one year with actual spending in a prior year, baseline budgeting raises the costs of monitoring budgetary practices and holding politicians accountable for budgetary outcomes. As Muris concludes in his analysis of baseline budgeting, by "raising the cost of understanding the budget, the current policy baseline reduces the capacity of voters to make informed electoral choices" (1994, 77). And that reduction in voter capacity always leads to higher spending and deficits.

Evidence from Multiyear Budget Deals

Although multiyear budgets have been common since the budget reconciliation process began in 1980, efforts to deal with soaring deficits brought about the government's most significant multiyear budget deals in the 1990s. Table 3 shows the CBO estimates of the impact on the federal budget of the 1990 Omnibus Budget Reconciliation Act, the 1993 Omnibus Budget Reconciliation Act, and the 1997 Balanced Budget and Taxpayer Relief Acts. Clearly, the estimated effects of those bills were significant. Nevertheless, the bills demonstrate a lack of transparency by promising large five-year deficit reductions in which most of the "fiscal pain" occurs near the end of the deal. Indeed, the 1997 budget acts actually raised the deficit by $21 billion in 1998, deferring all budget cuts to the last four years of the agreement.

Multiyear budget deals may lessen transparency in several ways. To begin, the forecasted effects of tax and spending policies become less certain as their time period extends into the future so that actual deficit reduction may never occur. Further, Congress and the president may ultimately yield to political pressures to renege on (future) legislated spending cuts and tax increases. In addition, delayed fiscal policies allow

Table 3. An Analysis of Multiyear Deficit-Reduction Bills						
CBO Estimates of Total Deficit Reduction (billions of dollars)		Percent of Total Deficit Reduction in Following Years				
		1	2	3	4	5
1990 Omnibus Budget Reconciliation Act	482	6.8	14.3	18.5	27.2	33.2
1993 Omnibus Budget Reconciliation Act	432.9	7.5	12.8	19.2	27.3	33.1
1997 Balanced Budget Act and Taxpayer Relief Act	137.9	n.a.	2.1	14.6	14.9	68.3

1990 OBRA *Source:* Congressional Budget Office, *The Economic and Budget Outlook: Fiscal Years 1992–1996* (Washington, D.C.: CBO, January 1991).

1993 OBRA *Source:* Congressional Budget Office, *The Economic and Budget Outlook: An Update* (Washington, D.C.: CBO, September 1993).

1997 BBA and TRA *Source:* Congressional Budget Office, *The Economic and Budget Outlook: An Update* (Washington, D.C.: CBO, September 1997).

politicians, at times, to escape accountability to voters. Noting the backloaded deficit-reduction provisions in the 1997 budget acts, former CBO director Robert D. Reischauer commented that "'President Clinton and the 105th Congress agreed that President Gore and the 107th Congress should sacrifice'" (see "Five-Year" 1997, 2–18).

Evidence from Budget Legislation

To further assess U.S. budgetary transparency, I examine the budgetary provisions of key fiscal legislation passed since the institution of modern budget practices by the Budget and Impoundment Control Act of 1974.[10] Specifically, I explore the Balanced Budget and Emergency Deficit Control Act of 1985, the Omnibus Budget Reconciliation Act of 1990, and the Balanced Budget Act and Taxpayer Relief Act of 1997, to determine whether budgetary practices and legislated provisions were consistent with budgetary transparency.

Balanced Budget and Emergency Deficit Control Act of 1985

Facing $200 billion deficits in the early to mid-1980s, Congress passed the Balanced Budget and Emergency Deficit Control Act of 1985, commonly known as the Gramm-Rudman-Hollings Act (GRH), in an effort to rein in deficits. The act had the appearance of serious deficit-reduction legislation, in part because it specified outcomes (deficit

---

10. The Budget and Impoundment Control Act significantly changed the budgeting process by shifting dates of the fiscal year, establishing the CBO, establishing the House and Senate budget committees, establishing overall targets for spending, establishing the budget reconciliation process, and forcing the president to spend impounded funds.

targets) rather than procedural reforms. Specifically, it set a deficit target of $172 billion in 1986, to decline by $36 billion per year until the budget was balanced in 1991. If deficits were not within $10 billion of targets, automatic spending cuts of an identical percentage would apply to all nonexempt programs to enforce compliance.[11]

Nevertheless, the act failed to achieve its deficit-reduction goals. Deficits were consistently above targets, reaching an unprecedented $269 billion in 1991, the year in which the budget was supposed to be balanced. These figures alone suggest the act was not a serious deficit-reduction effort, and examination of the legislated policies and budgetary practices carried out under it corroborate that conclusion. First, the act exempted from automatic cuts such mandatory spending as Social Security, the Earned Income Tax Credit, federal retirement programs, veterans benefits, Medicaid, Aid to Families with Dependent Children, and food stamps, along with other programs and interest on the national debt.[12] According to Davis, "about two-thirds of all spending was exempt from automatic reductions," so that "the category of spending most responsible for spending growth was unaffected by the procedural device intended to bring total spending under control" (1997, 18–19). By limiting the expenditures subject to sequestration, pressure mounted on the nonexempt expenditures and the required cuts became politically untenable. In the end, only two partial sequestrations were implemented, totaling $11.7 billion in 1986 and $4.6 billion in 1989 (Doyle and McCaffery 1991), and in 1987 the act was revised by raising deficit targets and extending the time required to meet them (see Thelwell 1990 for details). When the deficit was cut, budgetary gimmicks such as asset sales and intertemporal cost shifting were favored over long-term, substantive spending cuts or tax increases (Thelwell 1990, 192–94).[13]

The failure of GRH is not surprising. Any long-term deficit-reduction plan allows members of Congress who have left office to escape accountability. And as electoral pressures to sustain spending mount, rules fail. As William Keech concludes in his analysis of fiscal constraints, "it appears that the formal institutions and the informal norms of fiscal policy have not provided adequate restraints against the temptation to let expenditures outpace revenues" (1995, 182–83).

In sum, GRH, in origination and implementation, arguably reduced budgetary transparency by proposing unrealistic deficit targets, exempting the majority of the budget from the sequestration process, employing accounting gimmickry, and permitting some members of Congress to escape accountability. Thelwell argues that the

---

11. For a detailed account of negotiations leading to Gramm-Rudman-Hollings, see Miller 1994.

12. For additional details, see "Congress Enacts" 1985, 464.

13. Sperry 1999 lists a number of accounting gimmicks, including changed pay days, underfunded accounts, deferred obligations, leveraged spending, mandatory spending, off-budget programs, and—the most popular—emergency spending.

act's "inflexibility of mandatory deficit reductions, no tax increases, and equal cuts between defense and domestic programs invites cheating in a form that misleads the public" (1990, 197).

Omnibus Budget Reconciliation Act of 1990

With the failure of GRH to reduce the deficit, Congress took up the budget deficit again in the 1990 Omnibus Budget Reconciliation Act (OBRA). The act was estimated to reduce the deficit by approximately $500 billion over five years through a combination of tax increases and spending cuts. To ensure significant and lasting deficit reduction, the act set five-year caps for discretionary spending and required new entitlement programs to be funded by tax increases or cuts in existing programs, a procedure known as *pay-as-you-go* (PAYGO). The act also introduced a host of budgetary complexities, contingencies, and uncertainties, along with providing ample cover to politicians. Transparency was not well served.

Like Gramm-Rudman-Hollings, the OBRA set unrealistic deficit targets that were not met. However, unlike for GRH, attaining deficit targets was never of primary importance for this act. From the beginning, it permitted revisions of deficit targets if "tax revenues are overestimated, or program costs are underestimated due to inflation or clientele growth, or the economic assumptions turn out to be incorrect" (Doyle and McCaffery 1991, 33), rendering deficit targets meaningless and thwarting citizens' attempts to monitor compliance.

The primary focus of the OBRA was spending control rather than deficit control. Yet, its caps on discretionary spending were hardly a serious deficit-reduction provision. Schick's (1992) analysis shows that although discretionary defense spending was cut compared to baseline figures, the baseline was inflated and allowed president Bush to circumvent still deeper cuts desired by congressional Democrats. But congressional Democrats also had their interests served: over 1991–93, discretionary domestic spending was capped at $41.7 billion over the baseline. In the end, the "president got more for defense, the Democrats got more for domestic programs, and both sides celebrated their gutsy decision to curtail the deficit" (Schick 1992, 27).

Further, the caps were, from the beginning, subject to revision for "emergencies." In nominal dollars, budgetary authority for emergency spending from 1991–2000 equals $146.6 billion.[14] Qualified emergencies include refugee aid, relief for natural disasters, and defense operations in the Persian Gulf and Kosovo. Although the act implemented some cuts in entitlement spending, including a $44.2 billion reduction in Medicare spending, its PAYGO procedure permitted the cost of

---

14. See "Emergency Spending Under the Budget Enforcement Act: An Update," published by the CBO, at <www.cbo.gov>.

existing programs to continue their upward spiral, yielding further evidence that the OBRA was never a sincere deficit-reduction effort.

Through revised deficit targets, caps for discretionary spending, inflated baselines, and provisions for emergency spending, the OBRA of 1990 lessened budgetary transparency. It complicated not only the budget process, but also any attempt to evaluate budgetary outcomes.

Balanced Budget Act and Taxpayer Relief Act of 1997

The 1997 budget deal consisted of two reconciliation bills, the Balanced Budget Act (BBA) and the Taxpayer Relief Act (TRA), designed to cut the deficit by a CBO-estimated $116 billion (net) over five years and to achieve a balanced budget by 2002. The path to budget balance was eased by a rapidly growing economy that poured so much revenue into government coffers that the CBO, between January and March of 1997, "revised their deficit forecasts, 'finding' $225 billion over five years" (LeLoup, Long, and Giordano 1998, 5). Yet even those revisions underestimated deficit reduction, and in 1998 the federal government ran a fiscal surplus. Although the BBA, like its predecessors in 1990 and 1993, extended caps on discretionary spending and the PAYGO provision for entitlement spending, economic growth more so than legislative provision was responsible for achieving budget balance four years prior to the target of these acts.

The BBA and the TRA arguably are not serious deficit-reduction measures, nor do they enhance budgetary transparency and accountability. Although the BBA did cut Medicare spending by $100 billion over five years, these acts do little else to curb entitlement spending, which will escalate as baby boomers place greater demands on Social Security and Medicare (see the "Five-Year" 1997, 2–19). As noted before, politically unpopular spending cuts are back loaded, with the greater part scheduled for 2002, allowing the president and members of Congress out of office to escape blame.

Yet, even before 2002, it proved too great a temptation to spend more than these acts appropriated. Politicians spent "more than $30 billion more than allocated for Fiscal Year 2000," largely by categorizing funding for the 2000 census and the Head Start program as emergency spending (Graham 1999), as well as by extending "the current fiscal year three days to capture $2 billion from next fiscal year's revenues for this year" (see "Budget Caps" 1999, 14A). Further, Congress has already voted to rescind $16 billion in Medicare cuts, and calls to restore tens of billions more of Medicare funding came forth from the health-care sector to the halls of Congress.[15] Eviscerating fiscal discipline for fiscal years 2000 and 2001 greatly diminished the likelihood of maintaining it in future years.

---

15. See Janelle Carter, "Health Care Issues Plague Congress," September 25, 2000, at <infobeat.com>, and Janelle Carter, "Lawmakers Near Medicare Restoration," October 3, 2000, at <infobeat.com>.

Conclusions

Analysis of U.S. budgetary policies and practices is complex. This investigation of past policies and practices yields a mixed view of budgetary transparency. OMB and CBO macroeconomic and deficit forecasts have been generally unbiased, with the exception of OMB long-term deficit projections. On the other hand, many budgetary processes and practices lack transparency and accountability: the use of off-budget Social Security surpluses to reduce total-budget deficit figures; baseline budgeting; the backloading of politically unpopular spending cuts and tax increases in multiyear budget deals; specification of unrealistic and unattained deficit targets in GRH and the 1990 OBRA; an inflated defense baseline in the 1990 OBRA; violated spending caps in the 1997 BBA; and avoidance of significant entitlement-program reform in all budgetary legislation. Whether suffering from fiscal illusion or information asymmetry, citizen-voters can hardly be expected to understand the effects or to decipher the details of U.S. public budgets.

Although a lack of transparency and accountability might be expected in an era of fiscal deficits, current fiscal surpluses yield no evidence of increased transparency or accountability. The lack of transparency evident in past budgets, combined with current proposals to spend more for prescription drugs under Medicare and simultaneously cut taxes, casts doubt on the viability of the estimated budget surpluses. Indeed, even if the current proposals are not adopted, so that all of the projected surpluses are saved, a recent CBO report projects that without reform of Medicaid, Medicare, and Social Security, deficits will recur by 2040 and debt levels will eventually become "unsustainable."[16] In addition, forecasted economic conditions and surpluses, although statistically unbiased, may err, causing a return to deficits.[17]

The salient conclusion is that the political incentives that lead to obfuscated budgetary practices and greater spending in an era of deficits also apply in an era of surpluses. Regardless of the budget's balance, politicians will continue to use budget legislation and practices that obfuscate citizens' ability to understand budgetary provisions, monitor compliance, or hold politicians accountable.

References

Alesina, A., and A. Cukierman. 1990. The Politics of Ambiguity. *Quarterly Journal of Economics* 105: 829–50.

Alesina, A., R. Hausmann, R. Hommes, and E. Stein. 1996. *Budget Institutions and Fiscal Performance in Latin America*. National Bureau of Economic Research Working Paper no. 5586. Cambridge, Mass.: National Bureau of Economic Research.

---

16. If only off-budget surpluses are saved, deficits will recur in 2030. If none of the budget surplus is saved, deficits will recur in 2020. See "The Long-Term Budget Outlook," at <www.cbo.gov>.

17. See "Counting Their Chickens" 1999, 27–28.

Alesina, A., and R. Perotti. 1996. Fiscal Discipline and the Budget Process. *American Economic Review Papers and Proceedings* 86: 401–07.

Alesina, A., and N. Roubini, with G. Cohen. 1997. *Political Cycles and the Macroeconomy.* Cambridge, Mass.: MIT Press.

Bennett, J. T., and T. J. DiLorenzo. 1982. Off-Budget Activities of Local Government: The Bane of the Tax Revolt. *Public Choice* 39: 333–42.

Boudreaux, D. J. 1996. Was Your High-School Civics Teacher Right After All? Review Essay of Donald Wittman's *The Myth of Democratic Failure. Independent Review* 1: 111–28.

Brennan, G., and J. M. Buchanan. 1980. *The Power to Tax: Analytical Foundations of a Fiscal Constitution.* Cambridge.: Cambridge University Press.

Buchanan, J. M., and R. E. Wagner. 1977. *Democracy in Deficit.* New York: Academic.

Budget Caps Quietly Killed. *Greenville News,* November 20, 1999, A14.

Congress Enacts Strict Anti-Deficit Measure. 1985. In *Congressional Quarterly Almanac 1985,* 459–68. Washington, D.C.: Congressional Quarterly.

Counting Their Chickens. 1999. *The Economist,* February 6, 27–28.

Davis, E. 1997. The Evolution of Federal Spending Controls: A Brief Overview. *Public Budgeting and Finance* 17: 10–24.

Doyle, R., and J. McCaffery. 1991. The Budget Enforcement Act of 1990: The Path to No Fault Budgeting. *Public Budgeting and Finance* 11: 25–40.

Five-Year Balanced-Budget Deal Shapes Year's Fiscal Debate. 1997. In *Congressional Quarterly Almanac 1997,* 2–3—2–61. Washington, D.C.: Congressional Quarterly.

Graham, Lindsey. 1999. Congress Destroys Discipline in Planning Budget for 2000. *Greenville News,* November 26, A9.

Keech, W. 1995. *Economic Politics and the Costs of Democracy.* Cambridge: Cambridge University Press.

LeLoup, L. T., C. N. Long, and J. N. Giordano. 1998. President Clinton's Fiscal 1998 Budget: Political and Economic Paths to Balance. *Public Budgeting and Finance* 18: 3–32.

Light, Paul C. 1999. *The True Size of Government.* Washington, D.C.: Brookings Institution Press.

Merrifield, J. 1994. Factors That Influence the Level of Underground Government. *Public Finance Quarterly* 22: 462–82.

Miller, J. C. 1994. *Fix the Budget! Urgings of an "Abominable No-Man."* Stanford, Calif.: Hoover Institution.

Mixon, F. G., Jr., and J. B. Wilkinson. 1999. Maintaining the Status Quo: Federal Government Budget Deficits and Defensive Rent-Seeking. *Journal of Economic Studies* 26: 5–14.

Muris, T. J. 1994. The Uses and Abuses of Budget Baselines. In *The Budget Puzzle: Understanding Federal Spending,* edited by J. F. Cogan, T. J. Muris, and Allen Schick. Stanford, Calif.: Stanford University Press.

———. 2000. Ronald Reagan and the Rise of Large Deficits: What Really Happened in 1981? *Independent Review* 4 (winter): 365–76.

Niskanen, W. A. 1992. The Case for a New Fiscal Constitution. *Journal of Economic Perspectives* 6: 13–24.

Persson, T., and L. Svensson. 1989. Why a Stubborn Conservative Would Run a Deficit: Policy with Time-Inconsistent Preferences. *Quarterly Journal of Economics* 104: 325–45.

Schick, A. 1992. Deficit Budgeting in the Age of Divided Government. In *Fiscal Politics and the Budget Enforcement Act,* edited by Marvin Kosters. Washington, D.C.: AEI.

Schultze, C. L. 1992. Is There a Bias Towards Excess in U.S. Budgets or Deficits? *Journal of Economic Perspectives* 6 (spring): 25–43.

Sperry, P. 1999. *Breach of Faith: How Washington Is Poised to Shatter the Budget Agreement and Squander the Surplus.* Paper 1321. Washington, D.C.: Heritage Foundation.

Thelwell, R. 1990. Gramm-Rudman-Hollings Four Years Later: A Dangerous Illusion. *Public Administration Review* 50 (March–April): 190–98.

Twight, C. 1988. Government Manipulation of Constitutional-Level Transactions Costs: A General Theory of Transaction-Cost Augmentation and the Growth of Government. *Public Choice* 56: 131–52.

———. 1994. Political Transaction-Cost Manipulation: An Integrating Approach. *Journal of Theoretical Politics* 6: 189–216.

U.S. Council of Economic Advisers (CEA). 2000. *Annual Report.* Washington, D.C.: U.S. Government Printing Office.

Acknowledgments: I thank Franklin G. Mixon Jr., Jerry K. Slice, and Bruce Yandle for helpful suggestions on earlier drafts. Any remaining errors are my own.

Part II
Classical Public Debt Theory

Part II: An Overview

The classical economists wrote over the period 1776–1848, primarily in the setting of the economy of Great Britain, and they wrote generally about economic life and how it was and should be organized from the perspective of increasing the welfare of the average citizen (per capita income). One of their primary focal points was the process of economic growth.

In the area of public finance the classical economists, for the most part, were pragmatists. The issuance of public debt was seen as an emergency measure required for financing wartime spending. Once the emergency was at an end, the state was obliged to retire the public debt. That goal was best accomplished through the creation of sinking funds financed through peacetime budget surpluses.

Deficit spending during wars and other national crises was justified not by any intrinsic property of that method of public finance, but in recognition of the harsh reality that the additional revenues needed quickly to mobilize military forces would lag seriously behind the enactment of emergency tax measures. As Adam Smith put it, 'the want of parsimony in time of peace imposes the necessity of contracting debt in time of war'. Moreover, the classicals appreciated that governments in general would be unable or unwilling to impose new taxes at levels high enough fully to defray the cost of the war effort while simultaneously currying popular support for bellicose foreign policies. Hence, debt issue was grudgingly seen as a second-best fiscal policy alternative.

For the most part, the classical economists favored extinguishing debt incurred to finance wars as soon as practicable following the cessation of hostilities. John Stuart Mill, for example, thought that peacetime budget surpluses should first be disposed of by repealing the most objectionable of a nation's existing taxes. Nevertheless, they were properly skeptical of the notion that sinking funds would accomplish their stated purposes. Adam Smith, in particular, feared that funds instituted for the payment of old debts would be used instead to contract new ones. With typical insight, Smith argued that even 'during the most profound peace, various events occur which require an extraordinary expence, and government finds it always more convenient to defray this expence by misapplying the sinking fund than by imposing a new tax'.

Smith supported these fears by evidence he gathered from the British experience of the eighteenth century, where 'from the first time we had recourse to the ruinous expedient of perpetual funding, the reduction of the publick debt in time of peace, has never borne any proportion to its accumulation in time of war'. Smith's judgment on this issue is as relevant today as it was in the late eighteenth century. With the Cold War over, successive US governments continue to borrow against the so-called social security 'trust fund' as a means of financing deficit spending while creating the illusion of budget surplus.

Neither was David Ricardo sanguine about the prospects for peacetime debt retirement, observing that 'no sinking fund can be efficient for the purpose of diminishing the debt, if it not be derived from the excess of the public revenue over the public expenditure. It is to be regretted, that the sinking fund in this country is only such in name; for there is no excess of revenue above expenditure'. Similarly, John Stuart Mill thought that liquidation of wartime debt would be effected only if designated taxes were earmarked specifically to that end, thereby preventing monies destined for the sinking fund from being commingled 'with the general revenues of the state'.

Beyond supporting a limited, 'night-watchman' state (defense, justice, police), the classical economists did not view public spending as being productive relative to the alternative of private capital investments. Private investment, not public investment, drove the classical engine of economic growth. So the classical economists did not envisage any significant role for government that would entail competition between the public and private sectors for scarce loanable funds.

Thomas Malthus and David Ricardo both thought (incorrectly) that the payment of interest on the public debt constituted a pure transfer of income from taxpayers to the government's creditors and, hence, did not reduce the wealth of the nation. Indeed, Malthus went so far as to assert that any reduction in private demand caused by an increase in the public debt would be counterbalanced *exactly* by an increase in demand on the part of the government and the holders of its bonds.

To be sure, none of the classical economists seem to have understood that, except when levied lump sum, taxes inevitably produce deadweight social costs. Nevertheless, Adam Smith had a better understanding of the issue than either Ricardo or Malthus, recognizing that while the government's creditors have a general regard for the national welfare, in so far as their interest income is contingent on continued prosperity, the holders of the public debt do not have the same incentives for deploying resources to their highest valued uses as the owners of those resources, who are taxed to service the debt. An income transfer between these two groups therefore 'must, in the long-run, occasion both the neglect of land, and the waste or removal of capital stock'.

Smith's reasoning explodes the hoary myth – hoary apparently even in 1776 – that the payment of interest on the public debt has no real economic consequences because 'it is the right hand which pays the left' or because 'we owe it to ourselves'. That 'apology for the public debt' was also wrong as a factual matter, then as now, 'the Dutch, as well as several foreign nations, having a considerable share of our publick funds'.

So in this great formative period of the British state, various pro-growth policies appear in tandem. Britain moved strongly to endorse policies of free trade, deregulation, and lower taxes, thereby spawning the Industrial Revolution. Part of this policy was an antagonism to public debt and a view that governments should balance their budgets on an annual basis. Again quoting Adam Smith, 'if [government] cannot raise its revenue in proportion to its expence, it ought, at least, to accommodate its expence to its revenue'.

Finally, it was in the classical period that David Ricardo proposed his famous equivalence theorem, arguing that debt and taxes are perfectly substitutable as means of public finance. Ricardo reasoned that individuals would respond to an increase in public indebtedness by cutting their current consumption spending by exactly the amount necessary to pay their proportionate shares of the expectedly higher future tax bills required to service and retire the debt.

In present value terms, borrowing by government reduces disposable income to the same extent as an equal increase in current taxes. The doctrine of *Ricardian equivalence* thus implies that the public sector's burden on the private economy can be gauged solely by the current level of public spending, without regard to the sources of the funds used to finance those expenditures. Ricardo's theoretical proposition (a proposition, incidentally, concerning which he expressed some skepticism in the world of *realpolitik*) has provoked much discussion among modern economic theorists.

Charles K. Rowley
William F. Shughart II
Robert D. Tollison

[6]

Of publick Debts

1 IN that rude state of society which precedes the extension of commerce
and the improvement of manufactures, when those expensive luxuries
which commerce and manufactures can alone introduce, are altogether
unknown, the person who possesses a large revenue, I have endeavoured
to show in [395] the third book of this enquiry, can spend or enjoy that
revenue in no other way than by maintaining nearly as many people as it
can maintain.[1] A large revenue may at all times be said to consist in the
command of a large quantity of the necessaries of life. In that rude state
of things it is commonly paid in a large quantity of those necessaries, in
the materials of plain food and coarse cloathing, in corn and cattle, in
wool and raw hides. When neither commerce nor manufactures furnish
any thing for which the owner can exchange the greater part of those
materials which are over and above his own consumption, he can do nothing
with the surplus but feed and cloathe nearly as many people as it will
feed and cloathe. A hospitality in which there is no luxury, and a liberality
in which there is no ostentation, occasion, in this situation of things, the
principal expences of the rich and the great. But these, I have likewise
endeavoured to shew in the same book, are expences by which people
are not very apt to ruin themselves.[2] There is not, perhaps, any selfish
pleasure so frivolous, of which the pursuit has not sometimes ruined even
sensible men. A passion for cock-fighting has ruined many. But the
instances, I believe, are not very numerous of people who have been
ruined by a hospitality or liberality of this kind; though the hospitality
of luxury and the liberality of ostentation have ruined many. Among our
feudal ancestors, the long time during which estates used to continue in
the same family, sufficiently demonstrates the general disposition of people
[396] to live within their income.[3] Though the rustick hospitality, constantly exercised by the great land-holders, may not, to us in the present
times, seem consistent with that order, which we are apt to consider as
inseparably connected with good œconomy, yet we must certainly allow
them to have been at least so far frugal as not commonly to have spent
their whole income. A part of their wool and raw hides they had generally an opportunity of selling for money. Some part of this money, perhaps, they spent in purchasing the few objects of vanity and luxury, with
which the circumstances of the times could furnish them; but some part
of it they seem commonly to have hoarded. They could not well indeed
do any thing else but hoard whatever money they saved. To trade was

[1] See above, III.iv.   [2] Above, III.iv.16.   [3] See above, III.iv.16, and III.ii.7.

disgraceful to a gentleman, and to lend money at interest, which at that time was considered as usury and prohibited by law, would have been still more so.[4] In those times of violence and disorder, besides, it was convenient to have a hoard of money at hand, that in case they should be driven from their own home, they might have something of known value to carry with them to some place of safety. The same violence, which made it convenient to hoard, made it equally convenient to conceal the hoard.[5] The frequency of treasure-trove, or of treasure found of which no owner was known, sufficiently demonstrates the frequency in those times both of hoarding and of concealing the hoard. Treasure-trove was then considered as an important branch of the revenue of the so-[397] vereign. All the treasure-trove of the kingdom would scarce perhaps in the present times make an important branch of the revenue of a private gentleman of a good estate.

2   The same disposition to save and to hoard prevailed in the sovereign, as well as in the subjects. Among nations to whom commerce and manufactures are little known, the sovereign, it has already been observed in the fourth book,[6] is in a situation which naturally disposes him to the parsimony requisite for accumulation. In that situation the expence even of a sovereign cannot be directed by that vanity which delights in the gaudy finery of a court. The ignorance of the times affords but few of the trinkets in which that finery consists. Standing armies are not then necessary, so that the expence even of a sovereign, like that of any other great lord, can be employed in scarce any thing but bounty to his tenants, and hospitality to his retainers.[7] But bounty and hospitality very seldom lead to extravagance; though vanity almost always does.[8] All the antient sovereigns of Europe accordingly, it has already been observed, had treasures. Every Tartar chief in the present times is said to have one.

3   In a commercial country abounding with every sort of expensive luxury, the sovereign, in the same manner as almost all the great proprietors in his dominions, naturally spends a great part of his revenue in purchasing those luxuries. His own and the neighbouring countries supply him abundantly with all the costly trinkets which [398] compose the splendid, but insignificant pageantry of a court. For the sake of an inferior pageantry of the same kind, his nobles dismiss their retainers, make their tenants independent, and become gradually themselves as insignificant as the greater part of the wealthy burghers in his dominions.[9] The same frivo-

---

[4] It is remarked in LJ (B) 300, ed. Cannan 231–2, that 'In a rude society nothing is honourable but war' and that trade in particular is held in low esteem; a feeling which is not completely extinguished even in more refined societies. Smith adds at 302, ed. Cannan 233, with reference to ruder ages that the 'mean and despicable idea which they had of merchants greatly obstructed the progress of commerce'. Cf. III.iii.1–2.
[5] See above, II.i.31.   [6] Above, IV.i.30.   [7] See above, III.iv.5.
[8] Repeated from IV.i.30.   [9] See above, III.iv.15.

lous passions, which influence their conduct, influence his. How can it be supposed that he should be the only rich man in his dominions who is insensible to pleasures of this kind?[10] If he does not, what he is very likely to do, spend upon those pleasures so great a part of his revenue as to debilitate very much the defensive power of the state, it cannot well be expected that he should not spend upon them all that part of it which is over and above what is necessary for supporting that defensive power. His ordinary expence becomes equal to his ordinary revenue, and it is well if it does not frequently exceed it. The amassing of treasure can no longer be expected, and when extraordinary exigencies require extra-ordinary expences, he must necessarily call upon his subjects for an extraordinary aid. The present and the late king of Prussia are the only great princes of Europe who, since the death of Henry IV. of France in 1610, are supposed to have amassed any considerable treasure.[11] The parsimony which leads to accumulation has become almost as rare in republican as in monarchical governments. The Italian republicks, the United Provinces of the Netherlands, are all in debt. The canton of Berne is the single republick in Europe which [399] has amassed any considerable treasure. The other Swiss republicks have not.[12] The taste for some sort of pageantry, for splendid buildings, at least, and other publick ornaments, frequently prevails as much in the apparently sober senate-house of a little republick, as in the dissipated court of the greatest king.

4   The want of parsimony in time of peace, imposes the necessity of con-tracting debt in time of war. When war comes, there is no money in the treasury but what is necessary for carrying on the ordinary expence of the peace establishment. In war an establishment of three or four times that expence becomes necessary for the defence of the state, and con-sequently a revenue three or four times greater than the peace revenue. Supposing that the sovereign should have, what he scarce ever has, the immediate means of augmenting his revenue in proportion to the augmen-tation of his expence, yet still the produce of the taxes, from which this increase of revenue must be drawn, will not begin to come into the treasury till perhaps ten or twelve months after they are imposed. But the moment in which war begins, or rather the moment in which it appears likely to begin, the army must be augmented, the fleet must be fitted out, the garrisoned towns must be put into a posture of defence; that army, that fleet, those garrisoned towns must be furnished with arms, ammuni-tion and provisions. An immediate and great expence must be incurred in that moment of immediate danger, which will not wait for the gradual and slow re-[400]turns of the new taxes. In this exigency government can have no other resource but in borrowing.

[10] See above, V.i.h.2.   [11] See above, IV.i.25.   [12] See above, V.i.g.41, V.ii.a.9.

5   The same commercial state of society which, by the operation of moral causes, brings government in this manner into the necessity of borrowing, produces in the subjects both an ability and an inclination to lend. If it commonly brings along with it the necessity of borrowing, it likewise brings *along* with it the facility of doing so.

6   A country abounding with merchants and manufacturers, necessarily abounds with a set of people through whose hands not only their own capitals, but the capitals of all those who either lend them money, or trust them with goods, pass as frequently, or more frequently, than the revenue of a private man, who, without trade or business, lives upon his income, passes through his hands. The revenue of such a man can regularly pass through his hands only once in *a* year. But the whole amount of the capital and credit of a merchant, who deals in a trade of which the returns are very quick, may sometimes pass through his hands two, three, or four times in a year.[13] A country abounding with merchants and manufacturers, therefore, necessarily abounds with a set of people who have it at all times in their power to advance, if they chuse to do so, a very large sum of money to government. Hence the ability in the subjects of a commercial state to lend.

7   Commerce and manufactures can seldom flourish long in any state which does not enjoy a regular administration of justice, in which the [401] people do not feel themselves secure in the possession of their property, in which the faith of contracts is not supported by law, and in which the authority of the state is not supposed to be regularly employed in enforcing the payment of debts from all those who are able to pay. Commerce and manufactures, in short, can seldom flourish in any state in which there is not a certain degree of confidence in the justice of government.[14] The same confidence which disposes great merchants and manufacturers, upon ordinary occasions, to trust their property to the protection of a particular government; disposes them, upon extraordinary occasions, to trust that government with the use of their property. By lending money to government, they do not even for a moment diminish their ability to carry on their trade and manufactures. On the contrary, they commonly augment it. The necessities of the state render government upon most occasions willing to borrow upon terms extremely advantageous to the lender. The security which it grants to the original creditor, is made transferable to any other creditor, and, from the universal confidence in the justice of the state, generally sells in the market for more than was originally paid for it. The merchant or monied man makes money by lending money to government, and instead of diminishing, increases

---

a–a om. 5–6   *b–b* the *1*

[13] See above, II.v.27.   [14] See, for example, III.iii.12, II.i.30.

his trading capital. He generally considers it as a favour, therefore, when the administration admits him to share in the first subscription for a new [402] loan. Hence the inclination or willingness in the subjects of a commercial state to lend.

8   The government of such a state is very apt to repose itself upon this ability and willingness of its subjects to lend it their money on extraordinary occasions. It foresees the facility of borrowing, and therefore dispenses itself from the duty of saving.

9   In a rude state of society there are no great mercantile or manufacturing capitals. The individuals who hoard whatever money they can save, and who conceal their hoard, do so from a distrust of the justice of government, from a fear that if it was known that they had a hoard, and where that hoard was to be found, they would quickly be plundered. In such a state of things few people would be able, and nobody would be willing, to lend their money to government on extraordinary exigencies. The sovereign feels that he must provide for such exigencies by saving, because he foresees the absolute impossibility of borrowing. This foresight increases still further his natural disposition to save.[15]

10   The progress of the enormous debts which at present oppress, and will in the long-run probably ruin, all the great nations of Europe, has been pretty uniform. Nations, like private men, have generally begun to borrow upon what may be called personal credit, without assigning or mortgaging any particular fund for the payment of the debt; and when this resource has [403] failed them, they have gone on to borrow upon assignments or mortgages of particular funds.

11   What is called the unfunded debt of Great Britain, is contracted in the former of those two ways. It consists partly in a debt which bears, or is supposed to bear, no interest, and which resembles the debts that a private man contracts upon account; and partly in a debt which bears interest, and which resembles what a private man contracts upon his bill or promissory note. The debts which are due either for extraordinary services, or for services either not provided for, or not paid at the time when they are performed; part of the extraordinaries of the army, navy, and ordnance, the arrears of subsidies to foreign princes, those of seamens wages, &c. usually constitute a debt of the first kind. Navy and Exchequer bills, which are issued sometimes in payment of a part of such debts and sometimes for other purposes, constitute a debt of the second kind; Exchequer bills bearing interest from the day on which they are issued, and navy bills six months after they are issued. The bank of England, either by voluntarily discounting those bills at their current value, or by agreeing with government for certain considerations to circulate Exchequer bills, that is, to receive them at par, paying the interest which

[15] See above, IV.i.30. Hume develops this theme in his essay 'Of Public Credit'.

happens to be due upon them, keeps up their value and facilitates their circulation, and thereby frequently enables government to contract a very large debt of this kind. In France, where there is no bank, the state bills (billets d'état)* have [404] sometimes sold at sixty and seventy per cent. discount. During the great re-coinage in king William's time, when the bank of England thought proper to put a stop to its usual transactions, Exchequer bills and tallies are said to have sold from twenty-five to sixty per cent. discount;[16] owing partly, no doubt, to the supposed instability of the new government established by the Revolution, but partly too to the want of the support of the bank of England.[17]

12　　When this resource is exhausted, and it becomes necessary, in order to raise money, to assign or mortgage some particular branch of the publick revenue for the payment of the debt, government has upon different occasions done this in two different ways. Sometimes it has made this assignment or mortgage for a short period of time only, a year, or a few years, for example; and sometimes for perpetuity. In the one case the fund was supposed sufficient to pay, within the limited time, both principal and interest of the money borrowed. In the other it was supposed sufficient to pay the interest only, or a perpetual annuity equivalent to the interest, government being at liberty to redeem at any time this annuity, upon paying back the principal sum borrowed. When money was raised in the one way, it was said to be raised by anticipation; when in the other, by perpetual funding, or, more shortly, by funding.

13　　In Great Britain the annual land and malt taxes are regularly anticipated every year, by virtue of a borrowing clause constantly inserted [405] into the acts which impose them. The bank of England generally advances at an interest, which since the Revolution has varied from eight to three per cent. the sums for which those taxes are granted, and receives payment as their produce gradually comes in. If there is a deficiency, which there always is, it is provided for in the supplies of the ensuing year. The only considerable branch of the publick revenue which yet remains unmortgaged is thus regularly spent before it comes in. Like an cimprovidentc spendthrift, whose pressing occasions will not allow him to wait for the regular payment of his revenue, the state is in the constant practice of borrowing of its own factors and agents, and of paying interest for the use of its own money.

14　　In the reign of King William, and during a great part of that of Queen

---

* See Examen des Reflexions politiques sur les finances. [J. P. Duverney, *Examen du livre intitulé Réflexions politiques sur les finances et le commerce*, i.225.]

---

c–c unprovident *1*

---

[16] J. Postlethwayt, *History of the Public Revenue*, 14–15, and 301. See above, II.ii.80, n.

[17] See above, II.ii.79.

Anne, before we had become so familiar as we are now with the practice of perpetual funding, the greater part of the new taxes were imposed but for a short period of time (for four, five, six, or seven years only), and a great part of the grants of every year consisted in loans upon anticipations of the produce of those taxes.[18] The produce being frequently insufficient for paying within the limited term the principal and interest of the money borrowed, deficiencies arose, to make good which it became necessary to prolong the term.

15   In 1697, by the 8th of William III. c. 20. the deficiencies of several taxes were charged upon what was then called the first general mortgage or fund, consisting of a prolongation to the first [406] of August, 1706, of several different taxes, which would have expired within a shorter term, and of which the produce was accumulated into one general fund.[19] The deficiencies charged upon this prolonged term amounted to 5,160,459*l.* 14*s.* 9¼*d.*[20]

16   In 1701 those duties, with some others, were still further prolonged for the like purposes till the first of August 1710, and were called the second general mortgage or fund. The deficiencies charged upon it amounted to 2,055,999*l.* 7*s.* 11½*d.*

17   In 1707, those duties were still further prolonged, as a fund for new loans, to the first of August 1712, and were called the third general mortgage or fund. The sum borrowed upon it was 983,254*l.* 11*s.* 9¼*d.*

18   In 1708, those duties were all (except the old subsidy of tonnage and poundage, of which one moiety only was made a part of this fund, and a duty upon the importation of Scotch linen, which had been taken off by the articles of union) still further continued, as a fund for new loans, to the first of August 1714, and were called the fourth general mortgage or fund. The sum borrowed upon it was 925,176*l.* 9*s.* 2¼*d.*

19   In 1709, those duties were all (except the old subsidy of tonnage and poundage, which was now left out of this fund altogether) still further continued for the same purpose to the first of August 1716, and were called the fifth general mortgage or fund. The sum borrowed upon it was 922,029*l.* 6*s.* 0*d.*

20   [407] In 1710, those duties were again prolonged to the first of August 1720, and were called the sixth general mortgage or fund. The sum borrowed upon it was 1,296,552*l.* 9*s.* 11¾*d.*

21   In 1711, the same duties (which at this time were thus subject to four

---

[18] LJ (B) 320, ed. Cannan 247, comments that 'Soon after the Revolution, on account of the necessities of government, it was necessary to borrow money from subjects, generaly at a higher rate than common interest, to be repaid in a few years.' Smith comments on the issue of funding at 320-4, ed. Cannan 247-51.

[19] 8 and 9 William III, c. 20 (1696).

[20] The information in this paragraph and in the nine following is taken from J. Postlethwayt, *History of Public Revenue*, 38, 40, 59, 63, 64, 68, 71, 303, 305, 311, 319, 320.

different anticipations) together with several others were continued for ever, and made a fund for paying the interest of the capital of the South Sea company, which had that year advanced to government, for paying debts and making good deficiencies, the sum of 9,177,967*l.* 15*s.* 4*d.*; the greatest loan which at that time had ever been made.

22 Before this period, the principal, so far as I have been able to observe, the only taxes which in order to pay the interest of a debt had been imposed for perpetuity, were those for paying the interest of the money which had been advanced to government by the Bank and East India company, and of what it was expected would be advanced, but which was never advanced, by a projected land-bank. The bank fund at this time amounted to 3,375,027*l.* 17*s.* 10½*d.* for which was paid an annuity or interest of 206,501*l.* 13*s.* 5*d.*[21] The East India fund amounted to 3,200,000*l.* for which was paid an annuity or interest of 160,000*l.*; the bank fund being at six per cent., the East India fund at five per cent. interest.

23 In 1715, by the first of George I. c. 12.[22] the different taxes which had been mortgaged for paying the bank annuity, together with several others which by this act were likewise rendered perpetual, were accumulated into one common [408] fund called The Aggregate Fund, which was charged, not only with the *d*payments*d* of the bank annuity, but with several other annuities and burdens of different kinds. This fund was afterwards augmented by the third of George I. c. 8. and by the fifth of George I. c. 3. and the different duties which were then added to it were likewise rendered perpetual.

24 In 1717, by the third of George I. c. 7.[23] several other taxes were rendered perpetual, and accumulated into another common fund, called The General Fund, for the payment of certain annuities, amounting in the whole to 724,849*l.* 6*s.* 10½*d.*

25 In consequence of those different acts, the greater part of the taxes which before had been anticipated only for a short term of years, were rendered perpetual as a fund for paying, not the capital, but the interest only, of the money which had been borrowed upon them by different successive anticipations.

26 Had money never been raised but by anticipation, the course of a few years would have liberated the publick revenue, without any other attention of government besides that of not overloading the fund by charging it with more debt than it could pay within the limited term, and of not anticipating a second time before the expiration of the first anticipation. But the greater part of European governments have been incapable of

---

d-d payment *1*

[21] Above, II.ii.81.

[22] 1 George I, c. 12 (1714), to become effective in 1715; continued by 3 George I, c. 8 (1716) and 5 George I, c. 3 (1718).

[23] 3 George I, c. 7 (1716) to become effective in 1717.

those attentions. They have frequently overloaded the fund even upon the first anticipation; and when this happened not to be [409] the case, they have generally taken care to overload it, by anticipating a second and a third time before the expiration of the first anticipation. The fund becoming in this manner altogether insufficient for paying both principal and interest of the money borrowed upon it, it became necessary to charge it with the interest only, or a perpetual annuity equal to the interest, and such unprovident anticipations necessarily gave birth to the more ruinous practice of perpetual funding. But though this practice necessarily puts off the liberation of the publick revenue from a fixed period to one so indefinite that it is not very likely ever to arrive; yet as a greater sum can in all cases be raised by this new practice than by the old one of anticipations, the former, when men have once become familiar with it, has in the great exigencies of the state been universally preferred to the latter. To relieve the present exigency is always the object which principally interests those immediately concerned in the administration of publick affairs. The future liberation of the publick revenue, they leave to the care of posterity.

27   During the reign of queen Anne, the market rate of interest had fallen from six to five per cent., and in the twelfth year of her reign five per cent. was declared to be the highest rate which could lawfully be taken for money borrowed upon private security.[24] Soon after the greater part of the temporary taxes of Great Britain had been rendered perpetual, and distributed into the Aggregate, South Sea, and [410] General Funds, the creditors of the publick, like those of private persons, were induced to accept of five per cent. for the interest of their money, which occasioned a saving of one per cent. upon the capital of the greater part of the debts which had been thus funded for perpetuity, or of one-sixth of the greater part of the annuities which were paid out of the three great funds above mentioned. This saving left a considerable surplus in the produce of the different taxes which had been accumulated into those funds, over and above what was necessary for paying the annuities which were now charged upon them, and laid the foundation of what has since been called the Sinking Fund. In 1717, it amounted to 323,434*l.* 7*s.* 7½*d.*[25] In 1727, the interest of the greater part of the publick debts was still further reduced to four per cent.;[26] and in 1753[27] and 1757,[28] to three and a half and three per cent.; which reductions still further augmented the sinking fund.[29]

[24] 13 Anne, c. 15 (1713) in *Statutes of the Realm*, ix.928; 12 Anne, st. 2, c. 16 in Ruffhead's edition. See above, I.ix.5 and V.ii.f.8.

[25] A. Anderson, *Origin of Commerce* (1764), ii.273.

[26] 'At Midsummer this Year, the Reduction of the Interest on the National Debt from 5 to 4 per cent took place; whereby the famous Sinking-Fund was increased to above one Million per Annum.' (Ibid. ii.316.)   [27] 26 George II, c. 1 (1753).

[28] 30 George II, c. 4 (1757). See also A. Anderson, *Origin of Commerce* (1764), ii.391.

[29] In 1750 Henry Pelham 'cut the rate of interest on certain annuities held by the Bank

28   A sinking fund, though instituted for the payment of old, facilitates very much the contracting of new debts. It is a subsidiary fund always at hand to be mortgaged in aid of any other doubtful fund, upon which money is proposed to be raised in any exigency of the state. Whether the sinking fund of Great Britain has been more frequently applied to the one or to the other of those two purposes, will sufficiently appear by and by.

29   Besides those two methods of borrowing, by anticipations and by perpetual funding, there [411] are two other methods, which hold a sort of middle place between them. These are, that of borrowing upon annuities for terms of years, and that of borrowing upon annuities for lives.

30   During the reigns of king William and queen Anne, large sums were frequently borrowed upon annuities for terms of years, which were sometimes longer and sometimes shorter. In 1693, an act was passed for borrowing one million upon an annuity of fourteen per cent., or of 140,000*l.* a year for sixteen years. In 1691, an act was passed for borrowing a million upon annuities for lives, upon terms which in the present times would appear very advantageous. But the subscription was not filled up. In the following year the deficiency was made good by borrowing upon annuities for lives at fourteen per cent., or at little more than seven years purchase.[30] In 1695, the persons who had purchased those annuities were allowed to exchange them for others of ninety-six years, upon paying into the Exchequer sixty-three pounds in the hundred; that is, the difference between fourteen per cent. for life, and fourteen per cent. for ninety-six years, was sold for sixty-three pounds, or for four and a half years purchase.[31] Such was the supposed instability of government, that even these terms procured few purchasers.[32] In the reign of queen Anne, money was upon different occasions borrowed both upon annuities for lives, and upon annuities for terms of thirty-two, of eighty-nine, of ninety-eight, and of ninety-nine years. In 1719, the proprietors of [412]

[of England] to 3½, with a promise of 3 to come. In 1751 he grouped together a number of funds already, or about to be put, on a 3 per cent basis into the "three per cent consolidated annuities", the original Consols. These remained above par until 1755, and during this peaceful interval touch the highest price in the whole history of Consols down to the eighties of the nineteenth century`. . .` the last of the annuities due to the Bank [were brought] into line with Consols at 3 per cent as from Christmas 1757.' (J. H. Clapham, *The Bank of England*, i.97–8.)

[30] It is not clear to which acts Smith refers. 4 William and Mary, c. 3 (1692) aimed at raising £1,000,000 and offered annuitants *either* 10 per cent until 1700, then an increasing share of a fixed total sum as annuitants died *or*, if the entire £1,000,000 was not raised by May 1693, an annuity of 14 per cent. As only £881,494 was contributed, attempts were made to raise more by 5 William and Mary, c. 5 (1693) and 5 and 6 William and Mary, c. 20 (1694).

[31] 6 and 7 William and Mary, c. 5 (1694) and 7 and 8 William III, c. 2 (1695).

[32] Cf. LJ (B) 322, ed. Cannan 249: 'In the reigns of King William, Q. Ann, and in the begining of that of K. George the 1st, the funds rose and fell according to the credit of the government, as there was still some risk of a revolution.'

the annuities for thirty-two years were induced to accept in lieu of them South-sea stock to the amount of eleven and a half years purchase of the annuities, together with an additional quantity of stock equal to the arrears which happened then to be due upon them.[33] In 1720, the greater part of the other annuities for terms of years both long and short were subscribed into the same fund.[34] The long annuities at that time amounted to 666,821*l.* 8*s.* 3½*d.* a year.[35] On the 5th of January, 1775, the remainder of them, or what was not subscribed at that time, amounted only to 136,453*l.* 12*s.* 8*d.*

31   During the two wars which begun in 1739 and in 1755, little money was borrowed either upon annuities for terms of years, or upon those for lives. An annuity for ninety-eight or ninety-nine years, however, is worth nearly as much money as a perpetuity, and should, therefore, one might think, be a fund for borrowing nearly as much. But those who, in order to make family settlements, and to provide for remote futurity, buy into the publick stocks, would not care to purchase into one of which the value was continually diminishing; and such people make a very considerable proportion both of the proprietors and purchasers of stock. An annuity for a long term of years, therefore, though its intrinsick value may be very nearly the same with that of a perpetual annuity, will not find nearly the same number of purchasers. The subscribers to a new loan, who mean generally to sell their subscription as soon as possible, [413] prefer greatly a perpetual annuity redeemable by parliament, to an irredeemable annuity for a long term of years of only equal amount. The value of the former may be supposed always the same, or very nearly the same; and it makes, therefore, a more convenient transferable stock than the latter.

32   During the two last mentioned wars, annuities, either for terms of years or for lives, were seldom granted but as premiums to the subscribers to a new loan, over and above the redeemable annuity or interest upon the credit of which the loan was supposed to be made. They were granted, not as the proper fund upon which the money was borrowed; but as an additional encouragement to the lender.

33   Annuities for lives have occasionally been granted in two different ways; either upon separate lives, or upon lots of lives, which in French are called Tontines, from the name of their inventor. When annuities are granted upon separate lives, the death of every individual annuitant disburthens the publick revenue so far as it was affected by his annuity. When annuities are granted upon tontines, the liberation of the publick revenue does not commence till the death of all the annuitants comprehended in one lot, which may sometimes consist of twenty or thirty persons, of whom

---

[33] 5 George I, c. 19 (1718).   [34] 6 George I, c. 4 (1719).
[35] A. Anderson, *Origin of Commerce* (1764), ii.286.

the survivors succeed to the annuities of all those who die before them; the last survivor succeeding to the annuities of the whole lot. Upon the same revenue more money can always be raised by ton-[414]tines than by annuities for separate lives. An annuity, with a right of survivorship, is really worth more than an equal annuity for a separate life, and from the confidence which every man naturally has in his own good fortune, the principle upon which is founded the success of all lotteries, such an annuity generally sells for something more than it is worth.[36] In countries where it is usual for government to raise money by granting annuities, tontines are upon this account generally preferred to annuities for separate lives. The expedient which will raise most money, is almost always preferred to that which is likely to bring about in the speediest manner the liberation of the publick revenue.

34   In France a much greater proportion of the publick debts consists in annuities for lives than in England. According to a memoir presented by the parliament of Bourdeaux to the king in 1764, the whole publick debt of France is estimated at twenty-four hundred millions of livres; of which the capital for which annuities for lives had been granted, is supposed to amount to three hundred millions, the eighth-part of the whole publick debt. The annuities themselves are computed to amount to thirty millions a year, the fourth part of one hundred and twenty millions, the supposed interest of that whole debt. These estimations, I know very well, are not exact, but having been presented by so very respectable a body as approximations to the truth, they may, I apprehend, be considered as such. It is not the different degrees of anxiety [415] in the two governments of France and England for the liberation of the publick revenue, which occasions this difference in their respective modes of borrowing. It arises altogether from the different views and interests of the lenders.

35   In England, the seat of government being in the greatest mercantile city in the world, the merchants are generally the people who advance money to government.[37] By advancing it they do not mean to diminish, but, on the contrary, to increase their mercantile capitals; and unless they expected to sell with some profit their share in the subscription for a new loan, they never would subscribe.[38] But if by advancing their money they were to purchase, instead of perpetual annuities, annuities for lives

[36] Above, I.x.b.26, 27.

[37] See above, II.iv.5, where Smith draws a distinction between the mercantile and the monied interest.

[38] Cf. LJ (B) 323–4, ed. Cannan 250: 'there are a great many stockholders who are merchants, and who keep their stocks in the hands of the government that they may be ready to sell out on any sudden demand and take advantage of a good bargain when it casts up'. Smith examines the fluctuations in stock prices, reflecting the expectations of their holders, at 323–4, ed. Cannan 249–51. Stock jobbing as such, including the activities of bulls and bears, is considered at 324–6, ed. Cannan 251–2, where Smith also examines the effects of speculative jobbing on the price of new issues.

only, whether their own or those of other people, they would not always be so likely to sell them with a profit. Annuities upon their own lives they would always sell with loss; because no man will give for an annuity upon the life of another, whose age and state of health are nearly the same with his own, the same price which he would give for one upon his own. An annuity upon the life of a third person, indeed, is, no doubt, of equal value to the buyer and the seller; but its real value begins to diminish from the moment it is granted, and continues to do so more and more as long as it subsists. It can never, therefore, make so convenient a transferable stock as a perpetual annuity, of which the real value may be supposed always the same, or very nearly the same.

36   [416] In France, the seat of government not being in a great mercantile city, merchants do not make so great a proportion of the people who advance money to government. The people concerned in the finances, the farmers general, the receivers of the taxes which are not in farm, the court bankers, &c. make the greater part of those who advance their money in all publick exigencies. Such people are commonly men of mean birth, but of great wealth, and frequently of great pride. They are too proud to marry their equals, and women of quality disdain to marry them. They frequently resolve, therefore, to live bachelors, and having neither any families of their own, nor much regard for those of their relations, whom they are not always very fond of acknowledging, they desire only to live in splendor during their own time, and are not unwilling that their furtune should end with themselves.[39] The number of rich people, besides, who are either averse to marry, or whose condition of life renders it either improper or inconvenient for them to do so, is much greater in France than in England. To such people, who have little or no care for posterity, nothing can be more convenient than to exchange their capital for a revenue, which is to last just as long *e*, and no longer than they wish it to do.

37   The ordinary expence of the greater part of modern governments in time of peace being equal or nearly equal to their ordinary revenue, when war comes they are both unwilling and unable to increase their revenue in proportion [417] to the increase of their expence. They are unwilling, for fear of offending the people, who, by so great and so sudden an increase of taxes, would soon be disgusted with the war; and they are unable, from not well knowing what taxes would be sufficient to produce the revenue wanted. The facility of borrowing delivers them from the embarrassment which this fear and inability would otherwise occasion. By means of borrowing they are enabled, with a very moderate increase

e as *1–2*

[39] Smith comments at V.ii.k.73 on the attitude to upstart fortunes and on the 'foolish ostentation' of the tax-farmers.

of taxes, to raise, from year to year, money sufficient for carrying on the war, and by the practice of 'perpetual' funding they are enabled, with the smallest possible increase of taxes, to raise annually the largest possible sum of money. In great empires the people who live in the capital, and in the provinces remote from the scene of action, feel, many of them scarce any inconveniency from the war; but enjoy, at their ease, the amusement of reading in the newspapers the exploits of their own fleets and armies. To them this amusement compensates the small difference between the taxes which they pay on account of the war, and those which they had been accustomed to pay in time of peace. They are commonly dissatisfied with the return of peace, which puts an end to their amusement, and to a thousand visionary hopes of conquest and national glory, from a longer continuance of the war.[40]

38   The return of peace, indeed, seldom relieves them from the greater part of the taxes imposed during the war. These are mortgaged for the [418] interest of the debt, contracted in order to carry it on. If, over and above paying the interest of this debt, and defraying the ordinary expence of government, the old revenue, together with the new taxes, produce some surplus revenue, it may perhaps be converted into a sinking fund for paying off the debt. But, in the first place, this sinking fund, even supposing it should be applied to no other purpose, is generally altogether inadequate for paying, in the course of any period during which it can reasonably be expected that peace should continue, the whole debt contracted during the war; and, in the second place, this fund is almost always applied to other purposes.

39   The new taxes were imposed for the sole purpose of paying the interest of the money borrowed upon them. If they produce more, it is generally something which was neither intended nor expected, and is therefore seldom very considerable. Sinking funds have generally arisen, not so much from any surplus of the taxes which was over and above what was necessary for paying the interest or annuity originally charged upon them, as from a subsequent reduction of that interest. That of Holland in 1655, and that of the ecclesiastical state in 1685, were both formed in this manner.[41] Hence the usual insufficiency of such funds.

40   During the most profound peace, various events occur which require an extraordinary expence, and government finds it always more convenient to defray this expence by misapplying [419] the sinking fund than by imposing a new tax. Every new tax is immediately felt more or less by the people. It occasions always some murmur, and meets with

---

1-1 perpetually 3–4, ⟨corrected 4e–6⟩

[40] The American war would appear to have been an exception in that it touched directly on the economic interest of the mercantile classes. See above, IV.vii.c.43.

[41] A. Anderson, *Origin of Commerce* (1764), ii.273.

some opposition. The more taxes may have been multiplied, the higher they may have been raised upon every different subject of taxation; the more loudly the people complain of every new tax, the more difficult it becomes too either to find out new subjects of taxation, or to raise much higher the taxes already imposed upon the old. A momentary suspension of the payment of debt is not immediately felt by the people, and occasions neither murmur nor complaint. To borrow of the sinking fund is always an obvious and easy expedient for getting out of the present difficulty. The more the publick debts may have been accumulated, the more necessary it may have become to study to reduce them, the more dangerous, the more ruinous it may be to misapply any part of the sinking fund; the less likely is the publick debt to be reduced to any considerable degree, the more likely, the more certainly is the sinking fund to be misapplied towards defraying all the extraordinary expences which occur in time of peace. When a nation is already over burdened with taxes, nothing but the necessities of a new war, nothing but either the animosity of national vengeance, or the anxiety for national security, can induce the people to submit, with tolerable patience, to a new tax. Hence the usual misapplication of the sinking fund.

41   [420] In Great Britain, from the time that we had first recourse to the ruinous expedient of perpetual funding, the reduction of the publick debt in time of peace, has never borne any proportion to its accumulation in time of war. It was in the war which began in 1688, and was concluded by the treaty of Ryswick in 1697, that the foundation of the present enormous debt of Great Britain was first laid.

42   On the 31st of December, 1697, the publick debts of Great Britain, funded and unfunded, amounted to 21,515,742*l.* 13*s.* 8½*d.*[42] A great part of those debts had been contracted upon short anticipations, and some part upon annuities for lives; so that before the 31st of December, 1701, in less than four years, there had partly been paid off, and partly reverted to the publick, the sum of 5,121,041*l.* 12*s.* 0¾*d.*; a greater reduction of the publick debt than has ever since been brought about in so short a period of time. The remaining debt, therefore, amounted only to 16,394,701*l.* 1*s.* 7¼*d.*

43   In the war which began in 1702, and which was concluded by the treaty of Utrecht,[43] the publick debts were still more accumulated. On the 31st of December, 1714, they amounted to 53,681,076*l.* 5*s.* 6¹⁄₁₂*d.* The subscription into the South Sea fund of the *ᵍ*short and long*ᵍ* annuities increased the capital of the publick debts, so that on the 31st of December,

ᵍ⁻ᵍ long and short *1*

---

[42] The information in this and the two subsequent paragraphs is from James Postlethwayt, *History of the Public Revenue,* 42, 145, 147, 224, 300.

[43] In LJ (A) v.141 the peace of Utrecht is mentioned as one of 'many foolish peaces'.

1722, it amounted to 55,282,978*l*. 1*s*. 3$\frac{5}{6}$*d*. The reduction of the debt began in 1723, and went on so slowly that, on the 31st of December, 1739, [421] during seventeen years of profound peace, the whole sum paid off was no more than 8,328,354*l*. 17*s*. 11$\frac{1}{12}$*d*. the capital of the publick debt at that time amounting to 46,954,623*l*. 3*s*. 4$\frac{7}{12}$*d*.

44   The Spanish war, which began in 1739, and the French war which soon followed it, occasioned a further increase of the debt, which, on the 31st of December, 1748, after the war had been concluded by the treaty of Aix la Chapelle, amounted to 78,293,313*l*. 1*s*. 10$\frac{3}{4}$*d*. The most profound peace of seventeen years continuance had taken no more than 8,328,354*l*. 17*s*. 11$\frac{3}{12}$*d*. from it. A war of less than nine years continuance added 31,338,689*l*. 18*s*. 6$\frac{1}{2}$*d*. to it*.

45   During the administration of Mr. Pelham,[44] the interest of the publick debt was reduced, or at least measures were taken for reducing it, from four to three per cent.;[45] the sinking fund was increased, and some part of the publick debt was paid off. In 1755, before the breaking out of the late war, the funded debt of Great Britain amounted to 72,289,673*l*. On the 5th of January, 1763, at the conclusion of the peace, the funded debt amounted to 122,603,336*l*. 8*s*. 2$\frac{1}{4}$*d*. The unfunded debt has been stated at 13,927,589*l*. 2*s*. 2*d*. But the expence occasioned by the war did not end with the conclusion of the peace; so that though, on the 5th of January, 1764, the funded debt was increased (partly by a new loan, and partly by funding a part of the unfunded debt) to 129,586,789*l*. [422] 10*s*. 1$\frac{3}{4}$*d*. there still remained (according to the very well informed author of the Considerations on the trade and finances of Great Britain) an unfunded debt which was brought to account in that and the following year, of 9,975,017*l*. 12*s*. 2$\frac{15}{44}$*d*.[46] In 1764, therefore, the publick debt of Great Britain, funded and unfunded together, amounted, according to this author, to ^{h}139,516,807*l*.^{h} 2*s*. 4*d*.[47] The annuities for lives too, which had been granted as premiums to the subscribers to the new loans in 1757, estimated at fourteen years purchase, were valued at 472,500*l*.;

---

* See James Postlethwaite's history of the publick revenue.

$^{h-h}$ 139,561,807 *l*. *1*

[44] In LJ (A) vi.168 Pelham is mentioned as having raised 10 millions in one year, and Pitt is said to have raised 23 millions with 'greater ease than it had ever been done before'. The same point is made in LJ (B) 265, ed. Cannan 207, where it is stated that 'A late Minister of State levied in one year 23 millions with greater ease than Lord Godolphin could levy 6 in Q. Ann's time.'

[45] Above, V.iii.27.

[46] *Considerations on the Trade and Finances of the Kingdom* (London, 1766), 22, attributed to Thomas Whately and often ascribed to George Grenville. Most of the information in this paragraph is from the book.

[47] Not stated in *Considerations on the Trade and Finances of the Kingdom* but derived from it by adding together £129,586,789 10*s*. 1$\frac{3}{4}$*d*. and £9,975,017 12*s*. 2$\frac{15}{44}$*d*., giving £139,561,807 2*s*. 4*d*. as in Ed. 1.

and the annuities for long terms of years, granted as premiums likewise, in 1761 and 1762, estimated at 27½ years purchase, were valued at 6,826,875*l.* During a peace of about seven years continuance, the prudent and truly patriot administration of Mr. Pelham, was not able to pay off an old debt of six millions. During a war of nearly the same continuance, a new debt of more than seventy-five millions was contracted.

46   On the 5th of January, 1775, the funded debt of Great Britain amounted to 124,996,086*l.* 1*s.* 6¼*d.* The unfunded, exclusive of a large civil list debt, to 4,150,236*l.* 3*s.* 11⅞*d.* Both together, to 129,146,322*l.* 5*s.* 6*d.* According to this account the whole debt paid off during eleven years profound peace amounted only to 10,415,474*l.* 16*s.* 9⅞*d.* Even this small reduction of debt, however, has not been all made from the savings out of the ordinary revenue of the state. Several extraneous sums, [423] altogether independent of that ordinary revenue, have contributed towards it. 'Amongst' these we may reckon an additional shilling in the pound land tax for three years; the two millions received from the East India company, as indemnification for their territorial acquisitions; and the one hundred and ten thousand pounds received from the bank for the renewal of their charter. To these must be added several other sums which, as they arose out of the late war, ought perhaps to be considered as deductions from the expences of it. The principal are

	l.	*s.*	*d.*
The produce of French prizes	690,449	18	9
Composition for French prisoners[48]	670,000	0	0
What has been received from the sale of the ceded islands[49]	95,500	0	0
Total,	1,455,949	18	9

If we add to this sum the balance of the earl of Chatham's and Mr. Calcraft's accounts, and other army savings of the same kind, together with what has been received from the bank, the East India company, and the additional shilling in the pound land tax; the whole must be a good deal more than five millions. The debt, therefore, which since the peace has been paid out of the savings from the ordinary revenue of the state, has not, one year with another, amounted to half a million a year. The sink-

---

ᶦ⁻ᶦ Among ᴵ

[48] In LJ (B) 346–7, ed. Cannan 271, cartel agreements are cited as evidence of a growing humanity in the treatment of prisoners-of-war. In such treaties, Smith pointed out, 'soldiers and sailors are valued at so much and exchanged at the end of every campaign'. He added that 'In the late war indeed, we refused to enter into any such treaty with France for sailors, and by this wise regulation soon unman'd their navy, as we took a great many more than they.'

[49] The ceded islands are mentioned above, IV.vii.b.31.

ing fund, has, no doubt, been considerably augmented since the peace, by the debt which has been paid [424] off, by the reduction of the redeemable four per cents. to three per cents, and by the annuities for lives which have fallen in, and, if peace ʲwasʲ to continue, a million, perhaps, might now be annually spared out of it towards the discharge of the debt. Another million, accordingly, was paid in the course of last year; but, at the same time, a large civil list debt was left unpaid, and we are now involved in a new war which, in its progress, may prove as expensive as any of our former wars*. The new debt which will probably be contracted before the end of the next campaign, may perhaps be nearly equal to all the old debt which has been paid off from the savings out of the ordinary revenue of the state. It would be altogether chimerical, therefore, to expect that the publick debt should ever be completely discharged by any savings which are likely to be made from that ordinary revenue as it stands at present.

47   The publick funds of the different indebted nations of Europe, particularly those of England, have by one author been represented as the accumulation of a great capital superadded to the other capital of the country, by means of which its trade is extended, its manufactures multiplied, and its lands cultivated and im-[425]proved much beyond what they could have been by means of that other capital only[50]. He does not consider that the capital which the first creditors of the publick advanced to government, was, from the moment in which they advanced it, a certain portion of the annual produce turned away from serving in the function of a capital, to serve in that of a revenue; from maintaining productive labourers to maintain unproductive ones, and to be spent and wasted, generally in the course of the year, without even the hope of any future reproduction. In return for the capital which they advanced they obtained, indeed, an annuity in the publick funds in most cases of more than equal value. This annuity, no doubt, replaced to them their capital, and enabled them to carry on their trade and business to the same or perhaps to a greater extent than before; that is, they were enabled either to borrow of other people a new capital upon the credit of this annuity, or by selling it to get from other people a new capital of their own, equal or superior to that which they had advanced to government. This new capital, however, which they in this manner either bought or borrowed of other people, must have existed in the country before, and must have been

ᵏ* It has proved more expensive than any of our former wars; and has involved us in an additional debt of more than one hundred millions. During a profound peace of eleven years, little more than ten millions of debt was paid; during a war of seven years, more than one hundred millions was contracted.ᵏ

ʲ⁻ʲ were 4–6   ᵏ⁻ᵏ 3–6

⁵⁰ Cf. J. F. Melon, *Essai politique sur le Commerce* (1734), trans. D. Bindon (Dublin 1738), 330.

employed, as all capitals are, in maintaining productive labour. When it came into the hands of those who had advanced their money to government, though it was in some respects a new capital to them, it was not so to the country; but was only a capital withdrawn from certain [426] employments in order to be turned towards others. Though it replaced to them what they had advanced to government, it did not replace it to the country. Had they not advanced this capital to government, there would have been in the country two capitals, two portions of the annual produce, instead of one, employed in maintaining productive labour.

48 When for defraying the expence of government a revenue is raised within the year from the produce of free or unmortgaged taxes, a certain portion of the revenue of private people is only turned away from maintaining one species of unproductive labour, towards maintaining another. Some part of what they pay in those taxes might no doubt have been accumulated into capital, and consequently employed in maintaining productive labour; but the greater part would probably have been spent and consequently employed in maintaining unproductive labour. The publick expence, however, when defrayed in this manner, no doubt hinders more or less the further accumulation of new capital; but it does not necessarily occasion the destruction of any actually existing capital.

49 When the publick expence is defrayed by funding, it is defrayed by the annual destruction of some capital which had before existed in the country; by the perversion of some portion of the annual produce which had before been destined for the maintenance of productive labour, towards that of unproductive labour. As in this case, however, the taxes are lighter than [427] they would have been, had a revenue sufficient for defraying the same expence been raised within the year; the private revenue of individuals is necessarily less burdened, and consequently their ability to save and accumulate some part of that revenue into capital is a good deal less impaired. If the method of funding ¹destroys¹ more old capital, it at the same time hinders less the accumulation or acquisition of new capital, than that of defraying the publick expence by a revenue raised within the year. Under the system of funding, the frugality and industry of private people can more easily repair the breaches which the waste and extravagance of government may occasionally make in the general capital of the society.⁵¹

50 It is only during the continuance of war, however, that the system of funding has this advantage over the other system. Were the expence of war to be defrayed always by a revenue raised within the year, the taxes

¹⁻¹ destroy 4-6

---

⁵¹ It is also remarked at II.iii.31 that the frugality of private people is generally capable of overcoming the extravagance of government. See also below, § 57.

from which that extraordinary revenue was drawn would last no longer
than the war. The ability of private people to accumulate, though less
during the war, would have been greater during the peace than under
the system of funding. War would not necessarily have occasioned the
destruction of any old capitals, and peace would have occasioned the
accumulation of many more new. Wars would in general be more speedily
concluded, and less wantonly undertaken. The people feeling, during the
continuance of *ᵐthe*ᵐ war, the complete burden of it, would soon grow
weary of it, [428] and government, in order to humour them, would not
be under the necessity of carrying it on longer than it was necessary to
do so. The foresight of the heavy and unavoidable burdens of war would
hinder the people from wantonly calling for it when there was no real or
solid interest to fight for. The seasons during which the ability of private
people to accumulate was somewhat impaired, would occur more rarely,
and be of shorter continuance. Those on the contrary, during which that
ability was in the highest vigour, would be of much longer duration than
they can well be under the system of funding.

51   When funding, besides, has made a certain progress, the multiplication
of taxes which it brings along with it sometimes impairs as much the
ability of private people to accumulate even in time of peace, as the
other system would in time of war. The peace revenue of Great Britain
amounts at present to more than ten millions a year. If free and unmortgaged, it might be sufficient, with proper management and without
contracting a shilling of new debt, to carry on the most vigorous war. The
private revenue of the inhabitants of Great Britain is at present as much
encumbered in time of peace, their ability to accumulate is as much impaired as it would have been in the time of the most expensive war, had
the pernicious system of funding never been adopted.

52   In the payment of the interest of the publick debt, it has been said, it
is the right hand which pays the left.[52] The money does not go out of

ᵐ⁻ᵐ *om.* 6

[52] In LJ (B) 269, ed. Cannan 210, Smith also refers to the apology for the public debt
offered by some (unspecified) authors: 'Say they, tho' we owe at present above 100 millions, we owe it to ourselves, or at least very little of it to forreigners. It is just the right
hand owing the left, and on the whole can be little or no disadvantage.' Smith rejected
this doctrine on the ground that the taxes paid by the industrious classes, such as the
merchants, in effect reduced their stocks: 'it is to be considered that the interest of this
100 millions is paid by industrious people, and given to support idle people who are employed in gathering it. Thus industry is taxed to support idleness. If the debt had not
been contracted, by prudence and œconomy the nation would have been much richer
than at present.' Smith went on to point out that the contemporary clamour against the
debt caused Sir Robert Walpole to try and show that 'the public debt was no inconvenience, tho' it is to be supposed that a man of his abilities saw the contrary himself'
(LJ (B) 270, ed. Cannan 210–11). In his essay 'Of Public Credit' Hume described the
doctrine as being based on 'loose reasonings and specious comparisons' (*Essays Moral,
Political and Literary*, ed. Green and Grose, i.366). Melon stated: "The Debts of a State
are Debts due from the right hand to the left'. *Essai*, trans. Bindon, 329.

[429] the country. It is only a part of the revenue of one set of the inhabitants which is transferred to another; and the nation is not a farthing the poorer. This apology is founded altogether in the sophistry of the mercantile system, and after the long examination which I have already bestowed upon that system, it may perhaps be unnecessary to say any thing further about it. It supposes, besides, that the whole publick debt is owing to the inhabitants of the country, which happens not to be true; the Dutch, as well as several other foreign nations, having a very considerable share in our publick funds.[53] But though the whole debt were owing to the inhabitants of the country, it would not upon that account be less pernicious.

53   Land and capital stock are the two original sources of all revenue both private and publick. Capital stock pays the wages of productive labour, whether employed in agriculture, manufactures, or commerce. The management of those two original sources of revenue belongs to two different setts of people; the proprietors of land, and the owners or employers of capital stock.

54   The proprietor of land is interested for the sake of his own revenue to keep his estate in as good condition as he can, by building and repairing his tenants houses, by making and maintaining the necessary drains and enclosures, and all those other expensive improvements which it properly belongs to the landlord to make and maintain.[54] But by different land-taxes the re-[430]venue of the landlord may be so much diminished; and by different duties upon the necessaries and conveniencies of life, that diminished revenue may be rendered of so little real value, that he may find himself altogether unable to make or maintain those expensive improvements. When the landlord, however, ceases to do his part, it is altogether impossible that the tenant should continue to do his. As the distress of the landlord increases, the agriculture of the country must necessarily decline.

55   When, by different taxes upon the necessaries and conveniencies of life, the owners and employers of capital stock find, that whatever revenue they derive from it, will not, in a particular country, purchase the same quantity of those necessaries and conveniencies, which an equal revenue would in almost any other; they will be disposed to remove to some other.[55] And when, in order to raise those taxes, all or the greater part of merchants and manufacturers; that is, all or the greater part of the employers of great capitals, come to be continually exposed to the mortifying and vexatious visits of the tax-gatherers;[56] this disposition to remove will soon be changed into an actual removal. The industry of the country will

---

[53] Though Smith indicated earlier that there was a tendency to exaggerate the amount held by the Dutch. See above, I.ix.10.
    [54] Cf. I.xi.a.2.   [55] See above, V.ii.f.6.   [56] Above, V.ii.b.6, V.ii.k.65 and V.iii.74.

necessarily fall with the removal of the capital which supported it, and the ruin of trade and manufactures will follow the declension of agriculture.

56   To transfer from the owners of those two great sources of revenue, land and capital stock, from the persons immediately interested in the good [431] condition of every particular portion of land, and in the good management of every particular portion of capital stock, to another set of persons (the creditors of the publick, who have no such particular interest) the greater part of the revenue arising from either, must, in the long-run, occasion both the neglect of land, and the waste or removal of capital stock. A creditor of the publick has no doubt a general interest in the prosperity of the agriculture, manufactures, and commerce of the country; and consequently in the good condition of its lands, and in the good management of its capital stock. Should there be any general failure or declension in any of these things, the produce of the different taxes might no longer be sufficient to pay him the annuity or interest which is due to him. But a creditor of the publick, considered merely as such, has no interest in the good condition of any particular portion of land, or in the good management of any particular portion of capital stock. As a creditor of the publick he has no knowledge of any such particular portion. He has no inspection of it. He can have no care about it. Its ruin may in ⁿsomeⁿ cases be unknown to him, and cannot directly affect him.

57   The practice of funding has gradually enfeebled every state which has adopted it. The Italian republicks seem to have begun it. Genoa and Venice, the only two remaining which can pretend to an independent existence, have both been enfeebled by it. Spain seems to have learned the practice from the Italian republicks, [432] and (its taxes being probably less judicious than theirs) it has, in proportion to its natural strength, been still more enfeebled. The debts of Spain are of very old standing. It was deeply in debt before the end of the sixteenth century, about a hundred years before England owed a shilling. France, notwithstanding all its natural resources, languishes under an oppressive load of the same kind. The republick of the United Provinces is as much enfeebled by its debts as either Genoa or Venice. Is it likely that in Great Britain alone a practice, which has brought either weakness or desolation into every other country, should prove altogether innocent?

58   The system of taxation established in those different countries, it may be said, is inferior to that of England. I believe it is so. But it ought to be remembered, that when the wisest government has exhausted all the proper subjects of taxation, it must, in cases of urgent necessity, have recourse to improper ones.[57] The wise republick of Holland has upon

ⁿ⁻ⁿ most *I*

---

[57] Above, V.ii.k.80.

some occasions been obliged to have recourse to taxes as inconvenient as the greater part of those of Spain. Another war begun before any considerable liberation of the publick revenue had been brought about, and growing in its progress as expensive as the last war, may, from irresistible necessity, render the British system of taxation as oppressive as that of Holland, or even as that of Spain. To the honour of our present system of taxation, indeed, it has hitherto given so little embarrassment to industry, that, during the [433] course even of the most expensive wars, the frugality and good conduct of individuals °seem° to have been able, by saving and accumulation, to repair all the breaches which the waste and extravagance of government had made in the general capital of the society.[58] At the conclusion of the late war, the most expensive that Great Britain ever waged, her agriculture was as flourishing, her manufacturers as numerous and as fully employed, and her commerce as extensive, as they had ever been before. The capital, therefore, which supported all those different branches of industry, must have been equal to what it had ever been before. Since the peace, agriculture has been still further improved, the rents of houses have risen in every town and village of the country, a proof of the increasing wealth and revenue of the people; and the annual amount of the greater part of the old taxes, of the principal branches of the excise and customs in particular, has been continually increasing, an equally clear proof of an increasing consumption, and consequently of an increasing produce, which could alone support that consumption. Great Britain seems to support with ease, a burden which, half a century ago, nobody believed her capable of supporting. Let us not, however, upon this account rashly conclude that she is capable of supporting any burden; nor even be too confident that she could support, without great distress, a burden a little greater than what has already been laid upon her.

59   [434] When national debts have once been accumulated to a certain degree, there is scarce, I believe, a single instance of their having been fairly and compleatly paid. The liberation of the publick revenue, if it has ever been brought about at all, has always been brought about by a bankruptcy; sometimes by an avowed one, but always by a real one, though frequently by a pretended payment.

60   The raising of the denomination of the coin has been the most usual expedient by which a real publick bankruptcy has been disguised under the appearance of a pretended payment.[59] If a sixpence, for example, should either by act of parliament or royal proclamation be raised to the denomination of a shilling, and twenty sixpences to that of a pound sterling; the

---

°–° seems *1–2*

[58] See for example, II.iii.31.   [59] See above, I.iv.10.

person who under the old denomination had borrowed twenty shillings, or near four ounces of silver, would, under the new, pay with twenty six-pences, or with something less than two ounces. A national debt of about a hundred and twenty-eight millions, nearly the capital of the funded and unfunded debt of Great Britain, might in this manner be paid with about sixty-four millions of our present money. It would indeed be a pretended payment only, and the creditors of the publick would really be defrauded of ten shillings in the pound of what was due to them. The calamity too would extend much further than to the creditors of the publick, and those of every private person would suffer a proportionable loss; and this without any advantage, but [435] in most cases with a great additional loss, to the creditors of the publick. If the creditors of the publick indeed were gener-ally much in debt to other people, they might in some measure compensate their loss by paying their creditors in the same coin in which the publick had paid them. But in most countries the creditors of the publick are, the greater part of them, wealthy people, who stand more in the relation of creditors than in that of debtors towards the rest of their fellow-citizens. A pretended payment of this kind, therefore, instead of alleviating, aggra-vates in most cases the loss of the creditors of the publick; and without any advantage to the publick, extends the calamity to a great number of other innocent people. It occasions a general and most pernicious subver-sion of the fortunes of private people; enriching in most cases the idle and profuse debtor at the expence of the industrious and frugal creditor, and transporting a great part of the national capital from the hands which were likely to increase and improve it, to those which are likely to dissipate and destroy it. When it becomes necessary for a state to declare itself bankrupt, in the same manner as when it becomes necessary for an individual to do so, a fair, open, and avowed bankruptcy is always the measure which is both least dishonourable to the debtor, and least hurtful to the creditor. The honour of a state is surely very poorly provided for, when, in order to cover the disgrace of a real bankruptcy, it has recourse to a juggling trick of this kind, so easily seen [436] through, and at the same time so extremely pernicious.

61   Almost all states, however, antient as well as modern, when reduced to this necessity, have, upon some occasions, played this very juggling trick. The Romans, at the end of the first Punic war, reduced the As, the coin or denomination by which they computed the value of all their other coins, from containing twelve ounces of copper to contain only two ounces; that is, they raised two ounces of copper to a denomination which had always before expressed the value of twelve ounces. The republick was, in this manner, enabled to pay the great debts which it had contracted with the sixth part of what it really owed. So sudden and so great a bankruptcy, we should in the present times be apt to imagine, must have occasioned a

very violent popular clamour. It does not appear to have occasioned any. The law which enacted it was, like all other laws relating to the coin, introduced and carried through the assembly of the people by a tribune, and was probably a very popular law. In Rome, as in all the other antient republicks, the poor people were constantly in debt to the rich and the great, who, in order to secure their votes at the annual elections, used to lend them money at exorbitant interest, which, being never paid, soon accumulated into a sum too great either for the debtor to pay, or for any body else to pay for him. The debtor, for fear of a very severe execution, was obliged, without any further gratuity, to vote [437] for the candidate whom the creditor recommended. In spite of all the laws against bribery and corruption, the bounty of the candidates, together with the occasional distributions of corn, which were ordered by the senate, were the principal funds from which, during the ᵖlatterᵖ times of the Roman republick, the poorer citizens derived their subsistence.⁶⁰ To deliver themselves from this subjection to their creditors, the poorer citizens were continually calling out either for an entire abolition of debts, or for what they called New Tables; that is, for a law which should entitle them to a complete acquittance, upon paying only a certain proportion of their accumulated debts. The law which reduced the coin of all denominations to a sixth part of its former value, as it enabled them to pay their debts with a sixth part of what they really owed, was equivalent to the most advantageous new tables. In order to satisfy the people, the rich and the great were, upon several different occasions, obliged to consent to laws both for abolishing debts, and for introducing new tables; and they probably were induced to consent to this law, partly for the same reason, and partly that, by liberating the publick revenue, they might restore vigour to that government of which they themselves had the principal direction. An operation of this kind would at once reduce a debt of a hundred and twenty-eight millions to twenty-one millions three hundred and thirty-three thousand three hundred and thirty-three pounds six shillings and eight-[438]pence. In the course of the second Punic war the As was still further reduced, first, from two ounces of copper to one ounce; and afterwards from one ounce to half an ounce; that is, to the twenty-fourth part of its original value.⁶¹ By combining the three Roman operations into one, a debt of a hundred and twenty-eight millions of our present money, might in this manner be reduced all at once to a debt of five millions three hundred and thirty-three thousand

ᵖ⁻ᵖ later *I-2*

⁶⁰ Smith comments at I.xi.b.12 on the adverse effect on Roman agriculture of the free distribution of corn. See also III.ii.21.
⁶¹ Pliny, *Natural History*, XXXIII.xiii, translated by H. Rackham in Loeb Classical Library (1952), ix.35-9. See above I.iv.10. These points are also made by Montesquieu, *Espirt*, XXII.xi, and see also xii.

three hundred and thirty-three pounds six shillings and eight-pence. Even the enormous debt of Great Britain might in this manner soon be paid.

62   By means of such expedients the coin of, I believe, all nations has been gradually reduced more and more below its original value, and the same nominal sum has been gradually brought to contain a smaller and a smaller quantity of silver.

63   Nations have sometimes, for the same purpose, adulterated the standard of their coin; that is, have mixed a greater quantity of alloy in it. If in the pound weight of our silver coin, for example, instead of eighteen penny weight, according to the present standard, there was mixed eight ounces of alloy; a pound sterling, or twenty shillings of such coin, would be worth little more than six shillings and eight-pence of our present money. The quantity of silver contained in six shillings and eight-pence of our present money, would thus be raised very nearly to the denomination of a pound sterling. The adulteration of the standard has exactly the same effect with what the French call an augmentation, [439] or a direct raising of the denomination of the coin.

64   An augmentation, or a direct raising of the denomination of the coin, always is, and from its nature must be, an open and avowed operation. By means of it pieces of a smaller weight and bulk are called by the same name which had before been given to pieces of a greater weight and bulk. The adulteration of the standard, on the contrary, has generally been a concealed operation. By means of it pieces were issued from the mint of the same denominations, and, as nearly as could be contrived, of the same weight, bulk, and appearance, with pieces which had been current before of much greater value. When king John of France*, in order to pay his debts, adulterated his coin, all the officers of his mint were sworn to secrecy. Both operations are unjust. But a simple augmentation is an injustice of open violence; whereas an adulteration is an injustice of treacherous fraud. This latter operation, therefore, as soon as it has been discovered, and it could never be concealed very long, has always excited much greater indignation than the former. The coin after any considerable augmentation has very seldom been brought back to its former weight; but after the greatest adulterations it has almost always been brought back to its former fineness. It has scarce ever happened that the fury and indignation of the people could otherwise be appeased.

65   [440] In the end of the reign of Henry VIII. and in the beginning of that of Edward VI. the English coin was not only raised in its denomination, but adulterated in its standard. The like frauds were practised in Scotland during the minority of James VI. They have occasionally been practised in most other countries.

* See Du Cange Glossary, voce Moneta; the Benedictine edition. [C. Du Fresne, Sieur du Cange, *Glossarium* (Paris, 1842), iv.493. See also Melon, *Essai*, trans. Bindon, 221–2.]

66   That the publick revenue of Great Britain can ᵠneverᵠ be compleatly liberated, or even that any considerable progress can ever be made towards that liberation, while the surplus of that revenue, or what is over and above defraying the annual expence of the peace establishment, is so very small, it seems altogether in vain to expect. That liberation, it is evident, can never be brought about without either some very considerable augmentation of the publick revenue, or some equally considerable reduction of the publick expence.⁶²

67   A more equal land-tax, a more equal tax upon the rent of houses, and such alterations in the present system of customs and excise as those which have been mentioned in the foregoing chapter, might, perhaps, without increasing the burden of the greater part of the people, but only distributing the weight of it more equally upon the whole, produce a considerable augmentation of revenue. The most sanguine projector, however, could scarce flatter himself that any augmentation of this kind would be such as could give any reasonable hopes, either of liberating the publick revenue altogether, or even of making such progress towards that liberation in time of peace, as [441] either to prevent or to compensate the further accumulation of the publick debt in the next war.

68   By extending the British system of taxation to all the different provinces of the empire inhabited by people ʳof eitherʳ British or European extraction, a much greater augmentation of revenue might be expected. This, however, could scarce, perhaps, be done, consistently with the principles of the British constitution, without admitting into the British parliament, or if you will into the states-general of the British Empire, a fair and equal representation of all those different provinces, that of each province bearing the same proportion to the produce of its taxes, as the representation of Great Britain might bear to the produce of the taxes levied upon Great Britain.⁶³ The private interest of many powerful individuals, the

---

ᵠ⁻ᵠ ever *I*   ʳ⁻ʳ either of *I*

⁶² In Letter 203 addressed to William Eden, dated 3 January 1780, Smith wrote 'It does not occur to me that much can be added to what you have already said. The difficulty of either inventing new taxes or increasing the old, is, I apprehend, the principal cause of our embarassment.' Smith suggested three possibilities, apart from a 'strict attention to Oeconomy' first, a repeal of the bounties on exportation which in some years had reached £600,000; second, a repeal of the prohibitions on importation and the substitution of 'moderate and reasonable duties in the room of them'; third, repeal of the prohibition of exporting wool and the substitution of 'a pretty high duty in the room of it'. The reference is to William Eden's *Four Letters to the Earl of Carlisle* (London, 1779).

⁶³ See above, IV.vii.c.75. Smith considered that this principle would eventually lead to a transfer of the seat of empire, IV.vii.c.79. LJ (A) v.134–5 refers to the connection between taxation and representation as a doctrine derived from Locke, and added that 'It is in Britain alone that any consent of the people is required and God knows it is but a very figurative metaphoricall consent which is given here'. Cf. LJ (B) 94, ed. Cannan 69 and WN IV.vii.b.51.

confirmed prejudices of great bodies of people seem, indeed, at present, to oppose to so great a change such obstacles as it may be very difficult, perhaps altogether impossible, to surmount.[64] Without, however, pretending to determine whether such a union be practicable or impracticable, it may not, perhaps, be improper, in a speculative work of this kind, to consider how far the British system of taxation might be applicable to all the different provinces of the empire; what revenue might be expected from it if so applied, and in what manner a general union of this kind might be likely to affect the happiness and prosperity of the different provinces comprehended within it. Such a specula-[442]tion can at worst be regarded but as a new Utopia, less amusing certainly, but not more useless and chimerical than the old one.

69 The land-tax, the stamp duties, and the different duties of customs and excise, constitute the four principal branches of the British taxes.

70 Ireland is certainly as able, and our American and West Indian plantations more able to pay a land-tax than Great Britain.[65] Where the landlord is subject neither to tithe nor poors rate, he must certainly be more able to pay such a tax, than where he is subject to both those other burdens. The tithe, where there is no modus, and where it is levied in kind, diminishes more what would otherwise be the rent of the landlord, than a land-tax which really amounted to five shillings in the pound. Such a tithe will be found in most cases to amount to more than a fourth part of the real rent of the land, or of what remains after replacing compleatly the capital of the farmer, together with his reasonable profit. If all moduses and all impropriations were taken away, the compleat church tithe of Great Britain and Ireland could not well be estimated at less than six or seven millions. If there was no tithe either in Great Britain or Ireland, the landlords could afford to pay six or seven millions additional land-tax, without being more burdened than a very great part of them are at present. America pays no tithe, and could therefore very well afford to pay a land-tax. The lands in America and the West Indies, indeed, are in general not tenanted ˢnorˢ leased out [443] to farmers. They could not therefore be assessed according to any rent-roll. But neither were the lands of Great Britain, in the 4th of William and Mary, assessed according to any rent-roll, but according to a very loose and inaccurate estimation.[66] The lands in America might be assessed either in the same manner, or according to an equitable valuation in consequence of an accurate survey, like that which was lately made in the Milanese, and in the dominions of Austria, Prussia, and Sardinia.[67]

ˢ⁻ˢ or *I*

[64] Above, IV.vii.c.77–9.
[66] See above, V.ii.c.2.

[65] This tax is described above, V.ii.c.2.
[67] Cf. V.ii.c.26.

71   Stamp-duties, it is evident, might be levied without any variation in all countries where the forms of law process, and the deeds by which property both real and personal is transferred, are the same or nearly the same.

72   The extension of the custom-house laws of Great Britain to Ireland and the plantations, provided it was accompanied, as in justice it ought to be, with an extension of the freedom of trade, would be in the highest degree advantageous to both.[68] All the invidious restraints which at present oppress the trade of Ireland, the distinction between the enumerated and non-enumerated commodities of America, would be entirely at an end.[69] The countries north of Cape Finisterre would be as open to every part of the produce of America, as those south of that Cape are to some parts of that produce at present. The trade between all the different parts of the British empire would, in consequence of this uniformity in the ʿcustom-house lawsʿ, be as free as the coasting trade of Great Britain is at present. The British [444] empire would thus afford within itself an immense internal market for every part of the produce of all its different provinces. So great an extension of market would soon compensate both to Ireland and the plantations, all that they could suffer from the increase of the duties of customs.

73   The excise is the only part of the British system of taxation, which would require to be varied in any respect according as it was applied to the different provinces of the empire. It might be applied to Ireland without any variation; the produce and consumption of that kingdom being exactly of the same nature with those of Great Britain. In its application to America and the West Indies, of which the produce and consumption are so very

---

ʿ⁻ʿ customhouse *1*

[68] See below, § 89. Smith expressed agreement with regard to the beneficial consequences of free trade with Ireland in Letter 201 addressed to Henry Dundas, dated 1 November 1779: 'I cannot believe that the manufactures of G.B. can, for a century to come, suffer much from the rivalship of those of Ireland ... Ireland has neither the Skill, nor the Stock which could enable her to rival England ... Ireland has neither coal nor Wood.' Smith went on to point out that it would be perfectly reasonable to grant Ireland freedom to export to the most favourable markets, and to relieve her from the 'unjust and unreasonable' restraints under which her glass and woollen industries laboured. Smith supported free trade between Ireland and Britain and concluded that 'Nothing, in my opinion, would be more highly advantageous to both countries than this mutual freedom of trade. It would help to break down that absurd monopoly which we have most absurdly established against ourselves in favour of almost all the different classes of our manufacturers.' Smith expressed similar arguments in Letter 202 addressed to Carlisle, dated 8 November 1779, wherein he also commented that in addition to the lack of raw materials, Ireland also 'wants order, police, and a regular administration of justice both to protect and restrain the inferior ranks of the people, articles more essential to the progress of Industry than both coal and wood put together, and which Ireland must continue to want as long as it continues to be divided between two hostile nations, the oppressors and the oppressed, the protestants and the Papists.'

[69] Above, IV.vii.b.25.

different from those of Great Britain, some modification might be necessary, in the same manner as in its application to the cyder and beer counties of England.

74   A fermented liquor, for example, which is called beer, but which, as it is made of melasses, bears very little resemblance to our beer, makes a considerable part of the common drink of the people in America. This liquor, as it can be kept only for a few days, cannot, like our beer, be prepared and stored up for sale in great breweries; but every private family must brew it for their own use, in the same manner as they cook their victuals. But to subject every private family to the odious visits and examination of the tax-gatherers,[70] in the same manner as we subject the keepers of alehouses and the brewers for publick sale, would be altogether inconsistent [445] with liberty. If for the sake of equality it was thought necessary to lay a tax upon this liquor,[71] it might be taxed by taxing the material of which it is made, either at the place of manufacture, or, if the circumstances of the trade rendered such an excise improper, by laying a duty upon its importation into the colony in which it was to be consumed. Besides the duty of one penny a gallon imposed by the British parliament upon the importation of melasses into America; there is a provincial tax of this kind upon their importation into Massachusets Bay, in ships belonging to any other colony, of eight-pence the hogshead; and another upon their importation, from the northern colonies, into South Carolina, of five-pence the gallon. Or if neither of these methods was found convenient, each family might compound for its consumption of this liquor, either according to the number of persons of which it consisted, in the same manner as private families compound for the malt-tax in England; or according to the different ages and sexes of those persons, in the same manner as several different taxes are levied in Holland; or nearly as Sir Matthew Decker proposes that all taxes upon consumable commodities should be levied in England. This mode of taxation, it has already been observed, when applied to objects of a speedy consumption, is not a very convenient one. It might be adopted, however, in cases where no better could be done.[72]

75   Sugar, rum, and tobacco, are commodities which are no where necessaries of life,[73] which are [446] become objects of almost universal consumption, and which are therefore extremely proper subjects of taxation. If a union with the colonies ᵘwasᵘ to take place, those commodities might be taxed either before they go out of the hands of the manufacturer or grower; or if this mode of taxation did not suit the circumstances of those persons,

ᵘ-ᵘ were *4-6*

[70] See above, V.ii.b.6, V.ii.k.65 and V.iii.55.   [71] Above, V.ii.k.45,55.
[72] See above, V.ii.k.18, where Decker's proposals are considered.
[73] Smith attempts to define the 'necessaries of life' at V.ii.k.3.

they might be deposited in publick warehouses both at the place of manu-facture, and at all the different ports of the empire to which they might afterwards be transported, to remain there, under the joint custody of the owner and the revenue officer, till such time as they should be delivered out either to the consumer, to the merchant retailer for home-consumption, or to the merchant exporter, the tax not to be advanced till such delivery. When delivered out for exportation, to go duty free; upon proper security being given that they should really be exported out of the empire. These are perhaps the principal commodities with regard to which a union with the colonies might require some considerable change in the present system of British taxation.

76   What might be the amount of the revenue which this system of taxation extended to all the different provinces of the empire might produce, it must, no doubt, be altogether impossible to ascertain with tolerable exact-ness. By means of this system there is annually levied in Great Britain, upon less than eight millions of people, more than ten millions of revenue.[74] Ireland contains more than two millions of people, and [447] according to the accounts laid before the congress, the twelve associated provinces of America contain more than three.[75] Those accounts, however, may have been exaggerated, in order, perhaps, either to encourage their own people, or to intimidate those of this country, and we shall suppose therefore that our North American and West Indian colonies taken together contain no more than three millions; or that the whole British empire, in Europe and America, contains no more than thirteen millions of inhabitants. If upon less than eight millions of inhabitants this system of taxation raises a revenue of more than ten millions sterling; it ought upon thirteen millions of inhabitants to raise a revenue of more than sixteen millions two hundred and fifty thousand pounds sterling. From this revenue, supposing that this system could produce it, must be deducted, the revenue usually raised in Ireland and the plantations for defraying the expence of their respective civil governments. The expence of the civil and military establishment of Ireland, together with the interest of the publick debt, amounts, at a medium of the two years which ended March 1775, to something less than seven hundred and fifty thousand pounds a year.[76] By a very exact account of the revenue of the principal colonies of America and the West Indies, it amounted, before the commencement of the *present* disturbances, to a hundred and forty-one thousand eight hundred pounds. In this account, however, the revenue of Maryland, of North Carolina, [448] and of all our

---

v–v late *1*

[74] The same figures are cited at V.ii.k.78.

[75] See above, IV.iii.c.12. Smith comments on the rapid rate of growth of population in America at I.viii.23.

[76] See above, IV.vii.b.20.

late acquisitions both upon the continent and in the islands, is omitted, which may perhaps make a difference of thirty or forty thousand pounds. For the sake of even numbers therefore, let us suppose that the revenue necessary for supporting the civil government of Ireland, and the plantations, may amount to a million. There would remain consequently a revenue of fifteen millions two hundred and fifty thousand pounds, to be applied towards defraying the general expence of the empire, and towards paying the publick debt. But if from the present revenue of Great Britain a million could in peaceable times be spared towards the payment of that debt, six millions two hundred and fifty thousand pounds could very well be spared from this improved revenue. This great sinking fund too might be augmented every year by the interest of the debt which had been discharged the year before, and might in this manner increase so very rapidly, as to be sufficient in a few years to discharge the whole debt, and thus to restore compleatly the at present debilitated and languishing vigour of the empire. In the mean time the people might be relieved from some of the most burdensome taxes; from those which are imposed either upon the necessaries of life, or upon the materials of manufacture. The labouring poor would thus be enabled to live better, to work cheaper, and to send their goods cheaper to market. The cheapness of their goods would increase the demand for them, and consequently for the labour of [449] those who produced them. This increase in the demand for labour, would both increase the numbers and improve the circumstances of the labouring poor. Their consumption would increase, and together with it the revenue arising from all those articles of their consumption upon which the taxes might be allowed to remain.

77   The revenue arising from this system of taxation, however, might not immediately increase in proportion to the number of people who were subjected to it. Great indulgence would for some time be due to those provinces of the empire which were thus subjected to burthens to which they had not before been accustomed, and even when the same taxes came to be levied every where as exactly as possible, they would not every where produce a revenue proportioned to the numbers of the people. In a poor country the consumption of the principal commodities subject to the duties of customs and excise is very small; and in a thinly inhabited country the opportunities of smuggling are very great. The consumption of malt liquors among the inferior ranks of people in Scotland is very small, and the excise upon malt, beer, and ale, produces less there than in England in proportion to the numbers of the people and the rate of the duties, which upon malt is different on account of a supposed difference of quality. In these particular branches of the excise, there is not, I apprehend, much more smuggling in the one country than in the other. The duties upon the distillery, and the greater part of the duties of customs, in [450] proportion

to the numbers of people in the respective countries, produce less in Scotland than in England, not only on account of the smaller consumption of the taxed commodities, but of the much greater facility of smuggling. In Ireland, the inferior ranks of people are still poorer than in Scotland, and many parts of the country are almost as thinly inhabited. In Ireland, therefore, the consumption of the taxed commodities might, in proportion to the number of the people, be still less than in Scotland, and the facility of smuggling nearly the same. In America and the West Indies the white people even of the lowest rank are in much better circumstances than those of the same rank in England, and their consumption of all the luxuries in which they usually indulge themselves is probably much greater. The blacks, indeed, who make the greater part of the inhabitants both of the southern colonies upon the continent and of the West *ʷIndia*ʷ islands, as they are in a state of slavery, are, no doubt, in a worse condition than the poorest people either in Scotland or Ireland. We must not, however, upon that account, imagine that they are worse fed, or that their consumption of articles which might be subjected to moderate duties, is less than that even of the lower ranks of people in England. In order that they may work well, it is the interest of their master that they should be fed well and kept in good heart, in the same manner as it is his interest that his working cattle should be so.[77] The blacks accordingly have almost every where their [451] allowance of rum and of melasses or spruce beer, in the same manner as the white servants; and this allowance would not probably be withdrawn, though those articles should be subjected to moderate duties. The consumption of the taxed commodities, therefore, in proportion to the number of inhabitants, would probably be as great in America and the West Indies as in any part of the British empire. The opportunities of smuggling, indeed, would be much greater; America, in proportion to the extent of the country, being much more thinly inhabited than either Scotland or Ireland. If the revenue, however, which is at present raised by the different duties upon malt and malt liquors, *ˣwas*ˣ to be levied by a single duty upon malt, the opportunity of smuggling in the most important branch of the excise would be almost entirely taken away: And if the duties of customs, instead of being imposed upon almost all the different articles of importation, were confined to a few of the most general use and consumption, and if the levying of those duties *ʸwas*ʸ subjected to the excise laws, the opportunity of smuggling, though not so entirely taken away, would be very much diminished. In consequence of those two, apparently, very simple and easy alterations, the duties of customs and excise might probably produce a revenue as great in proportion to the consumption of

---

ʷ⁻ʷ Indian *1*   ˣ⁻ˣ were *4–6*   ʸ⁻ʸ were *4–6*

[77] See above, IV.vii.b.54.

the most thinly inhabited province as they do at present in proportion to that of the most populous.

78   [452] The Americans, it has been said, indeed, have no gold or silver money; the interior commerce of the country being carried on by a paper currency, and the gold and silver which occasionally come among them being all sent to Great Britain in return for the commodities which they receive from us.[78] But without gold and silver, it is added, there is no possibility of paying taxes. We already get all the gold and silver which they have. How is it possible to draw from them what they have not?

79   The present scarcity of gold and silver money in America is not the effect of the poverty of that country, or of the inability of the people there to purchase those metals. In a country where the wages of labour are so much higher, and the price of provisions so much lower than in England, the greater part of the people must surely have wherewithal to purchase a greater quantity, if it *was* either necessary or convenient for them to do so. The scarcity of those metals therefore, must be the effect of choice, and not of necessity.

80   It is for transacting either domestick or foreign business, that gold and silver money is either necessary or convenient.

81   The domestick business of every country, it has been shewn in the second book of this inquiry, may, at least in peaceable times, be transacted by means of a paper currency, with nearly the same degree of conveniency as by gold and silver money.[79] It is convenient for the Americans, who could always employ with [453] profit in the improvement of their lands a greater stock than they can easily get, to save as much as possible the expence of so costly an instrument of commerce as gold and silver, and rather to employ that part of their surplus produce which would be necessary for purchasing those metals, in purchasing the instruments of trade, the materials of clothing, several parts of household furniture, and the iron-work necessary for building and extending their settlements and plantations; in purchasing, not dead stock, but active and productive stock. The colony governments find it for their interest to supply *the* people with such a quantity of paper-money as is fully sufficient and generally more than sufficient for transacting their domestick business. Some of those governments, that of Pennsylvania particularly, derive a revenue from lending this paper-money to their subjects at an interest of so much per cent.[80] Others, like that of Massachusett's Bay, advance upon extraordinary emergencies a paper-money of this kind for defraying the publick

---

z–z were 4–6   *a–a* 2–6

---

[78] See above, II.ii.100.   [79] See above, II.ii.

[80] Above, V.ii.a.11. Smith comments on the moderation of the Pennsylvania government at II.ii.102 with regard to the issue of paper money.

expence, and afterwards, when it suits the conveniency of the colony, redeem it at the depreciated value to which it gradually falls.[81] In 1747* that
colony paid, in this manner, the greater part of its publick debts, with the
tenth part of the money for which its bills had been granted. It suits the
conveniency of the planters to save the expence of employing gold and
silver money in their domestick trans-[454]actions; and it suits the conveniency of the colony governments to supply them with a medium, which,
though attended with some very considerable disadvantages, enables them
to save that expence. The redundancy of paper money necessarily banishes
gold and silver from the domestick transactions of the colonies, for the same
reason that it has banished those metals from the greater part of the domestick transactions [b]in[b] Scotland;[82] and in both countries it is not the poverty,
but the enterprizing and projecting spirit of the people, their desire of
employing all the stock which they can get as active and productive stock,
which has occasioned this redundancy of paper money.

82   In the exterior commerce which the different colonies carry on with
Great Britain, gold and silver are more or less employed, exactly in proportion as they are more or less necessary. Where those metals are not
necessary, they seldom appear. Where they are necessary, they are generally
found.

83   In the commerce between Great Britain and the tobacco colonies, the
British goods are generally advanced to the colonists at a pretty long credit,
and are afterwards paid for in tobacco, rated at a certain price.[83] It is more
convenient for the colonists to pay in tobacco than in gold and silver. It
would be more convenient for any merchant to pay for the goods which his
correspondents had sold to him in some other sort of goods which he might
happen to deal in, than in money. Such a merchant would have no oc-[455]
casion to keep any part of his stock by him unemployed, and in ready
money, for answering occasional demands. He could have, at all times, a
larger quantity of goods in his shop or warehouse, and he could deal to a
greater extent. But it seldom happens to be convenient for all the correspondents of a merchant to receive payment for the goods which they sell to
him, in goods of some other kind which he happens to deal in. The

---

* See Hutchinson's Hist. of Massachusett's Bay, Vol. II. page 436 & seq. [*History of
the Colony of Massachussett's Bay*, 2nd ed., 1765–8.]

[b-b] of *1*

---

[81] Douglass, always an opponent of paper money, commented on the practice in Massachusetts' Bay: 'There seems to be a standing faction consisting of *wrong heads* and *frau-
dulent debtors*; this faction endeavours to persuade us, that one of our *invaluable* charter
privileges, is *A liberty to make paper-money, or public bills of credit*, receivable in all dealings
(specialities excepted) as a legal tender.' (W. Douglass, *British Settlements in North
America*, i.510–13.)
[82] See above, II.ii.89, where Scottish experience is likened to that of America,
[83] See also IV.vii.c.38.

British merchants who trade to Virginia and Maryland happen to be a particular set of correspondents, to whom it is more convenient to receive payment for the goods which they sell to those colonies in tobacco than in gold and silver. They expect to make a profit by the sale of the tobacco. They could make none by that of the gold and silver. Gold and silver, therefore, very seldom appear in the commerce between Great Britain and the tobacco colonies. Maryland and Virginia have as little occasion for those metals in their foreign as in their domestick commerce. They are said, accordingly, to have less gold and silver money than any other colonies in America. They are reckoned, however, as thriving, and consequently as rich as any of their neighbours.

84   In the northern colonies, Pennsylvania, New York, New Jersey, the four governments of New England, &c. the value of their own produce which they export to Great Britain is not equal to that of the manufactures which they import for their own use, and for that of some of the other colonies to which they are the car-[456]riers. A balance, therefore, must be paid to the mother country in gold and silver, and this balance they generally find.

85   In the sugar colonies the value of the produce annually exported to Great Britain is much greater than that of all the goods imported from thence. If the sugar and rum annually sent to the mother country were paid for in those colonies, Great Britain would be obliged to send out every year a very large balance in money, and the trade to the West Indies would, by a certain species of politicians, be considered as extremely disadvantageous.[84] But it so happens, that many of the principal proprietors of the sugar plantations reside in Great Britain. Their rents are remitted to them in sugar and rum, the produce of their estates. The sugar and rum which the West India merchants purchase in those colonies upon their own account, are not equal in value to the goods which they annually sell there. A balance, therefore, must ᶜnecessarilyᶜ be paid to them in gold and silver, and this balance too is generally found.

86   The difficulty and irregularity of payment from the different colonies to Great Britain, have not been at all in proportion to the greatness or smallness of the balances which were respectively due from them. Payments have in general been more regular from the northern than from the tobacco colonies, though the former have generally paid a pretty large balance in money, while the latter have ᵈeither paidᵈ no balance, or a much [457] smaller one. The difficulty of getting payment from our different sugar colonies has been greater or less in proportion, not so much to

ᶜ⁻ᶜ generally *1*   ᵈ⁻ᵈ paid either *1*

[84] That is, the species of politician who measure national well-being in terms of the balance of trade. See V.ii.k.29.

the extent of the balances respectively due from them, as to the quantity of uncultivated land which they contained; that is, to the greater or smaller temptation which the planters have been under of over-trading, or of under-taking the settlement and plantation of greater quantities of waste land than suited the extent of their capitals. The returns from the great island of Jamaica, where there is still much uncultivated land, have, upon this account, been in general more irregular and uncertain than those from the smaller islands of Barbadoes, Antigua, and St. Christophers, which have for these many years been compleatly cultivated, and have, upon that account, afforded less field for the speculations of the planter. The new acquisitions of Grenada, Tobago, St. Vincents, and Dominica, have opened a new field for speculations of this kind; and the returns from those islands have of late been as irregular and uncertain as those from the great island of Jamaica.

87   It is not, therefore, the poverty of the colonies which occasions, in the greater part of them, the present scarcity of gold and silver money. Their great demand for active and productive stock makes it convenient for them to have as little dead stock as possible; and disposes them upon that account to content themselves with a cheaper, though less commodious instrument of commerce than gold and silver. They are [458] thereby enabled to convert the value of that gold and silver into the instruments of trade, into the materials of cloathing, into houshold furniture, and into the iron work necessary for building and extending their settlements and plantations. In those branches of business which cannot be transacted without gold and silver money, it appears that they can always find the necessary quantity of those metals; and if they frequently do not find it, their failure is generally the effect, not of their necessary poverty, but of their unnecessary and excessive enterprize. It is not because they are poor that their payments are irregular and uncertain; but because they are too eager to become excessively rich. Though all that part of the produce of the colony taxes, which was over and above what was necessary for defraying the expence of their own civil and military establishments, were to be remitted to Great Britain in gold and silver, the colonies have abundantly wherewithal to purchase the requisite quantity of those metals. They would in this case be obliged, indeed, to exchange a part of their surplus produce, with which they now purchase active and productive stock, for dead stock. In transacting their domestic business they would be obliged to employ a costly instead of a cheap instrument of commerce;[85] and the expence of purchasing this costly instrument might damp somewhat the vivacity and ardour of their excessive enterprize in the improvement of land. It might not, however, be necessary to remit any part of the American revenue in gold [459] and silver. It might be remitted in bills drawn upon and accepted by

[85] Paper is described as a cheaper instrument of commerce at II.ii.26.

particular merchants or companies in Great Britain, to whom a part of the surplus produce of America had been consigned, who would pay into the treasury the American revenue in money, after having themselves received the value of it in goods; and the whole business might frequently be transacted without exporting a single ounce of gold ᵉorᵉ silver from America.

88   It is not contrary to justice that both Ireland and America should contribute towards the discharge of the publick debt of Great Britain. That debt has been contracted in support of the government established by the Revolution, a government to which the protestants of Ireland owe, not only the whole authority which they at present enjoy in their own country, but every security which they possess for their liberty, their property, and their religion; a government to which several of the colonies of America owe their present charters, and consequently their present constitution, and to which all the colonies of America owe the liberty, security, and property which they have ever since enjoyed.[86] That publick debt has been contracted in the defence, not of Great Britain alone, but of all the different provinces of the empire; the immense debt contracted in the late war in particular, and a great part of that contracted in the war before, were both properly contracted in defence of America.[87]

89   [460] By a union with Great Britain, Ireland would gain, besides the freedom of trade, other advantages much more important, and which would much more than compensate any increase of taxes that might accompany that union. By the union with England, the middling and inferior ranks of people in Scotland gained a compleat deliverance from the power of an aristocracy which had always before oppressed them. By ᶠanᶠ union with Great Britain the greater part of the people of all ranks in Ireland would gain an equally compleat deliverance from a much more oppressive aristocracy; an aristocracy not founded, like that of Scotland, in the natural and respectable distinctions of birth and fortune;[88] but in the most odious of all distinctions, those of religious and political prejudices; distinctions which, more than any other, animate both the insolence of the oppressors and the hatred and indignation of the oppressed, and which commonly render the inhabitants of the same country more hostile to one another than those of different countries ever are. Without a union with Great Britain, the inhabitants of Ireland are not likely for many ages to consider themselves as one people.

90   No oppressive aristocracy has ever prevailed in the colonies.[89] Even they, however, would, in point of happiness and tranquillity, gain consider-

---

ᵉ⁻ᵉ and *1*   ᶠ⁻ᶠ a *1*

[86] The constitution of the colonies is described at IV.vii.b.51.   [87] See IV.vii.c.64.

[88] Birth and fortune as sources of authority are considered at V.i.b.11. See also TMS I.iii.2.

[89] Smith comments on the absence of an aristocracy in the colonies at IV.vii b.51.

ably by a union with Great Britain. It would, at least, deliver them from those rancorous and virulent factions which are inseperable from [461] small democracies, and which have so frequently divided the affections of their people, and disturbed the tranquillity of their governments, in their form so nearly democratical. In the case of a total separation from Great Britain, which, unless prevented by a union of this kind, seems very likely to take place, those factions would be ten times more virulent than ever.[90] Before the commencement of the present disturbances, the coercive power of the mother-country had always been able to restrain those factions from breaking out into any thing worse than gross brutality and insult. If that coercive power *g*was*g* entirely taken away, they would probably soon break out into open violence and bloodshed. In all great countries which are united under one uniform government, the spirit of party commonly prevails less in the remote provinces than in the centre of the empire. The distance of those provinces from the capital, from the principal seat of the great scramble of faction and ambition, makes them enter less into the views of any of the contending parties, and renders them more indifferent and impartial spectators of the conduct of all.[91] The spirit of party prevails less in Scotland than in England. In the case of a union it would probably prevail less in Ireland than in Scotland, and the colonies would probably soon enjoy a degree of concord and unanimity at present unknown in any part of the British empire. Both Ireland and the colonies, indeed, would be subjected to heavier taxes than any which they at present [462] pay. In consequence, however, of a diligent and faithful application of the publick revenue towards the discharge of the national debt, the greater part of those taxes might not be of long continuance, and the publick revenue of Great Britain might soon be reduced to what was necessary for maintaining a moderate peace establishment.

91   The territorial acquisitions of the East India company, the undoubted right of the crown, that is, of the state and people of Great Britain, might be rendered another source of revenue more abundant, perhaps, than all those already mentioned. Those countries are represented as more fertile, more extensive; and in proportion to their extent, much richer and more populous than Great Britain. In order to draw a great revenue from them, it would not probably be necessary, to introduce any new system of taxation into countries which are already sufficiently and more than sufficiently taxed. It might, perhaps, be more proper to lighten, than to aggravate, the burden of those unfortunate countries, and to endeavour to draw a

---

g–g were *4–6*

[90] While recognizing that it was now unlikely, Smith argued that union with the American colonies would 'complete' the British constitution, IV.vii.c.77.

[91] It is interesting to recall that in the TMS the impartial spectator faces a problem of perspective when 'at a distance' from the object of judgement. Cf. III.i.3.

revenue from them, not by imposing new taxes, but by preventing the embezzlement and misapplication of the greater part of those which they already pay.

92   If it should be found impracticable for Great Britain to draw any considerable augmentation of revenue from any of the resources above mentioned; the only resource which can remain to her is a diminution of her expence. In the mode of collecting, and in that of expending the pub-[463] lick revenue; though in both there may be still room for improvement; Great Britain seems to be at least as œconomical as any of her neighbours. The military establishment which she maintains for her own defence in time of peace, is more moderate than that of any European state which can pretend to rival her either in wealth or in power. None of those articles, therefore, seem to admit of any considerable reduction of expence. The expence of the peace establishment of the colonies was, before the commencement of the present disturbances, very considerable, and is an expence which may, and if no revenue can be drawn from them, ought certainly to be saved altogether. This constant expence in time of peace, though very great, is insignificant in comparison with what the defence of the colonies has cost us in time of war. The last war, which was undertaken altogether on account of the colonies, cost Great Britain, it has already been observed, upwards of ninety millions.[92] The Spanish war of 1739 was principally undertaken on their account; in which, and in the French war that was the consequence of it, Great Britain spent upwards of forty millions, a great part of which ought justly to be charged to the colonies. In those two wars the colonies cost Great Britain much more than double the sum which the national debt amounted to before the commencement of the first of them. Had it not been for those wars that debt might, and probably would by this time, have been compleatly paid; and had it not been for the [464] colonies, the former of those wars might not, and the latter certainly would not have been undertaken. It was because the colonies were supposed to be provinces of the British empire, that this expence was laid out upon them. But countries which contribute neither revenue nor military force towards the support of the empire, cannot be considered as provinces. They may perhaps be considered as appendages, as a sort of splendid and showy equipage of the empire. But if the empire can no longer support the expence of keeping up this equipage, it ought certainly to lay it down; and if it cannot raise its revenue in proportion to its expence, it ought, at least, to accommodate its expence to its revenue. If the colonies, notwithstanding their refusal to submit to British taxes, are still to be considered as provinces of the British empire, their defence in some future war may cost Great Britain as great an expence as it ever has done in any former war. The rulers of Great Britain have, for more than a

[92] Above, IV.i.26, IV.vii.c.64; see also II.iii.35 and IV.viii.53.

century past, amused the people with the imagination that they possessed a great empire on the west side of the Atlantic. This empire, however, has hitherto existed in imagination only. It has hitherto been, not an empire, but the project of an empire; not a gold mine, but the project of a gold mine; a project which has cost, which continues to cost, and which, if pursued in the same way as it has been hitherto, is likely to cost immense expence, without being likely to bring any profit; for the effects of the monopoly of the colony trade, it [465] has been shewn,[93] are, to the great body of the people, mere loss instead of profit. It is surely now time that our rulers should either realize this golden dream, in which they have been indulging themselves, perhaps, as well as the people; or, that they should awake from it themselves, and endeavour to awaken the people. If the project cannot be compleated, it ought to be given up. If any of the provinces of the British empire cannot be made to contribute towards the support of the whole empire, it is surely time that Great Britain should free herself from the expence of defending those provinces in time of war, and of supporting any part of their civil or military establishments in time of peace, and endeavour to accommodate her future views and designs to the real mediocrity of her circumstances.[94]

[93] See above, IV.vii.c.

[94] However, it is argued at IV.vii.c.66 that a voluntary withdrawal is a ridiculous if not a pious hope.

[7]

Of Poor-Laws, continued

The remarks made in the last chapter on the nature and effects of the poor-laws have been in the most striking manner confirmed by the experience of the years 1815, 1816 and 1817.[1] During these years, two points of the very highest importance have been established, so as no longer to admit of a doubt in the mind of any rational man.

The first is that the country does not in point of fact fulfil the promise which it makes to the poor in the poor-laws, to maintain and find in employment, by means of parish assessments, those who are unable to support themselves or their families, either from want of work or any other cause.

And secondly, that with a very great increase of legal parish assessments, aided by the most liberal and praiseworthy contributions of voluntary charity, the country has been wholly unable to find adequate employment for the numerous labourers and artificers who were able as well as willing to work.

It can no longer surely be contended that the poor-laws really perform what they promise, when it is known that many almost starving families have been found in London and other great towns, who are deterred from going on the parish by the crowded, unhealthy and horrible state of the workhouses into which they would be received, if indeed they could be received at all; when it is known that many parishes have been absolutely unable to raise the necessary assessments, the increase of which, according to the existing laws, have tended only to bring more and more persons upon the parish, and to make what was collected less and less effectual; and when it is known that there has been an almost universal cry from one end of the kingdom to the other for voluntary charity to come in aid of the parochial assessments.

These strong indications of the inefficiency of the poor-laws may merely[2] be considered not only as incontrovertible proofs of the fact that

---

[1] [In 1826 a footnote was added here:
This chapter was written in 1817.
[2] [In 1826 the word *merely* was omitted.]

Of Poor Laws, continued   **CHAP VII**

they do not perform what they promise, but as affording the strongest presumption that they cannot do it. The best of all reasons for the breach of a promise is the absolute impossibility of executing it; indeed it is the only plea that can ever be considered as valid. But though it may be fairly pardonable not to execute an impossibility, it is unpardonable knowingly to promise one. And if it be still thought advisable to act upon these statutes as far as is practicable, it would surely be wise so to alter the terms in which they are expressed, and the general interpretation given to them, as not to convey to the poor a false notion of what really is within the range of practicability.

It has appeared further as a matter of fact, that very large voluntary contributions, combined with greatly increased parochial assessments, and aided by the most able and incessant exertions of individuals, have failed to give the necessary employment to those who have been thrown out of work by the sudden falling off of demand which has occurred during the last two or three years.

It might perhaps have been foreseen that, as the great movements of society, the great causes which render a nation progressive, stationary or declining, for longer or shorter periods, cannot be supposed to depend much upon parochial assessments or the contributions of charity, it could not be expected that any efforts of this kind should have power to create in a stationary or declining state of things that effective demand for labour which only belongs to a progressive state. But to those who did not see this truth before, the melancholy experience of the last two years[3] must have brought it home with an overpowering conviction.

It does not however by any means follow that the exertions which have been made to relieve the present distresses have been ill directed. On the contrary, they have not only been prompted by the most praiseworthy motives; they have not only fulfilled the great moral duty of assisting our fellow-creatures in distress; but they have in point of fact done great good, or at least prevented great evil. Their partial failure does not necessarily indicate either a want of energy or a want of skill in those who

---

[3] [In 1826 a footnote was added here:

The years 1816 and 1817.

[The very wet summer of 1816 resulted in a bad harvest and an epidemic of typhus; the cessation of the Napoleonic wars led to a steep fall in demand, for labour, and for such commodities as had already been manufactured in anticipation of high profits. There were outbreaks of destructive violence all over the country, as well as more rational agitation for parliamentary reform.]

have taken the lead in these efforts, but merely that a part only of what has been attempted is practicable.

It is practicable to mitigate the violence and relieve the severe pressure of the present distress, so as to carry the sufferers through to better times, though even this can only be done at the expense of some sacrifices, not merely of the rich, but of other classes of the poor. But it is impracticable by any exertions, either individual or national, to restore at once that brisk demand for commodities and labour which has been lost by events that, however, they may have originated, are now beyond the power of control.

The whole subject is surrounded on all sides by the most formidable difficulties, and in no state of things is it so necessary to recollect the saying of Daniel de Foe quoted in the last chapter. The manufacturers all over the country, and the Spitalfields weavers in particular, are in a state of the deepest distress, occasioned immediately and directly by the want of demand for the produce of their industry, and the consequent necessity felt by the masters of turning off many of their workmen, in order to proportion the supply to the contracted demand. It is proposed however, by some well-meaning people, to raise by subscription a fund for the express purpose of setting to work again those who have been turned off by their masters, the effect of which can only be to continue glutting a market already much too fully supplied. This is most naturally and justly objected to by the masters, as it prevents them from withdrawing the supply, and taking the only course which can prevent the total destruction of their capitals, and the necessity of turning off all their men instead of a part.

On the other hand, some classes of merchants and manufacturers clamour very loudly for the prohibition of all foreign commodities which may enter into competition with domestic products, and interfere, as they intimate, with the employment of British industry. But this is most naturally and most justly deprecated by other classes of British subjects, who are employed to a very great extent in preparing and manufacturing those commodities which are to purchase our imports from foreign countries. And it must be allowed to be perfectly true that a court-ball, at which only British stuffs are admitted, may be the means of throwing out of employment in one quarter of the country just as many persons as it furnishes with employment in another.

Still, it would be desirable if possible to employ those that are out of work, if it were merely to avoid the bad moral effects of idleness, and of

Of Poor Laws, continued   CHAP VII

the evil habits which might be generated by depending for a considerable time on mere alms. But the difficulties just stated will show that we ought to proceed in this part of the attempt with great caution, and that the kinds of employment which ought to be chosen are those, the results of which will not interfere with existing capitals. Such are public works of all descriptions, the making and repairing of roads, bridges, railways,[4] canals, &c.; and now perhaps, since the great loss of agricultural capital, almost every sort of labour upon the land, which could be carried on by public subscription.

Yet even in this way of employing labour, the benefit to some must bring with it disadvantages to others. That portion of each person's revenue, which might go in subscriptions of this kind, must of course be lost to the various sorts of labour which its expenditure in the usual channels would have supported; and the want of demand thus occasioned in these channels must cause the pressure of distress to be felt in quarters which might otherwise have escaped it. But this is an effect which, in such cases, it is impossible to avoid; and, as a temporary measure, it is not only charitable but just to spread the evil over a larger surface, in order that its violence on particular parts may be so mitigated as to be made bearable by all.

The great object to be kept in view, is to support the people through their present distresses, in the hope (and I trust a just one) of better times. The difficulty is without doubt considerably aggravated by the prodigious stimulus which has been given to the population of the country of late years, the effects of which cannot suddenly subside. But it will be seen probably, when the next returns of the population are made, that the marriages and births have diminished, and the deaths increased in a still greater degree than in 1800 and 1801; and the continuance of this effect to a certain degree for a few years will retard the progress of the population, and combined with the increasing wants of Europe and America from their increasing riches, and the adaptation of the supply of commodities at home to the new distribution of wealth occasioned by the alteration of the circulating medium, will again give life and energy to all

---

[4] [In 1817 there were about 160 miles of rail-road in the United Kingdom, used mainly for the transport of coal, timber, limestone and iron-ore, in wagons pulled by horses. Malthus would certainly have heard of the early experiments with steam locomotives, made by Trevithick and Hedley in 1804 and 1813; their inventions were to some extent stimulated by the war-time shortage of horses and fodder.]

our mercantile and agricultural transactions, and restore the labouring classes to full employment and good wages.[5]

On the subject of the distresses of the poor, and particularly the increase of pauperism of late years, the most erroneous opinions have been circulated. During the progress of the war, the increase in the proportion of persons requiring parish assistance was attributed chiefly to the high price of the necessaries of life. We have seen these necessaries of life experience a great and sudden fall, and yet at the same time a still larger proportion of the population requiring parish assistance.

It is now said that taxation is the sole cause of their distresses, and of the extraordinary stagnation in the demand for labour; yet I feel the firmest conviction that if the whole of the taxes were removed to-morrow, this stagnation, instead of being at an end, would be considerably aggravated. Such an event would cause another great and general rise in the value of the circulating medium, and bring with it that discouragement to industry with which such a convulsion in society must ever be attended. If, as has been represented, the labouring classes now pay more than half of what they receive in taxes, he must know very little indeed of the principles on which the wages of labour are regulated, who can for a moment suppose that, when the commodities on which they are expended have fallen one half by the removal of taxes, these wages themselves would still continue of the same nominal value. Were they to remain but for a short time the same, while all commodities had fallen, and the circulating medium had been reduced in proportion, it would be quickly seen that multitudes of them would be at once thrown out of employment.

The effects of taxation are no doubt in many cases pernicious in a very high degree; but it may be laid down as a rule which has few exceptions, that the relief obtained by taking off a tax is in no respect equal to the injury inflicted in laying it on; and generally it may be said that the specific evil of taxation consists in the check which it gives to production,

---

[5] [In 1826 a footnote was added here:

   1825. This has, in a considerable degree, taken place; but it has been owing rather to the latter causes noticed than to the former. It appeared, by the returns of 1821, that the scarce years of 1817 and 1818 had but a slight effect in diminishing the number of marriages and births, compared with the effect of the great proportion of plentiful years in increasing them; so that the population proceeded with great rapidity during the ten years ending with 1820. But this great increase of the population has prevented the labouring classes from being so fully employed as might have been expected from the prosperity of commerce and agriculture during the last two or three years.

Of Poor Laws, continued   CHAP VII

rather than the diminution which it occasions in demand. With regard to all commodities indeed of home production and home demand, it is quite certain that the conversion of capital into revenue, which is the effect of loans, must necessarily increase the proportion of demand to the supply; and the conversion of the revenue of individuals into the revenue of the government, which is the effect of taxes properly imposed, however hard upon the individuals so taxed, can have no tendency to diminish the general amount of demand. It will of course diminish the demands of the persons taxed by diminishing their powers of purchasing; but to the exact amount that the powers of these persons are diminished, will the powers of the government and of those employed by it be increased. If an estate of five thousand a year has a mortgage upon it of two thousand, two families, both in very good circumstances, may be living upon the rents of it, and both have considerable demands for houses, furniture, carriages, broad-cloth, silks, cottons, &c. The man who owns the estate is certainly much worse off than if the mortgage-deed was burnt, but the manufacturers and labourers who supply the silks, broad-cloth, cottons, &c., are so far from being likely to be benefited by such burning, that it would be a considerable time before the new wants and tastes of the enriched owner had restored the former demand; and if he were to take a fancy to spend his additional income in horses, hounds and menial servants, which is probable, not only would the manufacturers and labourers who had before supplied their silks, cloths and cottons be thrown out of employment, but the substituted demand would be very much less favourable to the increase of the capital and general resources of the country.

The foregoing illustration represents more nearly than may generally be imagined the effects of a national debt on the labouring classes of society, and the very great mistake of supposing that, because the demands of a considerable portion of the community would be increased by the extinction of the debt, these increased demands would not be balanced, and often more than balanced, by the loss of the demand from the fundholders[6] and government.

It is by no means intended by these observations to intimate that a

---

[6] [The fund-holders were those who had money invested in government stock. In 1751 a number of public securities had been consolidated into a single fund, bearing interest at 3 per cent; those who derived their income from this source were regarded as parasites on the rest of the community by William Cobbett and other radical writers.]

national debt may not be so heavy as to be extremely prejudicial to a state. The division and distribution of property, which is so beneficial when carried only to a certain extent, is fatal to production when pushed to extremity. The division of an estate of five thousand a year will generally tend to increase demand, stimulate production and improve the structure of society; but the division of an estate of eighty pounds a year will generally be attended with effects directly the reverse.

But, besides the probability that the division of property occasioned by a national debt may in many cases be pushed too far, the process of the division is effected by means which sometimes greatly embarrass production. This embarrassment must necessarily take place to a certain extent in almost every species of taxation; but under favourable circumstances it is overcome by the stimulus given to demand.[7] During the late war, from the prodigious increase of produce and population, it may fairly be presumed that the power of production was not essentially impeded, notwithstanding the enormous amount of taxation; but in the state of things which has occurred since the peace, and under a most extraordinary fall of the exchangeable value of the raw produce of the land, and a great consequent diminution of the circulating medium, the very sudden increase of the weight and pressure of taxation must greatly aggravate the other causes which discourage production. This effect has been felt to a considerable extent on the land; but the distress in this quarter is already much mitigated;[8] and among the mercantile and manufacturing classes, where the greatest numbers are without employment, the evil obviously arises not so much from the want of capital and the means of production, as the want of a market for the commodity when produced – a want for which the removal of taxes, however proper, and indeed absolutely necessary as a permanent measure, is certainly not the immediate and specific remedy.

The principal causes of the increase of pauperism, independently of the present crisis, are, first, the general increase of the manufacturing system and the unavoidable variations of manufacturing labour; and secondly, and more particularly, the practice which has been adopted in some counties, and is now spreading pretty generally all over the

---

[7] [In 1826 Malthus inserted three words here:
    ... stimulus given to demand compared with supply.
[8] [In 1826 a footnote was added here:
    Written in 1817. It increased again afterwards from another great fall in the price of corn, subsequent to 1818.

kingdom, of paying a considerable portion of what ought to be the wages of labour out of the parish rates. During the war, when the demand for labour was great and increasing, it is quite certain that nothing but a practice of this kind could for any time have prevented the wages of labour from rising fully in proportion to the necessaries of life, in whatever degree these necessaries might have been raised by taxation. It was seen, consequently, that in those parts of Great Britain where this practice prevailed the least, the wages of labour rose the most. This was the case in Scotland, and some parts of the North of England, where the improvement in the condition of the labouring classes, and their increased command over the necessaries and conveniences of life, were particularly remarkable. And if, in some other parts of the country, where the practice did not greatly prevail, and especially in the towns, wages did not rise in the same degree, it was owing to the influx and competition of the cheaply raised population of the surrounding counties.

It is a just remark of Adam Smith, that the attempts of the legislature to raise the pay of curates had always been ineffectual, on account of the cheap and abundant supply of them, occasioned by the bounties given to young persons educated for the church at the universities. And it is equally true that no human efforts can keep up the price of day-labour so as to enable a man to support on his earnings a family of a moderate size, so long as those who have more than two children are considered as having a valid claim to parish assistance.

If this system were to become universal, and I own it appears to me that the poor-laws naturally lead to it, there is no reason whatever why parish assistance should not by degrees begin earlier and earlier; and I do not hesitate to assert that, if the government and constitution of the country were in all other respects as perfect as the wildest visionary thinks he could make them; if parliaments were annual, suffrage universal, wars, taxes and pensions unknown, and the civil list fifteen hundred a year,[9] the great body of the community might still be a collection of paupers.

[9] [The word *pension* here does not refer to the modern retirement pension, but to 'regular payments to persons of rank, royal favourites, etc., to enable them to maintain their state' (O.E.D.). The civil list was formerly a list of the charges to be defrayed by the government; in Malthus's time it meant the sum voted by parliament for what were traditionally the personal expenses of the monarch, including the payment of pensions, as above. Like the fund-holders (see n.6) the pensioners were not popular.]

BOOK III   *Of Poor Laws, continued*

I have been accused of proposing a law to prohibit the poor from marrying.[10] This is not true. So far from proposing such a law, I have distinctly said that, if any person chooses to marry without having a prospect of being able to maintain a family, he ought to have the most perfect liberty so to do; and whenever any prohibitory propositions have been suggested to me as advisable by persons who have drawn wrong inferences from what I have said, I have steadily and uniformly reprobated them. I am indeed most decidedly of opinion that any positive law to limit the age of marriage would be both unjust and immoral; and my greatest objection to a system of equality and the system of the poor-laws (two systems which, however different in their outset, are of a nature calculated to produce the same results) is, that the society in which they are effectively carried into execution, will ultimately be reduced to the miserable alternative of choosing between universal want and the enactment of *direct* laws against marriage.

What I have really proposed is a very different measure. It is the *gradual* and *very gradual* abolition of the poor-laws.[11] And the reason why I have ventured to suggest a proposition of this kind for consideration is my firm conviction that they have lowered very decidedly the wages of the labouring classes, and made their general condition essentially worse than it would have been if these laws had never existed. Their operation is every where depressing; but it falls peculiarly hard upon the labouring classes in great towns. In country parishes the poor do really receive some compensation for their low wages; their children, beyond a certain number, are really supported by the parish; and though it must be a most grating reflection to a labouring man, that it is scarcely possible for him to marry without becoming the father of paupers; yet if he can reconcile himself to this prospect, the compensation, such as it is, is no doubt made to him. But in London and all the great towns of the kingdom, the evil is suffered without the compensation. The population raised by bounties in the country naturally and necessarily flows into the towns, and as naturally and necessarily tends to lower wages in them; while, in point of fact, those who marry in towns, and have large families, receive no assistance from their parishes unless they are actually starving; and

---

[10] [In this and the following paragraph Malthus virtually assumes that readers of this chapter are familiar with earlier editions of the *Essay*, and know already about the plan for the gradual abolition of the poor laws which he had put forward in the quarto, chapter viii of Book IV in this edition.]

[11] So gradual as not to affect any individuals at present alive, or who will be born within the next two years.

Of Poor Laws, continued   CHAP VII

altogether the assistance which the manufacturing classes obtain for the support of their families, in aid of their lowered wages, is perfectly inconsiderable.

To remedy the effects of this competition from the country, the artificers and manufacturers in towns have been apt to combine, with a view to keep up the price of labour and to prevent persons from working below a certain rate. But such combinations are not only illegal,[12] but irrational and ineffectual; and if the supply of workmen in any particular branch of trade be such as would naturally lower wages, the keeping them up forcibly must have the effect of throwing so many out of employment, as to make the expense of their support fully equal to the gain acquired by the higher wages, and thus render these higher wages in reference to the whole body perfectly futile.

It may be distinctly stated to be an *absolute impossibility* that all the different classes of society should be both well paid and fully employed, if the supply of labour on the whole exceed the demand; and as the poor-laws tend in the most marked manner to make the supply of labour exceed the demand for it, their effect must be, either to lower universally all wages, or, if some are kept up artificially, to throw great numbers of workmen out of employment, and thus constantly to increase the poverty and distress of the labouring classes of society.

If these things be so (and I am firmly convinced that they are) it cannot but be a subject of the deepest regret to those who are anxious for the happiness of the great mass of the community, that the writers which are now most extensively read among the common people should have selected for the subject of reprobation exactly that line of conduct which can alone generally improve their condition, and for the subject of approbation that system which must inevitably depress them in poverty and wretchedness.

---

[12] [In 1826 a footnote was added here:

This has since been altered; but the subsequent part of the passage is particularly applicable to the present time – the end of the year 1825. The workmen are beginning to find that, if they could raise their wages above what the state of the demand and the prices of goods will warrant, it is absolutely impossible that all, or nearly all, should be employed. The masters could not employ the same number as before without inevitable ruin.

[The Combination Acts of 1799 and 1800 had amounted to a general law against all trade unions; there had previously been many statutes forbidding combinations of workmen in particular trades. All such Acts were repealed in 1825. Malthus himself had given evidence, in May 1824, to the Select Committee on Artisans and

They are taught that there is no occasion whatever for them to put any sort of restraint upon their inclinations, or exercise any degree of prudence in the affair of marriage; because the parish is bound to provide for all that are born. They are taught that there is as little occasion to cultivate habits of economy, and make use of the means afforded them by saving-banks, to lay by their earnings while they are single, in order to furnish a cottage when they marry, and enable them to set out in life with decency and comfort; because, I suppose, the parish is bound to cover their nakedness, and to find them a bed and a chair in a work-house.

They are taught that any endeavour on the part of the higher classes of society to inculcate the duties of prudence and economy can only arise from a desire to save the money which they pay in poor-rates; although it is absolutely certain that the *only* mode, consistent with the laws of morality and religion, of giving to the poor the largest share of the property of the rich, without sinking the whole community in misery, is the exercise on the part of the poor of prudence in marriage, and of economy both before and after it.

They are taught that the command of the Creator to increase and multiply is meant to contradict those laws which he has himself appointed for the increase and multiplication of the human race; and that it is equally the duty of a person to marry early, when, from the impossibility of adding to the food of the country in which he lives, the greater part of his offspring must die prematurely, and consequently no multiplication follow from it, as when the children of such marriages can all be well maintained, and there is room and food for a great and rapid increase of population.

They are taught that, in relation to the condition of the labouring classes, there is no other difference between such a country as England, which has been long well peopled, and where the land which is not yet taken into cultivation is comparatively barren, and such a country as America, where millions and millions of acres of fine land are yet to be had for a trifle, except what arises from taxation.

And they are taught, O monstrous absurdity! that the only reason why the American labourer earns a dollar a day, and the English labourer earns two shillings, is that the English labourer pays a great part of these two shillings in taxes.

Some of these doctrines are so grossly absurd that I have no doubt

Machinery that recommended the abolition of these restrictive laws, laws which were in any case almost impossible to enforce.]

they are rejected at once by the common sense of many of the labouring classes. It cannot but strike them that, if their main dependence for the support of their children is to be on the parish, they can only expect parish fare, parish clothing, parish furniture, a parish house and parish government, and they must know that persons living in this way cannot possibly be in a happy and prosperous state.

It can scarcely escape the notice of the common mechanic, that the scarcer workmen are upon any occasion, the greater share do they retain of the value of what they produce for their masters; and it is a most natural inference, that prudence in marriage, which is the only moral means of preventing an excess of workmen above the demand, can be the only mode of giving to the poor permanently a large share of all that is produced in the country.

A common man, who has read his Bible, must be convinced that a command given to a rational being by a merciful God cannot be intended so as to be interpreted as to produce only disease and death instead of multiplication; and a plain sound understanding would make him to see that if, in a country in which little or no increase of food is to be obtained, every man were to marry at eighteen or twenty, when he generally feels most inclined to it, the consequence must be increased poverty, increased disease and increased mortality, and not increased numbers, as long at least as it continues to be true (which he will hardly be disposed to doubt) that additional numbers cannot live without additional food.

A moderately shrewd judgment would prompt any labourer acquainted with the nature of land to suspect that there must be some great difference, quite independent of taxation, between a country such as America, which might easily be made to support fifty times as many inhabitants as it contains at present, and a country such as England, which could not without extraordinary exertions be made to support two or three times as many. He would at least see that there would be a prodigious difference in the power of maintaining an additional number of cattle, between a small farm already well stocked, and a very large one which had not the fiftieth part of what it might be made to maintain; and as he would know that both rich and poor must live upon the produce of the earth as well as all other animals, he would be disposed to conclude that what was so obviously true in one case could not be false in the other. These considerations might make him think it natural and probable that in those countries where there was a great want of people, the wages of labour would be such as to encourage early marriages and large

BOOK III   *Of Poor Laws, continued*

families, for the best of all possible reasons, because all that are born may
be very easily and comfortably supported; but that in those countries
which were already nearly full, the wages of labour cannot be such as to
give the same encouragement to early marriages, for a reason surely not
much worse, because the persons so brought into the world cannot be
properly supported.

There are few of our mechanics and labourers who have not heard of
the high prices of bread, meat and labour in this country compared with
the nations of the continent, and they have generally heard at the same
time that these high prices were chiefly occasioned by taxation, which,
though it had raised among other things the money wages of labour, had
done harm rather than good to the labourer, because it had before raised
the price of the bread and beer and other articles on which he spent his
earnings. With this amount of information, the meanest understanding
would revolt at the idea that the very same cause which had kept the
money price of labour in all the nations of Europe much lower than in
England, namely, the absence of taxation, had been the means of raising
it to more than double in America. He would feel quite convinced that,
whatever might be the cause of the high money wages of labour in
America, which he might not perhaps readily understand, it must be
something very different indeed from the mere absence of taxation,
which could only have an effect exactly opposite.

With regard to the improved condition of the lower classes of people
in France since the revolution, which has also been much insisted upon;
if the circumstances accompanying it were told at the same time, it would
afford the strongest presumption against the doctrines which have been
lately promulgated. The improved condition of the labouring classes in
France since the revolution has been accompanied by a greatly diminished proportion of births, which has had its natural and necessary
effect in giving to these classes a greater share of the produce of the
country, and has kept up the advantage arising from the sale of the
church lands and other national domains, which would otherwise have
been lost in a short time. The effect of the revolution in France has been
to make every person depend more upon himself and less upon others.
The labouring classes are therefore become more industrious, more
saving and more prudent in marriage than formerly; and it is quite
certain that without these effects the revolution would have done nothing
for them. An improved government has, no doubt, a natural tendency to
produce these effects, and thus to improve the condition of the poor. But

Of Poor Laws, continued   CHAP VII

if an extensive system of parochial relief, and such doctrines as have lately been inculcated, counteract them, and prevent the labouring classes from depending upon their own prudence and industry, then any change for the better in other respects becomes comparatively a matter of very little importance; and, under the best form of government imaginable, there may be thousands on thousands out of employment and half starved.

If it be taught that all who are born have a *right* to support on the land, whatever be their number, and that there is no occasion to exercise any prudence in the affair of marriage so as to check this number, the temptations, according to all the known principles of human nature, will inevitably be yielded to, and more and more will gradually become dependent on parish assistance. There cannot therefore be a greater inconsistency and contradiction than that those who maintain these doctrines respecting the poor should still complain of the number of paupers. Such doctrines and a crowd of paupers are unavoidably united; and it is utterly beyond the power of any revolution or change of government to separate them.

[8]

TAXES ON OTHER COMMODITIES
THAN RAW PRODUCE

ON the same principle that a tax on corn would raise the price
of corn, a tax on any other commodity would raise the price
of that commodity. If the commodity did not rise by a sum
equal to the tax, it would not give the same profit to the producer which he had before, and he would remove his capital
to some other employment.

The taxing of all commodities, whether they be necessaries
or luxuries, will, while money remains at an unaltered value,
raise their prices by a sum at least equal to the tax.* A tax on
the manufactured necessaries of the labourer would have the
same effect on wages as a tax on corn, which differs from other
necessaries only by being the first and most important on the
list; and it would produce precisely the same effects on the
profits of stock and foreign trade. But a tax on luxuries would

* It is observed by M. Say, "that a manufacturer is not enabled to
make the consumer pay the whole tax levied on his commodity, because
its increased price will diminish its consumption." Should this be the
case, should the consumption be diminished, will not the supply also
speedily be diminished? Why should the manufacturer continue in the
trade, if his profits are below the general level? M. Say appears here
also to have forgotten the doctrine which he elsewhere supports, "that
the cost of production determines the price, below which commodities
cannot fall for any length of time, because production would be then
either suspended or diminished."—Vol. ii. p. 26.

"The tax in this case falls then partly on the consumer who is obliged
to give more for the commodity taxed, and partly on the producer, who,
after deducting the tax, will receive less. The public treasury will be
benefited by what the purchaser pays in addition, and also by the sacrifice
which the producer is obliged to make of a part of his profits. It is the
effort of gunpowder, which acts at the same time on the bullet which it
projects, and on the gun which it causes to recoil."—Vol. ii. p. 333.

have no other effect than to raise their price. It would fall wholly on the consumer, and could neither increase wages nor lower profits.

Taxes which are levied on a country for the purpose of supporting war, or for the ordinary expenses of the State, and which are chiefly devoted to the support of unproductive labourers, are taken from the productive industry of the country; and every saving which can be made from such expenses will be generally added to the income, if not to the capital of the contributors. When, for the expenses of a year's war, twenty millions are raised by means of a loan, it is the twenty millions which are withdrawn from the productive capital of the nation. The million per annum which is raised by taxes to pay the interest of this loan, is merely transferred from those who pay it to those who receive it, from the contributor to the tax, to the national creditor. The real expense is the twenty millions, and not the interest which must be paid for it.* Whether the interest be or be not paid, the country will neither be richer nor poorer. Government might at once have required the twenty millions in the shape of taxes; in

---

* "Melon says,[1] that the debts of a nation are debts due from the right hand to the left, by which the body is not weakened. It is true that the general wealth is not diminished by the payment of the interest on arrears of the debt: The dividends are a value which passes from the hand of the contributor to the national creditor: Whether it be the national creditor or the contributor who accumulates or consumes it, is, I agree, of little importance to the society; but the principal of the debt—what has become of that? It exists no more. The consumption which has followed the loan has annihilated a capital which will never yield any further revenue. The society is deprived not of the amount of interest, since that passes from one hand to the other, but of the revenue from a destroyed capital. This capital, if it had been employed productively by him who lent it to the State, would equally have yielded him an income, but that income would have been derived from a real production, and would not have been furnished from the pocket of a fellow citizen."—*Say*, vol. ii. p. 357. This is both conceived and expressed in the true spirit of the science.

[1] *Essai politique sur le commerce*, 'nouvelle édition', 1761, p. 296.

which case it would not have been necessary to raise annual taxes to the amount of a million. This, however, would not have changed the nature of the transaction. An individual instead of being called upon to pay 100*l.* per annum, might have been obliged to pay 2000*l.* once for all. It might also have suited his convenience rather to borrow this 2000*l.*, and to pay 100*l.* per annum for interest to the lender, than to spare the larger sum from his own funds. In one case it is a private transaction between A and B, in the other Government guarantees to B the payment of interest[1] to be equally paid by A. If the transaction had been of a private nature, no public record would be kept of it, and it would be a matter of comparative indifference to the country whether A faithfully performed his contract to B, or unjustly retained the 100*l.* per annum in his own possession. The country would have a general interest in the faithful performance of a contract, but with respect to the national wealth, it would have no other interest than whether A or B would make this 100*l.* most productive; but on this question it would neither have the right nor the ability to decide. It might be possible, that if A retained it for his own use, he might squander it unprofitably, and if it were paid to B, he might add it to his capital, and employ it productively. And the converse would also be possible; B might squander it, and A might employ it productively. With a view to wealth only, it might be equally or more desirable that A should or should not pay it; but the claims of justice and good faith, a greater utility, are not to be compelled to yield to those of a less; and accordingly, if the State were called upon to interfere, the courts of justice would oblige A to perform his contract. A debt guaranteed by the nation, differs in no respect from the above transaction. Justice and good faith demand that the interest of the national debt should continue to be

---

[1] Ed. 1 'of the interest'.

paid, and that those who have advanced their capitals for the general benefit, should not be required to forego their equitable claims, on the plea of expediency.

But independently of this consideration, it is by no means certain, that political utility would gain any thing by the sacrifice of political integrity; it does by no means follow, that the party exonerated from the payment of the interest of the national debt would employ it more productively than those to whom indisputably it is due. By cancelling the national debt, one man's income might be raised from 1000*l.* to 1500*l.*, but another man's would be lowered from 1500*l.* to 1000*l.* These two men's incomes now amount to 2500*l.*, they would amount to no more then. If it be the object of Government to raise taxes, there would be precisely the same taxable capital and income in one case, as in the other. It is not, then, by the payment of the interest on the national debt, that a country is distressed, nor is it by the exoneration from payment that it can be relieved. It is only by saving from income, and retrenching in expenditure, that the national capital can be increased; and neither the income would be increased, nor the expenditure diminished by the annihilation of the national debt. It is by the profuse expenditure of Government, and of individuals, and by loans, that the[1] country is impoverished; every measure, therefore, which is calculated to promote public and private economy[2], will relieve the public distress; but it is error and delusion to suppose, that a real national difficulty can be removed, by shifting it from the shoulders of one class of the community, who justly ought to bear it, to the shoulders of another class, who, upon every principle of equity, ought to bear no more than their share.[3]

---

[1] Eds. 1-2 'a' in place of 'the'.
[2] Eds. 1-2 spell 'œconomy'.

[3] In ed. 1 this and the three subsequent paragraphs are joined together.

From what I have said, it must not be inferred that I consider the system of borrowing as the best calculated to defray the extraordinary expenses of the State. It is a system which tends to make us less thrifty—to blind us to our real situation. If the expenses of a war be 40 millions per annum, and the share which a man would have to contribute towards that annual expense were 100*l*., he would endeavour, on being at once called upon for his portion, to save speedily the 100*l*. from his income. By the system of loans, he is called upon to pay only the interest of this 100*l*., or 5*l*. per annum, and considers that he does enough by saving this 5*l*. from his expenditure, and then deludes himself with the belief, that he is as rich as before. The whole nation, by reasoning and acting in this manner, save only the interest of 40 millions, or two millions; and thus, not only lose all the interest or profit which 40 millions of capital, employed productively, would afford, but also 38 millions, the difference between their savings and expenditure. If, as I before observed, each man had to make his own loan, and contribute his full proportion to the exigencies of the State, as soon as the war ceased, taxation would cease, and we should immediately fall into a natural state of prices. Out of his private funds, A might have to pay to B interest for the money he borrowed of him during the war, to enable him to pay his quota of the expense; but with this the nation would have no concern.

A country which has accumulated a large debt, is placed in a most artificial situation; and although the amount of taxes, and the increased price of labour, may not, and I believe does not, place it under any other disadvantage with respect to foreign countries, except the unavoidable one of paying those taxes, yet it becomes the interest of every contributor to withdraw his shoulder from the burthen, and to shift this payment from himself to another; and the temptation to remove himself and his capital to another country, where he will be exempted from such burthens, becomes at last irresistible, and overcomes the natural reluctance which every man feels to quit the place of his birth, and the scene of his early associations. A country which has involved itself in the difficulties attending this artificial system, would act wisely by ransoming itself from them, at the sacrifice of any portion of its property which might be necessary to redeem its debt. That which is wise in an individual, is wise also in a nation. A man who has 10,000*l*., paying him an income of 500*l*., out of which he has to pay 100*l*. per annum towards the interest of the debt, is really worth only 8000*l*., and would be equally rich, whether he continued to pay 100*l*. per annum, or at once, and for only once, sacrificed 2000*l*. But where, it is asked, would be the purchaser of the property which he must sell to obtain this 2000*l*.? the answer is plain: the national creditor, who is to receive this 2000*l*., will want an investment for his money, and will be disposed either to lend it to the landholder, or manufacturer, or to purchase from them a part of the property of which they have to dispose. To such a payment[1] the stockholders themselves would largely contribute. This scheme[2] has been often recommended,[3] but we have, I fear, neither wisdom enough, nor virtue enough, to adopt it. It must, however, be admitted, that during peace, our unceasing efforts should be directed towards paying off that part of the debt which has been contracted during war; and that no temptation of relief, no desire of escape from present, and I hope temporary distresses, should induce us to relax in our attention to that great object.

No sinking fund can be efficient for the purpose of diminishing the debt, if it be not derived from the excess of the public

---

[1] Ed. 1 'To such an effect'.
[2] Ed. 1 'Such a scheme'.

[3] It was first proposed by Archibald Hutcheson in 1714; see below, V, 41, n. 1.

revenue over the public expenditure. It is to be regretted, that the sinking fund in this country is only such in name; for there is no excess of revenue above expenditure. It ought, by economy, to be made what it is professed to be, a really efficient fund for the payment of the debt. If, on the breaking out of any future war, we shall not have very considerably reduced our debt, one of two things must happen, either the whole expenses of that war must be defrayed by taxes raised from year to year, or we must, at the end of that war, if not before, submit to a national bankruptcy; not that we shall be unable to bear any large additions to the debt; it would be difficult to set limits to the powers of a great nation; but assuredly there are limits to the price, which in the form of perpetual taxation, individuals will submit to pay for the privilege merely of living in their native country.*

When a commodity is at a monopoly price, it is at the very highest price at which the consumers are willing to purchase it. Commodities are only at a monopoly price, when by no possible device their quantity can be augmented; and when therefore, the competition is wholly on one side—amongst the buyers. The monopoly price of one period may be much lower or higher than the monopoly price of another, because the com-

---

* "Credit, in general, is good, as it allows capitals to leave those hands where they are not usefully employed, to pass into those where they will be made productive: it diverts a capital from an employment useful only to the capitalist, such as an investment in the public funds, to make it productive in the hands of industry. It facilitates the employments of all capitals, and leaves none unemployed."—Economie Politique, p. 463. 2 Vol. 4th Edition.—This must be an oversight of M. Say. The capital of the stockholder can never be made productive—it is, in fact, no capital. If he were to sell his stock, and employ the capital he obtained for it, productively, he could only do so by detaching the capital of the buyer of his stock from a productive employment.[1]

---

[1] Eds. 1-2 do not contain this note. Say's reference to 'the public funds' appears first in his 4th ed., 1819; the passage was altered in the 5th ed., 1826, in a way that avoids Ricardo's objection.

petition amongst the purchasers must depend on their wealth, and their tastes and caprices. Those peculiar wines, which are produced in very limited quantity, and those works of art, which from their excellence or rarity, have acquired a fanciful value, will be exchanged for a very different quantity of the produce of ordinary labour, according as the society is rich or poor, as it possesses an abundance or scarcity of such produce, or as it may be in a rude or polished state. The exchangeable value therefore of a commodity which is at a monopoly price, is no where regulated by the cost of production.

Raw produce is not at a monopoly price, because the market price of barley and wheat is as much regulated by their cost of production, as the market price of cloth and linen. The only difference is this, that one portion of the capital employed in agriculture regulates the price of corn, namely, that portion which pays no rent; whereas, in the production of manufactured commodities, every portion of capital is employed with the same results; and as no portion pays rent, every portion is equally a regulator of price: corn, and other raw produce, can be augmented, too, in quantity, by the employment of more capital on the land, and therefore they are not at a monopoly price. There is competition among the sellers, as well as amongst the buyers. This is not the case in the production of those rare wines, and those valuable specimens of art, of which we have been speaking; their quantity cannot be increased, and their price is limited only by the extent of the power and will of the purchasers. The rent of these vineyards may be raised beyond any moderately assignable limits, because no other land being able to produce such wines, none can be brought into competition with them.

The corn and raw produce of a country may, indeed, for a time sell at a monopoly price; but they can do so permanently only when no more capital can be profitably employed on the lands, and when, therefore, their produce cannot be increased. At such time, every portion of land in cultivation, and every portion of capital employed on the land will yield a rent, differing, indeed, in proportion to the difference in the return. At such a time too, any tax which may be imposed on the farmer, will fall on rent, and not on the consumer. He cannot raise the price of his corn, because, by the supposition, it is already at the highest price at which the purchasers will or can buy it. He will not be satisfied with a lower rate of profits, than that obtained by other capitalists, and, therefore, his only alternative will be to obtain a reduction of rent, or to quit his employment.

Mr. Buchanan considers corn and raw produce as at a monopoly price, because they yield a rent: all commodities which yield a rent, he supposes must be at a monopoly price; and thence he infers, that all taxes on raw produce would fall on the landlord, and not on the consumer. "The price of corn," he says, "which always affords a rent, being in no respect influenced by the expenses of its production, those expenses must be paid out of the rent; and when they rise or fall, therefore, the consequence is not a higher or lower price, but a higher or a lower rent. In this view, all taxes on farm servants, horses, or the implements of agriculture, are in reality land-taxes; the burden falling on the farmer during the currency of his lease, and on the landlord, when the lease comes to be renewed. In like manner all those improved implements of husbandry which save expense to the farmer, such as machines for threshing and reaping, whatever gives him easier access to the market, such as good roads, canals and bridges, though they lessen the original cost of corn, do not lessen its market price. Whatever is saved by those improvements, therefore, belongs to the landlord as part of his rent."[1]

It is evident that if we yield to Mr. Buchanan the basis on

[1] Buchanan's ed. of *Wealth of Nations*, vol. IV, *Observations*, pp. 37–8.

which his argument is built, namely, that the price of corn always yields a rent, all the consequences which he contends for would follow of course. Taxes on the farmer would then fall not on the consumer but on rent; and all improvements in husbandry would increase rent: but I hope I have made it sufficiently clear, that until a country is cultivated in every part, and up to the highest degree, there is always a portion of capital employed on the land which yields no rent, and that it is this portion of capital, the result of which, as in manufactures, is divided between profits and wages that regulates the price of corn. The price of corn, then, which does not afford a rent, being influenced by the expenses of its production, those expenses cannot be paid out of rent. The consequence therefore of those expenses increasing, is a higher price, and not a lower rent.*

It is remarkable that both Adam Smith and Mr. Buchanan, who entirely agree that taxes on raw produce, a land-tax, and tithes, all fall on the rent of land, and not on the consumers of raw produce, should nevertheless admit that taxes on malt would fall on the consumer of beer, and not on the rent of the landlord. Adam Smith's argument is so able a statement of the view which I take of the subject of the tax on malt, and every other tax on raw produce, that I cannot refrain from offering it to the attention of the reader.

"The rent and profits of barley land must always be nearly equal to those of other equally fertile, and equally well cultivated land. If they were less, some part of the barley land would soon be turned to some other purpose; and if they were

---

* "Manufacturing industry increases its produce in proportion to the demand, and the price falls; *but the produce of land cannot be so increased*; and a high price is still necessary to prevent the consumption from exceeding the supply." *Buchanan*, vol. iv. p. 40. Is it possible that Mr. Buchanan can seriously assert, that the produce of the land cannot be increased, if the demand increases?

greater, more land would soon be turned to the raising of barley. When the ordinary price of any particular produce of land is at what may be called a monopoly price, a tax upon it necessarily reduces the rent and profit* of the land which grows it. A tax upon the produce of those precious vineyards, of which the wine falls so much short of the effectual demand, that its price is always above the natural proportion to that of[1] other equally fertile, and equally well cultivated land, would necessarily reduce the rent and profit* of those vineyards. The price of the wines being already the highest that could be got for the quantity commonly sent to market, it could not be raised higher without diminishing that quantity; and the quantity could not be diminished without still greater loss, because the lands could not be turned to any other equally valuable produce. The whole weight of the tax, therefore, would fall upon the rent and profit*; properly upon the *rent* of the vineyard." "But the ordinary price of barley has never been a monopoly price; and the rent and profit of barley land have never been above their natural proportion to those of other equally fertile and equally well cultivated land. The different taxes which have been imposed upon malt, beer, and ale, *have never lowered the price of barley*; have never reduced the rent and profit* of barley land. The price of malt to the brewer, has constantly risen in proportion to the taxes imposed upon it; and those taxes, together with the different duties upon beer and ale, have constantly either raised the price, or, what comes to the same thing, reduced the quality of those commodities to the consumer. The final payment of those taxes has fallen

---

* I wish the word "Profit" had been omitted. Dr. Smith must suppose the profits of the tenants of these precious vineyards to be above the general rate of profits. If they were not, they would not pay the tax, unless they could shift it either to the landlord or consumer.

[1] Adam Smith says 'of the produce of'.

constantly upon the consumer, and not upon the producer."[1]
On this passage Mr. Buchanan remarks, "A duty on malt never
could reduce the price of barley, because, unless as much could
be made of barley by malting it as by selling it unmalted, the
quantity required would not be brought to market. It is clear,
therefore, that the price of malt must rise in proportion to the
tax imposed on it, as the demand could not otherwise be supplied. The price of barley, however, is just as much a monopoly
price as that of sugar; they both yield a rent, and the market
price of both has equally lost all connexion with the original
cost."[2]

It appears then to be the opinion of Mr. Buchanan, that a
tax on malt would raise the price of malt, but that a tax on the
barley from which malt is made, would not raise the price of
barley; and, therefore, if malt is taxed, the tax will be paid by
the consumer; if barley is taxed, it will be paid by the landlord,
as he will receive a diminished rent. According to Mr. Buchanan
then, barley is at a monopoly price, at the highest price which
the purchasers are willing to give for it; but malt made of
barley is not at a monopoly price, and consequently it can be
raised in proportion to the taxes that may be imposed upon it.
This opinion of Mr. Buchanan of the effects of a tax on malt
appears to me to be in direct contradiction to the opinion he
has given of a similar tax, a tax on bread. "A tax on bread will
be ultimately paid, not by a rise of price, but by a reduction
of rent."* If a tax on malt would raise the price of beer, a tax
on bread must raise the price of bread.

The following argument of M. Say is founded on the same
views as Mr. Buchanan's: "The quantity of wine or corn which
a piece of land will produce, will remain nearly the same, what-

* Vol. iii. p. 355.

[1] Bk. v, ch. ii, pt. ii, art. iv; vol. ii,　　[2] Buchanan's ed. of the *Wealth of*
pp. 376–7.　　*Nations*, vol. iii, p. 386, note.

CH. XVII]   TAXES ON OTHER COMMODITIES   255

ever may be the tax with which it is charged. The tax may take away a half, or even three-fourths of its net produce, or of its rent if you please, yet the land would nevertheless be cultivated for the half or the quarter not absorbed by the tax. The rent, that is to say the landlord's share, would merely be somewhat lower. The reason of this will be perceived, if we consider, that in the case supposed, the quantity of produce obtained from the land, and sent to market, will remain nevertheless the same. On the other hand the motives on which the demand for the produce is founded, continue also the same.

"Now, if the quantity of produce supplied, and the quantity demanded, necessarily continue the same, notwithstanding the establishment or the increase of the tax, the price of that produce will not vary; and if the price do not vary, the consumer will not pay the smallest portion of this tax.

"Will it be said that the farmer, he who furnishes labour and capital, will, jointly with the landlord, bear the burden of this tax? certainly not; because the circumstance of the tax has not diminished the number of farms to be let, nor increased the number of farmers. Since in this instance also the supply and demand remain the same, the rent of farms must also remain the same. The example of the manufacturer of salt, who can only make the consumers pay a portion of the tax, and that of the landlord who cannot reimburse himself in the smallest degree, prove the error of those who maintain, in opposition to the economists, that all taxes fall ultimately on the consumer."—Vol. ii. p. 338.

If the tax "took away half, or even three-fourths of the net produce of the land," and the price of produce did not rise, how could those farmers obtain the usual profits of stock who paid very moderate rents, having that quality of land which required a much larger proportion of labour to obtain a given result, than land of a more fertile quality? If the whole rent were remitted, they would still obtain lower profits than those in other trades, and would therefore not continue to cultivate their land, unless they could raise the price of its produce. If the tax fell on the farmers, there would be fewer farmers disposed to hire farms; if it fell on the landlord, many farms would not be let at all, for they would afford no rent. But from what fund would those pay the tax who produce corn without paying any rent? It is quite clear that the tax must fall on the consumer. How would such land, as M. Say describes in the following passage, pay a tax of one-half or three-fourths of its produce?

"We see in Scotland poor lands thus cultivated by the proprietor, and which could be cultivated by no other person. Thus too, we see in the interior provinces of the United States vast and fertile lands, the revenue of which, alone, would not be sufficient for the maintenance of the proprietor. These lands are cultivated nevertheless, but it must be by the proprietor himself, or, in other words, he must add to the rent, which is little or nothing, the profits of his capital and industry, to enable him to live in competence. It is well known that land, though cultivated, yields no revenue to the landlord when no farmer will be willing to pay a rent for it: which is a proof that such land will give only the profits of the capital, and of the industry necessary for its cultivation."—*Say*, Vol. ii. p. 127.

[9]

Of a National Debt

§ 1. [*Is it desirable to defray extraordinary public expenses by loans?*]
The question must now be considered, how far it is right or expedient to
raise money for the purposes of government, not by laying on taxes to the
amount required, but by taking a portion of the capital of the country in
the form of a loan, and charging the public revenue with only the interest.
Nothing needs be said about providing for temporary wants by taking up
money; for instance, by an issue of exchequer bills, destined to be paid off,
at furthest in a year or two, from the proceeds of the existing taxes. This
is a convenient expedient, and when the government does not possess a
treasure or hoard, is often a necessary one, on the occurrence of extraordinary expenses, or of a temporary failure in the ordinary sources of
revenue. What we have to discuss is the propriety of contracting a national
debt of a permanent character; defraying the expenses of a war, or of any
season of difficulty, by loans, to be redeemed either very gradually and at
a distant period, or not at all.

This question has *already been* touched upon in the First Book.*
We *b* remarked, that if the capital taken in loans is abstracted from funds
either engaged in production, or destined to be employed in it, their
diversion from that purpose is equivalent to taking the amount from the
wages of the labouring classes. Borrowing, in this case, is not a substitute
for raising the supplies within the year. A government which borrows does
actually take the amount within the year, and that too by a tax exclusively
on the labouring classes: than which it could have done nothing worse, if
it had supplied its wants by avowed taxation; and in that case the transaction, and its evils, would have ended with the emergency; while by the
circuitous mode adopted, the value exacted from the labourers is gained,
not by the state, but by the employers of labour, the state remaining charged
with the debt besides, and with its interest in perpetuity. The system of
public loans, in such circumstances, may be pronounced the very worst
which, in the present state of civilization, is still included in the catalogue
of financial expedients.

*Supra, vol. i. pp. 77–8.

*a–a*48, 49   been already   *b*48, 49, 52, 57   there

We however remarked that there are other circumstances in which loans are not chargeable with these pernicious consequences: namely, first, when what is borrowed is foreign capital, the overflowings of the general accumulation of the world; or, secondly, when it is capital which either would not have been saved at all unless this mode of investment had been open to it, or after being saved, would have been wasted in unproductive enterprises, or sent to seek employment in foreign countries. When the progress of accumulation has reduced profits either to the ultimate or to the practical minimum,—to the rate, less than which would either put a stop to the increase of capital, or send the whole of the new accumulations abroad; government may annually intercept *these* new accumulations, without trenching on the employment or wages of the labouring classes in the country itself, or perhaps in any other country. To this extent, therefore, the loan system may be carried, without being liable to the utter and peremptory condemnation which is due to it when it overpasses this limit. What is wanted is an index to determine whether, in any given series of years, as during the last *great* war for example, the limit has been exceeded or not.

Such an index exists, at once a certain and an obvious one. Did the government, by its loan operations, augment the rate of interest? If it only opened a channel for capital which would not otherwise have been accumulated, or which, if accumulated, would not have been employed within the country; this implies that the capital, which the government took and expended, could not have found employment at the existing rate of interest. So long as the loans do no more than absorb this surplus, they prevent any tendency to a fall of the rate of interest, but they cannot occasion any rise. When they do raise the rate of interest, as they did in a most extraordinary degree during the *French* war, this is positive proof that the government is a competitor for capital with the ordinary channels of productive investment, and is carrying off, not merely funds which would not, but funds which would, have found productive employment within the country. To the full extent, therefore, to which the loans of government, during the *f* war, caused the rate of interest to exceed what it was before, and what it has been since, those loans *are chargeable with all the evils which have been described*. If it be objected that interest only rose because profits rose, I reply that this does not weaken, but strengthens, the argument. If the government loans produced the rise of profits by the great amount of capital which they absorbed, by what means can they have had this effect, unless by lowering the wages of labour? It will perhaps be said, that what kept profits high during the war was not the drafts made on the

c–c48, 49, 52   those
e–e48, 49   late] 52   last
g–g48, 49, 52   cannot be relieved from the severest condemnation

d–d+57, 62, 65, 71
f48, 49, 52   last

national capital by the loans, but the rapid progress of industrial improvements. This, in a great measure, was the fact; and it no doubt alleviated
the hardship to the labouring classes, and made the financial system which
was pursued less actively mischievous, but not *ʰless contrary to principleʰ*.
These very improvements in industry, made room for a larger amount of
capital; and the government, by draining away a great part of the annual
accumulations, did not indeed prevent that capital from existing ultimately,
(for it started into existence with great rapidity after the peace,) but
prevented it from existing at the time, and subtracted just so much, while
the war lasted, from distribution among productive labourers. If the
government had abstained from taking this capital by loan, and had allowed
it to reach the labourers, but had raised the supplies which it required by a
direct tax on the labouring classes, it would have produced *ⁱ(in every
respect but the expense and inconvenience of collecting the tax)ⁱ* the very
same economical effects *ʲ* which it did produce, except that we should not
now have had the debt. The course it actually took was therefore
worse *ᵏ* than the very worst mode which it could possibly have adopted of
raising the supplies within the year *ˡ*: and the only excuse, or justification,
which it admits of, (so far as that excuse could be truly pleaded,) was
hard necessity; the impossibility of raising so enormous an annual sum by
taxation, without resorting to taxes which from their odiousness, or from
the facility of evasion, it would have been found impracticable to enforce*ˡ*.

When government loans are limited to the overflowings of the national
capital, or to those accumulations which would not take place at all unless
suffered to overflow, they are at least not liable to this grave condemnation:
they occasion no privation to any one at the time, except by the payment
of the interest, and may even be beneficial to the labouring class during the
term of their expenditure, by employing in the direct purchase of labour,
as *ᵐthatᵐ* of soldiers, sailors, &c., funds which might otherwise have quitted
the country altogether. In this case therefore the question really is, what
it is commonly supposed to be in all cases, namely, a choice between a
great sacrifice at once, and a small one indefinitely prolonged. On this
matter it seems rational to think, that the prudence of a nation will
dictate the same conduct as the prudence of an individual; to submit
to as much of the privation immediately, as can easily be borne, and
only when any further burthen would distress or cripple them too much,
to provide for the remainder by mortgaging their future income. It is an
excellent maxim to make present resources suffice for present wants; the

ʰ⁻ʰ48, 49, 52   at all less indefensible
ⁱ⁻ⁱ+57, 62, 65, 71
ʲ48, 49, 52   , in every respect,
ᵏ48, 49, 52   , by the whole of that great fact,
ˡ⁻ˡ+57, 62, 65, 71   ᵐ⁻ᵐ+49, 52, 57, 62, 65, 71

future will have its own wants to provide for. On the other hand, it may reasonably be taken into consideration that in *a country increasing in wealth,* the necessary expenses of government do not increase in the same ratio as capital or population; any burthen, therefore, is always less and less felt: and since those extraordinary expenses of government which are fit to be incurred at all, are mostly beneficial beyond the existing generation, there is no injustice in making posterity pay a part of the price, if the inconvenience would be extreme of defraying the whole of it by the exertions and sacrifices of the generation which first incurred it.

§ 2. [*Not desirable to redeem a national debt by a general contribution*] When a country, wisely or unwisely, has burthened itself with a debt, *is it* expedient to take steps for redeeming that debt? In principle it is impossible not to maintain the affirmative. It is true that the payment of the interest, when the creditors are members of the same community, is no national loss, but a mere transfer. The transfer, however, being compulsory, is a serious evil, and the raising a great extra revenue by any system of taxation necessitates so much expense, vexation, disturbance of the channels of industry, and other mischiefs over and above the mere payment of the money wanted by the government, that to get rid of the necessity of such taxation is at all times worth a considerable effort. The same amount of sacrifice which would have been worth incurring to avoid contracting the debt, it is worth while to incur, at any subsequent time, for the purpose of extinguishing it.

Two modes have been contemplated of paying off a national debt: either at once by a general contribution, or gradually by a surplus revenue. The first would be incomparably the best, if it were practicable; and *it would be practicable* if it could justly be done by *e* assessment on property alone. If property bore the whole interest of the debt, property might, with great advantage to itself, pay it off; since this would be merely surrendering to a creditor the principal sum, the whole annual proceeds of which were already his by law; *and* would be equivalent to what a landowner does when he sells part of his estate, to free the remainder from a mortgage. But property, it needs hardly be said, does not pay, and cannot justly be required to pay, the whole interest of the debt. Some indeed affirm that it can, on the *e* plea that the existing generation is only bound to pay the debts of its predecessors from the assets it has received from them, and not from the produce of its own industry. But has no one received anything from previous generations except those who have succeeded to property? Is the whole difference between the earth as it is, with its clearings and improvements, its roads

---

*n–n*48, 49   an improving country
*b–b*48, 49, 52, 57   practicable it would be
*d–d*48, 49, 52   or

*a–a*49   it is [*printer's error?*]
*c*48, 49, 52, 57   an
*e*48, 49   specious

and canals, its towns and manufactories, and the earth as it was when the
first human being set foot on it, of no benefit to any but those who are
called the owners of the soil? Is the capital accumulated by the labour and
abstinence of all former generations, of no advantage to any but those
who have succeeded to the legal ownership of part of it? And have we not
inherited a mass of acquired knowledge, both scientific and empirical, due
to the sagacity and industry of those who preceded us, the benefits of
which are the common wealth of all? Those who are born to the ownership
of property have, in addition to these common benefits, a separate inheritance, and to this difference it is right that advertence should be had in
regulating taxation. *It belongs to the general financial system of the
country to take* due account of this principle, and I have indicated, as in
my opinion a proper mode of taking account of it, a considerable tax on
legacies and inheritances. Let it be determined directly and openly what
is due from property to the state, and from the state to property, and let
the institutions of the state be regulated accordingly *g* . Whatever is the
fitting contribution from property to the general expenses of the state, in
the same and in no greater proportion should it contribute towards either
the interest or the repayment of the national debt.

This, however, if admitted, is fatal to any scheme for the extinction of
the debt by a general assessment on the community. Persons of property
could pay their share of the amount by a sacrifice of property, and have
the same net income as before; but if those who have no accumulations,
but only incomes, were required to make up by a single payment the
equivalent of the annual charge laid on them by the taxes maintained to
pay the interest of the debt, they could only do so by incurring a private
debt equal to their share of the public debt; while, from the insufficiency, in
most cases, of the security which they could give, the interest would amount
to a much larger annual sum than their share of that now paid by the state.
Besides, a collective debt defrayed by taxes, has over the same debt
parcelled out among individuals, the immense advantage, that it is virtually
a mutual insurance among the contributors. If the fortune of a contributor
diminishes, his taxes diminish; if he is ruined, they cease altogether, and
his portion of the debt is wholly transferred to the solvent members of
the community. If it were laid on him as a private obligation, he would
still be liable to it even when penniless.

When the state possesses property, in land or otherwise, which there
are not strong reasons of public utility for its retaining at its disposal, this

---

*f–f*48, 49   We are at liberty to assume that the general financial system of the
country takes
*g*48, 49   ; but let not principles, admitted in theory, be wounded mortally by a
back-handed blow

should be employed, as far as it will go, in extinguishing debt. Any casual gain, or godsend, is naturally devoted to the same purpose. Beyond this, the only mode which is both just and feasible, of extinguishing or reducing a national debt, is by means of a surplus revenue.

§ 3. [*In what cases it is desirable to maintain a surplus revenue for the redemption of debt*] The desirableness, *per se*, of maintaining a surplus for this purpose, does not, I think, admit of a doubt. We sometimes, indeed, hear it said that the amount should rather be left to "fructify in the pockets of the people." This is a good argument, as far as it goes, against levying taxes unnecessarily for purposes of unproductive expenditure, but not against paying off a national debt. For, what is meant by the word fructify? If it means anything, it means productive employment; and as an argument against taxation, we must understand it to assert, that if the amount were left with the people they would save it, and convert it into capital. It is probable, indeed, that they would save a part, but extremely improbable that they would save the whole: while if taken by taxation, and employed in paying off debt, the whole is saved, and made productive. To the fund-holder who receives the payment it is already capital, not revenue, and he will make it "fructify," that it may continue to afford him an income. The objection, therefore, is not only groundless, but the real argument is on the other side: the amount is much more certain of fructifying if it is *a*not*a* "left in the pockets of the people."

It is not, however, advisable in all cases to maintain a surplus revenue for the extinction of debt. The advantage of paying off the national debt of Great Britain, for instance, is that it would enable us to get rid of the worse half of our *b* taxation. But of this worse half some portions must be worse than others, and to get rid of those would be a greater benefit proportionally than to get rid of the rest. If renouncing a surplus revenue would enable us to dispense with a tax, we ought to consider the very worst of all our taxes as precisely the one which we are keeping up for the sake of ultimately abolishing taxes not so bad as itself. In a country advancing in wealth, whose increasing revenue gives it the power of ridding itself from time to time of the most inconvenient portions of its taxation, I conceive that the increase of revenue should rather be disposed of by taking off taxes, than by liquidating debt, as long as any very objectionable imposts remain. In the present state of England, therefore, I hold it to be good policy in the government, when it has a surplus of an apparently permanent character, to take off taxes, provided these are rightly selected. Even when no taxes remain but such as are not unfit to form part of a permanent system, it is wise to continue the same policy by experimental reductions

*a–a*48, 49, 52, 57 *not*   *b*48, 49, 52, 57 present

of those taxes, until the point is discovered at which a given amount of revenue can be raised with the smallest pressure on the contributors. After this, such surplus revenue as might arise from any further increase of the produce of the taxes, should not, I conceive, be remitted, but applied to the redemption of debt. Eventually, it might be expedient to appropriate the entire produce of particular taxes to this purpose; since there would be more assurance that the liquidation would be persisted in, if the fund destined to it were kept apart, and not blended with the general revenues of the state. The ^{c}succession duties^c would be peculiarly suited to such a purpose, since taxes paid as they are, out of capital, would be better employed in reimbursing capital than in defraying current expenditure. If this separate appropriation were made, any surplus afterwards arising from the increasing produce of the other taxes, and from the saving of interest on the successive portions of debt paid off, might form a ground for ^{d}a^d remission of taxation.

It has been contended that some amount of national debt is desirable, and almost indispensable, as an investment for the savings of the poorer or more inexperienced part of the community. Its convenience in that respect is undeniable; but (besides that the progress of industry is gradually affording other modes of investment almost as safe and untroublesome, such as the shares or obligations of great public companies) the only real superiority of an investment in the funds consists in the national guarantee, and this could be afforded by other means than that of a public debt, involving compulsory taxation. One mode which would answer the purpose, would be a national bank of deposit and discount, with ramifications throughout the country; which might receive any money confided to it, and either fund it at a fixed rate of interest, or allow interest on a floating balance, like the joint stock banks; the interest given being of course lower than the rate at which individuals can borrow, in proportion to the greater security of a government investment; and the expenses of the establishment being defrayed by the difference between the interest which the bank would pay, and that which it would obtain, by lending its deposits on mercantile, landed, or other security. There are no insuperable objections in principle, ^{e}nor, I should think,^{e} in practice, to an institution of this sort, as a means of supplying the same convenient mode of investment now afforded by the public funds. It would constitute the state a great insurance company, to insure that part of the community who live on the interest of their property, against the risk of losing it by the bankruptcy of those to whom they might otherwise be under the necessity of confiding it.

$^{c-c}$48, 49, 52 taxes on legacies and inheritances
$^{d-d}$+49, 52, 57, 62, 65, 71
$^{e-e}$48, 49, 52, 57 and I should think none

Part III
Keynesian Public Debt Theory

Part III: An Overview

John Maynard Keynes wrote *The General Theory of Employment, Interest and Money* (1936) at a time when the global economy seemed to be in free fall and his grim predictions of the economic consequences of Versailles were being confirmed by events in Germany. Armies of unemployed workers in the United States and Europe, representing upwards of one-quarter of the labor force, were queuing for relief while Adolf Hitler was starting down the path that would end not in a glorious 'triumph of the will', but in a Berlin bunker with a pistol shot to the head.

Failing to understand the fundamental monetary causes of the unprecedented economic collapse (Friedman and Schwartz, 1963, pp. 299–419), Keynes thought that full employment would be restored – and the capitalist economic system thereby rescued from itself – only if Western governments intervened aggressively, using their fiscal policy tools to offset the calamitous and apparently permanent decline in private investment spending that began in 1929. For Keynes and his disciples, the depth and persistence of the Great Depression proved that exclusive reliance on the self-correcting tendencies of unfettered markets would not guarantee stability and prosperity in highly complex industrial economies. *Laissez-faire* was no longer acceptable. The public sector must act.

Keynes prescribed an increase in government spending – on useful public works if possible, but on pyramids if need be – in order to inject purchasing power into the economy and put people back to work. Every new dollar spent by the public sector would increase national income several times over through the operation of a 'multiplier effect' as consumption spending by the initial recipients passes into the hands of merchants who, in turn, spend a portion of their now higher incomes, enriching others who increase their expenditures, and so on and so on. If, in addition, the increase in government spending is financed by debt (what Keynes called 'loan expenditure'), the holders of the bonds will feel wealthier, and this 'wealth effect' will generate further increases in private consumption and investment spending. Economic stagnation will thus be overcome and all who want work at ruling wage rates will find jobs.

Keynesian public debt theory challenged the orthodoxy of classical economics, not least by suggesting that public debt augments private wealth. That conclusion, which sets the doctrine of Ricardian equivalence on its head, has not gone uncontested, as later sections of these volumes show. However, it was Keynes's disciples, notably Alvin Hansen and Abba Lerner, who took his ideas to their logical extreme, provoking later generations of scholars to ponder whether Keynes was in fact a Keynesian.

The logical extremity is reached in Lerner's concept of 'functional finance' (see Chapter 11), which rejects completely what, in Paul Samuelson's derisive terms, is the 'oldfangled shirt-sleeve economics' of the classicals and their 'shibboleth of a balanced budget'. As Lerner defined it, 'the central idea [of functional finance] is that government fiscal policy, its spending and taxing, its borrowing and repayment of loans, its issue of new money and its withdrawal of money, shall all be undertaken with an eye only to the *results* of these actions on the economy and not to any established traditional doctrine about what is sound or unsound' (emphasis in original). In other words, fiscal policy is to be judged by whether it produces economic stability and promotes prosperity rather than by some old-fashioned 'principle of trying to balance the budget over a solar year or any other arbitrary period'.

Functional finance is part-and-parcel of a privileged scholar's mind-set, which presumes that macroeconomic policy decisions are taken by philosopher-king-economists who intervene appropriately so as to counterbalance the normal peaks and troughs of the business cycle and maintain the economy at full employment. The budgetary consequences of this balancing act are mere inconsequential by-products of the conduct of fiscal policy. If higher taxes and reduced government spending are needed to quell 'the animal spirits' fueling unsupportable economic expansion (what Alan Greenspan has called 'irrational exuberance'), then the public budget will show a surplus. On the other hand, if lower taxes and increased public spending are needed to prime the economic pump, then the government budget will be in deficit.

The precepts of functional finance go well beyond routine compensatory or counter-cyclical fiscal smoothing. Chronic economic stagnation, such as that of the decade before the Second World War, calls for chronic budget deficits. Governments should not be deterred from appropriate fiscal policy responses by worries about persistent budget imbalance. Indeed, Lerner argued that the supposed adverse effects of public debt were largely 'imaginary' and that governments could, in essence, borrow *ad libitum* and *ad infinitum*. To be sure, the public debt might impose a burden on the economy if taxes were ever raised to service or retire it; but these expenses could always be met by yet more government borrowing!

Lerner went to great lengths in attempting to dispel the 'fairy-tales of terrible consequences' from undertaking a prolonged program of deficit spending. He argued forcefully, that because 'we owe it to ourselves', the financial transactions involved in issuing public debt and making interest payments on it are pure transfers with no worrisome economic effects. Even intergenerational income transfers associated with public borrowing have no sting because 'if our children or grandchildren repay some of the national debt these payments will be made *to* our children or grandchildren and to nobody else' (emphasis in original).

While 'some people will be made better off and some people will be worse off' in the process, such 'redistribution can be ignored because we have no more reason for supposing that the new distribution is worse than the old one than for assuming the opposite'. For Lerner, only 'external debt' (government bonds purchased by foreigners) imposes a real burden on a nation's citizens. It is as if deficit spending is a carnival shell-game where players lose only when the pea ends up on the other side of an imaginary line on the table.

Thus the public debt in Keynesian economics came to be seen, for the most part, as beneficent – increasing the national income directly through the spending programs it financed, and indirectly through the wealth effects experienced by bondholders. Income and wealth can be conjured by government out of thin air as a perfectly free lunch. Although Samuelson and other Keynesians gradually acknowledged that the taxes levied to amortize or service the national debt would indeed have real consequences, these effects were a small price to pay for the full employment and healthy economic growth promised by the wise application of the government's fiscal policy tools. For Samuelson, the only thing wrong with the New Deal was that it was too timid.

Schooled in Keynesian macroeconomic policy prescriptions by successive editions of Samuelson's influential college textbook, generations of college sophomores learned that budget deficits were nothing to fear, particularly if the public debt does not grow faster than GDP grows. Britain experienced its greatest material progress in the century before the First World War, when its internal debt ranged between two and three times its national income and when interest charges were correspondingly high. Today, the national debt of the United States is a mere bagatelle by this measure, or so the Keynesians would have it.

Projected budget surpluses at the dawn of the twenty-first century notwithstanding, the legacy of Lord Keynes has been an erosion of the norm of fiscal responsibility in public finance and a political bias toward deficits that, over the past 30 years, have built a public debt pyramid of massive proportions throughout the Western democracies.

References

Friedman, M. and Schwartz, A.J. (1963), *A Monetary History of the United States, 1867-1960*. Princeton, NJ: Princeton University Press.

Keynes, J.M. (1936), *The General Theory of Employment, Interest and Money*. London: Macmillan.

Charles K. Rowley
William F. Shughart II
Robert D. Tollison

[10]

THE MARGINAL PROPENSITY TO CONSUME AND THE MULTIPLIER

We established in chapter 8 that employment can only increase *pari passu* with investment unless there is a change in the propensity to consume. We can now carry this line of thought a stage further. For in given circumstances a definite ratio, to be called the *multiplier*, can be established between income and investment and, subject to certain simplifications, between the total employment and the employment directly employed on investment (which we shall call the *primary employment*). This further step is an integral part of our theory of employment, since it establishes a precise relationship, given the propensity to consume, between aggregate employment and income and the rate of investment. The conception of the multiplier was first introduced into economic theory by Mr R. F. Kahn in his article on 'The Relation of Home Investment to Unemployment' (*Economic Journal*, June 1931). His argument in this article depended on the fundamental notion that, if the propensity to consume in various hypothetical circumstances is (together with certain other conditions) taken as given and we conceive the monetary or other public authority to take steps to stimulate or to retard investment, the change in the amount of employment will be a function of the net change in the amount of investment; and it aimed at laying down general principles by which to estimate the actual quantitative relationship between an incre-

THE GENERAL THEORY OF EMPLOYMENT

ment of net investment and the increment of aggregate employment which will be associated with it. Before coming to the multiplier, however, it will be convenient to introduce the conception of the *marginal propensity to consume*.

I

The fluctuations in real income under consideration in this book are those which result from applying different quantities of employment (i.e. of labour-units) to a given capital equipment, so that real income increases and decreases with the number of labour-units employed. If, as we assume in general, there is a decreasing return at the margin as the number of labour-units employed on the given capital equipment is increased, income measured in terms of wage-units will increase more than in proportion to the amount of employment, which, in turn, will increase more than in proportion to the amount of real income measured (if that is possible) in terms of product. Real income measured in terms of product and income measured in terms of wage-units will, however, increase and decrease together (in the short period when capital equipment is virtually unchanged). Since, therefore, real income, in terms of product, may be incapable of precise numerical measurement, it is often convenient to regard income in terms of wage-units (Y_w) as an adequate working index of changes in real income. In certain contexts we must not overlook the fact that, in general, Y_w increases and decreases in a greater proportion than real income; but in other contexts the fact that they always increase and decrease together renders them virtually interchangeable.

Our normal psychological law that, when the real income of the community increases or decreases, its consumption will increase or decrease but not so fast, can, therefore, be translated—not, indeed, with absolute accuracy but subject to qualifications which are obvious

THE MARGINAL PROPENSITY TO CONSUME

and can easily be stated in a formally complete fashion—into the propositions that ΔC_w and ΔY_w have the same sign, but $\Delta Y_w > \Delta C_w$, where C_w is the consumption in terms of wage-units. This is merely a repetition of the proposition already established on p. 29 above.

Let us define, then, $\dfrac{dC_w}{dY_w}$ as the *marginal propensity to consume*.

This quantity is of considerable importance, because it tells us how the next increment of output will have to be divided between consumption and investment. For $\Delta Y_w = \Delta C_w + \Delta I_w$, where ΔC_w and ΔI_w are the increments of consumption and investment; so that we can write $\Delta Y_w = k\Delta I_w$, where $1 - \dfrac{1}{k}$ is equal to the marginal propensity to consume.

Let us call k the *investment multiplier*. It tells us that, when there is an increment of aggregate investment, income will increase by an amount which is k times the increment of investment.

II

Mr Kahn's multiplier is a little different from this, being what we may call the *employment multiplier* designated by k', since it measures the ratio of the increment of total employment which is associated with a given increment of primary employment in the investment industries. That is to say, if the increment of investment ΔI_w leads to an increment of primary employment ΔN_2 in the investment industries, the increment of total employment $\Delta N = k'\Delta N_2$.

There is no reason in general to suppose that $k = k'$. For there is no necessary presumption that the shapes of the relevant portions of the aggregate supply functions for different types of industry are such that the ratio of the increment of employment in the one set of industries to the increment of demand which has

THE GENERAL THEORY OF EMPLOYMENT

stimulated it will be the same as in the other set of industries.[1] It is easy, indeed, to conceive of cases, as, for example, where the marginal propensity to consume is widely different from the average propensity, in which there would be a presumption in favour of some inequality between $\dfrac{\Delta Y_w}{\Delta N}$ and $\dfrac{\Delta I_w}{\Delta N_2}$, since there would be very divergent proportionate changes in the demands for consumption-goods and investment-goods respectively. If we wish to take account of such possible differences in the shapes of the relevant portions of the aggregate supply functions for the two groups of industries respectively, there is no difficulty in rewriting the following argument in the more generalised form. But to elucidate the ideas involved, it will be convenient to deal with the simplified case where $k = k'$.

It follows, therefore, that, if the consumption psychology of the community is such that they will choose to consume, e.g. nine-tenths of an increment of income,[2] then the multiplier k is 10; and the total employment caused by (e.g.) increased public works will be ten times the primary employment provided by

---

[1] More precisely, if e_e and e'_e are the elasticities of employment in industry as a whole and in the investment industries respectively, and if N and N_2 are the numbers of men employed in industry as a whole and in the investment industries, we have

$$\Delta Y_w = \frac{Y_w}{e_e . N} \Delta N$$

and

$$\Delta I_w = \frac{I_w}{e'_e . N_2} \Delta N_2,$$

so that

$$\Delta N = \frac{e_e I_w N}{e'_e N_2 Y_w} k . \Delta N_2,$$

i.e.

$$k' = \frac{I_w}{e'_e N_2} . \frac{e_e N}{Y_w} k.$$

If, however, there is no reason to expect any material relevant difference in the shapes of the aggregate supply functions for industry as a whole and for the investment industries respectively, so that $\dfrac{I_w}{e'_e . N_2} = \dfrac{Y_w}{e_e . N}$, then it follows that $\dfrac{\Delta Y_w}{\Delta N} = \dfrac{\Delta I_w}{\Delta N_2}$ and, therefore, that $k = k'$.

[2] Our quantities are measured throughout in terms of wage-units.

THE MARGINAL PROPENSITY TO CONSUME

the public works themselves, assuming no reduction of investment in other directions. Only in the event of the community maintaining their consumption unchanged in spite of the increase in employment and hence in real income, will the increase of employment be restricted to the primary employment provided by the public works. If, on the other hand, they seek to consume the whole of any increment of income, there will be no point of stability and prices will rise without limit. With normal psychological suppositions, an increase in employment will only be associated with a decline in consumption if there is at the same time a change in the propensity to consume—as the result, for instance, of propaganda in time of war in favour of restricting individual consumption; and it is only in this event that the increased employment in investment will be associated with an unfavourable repercussion on employment in the industries producing for consumption.

This only sums up in a formula what should by now be obvious to the reader on general grounds. An increment of investment in terms of wage-units cannot occur unless the public are prepared to increase their savings in terms of wage-units. Ordinarily speaking, the public will not do this unless their aggregate income in terms of wage-units is increasing. Thus their effort to consume a part of their increased incomes will stimulate output until the new level (and distribution) of incomes provides a margin of saving sufficient to correspond to the increased investment. The multiplier tells us by how much their employment has to be increased to yield an increase in real income sufficient to induce them to do the necessary extra saving, and is a function of their psychological propensities.[1] If saving is the pill and consumption is the jam, the extra jam has to be proportioned to the size of the

---

[1] Though in the more generalised case it is also a function of the physical conditions of production in the investment and consumption industries respectively.

117

THE GENERAL THEORY OF EMPLOYMENT

additional pill. Unless the psychological propensities of the public are different from what we are supposing, we have here established the law that increased employment for investment must necessarily stimulate the industries producing for consumption and thus lead to a total increase of employment which is a multiple of the primary employment required by the investment itself.

It follows from the above that, if the marginal propensity to consume is not far short of unity, small fluctuations in investment will lead to wide fluctuations in employment; but, at the same time, a comparatively small increment of investment will lead to full employment. If, on the other hand, the marginal propensity to consume is not much above zero, small fluctuations in investment will lead to correspondingly small fluctuations in employment; but, at the same time, it may require a large increment of investment to produce full employment. In the former case involuntary unemployment would be an easily remedied malady, though liable to be troublesome if it is allowed to develop. In the latter case, employment may be less variable but liable to settle down at a low level and to prove recalcitrant to any but the most drastic remedies. In actual fact the marginal propensity to consume seems to lie somewhere between these two extremes, though much nearer to unity than to zero; with the result that we have, in a sense, the worst of both worlds, fluctuations in employment being considerable and, at the same time, the increment in investment required to produce full employment being too great to be easily handled. Unfortunately the fluctuations have been sufficient to prevent the nature of the malady from being obvious, whilst its severity is such that it cannot be remedied unless its nature is understood.

When full employment is reached, any attempt to increase investment still further will set up a tendency in money-prices to rise without limit, irrespective of the marginal propensity to consume; i.e. we shall

THE MARGINAL PROPENSITY TO CONSUME

have reached a state of true inflation.[1] Up to this point, however, rising prices will be associated with an increasing aggregate real income.

III

We have been dealing so far with a *net* increment of investment. If, therefore, we wish to apply the above without qualification to the effect of (e.g.) increased public works, we have to assume that there is no offset through decreased investment in other directions,—and also, of course, no associated change in the propensity of the community to consume. Mr Kahn was mainly concerned in the article referred to above in considering what offsets we ought to take into account as likely to be important, and in suggesting quantitative estimates. For in an actual case there are several factors besides some specific increase of investment of a given kind which enter into the final result. If, for example, a government employs 100,000 additional men on public works, and if the multiplier (as defined above) is 4, it is not safe to assume that aggregate employment will increase by 400,000. For the new policy may have adverse reactions on investment in other directions.

It would seem (following Mr Kahn) that the following are likely in a modern community to be the factors which it is most important not to overlook (though the first two will not be fully intelligible until after Book IV has been reached):

(i) The method of financing the policy and the increased working cash, required by the increased employment and the associated rise of prices, may have the effect of increasing the rate of interest and so retarding investment in other directions, unless the monetary authority takes steps to the contrary; whilst, at the same time, the increased cost of capital goods will reduce their marginal efficiency to the private in-

---

[1]   Cf. chapter 21, p. 303, below.

THE GENERAL THEORY OF EMPLOYMENT

vestor, and this will require an actual *fall* in the rate of interest to offset it.

(ii) With the confused psychology which often prevails, the government programme may, through its effect on 'confidence', increase liquidity-preference or diminish the marginal efficiency of capital, which, again, may retard other investment unless measures are taken to offset it.

(iii) In an open system with foreign-trade relations, some part of the multiplier of the increased investment will accrue to the benefit of employment in foreign countries, since a proportion of the increased consumption will diminish our own country's favourable foreign balance; so that, if we consider only the effect on domestic employment as distinct from world employment, we must diminish the full figure of the multiplier. On the other hand our own country may recover a portion of this leakage through favourable repercussions due to the action of the multiplier in the foreign country in increasing its economic activity.

Furthermore, if we are considering changes of a substantial amount, we have to allow for a progressive change in the marginal propensity to consume, as the position of the margin is gradually shifted; and hence in the multiplier. The marginal propensity to consume is not constant for all levels of employment, and it is probable that there will be, as a rule, a tendency for it to diminish as employment increases; when real income increases, that is to say, the community will wish to consume a gradually diminishing proportion of it.

There are also other factors, over and above the operation of the general rule just mentioned, which may operate to modify the marginal propensity to consume, and hence the multiplier; and these other factors seem likely, as a rule, to accentuate the tendency of the general rule rather than to offset it. For, in the first place, the increase of employment will tend, owing

THE MARGINAL PROPENSITY TO CONSUME

to the effect of diminishing returns in the short period, to increase the proportion of aggregate income which accrues to the entrepreneurs, whose individual marginal propensity to consume is probably less than the average for the community as a whole. In the second place, unemployment is likely to be associated with negative saving in certain quarters, private or public, because the unemployed may be living either on the savings of themselves and their friends or on public relief which is partly financed out of loans; with the result that re-employment will gradually diminish these particular acts of negative saving and reduce, therefore, the marginal propensity to consume more rapidly than would have occurred from an equal increase in the community's real income accruing in different circumstances.

In any case, the multiplier is likely to be greater for a small net increment of investment than for a large increment; so that, where substantial changes are in view, we must be guided by the average value of the multiplier based on the average marginal propensity to consume over the range in question.

Mr Kahn has examined the probable quantitative result of such factors as these in certain hypothetical special cases. But, clearly, it is not possible to carry any generalisation very far. One can only say, for example, that a typical modern community would probably tend to consume not much less than 80 per cent of any increment of real income, if it were a closed system with the consumption of the unemployed paid for by transfers from the consumption of other consumers, so that the multiplier after allowing for offsets would not be much less than 5. In a country, however, where foreign trade accounts for, say, 20 per cent of consumption and where the unemployed receive out of loans or their equivalent up to, say, 50 per cent of their normal consumption when in work, the multiplier may fall as low as 2 or 3 times the employment pro-

THE GENERAL THEORY OF EMPLOYMENT

vided by a specific new investment. Thus a given fluctuation of investment will be associated with a much less violent fluctuation of employment in a country in which foreign trade plays a large part and unemployment relief is financed on a larger scale out of borrowing (as was the case, e.g. in Great Britain in 1931), than in a country in which these factors are less important (as in the United States in 1932).[1]

It is, however, to the general principle of the multiplier to which we have to look for an explanation of how fluctuations in the amount of investment, which are a comparatively small proportion of the national income, are capable of generating fluctuations in aggregate employment and income so much greater in amplitude than themselves.

IV

The discussion has been carried on, so far, on the basis of a change in aggregate investment which has been foreseen sufficiently in advance for the consumption industries to advance *pari passu* with the capital-goods industries without more disturbance to the price of consumption-goods than is consequential, in conditions of decreasing returns, on an increase in the quantity which is produced.

In general, however, we have to take account of the case where the initiative comes from an increase in the output of the capital-goods industries which was not fully foreseen. It is obvious that an initiative of this description only produces its full effect on employment over a period of time. I have found, however, in discussion that this obvious fact often gives rise to some confusion between the logical theory of the multiplier, which holds good continuously, without time-lag, at all moments of time, and the consequences of an expansion in the capital-goods industries which take gradual effect, subject to time-lag and only after an interval.

[1] Cf. however, below, p. 128, for an American estimate.

THE MARGINAL PROPENSITY TO CONSUME

The relationship between these two things can be cleared up by pointing out, firstly that an unforeseen, or imperfectly foreseen, expansion in the capital-goods industries does not have an instantaneous effect of equal amount on the aggregate of investment but causes a gradual increase of the latter; and, secondly, that it may cause a temporary departure of the marginal propensity to consume away from its normal value, followed, however, by a gradual return to it.

Thus an expansion in the capital-goods industries causes a series of increments in aggregate investment occurring in successive periods over an interval of time, and a series of values of the marginal propensity to consume in these successive periods which differ both from what the values would have been if the expansion had been foreseen and from what they will be when the community has settled down to a new steady level of aggregate investment. But in every interval of time the theory of the multiplier holds good in the sense that the increment of aggregate demand is equal to the product of the increment of aggregate investment and the multiplier as determined by the marginal propensity to consume.

The explanation of these two sets of facts can be seen most clearly by taking the extreme case where the expansion of employment in the capital-goods industries is so entirely unforeseen that in the first instance there is no increase whatever in the output of consumption-goods. In this event the efforts of those newly employed in the capital-goods industries to consume a proportion of their increased incomes will raise the prices of consumption-goods until a temporary equilibrium between demand and supply has been brought about partly by the high prices causing a postponement of consumption, partly by a redistribution of income in favour of the saving classes as an effect of the increased profits resulting from the higher prices, and partly by the higher prices causing a depletion

THE GENERAL THEORY OF EMPLOYMENT

of stocks. So far as the balance is restored by a post-ponement of consumption there is a temporary reduction of the marginal propensity to consume, i.e. of the multiplier itself, and in so far as there is a depletion of stocks, aggregate investment increases for the time being by less than the increment of investment in the capital-goods industries,—i.e. the thing to be multiplied does not increase by the full increment of investment in the capital-goods industries. As time goes on, however, the consumption-goods industries adjust themselves to the new demand, so that when the deferred consumption is enjoyed, the marginal propensity to consume rises temporarily above its normal level, to compensate for the extent to which it previously fell below it, and eventually returns to its normal level; whilst the restoration of stocks to their previous figure causes the increment of aggregate investment to be temporarily greater than the increment of investment in the capital-goods industries (the increment of working capital corresponding to the greater output also having temporarily the same effect).

The fact that an unforeseen change only exercises its full effect on employment over a period of time is important in certain contexts;—in particular it plays a part in the analysis of the trade cycle (on lines such as I followed in my *Treatise on Money*). But it does not in any way affect the significance of the theory of the multiplier as set forth in this chapter; nor render it inapplicable as an indicator of the total benefit to employment to be expected from an expansion in the capital· goods industries. Moreover, except in conditions where the consumption industries are already working almost at capacity so that an expansion of output requires an expansion of plant and not merely the more intensive employment of the existing plant, there is no reason to suppose that more than a brief interval of time need elapse before employment in the consumption industries is advancing *pari passu* with

THE MARGINAL PROPENSITY TO CONSUME

employment in the capital-goods industries with the multiplier operating near its normal figure.

V

We have seen above that the greater the marginal propensity to consume, the greater the multiplier, and hence the greater the disturbance to employment corresponding to a given change in investment. This might seem to lead to the paradoxical conclusion that a poor community in which saving is a very small proportion of income will be more subject to violent fluctuations than a wealthy community where saving is a larger proportion of income and the multiplier consequently smaller.

This conclusion, however, would overlook the distinction between the effects of the marginal propensity to consume and those of the average propensity to consume. For whilst a high marginal propensity to consume involves a larger *proportionate* effect from a given percentage change in investment, the *absolute* effect will, nevertheless, be small if the *average* propensity to consume is also high. This may be illustrated as follows by a numerical example.

Let us suppose that a community's propensity to consume is such that, so long as its real income does not exceed the output from employing 5,000,000 men on its existing capital equipment, it consumes the whole of its income; that of the output of the next 100,000 additional men employed it consumes 99 per cent, of the next 100,000 after that 98 per cent, of the third 100,000 97 per cent and so on; and that 10,000,000 men employed represents full employment. It follows from this that, when $5,000,000 + n \times 100,000$ men are employed, the multiplier at the margin is $\dfrac{100}{n}$, and $\dfrac{n(n+1)}{2(50+n)}$ per cent of the national income is invested.

THE GENERAL THEORY OF EMPLOYMENT

Thus when 5,200,000 men are employed the multiplier is very large, namely 50, but investment is only a trifling proportion of current income, namely, 0·06 per cent; with the result that if investment falls off by a large proportion, say about two-thirds, employment will only decline to 5,100,000, i.e. by about 2 per cent. On the other hand, when 9,000,000 men are employed, the marginal multiplier is comparatively small, namely $2\frac{1}{2}$, but investment is now a substantial proportion of current income, namely, 9 per cent; with the result that if investment falls by two-thirds, employment will decline to 6,900,000, namely, by 19 per cent. In the limit where investment falls off to zero, employment will decline by about 4 per cent in the former case, whereas in the latter case it will decline by 44 per cent.[1]

In the above example, the poorer of the two communities under comparison is poorer by reason of under-employment. But the same reasoning applies by easy adaptation if the poverty is due to inferior skill, technique or equipment. Thus whilst the multiplier is larger in a poor community, the effect on employment of fluctuations in investment will be much greater in a wealthy community, assuming that in the latter current investment represents a much larger proportion of current output.[2]

---

[1] Quantity of investment is measured, above, by the number of men employed in producing it. Thus if there are diminishing returns per unit of employment as employment increases, what is double the quantity of investment on the above scale will be less than double on a physical scale (if such a scale is available).

[2] More generally, the ratio of the proportional change in total demand to the proportional change in investment

$$= \frac{\Delta Y}{Y} \Big/ \frac{\Delta I}{I} = \frac{\Delta Y}{Y} \cdot \frac{Y-C}{\Delta Y - \Delta C} = \frac{1 - \dfrac{C}{Y}}{1 - \dfrac{dC}{dY}}.$$

As wealth increases $\dfrac{dC}{dY}$ diminishes, but $\dfrac{C}{Y}$ also diminishes. Thus the fraction increases or diminishes according as consumption increases or diminishes in a smaller or greater proportion than income.

THE MARGINAL PROPENSITY TO CONSUME

It is also obvious from the above that the employment of a given number of men on public works will (on the assumptions made) have a much larger effect on aggregate employment at a time when there is severe unemployment, than it will have later on when full employment is approached. In the above example, if, at a time when employment has fallen to 5,200,000, an additional 100,000 men are employed on public works, total employment will rise to 6,400,000. But if employment is already 9,000,000 when the additional 100,000 men are taken on for public works, total employment will only rise to 9,200,000. Thus public works even of doubtful utility may pay for themselves over and over again at a time of severe unemployment, if only from the diminished cost of relief expenditure, provided that we can assume that a smaller proportion of income is saved when unemployment is greater; but they may become a more doubtful proposition as a state of full employment is approached. Furthermore, if our assumption is correct that the marginal propensity to consume falls off steadily as we approach full employment, it follows that it will become more and more troublesome to secure a further given increase of employment by further increasing investment.

It should not be difficult to compile a chart of the marginal propensity to consume at each stage of a trade cycle from the statistics (if they were available) of aggregate income and aggregate investment at successive dates. At present, however, our statistics are not accurate enough (or compiled sufficiently with this specific object in view) to allow us to infer more than highly approximate estimates. The best for the purpose, of which I am aware, are Mr Kuznets' figures for the United States (already referred to, p. 103 above), though they are, nevertheless, very precarious. Taken in conjunction with estimates of national income these suggest, for what they are worth, both a lower figure and a more stable figure for the investment multiplier

THE GENERAL THEORY OF EMPLOYMENT

than I should have expected. If single years are taken
in isolation, the results look rather wild. But if they
are grouped in pairs, the multiplier seems to have been
less than 3 and probably fairly stable in the neighbour-
hood of 2·5. This suggests a marginal propensity to
consume not exceeding 60 to 70 per cent—a figure
quite plausible for the boom, but surprisingly, and, in
my judgment, improbably low for the slump. It is
possible, however, that the extreme financial conservatism of corporate finance in the United States,
even during the slump, may account for it. In other
words, if, when investment is falling heavily through a
failure to undertake repairs and replacements, financial
provision is made, nevertheless, in respect of such wastage, the effect is to prevent the rise in the marginal propensity to consume which would have occurred otherwise. I suspect that this factor may have played a
significant part in aggravating the degree of the recent
slump in the United States. On the other hand, it is
possible that the statistics somewhat overstate the decline in investment, which is alleged to have fallen off
by more than 75 per cent in 1932 compared with 1929,
whilst net 'capital formation' declined by more than 95
per cent;—a moderate change in these estimates being
capable of making a substantial difference to the multiplier.

VI

When involuntary unemployment exists, the marginal disutility of labour is necessarily less than the
utility of the marginal product. Indeed it may be
much less. For a man who has been long unemployed some measure of labour, instead of involving
disutility, may have a positive utility. If this is
accepted, the above reasoning shows how 'wasteful'
loan expenditure[1] may nevertheless enrich the com-

---

[1] It is often convenient to use the term 'loan expenditure' to include
the public investment financed by borrowing from individuals and also

THE MARGINAL PROPENSITY TO CONSUME

munity on balance. Pyramid-building, earthquakes, even wars may serve to increase wealth, if the education of our statesmen on the principles of the classical economics stands in the way of anything better.

It is curious how common sense, wriggling for an escape from absurd conclusions, has been apt to reach a preference for *wholly* 'wasteful' forms of loan expenditure rather than for *partly* wasteful forms, which, because they are not wholly wasteful, tend to be judged on strict 'business' principles. For example, unemployment relief financed by loans is more readily accepted than the financing of improvements at a charge below the current rate of interest; whilst the form of digging holes in the ground known as gold-mining, which not only adds nothing whatever to the real wealth of the world but involves the disutility of labour, is the most acceptable of all solutions.

If the Treasury were to fill old bottles with banknotes, bury them at suitable depths in disused coal-mines which are then filled up to the surface with town rubbish, and leave it to private enterprise on well-tried principles of *laissez-faire* to dig the notes up again (the right to do so being obtained, of course, by tendering for leases of the note-bearing territory), there need be no more unemployment and, with the help of the repercussions, the real income of the community, and its capital wealth also, would probably become a good deal greater than it actually is. It would, indeed, be more sensible to build houses and the like; but if there are political and practical difficulties in the way of this, the above would be better than nothing.

The analogy between this expedient and the gold-

any other current public expenditure which is so financed. Strictly speaking, the latter should be reckoned as negative saving, but official action of this kind is not influenced by the same sort of psychological motives as those which govern private saving. Thus 'loan expenditure' is a convenient expression for the net borrowings of public authorities on all accounts, whether on capital account or to meet a budgetary deficit. The one form of loan expenditure operates by increasing investment and the other by increasing the propensity to consume.

129

THE GENERAL THEORY OF EMPLOYMENT

mines of the real world is complete. At periods when gold is available at suitable depths experience shows that the real wealth of the world increases rapidly; and when but little of it is so available our wealth suffers stagnation or decline. Thus gold-mines are of the greatest value and importance to civilisation. Just as wars have been the only form of large-scale loan expenditure which statesmen have thought justifiable, so gold-mining is the only pretext for digging holes in the ground which has recommended itself to bankers as sound finance; and each of these activities has played its part in progress—failing something better. To mention a detail, the tendency in slumps for the price of gold to rise in terms of labour and materials aids eventual recovery, because it increases the depth at which gold-digging pays and lowers the minimum grade of ore which is payable.

In addition to the probable effect of increased supplies of gold on the rate of interest, gold-mining is for two reasons a highly practical form of investment, if we are precluded from increasing employment by means which at the same time increase our stock of useful wealth. In the first place, owing to the gambling attractions which it offers it is carried on without too close a regard to the ruling rate of interest. In the second place the result, namely, the increased stock of gold, does not, as in other cases, have the effect of diminishing its marginal utility. Since the value of a house depends on its utility, every house which is built serves to diminish the prospective rents obtainable from further house-building and therefore lessens the attraction of further similar investment unless the rate of interest is falling *pari passu*. But the fruits of gold-mining do not suffer from this disadvantage, and a check can only come through a rise of the wage-unit in terms of gold, which is not likely to occur unless and until employment is substantially better. Moreover, there is no subsequent reverse effect on account of provision for

THE MARGINAL PROPENSITY TO CONSUME

user and supplementary costs, as in the case of less durable forms of wealth.

Ancient Egypt was doubly fortunate, and doubtless owed to this its fabled wealth, in that it possessed *two* activities, namely, pyramid-building as well as the search for the precious metals, the fruits of which, since they could not serve the needs of man by being consumed, did not stale with abundance. The Middle Ages built cathedrals and sang dirges. Two pyramids, two masses for the dead, are twice as good as one; but not so two railways from London to York. Thus we are so sensible, have schooled ourselves to so close a semblance of prudent financiers, taking careful thought before we add to the 'financial' burdens of posterity by building them houses to live in, that we have no such easy escape from the sufferings of unemployment. We have to accept them as an inevitable result of applying to the conduct of the State the maxims which are best calculated to 'enrich' an individual by enabling him to pile up claims to enjoyment which he does not intend to exercise at any definite time.

[11]

FUNCTIONAL FINANCE AND THE FEDERAL DEBT

BY ABBA P. LERNER

APART from the necessity of winning the war, there is no task facing society today so important as the elimination of economic insecurity. If we fail in this after the war the present threat to democratic civilization will arise again. It is therefore essential that we grapple with this problem even if it involves a little careful thinking and even if the thought proves somewhat contrary to our preconceptions.

In recent years the principles by which appropriate government action can maintain prosperity have been adequately developed, but the proponents of the new principles have either not seen their full logical implications or shown an over-solicitousness which caused them to try to save the public from the necessary mental exercise. This has worked like a boomerang. Many of our publicly minded men who have come to see that deficit spending actually works still oppose the permanent maintenance of prosperity because in their failure to see *how* it all works they are easily frightened by fairy tales of terrible consequences.

I

As formulated by Alvin Hansen and others who have developed and popularized it, the new fiscal theory (which was first put forward in substantially complete form by J. M. Keynes in England) sounds a little less novel and absurd to our preconditioned ears than it does when presented in its simplest and most logical form, with all the unorthodox implications expressly formulated. In some cases the less shocking formulation may be intentional, as a tactical device to gain serious attention. In other cases it is due not to a desire to sugar the pill but to the fact that the writers them-

FUNCTIONAL FINANCE 39

selves have not seen all the unorthodox implications—perhaps sub-consciously compromising with their own orthodox education. But now it is these compromises that are under fire. Now more than ever it is necessary to pose the theorems in the purest form. Only thus will it be possible to clear the air of objections which really are concerned with awkwardnesses that appear only when the new theory is forced into the old theoretical framework.

Fundamentally the new theory, like almost every important dis-covery, is extremely simple. Indeed it is this simplicity which makes the public suspect it as too slick. Even learned professors who find it hard to abandon ingrained habits of thought have complained that it is "merely logical" when they could find no flaw in it. What progress the theory has made so far has been achieved not by simpli-fying it but by dressing it up to make it more complicated and accompanying the presentation with impressive but irrelevant sta-tistics.

The central idea is that government fiscal policy, its spending and taxing, its borrowing and repayment of loans, its issue of new money and its withdrawal of money, shall all be undertaken with an eye only to the *results* of these actions on the economy and not to any established traditional doctrine about what is sound or unsound. This principle of judging only by *effects* has been applied in many other fields of human activity, where it is known as the method of science as opposed to scholasticism. The principle of judging fiscal measures by the way they work or function in the economy we may call *Functional Finance*.

The first financial responsibility of the government (since no-body else can undertake that responsibility) is to keep the total rate of spending in the country on goods and services neither greater nor less than that rate which at the current prices would buy all the goods that it is possible to produce. If total spending is allowed to go above this there will be inflation, and if it is allowed to go below this there will be unemployment. The government can in-crease total spending by spending more itself or by reducing taxes so that the taxpayers have more money left to spend. It can reduce total spending by spending less itself or by raising taxes so that tax-payers have less money left to spend. By these means total spending can be kept at the required level, where it will be enough to buy the goods that can be produced by all who want to work, and yet not enough to bring inflation by demanding (at current prices) *more* than can be produced.

In applying this first law of Functional Finance, the government may find itself collecting more in taxes than it is spending, or spending more than it collects in taxes. In the former case it can keep the difference in its coffers or use it to repay some of the national debt, and in the latter case it would have to provide the difference by borrowing or printing money. In neither case should the government feel that there is anything especially good or bad about this result; it should merely concentrate on keeping the total rate of spending neither too small nor too great, in this way preventing both unemployment and inflation.

An interesting, and to many a shocking, corollary is that taxing is *never* to be undertaken merely because the government needs to make money payments. According to the principles of Functional Finance, taxation must be judged only by its effects. Its main effects are two: the taxpayer has less money left to spend and the government has more money. The second effect can be brought about so much more easily by printing the money that only the first effect is significant. Taxation should therefore be imposed only when it is desirable that the taxpayers shall have less money to spend, for example, when they would otherwise spend enough to bring about inflation.

The second law of Functional Finance is that the government should borrow money only if it is desirable that the public should have less money and more government bonds, for these are the *effects* of government borrowing. This might be desirable if otherwise the rate of interest would be reduced too low (by attempts on the part of the holders of the cash to lend it out) and induce too much investment, thus bringing about inflation. Conversely, the government should lend money (or repay some of its debt) only

FUNCTIONAL FINANCE   41

if it is desirable to increase the money or to reduce the quantity of government bonds in the hands of the public. When taxing, spending, borrowing and lending (or repaying loans) are governed by the principles of Functional Finance, any excess of money outlays over money revenues, if it cannot be met out of money hoards, must be met by printing new money, and any excess of revenues over outlays can be destroyed or used to replenish hoards.

The almost instinctive revulsion that we have to the idea of printing money, and the tendency to identify it with inflation, can be overcome if we calm ourselves and take note that this printing does not affect the amount of money *spent*. That is regulated by the first law of Functional Finance, which refers especially to inflation and unemployment. The printing of money takes place only when it is needed to implement Functional Finance in spending or lending (or repayment of government debt).[1]

In brief, Functional Finance rejects completely the traditional doctrines of "sound finance" and the principle of trying to balance the budget over a solar year or any other arbitrary period. In their place it prescribes: first, the adjustment of total spending (by everybody in the economy, including the government) in order to eliminate both unemployment and inflation, using government spending when total spending is too low and taxation when total spending is too high; second, the adjustment of public holdings of money and of government bonds, by government borrowing or debt repayment, in order to achieve the rate of interest which results in the most desirable level of investment; and, third, the printing, hoarding or destruction of money as needed for carrying out the first two parts of the program.

II

In judging the formulations of economists on this subject it is difficult to distinguish between tact in smoothing over the more stag-

---

[1]Borrowing money from the banks, on conditions which permit the banks to issue new credit money based on their additional holdings of government securities, must be considered for our purpose as printing money. In effect the banks are acting as agents for the government in issuing credit or bank money.

gering statements of Functional Finance and insufficient clarity on
the part of those who do not fully realize the extremes that are implied in their relatively orthodox formulations. First there were the
pump-primers, whose argument was that the government merely
had to get things going and then the economy could go on by itself.
There are very few pump-primers left now. A formula similar in
some ways to pump-priming was developed by Scandinavian economists in terms of a series of cyclical, capital and other special budgets which had to be balanced not annually but over longer periods.
Like the pump-priming formula it fails because there is no reason
for supposing that the spending and taxation policy which maintains full employment and prevents inflation must necessarily balance the budget over a decade any more than during a year or at the
end of each fortnight.

As soon as this was seen—the lack of any guarantee that the maintenance of prosperity would permit the budget to be balanced even
over longer periods—it had to be recognized that the result might be
a continually increasing national debt (if the additional spending
were provided by the government's borrowing of the money and
not by printing the excess of its spending over its tax revenues).
At this point two things should have been made clear: first, that
this possibility presented no danger to society, no matter what un-
imagined heights the national debt might reach, so long as Functional Finance maintained the proper level of total demand for
current output; and second (though this is much less important),
that there is an automatic tendency for the budget to be balanced
in the long run as a *result* of the application of Functional Finance,
even if there is no place for the *principle* of balancing the budget.
No matter how much interest has to be paid on the debt, taxation
must not be applied unless it is necessary to keep spending down
to prevent inflation. The interest can be paid by borrowing still
more.

As long as the public is willing to keep on lending to the government there is no difficulty, no matter how many zeros are added to
the national debt. If the public becomes reluctant to keep on lend-

ing, it must either hoard the money or spend it. If the public hoards, the government can print the money to meet its interest and other obligations, and the only effect is that the public holds government currency instead of government bonds and the government is saved the trouble of making interest payments. If the public spends, this will increase the rate of total spending so that it will not be necessary for the government to borrow for this purpose; and if the rate of spending becomes too great, *then* is the time to tax to prevent inflation. The proceeds can then be used to pay interest and repay government debt. In every case Functional Finance provides a simple, quasi-automatic response.

But either this was not seen clearly or it was considered too shocking or too logical to be told to the public. Instead it was argued, for example by Alvin Hansen, that as long as there is a reasonable ratio between national income and debt, the interest payment on the national debt can easily come from taxes paid out of the increased national income created by the deficit financing.

This unnecessary "appeasement" opened the way to an extremely effective opposition to Functional Finance. Even men who have a clear understanding of the mechanism whereby government spending in times of depression can increase the national income by several times the amount laid out by the government, and who understand perfectly well that the national debt, when it is not owed to other nations, is not a burden on the nation in the same way as an individual's debt to other individuals is a burden on the individual, have come out strongly against "deficit spending."[2] It has been argued that "it would be impossible to devise a program better adapted to the systematic undermining of the private-enterprise system and the hastening of the final catastrophe than 'deficit spending.'"[3]

These objections are based on the recognition that although every dollar spent by the government may create several dollars of

[2]An excellent example of this is the persuasive article by John T. Flynn in *Harper's Magazine* for July 1942.
[3]Flynn, *ibid.*

income in the course of the next year or two, the effects then disappear. From this it follows that if the national income is to be maintained at a high level the government has to keep up its contribution to spending for as long as private spending is insufficient by itself to provide full employment. This might mean an indefinite continuation of government support to spending (though not necessarily at an increasing rate); and if, as the "appeasement" formulation suggests, all this spending comes out of borrowing, the debt will keep on growing until it is no longer in a "reasonable" ratio to income.

This leads to the crux of the argument. If the interest on the debt must be raised out of taxes (again an assumption that is unchallenged by the "appeasement" formulation) it will in time constitute an important fraction of the national income. The very high income tax necessary to collect this amount of money and pay it to the holders of government bonds will discourage risky private investment, by so reducing the net return on it that the investor is not compensated for the risk of losing his capital. This will make it necessary for the government to undertake still more deficit financing to keep up the level of income and employment. Still heavier taxation will then be necessary to pay the interest on the growing debt—until the burden of taxation is so crushing that private investment becomes unprofitable, and the private enterprise economy collapses. Private firms and corporations will all be bankrupted by the taxes, and the government will have to take over all industry.

This argument is not new. The identical calamities, although they are now receiving much more attention than usual, were promised when the first income tax law of one penny in the pound was proposed. All this only makes it more important to evaluate the significance of the argument.

III

There are four major errors in the argument against deficit spending, four reasons why its apparent conclusiveness is only illusory.

FUNCTIONAL FINANCE   45

In the first place, the same high income tax that reduces the re-turn on the investment is deductible for the loss that is incurred if the investment turns out a failure. As a result of this the *net* return on the risk of loss is unaffected by the income tax rate, no matter how high that may be. Consider an investor in the $50,000-a-year income class who has accumulated $10,000 to invest. At 6 per-cent this would yield $600, but after paying income tax on this addition to his income at 60 cents in the dollar he would have only $240 left. It is argued, therefore, that he would not invest because this is insufficient compensation for the risk of losing $10,000. This argument forgets that if the $10,000 is all lost, the net loss to the investor, after he has deducted his income tax allowance, will be only $4,000, and the rate of return on the amount he actually risks is still exactly 6 percent; $240 is 6 percent of $4,000. The effect of the income tax is to make the rich man act as a kind of agent work-ing for society on commission. He receives only a part of the return on the investment, but he loses only a part of the money that is invested. Any investment that was worth undertaking in the absence of the income tax is still worth undertaking.

Of course, this correction of the argument is strictly true only where 100 percent of the loss is deductible from taxable income, where relief from taxation occurs at the same rate as the tax on returns. There is a good case against certain limitations on permis-sible deduction from the income tax base for losses incurred, but that is another story. Something of the argument remains, too, if the loss would put the taxpayer into a lower income tax bracket, where the rebate (and the tax) is at a lower rate. There would then be some reduction in the net return as compared with the potential net loss. But this would apply only to such investments as are large enough to threaten to impoverish the investor if they fail. It was for the express purpose of dealing with this problem that the cor-poration was devised, making it possible for many individuals to combine and undertake risky enterprises without any one person having to risk all his fortune on one venture. But quite apart from corporate investment, this problem would be met almost entirely if the maximum rate of income tax were reached at a relatively low level, say at $25,000 a year (low, that is, from the point of view of the rich men who are the supposed source of risk capital). Even if all income in excess of $25,000 were taxed at 90 percent there would be no discouragement in the investment of any part of income over this level. True, the net return, after payment of tax, would be only one-tenth of the nominal interest payments, but the amount risked by the investors would also be only ten percent of the actual capital invested, and therefore the net return on the capital actually risked by the investor would be unaffected.

In the second place, this argument against deficit spending in time of depression would be indefensible even if the harm done by debt were as great as has been suggested. It must be remembered that spending by the government increases the *real* national income of goods and services by several times the amount spent by the government, and that the burden is measured not by the amount of the interest payments but only by the inconveniences involved in the process of transferring the money from the taxpayers to the bondholders. Therefore objecting to deficit spending is like arguing that if you are offered a job when out of work on the condition that you promise to pay your wife interest on a part of the money earned (or that your wife pay it to you) it would be wiser to continue to be unemployed, because in time you will be owing your wife a great deal of money (or she will be owing it to you), and this might cause matrimonial difficulties in the future. Even if the interest payments were really lost to society, instead of being merely transferred within the society, they would come to much less than the loss through permitting unemployment to continue. That loss would be several times as great as the *capital* on which these interest payments have to be made.

In the third place, there is no good reason for supposing that the government would have to raise all the interest on the national debt by current taxes. We have seen that Functional Finance permits taxation only when the *direct* effect of the tax is in the social interest, as when it prevents excessive spending or excessive invest-

FUNCTIONAL FINANCE 47

ment which would bring about inflation. If taxes imposed to prevent inflation do not result in sufficient proceeds, the interest on the debt can be met by borrowing or printing the money. There is no risk of inflation from this, because if there were such a risk a greater amount would have to be collected in taxes.

This means that the absolute size of the national debt does not matter at all, and that however large the interest payments that have to be made, these do not constitute any burden upon society as a whole. A completely fantastic exaggeration may illustrate the point. Suppose the national debt reaches the stupendous total of ten thousand billion dollars (that is, ten trillion, $10,000,000,-000,000), so that the interest on it is 300 billion a year. Suppose the real national income of goods and services which can be produced by the economy when fully employed is 150 billion. The interest alone, therefore, comes to twice the real national income. There is no doubt that a debt of this size would be called "unreasonable." But even in this fantastic case the payment of the interest constitutes no burden on society. Although the real income is only 150 billion dollars the money income is 450 billion—150 billion in income from the production of goods and services and 300 billion in income from ownership of the government bonds which constitute the national debt. Of this money income of 450 billion, 300 billion has to be collected in taxes by the government for interest payments (if 10 trillion is the legal debt limit), but after payment of these taxes there remains 150 billion dollars in the hands of the taxpayers, and this is enough to pay for all the goods and services that the economy can produce. Indeed it would do the public no good to have any more money left after tax payments, because if it spent more than 150 billion dollars it would merely be raising the prices of the goods bought. It would not be able to obtain more goods to consume than the country is able to produce.

Of course this illustration must not be taken to imply that a debt of this size is at all likely to come about as a result of the application of Functional Finance. As will be shown below, there is a natural tendency for the national debt to stop growing long before it comes

48   SOCIAL RESEARCH

anywhere near the astronomical figures that we have been playing with.

The unfounded assumption that current interest on the debt must be collected in taxes springs from the idea that the debt must be kept in a "reasonable" or "manageable" ratio to income (whatever that may be). If this restriction is accepted, *borrowing* to pay the interest is eliminated as soon as the limit of "reasonableness" is reached, and if we further rule out, as an indecent thought, the possibility of *printing* the money, there remains only the possibility of raising the interest payments by taxes. Fortunately there is no need to assume these limitations so long as Functional Finance is on guard against inflation, for it is the fear of inflation which is the only rational basis for suspicion of the printing of money.

Finally, there is no reason for assuming that, as a result of the continued application of Functional Finance to maintain full employment, the government must always be borrowing more money and increasing the national debt. There are a number of reasons for this.

First, full employment *can* be maintained by printing the money needed for it, and this does not increase the debt at all. It is probably advisable, however, to allow debt and money to increase together in a certain balance, as long as one or the other has to increase.

Second, since one of the greatest deterrents to private investment is the fear that the depression will come before the investment has paid for itself, the guarantee of permanent full employment will make private investment much more attractive, once investors have got over their suspicions of the new procedure. The greater private investment will diminish the need for deficit spending.

Third, as the national debt increases, and with it the sum of private wealth, there will be an increasingly yield from taxes on higher incomes and inheritances, even if the tax rates are unchanged. These higher tax payments do not represent reductions of spending by the taxpayers. Therefore the government does not have to use these proceeds to maintain the requisite rate of spending, and it can devote them to paying the interest on the national debt.

FUNCTIONAL FINANCE   49

Fourth, as the national debt increases it acts as a self-equilibrating force, gradually diminishing the further need for its growth and finally reaching an equilibrium level where its tendency to grow comes completely to an end. The greater the national debt the greater is the quantity of private wealth. The reason for this is simply that for every dollar of debt owed by the government there is a private creditor who owns the government obligations (possibly through a corporation in which he has shares), and who regards these obligations as part of his private fortune. The greater the private fortunes the less is the incentive to add to them by saving out of current income. As current saving is thus discouraged by the great accumulation of past savings, spending out of current income increases (since spending is the only alternative to saving income). This increase in private spending makes it less necessary for the government to undertake deficit financing to keep total spending at the level which provides full employment. When the government debt has become so great that private spending is enough to provide the total spending needed for full employment, there is no need for any deficit financing by the government, the budget is balanced and the national debt automatically stops growing. The size of this equilibrium level of debt depends on many things. It can only be guessed at, and in the very roughest manner. My guess is that it is between 100 and 300 billion dollars. Since the level is a result and not a principle of Functional Finance the latitude of such a guess does not matter; it is not needed for the application of the laws of Functional Finance.

Fifth, if for any reason the government does not wish to see private property grow too much (whether in the form of government bonds or otherwise) it can check this by taxing the rich instead of borrowing from them, in its program of financing government spending to maintain full employment. The rich will not reduce their spending significantly, and thus the effects on the economy, apart from the smaller debt, will be the same as if the money had been borrowed from them. By this means the debt can be reduced to any desired level and kept there.

50   SOCIAL RESEARCH

The answers to the argument against deficit spending may thus be summarized as follows:

The national debt does not have to keep on increasing;

Even if the national debt does grow, the interest on it does not have to be raised out of current taxes;

Even if the interest on the debt is raised out of current taxes, these taxes constitute only the interest on only a fraction of the benefit enjoyed from the government spending, and are not lost to the nation but are merely transferred from taxpayers to bond-holders;

High income taxes need not discourage investment, because appropriate deductions for losses can diminish the capital actually risked by the investor in the same proportion as his net income from the investment is reduced.

IV

If the propositions of Functional Finance were put forward without fear of appearing too logical, criticisms like those discussed above would not be as popular as they now are, and it would not be necessary to defend Functional Finance from its friends. An especially embarrassing task arises from the claim that Functional Finance (or deficit financing, as it is frequently but unsatisfactorily called) is primarily a defense of private enterprise. In the attempt to gain popularity for Functional Finance, it has been given other names and declared to be essentially directed toward saving private enterprise. I myself have sinned similarly in previous writings in identifying it with democracy,[*] thus joining the army of salesmen who wrap up their wares in the flag and tie anything they have to sell to victory or morale.

Functional Finance is not especially related to democracy or to private enterprise. It is applicable to a communist society just as well as to a fascist society or a democratic society. It is applicable to any society in which money is used as an important element in the economic mechanism. It consists of the simple principle of

[*]In "Total Democracy and Full Employment," *Social Change* (May 1941).

FUNCTIONAL FINANCE 51

giving up our preconceptions of what is proper or sound or traditional, of what "is done," and instead considering the *functions* performed in the economy by government taxing and spending and borrowing and lending. It means using these instruments simply as instruments, and not as magic charms that will cause mysterious hurt if they are manipulated by the wrong people or without due reverence for tradition. Like any other mechanism, Functional Finance will work no matter who pulls the levers. Its relationship to democracy and free enterprise consists simply in the fact that if the people who believe in these things will not use Functional Finance, they will stand no chance in the long run against others who will.

[12]

The Burden of the
National Debt

⇒⇒ BY ⇐⇐

ABBA P. LERNER

MILLIONS of people are now taking time off from worrying about the prospects of atomic warfare to do some worrying on account of the burden of a growing national debt. But there are many quite different concepts of the nature of this burden. The purpose of this article is to examine the most important of these worries and to see to what extent they are justified and to what extent they are about imaginary burdens which only confuse the real issues.

I. IMAGINARY EFFECTS OF NATIONAL DEBT

1. By far the most common concern about the national debt comes from considering it as exactly the same kind of thing as a private debt which one individual owes to others. Every dollar of an individual's indebtedness must be subtracted from his assets in arriving at a measure of his net wealth. Indebtedness is impoverishment. It places the debtor in the hands of the creditor and threatens him with hardship and ruin. To avoid indebtedness as far as possible is undoubtedly an eminently well-established rule of private prudence.

The simple transferability of this rule to national debt is denied by nearly all economists. But nearly everybody who has ever suffered the oppressions of private indebtedness is tempted to apply the analogy directly, and the primary orthodoxy of the edi-

Abba P. Lerner

torial writers, the dogma that sound government finance means balancing the budget, has no other basis.

One of the most effective ways of clearing up this most serious of all semantic confusions is to point out that private debt differs from national debt in being *external*. It is owed by one person to *others*. That is what makes it burdensome. Because it is *interpersonal* the proper analogy is not to national debt but to *international* debt. A nation owing money to other nations (or to the citizens of other nations) *is* impoverished or burdened in the same kind of way as a man who owes money to other men. But this does not hold for national debt which is owed by the nation to citizens of the *same* nation. There is then no external creditor. "We owe it to ourselves."

This refutation of the validity of the analogy from *external* to *internal* debt must not be interpreted as a denial that any significant problems can be raised by internal national debt. When economists are sufficiently irritated by the illegitimate analogy they are liable to say that the national debt does not matter at all. But this must be understood in the same sense as when a man who finds that rumor has converted a twisted ankle into a broken neck tells his friends that he is perfectly all right.

2. A variant of the false analogy is the declaration that national debt puts an unfair burden on our children, who are thereby made to pay for our extravagances. Very few economists need to be reminded that if our children or grandchildren repay some of the national debt these payments will be made *to* our children or grandchildren and to nobody else. Taking them altogether they will no more be impoverished by making the repayments than they will be enriched by receiving them.

Unfortunately the first few times people see this argument destroyed they feel tricked rather than convinced. But the resistance to conceding the painlessness of repaying national debt can be diminished by pointing out that it only corresponds to the relative uselessness of incurring it. An *external* loan enables an individual or a nation to get things from others without having to

The Burden of the National Debt

give anything in return, for the time being. The borrower is enabled to consume more than he is producing. And when he repays the external debt he has to consume less than he is producing. But this is not true for *internal* borrowing. However useful an internal loan may be for the health of the economy, it does *not* enable the nation to consume more than it produces. It should therefore not be so surprising that the repayment of internal debt does not necessitate a tightening of the belt. The internal borrowing did not permit the belt to be loosened in the first place.

3. Many who recognize that national debt is no substraction from national wealth are nevertheless deeply concerned about the interest payments on the national debt. They call this the *interest burden* almost as if the interest payments constituted subtractions from the national income.

This involves exactly the same error. The interest payments are no more a subtraction from the national income than the national debt itself is a subtraction from the national wealth. This can be shown most clearly by pointing out how easy it is, by simply borrowing the money needed to make the interest payments, to convert the "interest burden" into some additional national debt. The interest need therefore never be more onerous than the additional principal of the debt into which it can painlessly be transformed.

Borrowing money to make the interest payments sounds much worse than simply getting into debt in the first place. Popular feeling on this score seems so strong that economists who are themselves quite free from the erroneous analogy have felt themselves constrained by the power of the prejudice to assume that the interest payments on national debt are never borrowed but raised by taxes.[1]

---

[1] E.g., Evsey D. Domar, "The Burden of the Debt and the National Income," *American Economic Review*, December, 1944, p. 799. "This assumption (that all funds for payment of interest charges are to be raised by taxation) is made both to simplify the argument and to protect the reader from a shock. To many, government investment financed by borrowing sounds so bad that the thought of borrowing to pay the interest is simply unbearable." (Reprinted by permission.)

Abba P. Lerner

The strict application of such a secondary orthodoxy would mean much more than these economists intend to concede to the popular prejudice. It would mean nothing less than the prohibition of all borrowing, and a meticulous adherence to the primary orthodoxy of balancing the budget at all times. For as soon as there is any national debt at all on which any interest has to be paid, *any* further government borrowing is indistinguishable from borrowing to pay the interest—unless we are taken in by book-keeping fictions of financial earmarking which say that the money borrowed goes for other purposes so that the particular dollars used to pay the interest come from taxation.[2]

4. Once the analogy with external debt is removed from the scene it is possible to consider various alleged effects of national debt on the economy to see whether they are real or important.

One of these is an alleged deflationary effect of the interest on the national debt. If the money to pay the interest is raised by additional taxes, these would probably reduce spending by more than the interest payments would increase spending. The net effect would be to aggravate any existing deficiency of spending or to alleviate any existing excess of spending. It would tend to deepen a depression or to mitigate an inflation.

But this deflationary effect is not really the effect of the interest payments. It only appears to be such because of a silent acceptance of the secondary orthodoxy of not borrowing to pay interest, but raising the money by additional taxation.[3] The deflationary effect of such additional taxation is then misleadingly attributed to the national debt or to the interest payments.

---

[2] If we did permit ourselves to indulge in such make-believe, the secondary orthodoxy would be reduced to declaring that everything is all right as long as the interest paid on the national debt does not exceed the total tax revenue. It could then be declared that the interest payments all come out of taxes even if all other expenditures are financed by borrowing!

[3] This is on a third interpretation of the secondary orthodoxy which would call for an *increase* in tax revenue to match any *increase* in interest payments on the national debt. While this is perhaps more in accord with the feelings behind the injunction, it is supported by neither reason nor tradition and fails to give a practical guide because there is no way of knowing what would be the level of tax revenue in the absence of the national debt.

The Burden of the National Debt

With the unmasking of the implicit secondary orthodoxy it becomes clear that the interest payments are *inflationary*. They constitute additional income to the recipients and *increase* the rate of spending. If any additional taxes are imposed, their normally deflationary effects must of course be taken into consideration; but there is no reason for attributing these effects to the interest payments, since we need not impose such taxes if their effects are not desired.

5. The rational alternative principle to the orthodox one of balancing the budget, which means keeping tax revenues equal to government spending, is the Functional Finance principle of keeping total spending in the economy at a level which is high enough to prevent depression yet low enough to prevent inflation.

This is to aim policy *directly* at the real problems in terms of which any policy—including the orthodox policy of balancing the budget—must ultimately be justified: the prevention of both inflation and depression.

Whether the budget will be balanced or underbalanced or over-balanced will then be a *result*, more or less foreseen, of the application of the Functional Finance principle, depending on which of these is necessary for the prevention of inflation and depression.

Our main problem can then be reformulated in this way:— Could we get into serious trouble from real effects of a growing national debt if we follow the principle of Functional Finance?

II. REAL EFFECTS OF NATIONAL DEBT

6. Since the interest payments on the national debt increase private spending, a fiscal program which would have led to the right level of total spending in the absence of the national debt and the interest payments on it would now result in too much spending. Any increase in national debt (which increases money income and therefore also the spending out of income) must therefore be accompanied by a decrease in government spending or by an increase in taxation (or both). If this involves the abandonment of useful government undertakings or the enactment of harmful

259

Abba P. Lerner

taxes, we really have a bad effect or "burden" of national debt.

This looks somewhat like the secondary orthodoxy which says that the money to make interest payments on the national debt must be raised from taxes, but the resemblance is only superficial. Since Functional Finance is interested only in total spending, it does not care whether the additional revenues from the taxes are equal to the interest payments. If more than an additional dollar is collected from the taxes needed to offset the extra spending due to an additional dollar of interest payments, tax revenue will have to be increased by more than the additional interest payments. On the other hand, if the efficiency of a dollar of tax revenue in reducing spending is greater than the efficiency of a dollar of interest payment in increasing spending, no increase in total spending will occur even though additional tax revenues are less than the additional interest payments.

But it is not really satisfactory to speak of tax revenues at all. Spending is affected by the tax *rates*, not by the tax *revenues*. The revenues are themselves effects of the taxes, and the efficiency of a tax in reducing spending is only indirectly connected with its efficiency in raising revenue. An increase in sales taxes which sharply diminished spending, for instance, might actually reduce the tax revenue. Functional Finance would then be served by additional taxes which offset the spending induced by the interest payments, even though tax revenues would actually be diminished just when the interest disbursements are increased.

7. In attempts to discredit the argument that we owe the national debt to ourselves it is often pointed out that the "we" does not consist of the same people as the "ourselves." The benefits from interest payments on the national debt do not accrue to every individual in exactly the same degree as the damage done to him by the additional taxes made necessary. That is why it is not possible to repudiate the whole national debt without hurting anybody.

While this is undoubtedly true, all it means is that some people will be better off and some people will be worse off. Such a redistribution of wealth is involved in every significant happening

The Burden of the National Debt

in our closely interrelated economy, in every invention or discovery or act of enterprise. If there is some good general reason for incurring debt, the redistribution can be ignored because we have no more reason for supposing that the new distribution is worse than the old one than for assuming the opposite. That the distribution will be *different* is no more an argument against national debt than it is an argument in favor of it.

8. The growth of national debt may not only make some people richer and some people poorer, but may increase the inequality of distribution. This is because richer people can buy more government bonds and so get more of the interest payments without incurring a proportionately heavier burden of the taxes. Most people would agree that this is bad. But it is no necessary effect of an increasing national debt. If the additional taxes are more progressive—more concentrated on the rich—than the additional holdings of government bonds, the effect will be to *diminish* the inequality of income and wealth.

9. There are also effects on investment. Additional taxes reduce the net yield from investment, after taxes, and make socially useful investments unprofitable to the investor.

This effect is cancelled whenever there is the possibility of balancing losses against profits for tax purposes. If such offsetting were universally possible the taxation would not discourage investment at all.[4] But the opportunity of loss offset is not universal, so that the interest payments on the national debt, by making more taxation necessary for the prevention of inflation, interferes with the efficiency of the economy by discouraging useful investments.

[4] See "Functional Finance and the Federal Debt," *Social Research*, February, 1943, (reprinted in *International Postwar Problems*, October, 1945) and "An Integrated Full Employment Policy," *International Postwar Problems*, January, 1946, and reprinted in Lerner and Graham, *Planning and Paying for Full Employment*, Princeton University Press, 1946. On the assumption of perfect loss offset, taxation might even *encourage* investment by impoverished investors willing to take more chances in attempts to maintain their standards, but this does not invalidate the general argument that a social loss is involved. See Musgrave and Domar, "Proportional Income Taxation and Risk Taking," *Quarterly Journal of Economics*, May, 1944.

Abba P. Lerner

A failure to consider the cancelling effects of loss offsets is partially responsible for a common exaggeration of the bad effect of national debt on investment. This sometimes takes the form of a vivid nightmare of a vicious circle. Government investment to maintain prosperity by filling the gap left by discouraged private investment is financed by loans which increase the national debt still further. This calls for still more taxes, still greater discouragement of private investment, and the need for still more government investment to prevent depression with still more government borrowing—the cycle going on until by this insidious mechanism the economy is unwittingly led to complete collectivism.

Here it must be pointed out that as long as it is necessary for the government to prevent depression by filling a gap in investment, the economy is suffering from *too little spending*. There is therefore no need for more taxation and its possible bad effect on investment. Such extra taxation is necessary only if the economy is suffering from the opposite trouble—from *too much spending*. The vicious circle, apart from some other weaknesses, depends on supposing the economy to suffer at the same time from too much spending and from too little spending.

10. An increase in national debt, with its accompanying accumulation of government bonds by the individuals to whom the debt is owed, can make the owners of the government bonds less willing to work. One of the reasons for working, the earning of money to put away for a rainy day, is weakened (from the point of view of these bondholders) because there is more put away already for rainy days.

This has been pointed out as a bad effect of national debt. But work is only a *means* for producing the things that people want and is not desirable as an end in itself. (Any work that is so enjoyed would not be reduced for the reasons here discussed.) The decrease takes place because people *prefer* the leisure to the products of labor, and the change represents an *increase* in the welfare of the people.

The increase in leisure would be accompanied by an increase in

262

The Burden of the National Debt

consumption, both this and the increased leisure coming out of a reduction in *saving*. This saving which is prevented by the increase in national debt would have taken place not for the sake of permitting an increase in future consumption but for the sake of the security yielded by the savings. It would have made necessary an increase in investment to prevent depression. This shift of resources from consumption (including leisure) to investment is unnecessary, because the desired security is provided without it by the ownership of the additional national debt. Anybody who still wants to save for the sake of the interest yield (reflecting the marginal efficiency of investment) is free to do so. But the increased consumption and reduced efforts by people who are enjoying the ownership of government bonds is merely the result of the elimination, by the national debt, of an uneconomic, because undesired, shifting of resources from present to future uses.

Of real importance is the consideration that the taxes necessary to offset the inflationary effects of the interest payments may reduce the net reward for work below the value of the marginal net product. This would reduce the amount of work done below the optimum, and constitute a real impairment of the efficiency of the economy.[5]

11. The effects of the national debt in discouraging its owners from working and in necessitating anti-inflationary taxes which may reduce the reward for work and for investment can be dramatized by imagining a fantastically large national debt.

If the national debt is so large that the interest on it comes to many times the national income from work (and if the interest payments are fairly widely distributed among the population), very little work will be done over and above that which is done for the pleasure of doing it.

This in itself is not anything bad. If such a state of affairs could be maintained without heavy taxation (which will be discussed

---

[5] The fact that our economy is not perfectly competitive, so that workers receive less than the value of their marginal product in any case, only increases the amount of harm that would be done by taxes which would reduce the net reward for work still further below the value of the marginal net product.

Abba P. Lerner

below), nearly all goods will be free, and we will have approached the ideal of plenty where Marxism and Anarchism converge and economy is no longer necessary. This is perhaps not quite as far of attainment as one tends to suppose. In a rich country like the United States, if everybody had such an accumulation of government bonds that conspicuous consumption and display lost their significance, needs of material goods could be so simplified and reduced as to make their complete satisfaction feasible by the few hours' work that are necessary for health or may become necessary for social approbation.

The age of plenty is, however, not imminent. An income from interest on the national debt many times as large as the income from other sources would result in expenditure on goods and services many times as large as the available supply of goods and services. There would therefore have to be very heavy taxes to keep the demand from exceeding the supply and thus bringing about inflation. If these taxes approached 100 per cent of the income, they would so reduce the net reward for effort that all work producing income subject to the tax (either when earning it or when spending it) would come to a stop, and the whole economy would break down. The continuation of life would depend entirely on the degree to which black markets could avoid the taxation, for only such activities would be worth while. Such heavy taxation would be much more destructive than the inflation from which it was supposed to protect the economy.[6]

III. THE EQUILBRIUM LEVEL OF NATIONAL DEBT

12. Although this shows that too large a national debt can be a most serious matter, it does not mean that Functional Finance has to be supplemented by additional precautions to prevent the national debt from growing too large. Functional Finance does this *automatically*.

A tendency to depression exists only when people do not spend enough—they are too eager to save. The amount they would save

[6] I am indebted on these points to correspondence with Richard A. Musgrave.

The Burden of the National Debt

if fully employed is greater than the amount privately being invested, so that unless the government augments investment or consumption expenditure we have a depression which prevents people from saving more than is being invested.

The people want to save so much because they do not have enough already saved up. The growth of national debt is an increase in the holdings of wealth, the past savings of the people, and so it relieves the pressure to save. If we assume that the government borrows the money for its augmentation of spending,[7] there is an automatic growth of the national debt as long as people want to save more than is being invested. This goes on until an *equilibrium level of national debt* is reached when people are so rich in claims to wealth that they no longer want to save more than is compatible with the maintenance of full employment with a balanced budget. At that point the application of Functional Finance calls for a balanced budget, and the national debt will not grow any more.

If the national debt is above the equilibrium level, Functional Finance calls for an overbalanced budget to prevent the excess demand for goods that this would bring about. The budgetary surplus could then go to repaying some of the debt, and so again there will be a tendency for the equilibrium level of national debt to be approached—this time from the other side.

This balancing of the budget is a *result* or symptom of long run equilibrium. The error of those who cling to the fiscal principle of balancing the budget lies in their prescribing as a *rule* for the short period what is properly only a *result* of the achievement of long period equilibrium.

If we assume a national debt many times greater than the equilibrium level, the taxes needed to prevent inflation may have to be so heavy, and their effects on the efficiency of the economy

---

[7] We shall see below that this is not the only or the best way of reaching an equilibrium. The assumption that budget deficits must be covered by borrowing is due to an even greater phobia against simply reducing monetary stocks and issuing more money if these should be exhausted. Mr. Musgrave, in correspondence, has aptly called this the tertiary orthodoxy.

Abba P. Lerner

so pernicious, that this Functional Finance cure for inflation would be worse than the disease. Other and more drastic measures may then be proper, such as a capital levy to reduce the national debt once for all to something near the equilibrium (where Functional Finance could manage it) or perhaps to achieve the same thing by permitting inflation to wipe out the excessive national debt. In such an extreme situation the normal operation of Functional Finance may not be adequate.

It is, however, important to remember that such an extreme situation could never be the result of Functional Finance because Functional Finance would not permit so great a movement beyond the equilibrium level in the first place. Functional Finance, if it is not given too great a job, works steadily to move the economy toward the equilibrium where the budget would be balanced. From that point there would be adjustments only to the extent that the equilibrium position is affected by movements in the level of income, the age distribution of the population, the distribution of wealth in the population, and other such slow moving secular determinants.

13. It should be noted that the equilibrium level of national debt is quite different from the "manageable" or "reasonable" levels of national debt which Professor Hansen and others insist on as limits to guide us in fiscal policy. The latter limits are *prescribed* limits which we are told not to pass because of dangers that lie on the other side. Sometimes they are accompanied by prognoses and estimates which indicate that there will be no tendency for these limits to be passed by a policy of maintaining full employment by borrowing to maintain adequate demand. But essentially they are signposts to guard against the dangers of permitting the national debt to go beyond the "manageable" or "reasonable" limit. Our equilibrium level is not a prescribed limit to policy. It describes an automatic tendency for the national debt to reach an equilibrium if we do nothing about it except merely follow the basic Functional Finance principle of keeping total demand at the proper level to prevent inflation or depression.

The Burden of the National Debt

14. The equilibrium level of the national debt, with its balanced budget, is reached when the Functional Finance policy of preventing inflation and depression results in a yield from taxes just sufficient to pay all the expenses of government including the interest payments on the national debt.

These taxes may have serious effects on the economy even before the equilibrium level of national debt is reached. If there is not a proper arrangement for loss offset, the taxes may interfere seriously with useful investment. If the taxes fall heavily on the reward for marginal effort, they will prevent useful work from being done, diminishing the real level of national income. If the government has to restrict its own expenditures, many socially useful undertakings will be killed in the efforts to prevent inflation. And the diminishing desire to work, accompanied by an increasing desire to spend (which accompanies the growth of individual wealth in the form of ownership of national debt), will decrease the supply of goods on the market even while it increases the demand for them. Even though this last item must not be counted as a social loss, it does contribute to the inflationary pressures, and necessitates more taxation and greater government economies, both of which can mean real diminutions in the national income.

It is true that all these bad effects come only from the imposition of "bad taxes." If the additional taxes did not fall on the income from additional effort, the bad effects would be avoided. But it is probably impossible to avoid all "bad taxes," especially if the good ones are already being exploited to the utmost—so that the problem cannot be dismissed by simply recommending good taxes instead of bad taxes.

It is conceivable that even before the equilibrium level of national debt is reached a vicious circle would be encountered in which additional taxation failed to check the increasing inflationary pressure because, by its interference with the reward for extra effort, it reduced supply more than it reduced demand.

In such an extreme and very unlikely situation, there is a very easy and extremely satisfactory way out. The solution is to *reduce*

267

Abba P. Lerner

taxes. This would increase supply more than it increased demand, and so would work to check the inflationary pressure even while it raised the national income.

More serious is the less extreme case where taxation reduces supply seriously but not more than it reduces demand. The tax increases needed to check the inflation might so reduce the efficiency of the economy and the real income that it would be better to suffer the evils of inflation. It may even happen that the increased tax rates resulted in a diminished yield because of the reduction in output so that the budget, instead of getting nearer and nearer to balancing, got more and more unbalanced. As the difference is added (we assume) annually to the national debt, the interest payments would increase year by year, while the tax collections lag further and further behind the government expenditures (including these interest payments) so that there is no tendency to equilibrium. The national debt would grow indefinitely—ultimately leading to all the evils of national debt much greater than the equilibrium level.

15. All these troubles not only assume extremely bad taxes, but depend on a basic misunderstanding of the function of government borrowing. The government is supposed to fight chronic depression by expenditure of money which it borrows at interest, so continually increasing the national debt until it becomes "unmanageable." Borrowing is thus seen as an inflationary activity, necessary to combat the tendency to chronic depression, and later necessary to raise the money to keep up interest payments on national debt even when the danger is one of inflation rather than of depression.

But borrowing is not inflationary. It is deflationary. It looks inflationary only if one fails to distinguish it from the expenditure of the borrowed money. This expenditure is more inflationary as a rule than the borrowing is deflationary, so that the net effect of the borrowing-plus-spending is inflationary.

Borrowing is deflationary because it takes money out of the hands of the lenders and puts government bonds there instead.

268

The Burden of the National Debt

People are somewhat less likely to want to buy other things when they have spent their money on government bonds. The sale of government bonds diminishes liquidity, tends to raise interest rates, and discourages investment. The government should therefore not borrow unless it wishes to bring about these deflationary effects. It can keep on making all the expenditures and investments it finds desirable without borrowing, merely by paying for these out of its stocks of money or creating new money if it should run short.

16. The government should therefore not borrow any money until the economy has passed out of the range of threatening depression into the range of threatening inflation. This will occur even without any incurrence of national debt simply as a result of the increase in the amount of money which gets into the hands of the public as the government spends it. As the amount of money in the hands of the public increases, the public feels itself wealthier —just as if they had more government bonds or other property. This is part of the "wealth effect." It diminishes the tendency to save, and to work for the sake of saving, and increases demand while it diminishes supply. The owners of the money do not get interest on their holdings as they would if there had been an increase in national debt instead of an increase in the amount of money. But in place of this there will be the increased liquidity of the economy, tending to lower the rate of interest, and thus to increase investment—and perhaps also some spending out of income by such as are discouraged from saving by the fall in the rate of interest. Instead of the "income effect" that would accompany the interest payments on the national debt there will be the "liquidity effect" of the increase in the amount of money, also tending to increase total demand. This is the other equilibrating mechanism. When the amount of money has increased sufficiently the deficiency of demand which called for the government deficit will have to come to an end, and the volume of money will cease to grow. Full employment is maintained by an equilibrium level in the amount of money. There is no danger of in-

269

Abba P. Lerner

flation from the increase in the amount of money because the first signs of inflation are at the same time signs that the increase in the amount of money has gone too far. It will be a sign that the government must spend less money than it collects in taxes (or otherwise), and so bring back the amount of money to the equilibrium level.

17. The effect of government borrowing (in the sense of simply borrowing, not borrowing-and-spending) is to diminish the liquidity of the economy, to raise the rate of interest, and to discourage investment. The government should therefore borrow only when it wishes to diminish liquidity. This will happen whenever the government thinks it better to check low-yield investment than to check consumption by imposing more taxes, or to check useful government expenditures. Borrowing is a deflationary instrument like taxation and government economy, competitive with these in the battle against inflation.

But while the *act* of government borrowing is deflationary, the resulting *fact* of the existence of government debt is inflationary, because of both the "wealth effect" and the "income effect" on spending. The "wealth effect" is also produced by the *fact* of existence of money. If both the national debt and the amount of money increase together, the long period equilibrium will be the result of *both* influences on the rate of spending, and will be reached at the point where the "wealth effects" of both the national debt and the amount of money, together with the "income effect" of the national debt and the "liquidity effect" of the new money, bring about the required total rate of spending for full employment. The budget is balanced, and neither the national debt nor the amount of money need change any more (except in adjusting to secular changes in the determinants of the equilibrium).

18. The difference between government borrowing and the other deflationary instruments, government economy and taxation, is that while the other instruments have a once-for-all deflationary effect, borrowing only temporarily offsets inflationary

The Burden of the National Debt

effects until the time when the debt is to be repaid, and then the inflationary pressure returns with interest—literally.[8] And even before the debt is repaid, and even if the debt is destined to remain on the books indefinitely, the inflationary pressures come back in the form of inflationary interest payments in the "income effect" of the national debt and the constant "wealth effect" from the mere existence of the national debt. The deflationary effect of government borrowing is weaker than that of the other instruments, partly because it is offset by the inflationary effects of the extra national debt which follows every dollar of government borrowing.

What this means is that government borrowing is not a real alternative to taxation or economy, but only a way of postponing these really deflationary instruments to a more convenient time in the future. Exactly the same relationships hold in reverse for the repayment of debt with its immediate inflationary effect through the increase in liquidity and its long run deflationary effect from the absence of the liquidated national debt.

19. The importance of this peculiarity of government borrowing as a deflationary instrument (and of repaying debt as an inflationary instrument) comes to light when we consider some attempts to derive rules for policy about national debt. It is pointed out for example that it is better for an economy to have a smaller rather than a larger national debt because the "wealth effect" and the "income effect" of the larger national debt cause more spending so that more taxes are necessary to prevent inflation. Since the taxes are not ideal taxes, they will to some extent fall on the marginal pay for effort, and they will also discourage useful investment and useful government spending. The national debt thus has a bad effect.

But is this remark of any use as a guide for policy? Hardly at

[8] Government economy can be temporary too if it consists of the postponement of necessary replacements which will only accumulate in the future. Such "economies" can be considered as equivalent to "borrowing" from the deteriorated equipment which will demand "repayment" in the future, perhaps with very high "interest."

Abba P. Lerner

all. For it is surely not intended to suggest that the debt or a part of it should be repudiated. The effects of this particularly arbitrary form of taxation would certainly be worse even than the imperfect taxes needed to prevent inflation, the bad effects of which it is hoped to avoid. Nor can it be intended to suggest that the borrowing should not have taken place in the past, if this borrowing was considered less harmful than the alternative deflationary instruments of taxation or government economies at the time. At the most it can tell us that the borrowing, which meant a postponement of the taxation or economy, was not wise if the taxation and economies would do more harm in the future than at the time from which they were postponed. The postponement was then a mistake. But that surely is no *general* reason for not incurring debt, since the postponement can very well be a very good policy. Certainly it is not intended to argue that it is better to permit unemployment if its prevention entails borrowing (the issue of new money being too shocking). Yet this is the lesson most likely to be derived by practical politicians from careless declarations that it is better to have a smaller than a larger debt. The statement is of the same category which says that it is better to have a larger than a smaller national income. Until it is shown what measures are proposed to increase the national income or to decrease the national debt, the statement is academic in the worst sense of the term.

The national debt cannot be made smaller by just wishing it so. It can be reduced only by repudiation, or by increased taxation, or by increased government economies on what are presumably useful activities. All of these steps immediately bring about in a more severe degree the very evils which the existence of the national debt threatens in the future.

IV. NATIONAL DEBT AND NATIONAL WEALTH

20. It might be supposed that national debt could be avoided if appropriate and wise fiscal policy would result in *private* borrowing and investment taking place instead of government borrowing and investment or other expenditure. (This is independent

272

The Burden of the National Debt

of whether the activity is conceived as helping to prevent depression by providing investment, or helping to prevent inflation by borrowing.) There will then be no government debt. Is this a way in which the evils of national debt could be avoided without giving up the fight to prevent inflation and depression?

To suppose this to be the case is to make a most serious mistake. For the whole of the analysis of this article, *all* the effects of government borrowing and of national debt apply just as much to private borrowing and to private debt. We have seen that what is important about national debt is that individuals feel rich and have more income—the "wealth effect" and the "income effect." These effects are just as much in evidence if the public, instead of owning government stock, owns stock in the private corporations which have done the investing instead of the government. The ownership of shares in private corporations has just as great a "wealth effect," and insofar as the yield in private investment is on the average greater than the interest on government bonds, it has a greater "income effect" even after allowing for bankruptcies. There will therefore be at least as great an inflationary pressure as if there had been the same amount of national debt; at least as much taxation will be necessary to prevent inflation, and at least as much harm will be done to the efficiency of the economy as in the other case. The evils cannot be avoided by having private instead of public debt.

All the other arguments developed above in relation to national debt will also be applicable in the same way to private debt. There will be an equilibrium level of *wealth* in the long run which will permit a balancing of the budget, though the wealth will consist of public and private debts, as well as money and real, physical goods.

Against this it has been argued that private investment results in an increase in the output of goods in the future to match the increase of demand out of the income of the recipients of dividends. But public investment may be just as useful in increasing future output, and it often may be more useful. Of course it is better to

273

Abba P. Lerner

have useful private investment than useless public investment. It is similarly better to have useful public investment than useless private investment. In fact it is simply better to have relatively useful investments than relatively useless investments, irrespective of whether they are public or private. But this residual proposition is not really very helpful.

21. A final argument takes the form of pointing out that private investment is always built on the expectation of being able to charge sufficient for the product to be able to pay dividends to the shareholders, while public investment is often directed to enterprises which, however useful they may be socially, do not collect sufficient from the consumers to pay the whole cost of the investment and the interest on the money invested. Indeed it is just such enterprises which do not permit the consumer to be charged the whole cost of the undertaking that are by definition the Public Utilities which tend to be run by public enterprise. It is therefore true that private enterprise is more likely to be less inflationary in the long run than public enterprise, and to need less taxation to prevent inflation.

But it does not in the least follow from this that it would be better to encourage private enterprise to undertake fully self-liquidating enterprise than for the government to undertake activities which are equally useful but would make more taxation necessary. For if these useful "Public Utilities," instead of being undertaken by the government and run on the socially most desirable scale (which results in losses and the need for more taxes), are undertaken by private enterprise (which will do so only if they can apply at least enough monopolistic restriction to get a normal return on their investment), the price will be raised above the marginal social cost to the average private cost. This inflicts exactly the same kind of social loss on the economy, interfering with its efficiency in serving the needs of the consumers, as is done by a very bad tax. Since the taxes imposed to prevent inflation are at least designed to some extent to avoid the evils of bad taxes, it would be most unreasonable to prefer the clearly bad "taxes" im-

The Burden of the National Debt

posed by monopolists to make "Public Utilities" self-liquidating.

22. We see then that the kinds of evil most popularly ascribed to national debt are wholly imaginary; that some less serious evils are more real, but are not to be avoided by the obvious policies of avoiding national debt; and that the direct application of the basic principles of Functional Finance are an adequate general guide to fiscal policy. If the short run equilibrium is taken care of so that there is neither too much spending nor too little spending, and so neither inflation or depression, and a normal amount of reasonableness is applied in choosing between the different ways of achieving this short run equilibrium, the long run equilibrium of the size of the national debt will look after itself.

[13]

FISCAL POLICY

AND FULL EMPLOYMENT

WITHOUT INFLATION

WE have seen in earlier chapters that the behavior of saving and investment determines the level of national income and employment. We have seen that private investment often fluctuates widely from year to year and that the same is true of foreign lending. History shows how painful and wasteful the business cycle has been in the past; today everyone is in agreement that, unless we succeed in laying the ghost of instability in the future, American free enterprise will be in jeopardy.

What prescription follows from our economic diagnosis? No single answer can be given; there is no single cure-all for the economic ills of society. Business, labor, and agriculture must all attempt to pursue price and wage policies aimed at maintaining a stable, high-employment economy. The Federal reserve system can also do a little, by way of interest and monetary policy, to prevent an aggravation of the business cycle. But, if all these measures have been tried and they still do not succeed in avoiding the perils of heavy unemployment or extreme inflation, then there is still the public weapon of fiscal policy. This is not to say that fiscal policy, alone, is a cure-all, but it is an important part of any economic program.

The reader is warned that the subject matter of this chapter is still in a controversial stage. While stress has been placed on limitations as well as on advantages of different fiscal policies, it is idle to believe that, in the present inadequate state of our scientific economic knowledge, economists are in agreement as to the importance of the pros and cons. No reader should form his opinions upon the basis of a hasty reading of some superficially persuasive argument.

409

410   FISCAL POLICY AND FULL EMPLOYMENT

A. *SHORT-RUN AND LONG-RUN FISCAL POLICY*

By a positive fiscal policy, we mean the process of shaping public *taxation* and public *expenditure* so as (1) to help dampen down the swings of the business cycle and (2) to contribute toward the maintenance of a progressive, high-employment economy free from excessive inflation or deflation.

The war years have shown fiscal policy to be a very powerful weapon. Indeed, some would argue that it is like the atomic bomb, too powerful a weapon to let men and governments play with; that it would be better if fiscal policy were never used. However, it is absolutely certain that, just as no nation will sit idly by and let smallpox decimate the population, so too in every country fiscal policy always comes into play whenever depressions gain headway. There is no choice then but to attempt to lead fiscal policy along economically sound rather than destructive channels. Every government always has a fiscal policy whether it realizes it or not. The real issue is whether this shall be a constructive one or an unconscious, bumbling one.

COUNTERCYCLICAL COMPENSATION VERSUS LONG-RANGE FISCAL POLICY

There are two main programs of fiscal policy. The first is the least controversial and involves nothing more than the attempt to dampen down the amplitude of the business cycle. This is called a purely "countercyclical compensatory," or "anticyclical" fiscal policy. It involves a budget that is balanced over the business cycle. The second and more controversial part of fiscal policy involves long-range action designed to lift the average level of purchasing power and employment throughout the business cycle as a whole; or, if the long-range situation is inflationary, it involves continued action designed to reduce the average level of purchasing power over the whole cycle.

COUNTERCYCLICAL COMPENSATORY POLICY

When private investment shoots up too high, it seems natural to ask that the government should try to compensate by curtailing public investment and expenditure and increasing its tax collections. On the other hand, when private investment and consumption go off into a slump, the government is then to compensate by stepping up its previously postponed expenditures and by reducing its tax collections. According to the countercyclical view, the government budget need not be in balance in each and every month or year; on the

SHORT-RUN AND LONG-RUN FISCAL POLICY 411

contrary, during inflationary times, the budget should show a surplus of tax receipts over expenditures so that the public debt can be reduced. But when bad times come, then the budget should show a deficit of taxes over expenditures, with the public debt returning to its previous level. Only over the whole business cycle need the budget be in balance.

In a nutshell, that is all there is to counter-cyclical compensatory fiscal policy. Stated in this way, it is seen to be a rather conservative doctrine—too conservative, some of the present generation of economists would be inclined to argue.

TYPES OF COUNTERCYCLICAL POLICY

Public Works. This principle of countercyclical finance with respect to public works was introduced into the American system by Herbert Hoover, while he was Secretary of Commerce to Republican President Coolidge. Hoover argued, and rightly, that inasmuch as the government finds it necessary to build a certain amount of roads, hospitals, schools, post offices, etc., then surely it would be better if these projects were intelligently planned so as not all to fall at a time when private construction is booming and manpower is scarce. Instead, they should be postponed until the time when private industry releases materials and men.

In consequence, there will result a relative stabilization of total business activity, since the peak of construction will be cut down and since the depression trough of construction will be at least partly filled in. Not only will jobs be created when needed most, but more than that, the government will be getting its necessary public works at lower prices and through efficient production. All this is so obviously sensible that no one was surprised when in 1931 Hoover and a Democratic Congress passed a law requiring the Federal government to set up a "permanent shelf of public-works projects" with long-range plans and blueprints always at hand, drawn up in such a way as to permit the anticyclical timing of public works.

Figure 1 illustrates how a countercyclical compensatory fiscal policy stabilizes business activity by "chopping off the hills and filling in the valleys." The solid line, *ABCD*, shows the business cycle as it would be if the government did nothing about it and pursued a neutral policy. The dotted line, *A'B'C'D'*, shows the government's budget. Note that this is not in balance in every year, but only over the whole cycle. Note too that the government's activity is just *opposite* in phase to the private cycle, so that it can compensate and dampen down the cycle. The shaded areas show how, as a result, the boom is reduced and how the depression is mitigated. Note too that the black areas

412   FISCAL POLICY AND FULL EMPLOYMENT

are greater than the volume of public expenditure or deficit; this is because the familiar multiplier is at work both in boom and in depression. The final resulting pattern of national income, after the government's compensatory policy, is given by *abcd*, which is much more nearly stable than was the original.

The private economy is not unlike a machine without an effective steering wheel or governor. Compensatory fiscal policy tries to introduce such a governor or thermostatic control device. As shown in the figure, compensatory

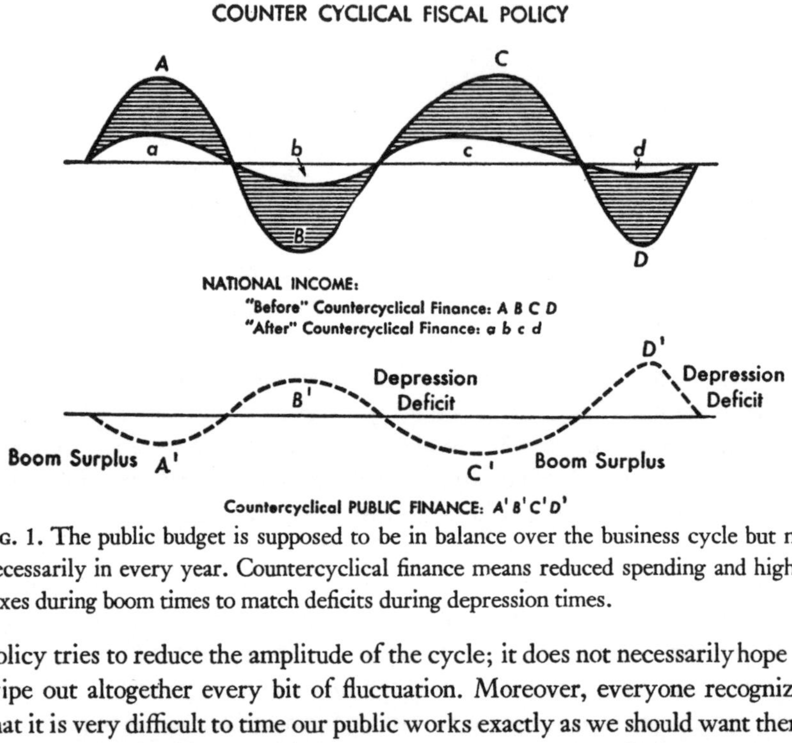

COUNTER CYCLICAL FISCAL POLICY

NATIONAL INCOME:
"Before" Countercyclical Finance: A B C D
"After" Countercyclical Finance: a b c d

Countercyclical PUBLIC FINANCE: A' B' C' D'

FIG. 1. The public budget is supposed to be in balance over the business cycle but not necessarily in every year. Countercyclical finance means reduced spending and higher taxes during boom times to match deficits during depression times.

policy tries to reduce the amplitude of the cycle; it does not necessarily hope to wipe out altogether every bit of fluctuation. Moreover, everyone recognizes that it is very difficult to time our public works exactly as we should want them. We can't simply throw a switch when we want more purchasing power and reverse the dial when we want less. Time is required to get a project under way, especially if it is a big one. Once under way, it would be difficult and expensive to abandon it. Because of these technical difficulties of starting and stopping public works and because we need time to discover whether we are really in a boom or a depression, our ambition must be less pretentious than that of creating 100 per cent stability of national income.

Welfare and Other Expenditure.   Fortunately, these difficulties are not insurmountable. Fortunately, too, public-works planning is only one of a number of anticyclical devices. Even without any planning at all, government expenditures

SHORT-RUN AND LONG-RUN FISCAL POLICY   413

on relief and unemployment automatically rise when people get thrown out of work, and automatically tend to fall when jobs again become plentiful.

In country after country all over the world the Great Depression caused budgets to become automatically unbalanced, in part because of an automatic increase in expenditures. Our own 48 states tend to build up in good times an Unemployment Compensation Reserve Fund, less being paid out in benefits to the unemployed than is being collected in payroll taxes. During bad times,

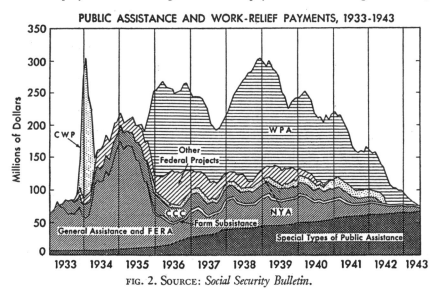

FIG. 2. SOURCE: *Social Security Bulletin.*

the reverse is true: payments to unemployed workers exceed tax collections, and purchasing power is partly maintained by spending out of the accumulated reserve funds.

During the depressed 1930's, the WPA provided work relief on public projects (schools, swimming pools, road building, writers' and drama projects, etc.). The PWA provided funds for privately contracted Federal and state projects. Home relief was provided for the unemployed and needy. Not all these projects were ideal; some were hastily improvised and unwisely administered. But they did patch up a potentially revolutionary situation and provide for basic human needs, at the same time contributing (with multiplier effects as well) to purchasing power and employment. Figure 2 shows a breakdown of emergency expenditure during the 1930's.

Automatic Changes in Tax Receipts. In addition to public-works expenditure and welfare expenditure, countercyclical compensatory fiscal policy can also rely on cyclically timed tax policies. We have already seen in the earlier

414   FISCAL POLICY AND FULL EMPLOYMENT

chapters on public finance (Chaps. 7 and 8) that our Federal tax system has important income elements in it, so that tax collections tend to vary strongly with national income. Even without Congress or the state legislatures changing any laws, it turns out that governmental tax collections tend to rise automatically when national income rises and to a fall off when national income falls off;[1] and because of the progressive elements in our tax structure, our relative tax collections vary even more sharply than income itself.

A century ago, writers thought that stability of tax revenue was a good thing, and they would have looked with disapproval on the present-day tendency for tax receipts to rise and fall with national income. Today, most believe that the truth is just the reverse. To dampen down a boom, a budgetary surplus is needed. Now there are two ways to produce a surplus: by a reduction in government expenditure, yes; but also by an increase in tax receipts. Indeed, from the standpoint of free private enterprise, tax changes represent the more conservative policy. How lucky we are, therefore, that our present tax system to some degree has "automatic flexibility," with its collections tending to rise in inflationary times and to fall in times of depression. This is a powerful factor stabilizing the whole economy and moderating the business cycle.

Countercyclical Tax-rate Changes. Even this is not all. Congress can also change tax rates. Back before World War I (and still in a few quarters even today), people thought it obviously desirable to balance the budget *in each and every year.* Therefore, they tried to raise tax rates whenever the public was experiencing falling incomes, and to reduce tax rates when incomes were becoming inflated. Once again, the pendulum of expert opinion has swung completely around; today, all but the most conservative students of public finance are opposed to such "preverse flexibility" of tax rates. Those who believe in a countercyclical compensatory fiscal policy argue that the time to reduce tax rates is in depression, when over-all purchasing power is too low; and the time to step up tax rates is during boom times.

Thus taxes as well as expenditures are important for a countercyclical compensatory policy.

LIMITATIONS ON COUNTERCYCLICAL COMPENSATORY POLICY

We have already mentioned (1) some of the difficulties in planning large public-works projects so that they can be quickly got under way or curtailed, and also (2) some of the forecasting difficulties in deciding just exactly when the time has come to step on the gas rather than the brakes. In addition to these

[1] For each 10 billion dollars of change in national income, the collections of our postwar tax system change by more than 2½ billion dollars.

SHORT-RUN AND LONG-RUN FISCAL POLICY 415

two, there are still other limitations on a perfectly effective countercyclical policy.

Effects on Private Investment. A third limitation has to do with changes in private investment. For example, some would argue that government expenditure or deficits may not really add much to purchasing power during depressions. If private investment could be assumed constant, then public expenditures would of course have favorable primary effects upon income and employment; more than that, the consumption respending of successive portions of income would give rise to the familiar multiplier chain of favorable secondary effects. What if private investment is frightened off by government expenditure or by the deficit?

This is certainly a possibility. Businessmen may say, "With that man in the White House spending recklessly, we're going to abandon even the little private investment we had planned." Or a private utility company may curtail investment because it fears the threat of public hydroelectric projects. Or when the government spending gives people money to buy in retail stores, the effect in time of deep depression may simply be to permit the merchant to work down his inventory of surplus merchandise; if he does not reorder production goods, the public investment has been just about neutralized by induced private *dis*investment (in inventory) and the multiplier chain is stopped dead in its tracks.

On the other hand, there may be favorable effects on private investment which are just the opposite to these unfavorable repercussions of government finance. When current production is at a low ebb and there is excess plant capacity, no prudent businessman feels like undertaking new capital formation. If the government is able to boost retail sales and the production of consumption goods, then businessmen will have the financial ability and at least some motive to renew equipment and build new plant. (An example of this was provided by the discussion in Chap. 17 of the acceleration principle relating induced investment to the upward change in sales.)

Where there are two such opposing tendencies—favorable and unfavorable effects upon private investment—facts rather than arguments must be our guide. Although economics does not permit us to make controlled experiments to settle the point conclusively, the bulk of the statistical data that have come to the attention of this writer suggests that private investment tends to move on the whole sympathetically with the level of national income. The cash register calls the tune, and in a free-enterprise society, rightly so.

This does not mean that we can neglect unfavorable psychological reactions to deficit financing. But these adverse reactions are of much greater importance in connection with long-range deficit financing than with the purely counter-cyclical case where the budget is balanced over the cycle. We may profitably defer this topic to later sections.

Fiscal Perversity of Local Finance. A fourth limitation on compensatory finance arises from the behavior of state and local governments. Unlike the Federal government, they have a tendency toward a perverse cyclical pattern—borrowing for hospitals and schools in good times and reducing their debts in bad times. This serves to aggravate rather than dampen down the business cycle.

However, it would be unfair to criticize them too harshly for this. The credit of the Federal government actually improves in bad times; also it has the constitutional powers to issue currency and to use the Central Bank to float its loans if Congress deems this necessary. The states and localities, on the other hand, are subject to greater credit difficulties when it comes to borrowing —although in recent years Federal grants-in-aid have been an important source of finance for local public works. Also, states and localities are often ham-strung by constitutional limitations upon their depression borrowing.

On the whole, it is probably too much to expect the states and localities to pursue a militant anticyclical spending policy. But at the very least, we can set for them the goal of being neutral with respect to the cycle rather than aggra-vating it by buying new fire engines and war monuments during inflation and cutting all services to the bone during depression. Also, it is to be hoped that local governments will avoid *perverse cyclical flexibility* with respect to tax rates, such as introducing deflationary, regressive sales taxes during depression times and cutting income tax rates during prosperity.

The "Pump-priming" Confusion. In addition to the above four criticisms, a number of other limitations upon countercyclical compensatory fiscal policy could be listed. But only one last criticism will be mentioned here. Many people are disappointed to find that *after the government curtails its depression spending, the national income may again fall back to a low level.* Really this is not a criticism of compensatory policy, but rather a case of confusing it with what is popularly called government "pump priming."

When the New Deal was still very new, many people thought that, if the government would only spend a little money, the economy would be lifted from the doldrums and would carry on forever after on its own steam. If only you pour a little water into the pump to prime it, it will repay you with an endless stream of water.

Actually, countercyclical compensatory fiscal policy is as different from pump priming as a gasoline engine is from a perpetual-motion machine. Stop

SHORT-RUN AND LONG-RUN FISCAL POLICY   417

feeding gas and the motor stops; stop eating and you will waste away. So with compensatory finance: public spending may have powerful secondary effects; still, like private investment itself, its effects cease soon after it ceases. In economics, there are few magical ways of getting something for nothing.[1]

So much for the limitations to countercyclical fiscal policy. In conclusion, we may simply note that few people would object in theory to its precepts. What they do occasionally object to is the tendency or danger that what starts out as an innocent-looking countercyclical fiscal policy may turn into a policy of long-range spending. For example, consider the period 1933 to 1938 as a complete cycle. Certainly 1935 and 1937 were in retrospect its best years, and according to the purely countercyclical view should have been years of budgetary surplus. But at the time, with almost 10 million unemployed, putting on the fiscal brakes hardly seemed rational or "political."

LONG-RUN FISCAL POLICY

Let us turn, therefore, to the longer run problem. If we could always be sure of 5 lean years of too small private investment to maintain high employment, followed by 5 fat years in which investments were too large to permit high employment at stable prices, then counter-cyclical finance might be perfect. But what if we move into a postwar era where the years of high boom tend always to *outnumber* those of depression? Then, in such a period of "secular exhilaration," many would argue that the government should not balance the budget over each business cycle. Instead, it should average a "budgetary surplus" (of taxes over expenditure) throughout most of each business cycle and over a long period of years.

This is clearly something quite different from a countercyclical policy aimed at smoothing out fluctuations; it is a policy of *continuous long-run surplus financing* aimed at reducing the average level of purchasing power and inflation.

On the other hand, suppose that the level and fluctuations in private investment were such as to give us a pattern of national income like that shown in Fig. 3. Although our manpower, resources, and know-how are such as to make it possible for the American economy to produce the indicated *potential* pattern of real product, suppose that the balance of saving and investment tends to give the *actual* pattern shown by *ABCDEFG*. The reader can draw in a third line

---

[1] One way of getting a pump-priming situation would be to consider a system where a dollar of expenditure did not create a multiplier chain of $3 = 1 + \frac{2}{3} + (\frac{2}{3})^2 + \cdots$, but rather created a chain of the form: infinity $= 1 + 1 + 1 + 1 + \cdots + 1 + \cdots$. Without any "saving leakages," the pump would give you any amount of water in return for the original amount used for priming.

418   FISCAL POLICY AND FULL EMPLOYMENT

showing what would be the pattern of income if only a countercyclical smoothing-out policy were pursued. Obviously, there would still be a wastage of resources and product most of the time, even if the contortions of the business cycle were partly ironed out.

Many modern writers would argue for a *long-run policy of full compensation* in such a case. According to them, it would not necessarily be desirable to pull the brakes at *A*, or at *C*, or at *G*. Only at *E* would a strongly contracting spending policy be called for.

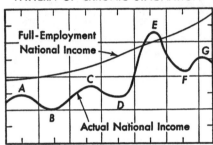

PATTERN OF CHRONIC STAGNATION

FIG. 3. Hypothetical data to illustrate case where simple countercyclical finance is held inadequate to achieve stable high employment.

According to this new school of fiscal theorists, fiscal policy ought —in such a period of "secular stagnation"—to be expansionary much if not most of the time. Over the business cycle as a whole, the budget might not be in balance, because the lean years would be outnumbering the good ones. As national income grows, so too might the public debt. All this is still controversial, and the reader is warned that many eminent economists are opposed to any policy of continuous deficits.[1]

Long-run surplus financing and long-run deficit financing both differ from a purely countercyclical policy. Which will be appropriate depends upon the happenstance of the long-run balance of saving and investment. Let us first turn to the more pessimistic view of stagnant investment opportunities relative to full-employment saving.

SECULAR STAGNATION?

Countercyclical fiscal policy, with the budget balanced over the cycle, is designed to even out the bumps in business activity, but not to alter the average level of employment very much. Continuous long-run surplus financing is designed to lower the average level of purchasing power in order to curb the inflation that would result from an era of "secular exhilaration" when domestic and foreign investment are tending to run beyond full-employment saving. The third possibility we must now explore: May there not be a tendency in the next few decades for full-employment saving to run ahead of investment

[1] See the lengthy study, "The American Industrial Enterprise System," Vol. II, Chap. XVIII, National Association of Manufacturers, New York, 1946.

SHORT-RUN AND LONG-RUN FISCAL POLICY   419

opportunities, with the inevitable result of more years of slump than of high employment, of long-lived depressions and brief, anemic recoveries?

Such a view is often called "secular stagnation." It is associated with the name of Prof. Alvin H. Hansen of Harvard University. According to Hansen, dynamic investment is the mainspring of economic fluctuations. As investment shifts to high gear, total demand is high and jobs are plentiful; when the capricious factors making for investment happen to be unfavorable for a long time, the economic system may go through years or decades of considerable unemployment.

So far, almost all economists would agree with Hansen. But a number would get off the band wagon when he goes on to express his opinion that there are a number of long-run factors in the American situation which make it possible or even probable that investment will be a lagging factor relative to full-employment saving. He thinks that a relatively "mature economy" like the United States is especially susceptible to stagnant investment and unemployment. Some of his reasons are as follows:

Investment Prospects.   In the past the principal determinants of investment have been these dynamic—not static!—elements: *rapid population growth, discovery and settlement of new territory,* and *technological innovation.* The geographical frontier is long since gone. Even before World War I the first two of these investment determinants were beginning to slow down. After World War I, and particularly in the decade of the 1930's, almost the full brunt was thrown upon technological innovation. This will be even more true in the decades ahead when immigration and birth rates are sure to be so much less than they were in the nineteenth century.

A full-employment economy, like an airplane, cannot stand still; it must go forward if disaster is to be avoided. An airplane traveling on only one engine instead of three may possibly make out all right, but as a betting proposition the chances of its encountering trouble are increased.

Moreover, Hansen believes that the third dynamic factor behind investment, technological innovation, will go on at a more brilliant pace than ever before in our history, but may to a considerable extent take the form of inventions that *lessen rather than increase the amount of needed investment.* Thus the invention of the airliner may make possible the development of Siberia without billions and billions of dollars of investment in public roads and railroads. The invention of wireless radio or of the multiple-message cable all economize on the tremendous amount of investment needed in capital installations. Atomic energy may minimize the need in many parts of the world for costly hydroelectric reclamation projects. Science gives and takes as far as investment is concerned, and

420   FISCAL POLICY AND FULL EMPLOYMENT

Hansen thinks there may continue to be—what he believes to have been true of the 1930's—a preponderance of "capital-saving invention."

Personal and Corporate Saving Prospects.   Hansen's views with respect to the future of saving round out his theory. He believes that people tend to divide their extra income between consumption and saving. Our incredibly creative scientists and engineers can be expected to increase our full-employment real incomes at a rapid rate. Probably, real wages and productivity will continue to grow at the compound-interest rate of 2 to 3 per cent per year, or even faster than in the past.

If people's tastes and standards of consumption remained the same, this vast increase in income would probably mean an even greater proportionate increase in saving. Fortunately for the prospects of avoiding mass unemployment, people's consumption standards do not remain constant. Their needs and desires are constantly expanding, because of new products invented, because of advertising, because of social custom and imitation.

Throughout all our history the Consumption-income schedule has been shifting upward; the Propensity-to-save schedule has been shifting downward. We now have pretty good statistical records going back more than half a century. These show, rather than an increase in the ratio of saving to income, a remarkable constancy of the proportion which the American people have saved out of past full-employment incomes. Hansen sees no reason why the same should not continue to be true in the years ahead. If rising living standards keep pace with rising productivity, then the percentage of personal saving that has to be offset by investment need not get worse—especially if progressive tax and expenditure policies help to maintain a high consumption economy, and if bold and vigorous attacks on unemployment are effective in forestalling any tendency for people to get frightened into oversaving and to fall behind in their acquiring of higher living standards.

Personal savings are only part of the picture. Increasingly, corporate saving is growing in importance, and here Hansen is less optimistic. It is sound business management for corporations to make full accounting allowances for depreciation and obsolescence; it is sound practice to withhold part of dividends and plow back earnings into a growing business. Hansen thinks that these business savings may be more than enough to finance replacement of capital equipment and new capital formation. And to the extent that corporate investment is completely financed by additional net (or gross) corporate saving, to that extent such investment is not available to offset personal saving and cannot add very much to jobs and purchasing power.

Hansen, who is by nature a confirmed optimist, hopes that the maintenance

SHORT-RUN AND LONG-RUN FISCAL POLICY 421

of continued full employment will cause businessmen to be contented with low unit profits on a high volume of production and with moderate rates of profit and saving.

Some of Hansen's followers are less guarded than he is. Also, there is a sizable body of conservative opinion which is much more pessimistic than he is, in that they agree with him as to the pattern of future and past facts but disagree as to the basic cause of stagnation. They are inclined to attribute the failure of investment in the pre- and postwar to the interference of government with business and to reform legislation. With nations all over the world moving increasingly toward a planned state, and with the American electorate showing a willingness to adjust the minute hand of the clock of history but apparently unwilling to turn the hour hand back toward *laissez faire*, holders of this view naturally tend to be rather despondent.

Before turning to criticisms of the Hansen stagnation thesis, let us beware of one of its common misunderstandings. It is not the growth of our productive potentialities that is believed likely to be stagnant. As Fig. 3 clearly shows, the secular stagnationists believe that our scientists will be more productive than ever—inventing glass neckties and causing 1 man-hour to do the work previously required of 2. As we have seen, Hansen believes that productivity and full-employment production may grow at a compound interest rate, doubling at every generation. The only thing that he thinks is likely to stagnate—if nothing is done about it—is our ability to keep everybody employed so as to realize our potentialities; or to put the matter differently, the level of investment relative to full-employment saving may stagnate in a wealthy, mature economy.

STAGNATION A BOGEY?

By no means are all, or most, economists prepared to regard the stagnation theory as proved or even probable. But surprisingly little vigorous and detailed opposition appeared in print until the Machinery and Allied Products Institute, a federation of trade associations in the industrial equipment field, published a full-size volume entitled "The Bogey of Economic Maturity." This was prepared by George Terborgh, an able economist, and constitutes the fullest reference source for anyone interested in the arguments against the stagnation viewpoint. Without going into details, some of his viewpoints can be briefly mentioned here.

Terborgh believes that the stagnation and mature-economy thesis is a bogey without sound factual or theoretical basis. It is a child of the pessimistic depression period. Prior to 1929, there was little or no evidence of senility of

422 FISCAL POLICY AND FULL EMPLOYMENT

the American economy; and just as one swallow doesn't make a summer, so one depression, even a great one, cannot establish a presumption toward stagnation. Terborgh also believes that the income analysis along saving and investment lines is in itself neutral and establishes no presumption in favor of stagnation. Of course, misuse of the analysis may seem to favor stagnation; *e.g.*, at any time in the past century it would have been difficult to name the industries that would provide us with investment, so that a simple-minded calculator of savings might at any time have come to pessimistic and incorrect conclusions.

Turning to specific facts, Terborgh admits that population growth provides an important quantitative source for investment; but that does not prove that investment would fail to go elsewhere if there were no population growth. Moreover, when population growth slows down, the elderly, retired portion of the population grows in relative importance. Therefore, the slowing down of population growth reduces saving at the same time that it may have diminishing tendencies on investment. Finally, and this is perhaps most important of all, the percentage decline in population has been going on for a century. Why, then, did stagnation not develop years and years ago?

So too with the disappearing frontier. The geographical frontier disappeared in the 1890's. Why no stagnation at that time? Why should new people on new land lead to more investment than new people on old settled land?

Turning to the third source of investment, technological innovation, Terborgh questions the vital importance of a few great and dramatic industries.

The important thing is the total flow of technological development, not its degree of concentration. Given an abundance of rising industries like aviation, mechanical refrigeration, air-conditioning, radio, television, rayon, plastics, quick-freezing, prefabricated housing, light metals, powdered metals, high-octane gasoline, gas turbines, jet propulsion, spun glass, cotton pickers, combined harvesters, electronics—to name only a few at random—the total volume of direct and induced investment can be tremendous. . . . There is . . . no evidence of an increasing proportion of capital-saving innovation.[1]

Terborgh also disbelieves in the bogey of an increase in self-financed business investment. His studies lead him to believe that the Great Depression of the 1930's must be explained in other terms, and that the immediate outlook is a relatively favorable one:

If . . . we suffer from a chronic insufficiency of *consumption and investment combined*, it will not be, in our judgment, because investment opportunity in a physical

[1] GEORGE TERBORGH, "The Bogey of Economic Maturity," pp. 89, 96, Machinery and Allied Products Institute, Chicago, 1945.

and technological sense is persistently inadequate to absorb our unconsumed income; but rather because of political and economic policies that discourage investment justi-fied, under more favorable policies, by these physical factors.[1]

The task of cyclical stabilization is difficult enough without the distraction of stag-nationist soothsaying. Even if we renounce the fatuous perfectionism of "sixty million guaranteed jobs," aspiring rather to the more modest immediate goal of relative sta-bility, the task is still difficult. It is not, however, impossible. To its accomplishment, haunted no longer by the demons of economic maturity, we can proceed with courage and resolution.[1]

We shall not attempt here to weigh the relative merits of the stagnation viewpoint. Economic analysis must be prepared to understand the policies called for by stagnation; it must be no less prepared to meet the opposite situation of long-range inflationary conditions. The next section discusses some of these problems and introduces us to some of the important features of our postwar public debt. The final section deals with the problems of an advancing full-employment economy.

SECULAR EXHILARATION, LONG-RUN SURPLUS FINANCING, AND DEBT RETIREMENT

Suppose that private investment demand and the propensity to consume should be so buoyant after the war that the schedules of saving and investment tend to intersect at an income higher than we have the manpower to produce. There would then be a tendency toward "overfull employment." There would be more than a tendency toward inflation, there would be actual inflation. The dollar shrinks in value as prices soar. People want to buy more goods than can be produced; prices are bid up and for the moment may seem to discourage excessive purchases. But the higher prices do not permanently equate supply and demand. The higher prices constitute someone's income—a farmer's, a businessman's, or a worker's. Again demand is excessive, again prices rise, and we have the familiar case of an inflationary spiral which cannot burn itself out so long as the savings and investment schedules fail to intersect at full employment.[2]

There is one thing to do. The government must cut its expenditures in order to reduce purchasing power; it must increase its tax collections so as to produce a surplus. It is not enough to do this for a day or a year; it must continue to run a surplus for as long as total demand remains excessive.

---

[1] *Ibid.*, pp. 213, 226.
[2] See the earlier discussion of inflation in Chap. 13.

B. *THE PUBLIC DEBT AND POSTWAR FISCAL POLICY*

Under such conditions of secular exhilaration, the Federal debt, which is around 250 billion dollars in 1948, would be gradually retired—not in each and every year, but in all but a few years of depression. If "secular (or long-term) exhilaration" continues for the next few decades, then the debt might be cut at least in half over the next quarter of a century. This is in contrast to a purely countercyclical policy, where the budget is balanced over every cycle and where the debt would dip down every decade to, say, 200 billion dollars and bob back up again to around 250 billion dollars.

Let us analyze the economic process of retiring debt. The government may use its surplus of taxes to retire bonds held by the banks or by the nonbanking public. The second case is the simpler and may be described first.

Retiring Nonbank Debt. Tax collections will reduce people's disposable income, which is just what the doctor orders for inflation. The government could simply let its deposits and cash balances grow at the expense of the rest of the community. More likely, it will use the money to retire bonds and reduce the public debt.

Even if the surplus tax funds are used in this way, the net effect will be deflationary. This is so because the taxes collected directly reduce disposable income and therefore consumption expenditure. But the payment of these taxes to bondholders is a capital rather than a current transaction. They cannot, and ordinarily will not, treat these sums as part of their recurring income to be spent upon consumption, any more than would a man who had sold his house on Wednesday for $15,000 treat that as his day's income.[1]

The public gives up bonds from its lockboxes and mattresses, and in effect it is left with receipted tax bills among its souvenirs. By running the movie camera backward, we see that the disappearance of the debt is an exact reversal of the process by which the war debt was created—out of thin air, so to speak. Instead of taxing the public to pay for battleships and guns, the government in

---

[1] Cashing in of war bonds by relatively poor spenders would, of course, be a different story. Also, using a tax surplus to retire debt may have some downward effects on the interest rate as compared to a policy of letting tax surplus accumulate in the government's bank accounts. Therefore, in an occasional boom period of the type where private investment would respond readily to such an availability of capital funds, the Treasury and the Federal reserve authorities will have to adopt contractionary monetary policies while reducing debt.

THE PUBLIC DEBT AND POSTWAR FISCAL POLICY   425

effect paid them in government bonds; more precisely, it paid them income which they saved in order to buy bonds.

Retiring Bank Debt.   What if the government surplus is used to retire bank-held debt? Then instead of killing off the public's bond assets, we shall be killing off their bank deposits and cash assets. How does this come about? First, I give the government cash or a check to pay my taxes. The government uses its enlarged bank account to buy back a bank-held government bond. The bank loses an asset and at the same time a deposit liability. The public ends up permanently with smaller bank deposits or currency.[1]

In short, retiring bank-held public debt would kill off a substantial part of our supply of money, by exactly reversing the process whereby our wartime expansion of debt vastly increased our supply of deposits and currency. Retiring nonbank government bonds will kill off an important part of the public's holdings of liquid government bonds. Thus, we see how reducing 125 billion dollars, or half of the war debt, would halve the public's liquid wealth (currency, deposits, or government securities).

The Debt and the Propensity to Consume.   In fact, after the debt had been dropping for a long time, people might finally begin to feel so poor as to cause the propensity to consume to fall far enough to end secular exhilaration—at which point large surplus tax collections would cease to be defensible.

Nobody knows how important would be the depressing effects upon consumption of a reduction in people's assets of financial wealth, or how significant upon consumption spending has been the great wartime growth of the public debt. The answer depends in part upon whether poor people who are ready spenders hold appreciable amounts of government bonds. It also depends upon whether people's income rather than their wealth most importantly influences consumption, and upon whether people tend to save more or less once they have accumulated a certain amount of saving. It is a little ironical that some writers who were most critical of deficit financing before the war are now the most ardent champions of the notion that the individual postwar holding of government bonds will increase consumption and prosperity.

Debt Retirement and Interest.   As another effect of debt retirement, the 5 billion dollars of interest, which the government must now annually pay out to

---

[1] For every 5 billion dollars of bonds bought from the commercial banks, the Treasury will have to buy 1 billion dollars from the 12 Federal Reserve Banks. This is in order to reduce commercial-bank reserve balances in step with their reduced deposits and to keep "excess reserves" from coming into being. The reader is referred to the discussion of central banking in Chap. 15 to refresh his memory on this exact reversal of the wartime pattern.

426   FISCAL POLICY AND FULL EMPLOYMENT

bondholders, might be considerably reduced. It is true that in 1947 this transfer payment amounted to less than 3 per cent of the national income, but nevertheless every dollar of government expense saved makes possible just that much lower taxes or increased expenditure elsewhere.

Even if the debt were cut in half over the next 25 years, the interest charges on the debt would not have to fall by an equal proportion. The cries of anguish of banks, insurance companies, widows, universities, and other coupon clippers would probably combine with the concomitant brisk demand of business investors to force some upward revision in interest rates. Because of the paradox that the government's credit (as measured by the interest rate that it must pay on its loans) improves in depressed times and deteriorates in good, the average rate of interest on the public debt might increase from today's 2 per cent to 3 or 4 per cent. Thus a halving of the debt could conceivably be fully canceled out by a doubling of the interest rate, with no appreciable change in total interest charge. However, if technological progress and population growth continue to cause our real national product almost to double every generation, then even 5 billion dollars of interest charges would fall to less than 2 per cent of the national income.

THE PUBLIC DEBT AND ITS LIMITATIONS

Now that we have surveyed the effects of retiring the public debt, we are in a good position to analyze some of its economic disadvantages and advantages.

In appraising the burdens involved in a public debt, we must carefully avoid the unscientific practice of making up our minds in advance that whatever is true of one small merchant's debt is also necessarily true of the government's debt. Prejudging the problem in this way might come perilously close to the logical fallacy of composition; and, instead of permitting us to isolate the true— all too real!—burdens of the public debt, might only confuse the issue.

External versus Internal Debt. A large *external* public debt, owed to people outside of the United States, would be a real burden and limitation upon the American economy. This is because as a nation we would be forced to ship valuable goods and services abroad to meet the interest charges on the external debt and possibly to amortize some of its principal. If 10 per cent of the national income had to go abroad in this way, the burden would be—if not an intolerable one—nevertheless a weighty one. The American people would have to work harder and longer, and they would have to do without.

There are also burdens involved in an internally held public debt like our present one, *but the burdens of an internal debt are qualitatively and quantitatively*

THE PUBLIC DEBT AND POSTWAR FISCAL POLICY   427

different from those of an external debt. This is the first and most important lesson to be grasped, without which nobody can go far in understanding the economics of the public debt. The interest on an internal debt is paid by Americans to Americans; there is no *direct* loss of goods and services. When interest on the debt is paid out of taxation, there is no *direct* loss of disposable income; Paul receives what Peter loses, and sometimes—but only sometimes—Paul and Peter are one and the same person.

Borrowing and Shifting Economic Burdens through Time. Still another confusion between an external and internal debt is involved in the often-met statement: "When we borrow rather than tax in order to fight a war, then the true economic burden is really being shifted to the future generations who will have to pay interest and principal on the debt." As applied to an external debt, this shift of burden through time might be true. It is unmistakably false in reference to an internal debt. Why?

To fight a war now, we must hurl present-day munitions at the enemy; not dollar bills and not future goods and services. If we borrow munitions from some neutral country and pledge our children and grandchildren to repay them in goods and services, then it may truly be said that external borrowing permits a shift of economic burden between present and future generations.

But suppose there is no outside nation to lend us goods. Suppose that our direct controls have cut civilian capital formation down to the bone, but still our government needs more resources for the war effort. Suppose that Congress is not willing to vote taxes large enough to permit the government to balance its swollen budget or stringent enough to reduce people's spending to where they will release resources for the war effort and stop bidding up prices. The government will then be running a deficit and will build up a huge debt. (It may also have to pass price-control and rationing laws, but that need not concern us here.)

Can it be truthfully said that "internal borrowing shifts the war burden to future generations while taxing places it on the present generation"? A thousand times no! The present generation must still give up resources to produce the munitions hurled at the enemy. In the future, some of our grandchildren will be giving up goods and services to other grandchildren. That is the nub of the matter. The only way in which we can impose a direct burden on the future nation as a whole is by incurring an external debt or by passing along less capital equipment to our posterity.

This explains why the British are a great deal more worried about their small external debt than they are over their vastly greater internal debt; the former directly impoverishes the British Isles. Fortunately, the United States has come out of the most costly war in all history with little impairment of capital equipment and external debt.

"We All Owe It to Ourselves."   If an internal debt is simultaneously owed and owned by Americans, why do some people think that the wartime creation of 250 billion dollars of government bonds makes the public more wealthy and more ready to spend? If we draw up a consolidated balance sheet for the nation as a whole, we see that the (internal) debt represents a kind of fictitious financial wealth, which cancels out as a liability and asset.

Even purely financial assets have important effects. Every citizen who owns government bonds includes them when drawing up his periodic balance sheet, along with his other assets. But he is a very rare man indeed if he also includes as a present liability the amount of *future* taxes which he may have to pay to finance government interest payments or debt retirement. He does not even have a way of estimating his share of these taxes. The result is that the internal debt, which as a liability should exactly cancel out itself as an asset, tends instead to be counted by people primarily as an asset. Given a nest egg of bonds which they can either sell or cash in, people *feel* richer and more secure and perhaps, therefore, tend to have a higher propensity to consume out of current income.

Debt Management and Monetary Policy.   The existence of a large outstanding public debt may also have an influence on the interest rate and on its use to fight the business cycle. Some writers fear that channeling investment funds into the purchase of government bonds will raise the rate of interest to private borrowers. Alexander Hamilton, the spokesman of the conservative Federalist party, had just the opposite opinion. He felt that, rightly managed and in the right amounts, a public debt would be "a national blessing" because it would provide a secure gilt-edge asset that would give businessmen an income and enable them to trade for smaller profits.

As was shown in Chap. 16 on Central Banking, the Federal reserve authorities have strong powers to regulate rates of interest on government bonds. Therefore, any undue upward or downward pressure of the debt upon interest rates can be offset by open-market purchases and sale of government securities. But, and this is an ironic paradox, the existence of the vast public debt, while it enhances their power, at the same time serves to inhibit the exercise of effective monetary and interest policy by the Federal Reserve Banks.

It will be recalled that monetary policy is supposed to act so as to raise interest rates and tighten credit conditions when over-all demand threatens to be inflationary. But with large amounts of bonds in the hands of banks and the

THE PUBLIC DEBT AND POSTWAR FISCAL POLICY   429

public, the governmental authorities have a strong incentive toward keeping up the selling price of government bonds—in order to keep interest charges on the debt low and prevent financial embarrassment of financial institutions holding government bonds. If government bonds cannot fall in price, then interest rates cannot be tightened; people and banks are always able to convert their bonds into the cash they need for consumption or investment spending. A large debt, therefore, tends to discourage the use of monetary policy to control the business cycle and serves to throw an even larger burden on fiscal policy.[1] It is true that many modern writers do not think that this is much of an evil, since interest rate changes are supposed to have minor influence on consumption and investment expenditure; but still it is an evil.

The True Indirect Burden of Interest Charges.   When taxes are used to pay interest charges on the public debt, then money goes from one pocket into another. No direct burden like that of an external debt is involved. But it would be wrong to jump to the hasty conclusion that no burden of any kind is involved. There is an indirect burden which may be very important.

In the first place, although money merely goes out from one pocket and into another, the trousers in question may be worn by different people. The present national debt is very widely held, so that almost every individual has some share, either through outright holdings or through bank deposits and insurance policies. Nevertheless, the statistical evidence suggests that the people who receive bond interest are *on the average* not in the lower income brackets. Thus interest on the public debt constitutes a regressive (Robin Hood in reverse) element in our fiscal system. "Soaking the poor to pay the rich" tends to reduce purchasing power and runs counter to many modern notions of equity. Nevertheless, it is a necessary evil if past commitments with respect to the public debt are to be scrupulously honored, as they must be.

However, with our present public debt this transfer from one income class to another is probably not its single most important indirect burden. More important, *transfering tax money from Peter to pay bond interest to the same Peter will involve a heavy indirect burden on the economy!* This is because taxation always has some distorting effects on people's economic behavior. Centuries ago houses were taxed on their windows, with the result that people built dark houses, even though the government still collected the same revenue by simply raising rates on the few remaining windows. Similarly, taxing people's

---

[1] The effects upon consumption of the large outstanding amount of government bond assets may make matters worse. Consumption becomes less responsive to disposable income and may become more changeable. Fiscal policy then has more work to do and has less leverage to do it.

430   FISCAL POLICY AND FULL EMPLOYMENT

income may cause them to work too little, or in many cases too hard, in their attempt to maintain the same standard of living. Perhaps of even more importance, high corporation or personal income taxes will often have adverse effects upon people's willingness to venture their capital on risky enterprises. The result: less technological progress and fewer jobs.

At this point, the reader may protest that this is all nonsense and that there is no net tax burden involved in an internal transfer since it is being assumed that we all own bonds in proportion to our share of taxes, and in effect are only paying to ourselves. This reasoning is quite mistaken. *Taxes on each individual matched by exactly equal interest payments to him do not cancel out!*

This is so because what is true of all is not true for each individual. Suppose for simplicity that all Americans earn $4,500 a year in wages. Suppose that each owns $25,000 in government bonds, which at 2 per cent bring in a yield of $500 per year. To pay this interest the government, let us say, adds 10 per cent (in addition to existing taxes) on total income of $5,000 ($4,500 + $500). Previously it just paid me to work an extra bit of overtime to earn the last dollar of my $5,000. But now the government takes another dime out of that dollar. I (and every American like me) may now feel that it doesn't pay to work such long hours. By cutting out, say, one-third of my working hours, my income is now only $3,500. The tax has distorted national effort and production.

The unconvinced reader will say at this point: "What if everybody else does what you do? Then the extra tax rate will have to be raised from 10 per cent to almost 15 per cent if the total of bond interest is to be covered." True enough. But this only proves the point. The final situation may end up with even a greater distortion of effort and risk taking, and with an even higher tax rate. This all happens because, although the nation cannot avoid raising taxes equal to the interest payment, each individual knows that he can affect his taxes by varying his effort, with his own small interest payments going on anyway, regardless of what he or a single small person does.

The above example is oversimplified and undoubtedly exaggerates the harmful effects of internal transfers. Also, different kinds of taxes differ in their harmful effects, but in any case with our taxes already so high, any further burden due to interest on the public debt is just that much more harmful.

Moreover, we have neglected the beneficial effects of interest payments to banks, universities, widows, and other *rentiers*. If there were no public debt or if interest rates were to fall substantially, then (1) charitable institutions would have to be supported by public and private current contributions more than by interest on perpetual endowments, (2) social security and annuities would have to take the place of *rentier* interest, and (3) service charges by

THE PUBLIC DEBT AND POSTWAR FISCAL POLICY   431

banks would have to be increasingly relied upon instead of government bond interest.

THE QUANTITATIVE PROBLEM OF THE DEBT

We may summarize the above section on the economics of a public debt as follows: (1) Our internal debt does not involve the direct burden of an external debt nor the same possibility of shifting real burdens between generations. (2) Although we all owe it to ourselves, people tend to treat bonds as a safe liquid asset which increases their willingness to consume out of current income. The huge volume of outstanding debt hampers an anticyclical interest rate policy because the authorities are loath to see bond prices fluctuate. (3) An internal debt involves an important *indirect* burden whenever new taxes have to be raised to meet interest payments. This would be true even if the typical person was taxed by as much as his own interest payments, but it is further aggravated by the fact that interest receivers appear to be somewhat more wealthy than average taxpayers.

To assess the importance of the public debt, we must turn to the facts. Do interest payments on it swallow up most of the national income? How does the total of all interest payments, public and private, compare with past years and with the experience of other countries? What about foreseeable future trends?

In Chap. 7 (Fig. 1, page 151) the historic growth of our national debt was pictured.[1]

To see how the present quarter of a trillion dollar debt compares with the past and some other countries, Table 1 has been drawn up. It shows for selected times and places the size of national debts and their relationship to size of national income and interest payments. Thus, early in 1947 our national debt of 257 billion dollars represented less than 1½ years of national income, and its interest payments represented less than 3 per cent of national income. Note that England, in 1818, 1923, and 1946 had an internal debt estimated at more than twice national income, and her interest on the debt as a percentage of national income far exceeded anything that we need look forward to. Yet, the

[1] The approximate ownership of the total of 257 billion dollars of outstanding Federal debt early in 1947 was as follows (in billions of dollars):

Commercial and mutual savings banks	$84
Federal Reserve Banks	24
Insurance companies	25
Individuals	64
Corporations and miscellaneous	23
Federal, state, and local governments	37

About 51 billion dollars of the total was in the form of familiar United States savings bonds.

432   FISCAL POLICY AND FULL EMPLOYMENT

century before World War I was England's greatest century—greatest in power and material progress. Nevertheless, as the table shows, her national debt was not substantially reduced; but with the steady growth of her national income, the debt and its interest charges shrank to almost nothing in relative quantitative magnitude.

TABLE 1. *National Debt and Interest·Charges Relative to National Income*

Year	National debt	Interest charges on national debt	National income	Size of debt in years of national income	Interest charges as a per cent of national income
				(5) =	(6) ÷ 100 =
(1)	(2)	(3)	(4)	(2) ÷ (4)	(3) ÷ (4)
United States	(Billions)	(Billions	(Billions)		
1947*	$257	$5	$200	1.3	2.5
1939	34.9	0.97	68.5	0.5	1.4
1932	18.2	0.64	46.7	0.4	1.4
1929	15.1	0.67	79.5	0.2	0.8
1920	23.5	1.06	68.4	0.3	1.5
1916	1.2	0.02	38.7	0.0+	0.0+
1868	2.6	0.13	6.8	3.8	2.0
Britain:	(Millions)	(Millions)	(Millions)		
1946*	£24,500	£500	£8,000	3.1	6.2+
1923	7,700	271	3,800	2.0+	7.1
1913	656	17	2,300	0.3	0.7
1818	840	31	400	2.1	7.7

SOURCE: "Economic Almanac," Department of Commerce, U.S. Treasury; "Colwyn Report," Statistical Abstract of United Kingdom. Data rounded off.
    * Estimated.

In view of these statistics and careful qualitative analysis, it is perhaps fair to conclude that the national debt does not yet constitute a problem of the first magnitude in comparison with the problem of the peace, the atomic bomb, or unemployment. Whether productivity will continue to rise in the future, whether labor and management can learn to bargain collectively without strikes and inflation—all these are more important than the debt itself.

THE PUBLIC DEBT AND POSTWAR FISCAL POLICY   433

Yet there is a tremendous amount of emotion involved in people's attitudes toward the debt, and this we must not dismiss lightly. Like sex or religion, the public debt is a subject that it does little good to argue about, and yet nobody can help doing so. Many people used to predict the end of the world when the debt reached one-hundredth, one-tenth, and one-fifth of its present level; each year when the dire disaster had not appeared, they renewed their predictions for the following years.

In dispassionately analyzing the growth of the debt, one error we must avoid: *we must not forget that the real national product of the United States is an ever-growing thing.*

Population increase has slowed down some, but for a long time our numbers will continue to grow. As to productivity, there is absolutely no indication that man-hour efficiency and new techniques have begun to slacken off. Upon this, stagnationists and exhilarationists both agree. What seemed like a big debt in 1790 would be nothing today. What our children will come to regard as a big debt, our great grandchildren may consider relatively unimportant.

This explains why England and France, in the crucially formative years of the capitalistic system and industrial revolution, were able to go on—not only decade after decade but almost century after century with their budgets in balance less than half the time. This same factor of growth explains why in the United States, where real national production doubles every generation or so, the public debt might increase by 250 billion dollars in 25 years without its relative percentage burden growing.

This would give the wildest believer in government spending an average deficit of some 10 billion dollars per year before he would have to turn to such even more unorthodox financial expedients as printing money or selling interest-free bonds to the Federal Reserve Banks. Moreover, before turning to such expedients, he would still have open to him the now familiar process of forcing down interest rates on government bonds by a conventional easy-money banking policy.

In short, there is no technical financial reason why a nation fanatically addicted to deficit spending should not pursue such a policy for the rest of our lives, and even beyond. The real question is only whether such a policy will impinge on an economy that is inflationary or deflationary. So long as private and government spending are only enough to offset saving, that is one thing. If a nation or Congress is misguided enough to continue heavy spending and light taxing after total consumption and private investment have become too large, then inflation will be the outcome.

434   FISCAL POLICY AND FULL EMPLOYMENT

USEFUL VERSUS WASTEFUL FISCAL POLICY

Those who believe in an active fiscal policy set up a perfectionist goal: the maintenance of total effective demand at a level high enough to prevent the wastes of mass unemployment, and low enough so as not to lead to a level of inflationary total spending in excess of total producible goods.

Or, to put the matter in technical terms, they argue that fiscal policy should shape taxes and expenditure, quantitatively and qualitatively, so that the economy's Saving and Investment schedules will intersect neither to the right nor to the left of the region of high (or full) employment. Many equally competent economists insist that there are other goals of equal or greater importance.

It cannot be repeated too often that building pyramids or digging holes and filling them up is indefensible. True, in comparison with a policy of doing nothing about a deep depression, such boondoggling might seem in some ways preferable, because of the favorable respending effects of those who receive government expenditures. But such a policy is surely only the lesser of two evils. Properly planned useful public works have just as favorable secondary effects, and in addition they fill important human needs.

Nor is it necessary or always desirable to fight a depression with useful public works. If the American people feel that private consumption should have a higher social priority, tax reduction or transfer expenditure should be relied upon. The extra income available from the conquest of unemployment will then be going for privately produced and purchased goods.

Which of the alternatives of government expenditure or tax reduction should be followed if private investment and consumption are lacking? The answer should not be given simply in terms of financial orthodoxy: the size of the deficit.[1] It should be given in terms of what the American people consider to be the pressing postwar social priorities. If 10 billion dollars of resources were to be released from investment purposes, the American people would wish to use part of this for extra food, extra clothes, extra leisure, etc. This suggests tax reduction (or increase in transfer expenditure).

But the American people may also want to spend part of their newly available income on education, on public health, on urban redevelopment projects, on roads, etc. This suggests some use of government expenditure in depressed times.

The one way that the American people should not want to spend their

[1] The reader is referred to the Appendix to this chapter, which analyzes in quantitative terms four different paths to full employment.

THE PUBLIC DEBT AND POSTWAR FISCAL POLICY   435

income is upon involuntary unemployment. There should never be any need to indulge in wasteful or inefficient government expenditure; the government should always get something useful for the resources it uses up. If collective consumption projects have a lower social priority than private consumption, then the proper fiscal policy is one of tax reduction and transfer expenditure.

A FUNDAMENTAL DIFFICULTY WITH FULL EMPLOYMENT

One last and important set of qualifications must be made before completing the discussion of fiscal policy and, indeed, of the whole problem of national income determination. In a rough way, we know what is meant by full or high employment; but only in a rough way.

Of course, full employment doesn't mean that every man, woman, and child should be out at work every hour of a 24-hour day. It doesn't mean that I can hold out for a job as pitcher with the New York Yankees, or as a $100-a-day carpenter. But it does mean that reasonably efficient workers, willing to work at the currently prevailing ("fair") wage rates, need not find themselves unemployable as a result of too little general demand. Women who want to do so can work in the home, youths can go to school if they prefer to, and the aged or unwell can retire from the labor force; but none of these are to be forced to do so because of job shortages.

The real difficulty with full employment lies not in its rough definition but in the fact that *wages and prices may begin to soar while there is still considerable unemployment and excess capacity.* An increase in private investment spending or in government spending may be prevented from effectuating full employment, its favorable dollar effects being wasted by a paper rise in prices.

If businessmen and trade-unions react perversely to an increased demand, fiscal policy cannot be relied upon to achieve and maintain full employment. Some pessimists have argued that there is nothing to do but hope for a large enough "army of the unemployed" to keep laborers from making unreasonable wage demands; thus, a reserve army of 10 million jobless hanging around factory gates might keep wages from rising and labor from becoming obstreperous. Still others might see no escape from the dilemma other than to have some degree of inflation most of the time.

Still other writers would then advocate the use of direct price and wage controls to keep prices from spiraling upward at high employment levels. In the present writer's personal opinion, efficient peacetime over-all price controls would involve a degree of planning incompatible with past, and perhaps present, philosophical beliefs of the great majority of the American people. For, as we shall see in Part Three, the problem of setting appropriate social

436   FISCAL POLICY AND FULL EMPLOYMENT

prices is a tremendously complex one—so complex that the whole nature of our economic system would have to be different, once we had decided not to rely upon market forces.

It is hardly too much to say that this price-wage question is the biggest unsolved economic problem of our time: *Can business, labor, and agriculture learn to act in such a way as to avoid inflation whenever private or public spending brings us anywhere near to full employment?* A wage and price policy for full employment—that is America's greatest problem and challenge.

THE EMPLOYMENT ACT OF 1946

Obviously no one has a crystal ball to read the future, particularly the distant future. The case for and against secular stagnation cannot be definitively assessed. But fortunately—and this requires great emphasis—it is not necessary for Congress or the experts to be able to see a decade or more into the future in order to pursue correct economic policies currently.

In the momentous Employment Act of 1946, both political parties in Congress affirmed the responsibility of the government, and of private enterprise, to fight mass unemployment and inflation. This law provided for a Council of Economic Advisers which each year is to keep Congress and the President informed as to the state of "employment, production, and purchasing power"; also a Joint Congressional Committee is set up whose duty it is to study and evaluate the recommendations contained in the President's Annual Economic Report.

By itself, fiscal policy is not enough to create a healthy state of stable high employment with rising productivity and efficient use of economic resources in production. In fact, the eight chapters of Part Three are concerned with the proper relations of prices and different branches of production in a world where the problem of over-all effective demand is nonexistent. If ever the curse of general inflation or deflation has been banished, there will rise to the top of our national policy agenda—and properly so—the true and abiding universal economic problems which every economic society has had to face since the Garden of Eden.

SUMMARY

A. SHORT-RUN AND LONG-RUN FISCAL POLICY

1. Fiscal policies with respect to government spending and taxing fall into two categories: the less controversial problem of countercyclical compensatory spending aimed simply at ironing out the worst swings of the business cycle but not at altering the average level of spending over the whole cycle; and long-run fiscal policy aimed at raising or lowering the average level of income so as to maintain high employment without inflation.

2. Four aspects of a countercyclical policy involve (*a*) careful planning of public-works projects; (*b*) proper timing of welfare and other government spending; (*c*) quasi-automatic changes in tax collections brought about by income changes even with no alterations in tax rates; (*d*) quantitative (and qualitative) changes in tax rates so as to increase tax receipts in prosperity and decrease them in bad times.

The reader should be acquainted with the difficulties of countercyclical finance, and appreciate the difference between it and the special theory of pump priming.

3. We go beyond the realm of countercyclical finance when we argue for a long-run policy of tax surplus and debt retirement if there should turn out to be a postwar era of excessive total demand, *i.e.*, an era of secular exhilaration.

4. If, instead of there being too much demand, there should turn out to be unemployment and too little "offsets to saving," the same reasoning would advocate a long-run increase in the average level of government spending, or decrease in tax collections. It would not insist upon the budget's necessarily being balanced over the cycle, arguing that the public debt will grow with the growth of the whole economy.

B. DEBT AND POSTWAR POLICY

5. The reader should understand the economic effects of debt reduction and also the economics of an internal debt: (*a*) the difference between the direct burden of an external and internal debt, and the ability of a country to shift burdens through time in the two cases; (*b*) the effect of the public debt on people's financial wealth and consumption habits; (*c*) the difficulties created by the debt for a countercyclical interest rate policy because of the desire of government authorities to stabilize bond prices; (*d*) the important indirect

438   FISCAL POLICY AND FULL EMPLOYMENT

burden of collecting taxes to pay interest on a debt, even if we all owe it to ourselves.

It is important, also, to know roughly what the size of the postwar Federal debt is in relation to national income and interest charges, in order to assess the present, both in terms of the past and in terms of the future. The growth of the debt must be appraised in terms of the growth of the economy as a whole.

6. A full (or high) employment program has as its goal a level of total spending which is neither too little nor too great—so that the Saving and Investment schedules intersect in the region of full employment. The Employment Act of 1946 represents an important innovation in our national government, affirming responsibility of the government for employment opportunities and setting up executive and congressional machinery for policy action.

7. Our economy is still confronted with the dilemma that any approach to full employment—whether brought about publicly or privately—may be followed by wage increases and price rises even before unemployment disappears or idle capacity comes into use. A wage-price policy for full employment provides a fundamental challenge to our mixed system of private enterprise and public responsibility.

QUESTIONS FOR DISCUSSION

1. "No nation can avoid having a fiscal policy. With the government such an important part of the present-day economy, it is almost impossible even to define a 'neutral fiscal policy.' It is even harder to give rational reasons for preferring such a policy to an active fiscal program aimed at preventing inflation and deflation." Subject this statement to critical examination, possibly bringing in some noneconomic considerations.

2. Draw up a list of new college buildings and projects that might be made part of a planned countercyclical program. What would some of the difficulties and disadvantages be in carrying this out?

3. What phase of the business cycle are you now in? What taxation policies would seem appropriate? what expenditure policies?

4. Qualitatively, how would you vary the relative importance of different kinds of taxes (such as income tax rates and exemptions, sales tax rates, or property taxes) so as to compensate for unemployment or inflation?

5. From the early 1870's to the middle 1890's, depressions were deep and prolonged, booms were short-lived and relatively anemic, the price level was declining. What long-run fiscal policy do you think should have been followed in that quarter of a

THE PUBLIC DEBT AND POSTWAR FISCAL POLICY 439

century? Would your answer be the same for the following 20 years leading up to World War I, a period of rising prices and comparative prosperity?

6. Show step by step how the wartime growth of the public debt caused bank deposits and the public's liquid wealth to expand. Show how contraction of the debt would exactly reverse this process.

7. Comment on the following quotation from the English historian of the last century, Lord Macaulay:

"At every stage in the growth of that debt the nation has set up the same cry of anguish and despair. At every stage in the growth of that debt it has been seriously asserted by wise men that bankruptcy and ruin were at hand. Yet still the debt went on growing; and still bankruptcy and ruin were as remote as ever. . . .

"The prophets of evil were under a double delusion. They erroneously imagined that there was an exact analogy between the case of an individual who is in debt to another individual and the case of a society which is in debt to a part of itself. . . . They made no allowance for the effect produced by the incessant progress of every experimental science, and by the incessant efforts of every man to get on in life. They saw that the debt grew; and they forgot that other things grew as well as the debt."

8. Professor A. P. Lerner has set down the following (abbreviated) principles of "Functional Finance." Criticize:

"There are effective instruments in the hands of the government for maintaining full employment and preventing inflation, but their use is hindered by strong prejudices. The instruments are not available until it is recognized that the size of the national debt is relatively unimportant, that the interest on the debt is not a burden on the nation, and that the nation cannot be made "bankrupt" by internally held debt. Every debt has a corresponding credit. Only external debt is like individual debt and impoverishes the nation. The purpose of taxation is never to raise money but to leave less in the hands of the taxpayer. . . . There is no room for the *principle* of balancing the budget . . . ."

9. "Say what you will, graft keeps money in circulation and gets things done." What do you say?

10. The Council of Economic Advisers to the President, in its first report under the Employment Act of 1946, questions that "we can always create full employment by pumping enough purchasing power into the system," and the doctrine that we have only to "turn the faucet off and cause a contraction." According to the Council Report, " . . . we cannot assume that deficiency of demand in one particular area or of one particular character can be made up just by adding purchasing power in general, for instance through tax relief. . . . If labor is pricing itself out of jobs or manufacturers and farmers are pricing themselves out of a market, or capital is pricing itself out of investment, the basic remedy is the correction of these specific situations, not the injection of some aggregate purchasing power in a dose measured in size to offset an estimated future total of unemployment."

With how much of this would you agree? Why?

APPENDIX TO CHAPTER 18
FOUR QUANTITATIVE PATHS TO FULL
EMPLOYMENT

Concrete numbers often help to illustrate an abstract argument. In this section, four hypothetical quantitative paths to full employment are presented.
They are by no means the only ones; but being oversimplified, pure cases, each
exemplifies a different portion of the problem.

The first route is the private-enterprise maintenance of high employment:
through good luck or policies, it turns out that private consumption and private
net investment are just large enough to lead to full employment. This is by all
odds the simplest and, to most of us, the best way to have full employment.

But what if private investment is too small? What are other approaches to
full employment? The other three paths are designed to illustrate how a given
deficiency of private investment may be countered: by an increase in government spending on goods and services alone, by a reduction in net taxes alone,
or by a balanced increase in both spending and taxes.

In each of these last three cases, private net investment has been arbitrarily
written down by 10 billion dollars, purely for quantitative illustration; this is
not intended as a realistic prediction, since there is reason to be more optimistic
in the immediate postwar years and since the different fiscal policies might
have different effects upon private investment.

Let us turn to Table 2. It has eight lines altogether. Line 1 in every case
represents a full-employment *net national product* of 200 billion dollars (at
1947 market prices). Lines 5, 6, and 7 give the breakdown of this NNP into
the three components of consumption, private net capital formation or investment, and government expenditure on goods and services (including state and
local).

This last government expenditure item definitely excludes all government
transfer payments such as relief, veterans' bonuses, and bond interest. These
transfer payments which give people money rather than taking it away from
them are just like negative taxes. Therefore, all transfer payments have been
subtracted from all tax collections to arrive at what is called "net" taxes or
withdrawals and are shown in line 3. This means that, in Model I when
government expenditure on goods and services is just balanced by "net" taxes
or withdrawals at a level of 30 billion dollars, this really corresponds to a

THE PUBLIC DEBT AND POSTWAR FISCAL POLICY   441

combined Federal, state, and local governmental budget of that much plus more than a dozen billion dollars of transfer payments as well.

TABLE 2. *Four Paths to Full Employment (In billions of 1947 dollars)*

Line and item	Model I, private investment boom	Model II, deficit spending	Model III, tax-reduc-tion deficit	Model IV, balanced budget
1. Net national product (at 1947 market prices).............	$200	$200	$200	$200
2. Less net corporate saving......	−6	−6	−6	−6
3. Less "net" taxes (total state, local, and Federal taxes and social insurance contributions minus all govt. transfer expenditure)...................	**−30**	**−30**	**−17½**	**−80**
4. Disposable income (line 1 − line 2 − line 3).............	164	164	176½	114
5. Consumption expenditure (varies 80 cents for every $1 variation in disposable income)....	$148	$148	$158	$108
6. Private net capital formation (arbitrarily taken as constant).	**22**	**12**	**12**	**12**
7. Government expenditure on goods and services (excludes transfers such as relief and interest)..................	**30**	**40**	**30**	**80**
8. Government deficit (line 7 − line 3)....................	$ 0	$ 10	$ 12½	$ 0

Lines 6, 7, and 3 appear in bold-faced type because investment is assumed to be an arbitrary number in each model and because government spending and taxing are assumed arbitrarily as the definition of each model.

How do we arrive at consumption? Here we must first know what people's disposable income will be and then their propensity to consume out of disposable income. To get disposable income in line 4, we must always subtract from NNP in line 1 the net corporate saving (line 2) and the "net" taxes or

442   FISCAL POLICY AND FULL EMPLOYMENT

withdrawals (line 3). Throughout, net corporate saving (or plowed-back undistributed profits) has been made to depend on NNP and to be equal to 6 billion dollars.

Now that we have disposable income, what about the propensity to consume? A fairly optimistic assumption is made that at 164 billion dollars of disposable income, there will be as much as 148 billion dollars of consumption; and that for every dollar variation of disposable income there will be $\frac{4}{5}$ of a dollar "marginal propensity" for consumption to change. Our assumptions are now complete.

Model I: *Private Enterprise, Full Employment.*   In the first path, government expenditure (line 7) and "net" taxes (line 3) are both 30 billion dollars. Disposable income (line 4) is therefore (6 + 30) billion dollars less than the 200 billion dollars of NNP, or 164 billion dollars. According to the propensity to consume, consumption (line 5) is 148 billion dollars. Therefore, private net capital formation to maintain full employment (line 6) must necessarily be 22 billion dollars (200 − 148 − 30). By definition, there is a zero deficit, as can be seen by comparing lines 7 and 3.

If net investment were to fall below 22 billion dollars, say, to fall by as much as 10 billion dollars, then what would happen? If no legislative action were taken, NNP would, of course, fall and, because of the multiplier, by a good deal more than 10 billion dollars.[1] The next three models are designed to show what can be done to prevent this from happening.

Model II: *Deficit-spending Path to Full Employment.*   In this model, taxes do not change. Government expenditure on goods and services simply goes up by 10 billion dollars to counter the 10-billion-dollar drop in private investment. Except for lines 6 and 7, the second column of figures is just like the first. But now, of course, there is a 10-billion-dollar deficit.

Model III: *Tax-reduction Path to Full Employment.*   Here, taxes are cut (or transfer expenditure increased) until people's disposable income has grown enough to induce them to increase their consumption by as much as the 10-billion-dollar decline in investment. The government's use of resources remains at the 30-billion-dollar level of Model I. But to get people to consume an extra 80 cents, we must change their disposable income by $1; to get them to consume an extra 10 billion dollars, net taxes must be cut by $12\frac{1}{2}$ billion dollars, or in line 3 from 30 down to $17\frac{1}{2}$ billion dollars. This means a $12\frac{1}{2}$-

---

[1] The reader may test his proficiency by filling in a fifth column showing the result of a do-nothing policy. (HINT: Assume that net corporate savings go down 10 cents for every $1 drop in *NNP*, while "net" taxes go down by 25 cents. Show that the final drop in *NNP* is $10\frac{9}{48}$ times the 10-billion-dollar drop in investment.)

THE PUBLIC DEBT AND POSTWAR FISCAL POLICY 443

billion-dollar deficit (line 8). Note that Model III has a bigger deficit than Model II, that tax reduction or transfer expenditure tends to be weaker dollar for dollar—other things being equal—than extra expenditure on goods and services.[1]

Model IV: Balanced-budget path to Full Employment. Because of the slight extra "leverage" of spending over taxing, we can theoretically increase them both together and finally make up for the drop in private investment. But the government's expenditure on resources must now go up by 50 billion dollars to compensate for the 10 billion dollars of net investment! This tremendous expansion of the collective sector of the economy is necessary because insisting upon a balanced budget means that taxes must vastly increase and that private consumption must greatly contract, with government spending having to make up for both the investment and the consumption contractions in the private sector.

This financially orthodox approach is actually most radical from the standpoint of free and individualistic private enterprise. The tax-reduction model, Model III, which is philosophically most consistent with rugged individualism, is financially most heretical. That is why some conservatives are now becoming of the opinion that there are worse things than deficits—*e.g.*, high taxes. And that is why, when investment is for any reason stagnant, only a socialist can afford to be financially orthodox and preach the thrift doctrine of "Poor Richard's Almanac."

[1] There is another way of seeing this. For example, suppose that $1 of expenditure has, counting in all secondary multiplier effects, a $3 effect on income; then a $1 change in taxes is likely—other things being equal—to have less than $3 effect all together, probably only about a $2 total effect. This means that, if we expand both expenditure and taxes by $1 with no deficit at all, there will still be a $1 increase in total national income. The increase of $1 in expenditure gives rise to $3 = 1 + \frac{2}{3} + (\frac{2}{3})^2 + \cdots$. The increase in taxes gives rise to a reduction of $-2 = 0 - \frac{2}{3} - (\frac{2}{3})^2 - \cdots$. The combined effect is $3 - 2 = 1$, the difference being due to the fact that the effect of taxes does not enter into national income on the first round, but affects employment and production only on the successive rounds of respending.

[14]

Fiscal Policy and Full Employment without Inflation

The Congress declares that it is the continuing responsibility of the federal government to . . . promote maximum employment, production, and purchasing power.
EMPLOYMENT ACT OF 1946

We have seen in earlier chapters that the behavior of saving and investment determines the level of national income and employment. We have seen that investment and other spending often fluctuate widely from year to year. History shows how painful and wasteful the business cycle has been in the past. Today everyone is in agreement that we must continue to succeed in laying to rest the ghost of instability, chronic slump, and snowballing inflation. The historic Employment Act of 1946 brought the United States up to the other mixed economies in this respect. It set up a Council of Economic Advisers and a Joint Economic Committee to help ensure full employment and healthy growth.

What prescription follows from our economic diagnosis? Earlier chapters have shown that the Federal Reserve System can do much, by way of monetary policy and interest, to moderate instability. Reinforcing central bank actions, powerful help is still needed from the weapon of public *fiscal policy* (i.e., governmental tax and expenditure policies).

OLD-FASHIONED FINANCE

Forty years ago the chapter in an economic textbook dealing with public finance read just as it had in Adam Smith's time. From 1776 to 1929 there was little discernible progress. Moreover, the Democratic President Grover Cleveland differed not a bit in his ideology of finance from Republican William McKinley, or for that matter from Calvin Coolidge and Herbert Hoover.

What were the clichés of oldfangled shirt-sleeve economics, the doctrines our grandfathers were taught and preached? Here are a few:

1. The budget should be balanced in every year (and at a low level, with expenditure prudent and purposes strictly limited).

2. The public debt is a burden on the backs of our

330

children and grandchildren (just as though each of us has to carry on our shoulders heavy boulders). All debt is evil; public debt, absolutely evil.

3. Everything that is true of an individual or family is also true of the government. If a husband and wife spend more than their monthly income, they go bankrupt and misery follows. The same is true for Uncle Sam (or John Bull or Kaiser Wilhelm).

4. In agreement with one of Adam Smith's four fundamental "canons of taxation," a good tax is one that produces *the same revenues in good times as well as bad.*

You can extend the list in any club locker room or bar. What is interesting about it is that today no experts agree with it or the reasonings on which it relies. And no nations, even in the heyday of Victorian capitalism, came anywhere near to living up to it; for, fortunately, they could not do so. During each depression and recession, *automatically* budget deficits developed at the same time that the conventional wisdom was deploring the phenomenon. For centuries, in times of distress, local and national governments have resorted to work on the roads and other public works to relieve the distress. For centuries, poorhouse relief and other transfer expenditures have ebbed and risen with the dance of the business cycle.

As will be seen in this chapter, experienced researchers into the facts and the analytical principles of public finance have today, all over the world, quite different answers to these questions from those of our forefathers. The problem for an introductory text is to explain the logic and experience underlying modern doctrines, not indoctrinate the student into any one view. Objective analysis of the issues—both pros and cons—should be helpful in giving each person the materials from which he can form his own understanding of the fiscal practices followed by mixed economies all over the world.

A. SHORT-RUN AND LONG-RUN FISCAL POLICY

By a positive fiscal policy, we mean the process of shaping *taxation* and *public expenditure* in order (1) to help dampen down the swings of the business cycle and (2) to contribute toward the maintenance of a growing, high-employment economy free from excessive inflation or deflation.

Suppose the economic system in a particular year is threatened with a deflationary gap. Suppose private consumption and investment spending are too weak to provide adequate employment. What action would then be called for?

The Federal Reserve will use expansionary monetary policy to try to stimulate private investment. To the degree[1] that its efforts are not fully adequate, the fiscal authorities would still be faced by a deflationary gap. This would be the signal for Congress and the President to introduce tax and public-expenditure policies designed to help reachieve stable full employment.

Similar action would be called for in the case where private investment and consumption decisions were threatening the economy with an inflationary gap. With prices rising and employers vying desperately for nonexistent workers, the Fed would initiate contrac-

---

[1]How much of the stabilizing load is carried by monetary and how much by fiscal policy depends, as Chapter 41 will discuss, on public-growth targets and international-payments constraints. Also, the financing of deficits and surpluses can itself help shape the course of money-supply growth.

tionary credit programs aimed to reduce the inflationary gap. But if the saving-investment or $C + I + G$ intersections still threatened the economy with a sustained inflationary gap, it would then be the duty of Congress and the President to initiate higher tax rates and/or lower-public-expenditure programs in the attempt to restore a high-employment equilibrium without inflation.

In summary, fiscal policies dealing with taxes and public expenditure, in cooperation with stabilizing monetary policies, have for their goal a high-employment and growing economy—but one without price inflation. The fiscal and monetary authorities "lean against the prevailing economic winds," thereby helping provide a favorable economic environment within which the dynamic forces of private initiative can have the widest opportunity for achievement.

OUR IMPORTANT "BUILT-IN STABILIZERS"

One might get the impression from the above remarks that fiscal policy helps stabilize the economy only so long as government officials are carefully watching trends, are successfully anticipating future developments, and are meeting promptly to take decisive action. Such "discretionary fiscal policies," involving the making and changing of explicit decisions, are important; fortunately, they are but part of the story.

The modern fiscal system has great inherent *automatic stabilizing* properties. All through the day and night, whether or not the President is in the White House, the fiscal system is helping to keep our economy stable. If in 1975 a recession got under way while Congress was out of session, powerful automatic forces would go instantly into action to counteract it before there were any committee meetings or the exercise of special intelligence of any form.

What are these mysterious stabilizers? They are primarily the following:

1. *Automatic changes in tax receipts.* We saw in Chapters 8 and 9 that our federal tax system depends progressively on personal and corporate incomes. What does this mean for stability? It means that as soon as income begins to fall off, and even before Congress makes any changes in tax rates, the tax receipts of the government also fall off. (Today, for each 10-billion-dollar drop in NNP, total tax receipts drop by about $3\frac{1}{2}$ billion. After President Nixon's variant of the negative income tax becomes law, this fraction may become considerably larger.)

Now, reductions in tax receipts are just what the doctor prescribes in case of a dip in income. So our present tax system is a mighty and rapid built-in stabilizer.

NOTE: Taxes stabilize *against upward* as well as downward movements. In times of inflation, this is a good thing; but when built-in rises in taxes stand in the way of healthy real growth, we call it "fiscal drag"—a subject discussed on page 339.

A century ago, writers thought that *stability* of tax revenue was a good thing, and they would have looked with disapproval on the present-day tendency for tax receipts to rise and fall with national income. (Recall Adam Smith's canon of prudent taxation!) Today, most economists believe that just the reverse is the truth. Thus, to dampen a boom, a budgetary surplus is desirable. There are two ways to produce such a surplus: by a reduction in government expenditure, yes; but also by an increase in tax receipts. To fight a recession, there are likewise two ways open: raising expenditures, or cutting tax rates. How lucky we are, therefore, that our present tax system has to some degree "automatic flexibility," with its receipts tending to rise in inflationary times and to fall in times of depression. This is a powerful factor stabilizing the economy and moderating the business cycle.

2. *Unemployment compensation and other welfare transfers.* In the last 40 years we have built up an elaborate system of unemployment compensation. Soon after men are laid off, they begin to receive payments from the unemployment compensation funds. When they go back to work, the payments cease; and the taxes collected to finance unemployment compensation rise when employment is high. During boom years, therefore, the unemployment reserve funds grow and exert stabilizing pressure against too great spending; conversely, during years of slack employment, the reserve funds are used to pay out income to sustain consumption and moderate the decline.

Other welfare programs—such as family relief payments outside the Social Security system—also show an anticyclical automatic behavior of a stabilizing type.

3. *Farm aid programs.* The various parity programs to aid agriculture, which we shall discuss later in Part Three, act like built-in stabilizers. When dollar spending drops off and farm prices fall, the federal government pays out dollars to farmers and absorbs surpluses. When inflation brews and prices soar, the government warehouses put forth farm goods and absorb dollars, thus cushioning any movement.[2]

4. *Corporate savings and family savings.* Not all the applause goes to the government. Our private institutions also have built-in stabilizers. Thus, the custom of corporations' maintaining their dividends, even though their incomes change in the short run, does cause their retained savings to act like a shock absorber or built-in stabilizer.[3] And to the extent that families try to maintain previous living standards and are slow to adjust their living standards upward—to this extent, they too help stabilize. (To the extent that they rush out to spend extra income on down payments or hysterically cut down on consumption when economic clouds arise, they hinder stability.)

Still other stabilizers could be mentioned, but these are the main ones.[4]

LIMITATIONS OF AUTOMATIC STABILIZERS

Before leaving the subject of automatic stabilizers, we should stress two things. First, the built-in stabilizers are our first line of defense, but are not by themselves sufficient to maintain full stability. Second, reliance on them in preference to discretionary programs raises some philosophical and ethical questions. Let us examine these points.

---

[2] By pushing up the prices of raw materials, parity formulas can also have an "escalating," or destabilizing, effect; and to the extent that they simply limit supply at all times, they redistribute and lower rather than stabilize income. Defense stockpiling of metals is at times stabilizing, at times not.

[3] To the extent that corporate investment is itself linked to corporate saving, this stabilizing influence is negated. A rise in the wages-profits ratio is a stabilizer on dips, as Cambridge's Nicholas Kaldor insists (but which is only partial in the view of most of his critics).

[4] Many experts advocate increasing the stabilizers by having Congress pass a law making tax *rates* vary *automatically* with changes in various aggregative price and income indices. But Congress so far has not been willing even to vote discretionary power over tax rates to the President, as the Commission on Money and Credit had recommended.

The automatic tendency for taxes to take away a fraction of each extra dollar of NNP means that the size of the "multiplier" is cut down. Each dollar swing in investment—whether caused by sunspots, inventions, or anything else—will now have its stabilizing effect on the system reduced *but not wiped out completely*. Instead of such disturbances having their effects on NNP multiplied 3 or more times, there will now—because of the automatic stabilizing effect of taxes—be a multiplier effect of only 1.5 or 2 times.[5]

In short, a built-in stabilizer acts to *reduce part* of any fluctuation in the economy, but does not wipe out 100 per cent of the disturbance. It leaves the rest of the disturbance as a task for fiscal and monetary discretionary action.

Philosophically, some reformers dislike the need to have human beings decide policy. They speak of a "government of laws and not of men." They advocate setting up automatic rules and mechanisms that would go into action without ever depending on human decisions. At the present time an automatic gyropilot can keep an airplane pretty stable while the pilot catches a nap; but when something unusual comes up, the human pilot must still take over. No one has yet found a gadget with all the flexibility of man. Similarly in the social field: we have not yet arrived at a stage where any nation is likely to create for itself a set of constitutional procedures displacing the need for discretionary policy formation and responsible human intelligence.

DISCRETIONARY FISCAL POLICY

The principal weapons of discretionary fiscal policy—programs which involve explicit public decision making—are (1) varying public works and other expenditure programs, (2) varying transfer-expenditure programs, and (3) varying tax rates cyclically.

Public works   When governments first began to do something active about depressions, they tended to initiate work on public investment projects for the unemployed. Often these were hastily devised, and in that they aimed primarily to make work for people, they often were rather inefficient; e.g., road building using as little machinery as possible to make the work stretch, leaf raking during the Depression by the WPA relief workers, trumped-up pork-barrel projects of low utility and lacking careful planning. The extreme case is the mythical program where men dig holes and then refill them.

The day is long past when a modern nation will let its economy collapse to the point where its only rescue must come from hastily contrived and wasteful public-works spending. The modern emphasis has, rightly, shifted away from such "make work" projects. Indeed, where a recession is expected to be a short one, economists today would wish

---

[5]Intermediate texts show that in the simple multiplier formula $1/(1 - \text{MPC})$, we have to cut MPC down to .65 MPC now that .35 of each NNP dollar goes to taxes and only .65 to disposable income. What effect on the multiplier does this attenuation of MPC have? In the case of a multiplier of $3.0 = 1/(1 - \frac{2}{3})$, it cuts the $\frac{2}{3}$ down to .433 and the final multiplier down to only 1.8. (The propensity of corporations to distribute only a fraction of their earnings has similar attenuating effects on the multiplier; but their tendency to let a rise in income induce I and their tendency to increase their I merely because they have some retained profits will work to increase the multiplier.) Transfer expenditures on welfare, which tend to fall when NNP rises, act like taxes to reduce the multiplier.

to rely much more on a temporary reduction in tax rates than on an increase in public works.

Why this shift away from public works as a recession cure? Men now realize that it takes a long time to get a post office started or to put into effect a road-building and slum-clearance program. Plans must be made; blueprints drawn; land acquired by purchase and court condemnation; existing buildings razed; and then new structures and roads constructed. All this may take five or more years; and, at the least, half of this time may elapse before any sizable amount of money will get spent on labor and materials. Suppose the recession turns out to last a year at most, followed by two years of steady advance. Then, just in the third year, when the economy may have gone all the way from too little demand to too much demand, there will suddenly come onto the market the government spending that was intended to help a recession. Such timing would of course make fiscal policy an aggravator of instability, not a reducer.

The above remarks should not be construed as an argument against public works. Slum clearance, urban rehabilitation, road building, and public construction are deemed by the American people to represent urgent use of their social resources. Therefore, such programs should be pushed hard; but—and this is the point—they should not be pushed hard under the guise of a program designed *merely* to achieve short-run stabilization. They should be carried out for their own sake and over that long period of time which is necessary if they are to be done well and efficiently.

Of course, the case will often arise where the economy is in a recession or pause and where it may be possible to move ahead the date of carrying out a long-term public-expenditure program that the people had already agreed ought to get done anyway. An intelligently planned shelf of blueprints for desirable public-works projects, even though some costs would be involved in arranging them ahead of time and keeping them up to date, could much improve fiscal timing. As Secretary of Commerce and President, Herbert Hoover long advocated this, and since 1931 we have had such laws. Likewise, it was logical for President Nixon, during the 1969 Vietnam inflation, to freeze most of new federal construction programs.

Welfare expenditures We saw that existing welfare programs, such as unemployment compensation and old-age retirement payments, do act as automatic stabilizers, rising automatically when incomes fall and needs increase.

In addition to such built-in stabilizers, it is possible for the government to institute various discretionary programs of transfer expenditures that will stabilize further. Thus, the government could refrain from giving some pending veterans' bonus in inflationary times and push forward such disbursements in depressed times. If it intends to lower parity farm payments, Congress might hope to time the change to coincide with a boom period. Most important, in times of prolonged unemployment, the federal government has moderated the decline by aiding the states in prolonging the period for which the jobless can get paid unemployment compensation. It is precisely in times of *sustained* unemployment that the present system is most deficient, and it is in such times that there will be minimal harmful effects on job mobility and incentives from increasing unemployment disbursements.

Variation of tax rates   If there is good reason to think that a recession will be brief, a temporary cut in income-tax rates can be a very good way of keeping disposable incomes from falling and of preventing a decline from snowballing. Under our withholding system, the moment Congress or the executive branch decides the economy needs stimulus through tax reduction, employers can begin to withhold less from salary paychecks. Varying tax rates can be used also to help control an inflationary gap and long-run sluggishness. Thus, belatedly, Congress and both Presidents Johnson and Nixon relied on a 10 per cent tax surcharge to help moderate the Vietnam-induced inflation, and the investment tax credit was suspended to help curb the 1966 and 1969 investment booms.

Aside from the obvious political difficulty that it takes Congress a long time to debate and act to make tax changes, there is a minor weakness in the case for heavy reliance on discretionary varying of tax rates for stability purposes. An objection to "temporary" suspension of tax rates to counter a recession comes from the political fact of life that in a democracy it may be hard to get tax rates *back up* after the emergency decline is over. Political sentiment to fight unemployment is often easier to mobilize than senti-ment to fight inflationary gaps and more-than-full employment. (In long slumps this may be good.) Furthermore, if people know tax changes are to be temporary and will not be altering their permanent incomes much, they may not vary their consumption spending very much.

SURPLUS AND DEFICIT FINANCING: STAGNATION, EXHILARATION, AND CONTRIVED GROWTH

So far we have been talking only about ironing out the business cycle. If the business cycle were around some "normal" level, most people would not worry too much so long as the boom-time budgetary surplus were always matched by the depression budgetary deficit. With such regularity, *the budget would be balanced over the business cycle* even though not balanced in every single year or month. There would be no secular trend upward in the public debt, nor downward.

But how can one be sure that the cycle will be so regular? What if America is in for what in 1938 Harvard's Alvin Hansen called "secular stagnation"—which means a long period in which (1) slowing population increase, (2) passing of the frontier's free land, (3) high corporate saving, (4) the vast piling up of capital goods, and (5) a bias toward capital-saving inventions—all of which will imply depressed investment schedules relative to saving schedules? Will not an active fiscal policy designed to wipe out such deflationary gaps then result in running a deficit *most of the time*, leading to chronic growth in the public debt? The modern answer is, "Under these conditions, yes; and over the decades the budget should not necessarily be balanced."

Contrariwise, suppose population is proliferating, new inventions are zooming, and investment is generally excessive relative to full-employment saving. If this threatens to go on most of the time, will not active fiscal policy require a budgetary surplus most of the time? Hence, will not such a condition of "secular exhilaration" lead to a long-term *decline* in the public debt? The modern answer is, "Under these conditions, yes,—and a good thing."

In the longer run, deficits may cancel out or public debt may trend upward or downward:

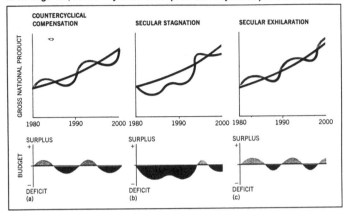

FIG. 19-1.   In every case the trend line of policy-achieved full-employment output is shown in gold. How the GNP would grow in absence of active fiscal policy is shown in brown. The indicated budget policy, of successful "leaning against the wind," is shown in blue below. In (*a*), the light areas of surplus cancel out the dark areas of deficit over the business cycle. In (*b*)'s case of secular stagnation, the dark deficits prevail over the surpluses and the debt trends upward. In (*c*), surpluses predominate on the average and debt declines.

A new, third possibility will be discussed in Chapter 41. Suppose a democracy is concerned to accelerate its own rate of growth. Suppose its representative government wishes to increase the fraction of its full-employment income that gets devoted to capital formation rather than to consumption. If public policy succeeds in stepping up net investment by militant easy credit or other policies, how can consumption spending be cut down to prevent excessive dollar demands from precipitating inflation? Primarily by having the government pursue an austere fiscal policy; raising tax rates and cutting down on marginal expenditures, thereby contriving a *chronic* budget surplus to offset easy money.

In brief, one cannot set in advance the optimal trend of surplus or deficit. A diagram can summarize long-term budget alternatives. Figure 19-1 illustrates three variants of modern fiscal policy, all in contrast to a budget balanced in every single year.

In 19-1(a), we see *simple compensatory finance* to iron out the business cycle, with boom surpluses canceling out depression deficits.

In 19-1(b), under secular stagnation, surplus periods are rarer and do not suffice to keep the public debt from having a tendency to grow chronically. (In the last half of the chapter, we study the consequences and true burdens of public-debt growth.)

In 19-1(c), with private $C + I$ spending either spontaneously strong or made strong by expansive Federal Reserve policy, the tendency for the system to run inflationary gaps much of the time is countered by budget surpluses most of the time, with the public debt tending to decline in the long run.

THE NEW ECONOMICS AT WORK

For 10 years after World War II, total demand was exuberant, real economic growth was unusually rapid, and by 1953 unemployment was down to what seems in retrospect a glorious minimal amount. During the 1950s unemployment became higher at each successive peak: 2½ per cent in 1953, 4 per cent in 1957, 5 per cent in 1960. Real growth was sluggish in the Eisenhower years: businessmen complained of a "profit squeeze"; and critics of the mixed economy began to wonder whether it was not subject to the debilitating disease of "structural unemployment" that could not be cured by macro-economic measures. Long-term stagnation had again reared its ugly head.

At this point President Kennedy introduced the "New Economics" into American public policy. Elected in 1961 on the pledge to "get the country moving again," he realized that this would require fiscal actions and not just words. In the first years of the 1960s, the United States government for the first time in its history *explicitly tried to add to a recession deficit in the interests of higher employment and better growth.*

At first, the New Frontier fiscal actions took the form primarily of an increase in government expenditure. But by the end of 1962 President Kennedy had become convinced that the country needed a massive tax cut. To cut taxes when there was already a budget deficit was indeed "new" economics. Only after a long campaign of education did businessmen, laborers, and the man in the street generally become persuaded of the following precepts:

1. To the extent that a tax cut succeeds in stimulating business, our progressive tax system will collect extra revenues out of the higher income levels. Hence, a tax cut *may* in the long run imply little (or even no) loss in federal revenues, and hence no substantial increase in the long-run public debt.

2. There is no need to balance the budget, or try to balance it, in every year. In a growing economy prudent policy does not even require that the budget be balanced over a decade, or over a business cycle. So long as continuous deficits do *not result in the public debt growing faster than GNP grows,* good economic health can prevail. For the economy, "balance" means full employment and healthy growth with no wasteful gap between our potential and our actual real output, and also no inflationary gap.

At first the nonexpert public remained skeptical about these new doctrines. But when President Johnson, after Kennedy's assassination, persuaded Congress to introduce a massive tax cut early in 1964, it worked well enough to impress even the most skeptical. What were the effects of the more than $10-billion tax cut? Scientists have studied this experiment more carefully than almost any other in our economic history, and here are their main conclusions.

The cut in taxes did not prove impotent to change consumption and investment spending, as extremists had argued. Nor did it succeed miraculously in producing full employment overnight, as other extremists had argued.

Instead, the tax cut resulted in just about the gradual rise in consumer spending that the propensity-to-consume concept had predicted. It also had the expected direct stimulus on investment spending. And then the multiplier doctrine worked very much as modern economic textbooks had suggested it would. Moreover, Federal Reserve actions reinforced the fiscal actions with the appropriate monetary policies needed for a steady return toward full employment.

In economics, of course, controlled experiments are not possible. Other things will not remain constant, and by 1966 the unplanned upswing in Vietnam military expenditures caused the economy to overshoot the goal of full employment and enter into a period of demand-pull inflationary gap. Despite advice of most economists to raise taxes, Congress procrastinated from mid-1965 to mid-1968 before introducing the 10 per cent tax surcharge, and by that time prices had been rising for so long that stubborn inflationary expectations were aroused. The resulting rise in $C + I$ spending and in prices proved hard to quell by monetary and fiscal policy.

FISCAL DRAG OR DIVIDEND[6]

In concluding this discussion of deficits and surpluses, and before taking up the issue of the public debt, we should notice some new principles which were developed in the 1960s. First, there is the important concept of "fiscal drag or dividend." Second, there is the related concept of the "full-employment budgetary surplus (or deficit)" as contrasted with the actual surplus or deficit experienced at whatever NNP actually happens to be.

We have seen that a progressive income-tax structure results in vast increases in tax revenues when incomes grow. Thus, every year that the American economy shows 6 or 7 per cent growth in money NNP, the government collects about $15 billion extra of revenue. Every year! Since existing government expenditures do not automatically grow by this amount, we are provided in effect with a "fiscal dividend" that can be used for public purposes.

If inflation is taking place, this built-in stabilizer is a great thing—just what the doctor ordered. But suppose the economy is in a normal healthy state of full employment without inflationary or deflationary gap? Then a collection of billions of new dollars of tax revenue can prove a *deflating* influence that may kill off full employment. And in this case we call it "fiscal drag," and know that we must get rid[7] of it either by cutting taxes, raising federal expenditures, or giving financial aid to the states and localities, with their burgeoning social needs and inflexible tax systems.

Definition: **"Fiscal drag or dividend" is the name for the automatic growth in tax revenues in an economy with a progressive tax structure and steady over-all growth. Unless needed to fight an inflationary gap, fiscal drag has to be offset by (1) federal-expenditure increase on public goods deemed vital, (2) tax-rate cuts that increase people's disposable incomes and expenditures in the private sector, (3) revenue sharing with the states and the localities, or (4) combinations of all of these.**

THE FULL-EMPLOYMENT BUDGET SURPLUS

As a way of dramatizing this ever-recurring problem of fiscal drag, economists have learned not to look at the actual budget deficit. When, as in 1961, we had 7 per cent

---

[6] The next two sections may be skipped in brief courses.

[7] As will be seen in Chapter 41, if there is no international constraint on expansionary monetary policy, fiscal drag can be offset by inducing higher private investment to accelerate national growth.

The New Economics introduces new concepts: full-employment budget and fiscal drag:

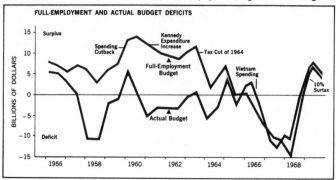

FIG. 19-2. Even though the brown curve shows that the actual budget was in deficit most of the time from 1958 to 1968, the blue curve shows that there was a surplus in the full-employment budget (which measures what the story would be if output and tax receipts were at the full-employment level). Growth of the economy would have enlarged the full-employment surplus every year and produced "fiscal drag," if the Kennedy-Johnson administrations had not deliberately raised expenditures at the beginning of the 1960s and deliberately cut taxes in the mid-1960s. To fight a post-1965 demand-pull inflation, can you show that you want to reinforce fiscal drag by raising the full-employment surplus through judicious tax-rate increases? (Source: Federal Reserve Bank of St. Louis; Council of Economic Advisers.)

unemployment and a large gap between our actual output and our full-employment potential, we were of course running a budget deficit.

But modern economists make a new calculation, asking: "Suppose we were now at high or full employment, say, with only $3\frac{1}{2}$-to-4 per cent of the labor force unemployed and with firms at their desired 95 per cent of capacity. With all the higher tax revenues that such an increase in GNP would bring, what then would our budget deficit be?"

Figure 19-2 shows by the blue curve that in the early 1960s there was really a "full-employment surplus," even though the brown line indicates an actual budget deficit at that time.

To summarize, the "full-employment budget surplus or deficit" measures what *would* be the budget position *if* the economy were at full employment and the legislated tax and spending structures were in effect. Unless tax rates are cut or expenditures increased, there would be in every healthily growing economy an increase in the full-employment surplus and a resulting fiscal drag.

By now we have come a long way from the old-fashioned views of the man in the street. Economic emphasis has been put on the economy's healthy growth without inflation and not on the balancing of the budget. But is this sound economics? Can the economic system *prudently bear the implied burden of the public debt?* To that vital question we turn for the remaining section of this chapter.

B. THE PUBLIC DEBT AND MODERN FISCAL POLICY

As a result primarily of World War II, the public debt of the federal government is about $360 billion—more than a third of a trillion dollars. What are the various economic problems created by such a debt? Are there any false problems associated with it? What are the important noneconomic factors that must be reckoned with in any discussion of this vital political issue?

In appraising the burdens involved in a public debt, we must carefully avoid the unscientific practice of making up our minds in advance that whatever is true of one small merchant's debt is also necessarily true of the government's debt. Prejudging the problem in this way comes perilously close to the logical fallacy of composition; and instead of permitting us to isolate the true—all too real—burdens of the public debt, it may only confuse the issue.

No introduction can go into all the intricacies involved in correct appraisal of the public debt. But modern economists give attention to the debt's true burden and diagnose its problems in a way significantly different from the approach the layman used to take.

BURDENS AND BENEFITS OF THE PUBLIC DEBT

The man in the street, if asked to make a list of important economic problems, will usually put the size of the public debt near the top of his list. A panel of economic experts, in this country or anywhere in the Western world, will usually put the debt toward the bottom of any such list, and indeed some will actually include it on the credit side as a positive blessing.

Why this difference of opinion? And why is it that in countries like Germany, Britain, Japan, and Holland, statesmen, editors, and the citizenry never even know what their current budgetary deficits (as *we* measure the concept) are? These are interesting *psychological* questions that do not belong primarily in a course on economics. It is our task here to make sure we understand in an objective and dispassionate way the *economic* effects of debts, deficits, and surpluses. The facts agreed on by economic scholars can be briefly summarized in the main body of this chapter. The Appendix will present a survey of the deeper analysis that underlies the economics of public debt.

As the Appendix shows,

The main way that one generation can put a burden on a later generation is by using up currently the nation's stock of capital goods, or by failing to add the usual investment increment to the stock of capital.

Thus, the bulk of our $360 billion of federal debt came from World War II. The primary burden of that war came from the need *then* to eat up capital goods without replacing them in order to maximize our effectiveness against the enemy and shorten the conflict. (Hence, it was the prohibition against car manufacture or building construction and repair that produced this real burden, and not the happenstance that Congress decided to finance part of the war effort on a loan-deficit basis rather than on a full tax-as-you-go basis.)

Looking to the future, we can say that (1) *increases in public debt which are incurred in time of full employment* and involve no government capital formation, but *which* (2) *do require that private investment be held down* (by Federal Reserve policy or by inflation itself), do in fact represent a "burden." On the other hand, incurring debt when there is no other feasible way to move the $C + I + G$ equilibrium intersection up toward full employment actually represents a *negative* burden on the immediate future to the degree that it induces more current capital formation than would otherwise take place!

There is a second aspect of the American public debt needing stress. An *external* debt (owed to foreigners), as the Appendix shows in detail, does involve a net subtraction from the goods and services available to the American people, to the degree that we have to send goods abroad to pay interest on that debt. An *internal* debt (owed by the government to its own citizens) is quite a different matter. Certainly one cannot blithely ignore an internal debt on the ground that "we all owe it to ourselves." There definitely are problems involved in an internal debt, but they do differ from those of an external debt.

Two internal-debt problems First, there are the *transfer* payments of interest that must be made to some people and the taxes that are levied upon all people for this purpose. To the degree that the people involved are different and that the interest receivers are wealthier, more thrifty, or deemed less in need of income, there will be some (admittedly minor) *redistributional* effects to reckon with. But even if the same people are taxed to pay on the average the same amounts they receive in interest, there will still be the *distorting effects on incentives* that are inescapably present in the case of any tax. (The Appendix shows that taxing Peter to pay Peter interest may make Peter work less hard or harder—and either of these may be a distortion of efficiency and well-being.[8]) Second, because we do not live forever, we tend as individuals to treat the public debt as something of an addition to our net worths (added onto the value of the land, structures, and machinery we own). This feeling of greater wealth may well cause us to consume a bit more and save a bit less. Thus the existence of a large outstanding public debt may have some long-run influence on interest-rate levels. Some writers fear that channeling investment funds into the purchase of government bonds will raise the rate of interest to private borrowers. Thus, if people want to hold a certain total of assets to provide for their old-age retirement, the existence of government bonds may substitute for ownership of deeds to machinery and buildings.

Alexander Hamilton, the spokesman of the conservative Federalist party, argued that the debt could lower interest rates. He felt that, rightly managed and in the right amounts, a public debt would be "a national blessing" because it would provide a secure gilt-edge asset that would give businessmen an income and enable them to trade for smaller profits. Notice, too, the beneficial effects of interest payments to banks, colleges, widows, and other *rentiers*. If there were no public debt, or if interest rates were to fall substantially, (1) charitable institutions would have to be supported by public and private current contributions more than by interest on endowments, (2) social security and annuities would have to take the place of *rentier* interest, and (3) service charges by banks would have to be relied upon instead of public bond interest.

[8] But recall that back on page 143, debt interest is listed as only one-twelfth of the total tax level.

Still other effects are analyzed in the Appendix. But in general, when economists evaluate the magnitude and trend of the public debt, with rare exceptions, they agree that its present level does not merit the psychological excitement that used to be accorded it and that often still is. They also agree, however, that *recklessness* concerning deficit spending and debt formation could become an important social evil if it emasculates all public self-discipline, and they point to historical instances of ruinous inflations.

EFFECTS ON PRIVATE EMOTIONS AND INVESTMENT

Never forget that there is a tremendous amount of emotion involved in people's attitudes toward the debt, and this we must not dismiss lightly. Like sex or religion, the public debt is a subject we all love to discuss. Many people used to predict the end of the world when the debt reached one-hundredth, one-tenth, and one-fifth of its present level; each year when the dire disaster had not appeared, they renewed their predictions for subsequent years.

Such attitudes may affect private investment. What if private investment is frightened off by government expenditure or by the deficit? This is certainly possible. Businessmen may say, "With that man in the White House spending recklessly, we're going to abandon even the little private investment we had planned." Or a private utility company may curtail investment because it fears the threat of public dam projects. Or when government spending giyes people money to buy in retail stores, the effect in time of deep depression may simply be to permit merchants to work off inventory of surplus merchandise; if they don't reorder production goods, the public expenditure has been just neutralized by induced private *disinvestment* (in inventory), and the multiplier chain is stopped dead in its tracks.

On the other hand, there are expansive effects on private investment that are just the opposite of these unfavorable repercussions of government finance. When current production is at a low ebb and there is excess plant capacity, no prudent businessman feels like undertaking new capital formation. If the government is able to boost retail sales and the production of consumption goods, then businessmen will have the financial ability and at least some motive to renew equipment and build new plants.[9] Sometimes purely psychological fears about the public debt and deficit could *accentuate* an inflation situation, even one with its origin outside the fiscal sphere.

Where there are two such opposing tendencies—expansive and contractionary effects upon private investment—facts rather than arguments must be our guide. Although economics does not permit us to make controlled experiments to settle the point conclusively, the bulk of the statistical data seems to suggest that private investment tends on the whole to move sympathetically with the level of national income. The cash register calls the tune.

Proof of the pudding   Some Congressmen have said, "Deficit financing was tried in the Great Depression and proved to be a failure." MIT's E. Cary Brown studied the fiscal

---

[9] An example of this was provided by the discussion in Chapter 14 of the acceleration principle relating induced investment to the upward change in sales.

facts of the 1930s to see whether this was true. His careful measurement of the actual statistics of NNP, *G*, and deficits showed that the historical facts agreed remarkably well with multiplier theory: despite the hysterical criticisms of the New Deal deficits as being gigantic, they in fact were what we would consider small today in relationship to the existent deflationary gap—much too small for any scientist to predict that they would restore full employment; but the fiscal actions of the 1930s did, *per dollar,* produce the expansionary effects predicted by multiplier theory.

THE QUANTITATIVE PROBLEM OF THE DEBT

To assess the importance of the present public debt, we must turn to the facts. Do interest payments on it swallow up most of the national income? How does the total of all interest payments, public and private, compare with past years and with the experience of other countries? What about the future?

To see how the present debt compares with the past and with Britain's debt, look at Table 19-1. It shows for selected times and places the size of national debts and their relationship to size of national income and interest payments. Thus, in 1970 our national debt of about \$360 billion represented little more than one-third year of our trillion-dollar GNP (or about 5 months of 1970 national income), and the debt's interest payments represented only about 2 per cent of national income. Note that England in

Growing debt holds little peril for a dynamically growing economy:

PUBLIC DEBT AND INTEREST CHARGES RELATIVE TO NATIONAL INCOME					
(1)	(2)	(3)	(4)	(5)	(6)
YEAR	NATIONAL DEBT	INTEREST CHARGES ON NATIONAL DEBT	NATIONAL INCOME	SIZE OF DEBT IN YEARS OF NATIONAL INCOME (5) = (2) ÷ (4)	INTEREST CHARGES AS A PERCENTAGE OF NATIONAL INCOME (6) ÷ 100 = (3) ÷ (4)
United States (billions):					
1970	\$360	\$16½	\$815	$\frac{5}{12}$	2.0
1945	278.7	3.66	181.5	1.5	2.0
1939	47.6	0.95	72.6	0.7	1.3
1929	16.3	0.66	86.8	0.2	0.7
1920	24.3	1.02	79.1	0.3	1.3
1916	1.2	0.02	38.7	0.0+	0.0+
1868	2.6	0.13	6.8	0.4	1.9
Britain (millions):					
1967	£31,986	£1,198	£31,148	1.0	3.8
1946	24,000	500	8,100	3.0	6.2
1923	7,700	325	3,950	1.9	8.2
1913	625	20	2,400	0.3	0.8
1818	840	31	400	2.1	7.7

TABLE 19-1. The \$40-billion debt that so worried people in the 1930s looks small against the subsequent rise in our income. (Sources: *Economic Almanac,* U.S. Department of Commerce; U.S. Treasury; United Nations; *Statistical Abstract of United Kingdom.*)

1818, 1923, and 1946 had an internal debt estimated at two or three times national income, and interest on the debt as a percentage of national income far exceeded anything that we need look forward to; yet the century before World War I was England's greatest century—greatest in power and material progress. Furthermore, as the table shows, her national debt was not substantially reduced; but with the steady growth of her national income, the debt and its charges shrank to almost nothing in relative magnitude!

In the light of these statistics and by careful qualitative analysis, the reader must form his own judgment as to whether the national debt can be rationally regarded as a problem of the first magnitude in comparison with the problems of national defense, the nuclear bomb, urban blight, racial tension, unemployment, and inflation. Whether productivity will continue to rise in the future, whether labor and management can learn to bargain collectively without strikes and inflation—to many observers these seem much more important than the debt itself.

Growth in the economy   In dispassionately analyzing the growth of the debt, there is one error we must avoid: *We must not forget that the real national product of the United States is an ever-growing thing.*

Our population grows lustily. As to productivity, there is no indication that man-hour efficiency and new techniques have begun to slacken off. Upon this, "stagnationists" and "exhilarationists" both agree. What seemed like a big debt in 1790 would be nothing today. What our children will come to regard as a big debt, our great-grandchildren will deem relatively unimportant.

This explains why England and France, in the crucially formative years of the capitalistic system and the Industrial Revolution, were able to go on—not only decade after decade, but century after century—with their budgets in balance less than half the time. The historian Thomas Macaulay, more than a century ago, said the last word on the debt and growth:

At every stage in the growth of that debt the nation has set up the same cry of anguish and despair. At every stage in the growth of that debt it has been seriously asserted by wise men that bankruptcy and ruin were at hand. Yet still the debt went on growing; and still bankruptcy and ruin were as remote as ever. . . .
The prophets of evil were under a double delusion. They erroneously imagined that there was an exact analogy between the case of an individual who is in debt to another individual and the case of a society which is in debt to a part of itself. . . . They made no allowance for the effect produced by the incessant progress of every experimental science, and by the incessant efforts of every man to get on in life. They saw that the debt grew; and they forgot that other things grew as well. . . .

Figure 19-3 on the next page shows that the growth of our economy since 1945 has drastically reduced the ratio of United States public debt to gross national product. (This, properly, excludes FRB and Treasury holdings; but the point would be the same if these exclusions had not been made.) This fact of growth explains why, in the United States, where money GNP doubles in less than 15 years, the public debt might increase by another $360 billion in that time without its relative percentage burden growing at all.

This would give the wildest believer in government spending an average deficit of tens of billions of dollars per year before he would have to turn to such even more

While private debt outstripped NNP growth, public-debt ratio fell steadily after World War II:

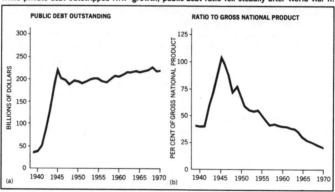

FIG. 19-3.   Most of the federal debt held by the public came from wars. In the last 25 years, its ratio to the growing GNP or NNP has declined steadily. (Source: U.S. Treasury. FRB and government holdings of bonds are excluded from the total of federal debt.)

unorthodox financial expedients as printing money or selling interest-free bonds to the Federal Reserve Banks.

Could a nation fanatically addicted to deficit spending pursue such a policy for the rest of our lives and beyond? Study of the mechanics of banking and income determination suggests that the barrier to this would not be financial. The barrier would have to be political; and the effects of such a policy depend crucially upon whether it impinges on an economy that is already inflationary or deflationary. And if the electorate and Congress learn the half-truth that expenditure is expansionary, while forgetting the fact that unpleasant taxes may be necessary to curb undue expansion, then the long-term outlook may indeed be in the direction of rising prices.

PRIVATE AND PUBLIC ANALOGIES[10]

Undoubtedly the major reason for concern about the public debt does not involve sophisticated questions of whether or not it affects the stock of real capital goods. The major concern has to do with the fact that people are uncomfortable at the prospect of anything that may go on growing forever. We all are made uncomfortable by infinity; we are all frightened of the way things grow at compound interest. Some psychologists attribute this to the fact that every child is frightened of the prospect of dying, of *not* living forever. The following case study of the public debt in comparison with the debt of the American Telephone and Telegraph Company adds little to sophisticated analysis of the economics of the matter; but it does bring psychological comfort where it is needed most, to those fearful of ultimate national bankruptcy.

[10] This section may be skipped by brief courses.

"How can the government go on running up debt? If I or my wife lived beyond our means and ran a debt, we'd soon learn what trouble is." The person speaking has overlooked the fallacy of composition: What is true for each unit may be false for the whole of society.

"Why do conservatives complain about the size of the public debt? Private debt has grown tremendously faster in the postwar period than public debt, and you don't hear complaints about that. All credit involves debt. The pyramid of credit could be called the pyramid of debt. If people are to have liquid assets, other people or institutions must have liabilities—d--t to the squeamish." The speaker here is also trying to use analogies with private finance, but this time to the advantage of a program for large deficits.

Both analogies are in principle suspect. Each contains some element of truth, but every strand of such arguments needs critical testing. Thus, it is true that private debt is more than twice the public debt, and that it more than doubled in the last 20 years, while federal debt grew little in absolute amount and has actually dropped from being 62 per cent of all debt in 1945 to being only 20 per cent in the late 1960s. But it is also true that the private assets to back up that private debt have gone up too. And it is true that one could imagine an economy—not ours!—where everything was financed by *equity* issues without fixed debt.

With the warning that no analogy is conclusive, here is an analogy between a private corporation like the American Telephone and Telegraph Company and the United States government.

AT&T has grown all this century. It has floated new debt throughout this century, with never an end to it. If our economy remains healthy, AT&T will undoubtedly have a rising bond debt for the rest of this century. This is prudent finance, not unsound finance. It is prudent to buy that bond debt, but not for the reason that the company has plants and equipment bought from that debt financing and which it could liquidate in a pinch. There is no one to whom AT&T could sell such specialized items in an emergency, since they are good only for the telephone business in which AT&T has complete local monopolies.

Why is never-ending growth in AT&T debt prudent? It is prudent because *the dollar receipts the company can earn from its telephone services are sure to grow along with the population and GNP.* The interest on the debt, and the occasional refunding (but not retirement) of the debt, can be paid for out of the revenues from the telephone company's customers. If they all became impoverished, say, by atomic war, AT&T would have to go bankrupt and not repay its debt. But in a growing economy, no going concern proceeds on the assumption that all the people will go bankrupt.

What does the federal government use to pay its debt interest and refundings? Obviously, *it is the taxable capacity of the country's national product that any government can rely on.*

So long as the money NNP (or GNP) grows at 5 or 6 per cent from now until kingdom come, the public debt of the federal government can grow at those rates, ultimately passing one, two, or any number of trillion dollars. No inflation need result if the process takes place in balance. And no bankruptcy or increase in relative tax burden. And no embarrassment to the Secretary of the Treasury. Like life itself, there is no end to the process.

The above analogy is given only for those who feel a psychological need for reassuring analogies and as an antidote to misleading pessimistic analogies. It says nothing about the great harm governments can do if they spend their taxed or borrowed funds rashly and feed fuel to inflationary gaps when such exist. It says nothing about the proper scope and efficiency of government, because those issues were already clarified in Chapter 8. It says nothing about the proper rate of capital formation and rate of current consumption.

Now we have looked carefully at the facts about the public debt here and abroad and have given the economic principles that underlie the burdens of a public debt. We have seen that there are certain definite problems involved, but that laymen often have mixed-up notions as to what are and are not genuine burdens.

There are many major problems ahead for our economy: inflation, slump, conservation and congestion, adequate growth, international balance of payments, and scores of others. Prudent fiscal and monetary policies impinge on them all; but in a sober man's list of grave problems, the present magnitude of the public debt does not come near the top.

CONCLUSION: MACROECONOMICS OF THE MIXED ECONOMY

The Employment Act of 1946 stated that the government had a responsibility to act to keep employment high and to moderate cyclical instability (and many have suggested that it be amended to mention explicitly a similar government concern for "reasonable stability" of the price level). Even if there were no such legislative proclamations, it is a fact all over the world that the populace of modern mixed economies require their representative governments to pursue economic policies that attempt to keep employment high, growth strong, and prices stable.

Part Two has presented the economic *tools of macroeconomics:* how the various schedules determine levels and movements in incomes and prices; and how monetary and fiscal policies can shift those schedules so as to avoid deflationary and inflationary gaps and promote growth. In Part Six certain special problems connected with the modern era—growth, demand-pull and cost-push inflation, and so forth—will be discussed in greater detail. The millennium has not yet arrived.

The finding of our macroeconomic analysis rejects both the classical faith that laissez faire must by itself lead to utopian stability and the pre–World War II pessimism that classical microeconomic principles have become inapplicable to the modern world. Instead we end with the reasoned prospect that appropriate monetary and fiscal policies can ensure an economic environment which will *validate* the verities of microeconomics—that society has to choose among its alternative high-employment production possibilities, that paradoxes of thrift and the fallacies of composition will not be permitted to create cleavages between private and social virtues or private and public vices.

By means of appropriately reinforcing monetary and fiscal policies, a mixed economy can avoid the excesses of boom and slump and can look forward to healthy progressive growth. This being understood, the paradoxes that robbed the older classical principles dealing with small-scale "microeconomics" of much of their relevance and validity will now lose their sting. The broad cleavage between microeconomics and macroeconomics has been closed by active public use of fiscal and monetary policy.

With good conscience we can turn to the analysis in Part Three of how the great social aggregates of national income and employment *get determined in their detailed parts* and to Part Four's analysis of *income distribution.*

SUMMARY

A. SHORT-RUN AND LONG-RUN FISCAL POLICY

1   When private investment and consumption spending create an inflationary (or deflationary) gap, it is the task of fiscal and monetary policy to offset the gap in the attempt to preserve price stability, high employment, and growth.

2   Fiscal weapons refer to taxation and expenditure policies. In this connection, the modern economy is blessed with important "built-in stabilizers." Requiring no discretionary action, tax receipts change *automatically* when income changes, thereby reducing the size of the multiplier and serving to wipe out part of any disturbance. (The same stabilizing effect is created by unemployment compensation and other welfare transfers that automatically grow as income falls, as well as by farm aid programs and the propensity of corporations to pay out in dividends only part of their current earnings.)

3   Because the automatic stabilizers never *fully* offset the instabilities of an economy, scope is left for *discretionary* programs. Public works and other expenditure on goods and services can involve such time lags in getting under way as to make their use to combat short recessions undesirable. Discretionary variations in transfer expenditures and in tax rates—politics aside—have greater short-run flexibility.

4   When men began to drop the notion that the government's budget had to be balanced in every year or month, they first thought that it would be in balance over the business cycle—with the boom-time surpluses just matching the depression deficits. It is today realized that only by coincidence would the prosperity years just balance in their intensity the recession years and with the desired mix of consumption and capital formation.

    If, as a few believe, we are faced by "secular stagnation," with private saving and investment schedules tending much of the time to produce deflationary gaps, fiscal policy will probably succeed in maintaining stable high employment only by having a *long-term* increase in the public debt. If, as others believe, we are in for "chronic exhilaration," with demand so brisk as to lead much of the time to inflationary gaps, then active fiscal policy will probably mean a bias toward surplus financing and a secular downward trend in the public debt. Perhaps the majority of economists feel there is no need to try to predict what the distant future has in store, being prepared to advocate programs that the developing situation calls for.

5   To get a better measure of changes in discretionary fiscal policy, economists supplement knowledge of the *actual* budget surplus or deficit with the hypothetical "full-employment budget surplus or deficit," which measures what the existing tax and spending structure *would* entail if GNP were at the full-employment level. In a growing economy, there would automatically be a steady growth in the size of the full-employment surplus and resulting "fiscal dividend" or "fiscal drag"—unless offset by expenditure increases, tax cuts, or sharing of tax revenues with states and localities. In time of inflation, automatic fiscal drag is a good thing; and at all times a dividend from genuine growth provides resources for new public or private activities.

B. THE PUBLIC DEBT AND MODERN FISCAL POLICY

6   The public debt does not burden the shoulders of a nation as if each citizen were made to carry rocks on his back. To the degree that we now follow policies of reduced capital formation which will pass on to posterity less capital goods, we can directly affect the production possibilities open to them. To the degree that we borrow from abroad for

some transitory consumption purposes and pledge posterity to pay back the interest and principal on such external debt, we do place upon that posterity a net burden, which will be a subtraction from what they can later produce. To the degree that we bequeath to posterity an internal debt but no change in capital stock beyond what would anyway have been given them, there may be various *internal transfer effects* as one group in the community receives a larger share of the goods then produced at the expense of another group. At any one time there is no "net burden" of such internal transfers quite like the net subtraction involved in the external debt payment, but at most important *transfer effects* between people of different ages then alive and certain effects within each generation's lifetime on how much they will receive of consumption and at what ages. And the process of taxing Peter to pay Paul, or taxing Peter to pay Peter, can have definite costs: these can involve various distortions of production and efficiency, but should not be confused with actually sending goods abroad.

Aside from the above "real" effects, there may also be psychological effects upon the minds of men, and men's resulting actions must of course be regarded as real. Moreover, the fact that there are more rather than less bonds being owned by people in the community can be expected to have quite real effects on their propensity to save and consume out of income. Each person regards his government bond as an asset, but the future taxes to service these bonds he does not count in fully as a current personal liability, even though all society will have to pay taxes equal to such debt service. (This is not irrational from his viewpoint, since the tax rates he will be subject to have little to do with his personal holding of the debt, as the Appendix discusses.)

This summary point has been written at some length to indicate the complexity of the problem. We see that a debt does have important impacts on the economy, even if they are not primarily those that orators and editors preach about.

It is important, also, to know roughly what the size of the post–World War II federal debt is in relation to national income and interest charges, in order to assess the present, both in terms of the past and in terms of the future. The growth of the debt must be appraised in terms of the growth of the economy as a whole. Since 1945 the ratio of public debt to private debt and national product has been substantially declining.

7   A full- (or high-) employment program has as its goal a level of total spending that is neither too little nor too great—so that the saving and investment schedules intersect in the region of full employment. The Employment Act of 1946 represents an important innovation, affirming responsibility of the government for employment opportunities and setting up executive and congressional machinery for policy action.

QUESTIONS FOR DISCUSSION

1   "No nation can avoid having a fiscal policy. With the government such an important part of the present-day economy, it is almost impossible even to define a 'neutral fiscal policy.' It is even harder to give rational reasons for preferring such a policy to an active fiscal program aimed at preventing inflation and deflation." Examine critically.

2   List various "built-in stabilizers." Show how they work in the 1970s.

3   What phase of the business cycle (if any) are you now in? What tax and expenditure policies would seem appropriate? Qualitatively, how would you vary the relative mix of taxes (income-tax rates and exemptions, sales taxes, property taxes) to fight unemployment or inflation?

4   From the early 1870s to the middle 1890s, depressions were deep and prolonged, booms were short-lived and relatively anemic, the price level was declining. What long-run fiscal policy should have been followed in that quarter of a century? Would your answer be the same for the following 20 years leading up to World War I, a period of rising prices?

5   "In the AT&T–debt versus public-debt analogy, it should be noted that along with the private debt went new capital goods—machines, buildings, etc.—which *themselves* enabled growth of real GNP. The same is not true of public-debt growth to finance current public-consumption programs." Verify the element of truth in this.

6   Show briefly why "burden of the debt" is a complicated economic issue.

7   Formulate and evaluate the "New Economics."

Review your understanding of the following concepts:

inflationary and deflationary gap	internal versus external debt
tax receipts and tax rates	present versus future generations and
government expenditure on goods	bequeathal of real capital
and transfer expenditures	debt-income ratios here and abroad,
built-in stabilizers and the reduced	today, yesterday, and tomorrow
multiplier	AT&T versus U.S.A.
discretionary fiscal programs	chronic stagnation, exhilaration, and
fiscal drag and fiscal dividend	trends in the public debt
the full-employment budget surplus	Employment Act of 1946

APPENDIX: False and Genuine Burdens of the Public Debt

We have seen that the public debt, prorated over the population, is sometimes regarded to be a load on each man's back. According to this same image, when Congress adds a dollar to the debt by running a current deficit of a dollar, that is like just one more rock added to the load our children or grandchildren will already have to carry on their backs.

This image is misleading in two ways. First, it exaggerates the burdens that are truly involved. Second, by giving a mistaken view of the debt burden, it lays itself open to refutation and thereby to the mistaken conclusion that there are, after all, *no* burdens connected with the public debt. In other words, superficial and wrong analysis offers genuine comfort neither to the conservatives, liberals, or radicals.

As a preview to a judicious appraisal, see how vulnerable the foregoing image is.

A DIALOGUE

Suppose all debt came from World War II. This war is over. Suppose all America's families (1) share equally in ideal nondistorting taxes, (2) hold equal shares of public-debt bonds, (3) all live forever (as individuals or as a cohesive family). With no debt held abroad, (4) "we all owe it to ourselves."

"Then such bonds are not rocks on our shoulders, or even paperweights. If we unanimously voted to abolish the bonds, there would be no real difference. If an enemy bombed our homes and factories, that would be a genuine personal and national burden. But if an enemy bombed our bond lockboxes out of existence, that would merely save us the red tape of taxing ourselves to pay each of us back in bond interest just what the extra tax took away."

So goes the argument. Notice how simple the above refutation is. And how clever in taking the wind out of the sails of those who use the oversimplified rock-burden image. Moreover, the refutation is—granted its assumptions—logically rigorous.

Has the refutation proved that the war involved no grievous burden? It has been cunningly silent on that matter. The Devil's Advocate who produced the refutation would, if pressed by a Tireless Truthseeker, have to concede much.

Devil's Advocate: Yes, the war did involve a grievous economic burden at the time. We had to work hard and long hours. We had to cut wartime consumption to the bone: do with little meat, no cars, no travel, no urban development—make do with few of the things that make life enjoyable rather than merely tolerable.

Tireless Truthseeker: With severe rationing controls, the contemporaneous wartime burden of sacrificed consumption would, according to your view, be much the same even if the war had been financed by pay-as-you-go wartime taxes instead of deficit?

D.A.:   Precisely. Postwar canceled tax receipts, instead of bonds, would make no difference.

T.T.:   But surely, we used up capital goods during the war by not replacing them. The enemy had to be fought with current 1941–1945 goods and not with 1970 goods. By using up capital goods *then*, we could throw more resources into the war effort. And that did put a real burden *on us in the postwar period* since we inherited less capital goods at war's end. In the postwar period we've had to consume less in order to rebuild those capital goods; and we've had to consume less than we could have if 1941–1945 had given us the normal peacetime increase in capital goods.

D.A.:   True. But wartime rationing produced that result. If no wartime deficits and bond indebtedness had been created, that *genuine burden* on the postwar group due to the war would still have had to take place.

T.T.:   I feel there must be a catch somewhere. Your argument sounds too facile.

   1. I can't help feeling that the existence of the public debt leads (*a*) to tax distortions as we collect taxes to pay its interest, and (*b*) to a lower consumption schedule when poor people with higher MPC pay taxes for bond interest to wealthier people with a lower MPC.

   2. Moreover, people don't live forever, and it is not irrational of them to feel wealthier because of the public debt (since they need count on paying taxes for debt interest *only through their remaining lifetime*). This increase in the *CC* propensity to consume could be at the expense of net capital formation in a full-employment postwar year, requiring contractionary M policy that hurts investment.

   3. Besides, a small part of our public debt (about 1 in 20) is external and held abroad: sending foreigners goods to cover the interest payments does constitute a definite subtraction from our GNP available for domestic consumption and investment.

   4. While it may be true that transfers of purchasing power—between individuals living at one time, between individuals at different ages of their life-spans, and between individuals alive today and yet unborn—can be engineered by the government without using the device of the public debt at all, yet I can't help believing that society is led by the presence of the debt to make some transfer decisions that it probably wouldn't otherwise have made.

   5. If the decision to have a deficit in depression times (or in times when the international balance of payments makes expansionary monetary policy infeasible) merely prevents unemployment, then I admit the implied deficit adds to, rather than subtracts from, the capital stock bequeathed to the postdepression times. (Maybe $50 billion of the depression deficit and some of the 1958–1964 deficit was such a blessing.) But when a decision to have a deficit leads to a compensating cut in private capital formation through inducing more restrictive FRB monetary policy than would otherwise be the case, I say that such a way of increasing the public debt does *itself* put a real burden on the backs of later citizens.

   6. Of course, I admit that floating a public debt to add to useful government capital is as legitimate as floating private debt to build useful private capital—because in each case the new paper assets are matched by real income-creating assets.

   7. But in a well-run full-employment system, I have to regard loan finance for *current* public consumption as putting a kind of burden on the future through its effective cutting down on net capital formation at the time, and subsequently through its wealth stimulus on consumption that may be competitive with investment.

D.A.:   I've never denied anything you are saying. I merely assumed away most of your genuine burdens. If I may say so, you are now shifting over to the side of the angels and are beginning to analyze the true and false burdens that obscure rather than illuminate the truth, the whole truth, and nothing but the truth.

SUMMARY OF DEBT BURDENS AND BENEFITS

1. Capital-bequeathed burden   The principal way one generation puts a burden on itself later or on a later generation is by bequeathing it less real capital than would otherwise have been the case. Any growth of public debt that has this effect—as in the case of full-employment borrowing for current public consumption that has to be offset by contractionary monetary policy which will lower investment—most definitely does involve a genuine "burden."

2. External-debt burden   Any public debt that is externally held does involve a current burden on the citizens at home, since in the end they have to send goods abroad corresponding to the interest payments and debt service. (Of course, if the original borrowing from abroad resulted in equivalent fruitful capital goods here, their fruits will cover the external-debt service; so the net effect of such external borrowing, taken as a complete package, would be favorable to our economy.)

3. Transfer effects   Taxing Peter to pay Paul bond interest, even if they are the same person, is certain to cause some harmful distortions of personal and business decisions. (EXAMPLE: Peter is taxed 10 per cent of his income to pay himself $1,000 of bond interest. He is under the illusion, and rightly so as an individual, that he can work less and cut down on his tax; but if all do so, we simply have to increase the tax rate. Result: We all end working less because taxes on each individual matched by exactly equal interest payments to him do not economically cancel out!)

Correlated with public-debt operations, but not always in an intrinsic way, are certain transfers that take place between different individuals living at the same time, between the same individual at different periods of life, and between successive generations.[1]

[1]EXAMPLES: Twin Jane Day worked hard in World War II; twin Rose did not. Because our government used deficit financing, Jane ended up in 1945 with bonds rather than tax receipts. (Jane may have been motivated to work harder by the bribe of postwar command over goods.) Since 1945 Jane has been receiving a larger share of consumption than Rose; Rose is being taxed more than would otherwise have been the case in order to help pay interest and principal to Jane. Moral: A public debt can definitely involve *internal transfer effects* between individuals of the same or different ages.

4. Wealth stimulus to consumption   The existence of public debt, for reasons already seen, makes the average man feel wealthier. For good or evil, it raises his propensity-to-consume schedule: this may, in a poorly functioning system, be a great thing to reduce unemployment and increase both consumption and investment. But in a system where employment can be counted on to remain full by virtue of price flexibility, luck, or monetary management, the increase in *C* may be at the expense of *I* and reinforce the less-capital-bequeathed burden.

5. Effects on interest and money policy   A large debt gives the Fed great leverage for massive open-market operations to achieve stabilization—unless, as in 1946–1951, the central bank is pressured by the government to sacrifice the goal of stabilization to the dubious goal of keeping down the interest charges on the public debt. Many experts believe that the existence of a broad market in government securities makes possible extensive open-market operations of a stabilizing type and tends to enhance the effectiveness of monetary policy. Debt management by the Treasury and Fed by a proper policy of open-market operations in bonds of all maturities that was properly carried out could enhance the stability of a modern system.

6. Effects on discipline and ideology   It would be a tragedy if people, in giving up their irrational fears of deficit spending, were thereby led to call the sky the limit. Unlimited spending can produce inflation, chaos, and waste.

It is to be hoped that the discipline of rationality can replace the discipline of superstition and misunderstanding. After the shibboleth of a balanced budget has lost its power to limit public spending, the good society will have to replace it by a calculus of cost-and-benefit.

Even if Jane Day had died in 1965, she could have consumed more in 1945–1965 by selling off her bonds. The burden of *this* extra consumption could be imposed on those born after 1965 (1) by causing a reduced capital stock after 1965 due to lowered investment in 1945–1965, but also (2) by having an intermediate generation of young postwar workers (employed in 1945–1965 and who have bought Jane's bonds out of their personal saving) supported in *their* old age by the 1980 workers who will then pay taxes on the public debt.

Part IV
The Burden of Debt Re-examined

Part IV: An Overview

Personally, I do not feel that any amount can be properly called a surplus as long as the nation is in debt. I prefer to think of such an item as a reduction on our children's inherited mortgage. (Dwight D. Eisenhower, 7 January 1960)

President Eisenhower's occasional remarks on the national debt, as exemplified by the epigraph from his last State of the Union Message, helped to provoke a scholarly reexamination of the incidence of loan-financed public expenditures. The revisionist literature of the late 1950s and 1960s took two divergent paths. One approach, illustrated in the selections reprinted here by James Meade, Richard Musgrave, and Franco Modigliani, remained squarely within the Keynesian tradition, analyzing the effects of public debt issue in terms of macroeconomic aggregates. The other approach, pioneered by James Buchanan, considered the problem of government loan expenditure from the perspectives of the microeconomic behavior of individuals and simple common sense.

Both of the new approaches led to the conclusion that public debt does indeed impose a burden on future generations. However, the reasoning of the two approaches differs markedly. Abba Lerner, to be sure, clung tenaciously to his earlier position, that because 'we owe it to ourselves', and because the resources redeployed from the private to the public sector are used up by a loan-financed project '*at the time it uses them up*, and not before or after' (emphasis in original), deficit spending has only socially inconsequential distributional effects. But his rejection of 'the baseless fear of impoverishing future generations by leaving them with a larger internal debt' by the early 1960s was clearly a minority opinion.

The revisionist literature produced agreement on various issues of second-order importance, including acknowledgment of the distortionary impact of taxes levied to service and amortize government bond issues. It was agreed further that a proper analysis of the burden of the public debt must take account of the benefits associated with the public goods and other programs financed by loan expenditures. The debate between Buchanan and the Keynesians was joined on questions concerning the first-order effects of government bond issues unsecured by any public assets (what Meade called the 'deadweight debt'), which is collateralized only by the public sector's 'full faith and credit' (i.e., its taxing power).

Neoclassical, post-Keynesian analyses of the national debt, for the most part, validated the classical economists' objections to deficit spending. To the extent that taxes levied to make interest payments on the debt or to retire it are met by drawing down savings, the nation's store of capital stock will be reduced. Future generations will therefore be poorer than otherwise by virtue of the smaller stock of capital bequeathed to them. It is the adverse impact on capital formation, not the higher future tax bills required to service or amortize government bond issues, that represents the main burden of the public debt.

Buchanan, on the other hand, analyzed the public debt problem from the perspective of the individual economic actors who, as citizens of a democratic polity, collectively must choose methods of financing the expenditures of government. Printing money aside, the public sector's expenses can be defrayed either by paying taxes in the present period or by borrowing, which defers a portion of the tax bill to future periods. The issue of debt, in other words, involves intergenerational distributional issues that are bound to influence political choices at the margin, not least because the future generations do not vote.

The commonsensical observation that deficit spending shifts tax liabilities forward in time raises the question whether that fiscal option inflicts a cost on future taxpayers. Buchanan answered in the affirmative, reasoning that 'the individual's income stream (his potential consumption) in future periods is reduced by the full amount of the debt service charges that are imposed upon him'. It is the reduction in future consumption opportunities, not the particular sources of the funds used either to purchase government bonds or to pay the interest charges on them, that represents the main burden of the public debt. Moreover, in so far as individuals are different – face different opportunities and different constraints – at different points in time, those costs will be felt even if the deferred taxes come due during the lifetimes of the taxpayers who participated in the decision to issue public debt: 'the individual who inherits the consequences of past commitments, even those made by himself ... will always consider "what might have been", and the alternatives as seen retrospectively must look different from those contemplated at the time of choice.'

Buchanan's analysis is simple and yet compelling. The fact that the national debt must be serviced and retired in the future implies a future tax liability. The burden of the debt is accordingly shouldered by future taxpayers, some living 'at the time of choice' but unable to vote and others yet unborn. The normative public finance issue is thus whether such taxes are 'fair' and 'efficient' (i.e. constitute reasonable and accurate charges for the public goods and services financed by government borrowing). The positive public choice issue is whether the opportunity to redistribute wealth from future to present taxpayers creates a political bias toward deficit spending and a mounting national debt, a bias that would be reinforced if taxpayers should suffer 'fiscal illusion' leading them for one reason or another to undervalue their future tax liabilities. In Buchanan's judgment, however, the incidence of the burden of the debt on future taxpayers does not depend on the existence of fiscal illusion.

Perhaps no greater testimony can be given to the import of Buchanan's reformulation of the public debt problem than today's clamoring of the political class in the United States to use the purported budget 'surplus' to retire past bond issues. Although Keynesian fiscal policy prescriptions have consistently presumed that government revenues in excess of the expenditures necessary to maintain full employment would always be used to pay off the national debt, the contemporary argument is fundamentally Buchananesque – why saddle future generations with the responsibility? It is ironic if not entirely surprising that the political pundits rush to endorse Buchanan's position, during a period of apparent budget surplus, having roundly denigrated it during the lengthy era of budget deficits.

Charles K. Rowley
William F. Shughart II
Robert D. Tollison

[15]

IS THE NATIONAL DEBT A BURDEN?

By J. E. MEADE

I

THE view is sometimes expressed that a domestic national debt means merely that citizens as potential taxpayers are indebted to themselves as holders of government debt, and that it can, therefore, have little effect upon the economy, except in so far as it may lead to a redistribution of income and wealth between taxpayers and owners of property. It is my purpose to refute this argument; to show that, quite apart from any distributional effects, a domestic debt may have far-reaching effects upon incentives to work, to save, and to take risks; and to examine the nature of these effects.

I shall say very little about the distribution of income and property. My thesis is that if the national debt could be removed in such a way as to leave the distribution of real income totally unchanged, then in certain specified ways it would improve economic incentives. In economic policy there is very frequently a conflict between the objectives of efficiency and of equality. Measures which improve incentives often increase inequalities; and measures which increase equality often blunt economic incentives. If it can be shown that the removal of the national debt in a way which did not affect the distribution of income would improve economic incentives, then it would not be difficult to show that the removal of the national debt in a way which did not affect incentives could be used to improve distribution.

This paper is concerned only with domestic debt. It is well known that an external debt is a burden on a community, since there must be a transfer of real goods and services from the debtor to the creditor country in payment of interest and sinking fund on the debt. A domestic debt, on the other hand, means merely a transfer from citizens as taxpayers to citizens as property-owners, so that there is no direct loss of real goods and services to the citizens as a whole.

But one must not conclude from this that a domestic debt has no adverse economic effects.[1] In order to examine these effects, a comparison

---

[1] Some excellent articles have been written to remove fears about the evils to be expected from an ever-growing debt. For example, Professor A. P. Lerner ('The Burden of the Debt' in *Income, Employment, and Public Policy*) shows that there is no reason to believe that the debt will grow without limit, even if a debt is always created to finance a budget deficit so long as total demand is deficient; for when the debt has grown to a certain size its 'Pigou-effect' (see p. 166 below) will serve to raise demand without further growth of debt. Professor Domar ('The Burden of the Debt and the National Income', *American Economic Review*, 1944) has shown that even if debt grows without limit, the rate of tax

will be made between two societies which are in every respect similar except that the one has a large domestic national debt and the other has no debt. This idea is a useful analytical device to isolate certain factors at work in society; but the concept is an artificial one and needs careful definition in particular in respect to the effect of the presence or absence of a national debt upon the distribution of income and property.

We can apply this concept by supposing that we move by means of a capital levy from a society with a national debt to a society without a national debt. But this capital levy is a purely analytical device.[1] We are really imagining two different societies, otherwise the same, except that history has left one with and the other without a national debt; and this is put in terms of assimilating the position of the former to that of the latter by means of a capital levy merely as a way of explaining in what sense they are otherwise the same.

Let us then consider a society with a large national debt. We will make one and only one simplifying assumption about distribution, namely that all citizens in any one given income bracket have the same ratio of income from work to income from property. The rich man may have a higher ratio than the poor man of unearned to earned income, but each rich man has the same ratio as every other rich man and each poor man has the same ratio as every other poor man. Suppose then that there is a capital levy of any degree of progression, the total levy being on a scale sufficient to redeem the whole debt. After the levy any citizen in any one income bracket will have a lower gross income according to the amount of income from property in that bracket and according to the progressiveness of the levy on property. Let us suppose that the scale of taxation on income is then so adjusted that each citizen in each income bracket gains in reduced taxation on income exactly what he loses in income from property.[2] Each citizen's net tax-free income remains exactly the same as before, so that the capital levy has left the distribution of personal incomes unchanged. If the capital levy was a proportionate one, it would also have left the distribution of property unchanged, in the sense that it would have

necessary to service it may not grow beyond a certain limit, if the national income is also growing. But these articles show only that the debt is unlikely to grow without limit relatively to the national income. They do not show that a given debt has no adverse effects.

[1] For the reasons given below (p. 180) I would not personally advocate an actual capital levy.

[2] This involves the assumption that each citizen is paying sufficient in income taxation for it to be possible to offset by a remission of such tax his loss of income from property resulting from the levy on his capital. But this assumption can be safely made in conditions in which (i) income taxation accounts for a large proportion of government revenue and debt interest for a small proportion of government expenditure, so that much revenue from income tax is needed even after the capital levy; and (ii) income taxation and the capital levy are both progressive and people with large incomes hold large amounts of property, so that the people who lose income from property are also the main payers of income taxation.

reduced all personal properties in the same proportion. If the capital levy was a progressive one, it would *pro tanto* have diminished the inequality of ownership of property.

There is, of course, a relationship between the degree of progression of the levy and the modification of the progressiveness of the existing taxation on income which is necessary to leave each citizen's net income unchanged.[1] But for our present purpose we can be content to conclude that on our assumptions in the society without the national debt (i) every citizen will own a smaller amount of property, (ii) every citizen's gross income will be lower, (iii) every citizen's average rate of taxation on income will be lower, but (iv) every citizen's net income will be unchanged.

II

What would be the effects of these changes on the citizen's behaviour? The first and foremost effect, but a strangely neglected effect, is the increased incentive to save which would be caused by the fact that each citizen's net income was unchanged while the value of his property had been reduced. Imagine the same individual in two situations; in both situations he has a tax-free income of £1,000 to spend or save; but in situation 1 he has £10,000 worth of property and in situation 2 he has only

---

[1] Let $e+pr$ be an individual's gross income, where e is income from work, p the value of property, and r the rate of interest on property. Let i be the rate of tax on his income before the capital levy, c the rate of levy on his capital, and i' the rate of tax on his income after the levy. For his net income to remain unchanged we have

$$(e+pr)(1-i) = \{e+(1-c)pr\}(1-i'),$$

or $\dfrac{1-i'}{1-i} = \dfrac{1}{1-ck}$ where $k = \dfrac{pr}{e+pr}$ or the proportion of his income which is unearned. Consider now an individual with a large total income denoted by subscript $_1$ and an individual with a small total income denoted by subscript $_2$. Then $\dfrac{1-i_1'}{1-i_1}$ is $> \dfrac{1-i_2'}{1-i_2}$ if $c_1 k_1 > c_2 k_2$. The modification in the degree of progression of the income tax is thus seen to depend on the progressiveness of the capital levy (c_1 and c_2), and on the factors determining k_1 and k_2 which are the distribution of income from work (e_1 and e_2), the distribution of property (p_1 and p_2), and the yield of income from property (r). Now if the rich man has a higher ratio of unearned to earned income ($k_1 > k_2$) and the capital levy is progressive ($c_1 > c_2$), then $c_1 k_1 > c_2 k_2$. In this case taxation of income must be so adjusted that the tax-free proportion of gross income goes up in a greater proportion for the rich than for the poor $\left(\text{i.e. } \dfrac{1-i_1'}{1-i_1} > \dfrac{1-i_2'}{1-i_2}\right)$. In this sense the taxation of income must become less progressive; and its degree of progression will be reduced the more, the more progressive *ceteris paribus* is the capital levy, i.e. the greater is c_1/c_2. But the mere fact that the rich man has a greater *absolute* amount of property than the poor man (even if the capital levy remains progressive) is not sufficient to cause the post-levy taxation of income to become less progressive in the sense defined above. A man with a large income may have a larger absolute income from property and yet a smaller proportion of his income coming from property than in the case of a poor man, i.e. k_2 can be greater than k_1. If the capital levy is only slightly progressive (c_1 only slightly $> c_2$), it is possible that $c_1 k_1 < c_2 k_2$.

166   IS THE NATIONAL DEBT A BURDEN ?

£5,000 worth of property against a rainy day, or for his old age, or to leave
to his family, or to supplement his present consumption by living on his
capital. The amount which he would spend on goods and services would
almost certainly be considerably greater in situation 1 than in situation 2;
or, to put the same thing another way, a man's net savings will be higher
or his net dissavings lower, the lower is the ratio of his capital to his tax-
free income. We may call this the Pigou-effect.[1]

Professor Hicks[2] has estimated that in 1947–9 the domestic indebtedness of the government which was uncovered by any real assets (which I
will call the 'deadweight debt') represented no less than 43 per cent. of
all privately owned property. The removal of the deadweight debt could
thus be considered as capable in those circumstances of reducing the
representative citizen's property by 43 per cent. without reducing his
tax-free income. This is what might be called a gigantic Pigou-effect and
would clearly raise the incentive to save very greatly.[3]

This increase in the incentive to save is almost certain to represent an
improvement from the point of view of society. If a reduction in the
demand for consumption goods is desired either to reduce an inflationary
pressure or to release resources so that investment can be raised in the
interests of economic growth, the advantage is obvious. But even if no
change in expenditure on consumption goods is desired, the increased
incentive to save can be made to have advantageous indirect effects. For,
in this case rates of taxation can be reduced so as to raise the citizens' tax-
free incomes to the extent necessary to restore their demand for consumption goods; and these reductions in rates of tax will improve incentives
for work and enterprise.[4]

Moreover, the fact that the removal of the deadweight debt would cause
all personal properties to be smaller than before is likely to improve
incentives for work and enterprise as well as for saving. Greater effort of
every kind is likely to be made to be in a position to build up private
fortunes when these are not already inflated by a deadweight debt.[5]

---

[1] See Pigou, 'Economic Progress in a Stable Environment', *Economica*, 1947.

[2] See Hicks, *The Social Framework*, 2nd ed., p. 109.

[3] We are not, of course, considering the effects of an actual capital levy, which might
have other psychological repercussions upon the incentive to save, particularly if it were
thought that the levy might be repeated. We are considering only how incentives in this
country might differ from what they are if the past history of the country had been such as
to leave it now with its present real income and real resources but without the deadweight
debt.

[4] It should be noted that these reductions of tax rates made possible by the Pigou-effect
are quite separate from, and additional to, any reductions in tax rates made possible through
a saving of interest payments from the State budget, which are the subject-matter of the
next section.

[5] Mr. N. K. Kaldor has suggested this point to me. I shall refer to it as the Kaldor-
extension of the Pigou-effect.

III

The second major effect of the disappearance of the deadweight debt is the familiar one most usually discussed in this connexion, namely the improvement to incentives to save, to work, and to risk brought about by the reduction in rates of taxation which it would make possible directly as a result of the saving of interest payments on the budget. The argument is in principle a very simple one. The redemption of the deadweight debt would mean a saving in budgetary expenditure on interest on the debt. This would make it possible to reduce rates of tax; and this would improve incentives to earn larger incomes by more effort and enterprise.

That there would be some incentive to more work and enterprise and that this would mark an improvement in economic arrangements is almost certain. We are assuming that when the deadweight debt disappears each citizen experiences a reduction in the rate of tax on his remaining income which exactly offsets his loss of income from property. So far he is in exactly the same real position with the same real income—neither better nor worse off. The only change is that if he earns an additional unit of income he will keep more of it. He will then take steps to earn more because he starts with the same real income and can get another unit of income more easily than before. And this change must be an improvement from his point of view because he could, had he so wished, have made no change in his income or leisure; and, so long as any positive rate of tax remains on income, he is likely by further effort to add more to the wealth of society than he takes from society after payment of tax on his additional earnings.

But how important are these effects of reduced rates of taxation on income likely to be? It has often been argued that they will be quantitatively very small if (i) the market rate of interest is low, (ii) the progressiveness of existing rates of taxation on income are high, (iii) there is a high correlation between large incomes and large properties, and (iv) the progressiveness of the capital levy is also high.[1] In these conditions a large redemption of debt is likely to lead only to a very small net saving of expenditure on the budget and so to make room for only a very small reduction of rates of taxation. If the rate of interest is low, a given

---

[1] We are using the capital levy merely as an analytical device for comparing two otherwise similar societies, whose histories have differed in one way or another so that in one a large national debt has been contracted and in the other no debt has been contracted. Since a national debt involves the inflation of the total amount of privately owned property, the histories of our two societies must have differed in such a way that over the past years in one of them private citizens have been able to accumulate more savings than in the other. The assumption that the capital levy is progressive corresponds, therefore, to a difference in the past histories of our two societies such that it is those who were able to accumulate the largest sums in the one society who were most denied the opportunity to accumulate in the other.

redemption of debt will cause only a small gross saving of interest payment in the budget; if the levy on capital is progressive, if large properties are held mainly by people with large incomes, and if the marginal rates of tax on these incomes are very high, then most of this small gross saving of interest will itself be absorbed by a loss of revenue from the taxation of income. The net saving to the budget and so the consequential reduction in tax rates and so the consequential improvement in incentives to be expected from a redemption of debt will be very small.

The conditions which I have just enumerated existed in this country in the years immediately after the war; and for these reasons the existence of a very large national debt was not considered to have any seriously adverse effects on incentives. But, quite apart from the very important Pigou-effect, there are at least three reasons why the deadweight debt has been a more serious impediment to economic incentives than was generally recognized.

In the first place, the rate of interest was kept at a low level in large measure because of the existence of the national debt. These were years of heavy inflationary pressure. Reluctance to use monetary policy as one of the instruments to restrain inflation was greatly increased by the fact that an all-round rise in interest rates would immediately increase the budgetary burden of expenditure of interest on treasury bills and other short-term debt and would gradually lead to a rise in expenditure on longer-dated debt as it fell due for repayment.[1] With low interest rates a removal of the debt might cause only a small gross saving on debt interest; but it would mean that a rise of interest rates as an anti-inflationary device would no longer be open to the objection that it would seriously increase the budgetary problem. The removal of the national debt would thus have made it much easier to use the instrument of monetary policy flexibly for the control of inflation and deflation. Now that, for better or worse, interest rates have been raised to really high levels the argument can, of course, be put once more in its direct form. Rates of interest being high the redemption of national debt would mean a large saving of interest on national debt.

Our attitude to a deadweight debt must be much influenced by the surrounding economic climate. In times of economic stagnation like the 1930's, low interest rates and cheap money were most desirable in them-

---

[1] It is not certain that a rise in interest rates increases the net burden of a given national debt. This depends greatly on the structure of the debt. If the debt consisted solely of short-term bills it would not affect the capital value of the debt but would add to the interest payments and so raise the rates of tax needed to service the debt. If the debt consisted solely of irredeemable bonds it would reduce the capital value of the debt without raising interest payments. In the former case there would be an unfavourable effect on tax rates with no favourable Pigou-effect; in the latter case there would be a favourable Pigou-effect with no adverse effects on tax rates.

selves to stimulate investment; this had the incidental result that a given national debt did not involve very high rates of tax for its service and, at the same time, the Pigou-effect of a high capital sum of the debt in discouraging savings was positively beneficial. But in the present (and so much more desirable) world climate of economic development and buoyancy, high interest rates may be desired as a means of discouraging the least productive investment projects, and the Pigou-effect of the debt in discouraging savings is most undesirable. A deadweight debt may have been a blessing in the 1930's, but it is a curse in the 1950's.

Secondly, the fact that a progressive capital levy combined with a progressive system of taxation of income means that there is little scope for subsequent reduction in the existing schedules of taxation on income does not mean that it gives no increased incentive at the margin for greater work and enterprise. A capital levy reduces the property-owner's gross income; with a progressive system of taxation of income the reduction in the amount of his gross income by putting him into a lower income bracket causes the rate of tax on his income to be reduced. For this reason, even if there were no reduction whatsoever in the schedules of taxation of income after the capital levy, there would nevertheless be an improvement in marginal incentive. Because he was now in a lower gross-income bracket the representative taxpayer could keep a larger proportion of each additional £1 which he earned.

Thirdly, there is some reason to believe that a given reduction in the marginal rate of tax will be more important from the point of view of economic incentives when tax rates are high than when they are low. Consider two situations which are otherwise the same. In situation 1 the rate of income tax is 19s. 6d. in the pound because the cold war is on and there is a great deal of government expenditure on armaments to finance in addition to interest on the national debt. In situation 2 real peace has broken out and the rate of income tax is only 2s. in the pound because there is little government expenditure on armaments, though expenditure on interest on debt remains unchanged. Now in situation 1 remove just sufficient national debt to make possible a reduction of 6d. in the pound in the income tax while leaving every citizen with the same real income as before because his loss of interest on debt is just compensated by the fall in the rate of income tax. Then in situation 2 make a similar change; that is to say, remove that amount of debt which in situation 2 will permit a reduction of 6d. in the pound while leaving every citizen with the same real income. In situation 1 out of every additional £100 which he now earns a citizen can keep £5 instead of only £2. 10s. In situation 2 out of every additional £100 which he now earns he can keep £92. 10s. instead of only £90. The same reduction of tax of 6d. in the pound has in both situations left the taxpayer's spendable income unchanged; but it has raised his *marginal* reward by 100 per cent. in situation 1 and by under 3 per cent. in situation 2. Since in the 'cold-war' situation our taxpayer is so much worse off than in the 'real-peace' situation we cannot say for certain that a 100 per cent. increase in his marginal reward without any change in his total reward will have a greater effect on the amount of work which he does in situation 1 than a 3 per cent. increase in his marginal reward without any change in his total reward in situation 2. But there is a strong presumption that he will increase his effort more in situation 1 than in situation 2.[1]

But even if he increased the amount of work which he did by the same amount in situation 1 when his marginal reward was doubled as in situation 2 when his marginal reward was increased by only 3 per cent., the reduction in tax would be much more important in situation 1 than in situation 2. In both cases his wage before tax measures the value of his marginal product, while his wage after tax measures the marginal disutility of effort to him. In situation 1 our citizen is working to a margin at which the value of his marginal product is no less than 40 times as great as the cost of his marginal effort (£100÷£2. 10*s.* = 40). In situation 2 the value of his marginal product is only $1\frac{1}{9}$ times as great as the cost of his marginal effort (£100÷£90 = $1\frac{1}{9}$). In the former case society as a whole stands to gain much more from additional work than it does in the latter case.

Thus it is certainly true that if the initial taxation of income is high and progressive, then a progressive capital levy will lead to only a small budgetary saving of interest on debt and will therefore permit only a small reduction in tax rates. But it is precisely when marginal rates of tax on income are high that a small reduction in tax rates may do much good.

IV

Up to this point the existence of death duties has been neglected. A removal of the deadweight debt would reduce the size of the average private holding of property; it would thus reduce the size of the average estate passing at death; and so with any given schedule of death duties it would reduce the annual revenue from such duties. This additional automatic loss of revenue, so it may be argued, still further weakens the

---

[1] If his elasticity of demand for income in terms of effort is equal to unity, then he is supplying the same amount of work in situation 1 as in situation 2. The outbreak of the cold war and the consequent increase in the rate of tax from 2*s.* to 19*s.* 6*d.* in the pound will have raised the marginal utility of money income to him (by reducing his tax-free income) in exactly the same proportion as it has lowered his tax-free wage in terms of money. Since he is doing the same amount of work, the marginal disutility of work is in this case the same to him in situation 1 as in situation 2. In both cases when debt is removed and the tax rate is lowered by 6*d.* the marginal utility of income is unchanged (because he loses in interest as much as he gains by paying his tax); but in situation 1 his net reward for doing more work is doubled and in situation 2 it is raised by less than 3 per cent. He will be certain in this case to increase his supply of work more in situation 1 than in situation 2.

case for a removal of the deadweight debt as a means of making possible a reduction of tax rates and so an improvement in incentives.

That one must be careful about this argument is forcibly demonstrated by the following consideration. If the rate of interest is sufficiently low, if the taxation of income is sufficiently high and progressive, if the capital levy itself is sufficiently progressive, if estates pass frequently enough by death from one owner to another, and if the rates of death duty are sufficiently high and progressive, then the removal of the deadweight debt may at existing tax rates cause budgetary revenue to fall by more than budgetary expenditure. The loss of death duties because of the reduction in the capital sum of personal properties may be greater than the small saving of interest after payment of income tax. To preserve the budgetary balance tax rates must be raised after the removal of the debt. The greater the national debt, the better the budgetary situation.

It is quite probable that in the years immediately after the war conditions were of this kind, so that the disappearance of the debt would have reduced budgetary expenditure less than budgetary revenue. Yet common sense rightly rebels against the conclusion that the great growth of debt during the war could have improved the budgetary situation in any basic sense. Where has the argument gone astray?

The answer is, of course, that there is no reason to believe that the balance between revenue and expenditure ought to remain unchanged when the deadweight debt is removed. In the modern economy the basic purpose of taxation is to restrain the demands of private citizens in order to release real resources from the production of goods and services for private consumption to the extent that they are needed to meet the demands of current government services and of the programme of capital development that, with given policies and institutions, the State and private enterprise plan to carry out. As a first approximation we should judge the extent to which tax rates can be reduced after the removal of the deadweight debt not by the criterion that the balance between budgetary revenue and expenditure should be unaffected, but by the criterion that the demand of private citizens for goods and services for private consumption should be unchanged. If this criterion is applied, there can be no doubt that the removal of the deadweight debt will permit some reduction of tax rates even in the extreme conditions which we have been envisaging, in which, because of the incidence of death duties, it will at unchanged rates of tax worsen the balance between budgetary revenue and expenditure.

This can be demonstrated by the following example. In both the pre-levy and the post-levy situations a representative citizen has a net tax-free income of £1,000, but in the former situation he possesses a property of

£10,000 and in the latter he possesses only £5,000 of property. His con
sumption will be greater in the first than in the second case simply becaus
he has so much more property; and if death duties are high and progressive
his consumption in the first situation may be higher still because he i
allowed to consume all his property during his lifetime but cannot hand
much of it on to his heirs. But in the first situation the State will be
enjoying a large revenue from death duties (since some citizens will be
dying each year and handing on their considerable properties), whereas in
the second situation the State will receive much less revenue from death
duties because there is only half as much private property to hand on at
death. Now, since *ex hypothesi* our citizen has the same tax-free income
in both situations, the State has already reduced rates of taxation of
income between the first and second situation sufficiently to leave him
with the same net tax-free income, even though he has lost half his income
from property. This in itself will have left the balance of revenue and
expenditure in the budget unchanged, since the State has lost in tax
payments by him exactly as much as it has reduced its interest payment to
him. But the State will also have lost a large part of its revenue from death
duties since there is now only half as much private property to pass at
death. Nevertheless, because of the Pigou-effect the reduction in our
citizen's property will have reduced his expenditure on consumption and
tax rates must be reduced still further if private consumption expenditure
is to be maintained. In other words, when the deadweight debt is removed
not merely should the loss of revenue from death duties be totally dis-
regarded, but in addition rates of taxation on income can properly be
reduced by more than would be sufficient to maintain the previous balance
between revenue and expenditure even if there had been no fall in revenue
from death duties.

V

The disappearance of the deadweight debt would also have a revolutionary effect in the capital and money markets through changes in the
amount and the structure of capital assets available to be held by the
banks and the rest of the private sector of the economy, and this would
have some marked effects upon economic incentives which we must now
examine.[1]

Let us divide the assets available to be held by the private sector of our
community into four categories, namely: Money, Bills, Bonds, and
Equities. Money includes coin, notes, and bank deposits, on all of which
no interest is paid but all of which are fixed in money value and can be

---

[1] See E. Nevin, *The Problem of the National Debt*, for a stimulating description and discussion of the effect of the debt upon the assets held by the various sectors of the United
Kingdom economy.

transferred at a moment's notice with negligible cost. Bills, of which the three-months treasury bill is the pure example, are reliable promises to pay a fixed sum of money in a short time; their capital value when that time comes will be certain, but there is some possibility of moderate variations in their value with variations in the rate of interest before they reach maturity. Bonds, of which 2½ per cent. Consols are the pure example, are reliable promises to pay a fixed annual money income with no obligation to repay the capital sum; income from them is certain but their future capital value may vary widely with variations in the rate of interest. Equities include ordinary shares and real assets like machines; the income from them is uncertain and the rate of interest at which that income should be capitalized is also uncertain; their future capital value is subject to a double risk.

We will for the moment make two simplifying assumptions, both of which we shall in due course modify. First, let us assume that the disappearance of the deadweight debt does not disturb the banking system and that the total amount of coins, notes, and deposits made available by the banking system to the rest of the private sector of the economy remains unchanged. Second, let us assume that there is no attempt to keep the balance of revenue and expenditure in the budget unchanged, but rather that tax rates are reduced sufficiently to keep the total demand for private consumption goods at its previous level. In this case, since the market for finished goods is undisturbed, we can assume that there is no change in the absolute level of earnings expected on Equities.

There are two main ways in which the disappearance of the national debt might in these circumstances affect the incentive to invest, the first operating directly through the change in the amount of Bills-and-Bonds existing in the market and the second operating through the consequential changes in the prices of Bills, Bonds, and Equities.

The Kaldor-extension of the Pigou effect (p. 166 above) suggests that people might make all sorts of efforts to rebuild their private fortunes if they had been diminished by the disappearance of the deadweight debt. Such efforts might include greater activity on the part of business men, involving an increased incentive to invest in capital equipment. But there is an important influence operating in the opposite direction. The disappearance of the deadweight debt means that the entrepreneur (whether he be a private business man or be taken to represent the managing body of a joint-stock company) will have at his command a much smaller amount of assets—and precisely of assets like government Bills-and-Bonds on the security of which, or through the sale of which, it is especially easy to raise funds for the finance of capital development. Both because the ratio of his total assets to liabilities will be lower and because the ratio of

174   IS THE NATIONAL DEBT A BURDEN ?

his readily realizable assets to other assets will be lower, the typical entrepreneur will be less able to finance projects of capital development, and the risks involved in doing so will be greater. Thus the incentive to invest may be increased, but the ability to finance investment is likely to be reduced, simply by the changes in the quantity of assets.[1]

VI

But the disappearance of the deadweight debt will affect the prices as well as the amounts of various assets; and these changes in price may also affect the level of investment. The disappearance of the deadweight debt represents, on the one side, a reduction by that amount in the total capital wealth of the private sector of the community and, on the other hand, an equal reduction in the Bills-and-Bonds available to be held by the private sector, the amounts of Money and of Equities available in the market, and the level of earnings expected on Equities being unchanged. But when a private citizen has £5,000 less capital to hold with asset prices and expectations unchanged, he is unlikely to choose to hold £5,000 less Bills-and-Bonds; although his reduction in holdings of Money, Bills, Bonds, and Equities will not necessarily all be in the same proportion, he is likely to want at current asset prices to hold somewhat less of each type of asset.[2] In other words the disappearance of the deadweight debt will cause a scarcity of Bills-and-Bonds relatively to Money and relatively to Equities; in an otherwise unchanged market situation, the price of Bills-and-Bonds will probably rise in terms of Money and in terms of Equities.

The rise of the price of Bills-and-Bonds in terms of Money represents a fall in the rate of interest. The rise in the price of Bills-and-Bonds relatively to that of Equities represents a rise in the risk-premium. The margin between the rate of yield on Equities, on the one hand, and on Bills-and-Bonds, on the other hand, will be increased. It will be easier to borrow for capital development by the issue of fixed interest debentures than by the issue of ordinary shares. There will be a premium on capital development of a safe kind.

It would, of course, always be possible for the government to offset this change in asset prices by itself supplying risk-bearing. This it could do by issuing Bills-and-Bonds and investing the proceeds in Equities, so that, while the deadweight debt was eliminated, there remained a considerable governmental liability in the form of government Bills-and-Bonds balanced

---

[1] The argument in this paragraph was suggested to me in discussion by Mr. N. Kaldor.

[2] He will presumably wish to reduce his holding of foreign assets as well as of domestic assets. In this way a reduction of domestic deadweight debt might cause some easement on the capital account of a country's balance of payments.

by an equal asset in the form of governmental investments in private industry.[1]

But suppose that the government took no such action. Then, as we have seen, there will be some rise in the price of Bills-and-Bonds in terms of Money; this will represent a fall in the pure rate of interest; and a lower pure rate of interest is a price change which may help to stimulate some extra investment in safe, long-term projects such as house-building.

But a change in the price of Equities (which represents the market valuation placed on machines and other real assets in industry) is more likely to affect investment than is a change in the price of Bills-and-Bonds. Bills-and-Bonds go up in terms of Money and in terms of Equities. But will Equities go up or down in terms of Money?

The outcome will depend upon whether Bills-and-Bonds are better substitutes for Money than for Equities or whether, on the contrary, they are better substitutes for Equities than for Money. When the government Bills-and-Bonds disappear, the amounts of Money and of Equities remaining unchanged, the representative private citizen has got to increase by a given amount the proportion of his assets which he holds in Money and by another given amount the proportion of his assets which he holds in Equities. If Bills-and-Bonds are a good substitute for Money, then only a small rise will be needed in the money price of Bills-and-Bonds to persuade the representative citizen to make the needful shift into Money; and if Bills-and-Bonds are a bad substitute for Equities, a large rise in the price of Bills-and-Bonds will be necessary in terms of Equities to bring about the needed shift into Equities. In these conditions there will be only a small rise in the money price of Bills-and-Bonds, i.e. only a small fall in the pure rate of interest; and the increase in the risk premium will be large and will be brought about by a fall in the price of Equities. Similarly, in the opposite conditions where Bills-and-Bonds are a bad substitute for Money but a good substitute for Equities, the price of Bills-and-Bonds will rise a lot and the rate of interest will fall a lot in order to cause the necessary shift to Money; but the risk premium will have to rise only a little to cause the necessary shift to Equities, so that the money price of Equities will rise almost as much as the money price of Bills-and-Bonds.

Which of these two things is likely to happen in fact? We must distinguish between Bills and Bonds. Bills are more like Money than are

---

[1] In terms of our analytical capital levy this result would be brought about and all asset prices would remain unchanged if those liable to the capital levy were allowed at their choice to pay in Money, Bills, Bonds, or Equities, and if the government after cancelling any government Bills-and-Bonds which the payers of the levy surrendered, itself held on to the other private assets handed over to it, leaving outstanding in private ownership any government Bills-and-Bonds which had not been surrendered to it in payment of the levy.

Bonds, and Bonds are more like Equities than are Bills. When the private citizen loses his Bills he is likely to go for Money. But in fact most government short-term debt is held by the banks. As long as we are assuming that the banks are not disturbed by the change but supply an unchanged amount of money, the effect of the disappearance of the national debt on the private sector's structure of assets will be mainly a loss of Bonds. When property-owners are starved of Bonds will they shift to Money or to Equities?

There is, I think, no simple answer to this question. One can imagine circumstances in a mature economy with a tendency to secular stagnation in which exceedingly low rates of interest are necessary to prevent deflation, so that a further fall in interest rates is almost out of the question. In this case an increased risk margin will show itself in a fall in the money price of Equities rather than in a rise in the money price of Bonds. The disappearance of the deadweight debt will have made an already deflationary situation still more deflationary. On the other hand, one can imagine a buoyant situation in which interest rates are very high and in which it is the scarcity of capital rather than of risk bearing and of profitable opportunities for investment which holds back further development. In these circumstances a scarcity of Bonds might well cause a substantial fall in the rate of interest which might carry upwards the money price of Equities; and in this case, in so far as price effects in the capital market are concerned, the disappearance of the national debt would have made an inflationary situation still more inflationary.

But the analysis in the last paragraph has not allowed for the fact that substantial deflations or inflations of the general level of prices may be in progress and may be expected to continue. The capital value of Bills and the interest payable on Bonds are fixed in terms of Money; in the case of Equities, neither capital value nor yield is fixed. For this reason in times of rapidly changing money prices Bills and Bonds are likely to be better substitutes for Money than for Equities. This is an added reason why the disappearance of the national debt is likely to exert a deflationary influence on the price of Equities.

VII

We have still to modify our two assumptions that the disappearance of the deadweight debt does nothing in itself to affect either the absolute level of earnings expected on Equities or the total supply of Money. In fact in both these respects also it might exert a strong deflationary force.

For the reasons developed in Section II above, the disappearance of the deadweight debt would be likely to increase the propensity to save. The effects of this we have so far assumed to be offset by a reduction of tax rates by the government sufficient to restore private expenditure to its previous level. But, of course, tax rates might not be reduced in this way. The increase in savings and decrease in expenditure on consumption goods caused by the disappearance of the deadweight debt might be acceptable to the government if there was initially a strong inflationary pressure which it was desired to counteract. Or the reduction in the demand for consumption goods might be acceptable even in the absence of any inflationary pressure, if it was thought that too much of the community's resources was being devoted to consumption and too little to investment. In this case the reduced expenditure on consumption, by causing a fall in the absolute level of earnings expected on Equities would cause an undesirable deflationary pressure. In order that this should not cause an actual deflation of total demand, it would then be necessary for there to be an increase in total investment expenditure equal to the reduction in expenditure on consumption goods. To engineer an increased expenditure on capital development, when the market for finished consumption goods was actually being contracted, might require a very large increase in monetary liquidity and fall in interest rates or risk premium. In such circumstances the disappearance of the deadweight debt might well be deflationary unless the total supply of Money were considerably increased.

But how would the supply of Money react to the disappearance of the deadweight debt? At present the supply of Money depends upon the liquidity of the banking system which depends upon the issue of a sufficient amount of liquid treasury bills to be shuffled about between the Bank of England, the Discount Houses, and the Clearing Banks. If these higher banking mysteries remain unchanged, then the disappearance of the deadweight debt including the disappearance of all government Bills would make the banking system highly illiquid and would cause a reduction in the supply of Money.[1] This deflationary effect could be offset if the government, while its net debt was zero, issued Bills to the banks and invested the money so borrowed in private Bonds or Equities. The government would buy private Bonds-and-Equities with government Bills in order that the banks might buy Bills with Money, unless there were a change in banking arrangements so that the banks themselves in these conditions bought Bonds and Equities with Money.

[1] If the national debt consisted entirely of Bills held partly by the banks and partly by private owners and if, as is probable, Bills are a good substitute for Money, then the disappearance of the national debt would cause a large reduction of Money-and-Bills with an unchanged stock of privately issued Bonds-and-Equities. In this case the money prices of Bonds and of Equities would fall. In other words, the pure rate of interest would rise because the change would be essentially one of reduced liquidity.

VIII

Whether the net effect of the disappearance of the deadweight debt would be inflationary or deflationary rests upon a complex balance of forces. The outstanding deflationary possibility would be its effect upon the banking system. If all treasury bills disappeared there would in present conditions be a catastrophic monetary deflation. Let us leave this on one side and assume that some alternative method is found for controlling the supply of Money. This is a *sine qua non* for the removal of the deadweight debt.

There would remain a number of conflicting forces at work.

(i) Because of the Pigou-effect people are likely to spend less on consumption and to save more, which in itself will be a deflationary force.

(ii) Because of the Kaldor-extension of the Pigou-effect and because of reductions in marginal rates of tax people are likely to produce more goods and services. Since producers are likely to increase their expenditures by less than their incomes (particularly when rates of taxation on incomes are high and progressive), this is likely to increase supplies relatively to demand and to exert a deflationary influence.

(iii) Entrepreneurs will have a smaller amount of easily realizable assets in their ownership and this will make the finance of investment more difficult.

(iv) If Bonds are a good substitute for Money and a poor substitute for Equities, then the disappearance of government Bonds is likely to cause only a small rise in the price of Bonds but a large fall in the price of Equities. This would probably exercise a deflationary effect upon investment. If, on the other hand, Bonds were a bad substitute for Money and a good substitute for Equities, the prices of Bonds and Equities would both rise with a consequential inflationary effect upon investment. But, as we have seen, in periods of rapid fluctuations in commodity prices, Bonds are unlikely to be a good substitute for Equities, and the inflationary effect upon Equity prices is not very probable in such circumstances.

(v) The desire to rebuild private fortunes which have been reduced by the disappearance of government debt might stimulate business men to greater risk-bearing and enterprise and thus to a higher level of expenditure on investment programs.

On balance it would appear probable that, even apart from any effects on the supply of Money through the banking system, the disappearance of the deadweight debt would exert a significant deflationary influence. But, provided always that the government has a firm grip upon monetary institutions and policies and is prepared so to control its monetary and fiscal policies as to stabilize the total demand for goods and services, this in present-day conditions must be counted a great advantage of the removal of the debt. In present-day conditions of economic expansion and buoyancy interest rates and rates of taxation have to be kept at otherwise undesirably high levels in order to avoid the threat of inflation. The disappearance of the deadweight debt could provide just the occasion for an otherwise desirable relaxation of monetary and fiscal conditions.

The danger might, however, remain that through the increased difficulty of finding finance for risky investment projects and through an increase in the risk premium on Equities, there would be a special deterrent to innovation and to the application of new and risky techniques. To counteract such a tendency it might be necessary for the government to relax its monetary and fiscal policies in ways which specially favoured innovation and enterprise (e.g. by tax allowances for new investment), and to introduce new arrangements for the provision of risk capital through public or semi-public institutions. But, given this, the disappearance of the deadweight debt could be made the occasion for a great improvement in economic incentives.

IX

This paper has been devoted to the question whether an internal national debt is an economic burden or not. The method of analysis of this problem has been to remove the debt by means of an imaginary capital levy to see what difference this would make to economic incentives, if everything also remained unchanged. Our analysis has suggested that in certain important respects the existence of a large deadweight debt seriously blunts economic incentives. But before we rush to rebuild society with a zero deadweight debt there are two further questions which would require extensive investigation. In this paper they can only be briefly mentioned.

The first remaining problem is this. Granted that a positive deadweight debt is a burden, it does not follow that the optimum size for the deadweight debt is zero. Perhaps a negative debt would be still better. Or in terms of our national capital levy, why should the total levy be just equal to the deadweight debt ? Might there not be advantages if it were still bigger and left the State a net creditor instead of a net debtor to the private sector of the economy ? The argument for such a development runs as follows. The government has expenditures to finance on defence, justice, police, education, health, and social security. For this it has to impose taxes. Rates of tax cause divergences between efforts and rewards and thus interfere with economic incentives. If the State was a net owner of property which it itself used productively or hired out to the private sector of the economy, it would itself obtain a net income from rents, interest, and profits which it could use to finance part of its expenditures so that

180   IS THE NATIONAL DEBT A BURDEN?

rates of tax could be further reduced. Provided that the State's property was devoted to uses where the marginal social return on it was at least as high as it would have been if it had been left in private ownership, the reduction in tax rates would represent a further net improvement in economic incentives; and there would, of course, be a still greater Pigou-effect stimulating private savings.

There would remain the question of the kind of assets which the State should hold. Some assets, like roads, schools, and the equipment of nationalized industries are obvious candidates. But for the rest should the State invest in private Bonds or in private Equities? If it invested its funds in fixed charges like ground rents, mortgages, and debentures, it would still further usurp the function of the private rentier. The private-property-owner would willy-nilly be forced to become more and more of a private risk bearer, if not an actual entrepreneur. If, on the other hand, this would reduce the supply of risk-bearing too seriously, the State would have to hold private Equities rather than private Bonds; and an arrangement which was devised in the first place to give the State an income from property would have the indirect effect of forcing the State into participation in the management of private industry.

But with the present gigantic deadweight debt these problems are all ones for a still far distant Utopia. We should be happy enough to see a substantial reduction in the debt without demanding even its total elimination, much less its replacement by a net ownership of property by the State. Even so, there remains the great practical question: how is the reduction to be effected? The fact that the deadweight debt is a serious and real economic burden does not itself prove that it should be removed or even reduced. It might be a good thing if it had never existed; but it does exist and the best cure might be worse than the disease.

The first possibility is to use the capital levy not merely as a tool of economic analysis, but also as a practical means of debt redemption. I have been persuaded that we should not.[1] We have to face the following dilemma. A levy can be successful only if it is not expected that it will be repeated, since the expectation of a further levy would destroy all incentives to save. A successful levy will lead to the expectation that it will be repeated unless it is on such a scale that there remains no case for a repeat. But a levy on this scale would present such problems of administration and valuation, would so disturb the structure of the capital market, and would involve such vast changes in personal wealth that it really lies outside the range of what is practicable or suitable in our evolutionary methods of social and economic reform.

---

[1] The argument is exceedingly well put by Mr. C. A. R. Crosland in pp. 311–18 of his *The Future of Socialism.*

J. E. MEADE   181

But alternative and less revolutionary methods are available to reduce the burden of the national debt. We may perhaps take the ratio of deadweight debt to total privately owned property as an index of the relative size of the debt. There remain three ways of reducing this proportion, namely: inflation, private savings, and public savings through budget surpluses.

First, it can be very effectively reduced by inflation. This has in fact been happening since the war. In the nine years since 1947–9 the general level of money prices of fixed assets in this country has risen by some 45 per cent. In 1947–9 43 per cent. of private property was deadweight debt.[1] If this 43 per cent. remains fixed in money values and the other 57 per cent. rises by 45 per cent. in money values, then the deadweight debt represents only 34 per cent. instead of 43 per cent. of total private property.[2]

Second, the relative importance of the deadweight debt can be reduced by the accumulation of private savings.[3] Such savings, matched by an expansion of the community's real capital assets, represent a growth of total privately owned property, so that any given amount of deadweight debt will represent a smaller proportion of total privately owned property. In the nine years 1948–57 total private savings reckoned at 1948 prices amounted to about £6,100 million, which represents an addition of some 15 per cent. to the £40,500 million of total privately owned property which was estimated to exist in 1947–9.[4] Such an increase would reduce the proportion of deadweight debt to total privately owned property from 43 per cent. to 38 per cent.

Third, there is the old-fashioned method of debt reduction through an annual surplus of revenue over expenditure in the State budget. Such public savings have a double effect in reducing the proportion of total privately owned property which takes the form of deadweight debt. Suppose that the government has an excess of revenue over current expenditure of £1 million. If the government invests this sum in new public works like schools, then £1 million of existing government debt ceases to be uncovered by real assets. Privately owned property remains

---

[1] J. R. Hicks, loc. cit.

[2] I would like to thank Mr. J. Longden of the Faculty of Economics and Politics, University of Cambridge, for help in the preparation of the estimates in this and the following paragraphs.

[3] For this and the following paragraph the total savings of the community have been divided between private and public savings. Private savings include the surpluses of public corporations as well as the undistributed profits of ordinary companies. The realization of assets for the payment of death duties has been treated as a reduction of private savings and accordingly the receipt of death duties has been allowed to swell the budget surplus. The current revenue of the public authorities and so their savings also includes the receipts of foreign aid. Public savings include the surpluses of local authorities as well as of the central government.

[4] J. R. Hicks, loc. cit.

182   IS THE NATIONAL DEBT A BURDEN?

unchanged in total, but it consists of £1 million less of deadweight debt and £1 million more of claims backed by real assets. If the government uses its surplus of £1 million to redeem outstanding national debt, then private owners must hold £1 million less of government debt and they must invest this sum in £1 million worth of additional private real assets. The ratio of the former to the latter has fallen both because the former has decreased and also because the latter has increased. During the nine years 1948–56 public savings amounted at 1948 prices to some £3,100 million. If we subtract this figure from the £17,500 million of deadweight debt outstanding in 1947–9 and add it to the £23,000 million of other privately owned property, outstanding at that time,[1] the ratio of deadweight debt to total privately owned property is reduced from 43 per cent. to 36 per cent.

Nowadays, the desirability of a budget surplus is often argued on one or both of two grounds: first, that high levels of taxation and low levels of governmental expenditure are desirable in order to exert a disinflationary pressure in an inflationary situation and, second, that public savings through a budget surplus are a desirable supplement to private savings in order that, in the interests of economic growth, more resources may be devoted to capital development at the expense of immediate consumption. I would like to restore a third old-fashioned argument for a budget surplus, namely, that it will help to reduce the national debt and thereby improve economic incentives in the future.

Additional taxation even if it were paid wholly out of savings (i.e. even if it caused no reduction at all in private consumption and therefore served no useful purpose in fighting inflation or promoting economic growth) would nevertheless serve a useful purpose in debt redemption. It would reduce the amount of national debt held by individuals even though it caused no net increase in their holding of other assets. Of course, taxes imposed for this purpose as for all others should have as little adverse effect as possible upon current incentives for work and enterprise; the point is only that if taxes are imposed for debt redemption, they are not to be ruled out because they are paid out of private savings. Death duties and annual taxes assessed not on income but on the value of privately owned property may fall into this category. Such taxes may have the smallest adverse effects upon work and enterprise (though it would be rash to claim that they have no such effects), but they are likely to be paid wholly or in large part out of private savings. It might be wise to build up a considerable budget surplus financed out of these taxes and to use it for the redemption of the national debt.[2]

---

[1] J. R. Hicks, loc. cit.

[2] Taxes of this sort (and in particular death duties) are not of the kind whose rates can appropriately be frequently varied. In so far as variations in tax rates are needed to

J. E. MEADE　　　　　183

A budget surplus can also be achieved by a reduction in budgetary expenditure in so far as this is not offset by a reduction in rates of taxation. If expenditure is reduced for the purpose of debt redemption, the future advantages of a lower national debt are gained at the expense of the present restriction of government expenditure below the level which would otherwise be considered desirable.

Indeed we are faced, as so often in economic policy, with a dilemma. There would be great future advantages in improved economic incentives if the debt were reduced. But the methods of doing this are likely to worsen economic conditions in the immediate present. Inflation is the great debt-reducer, but has many other bad marks to be set against it. Private savings may be stimulated, but after a point only by means of systems of taxation which involve a reduction in public savings or are undesirable on distributional or similar grounds.[1] A budget surplus can be achieved only by further increases in tax rates or by a reduction in other budgetary expenditures—when it is a main purpose of debt reduction to enable a given level of other budgetary expenditures to be maintained without the disincentive effects of high taxation. The purpose of this paper is the limited one of showing in what ways the existence of a large national debt blunts economic incentives; it has not attempted to assess the balance between the immediate costs and the ultimate gains of different methods of debt reduction.

CHRIST'S COLLEGE

CAMBRIDGE

---

control total expenditure in order to avoid inflations and deflations of demand, alterations in rates of taxation on income or on purchases are more appropriate. But if, over and above such taxes, there is a considerable and fairly stable revenue from death duties and other taxes which are paid out of savings, it should be possible normally to run a considerable budget surplus. Any reductions in other taxes which may then at any time be needed to offset the threat of a general deflation will involve the reduction of a budget surplus rather than the incurring of an actual deficit. Revenue from taxes paid out of savings thus allows fiscal measures to be used for reflationary purposes without a budget deficit and thus without building up once more a deadweight debt.

[1] I would exempt from this criticism any shift from a progressive tax on income to an equally progressive tax on expenditure which, if administratively practicable, should greatly stimulate savings without other seriously adverse effects.

[16]

IS THE NATIONAL DEBT A BURDEN?
A CORRECTION

By J. E. MEADE

In my article in the *Oxford Economic Papers* for June 1958 I made a serious mistake.[1] The point which I overlooked is one which would tend to raise the money price of privately held assets after their quantity had been reduced by the capital levy. The total value of the remaining capital assets would thus be greater than I allowed in my article; but, as I argue in this note, the rise in their price would not normally be great enough to restore the total value of privately held assets to their pre-levy value. Some element of the Pigou-effect (discussed in Section II of my article) would remain.

My blunder was as follows. In Section VI of my article I argued as if the functional relationship expressing the demands for Money, Bills, Bonds, and Equities in terms of the total Money value of assets to be held and of the Money prices of Bills, Bonds, and Equities would be the same before and after the levy. But this is not so because of the lower rate of tax on interest and dividends after the levy. The gross (or *cum* tax) and net (or *ex* tax) yield on Money is always zero; with a gross yield on Bonds of 4 per cent., the net yield is 2 per cent. with a rate of tax of 10s. in the £ and 3 per cent. with a rate of tax of 5s. in the £. This means that, after the levy, income-yielding assets become so much the more attractive at any given price in terms of Money. This will cause their price to be driven up (i.e. their gross yield or the rate of interest to be driven down) not only because they are now scarce relatively to Money (the point which I made) but also because their net yield is now higher while that on Money remains zero (the point which I overlooked in my article).

Nevertheless, I think that there remains a presumption that the price of income-yielding assets (Bills, Bonds, and Equities) will not rise to the extent necessary to restore the total value of such assets to the pre-levy total. The argument may be put in the form of a *reductio ad absurdum*. Suppose that the rate of interest did fall to the extent necessary to restore the pre-levy total value of all assets. Then there are two reasons why it would rise again.

First, the net rate of yield on such assets would now be *lower* than in the pre-levy situation and this would cause people to desert income-yielding assets for Money, i.e. would cause some rise in the rate of interest. The reason for this is that, while the loss of interest on the national debt is

[1] This mistake has come to light as a result of a correspondence with Mr. John Spraos, to whom I would like to acknowledge my indebtedness.

110   IS THE NATIONAL DEBT A BURDEN ? A CORRECTION

exactly counterbalanced by a reduction of income tax (assuming income tax to be the only form of tax and a balanced budget to be maintained), the loss of interest on debt is wholly a loss of income from property but the gain through lower tax is spread over earned and unearned income. Thus the tax-free income from property is lower post-levy than pre-levy, so that if the total market value of property is to be the same post-levy as pre-levy the net rate of return on income-yielding property must be lower post-levy than pre-levy. If the tax remission were confined to the remission of tax on income from property, it might be argued that the first presumption in the capital market is that the total value of income-yielding assets will be exactly restored by a fall in the rate of interest; for in this case the amount of Money, the value of other assets, and the net yield on other assets would all remain unchanged; but in so far as some of the tax remission is on earned income the net yield on income-yielding assets is reduced and their value will tend to fall.

Second, suppose that the tax remission were confined to taxation of income from property so that the above considerations would not prevent the value of assets being restored to their pre-levy level. There would now be no Pigou-effect to cause a rise in savings and so a deflation in the demand for consumption goods, and for exactly the same reason there would be no deflationary influence damping down investment of the kind which I mentioned at the bottom of page 173 and top of page 174 in my article. But in so far as the rate of interest affects investment, there would now be an inflationary demand for investment goods because it is the *gross* and not the *net* rate of yield which affects investment incentives. So far nothing would have happened to make people expect a lower gross rate of profit on any given new investment, but the gross rate of interest would have fallen so as to keep the net tax-free rate of yield unchanged. The fall in the rate of interest would cause an inflation; and if monetary policy and not budgetary policy were used to prevent this the amount of Money would have to be reduced and the rate of interest raised again somewhat, so that the total value of assets would fall. Indeed, if on these grounds monetary policy was so devised as to keep the gross rate of interest at its pre-levy level, there would be a completely unmitigated Pigou-effect; the total value of privately held assets would fall by the amount of the levy.

The net effect of this correction is, therefore, to suggest that, while there would still be a Pigou-effect, it might be less marked than I supposed it to be in my article.

[17]

❧

Concerning Future Generations

THE new orthodoxy of the public debt is based upon three propositions. If these propositions can be shown to be false, the modern conception of public debt must be radically revised. If these propositions can be shown to be true in reverse, the conception must be completely discarded. I shall attempt, in this and the following chapters, to accomplish this reversal. I shall try to prove that, in the most general case:

1. The primary real burden of a public debt is shifted to future generations.
2. The analogy between public debt and private debt is fundamentally correct.
3. The external debt and the internal debt are fundamentally equivalent.

THE ANALYTICAL FRAMEWORK

Initially I shall discuss public debt in what may be called its "classical" form. The existence of substantially full employment of resources is assumed. Secondly, I shall assume

31

32   *PUBLIC PRINCIPLES OF PUBLIC DEBT*

that the debt is to be created for real purposes, not to prevent or to promote inflation. The government desires to secure command over a larger share of economic resources in order to put such resources to use. This assumption suggests that debt instruments are purchased through a transfer of existing monetary units to the government. Thirdly, I shall assume that the public expenditure in question is of a reasonably limited size relative to both the total income and investment of the community, and, consequently, that the effects of the sale of government securities on the interest rate and the price structure are negligible. Fourthly, I shall assume that the funds used to purchase government securities are drawn wholly from private capital formation. I shall also assume that competitive conditions prevail throughout the economy. Finally, I shall make no specific assumption concerning the purpose of the expenditure financed. I shall show that this purpose is not relevant to the problem at this stage of the analysis.

These assumptions may appear at first glance to be unduly severe. They will, of course, be relaxed at later stages in the argument, but it is perhaps worthwhile to point out that these assumptions are largely applicable to the debt problem as it has been, and is being, faced in the 1950's. They apply, by and large, to the highway financing proposals advanced by the Clay Committee in early 1955. They apply, even more fully, to the debt problems facing state and local units of government, which alone borrowed more than five and one-half billions of dollars in 1956.

By contrast, the assumptions do not accurately reflect the conditions under which the greater part of currently outstanding public debt has been created. This qualification may appear to reduce somewhat the generality of the conclusions reached. Such is, however, not the case. The initial restriction of the analysis to public debt in the "classical" form allows the characteristic features of real debt to be examined; other forms of public debt are less "pure," and it is appropriate that they be introduced only at a second stage of analysis. When this is done in later chapters, the conclusions reached from the initial analysis will be found generally applicable, and the apparently contradictory conclusions stemming from the new orthodoxy will be explained on the basis of the methodological confusion discussed in Chapter 3.

The first of the three basic propositions will now be examined in the light of the specific assumptions stated above.

THE SHIFTING OF THE BURDEN
TO FUTURE GENERATIONS

Before we can proceed to discuss the question of the possible shifting of the debt burden, we must first define "future generations." I shall define a "future generation" as any set of individuals living in any time period following that in which the debt is created. The actual length of the time periods may be arbitrarily designated, and the analysis may be conducted in terms of weeks, months, years, decades or centuries. The length of the period *per se* is not relevant. If we choose an ordinary accounting period of one year and if we further call the year in which the borrowing operation takes place, t_0, then individuals living in any one of the years, t_1, t_2, t_3, . . . t_n, are defined as living in future "generations." An individual living in the year, t_0, will normally be living in the year, t_1, but he is a different individual in the two time periods, and, for our purposes, he may be con-

34   *PUBLIC PRINCIPLES OF PUBLIC DEBT*

sidered as such. In other words, I shall not be concerned
as to whether a public debt burden is transferred to our children or grandchildren as such. I shall be concerned with
whether or not the debt burden can be postponed. The real
question involves the possible shiftability or nonshiftability of the debt burden in time, not among "future generations" in the literal sense. Since, however, the "future generation" terminology has been used widely in the various discussions of the subject, I shall continue to employ it, although the particular definition here given should be kept
in mind.

What, specifically, do the advocates of the new approach
mean when they suggest that none of the primary real burden
of the public debt can be shifted to future generations? Perhaps the best clue is provided in a statement from Brownlee
and Allen: "The public project is *paid for* while it is being
constructed in the sense that other alternative uses for these
resources must be sacrificed during this period."[1] (Italics
mine.) The resources which are to be employed by the
government must be withdrawn from private employments
during the period, t_0, not during any subsequent period.

This last statement is obviously true, but the error lies in a
misunderstanding of precisely what is implied. The mere
shifting of resources from private to public employment does
not carry with it any implication of sacrifice or payment. If
the shift takes place through the voluntary actions of private
people, it is meaningless to speak of any sacrifice having
taken place. An elemental recognition of the mutuality of
advantage from trade is sufficient to show this. If an indi-

---

[1] O. H. Brownlee and E. D. Allen, *Economics of Public Finance* (2d ed.;
New York, 1954), p. 126. Also, see, Henry C. Murphy, *The National Debt in
War and Transition* (New York, 1950), p. 60.

vidual freely chooses to purchase a government bond, he is, presumably, moving to a preferred position on his utility surface by so doing. He has improved, not worsened, his lot by the transaction. This must be true for each bond purchaser, the only individual who actually gives up a current command over economic resources. Other individuals in the economy are presumably unaffected, leaving aside for the moment the effects of the public spending. Therefore, it is impossible to add up a series of zeroes and/or positive values and arrive at a negative total. The economy, considered as the sum of the individual economic units within it, undergoes no *sacrifice* or *burden* when debt is created.

This simple point has surely been obvious to everyone. If so, in what sense has the idea of burden been normally employed? The answer might run as follows: To be sure no single individual undergoes any sacrifice of utility in the public borrowing process because he subscribes to a voluntary loan. But in terms of the whole economy, that is, in a macro-economic model, the resources are withdrawn from private employment in the period of debt creation, not at some subsequent time. Therefore, if this sort of model is to be used, the economy must be treated as a unit, and we may speak of a *sacrifice* of resources during the initial time period. In the macro-economic model we are not concerned with individual utilities, but with macro-economic variables.

It is perhaps not surprising to find this essentially organic conception of the economy or the state incorporated in the debt theory of Adolf Wagner,[2] but it is rather strange that it could have found its way so readily into the fiscal theory of those countries presumably embodying democratic gov-

---

[2] *Finanzwissenschaft* (Leipzig, 1877), Vol. I, p. 122.

36   *PUBLIC PRINCIPLES OF PUBLIC DEBT*

ernmental institutions and whose social philosophy lies in
the individualistic and utilitarian tradition. The explanation
arises, of course, out of the almost complete absence of political sophistication on the part of those scholars who have
been concerned with fiscal problems. With rare exceptions,
no attention at all has been given to the political structure
and to the possibility of inconsistency between the policy
implications of fiscal analysis and the political forms
existent. Thus we find that, in explicit works of political
theory, English-language scholars have consistently eschewed
the image of the monolithic and organic state. At the same
time, however, scholars working in fiscal analysis have developed constructions which become meaningful only upon
some acceptance of an organic conception of the social
group.[8]

In an individualistic society which governs itself through
the use of democratic political forms, the idea of the
"group" or the "whole" as a sentient being is contrary to
the fundamental principle of social organization. The individual or the family is, and must be, the basic philosophical entity in this society. This being true, it is misleading to
speak of group sacrifice or burden or payment or benefit unless such aggregates can be broken down into component
parts which may be conceptually or actually imputed to
the individual or family units in the group. This elemental
and necessary step cannot be taken with respect to the primary real burden of the public debt. The fact that economic
resources are given up when the public expenditure is made

---

[8] For a further discussion of this point, see my "The Pure Theory of
Government Finance: A Suggested Approach," *Journal of Political Economy*,
LVII, (1949), 496–505.

does not, in any way, demonstrate the existence of a *sacrifice* or *burden* on individual members of the social group.

The error which is made in attributing a *sacrifice* to the individual who purchases a security, be it publicly or privately issued, has time-honored status. One of its sources, for there must be several, may lie in the classical doctrine of pain cost. Nassau Senior is generally credited with having popularized, among economists, the notion of abstinence. This concept was introduced in order to provide some philosophical explanation and justification for profits or returns to capital investment. The individual, in abstaining from consuming current income, undergoes the pain of abstinence which is comparable to that suffered by the laborer. Abstinence makes the receipt of profits, in an ethical sense, equally legitimate with wages in the distributive system of the late classical economists.

Traces of this real or pain-cost doctrine are still with us, notably in certain treatments of international trade theory, but neoclassical economic theory has, by and large, replaced this doctrine with the opportunity cost concept. Here the works of Wicksteed and Knight generally and of Ohlin in particular must be noted. In the neoclassical view, resources command a price not due to any pain suffered by their owners, but because these resources are able to produce alternative goods and services. Resources may be used in more than one line of endeavor. A price, that is, a payment to the resource owner, is necessary in order to secure the resource service. Its magnitude is determined by the marginal productivity of the resource in alternative uses.

This shift of emphasis from the real cost to the opportunity cost conception has profound implications, some of which have not yet been fully understood. The real cost doctrine suggests, for example, that a man is paid because he works, while the opportunity cost doctrine reverses this and suggests that a man works because he is paid. The emphasis is placed on the individual choice or decision, and the gain or benefit side of individual exchange is incorporated into the theory of market price. The classical economists did not clearly view the distributive share as a price and the distribution of real income as a pricing problem.[4] Neoclassical theory does interpret the distributive share as a price, and the factor market is subjected to standard supply and demand analysis. The mutuality of gain from trade becomes as real in this market as in any other.

It becomes irrelevant whether the individual undergoes "pain" as measured by some arbitrary calculus when he works. If he works voluntarily, he is revealing that his work, when coupled with its reward, enables him to move to a preferred position. The individual is in no sense considered to be *paying for* the output which he cooperates in producing, merely because his productive services enter into its production. I am not, in my capacity as a member of the faculty of the University of Virginia, *paying for* the education of young men merely because my time is spent in classroom instruction, time which I could spend alternatively in other productive pursuits. Clearly the only meaningful *paying for* is done by those parents, donors, and taxpayers, who purchase my services as a teacher. What I am paying for when I teach is the income which I earn and by means of this the

---

[4] For the best discussion of all these points see F. H. Knight, "The Ricardian Theory of Production and Distribution," *Canadian Journal of Economics and Political Science*, 1935. Reprinted in F. H. Knight, *On the History and Method of Economics* (Chicago, 1956), pp. 37–88.

real goods and services which I subsequently purchase. Only if a part of my income so earned is devoted to expenditure for education can I be considered to be *paying for* education.

All of this is only too obvious when carefully considered. It is a very elementary discussion of the wheel of income which every sophomore in economics learns, or should learn, on the first day of class. If *sacrifice* or *payment* is to be used to refer both to the producer and the final consumer of goods and services, we are double counting in the grossest of ways; we are *paying* double for each unit of real income. We are denying the existence of the circular flow of real income in an organized market economy.

It is not difficult to see, however, that this error is precisely equivalent to that committed by those who claim that the real payment or sacrifice of resources must be made by those living in the period of public debt creation. The purchaser of a government security does not *sacrifice* resources *for* the public project; that is, he does not *pay for* the project any more than I pay for the education of young men in Virginia. He *pays for* real income in some future time period; he exchanges current command over resources for future command over resources. No payment or sacrifice is involved in any direct sense. The public project is *purchased,* and *paid for,* by those individuals who will be forced to give up resources *in the future* just as those who give up resources to pay my salary at the University of Virginia pay for education. It is not the bond purchaser who sacrifices any real economic resources anywhere in the process. He makes a presumably favorable exchange by shifting the time shape of his income stream. This is not one bit different from the ordinary individual who presumably makes favor-

40   *PUBLIC PRINCIPLES OF PUBLIC DEBT*

able exchanges by shifting the structure of his real asset pattern within a single unit of time.

All of this may be made quite clear by asking the simple question: Who suffers if the public borrowing is unwise and the public expenditure wasteful? Surely if we can isolate the group who will be worse off in this case we shall have located the bearers of the primary real burden of the debt. But clearly the bondholder as such is not concerned as to the use of his funds once he has received the bond in exchange. He is guaranteed his income in the future, assuming of course that the government will not default on its obligations or impose differentially high taxes upon him through currency inflation. The taxpayer in period t_0 does not sacrifice anything since he has paid no tax for the wasteful project. The burden must rest, therefore, on the taxpayer in future time periods and on no one else. He now must reduce his real income to transfer funds to the bondholder, and he has no productive asset in the form of a public project to offset his genuine *sacrifice*. Thus, the taxpayer in future time periods, that is, the future generation, bears the full primary real burden of the public debt. If the debt is created for productive public expenditure, the benefits to the future taxpayer must, of course, be compared with the burden so that, on balance, he may suffer a net benefit or a net burden. But a normal procedure is to separate the two sides of the account and to oppose a burden against a benefit, and this future taxpayer is the only one to whom such a burden may be attributed.

Widespread intellectual errors are hard to trace to their source. We have indicated that the pain cost doctrine may have been responsible for some of the confusion which has surrounded public debt theory. But there are other possible, and perhaps more likely, sources for the future burden error. One of the most important of these is the careless use of national income accounting which has grown up in the new economics. Attention is focused on the national or community balance sheet rather than on individual or family balance sheets. In relation to debt theory, this creates confusion when future time periods are taken into account. There is no net change in the aggregative totals which make up the national balance sheet because the group includes both bondholders and taxpayers. The debits match the credits, so no net burden in the primary sense is possible. "Future generations" cannot be forced to *pay for* the resources which have already been used in past periods.

This simple sort of reasoning makes two errors. First, the effect on the national balance sheet is operationally irrelevant. As pointed out above, the nation or community is not a sentient being, and decisions are not made in any superindividual or organic way. Individuals and families are the entities whose balance sheets must be examined if the effects on social decisions are to be determined. The presumed canceling out on the national balance sheet is important if, *and only if*, this is accompanied by a canceling out among the individual and family balance sheets.

A moment's consideration will suggest that genuine canceling in the latter sense does not take place. The balance sheet of the bondholder will include an estimated present value for the bond, a value which is calculated on the certain expectation that the interest payments will be made and the bond amortized when due. These interest payments represent the "future" income which the bondholder or his forbears *paid for* by the *sacrifice* of resources in the initial period of debt creation. These payments are the *quo* part of his

42   *PUBLIC PRINCIPLES OF PUBLIC DEBT*

quid pro quo. They are presumably met out of tax revenues, and taxpayers give up command over the use of resources. This sacrifice of income has no direct *quid pro quo* implication; it is a sacrifice imposed compulsorily on the taxpayer by the decision makers living at some time in the past. To be sure, as pointed out above, if the public expenditure is "productive" and is rationally made, the taxpayer may be better off with the debt than without it. His share of the differential real income generated by the public project may exceed his share of the tax. But the productivity or unproductivity of the project is unimportant in itself. In either case, the taxpayer is the one who *pays*, who *sacrifices* real resources. He is the final "purchaser" of the public goods and services whether he is a party to the decision or not. His is the only sacrifice which is offset, if at all, by the income yielded by the public investment of resources made possible by the debt.

From this analysis it is easy to see that much of the recent discussion on the burden of transfer misses the point entirely. One senses as he reads the discussion, notably that of Ratchford, that underlying the argument for the existence of a transfer burden there is an implicit recognition that the primary real burden does fall on taxpayers of future generations.[5] But the transfer burden advocates were unable to escape the real sirens of the new orthodoxy, the national balance sheet and the false analogy. Their deep and correct conviction that all was not happy in the conceptual underpinnings of the newly rediscovered edifice properly led them

---

[5] Ratchford, *op. cit.*, Pt. IV. Abbott, in his work on debt management, appears also to recognize implicitly that the primary real burden of debt is borne by taxpayers of "future generations." He does not, however, discuss this aspect of the problem directly. See, Charles C. Abbott, *Management of the Federal Debt* (New York, 1946).

to re-examine the theory; but they accepted entirely too much before they started. They gave away their case, and their efforts resulted in little more than a slight modification of the theory. They did little more than to force a new emphasis on the secondary burden of making transfers.

The transfer burden analysis suffers the same methodological shortcomings as the more general approach of the new orthodoxy. If public debt issue is analyzed in terms of the whole set of relevant alternatives, in this case notably that of taxation, the burden associated with the making of an interest transfer cannot fail to be viewed as a primary one akin to that which is imposed through taxation. The failure to consider the position of the individual bondholder under each of the alternative situations led the "transfer burden" analysts to accept the fundamental premise of the new orthodoxy, that interest payments do, in a differential sense, represent a net "transfer" among individuals within the economy.

THE RICARDIAN APPROACH

We may now discuss the unique set of assumptions under which the primary real burden of the debt cannot be shifted forward in time. And surprisingly enough, this is not mentioned in the new orthodoxy at all. It is propounded by the classical economist, David Ricardo. Ricardo enunciated the proposition that the public loan and the extraordinary tax exert equivalent effects on the economy. His argument is as follows:

When, for the expenses of a year's war, twenty millions are raised by means of a loan, it is the twenty millions which are withdrawn from the productive capital of the nation. . . . Government might at

44   *PUBLIC PRINCIPLES OF PUBLIC DEBT*

once have required the twenty millions in the shape of taxes; in which case it would not have been necessary to raise annual taxes to the amount of a million. This, however, would not have changed the nature of the transaction. An individual instead of being called upon to pay 100£ per annum, might have been obliged to pay 2000£ once and for all.[6]

Under these Ricardian assumptions, the full burden of payment for the public project, whether it be a war or a royal ball, will be borne by the generation which lives at the time of the expenditure. But this is true only because Ricardo assumes that the creation of the debt, with its corresponding obligation to meet the service charges from future tax revenues, causes individuals to write down the present values of their future income streams. The tax reduces the individual's current assets directly; both the gross and net income streams over future time periods are reduced, these being equivalent in this case. The loan does not affect the gross income stream, but it does impose a differential between this and the net income stream. Capitalized values will be figured on the basis of income streams net of tax. Therefore, present values of assets will be immediately reduced by the present value of the tax obligations created by the future service charges. Present values will be identical in the two cases.

This Ricardian reasoning is correct within the framework of his assumptions. But it should be noted first that this is not at all the reasoning of the new orthodoxy. Ricardo places the primary burden of the public loan on the *tax-payer* not the bond purchaser. The primary burden is placed

---

[6] David Ricardo, "Principles of Political Economy and Taxation," *Works and Correspondence,* Vol. I, (Cambridge, 1951), pp. 244–45.

on the taxpayer because he writes down the value of his capital assets in anticipation of his obligation to pay future taxes to service the debt.

This Ricardian proposition has been much discussed in the Italian works on fiscal theory. This Italian contribution will be treated in some detail in the Appendix to Chapter 8. It will be sufficient at this point to indicate in general terms the deficiencies in the Ricardian proposition. The major objection which has been raised to the proposition is that individuals do not fully discount future taxes. While full discounting may take place for those individuals who own income-earning assets, this reasoning cannot be extended to individuals who own no assets. For the individual owning capital, it is possible that he will write down the value of his assets and transmit them to his heirs at the reduced value. In this case the burden of the tax required to service the debt can be said to be borne entirely by the individual in the initial period. The necessity of transferring income to bondholders will not reduce the present value of expected utilities for future taxpayers because this would have already been discounted for in the past.

For the individual who owns no capital assets, however, this analysis cannot fully apply. Since slavery is not an acceptable institution in the modern world, individuals are not treated as capital assets and traded in accordance with capitalized values. The individual human being as either a capital asset or a liability disappears at death, and his heirs inherit directly neither his asset characteristics nor his liabilities. For this reason, the individual who owns no capital assets will not fully capitalize the future tax burden involved in the interest charges. He will capitalize them, if at all, only within the limits imposed by his effective planning

46   *PUBLIC PRINCIPLES OF PUBLIC DEBT*

horizon, that is, only to the degree which he, individually, conceives that he will be a future taxpayer. And, since human life is short, much of the debt burden must remain uncapitalized. Therefore, even granting all of the other Ricardian assumptions, which are extremely restrictive, the burden must rest on "future generations," at least to some degree.

Insofar as other individuals who do own capital assets do not plan to submit these intact to their heirs, that is, insofar as family relationships do not make individuals act as if they will live forever, the Ricardian proposition is further weakened. And when the possibility of individual irrationality in discounting future tax payments is introduced, as Ricardo himself recognized, the location of the debt burden on future taxpayers is even more clear.

It must be concluded, therefore, that this Ricardian analysis, as amended, introduces only a slight modification of the conclusions earlier attained. The primary real burden of a public debt is borne by members of the current generation only insofar as they correctly anticipate their own or their heirs' roles as future taxpayers, and take action to discount future tax payments into reductions of present capital values. Insofar as the time horizons of individuals are not infinite, that is, insofar as future individuals are considered to be separated conceptually from present individuals, there must be some shifting of the primary real burden to future generations.

CONCLUSIONS

It has been shown in this chapter that the primary real burden of a public debt does rest largely with future generations, and that the creation of debt does involve the shifting of the burden to individuals living in time periods subsequent to that of debt issue. This conclusion is diametrically opposed to the fundamental principle of the new orthodoxy which states that such a shifting or location of the primary real burden is impossible. We have examined the reasons for the widespread acceptance of the nonshiftability argument. We have isolated at least some of the roots of the fallacy. Among these are the pain-cost doctrine and the use of national rather than individual balance sheets.

The primary real burden of the debt in the only sense in which this concept can be meaningful must rest with future generations at least in large part. These are the individuals who suffer the consequences of wasteful government expenditure and who reap the benefits of useful government expenditure. All other parties to the debt transactions are acting in accordance with ordinary economic motivations.

APPENDIX

❦

A Suggested Conceptual Revaluation of the National Debt

I. INTRODUCTION

THIS Appendix represents an attempt to apply the theory of public debt contained in the earlier chapters to the general problem of measuring the magnitude or size of the national debt. It is an exploratory effort designed to raise and to isolate the relevant issues rather than to resolve all of the complexities which may appear. With this quite limited objective in view, I have not tried to provide definitive solutions to the measurement problem. Insofar as the argument requires, I have used actual data on the national debt for illustrative purposes. But I should emphasize the illustrative usage as opposed to any presumed factual presentation or rearrangement of data.

II. THE GENERAL MEASUREMENT PROBLEM
AS APPLIED TO PRIVATE DEBT

Public debt has traditionally been measured in terms of the principal or maturity value, that is, the amount which

196

must be repaid at the maturity date, and, except for securities issued at a discount, the amount of funds transferred to the government when the debt is created.[1] This apparently simple measurement has its origin in the treatment of private debt. Since the principal represents the payment necessary to discharge fully the obligation of the debt, it seems appropriate that this be used in measuring debt size. The implications of this measurement procedure do not seem to have been thoroughly examined.

Let us initially suppose that a riskless private loan is contracted and that the structure of interest rates remains stable through time. The interest rate paid on this loan will be a "pure" rate unalloyed by any risk premium. Competition will insure that this rate approximates that paid on other riskless loans in the economy. Under these circumstances there can be no question but that the size of the debt is best shown by the maturity value. This indicates the value of an alternative capital asset of identical risk characteristics which would be required to provide a yield sufficient to cover fully the debt obligation. In a slightly different sense, the maturity value also represents the capitalized value of the future payments stream if this stream is capitalized at the pure rate of yield on investment. In this particular example, the stream of payments is capitalized at the internal rate, obviously yielding the maturity value as a capitalized sum.

Let us now introduce a second model in which a private loan of some riskiness is contracted. We shall continue to assume that the structure of interest rates remains stable

---

[1] All of the national debt of the United States is measured in this way except for Savings Bonds which are carried in the debt totals at current redemption values. For these securities the additional debt which accrues through time shows up also as expenditure, presumably in the interest item of the budget.

198   *PUBLIC PRINCIPLES OF PUBLIC DEBT*

over time. In this case, the interest rate paid must include some risk premium; it must exceed that paid on the no-risk investment. The maturity value of the debt will not be equal to the capitalized value of the stream of payments, capitalized at the pure rate of yield. For example, suppose that we are considering a loan of $100 (which we may convert to a loan in perpetuity by the assumption of refunding at the same rate) at an interest rate of 10 per cent while the pure rate of yield is 5 per cent. The capitalization of a $10-payments stream in perpetuity yields a total value of $200. The debt claim will, however, be worth only $100 in the market. In order words, $100 will be sufficient to purchase an asset of equivalent risk characteristics. The $100 purchase will not, of course, provide a certain yield which will guarantee that the initial debt can be fully serviced. If the borrower desires a perfect hedge against the debt, he must purchase that asset which will yield the $10 with certainty. This asset will command a market price of $200. But this $200 asset will more than remove the debt obligation represented by the original loan. It will also remove from either borrower or lender the risk which the lender assumed in the original transaction. The purchase of the $100 asset is sufficient to place both borrower and lender in a position identical to that which they enjoyed prior to the debt transaction.

The measure of the size of private debt in terms of maturity values is less appropriate when the assumption of stability in the structure of interest rates is dropped. If the pure rate of yield on private investment changes subsequent to the contraction of a private loan, the capitalization process suggested above will yield a different value for debt than the principal or maturity value. And, for many purposes, this capital value is more useful in indicating the real weight of the debt.

Suppose, to return to our first model, that a riskless loan of $100 is contracted at the pure rate of 5 per cent. Subsequently, the rate of yield on marginal investments in the economy falls to 4 per cent. The capitalization process now yields $125 as a measure of the debt rather than $100. This indicates that the full discharge of the debt obligation is now equivalent to the sacrifice of an alternative earning asset commanding a price of $125. The larger figure is obviously more appropriate as a measure if the debt instrument is marketable; but, when considered correctly, it is equally appropriate when debt instruments are not marketable.

III. MEASURING LOCAL GOVERNMENT DEBT

The maturity value measure is applicable only in a more restricted sense to local government debt. Initially, let us assume once again that the structure of interest rates does not change over time. In this case, as with private debt, the maturity value of the debt will represent the market value of resources which must be sacrificed in order to finance the purchase of a capital asset of characteristics identical to the debt obligation. But the special feature of local government debt is that income from local government securities is tax exempt. This means that such securities may be marketed at a rate which is lower than the pure rate of yield on marginal investment in the private sector. The effects of this feature on the measurement problem must be examined.

Again it will be helpful to consider a simplified numerical example. Suppose that some local government issues a bond for $100 at a rate of 3 per cent while the pure rate of yield on private investment is 4 per cent. Again we shall assume that the maturing issues are continually refunded, allowing the fixed maturity security to be converted conceptually into a security of no maturity date. The $3.00 annual interest payment discounts to a value of only $75 when this payments stream is capitalized at the pure yield rate. But the market will operate so as to insure that an equivalent asset commands a market price of $100. The local unit of government may, if it desires, purchase a no-risk asset for $75 which will yield an income sufficient to service the debt. This suggests that the $75 provides a more useful measure for the size of the debt than the $100 maturity value or, in the case of the no-maturity security, the principal.

Actually, however, both the $75 and the $100 measure must be used. It is true that a tax payment of only $75 would be required to offset the debt. But the discharge of the debt will also eliminate from the economy a tax exemption which has a capital value of $25 under our assumptions. Therefore, the market value of resources which must be given up, in present or future periods, by individuals in order to discharge fully the obligation represented by the debt is $100. The maturity value measure is the more useful one when the problem is considered in this light. However, when it is recognized that the local taxpaying group may be quite different from the bond purchasing group, the measure becomes less useful. The bonds issued by single local units of government are normally marketed nationally. The advantages of the tax exemption feature are secured by federal taxpayers scattered throughout the economy. The capital value of the tax exemption is held, not by local taxpayers of the borrowing jurisdiction, but by bond purchasers from the entire nation. Therefore, it is not proper to attribute to local taxpayers the supplementary capital value of the tax exemption.

The $75 figure more correctly measures the size of local government debt when the single local unit of government is considered in isolation.[2]

On the other hand, when aggregate local debt is considered, the use of maturity values seems necessary. Those individuals holding the bonds of any one jurisdiction must be taxpayers in some local unit, and, therefore, the capital value of the tax exemption must be added in when all local debts are taken into account.

Just as in the case of private debt, when the assumption of stability in the interest rate structure is dropped, the use of principal to measure debt size is not acceptable, even in the

---

[2] This is not the place to introduce an extended discussion of local government financing. But the above example does illustrate quite clearly how a local unit of government may (if its charter allows) finance expenditures without imposing any cost upon its own taxpayers, either present or future. Let us suppose that a local unit decides to construct a school building at a cost of $1 million. To finance this building, it issues bonds totaling $4 million at 3 per cent. It then devotes $1 million of the proceeds to the actual construction of the school. With the remaining $3 million it enters the private securities market and purchases assets which provide a pure yield of 4 per cent. These assets provide a sufficient income to enable the service charges on the local government debt to be fully offset. Local taxpayers are freed from any burden of payment when the school building is constructed, and they are not obligated to pay taxes to service the local debt. The cost of the project is shifted to federal government taxpayers in general and local citizens pay only in their capacities as federal taxpayers.

In such a situation, the local government is merely taking advantage of an opportunity to make a profit through arbitrage. The differential between the rate of yield on municipals and on private bonds is, of course, exaggerated in the example. But so long as any differential at all exists, the operation outlined here is possible.

Local units of government are normally prevented by charter from investing in private securities. They may be allowed, however, to invest in federal government securities. And here, too, if a differential in rate should be present, local taxpayers can be relieved of a large portion of their normal public expenditure burden through a similar operation.

The implication of this appears to be that, if federal income tax rates should remain high, the stiffening of debt limit laws restricting local government borrowing or the removal of all investing opportunities may prove desirable.

202   *PUBLIC PRINCIPLES OF PUBLIC DEBT*

measurement of aggregate local government debt. If interest
rates increase after the sale of local securities, the borrowing
jurisdiction may, if it chooses, repurchase its own securities
for a price below that indicated by the principal of the loan.
The size of the aggregate local government debt at any
moment in time seems to be best measured by the amount of
current tax collections which would be required to finance
the purchase of an earning asset which will yield an income
sufficient to service all outstanding debt plus the capital value
of the tax exemption feature. To return to the numerical example, let us suppose that the pure rate of yield on marginal
investment increases from 4 per cent to 5 per cent subsequent to the debt issue. The capitalization process yields a
sum of $60 instead of $75 as the amount of taxes required to
purchase an earning asset yielding a sum sufficient to service
the debt. If the local unit is considered in isolation, this
becomes the measure of the debt. If, on the other hand, the
aggregate local debt is to be measured, the capital value of
the tax exemption feature must also be calculated. The
differential yield of $1.00 capitalized at 5 per cent rather
than 4 per cent gives a total capital value of $20 rather than
$25. When aggregate local debt is measured, the appropriate
magnitude now becomes $80 instead of $100.

IV. THE NATIONAL DEBT

The two preceding sections have shown that the normally
accepted measurement procedures may not provide meaningful totals for private debt and for local government debt
under certain conditions. The use of principal or maturity
value to measure the magnitude of the debt obligation is

even less applicable for the national debt. The fundamental reason for the difference lies, of course, in the possession of money-creating powers by the central or national government. As earlier chapters have shown, the existence of this power, along with that of pure debt creation, has led to some confusion. In the discussion which follows I shall propose an alternative way of evaluating the debt, at least conceptually, which should be of some assistance in clarifying the distinction between real or pure debt and monetized debt.

How large is the national debt? As of July 31, 1957, official records indicate that the national debt of the United States amounted to $272.5 billion. What does this figure tell us? This is somewhat more difficult to answer. It may provide some information concerning the amount of purchasing power which was transferred to government at some time in the past by individuals and institutions. There is, however, no way of knowing whether or not this purchasing power was actually transferred *away* from the private economy. All, none, or any portion of this purchasing power may have been *created* in the process of debt issue. The $272.5 billion figure tells us nothing about the real debt which was created, nor does it tell us anything about the amount of real resources which must currently be given up if we choose to discharge fully the debt obligation.

The confusion generated by the use of this measure may be readily illustrated by frequently encountered popular statements which claim that each man, woman, and child in the United States owes a national debt of some $1,600. This is computed by dividing the debt total of $272 billion by some current estimate for population. From this the inference is often drawn, implicitly or explicitly, that the full discharge of the debt obligation would require that additional current taxes in the amount of $1,600 be levied on each individual (on the average).

If we neglect for the time being the fact that interest rates have risen sharply since the issue of large portions of the national debt, the inference would seem valid in terms of the analogy with private debt. When the adjustment to present market values is made (an adjustment which applies equally to private and public debt), such a per capita computation should indicate the market value of real resources which each individual would have to sacrifice to discharge fully his per capita share of the national debt obligation.

It is obvious, however, that the inference is almost wholly incorrect when applied to national debt. Here the analogy between public and private debt appears to be false. The explanation is not difficult to find. A large part of the national debt does not represent pure debt at all. This part is essentially "money" both when issued and as held by individuals and institutions. This being the case, full tax financing of debt retirement would act to destroy "money" in the system, thereby generating serious destabilizing effects. The analogy breaks down here only because of this mixture of pure debt and "money" in what we normally refer to as national debt. As the analysis of this book has demonstrated, the analogy fully holds when pure or real debt is considered. Quite obviously money is not debt.

Any meaningful measure of the national debt should reflect the same information as that which is provided by the accepted measure of private debt. That is, this measure should indicate the capital value of resources which must be given up or sacrificed in order to discharge fully the debt obligation. It should indicate the total tax collection, in real terms, which is required to retire all national debt without, at the same time, exerting significant over-all effects on the absolute price level. In other words, the conceptual retirement operation should be neutral in its effects on the level of economic activity. If the use of maturity values as adjusted to take account of changes in interest rates fails this test, how may such a meaningful measure be constructed?

The solution is to be found in the capitalization process discussed above for private debt and local government debt. If the interest payments stream is capitalized at a rate indicating the pure rate of yield on marginal investments in the private sector, the resultant capital value will provide an accurate measure of the national debt in some meaningful sense. This approach was shown to be faulty in application to private debt and to local government debt in the aggregative sense. The capital value, calculated in this manner, was shown to diverge from the principal of the debt in the one case because of the failure to include a differential risk premium and in the other because of its omission of a differential tax exemption feature. But the market appropriately places some values, negative or positive, on these features. And the private individual is forced to abide by market evaluations in purchasing equivalent assets or in re-purchasing debt instruments.

In the case of the national debt, however, the measure yielded by the capitalization process suggested is much more useful. Quite clearly, as Section V will demonstrate, the current interest charges capitalized at an estimated rate for the net or pure yield on capital investment will provide a figure far below either the maturity value of the national debt or for this latter value adjusted downward for the recent increases in the level of interest rates. It is equally clear that this difference is primarily due to the fact that the national debt instruments possess many characteristics of money. This being true, the adjusted maturity value does not reflect the value of real resources which would have to be given up to discharge the debt.

Money may be issued at zero cost. Therefore, that portion of the national debt which does represent "money" in its relevance to human behavior can be replaced with actual money, currency, without private people being forced to sacrifice real goods and services. The share of total debt, as measured, which represents genuine or pure debt can best be determined from the capitalization process suggested.

In the following section I shall attempt to apply this proposed measurement process to the national debt of the United States.

V. HOW LARGE IS THE NATIONAL DEBT?

As of July 31, 1957, the national debt, as measured, amounted to $272.5 billion. This may be called, for our purposes, the principal or the maturity value measure. Since interest rates have risen since much of the debt has been issued, the first step in any evaluation is that of adjusting this value downward to reflect the reduction in capital value which has taken place. The government debt may be conceptually repurchased for less than the principal sum outstanding.

An extremely rough calculation suggests that the adjusted market value of national debt as of July 31, 1957, was $257 billion.[3] This figure represents the cash outlay which

---

[3] The calculation is direct for marketable securities. The government could repurchase these below par. For nonmarketable issues, this sort of repurchase

will enable the government conceptually to repurchase all
outstanding debt, either directly through established markets
or indirectly through "hedging" sale and repurchase of additional debt sufficient to offset nonmarketable issues.[4]

There are two means through which the necessary cash outlay of $257 billion may be secured. Money may be printed
directly, or taxes may be levied. The $257 billion figure
tells us nothing concerning the breakdown between these two
sources. To secure such a breakdown, the capitalization process suggested above must be introduced.

The annual interest charge on the national debt as of
July, 1957, is estimated at $7.4 billion. This amounts to 2.7
per cent of the maturity value of $272.5 billion, and almost
2.9 per cent of the adjusted market value of $257 billion.
Quite clearly neither of these represents an appropriate

---

alternative is not open, but the government may, conceptually, convert this
nonmarketable debt to marketable debt by selling marketable securities at
current prices sufficient to offset fully the service and the amortization of the
nonmarketable issues. To estimate the appropriate capital value of the marketable securities which would have to be sold in such an operation, some present
market value must be applied to the nonmarketable securities. In the calculation here I have used the same market-to-maturity value ratio as that found
to apply for the whole of the marketable debt. I have applied this ratio to
all nonmarketable securities, including securities held by governmental trust
funds, except Savings Bonds which are already carried in debt totals at current redemption values.

All data employed in making this calculation were taken from *Treasury
Bulletin* for September, 1957.

[4] It is important to emphasize the conceptual nature of this repurchase
operation. If the government *actually* attempts to repurchase its own securities, prices will be driven up and current market values will provide no
measure of the actual money cost of retiring all debt. It does not seem appropriate, however, to include this adjustment in the calculations made. The
aim is that of deriving some measure which will be useful in indicating the
weight of carrying the debt, a measure which is in capital-value dimensions.
Whether or not an actual repurchase operation would exert significant effects
on bond prices will depend on the source of the funds and also upon the
degree of substitution between government bonds and private bonds. See Footnote 6 for further discussion.

208 *PUBLIC PRINCIPLES OF PUBLIC DEBT*

capitalization rate in the 1950's. This rate should be representative of the pure rate of yield on capital investment at the margin of use. Without making any detailed attempt to determine this rate accurately, I shall make the assumption that this rate is 4 per cent.[5] If the $7.4 billion (assumed to be the value of the interest payments stream in perpetuity) is capitalized at a 4 per cent rate, we get a capital value of $185 billion, not $257 billion. This figure comes much closer to providing a measure of national debt in some "pure" sense. By the current sacrifice of $185 billion in privately owned earning assets or in consumption goods, the national debt can be fully retired, provided we can neglect the possible secondary effects of the retirement process itself on the structure of interest rates.[6] A more direct statement can be made in a slightly different manner. The net yield from $185 billion of earning assets in the private economy is obligated to the service of the national debt.

The remaining $72 billion represent that portion of the national debt which is, for the most part, "money" in its relevance to human behavior.[7] This suggests that, secondary

---

[5] This is based on the average yield for July, 1957, on Moody's Aaa Corporation Bonds.

[6] These secondary effects may be easily exaggerated. The conceptual refunding operation proposed would change interest rates only insofar as the tax imposed to finance the pure debt retirement reduces consumption spending more than the retirement itself increases consumption spending. Since some effect in this direction seems probable, the whole operation will tend to reduce interest rates and to increase the capitalized value of real debt. This complication may be avoided by assuming that the capitalization rate used is some average of the initial pure rate of yield and that rate which would prevail after the conceptual refunding. The difference between these two rates would depend on the size of the debt and on the elasticity of demand for private investment funds.

[7] This differential may, in part, represent other features. For example, if "patriotism" should cause individuals to accept a lower rate on public than on private loans, the capital value of this feature would be included in the $72 billion. This, and other "nonmoneyness" features, might create some dif-

effects aside, the national debt could be wiped off the books with a capital levy of $185 billion and a direct currency creation of $72 billion. The additional currency would be needed to offset the deflationary impact of the debt retirement, and to keep the whole operation "neutral" in its stabilization effects. Having removed the debt instruments, possessing much "moneyness," there would have to be more nominal units of money introduced in order to prevent serious deflationary consequences. But this additional money needed may be created without cost, and, therefore, it should not be included in any estimate of "pure" debt.

It is to be emphasized that I am proposing a conceptual revaluation of the debt, not any actual attempt at retirement. Specifically, what is suggested is that the manner of measuring the debt be modified and that an additional and supplementary evaluation be made. The total process of debt measurement should look as follows:

NATIONAL DEBT AS OF JULY, 1957

Billions of Dollars

1. National debt, maturity value...................$272
2. National debt, present market value............. 257
3. National debt, "pure"...........$185
   National debt, "monetized"...... 72
   ————
   $257

This account would be useful in many respects. First of all, it would indicate more accurately the real burden of debt which is being shifted forward to future generations of taxpayers. This is the $185 billion, not the $257 or the

---

ficulties if the conceptual refunding discussed were to be actually attempted since these features could not be replaced by currency. Their introduction does not, however, change the appropriateness of measuring real or pure debt by the $185 billion. In the text, we assume that the differential is represented by "moneyness" alone.

210   *PUBLIC PRINCIPLES OF PUBLIC DEBT*

$275 billion. The burden of the $72 billion, if it existed, was not a burden of pure debt *but of inflation,* and, as such, *has already been shouldered.* Future generations will be little affected by this portion of the nominal debt. Similar conclusions follow for the $18 billion difference between the maturity value and the present market value. This no longer exists as a debt obligation; this portion has been "retired" through the levy of a "tax" on the holders of government securities.

VI. TREASURY REFUNDING OPERATIONS

One of the most important uses of this supplementary account would be that of providing an accurate check on the effects of Treasury refunding operations. Suppose that the Treasury succeeds in refunding a portion of the debt at a lower rate of interest. This is accomplished, assuming that the general pattern of rates is not changing, by replacing debt instruments possessing less "moneyness" with debt instruments possessing more "moneyness." Let us assume that a particular operation of this sort reduces the annual interest charge from $7.4 to $7 billion. We shall continue to assume that the pure rate of yield is 4 per cent. This operation reduces the value of pure debt from $185 to $175 billion, while the value of the monetized debt is increased by $10 billion. In this way it becomes obvious that the refunding operation is equivalent to the retirement of pure debt. Future generations of taxpayers are relieved of an annual interest charge of $.4 billion, and individuals living currently are subjected to a possible burden of an additional $10 billion. In the full-employment setting, a refunding of this sort will be inflationary, and the $10 billion may be considered a tax on the holders of cash balances and government securities. The refunding will have shifted a real burden of debt from future taxpayers to these groups. If unemployment should be present, the inflationary consequences need not occur. And here the burden may be removed from future taxpayers without placing substantial real cost on individuals currently living. Under these conditions, this type of refunding is, of course, to be recommended.

The opposing case may now be considered. We assume that the Treasury succeeds in increasing the total interest charge on the debt. This is accomplished by replacing debt instruments possessing considerable "moneyness" with others which more closely resemble pure debt. Again for purposes of illustration, suppose that a particular operation increases the annual interest charge from $7.4 to $7.8 billion. This will increase the value of pure debt from $185 billion to $195 billion, assuming the same capitalization rate of 4 per cent. The operation is equivalent to the issue of $10 billion additional pure debt. The monetized debt is reduced by $10 billion.

This operation will be deflationary, at least relative to what would have taken place in its absence. But the deflation itself must relieve present taxpayers at the expense of future taxpayers in this case. The government secures no greater share of resources than before the refunding; but it agrees to pay more future income than before. Individuals, after the operation, hold more claims to future income. The net value of claims, to current income ("money") and to future income (pure debt) has not been modified. But claims to current income have been reduced and claims to future income increased. Those who give up the claims to current incomes in exchange for greater claims on future incomes are not

212 *PUBLIC PRINCIPLES OF PUBLIC DEBT*

harmed by the operation. They are purchasing pure debt instruments. On the other hand, those who are unaffected directly by the operation gain by the deflation imposed, assuming that we may neglect distributional consequences.

This analysis may be clarified somewhat by a more specific example. Suppose that Individual A holds, prior to the refunding, a security with a maturity value of $100 yielding only 3 per cent interest because of specific redemption features which allow this security to fill a near-money role in his portfolio. The Treasury offers him in exchange a $100 security which yields 4 per cent but which does not carry with it these "moneyness" features. The individual accepts the offer and the exchange is made. Clearly, future taxpayers are charged with the additional $1.00 of interest. Individual A will find it necessary to reduce his rate of spending on current real goods and services sufficiently to restore his liquidity position. He will find it necessary to withdraw approximately $25 from circulation. The goods and services so released will become available to the whole social group. Other individuals will be benefited by the refunding while Individual A will have undergone merely a transformation of his assets. In this simple model, the net effect on the current generation must be beneficial.

The conclusions reached on such a simple model must be modified if we introduce leverage effects stemming from fractional reserve banking. For example, if the refunding operation should take the form of retiring debt held by the central bank and replacing it with debt held by individuals, the reduction in liquidity occasioned by the retirement may be some multiple of the actual maturity value of the debt involved. In this case the refunding operation has the effect of removing "powerful" money from the system and replacing it with "weak" money. Whether or not this is desirable will depend on the stage of the cycle in which the refunding operation takes place. Refunding at higher yields is equivalent to borrowing solely to prevent inflation. This case was analyzed somewhat more fully in Chapter 11.

The analysis to this point has assumed that the level or pattern of interest rates does not change with any Treasury refunding. But clearly interest rates do change, and this must now be taken into account. Let us return to the first example in which the total interest charge is reduced from $7.4 to $7 billion. In saying that this operation reduces pure debt from $185 to $175 billion, the old rate of 4 per cent for the net yield on private investment was employed. But a refunding of this magnitude would tend to reduce the level of interest rates, and thus the appropriate capitalization rate. And if the annual interest payments stream is reduced, but at the same time the capitalization rate is reduced, will the amount of pure debt, as calculated in the manner proposed, necessarily be changed? It may readily be demonstrated that the amount of pure debt must also be reduced under these conditions, although by less than in the previous example. It is true that the operation may reduce both the interest payment and the appropriate rate of capitalization. But it is impossible for the Treasury operation alone to reduce the rate of capitalization, defined as the estimated net yield on zero-risk investment *in the whole economy*, proportionately with the interest payment. The interest charge is calculated for the national debt alone; the rate of capitalization is taken from the whole economy. The refunding operation must, therefore, effect an increase in monetized debt and a decrease in real debt.

Similar conclusions follow when the opposite sort of re-

214   *PUBLIC PRINCIPLES OF PUBLIC DEBT*

funding is considered. Here the general level of interest rates will tend to increase, and thus the appropriate discount rate. But this rate cannot increase proportionately with the interest charge. Pure debt must increase and monetized debt decrease.

The necessity for taking the change in the rate of capitalization into account along with the change in the payments stream need not make the conceptual revaluation much more difficult. Since the purpose is that of allowing us to define somewhat more specifically the effects of a refunding operation, the revaluation can be conducted in an *ex poste* sense, that is, after both the payments stream and the capitalization rate have maintained their newer levels.

VII. RELATION WITH SIMONS' PROPOSAL

Henry Simons, in his famous paper on debt policy,[8] suggested that all of the national debt should be refunded into consols or transformed into currency. The revaluation proposed here is a means of accomplishing the purpose desired by Simons without necessarily undertaking the drastic steps which he suggested. The revaluation proposal is based on an acceptance of the fact that the public debt instruments, as issued, will continue to fall anywhere along the spectrum between currency and consols, or more properly put, between currency and pure debt instruments.[9] The revaluation serves to separate these two aspects of the national debt. In a sense

---

[8] Henry Simons, "On Debt Policy," *Journal of Political Economy*, LII (December, 1944), 356–61; reprinted in *Economic Policy for a Free Society* (Chicago, 1948), pp. 222–30.

[9] Consols themselves, insofar as they possess some "moneyness," do not represent pure debt in the full sense of the term as here discussed. But since consols do approach pure debt instruments closely, we may, for present purposes, largely disregard the difference.

it represents a conceptual refunding along the lines which Simons suggested. By revaluing debt through the capitalization of the annual interest charge on the basis of the net yield on no-risk investment, we are essentially isolating that portion of the debt which can be refunded as consols, that form of debt as far removed from currency as is possible. The remainder (subtracting the first item from present market rather than maturity value) can be considered as being refunded into currency. This step alone will clarify discussion of the debt, and it would seem to be relatively less important whether or not an actual refunding along these lines takes place. The confusion which has been based on the fact that actual debt instruments possess features of both currency and pure debt would be substantially eliminated by reference to the account proposed.

[18]

Richard A. Musgrave

Classical theory of public debt

Before proceeding with the discussion of debt policy as a stabilization device, let us pause to examine what may be called the classical aspects of debt theory, that is, the use of debt policy to serve objectives of the Allocation and the Distribution Branches. This is *the* problem of debt policy in a system where no stabilization is required. In a more realistic setting, allocation and distribution objectives cannot be divorced from the stabilization function. Indeed, they may prove incompatible with the latter. We shall consider internal debt first, leaving external debt for later examination.

A. INTERNAL DEBT IN THE CLASSICAL SYSTEM

In the classical system all private income is spent on either consumption or investment. Full employment is secured automatically. Price-level stability is maintained if the money supply is held stable or is increased at the same rate at which real income grows. In this setting there is no need for compensatory finance. Loan finance is as effective as tax finance in reducing aggregate demand, and debt retirement is as effective as goods and service expenditures of government in expanding demand. What role, then, can be assigned to public debt policy in such a system?[1]

The choice between tax and loan finance remains important because it determines the way in which the resource withdrawal from the private sector will be divided between consumption and capital formation. Let us define the classical system as one in which saving is a function of dis-

---

[1] For a somewhat similar discussion see James M. Buchanan, *Public Principles of Public Debt*, Richard D. Irwin, Inc., Homewood, Ill., 1958. Buchanan's volume became available after compilation of this manuscript and is not dealt with here.

CLASSICAL THEORY OF PUBLIC DEBT   557

posable income as well as of interest.   If the savings schedule is wholly
inelastic to interest while the investment schedule is elastic, the entire
resource withdrawal under loan finance will be from private capital
formation.   Private savings will be absorbed in part by public borrowing.
Private investment will fall and the interest rate will rise, but saving and
hence consumption will remain unchanged.   Tax finance will result in a
withdrawal from both private capital formation and consumption,
depending on the taxpayers' marginal propensity to consume.[1]

If the savings schedule is interest-elastic while the investment schedule
is wholly inelastic, the entire resource withdrawal for loan finance will be
from private consumption.   The rate of interest will rise until saving
increases by the amount of public borrowing.   Tax finance must give the
same result since investment remains unchanged.   If both the saving and
investment schedules are interest elastic, the resource withdrawal will be
spread between consumption and capital formation for both types of
finance.   The more interest elastic saving is, and the less elastic investment is, the larger the share contributed by capital formation will be.
However, the share contributed by consumption will be larger in the case
of tax finance than in the case of loan finance.

The result depends, moreover, on the type of expenditures the government makes.   If the government spends for investment, resource withdrawal will be more from private capital formation, provided that
government investment enters into the same total investment schedule as
does private investment.   Government investment will then drive down
the rate of interest and lower saving.   However, government investment
may raise the share contributed by private investment, if the public
investment does not draw on the same investment outlets but raises the
efficiency of private investment.[2]

The choice between loan finance and tax finance thus involves a choice
between a resource withdrawal largely from private capital formation and
one largely from private consumption.   A fiscal policy designed to
accentuate growth relies on tax finance, while a policy designed to support present consumption relies on loan finance.   If regulation of the rate
of growth is considered a function of budget policy, such regulation is the

---

[1] For convenience we shall assume a lump-sum tax, so that substitution effects need
not be considered.

[2] The same general principles apply, but the details differ, for a primitive classical
system in which saving is a function of the rate of interest only.   If government
expenditures are for consumption, resource withdrawal through taxation must always
come out of private consumption.   Since the rate of interest is not changed by the
imposition of the tax, private saving remains unchanged, as does private investment.
The results for borrowing depend again on the elasticities of the investment and saving schedules: and as before, the results may differ if government expenditures are for
investment.

crucial consideration in the choice between loan and tax finance. However, this is not the case in the classical system. Here the rate of growth may be determined by consumer preference between present and future consumption, and by the return on capital that is obtained in the market.[1] The government's choice between loan and tax finance is to be made as a part of this process; the purpose is not to interfere with the market-determined rate of growth, but to align the choice between present and future satisfaction of social wants, with the choice between present and future satisfaction of private wants.

Our argument has been that the budget of the Allocation Branch should be balanced, since the opportunity cost of resource withdrawal must be allocated to the individuals whose wants are satisfied; but we have also noted that annual balance was not necessary, since the cost of durable goods or of lasting services should be allocated over their useful life.[2] We must now consider more carefully just when loan finance is called for in the budget of the Allocation Branch.

Pay-as-you-use Finance

Let us suppose that people want to provide for the satisfaction of certain social wants involving initial capital expenditures. The facilities may be durable consumer goods such as playgrounds, capital goods such as highways, or productivity-increasing services such as investment in education. In these cases, present expenditures will provide for future benefits. Where the initial outlay is large, taxpayers may not wish to assume the entire cost at once and may prefer to pay over the years as the services of the new facility are enjoyed. This reflects the same motivation underlying the purchase of a house on a mortgage or of an automobile on an installment basis. The option of pay-as-you-use finance increases the flexibility of consumer budgeting and adds to the efficiency of private finance. Precisely the same results occur in public finance. The question is only how the principle can be implemented at the public level.

Matters are simple enough if we assume that there is a continuous stream of capital outlays. In such a case, tax finance of new projects becomes equivalent to pay-as-you-use finance of old projects. This solution is not open if we consider the financing of a single and discontinuous project. Here we are confronted with the inevitable fact that provision of a durable facility requires the full resource input in the *initial* period. Resources must be withdrawn from other uses, thus giving rise to a current opportunity cost that the community must assume at once. There is no escape from this, whatever the sources of internal finance. The government's internal borrowing, unlike external borrowing, does not increase

[1] See p. 553.
[2] See p. 16.

CLASSICAL THEORY OF PUBLIC DEBT   559

the supply of resources available to the group as a whole.   It cannot obviate the need for releasing resources from other uses.

However, it makes a difference whether this release is from present consumption or from capital formation.   The immediate burden of a heavy public outlay in terms of current consumption is cushioned if the resources are withdrawn from private capital formation.   This is accomplished by the use of loan finance.   In a perfect system, with rational taxpayer behavior and a pure credit market, it will be equally advantageous for the government to use tax or loan finance.   If the taxpayer wishes to spread his burden, he may secure a tax or consumer loan and thus obtain command over resources that otherwise would have gone into capital formation.   The outcome will be similar to that of public loan finance, the only difference being that private rather than public debt is issued.   In the real world, where credit facilities are not available on equal terms to all taxpayers, this equality does not apply.   Public loan finance may then be thought of as a means of enabling individual taxpayers to secure tax credit at equal terms.   By placing payment on a pay-as-you-use basis, loan finance remains a significant instrument of policy, even though it does not increase the total availability of resources.[1]   By the nature of the pay-as-you-use principle public debt issued for such purposes should be repaid as the benefits from the initial expenditure are being exhausted. The principle is the same as for consumer credit on the private level.

Proceeding on this basis, we may draw up a budget statement that divides the budget accounts into a current and a capital part.[2]   This is illustrated in Table 23-1.   The current budget should be tax-financed. On the expenditure side, we include expenditures to provide goods and services, the benefits from which accrue currently.   Also we include an

[1] This fact seems to be overlooked by A. C. Pigou, *A Study in Public Finance*, 3d ed., Macmillan & Co., Ltd., London, 1951, p. 38, who argues that there can be no transfer of costs by internal borrowing because the resource use must occur at once. However, in his *Political Economy of War*, 2d ed., Macmillan & Co., Ltd., London, 1940, chap. 7, Pigou notes that in the case of war finance the future is burdened if the "real war fund" is drawn from capital formation.   This, precisely, is the central point of our argument.

[2] Out of a considerable literature on capital budgets, see Erik Lindahl, *Studies in the Theory of Money and Capital*, Rinehart & Company, Inc., New York, 1939, pp. 367–384; Gunnar Myrdal, "Fiscal Policy in the Business Cycle," *American Economic Review*, vol. 29, Supplement, no. 1, pp. 183–193, March, 1939; Benjamin Higgins and R. A. Musgrave, "Deficit Finance: The Case Examined," *Public Policy*, Harvard University Press, Cambridge, Mass., 1941, vol. II, pp. 193–203; *Budgetary Structure and Classification of Government Accounts*, United Nations, Department of Public Information, New York, 1951; J. R. Hicks, *The Problem of Budgetary Reform*, Oxford University Press, New York, 1948; J. A. Maxwell, "The Capital Budget," *Quarterly Journal of Economics,* vol. 57, pp. 450–465, 1942–1943; Richard Goode and Eugene A. Birnbaum, "Government Capital Budgets," *International Monetary Fund Staff Papers*, vol. 5, pp. 23–46, February, 1956.

allowance for the current use of benefits purchased in past periods. This includes amortization charges against government assets, as well as against private assets created by past public services. Moreover, we include interest on funds borrowed for this purpose, thus allowing for the cost of placing payment on a pay-as-you-use basis.

TABLE 23-1. BUDGET FOR PAY-AS-YOU-USE FINANCE
(In dollars)

Current budget			
Taxes	83	Expenditures for current benefits	75
Deficit	17	Interest	5
		Amortization	20
		Surplus	0
Total	100	Total	100

Capital budget			
Amortization	20	Expenditures for future benefits:	
Sale of assets	3	Resulting in acquisition of assets	18
Net borrowing	24	Not resulting in acquisition of assets	12
Net increase in provision for future		Net decrease in provision for future	
benefits	0	benefits	17
Total	47	Total	47

The capital budget is to be loan-financed. On the expenditure side we include the cost of providing for goods and services, the benefits from which will accrue in the future. These expenditures may result in the acquisition of assets by government, such as buildings or highways; or they may create private assets, such as educational training. Either outlay provides for future benefits and is included. On the revenue side of the capital budget, we record charges against the provision for future benefits. These include amortization charges as recorded in the current budget, the sale of assets held by government, and proceeds from the sale of government debt. The last two items both absorb funds that otherwise would have been channeled into private investment.

The state of balance in the budget, as recorded in Table 23-1, is not in accord with pay-as-you-use finance. Tax receipts in the current budget fall short of the provision for current benefits. This deficit in the current budget reappears as a net decrease in the provision for future benefits in the capital budget. Unless justified by certain other considerations, a deficit or surplus in the current budget is not compatible with efficient budgeting.[1]

[1] Notwithstanding this lack of balance in the provision for future benefits, note that total cash outgo, or payments to the public, equals total cash inflow (including proceeds from borrowing) from the public. This will hold if total payments are to remain unchanged, since we are dealing with a classical system.

CLASSICAL THEORY OF PUBLIC DEBT   561

Now it is important to note that the deficit in the current budget, or the decrease in the provision for future benefits in the capital budget, does *not* equal the change in the net worth of the government.   Using the same figures as before, a budget statement designed to equate deficit with reduction in the government's net worth would look as follows:

TABLE 23-2. BUDGET FOR NET-WORTH APPROACH
(In dollars)

Current budget			
Taxes	83	Expenditures resulting in acquisition	
Deficit	29	of assets	87
		Interest	5
		Amortization	20
Total	112	Total	112

Capital budget			
Amortization	20	Expenditures not resulting in acquisi-	
Sale of assets	3	tion of assets	18
Net borrowing	24	Decrease in net worth	29
Increase in net worth	0		
Total	47	Total	47

Table 23-2 differs from Table 23-1 in that expenditures which provide for future benefits without involving the acquisition of assets are now recorded in the current budget.   As a result, the balance shows the change in the government's net worth, defined as assets minus liabilities.[1]

This formulation of the capital budget implies the proposition that a sound budget policy is one that does not permit net worth to fall; and that changes in net worth are the significant factor in determining the proper state of budgetary balance.   This proposition is based on an analogy to the finances of the private firm, an analogy that is applicable only for the

[1] This seems to be the approach followed in the budget system recommended by the United Nations, *Budgetary Structure and Classification of Government Accounts*, p. 15, where capital expenditures are defined as the purchase of assets with a long life expectancy.   At the same time, the UN statement holds (p. 14) that "there is neither a conceptual nor an institutional link between the capital account and borrowing for purposes of asset acquisition."   If this is the case, there is no reason for separating the balance of the current budget from the balance for the total budget.   The determination of capital costs involved in particular expenditure projects and the administration of government assets may be accomplished without an over-all division of the budget into a current and a capital budget, and without singling out the state of balance in the current budget.   If the division *is* made, its usefulness must derive from the policy significance of the concept of surplus or deficit used in the current budget. This is the crucial point in interpreting any budget statement.   See my "The Nature of Budgetary Balance and the Case for the Capital Budget," *American Economic Review*, vol. 29, no. 2, pp. 260–271, June, 1939.

562   COMPENSATORY FINANCE

special case of public enterprises but not for the general type of budgetary activity.   In order to be solvent, a private corporation must have assets that will match its debt.   If assets increase, debt can be increased, but not otherwise.   Applying this reasoning to the government, one is tempted to conclude that borrowing in the capital budget is sound, while borrowing in the current budget is unsound.   This is a fallacy that overlooks the essentially different nature of government and business firms.

The purpose of business finance is to increase net worth, but this is not the case for government finance.   Assets held by the firm are the collateral against the firm's debt, but no such reasoning applies to government assets.   The solvency of government depends on the productive powers of the economy and on the taxable capacity that they comprise. Government-held assets have little, if anything, to do with the matter. While the net-worth approach might serve to sell businessmen on the idea of unbalanced budgets, this is a point in fiscal politics rather than economics.[1]

As far as the economics of the matter are concerned, focus on the acquisition of assets as a criterion of budget planning only serves to disturb the proper allocation of budgetary resources.   It encourages the cement-and-steel concept of economic development and reinforces the ancient prejudice in favor of expenditures on hardware as distinct from services, a prejudice dating back to the physiocrats and Adam Smith's misleading use of the terms *productive* and *unproductive*.   The resulting damage to budget planning is especially serious in underdeveloped economies, where basic services are of primary importance, but the damage is by no means limited to such places.   It is only too frequent, in United States municipal finances, that elaborate school structures can be built on debt issue, while no adequate funds for teachers' salaries can be secured, since tax finance is required.

Notwithstanding a superficial similarity between the pay-as-you-use approach and the net-worth approach, the underlying philosophies are totally different.   The former approach presents a legitimate, if somewhat subtle, argument for loan finance in the provision of future benefits. The latter is based on a falacious analogy, and distorts fiscal planning. Since it is difficult in practice to separate the two approaches, great care must be taken if the pay-as-you-use approach is to be formalized in a double budget system.

Intergeneration Equity

The general principle of pay-as-you-use finance gains in importance if we allow for the fact that facilities provided for by government will be

---

[1] Such implications may be found in many places—for instance, in the previously noted paper by Myrdal.

CLASSICAL THEORY OF PUBLIC DEBT   563

used frequently by several generations of taxpayers.   This is particularly true in municipal finance, where the composition of the resident group is subject to more or less frequent change.   Here the principle of pay-as-you-use finance follows directly from that of benefit taxation, and loan finance is required to distribute costs among the various generations.

To illustrate the point, consider a project whose services become available in equal installments over three periods.   Also, suppose that the life (or residency) span of each generation covers three periods, and that the population is stable.   Finally, assume that loans advanced by any one generation must be repaid within its life span.   In each period the benefits accrue to three generations, including generations 1, 2, 3 in the first period; 2, 3, 4 in the second; and 3, 4, 5 in the third period.   To contribute their proper share, generations 1 and 5 should each pay $\frac{1}{6}$ of the cost; generations 2 and 4 should each pay $\frac{2}{6}$; and generation 3 should pay $\frac{3}{6}$. Let us now suppose that the total cost is $100, and that it is to be allocated accordingly.   To simplify matters, we will disregard the allocation of interest cost.[1]

The entire outlay of $100 must be raised and spent in the first period. Of this, $33.3 is obtained by taxation, divided equally between generations 1, 2, and 3.   The remainder is obtained by loans from generations 2 and 3.   There can be no loans from generation 1 owing to our rule that each generation must be repaid during its life span.   In the second period, tax revenue is again $33.3, contributed now by generations 2, 3, and 4; the debt held by generation 2 is retired in full, and loans of $16.6 are advanced by generation 4 to retire part of the debt held by generation 3.   In the third period, the tax revenue of $33.3 is contributed by generations 3, 4, and 5.   It is used to retire the remainder of the debt held by generations 3 and 4.   In retrospect, the total cost has been divided between the five generations in accordance with benefits received.   Loan finance in this case not only provided credit to taxpayers but resulted in a bona fide division of the cost between generations—a result impossible to secure through tax finance.[2]

Concerning the change in resource allocation in the private sector, let

---

[1] The interest will be divided between the generations in proportion to their share in the postponement of payment, so that $\frac{1}{4}$ is contributed by generations 2 and 4 each, while 3 pays $\frac{1}{2}$.

[2] Note that this financing pattern does not involve tax discrimination between generations.   The tax in any one period applies alike to the members of all generations living.   While the schedule of debt transactions in each period involves a distinction between generations, our scheme does not necessitate the use of bonds that are nontransferable among generations.   Rather, the government can borrow and retire debt independent of the particular holder.   The general pattern of Table 23-2 comes about on its own accord, provided that each generation consumes its assets while still present.

TABLE 23-3. INTERGENERATION EQUITY THROUGH LOAN FINANCE
(In dollars; figures rounded)

Period	Source of funds*	Payments for each generation					Total payments in period
		1	2	3	4	5	
1	Taxes..........	11.1	11.1	11.1	†	†	33.3
	Loans..........	.....	33.3	33.3	†	†	66.7
	Repayments.....	.....	......	....	†	†	
	ΔC...........	−8.3	−8.3	−8.3	†	†	−25.0
	ΔI............	−2.8	−36.1	−36.1	†	†	−75.0
2	Taxes..........	†	11.1	11.1	11.1	†	33.3
	Loans..........	†	......	......	16.6	†	16.6
	Repayments.....	†	33.3	16.6	......	†	49.9
	ΔC...........	†	−8.3	−8.3	−8.3	†	−25.0
	ΔI............	†	30.5	13.8	−19.4	†	25.0
3	Taxes..........	†	†	11.1	11.1	11.1	33.3
	Loans..........	†	†	......	......	.....	
	Repayments.....	†	†	16.6	16.6	.....	33.3
	ΔC...........	†	†	−8.3	−8.3	−8.3	−25.0
	ΔI............	†	†	13.8	13.8	−2.8	25.0
1-3	Taxes..........	11.1	22.2	33.3	22.2	11.1	100.0
	Loans..........	.....	33.3	33.3	16.6	.....	83.2
	Repayments.....	.....	33.3	33.3	16.6	.....	83.2
	ΔC...........	−8.3	−16.7	−25.0	−16.7	−8.3	−75.0
	ΔI............	−2.8	−5.5	−8.4	−5.5	−2.8	−25.0

* ΔC indicates change in consumption.
  ΔI indicates change in investment.
  † Unborn or deceased.

us assume that 75 per cent of tax receipts comes from consumption, and 25 per cent from saving. Since we are dealing with a system in which planned saving is matched by investment, the latter fraction is reflected in reduced capital formation in the private sector. Moreover, we assume that saving is inelastic to interest, so that the full amount of government borrowing is withdrawn from private capital formation. Repayment of government debt is reflected similarly in increased capital formation in the private sector. As shown in the last column of Table 23-3, we find private consumption reduced by $25 for each period, thus reflecting the principle of pay-as-you-use finance. Private capital formation is reduced by $75 in the first period and increased by $25 for each of the following periods. The net reduction in private capital formation for all periods as a whole equals $25. Thus the total cost is divided between consumption and capital formation in accordance with the marginal propensity to consume. This is true since we assume that saving is not elastic to interest. If interest elasticity is allowed for, the insertion of government demand in the loan market, by driving up the rate of interest, may lead to an increase in the rate of saving, with a corresponding transfer of part of the cost to private consumption.

Old-age Insurance

As far as the structure of the capital budget is concerned, the considerations of intergeneration equity lead to the same principles as those which underlie Table 23-1 and need not be repeated. However, one case of intergeneration equity, which has received special attention since the thirties, should be noted. This is the financing of a system of old-age insurance in which insurance benefits and contributions are on a strictly contributory and quid pro quo basis.

In such a plan, those who are aged when the system is introduced should receive no benefits since they have not contributed in the past; those who are middle-aged at the time of introduction should receive some benefits when they retire, since they have contributed for part of their working lives; but the full benefits should become available only to those who are at the beginning of their working lives when the plan is introduced. This requires contributions in excess of benefit payments for the early years, until a situation is reached where everyone has contributed over his entire working life. At that time, receipts from current taxes and interest in the reserve account will come into balance with benefit payments, and the system will be on a pay-as-you-go basis. The difficulty lies with the earlier period in which receipts are in excess of payments.[1]

These excess receipts may be hoarded, used to store goods, or invested. The first procedure would not accomplish the desired objective but would merely give rise to the inequities of price-level change. The second procedure would meet the requirement that those of working age should contribute while the aged should receive no benefits; nevertheless, it would be an absurd solution. Quite apart from storage cost and deterioration, the goods thus set aside would be lost to the community forever. Putting it differently, such a plan would fail to realize the earnings that might be derived by investing the resources set aside. The third and proper solution, therefore, is to return the initial surplus to the capital

---

[1] On the general problem of financing old-age insurance, see A. W. Willcox, "The Old-age Reserve Account: A Problem in Government Finance," *Quarterly Journal of Economics*, vol. 51, no. 3, p. 460, May, 1937; Seymour Harris, *Economics of Social Security*, McGraw-Hill Book Company, Inc., New York, 1941, chap. 9, pp. 199–227; Alan T. Peacock, *The Economics of National Insurance*, W. Hodge, London, 1952; and Ida C. Merriam, *Social Security Financing*, Federal Security Agency, Bureau Report no. 17, Washington, 1952, chap. 2, pp. 32–52.

market and to credit a reserve account or trust fund with the assets thus purchased.

As a result, resources are transferred from consumption to capital formation in the initial period; future income of the reserve fund will be supplemented by a corresponding capital income on this initial investment. Those of working age when the plan is introduced can be called upon to contribute the full amount of their future benefit, adjusted to an actuarial basis and discounted to its present value in the initial period. As the system matures, the contributions of those of working age, together with the capital income of the reserve account, will pay the benefits of the aged. At this point, a pay-as-you-go basis is achieved. The rate of tax required to finance the matured system will henceforth be less than it would be if a pay-as-you-go plan had been followed from the beginning. This is true because the income of the system is supplemented by the earnings obtained from the reserve. Throughout, the principle of inter-generation equity is complied with.

The principle remains the same whether the surplus of the initial period is returned to the capital market through government lending or whether it is used to retire government debt held by the public. In the latter case, government debt is shifted from the public to the reserve fund or trust account. According to the assumption of the classical system, funds made available through either channel flow into private investment. Thus, the effect of debt retirement on capital formation is the same as it would be if direct investments were made by the government. In the one case, the reserve fund receives income from private assets; in the other, it receives interest on public debt. Assuming the yield on government and on comparable private securities to be similar, the combined tax rate (that is, the rate for retirement contributions plus the rate of tax required to finance interest on public debt) will be the same in both cases. The taxes needed to finance interest payments to the reserve fund would have been needed otherwise to finance interest payments on public debt held outside the reserve fund.

Similarly, the principle remains the same if the surplus from the insurance operation is used to finance expenditures that otherwise would have been financed by borrowing. In the efficient system, it makes no difference whether new debt is issued to the reserve fund rather than to the public, or whether outstanding debt is transferred from the public to the reserve fund. However, the result differs if, as a matter of fiscal politics, the additional receipt *causes* an increase in public expenditures that otherwise would not have occurred.

These considerations apply to an insurance scheme that is on a strictly contributory basis. If the present aged are to receive benefit payments when the plan is introduced, a contribution from the general budget is required. If the coverage of the scheme by occupations is comprehensive, the resulting transfer is between generations only; if the coverage is limited, a wider set of transfers is involved. Where the relationship between tax and benefit formulas is such as to involve redistribution between income groups, as is the case with the United States system, the application of the contributory principle is limited to begin with, and objections to the initial inclusion of the aged are reduced accordingly.

Loan Finance to Adjust Distribution

So far we have been concerned with the use of loan finance in the budget of the Allocation Branch. We shall now turn to an application in the context of the Distribution Branch. Under conditions of war economy, it may be necessary for reasons of economic policy to secure a sharp reduction in consumption. This may render it necessary to obtain a larger share of total proceeds from the lower-income groups than seems desirable on grounds of distributional considerations. If so, wartime withdrawals may be arranged so as to provide for a subsequent adjustment after the war. Wartime withdrawals from the lower-income groups may take the form of refundable taxes or forced loans, to be repaid subsequently by transfers from the upper-income groups.[1] Thus loan finance may serve as a means of intertemporal redistribution between income brackets, as well as a means of intertemporal shifts between generations.

Loan Finance to Reduce Tax Friction

Let us now turn to still another function of loan finance—minimizing fluctuations in the level of tax rates due to fluctuations in the level of public expenditures. The avoidance of fluctuations in tax rates may be desirable because changes in rates introduce an element of uncertainty that is disruptive. More important, intermittant loan finance may be desirable where frictional effects of taxation become an increasingly serious problem as the level of taxation (the ratio of tax yield to income) rises. If we assume that friction rises at an increasing rate with the level of taxation, friction may be reduced over the years if a fairly stable rate of taxation can be maintained. This requires the use of loan finance.

At the level of state and local finance, the case of nonrecurrent, extraordinary expenditures largely coincides with that of lumpy outlays on durable goods. The objective of using loan finance so as to reduce tax friction thus supplements the objective of achieving intergeneration equity. At the level of national government, the most important case of extraordinary expenditure needs is that of war finance. Not only is this the most striking case of temporarily high expenditure needs, but also

[1] See the previous reference (p. 250) to Keynes's scheme for war finance.

the emergency setting of war economy accentuates the need for avoiding detrimental incentive effects. Effects on work incentives in particular tend to be less detrimental in response to loan finance than in response to taxation.[1]

Loan finance, unless wholly compulsory, is more flexible in its adaptation to the capacities of the individual contributors than is tax finance. Moreover, there is an asymmetry in the accounting rules of lenders and taxpayers; lenders find their net worth unchanged after making a loan, while taxpayers fail to reduce their net worth by the present value of the future burden of debt service. Considerable reliance on borrowing is thus a proper and inevitable instrument of war finance. Moreover, loan finance serves to reduce private capital formation, whereas taxes fall more heavily on consumption. Thus there occurs some degree of burden transfer to future generations, even though the resource input for war production cannot be postponed. However, this consideration is of secondary importance, since the war economy is usually one in which direct controls of private investment are required, and the logic of the classical system is suspended.

Considerations such as these lend some validity to the argument for dividing the budget into an "ordinary" and an "extraordinary" part, and for requiring tax finance of the former only. However, the validity is limited indeed. By the logic of the case, the extraordinary budget must be balanced over a longer period, matching a surplus when expenditures are unusually low with a deficit when they are unusually high. Since it is difficult to determine what is usual or unusual, the institution of the extraordinary budget is open to abuse; and where such budgets have been used, the result has generally been detrimental. The rule that ordinary expenditures must be tax-financed leads, in times of stringency, to curtailment of precisely those expenditures that are most basic to governmental functions, as well as to overexpansion of outlays that may claim classification as extraordinary.

Indeed, it may well be argued that the entire concept of the extraordinary budget involves an inherent fallacy. If it is the objective to stabilize the level of tax rates, it does not follow that ordinary outlays should be tax-financed while extraordinary outlays should be loan-financed, but rather that a fraction of *total* financing should be loan-financed when *total* expenditures are unusually high, and that there should be debt retirement when they are unusually low. Thus the logic of the argument points to the planning of total annual budgets in the context of, say, a ten-year budget rather than to a division of annual budgets into an ordinary and an extraordinary part. This bears some

---

[1] See p. 250.

CLASSICAL THEORY OF PUBLIC DEBT   569

similarity to the proposal, made in the context of the compensatory setting, that the budget should be balanced over the cycle.[1]

Loan Finance of Self-liquidating Projects

Let us now consider the use of loan finance for self-liquidating projects. Self-liquidating projects may be defined narrowly as investments in public enterprises that provide a fee or sales income sufficient to service the debt incurred in their financing; or they may be defined broadly as expenditure projects that increase future income and the tax base. Such projects permit servicing (interest and amortization) of the debt incurred in their financing without requiring an increase in the future level of tax rates.

Public Enterprise. Self-liquidating investments of the narrower type are a special case where an analogy to business finance is appropriate. Public enterprises may be considered part of the private rather than public sector of the economy. The initial outlay cannot be financed by the advance collection of fees. As in private investment, the required capital is obtained properly on a loan basis and must be amortized out of subsequent sales proceeds. This procedure is in compliance with pay-as-you-use finance as well as intergeneration equity. Thus there is good reason for separating the accounts of public enterprises from the general budget. However, a link is provided by enterprise losses that appear as a subsidy on the expenditure side of the current sector of the general budget, and by enterprise profits that appear on the revenue side as an excise tax.[2] Notwithstanding the separation of basic accounts, the enterprise and general budgets may be combined subsequently in an over-all budget, which in turn may be divided into a current and a capital account.

Reproductive Expenditures. Self-liquidating investments of the broader type do not permit this analogy to business finance. Nevertheless, they provide for future benefits; thus the arguments for pay-as-you-use finance and intergeneration equity apply. Moreover, taxable income is increased in the future so that the debt may be retired without an increase in tax rates, or with a lesser increase than would be needed for immediate tax finance. Thus, loan finance of outlays that raise the future level of taxable income is sustained on grounds of tax friction as well as considerations of intergeneration equity. Expenditures for resource development offer a good illustration. The loan finance of outlays that provide for future benefits but do not raise the level of future taxable income involves justification by intergeneration equity only—as, for instance, in the construction of playgrounds. While the benefits thus

---

[1] See p. 523.

[2] For a general discussion of the relationship between enterprise accounts and general budget, see J. R. Hicks, *The Problem of Budgetary Reform*, Oxford University Press, New York, 1948.

provided for increase future real income, this income is not imputed to the tax base.

The Capital-formation Approach

A final view of the capital budget is focused on the contribution of budget policy to total capital formation, public or private, in the economy. For this purpose, the balance of the current budget must be defined to show the net addition (surplus) or reduction (deficit) in capital formation that results.

We shall now record, on the receipt side of the current budget, all receipts drawn from private consumption. This will include varying shares of different taxes, depending on the taxpayers' marginal propensity to consume and on possible substitution effects. In the case of death duties, no revenue is counted, whereas for a spendings tax, a multiple of the yield is entered. On the expenditure side of the current budget we must include public outlays that provide for current services in the nature of consumption. Also, we include amortization of government assets and private-consumption expenditures out of public transfer payments.

On the receipt side of the capital budget we record the surplus from the current budget, amortization charges, and receipts from funds that otherwise would have been channeled into capital formation in the private sector.[1] This includes varying shares of taxes, profits, or borrowing, depending on their origin. On the expenditure side we record government outlays on capital formation whether or not they result in the acquisition of assets, as well as private capital formation out of public transfers. Capital formation in this sense includes provision for durable consumer goods as well as for capital goods that are means of production. However, a division should be made between the two, since only the latter are investments as the term is used in measuring the effects of budget activity upon economic growth.[2]

The existence of a deficit or surplus under the capital-formation approach is of great importance to the fiscal planning of underdeveloped countries, where the contribution to economic growth may be the very focus of budget policy. Indeed, it may well be the most important concept of budgetary balance, next to the totally different concept of net contribution to aggregate demand that arises in the compensatory system. If it can be assumed that tax finance comes largely from consumption, whereas loan finance (drawn from the nonbank public) comes

---

[1] A partial allowance for this point of view is reflected in the United Nations' (*Budgetary Structure and Classification of Government Accounts*, United Nations, Department of Public Information, New York, 1951, p. 41) receipts from death duties in the capital account.

[2] See p. 484.

CLASSICAL THEORY OF PUBLIC DEBT   571

largely from private capital formation, the requirement of tax finance for current expenditures implies that budget policy should not retard total capital formation.

B. INTERNAL DEBT IN THE COMPENSATORY SYSTEM

We must now inquire how the preceding arguments for debt finance stand up in the more realistic context of a system where liquidity preference exists and where there is no necessary equality between saving and investment at a full-employment income. While the choice between tax and loan finance did not affect the level of aggregate demand in the preceding system, substitution of tax for loan finance now reduces the level of demand. Therefore we must examine how the foregoing argument can be reconciled with the requirements of compensatory finance.[1]

Fixed-investment Model

Let us begin with the extreme case of an economy where saving is inelastic to interest and the level of private investment is fixed. In such a system the proper level of aggregate expenditure must be maintained by stabilization policy.

Since private investment is fixed, any increase in public expenditures must be offset by a corresponding decrease in private expenditures on consumption. If we assume that public borrowing leaves private consumption unchanged, loan finance raises aggregate demand by the same amount as does finance out of new money. Given an initial situation where the budget is adjusted to provide for the proper level of private demand, *any* increase in public expenditure must be accompanied by increased taxation so that $\Delta T = \Delta G/c$, where c is the taxpayers' marginal propensity to consume. This rule applies whether such expenditures are for current services or for capital outlays.

Pay-as-you-use Finance. It follows that borrowing cannot be used as a means of pay-as-you-use finance. Any increase in public goods and service expenditures, whether for current services or durable goods, now requires that there be a corresponding adjustment in taxation. If loan finance is used in the first period, as shown in Table 23-3, prices will rise, and the entire burden falls on generations 1, 2, and 3. If tax proceeds are

[1] For a discussion of this problem, see Arthur Smithies, "Federal Budgeting and Fiscal Policies," in Howard S. Ellis (ed.), *Survey of Contemporary Economics*, American Economic Association, Richard D. Irwin, Inc., Homewood, Ill., 1948, pp. 174–210, whose argument is based on the implicit assumption of a fixed-investment model; and Paul A. Samuelson, "Principles and Rules in Modern Fiscal Policy: A Neo-classical Reformation," in *Money, Trade, and Economic Growth: In Honor of John Henry Williams*, The Macmillan Company, New York, 1951, pp. 170ff., who argues that—for the long run, at least, the classical model is more or less applicable.

used in the second period to retire debt, this transaction will cause a reduction in employment and real income rather than secure a transfer out of full-employment income.

By the very nature of the present model, current expenditures of government must come out of a reduction of current consumption in the private sector. Pay-as-you-use finance for the group as a whole is impossible. The rationale of capital budgeting, as shown in Tables 23-1 and 23-3, is inapplicable. There is no logical link, in this case, between the appropriateness of (1) tax or loan finance and (2) the distinction between public expenditures for current benefits and public expenditures for future benefits. There remains a justification for loan finance of public expenditures that raise future taxable income—a justification based on the proposition that it is desirable to avoid temporary changes in tax rate.

Intergeneration Equity. While pay-as-you-use finance is impossible, intergeneration equity may still be applied. To be sure, it cannot be achieved in the present setting through loan finance, but it may be accomplished through a tax-transfer scheme. Let us return to the case of Table 23-3 and the task of allocating the cost of $100 between our five generations; as before, generations 1 and 5, must bear $\frac{1}{8}$ of the cost, while generations 2 and 4 contribute $\frac{2}{8}$, and generation 3 contributes $\frac{3}{8}$. We now obtain the picture of Table 23-4.

In order to reduce consumption by $100 in the first period, and assuming the marginal propensity to consume at $\frac{3}{4}$, $133.3 must be paid in taxes. In all subsequent periods tax payments and transfers must cancel so as to maintain total consumption unchanged. For the three periods as a whole, the reduction of consumption of $100 is divided between the five generations in the required proportions, as is the net-tax bill of $133.3. While intergeneration equity cannot be secured through loan finance, it can be secured through a tax and transfer scheme. However, this is subject to the condition that consumers respond to refundable taxes as if they were outright taxes, and to the refund as if it were an addition to income. If such taxes and refunds are considered loans, without effect on current consumption, intergeneration equity does not work.

Old-age Insurance. Similar difficulties arise in the financing of old-age security. Lending out the surplus or retirement of public debt in the initial period will not raise the level of private investment. Whatever is done with the surplus, an excess of receipts over payments reduces aggregate demand and necessitates expansionary fiscal measures somewhere else. Such measures may take the form of reduced taxation or increased expenditures. In both cases the decrease in publicly held debt owing to reserve finance must be offset fully, or nearly so, by new borrowing needed to finance an additional deficit in the general budget.

CLASSICAL THEORY OF PUBLIC DEBT   573

TABLE 23-4. INTERGENERATION EQUITY THROUGH TAX-TRANSFER PLAN
(In dollars; figures rounded)

Period	Source of funds*	Payments for each generation					Total payments in period
		1	2	3	4	5	
1	Taxes........	14.8	59.2	59.2	†	†	133.3
	Transfers....	......	......	......	†	†	
	ΔC........	−11.1	−44.4	−44.4	†	†	−100.0
2	Taxes........	†	......	......	29.6	†	33.4
	Transfers....	†	29.6	......	......	†	33.4
	ΔC........	†	22.2	......	−22.2	†	
3	Taxes........	†	†	......	......	14.8	14.8
	Transfers....	†	†	14.8	......	......	14.8
	ΔC........	†	†	11.1	......	−11.1	
1–3	Taxes........	14.8	59.2	59.2	29.6	14.8	177.6
	Transfers....	......	29.6	14.8	......	......	44.4
	Net Tax.....	14.8	29.6	44.4	29.6	14.8	133.2
	ΔC........	−11.1	−22.2	−33.3	−22.2	−11.1	100.0

* ΔC indicates change in consumption.
† Unborn or deceased.

Whether publicly held debt is reduced or increased on balance depends on the extent to which private demand is reduced per dollar of insurance contribution, and the extent to which it is increased per dollar of tax reduction or additional public expenditure.

Suppose that the offsetting measure in the initial period is through tax reduction. The resulting benefits will accrue either to the very people who pay the contribution, in which case the transaction cancels or to others, in which case there is a spurious redistribution no less objectionable than a payment of old-age benefits to noncontributors in the initial period.

Suppose, now, that the government offsets the deflationary effect of the initial surplus by increasing goods and service expenditures. In other words, the surplus receipts of the reserve account are used to finance additional expenditures. If such expenditures are for purposes of current consumption, no contribution is made to the solution of our problem.[1] However, something might be accomplished through public capital forma-

[1] To the extent that the aged in the initial period are benefited, we may as well start out on a pay-as-you-go basis. To the extent that the benefits accrue to the contributors in the initial period, no resources are surrendered, and the transaction cancels.

tion. If contributors are called upon to finance public investments in the
initial period, the benefits from such investments can be enjoyed by those
of working age in the subsequent period. This second group might then
be called upon to pay for such services by sustaining the retirement
benefits of the aged, who, as contributors in the preceding period, provided
for the second group's benefits. However, such an approach is workable
only within the limits set by the existence of a legitimate demand for
durable public goods in the initial period.

Mixed System

In the more realistic intermediary case, changes in the supply of funds
have some bearing on the level of investment, with varying degrees of
effectiveness, depending on economic conditions at any particular time.

In such a setting, the classical principles of loan finance may be applied,
but with qualifications. While loan finance will affect the level of
expenditure, it will not do so on a 1:1 basis. Returning to Table 23-1,
the level of debt transactions must now be higher than it was in the
classical model. In other words, loan finance of additional public
expenditures must be supplemented by restrictive liquidity measures so
as to obtain the proper release of resources from private capital formation.

In the case of social-security finance, we now find that the net effect of
retiring public debt out of tax surplus in the initial period will not be so
deflationary as in the fixed-investment model. Some of the funds paid
out in redemption of public debt will be channeled into private investment, but the net effect is likely to remain deflationary. Some adjustment must be made to offset this. Policy may move from more to less
deflationary types of taxes, thus raising private consumption. Where
this interferes with the objectives of the Distribution Branch, a gain in
the equity of allocating retirement cost is traded against a loss in equity
in the remainder of the tax structure. The offset, therefore, must be
provided by an expansionary liquidity policy, that is, a substitution of
money for debt in the initial period, thus raising private investment. On
balance, reserve finance involves a change in the mix of stabilization
policy toward sharper tax and slighter liquidity restriction, thus providing
for a consequent shift of resources from private consumption to capital
formation. Reserve finance will be effective only to the extent that this
shift can be accomplished.[1]

[1] As a practical matter, the choice between the pay-as-you-go and the reserve
approach to old-age security might be determined by considerations of fiscal politics
rather than fiscal theory. Thus it can be argued for the reserve approach that the
contractual framework of the reserve system protects it against political raids; but
it can be argued against the reserve approach that additional tax receipts tend to
encourage nonessential additions to expenditures, and that a surplus in the reserve
plan makes it more difficult to obtain adequate deficits when needed.

We conclude that the principles of intergeneration equity and reserve finance, while largely inoperative in the fixed-investment model, are not without basis in the mixed system. At the same time, the case is not so clear-cut as in the classical system. For the case of central finance, which must carry the responsibility of stabilization policy, it may be the better part of wisdom to conclude that there should be no association between types of expenditure and the choice between internal loan or tax finance. The capital-budget approach is more generally applicable to the case of local finance, where there is no immediate concern with stabilization policy. Moreover, local borrowing usually involves a draft on external resources.

C. EXTERNAL DEBT

We now turn to the case of external borrowing—either external borrowing by local government or foreign borrowing by national government. The crucial difference between internal and external finance is that the latter permits an import of real resources, thereby enabling the government to provide additional facilities without an immediate reduction in other uses of resources, whether for consumption or capital formation. That is, the realization of opportunity cost is postponed until later, when the debt is serviced and repaid, thus giving rise to an outflow of resources at that time.

Local Finance

All this is of particular importance for borrowing by local governments, because such borrowing is largely in the nature of external borrowing.

Pay-as-you-use finance may now be supplemented by external borrowing, as durable facilities may be provided for without a reduction in other types of domestic capital formation. We have, in this case, a perfect analogy between the individual consumer who increases the volume of immediately available resources through the use of installment credit, and the group that borrows from abroad to provide for capital investment in durable consumer goods. Similarly, intergeneration equity in the provision of durable goods may be implemented by initial finance through external borrowing and by amortization of the debt in line with the accretion of benefits to subsequent generations.

External borrowing, in terms of this reasoning, requires that the capital be obtained from abroad but not that the public facility as such be imported from abroad.[1] If, for example, the internal public expenditure is the local purchase of bricks for a school building, the import results from

[1] Capital may be obtained from abroad by selling debt abroad or by selling debt at home to lenders who withdraw the necessary funds from abroad.

the brick producer's expenditures on externally supplied goods and services, or on internally produced goods and services that otherwise would have been exported.

National Finance

Foreign borrowing by national government accomplishes the same import of resources as does external borrowing by local government. Where national government can draw on foreign borrowing, the logic of the capital budget applies with regard to both pay-as-you-use finance and provision for intergeneration equity. This holds even if the domestic setting is more or less similar to that of our fixed-investment model.

However, national borrowing abroad poses a transfer problem in foreign exchange—a problem that does not arise in the case of external borrowing by local government.[1] Borrowing from abroad, especially if put to unproductive use, not only may result in a burdensome drain of resources in subsequent periods when the debt must be serviced, but may also give rise to difficulties in the balance of payment. At the same time, foreign borrowing, if used to secure economic growth, will create the export capacity necessary to service the debt at a future date.[2] The role of foreign borrowing or other forms of capital import is vital in the early stages of economic development. It permits capital formation without reduction in the current level of consumption, which may be close to subsistence standards. It also provides the foreign exchange needed to secure capital equipment that cannot be secured at home. The extent to which budget transactions ease or curtail the scarce supply of foreign exchange thus constitutes another important type of budgetary balance.

Conclusion on Concepts of Balance

In concluding this discussion, it must be emphasized that there is no single type of budgetary management or concept of budgetary balance that serves all purposes of fiscal planning. There are many useful concepts that may be used side by side; there are other concepts that are misleading and should be discarded.

Among the useful concepts, we have noted those associated with pay-as-you-use finance and total capital formation in the economy. Further considerations involve the avoidance of unnecessary changes in tax rates, the finance of self-liquidating expenditures, and the supply of foreign exchange. In the compensatory system, there is the additional concept

[1] At the same time, interregional capital movements may result in transfer burdens and gains in the sense of changes in employment or terms of trade associated with resulting changes in the allocation of resources.

[2] See Evsey D. Domar, "Foreign Investment and Balance of Payments," *American Economic Review*, vol. 40, pp. 805–826, December, 1950.

of balance that measures the budget's net contribution to the income scheme—a concept dealt with in preceding chapters, which need not be recalled here. There are other applied concepts, such as a balance that measures financing requirements for purposes of debt management.

Whatever the specific purpose of the concept of balance, the crux of the problem is always the policy meaning of the concept to be used. This must be defined first, and from the definition the detailed grouping of various revenue and expenditure items must be derived.

D. THE BURDEN OF DEBT

The preceding discussion throws some light on the frequently used concept of burden of debt. Assuming that a debt has been incurred in the past, let us consider whether, and in what sense, the existence of such a debt involves a burden.

Wasteful Use of Foreign Loans

The existence of external debt involves a burden for the group as a whole, since resources must be surrendered in servicing it. Taxpayers as a group would be better off if the debt was forgiven. At the same time, the present generation might be better off after allowance for debt service than it would have been without past borrowing. Past investments of the resources thus gained may more than pay for the debt service. By the same token, the present generation will be worse off if past imports have been used for consumption. This is but the counterpart of our earlier conclusion that outside borrowing is a means of transferring resources between generations.

The argument applies to the outside debt of local governments and to the foreign debt of national governments. It does not apply in this form to internally held public debt. The collection of taxes to finance amortization or interest charges on domestically held debt does not reduce the availability of resources for the group as a whole. Yet it does not follow that domestic debt is irrelevant just because its service involves a mere transfer within the group.

Interest as Social Cost

Let us return to a classical model where loan finance curtails the scarce supply of savings available for private capital formation. Here interest on public debt may be considered the opportunity cost of previous earnings from private investment. Debt retirement in turn increases the supply of funds available to private capital formation, provided that the funds are obtained from taxes that reduce consumption.

In this setting, the existence of public debt implies a burden in that current national income would have been higher if past outlays of government had been tax- rather than loan-financed.   The principle is similar to that observed previously in the use of domestic borrowing to implement pay-as-you-use finance.   At the same time, it does not follow that current income would be higher had past loan-financed expenditures not been made.   Current income would be higher only if public borrowing served to finance past consumption, of if public investment was less productive than private investment would have been.

These considerations do not apply in the fixed-investment model, where public borrowing does not affect the level of private capital formation. Here debt service is a distributional phenomenon, which does not involve a draft on scarce resources.   Public debt in this case does not involve an opportunity cost of previous private investment.

In the mixed model, the significance of public debt is more difficult to interpret.   Loan finance, as distinct from tax finance, may raise the rate of interest and impair private investment.   But the change in private investment may be a mere fraction of the debt issued.   Moreover, the issuance of debt may be matched by an offsetting increase in money supply so that the rate of interest remains unchanged.[1]   Thus interest payments on public debt become a price paid for choosing one particular type of stabilization policy, and cease to be an index of the opportunity cost incurred in reduced private investment.   At the same time, the choice between tax finance and loan finance retains some bearing on the level of private investment, and the argument of the classical model remains applicable to some degree.

Tax Friction

Setting aside, for the moment, the type of cost dealt with in the preceding section, the transfer process of debt service may be burdensome in another sense: It may cause dislocations in the functioning of the private sector; or, to put it differently, the transfer process of debt service may pre-empt taxable capacity, thus forcing budgetary retrenchment along other lines.   This may be readily seen if we visualize a situation where, say, 90 per cent of taxable income (including national income and interest payments) is absorbed in taxes needed to finance interest charges; such taxes may be a multiple of national income.   As shown in the discussion of growth, it is most unlikely that a situation of this type would arise under peacetime conditions, since an extreme degree of stagnation would be required.[2]   Nevertheless, the problem may arise as the result of war finance.

[1] See p. 527.
[2] See p. 500.

CLASSICAL THEORY OF PUBLIC DEBT   579

At first sight one might be inclined to argue that tax finance of interest charges creates no problem of tax burden, since any increase in the interest bill also leads to an increase in taxable income and, hence, in the tax base. This proposition implies that tax friction remains unchanged when equal absolute amounts are added to the tax bill and the tax base. The situation differs if we accept the more reasonable hypothesis that tax friction depends on the level of tax *rates*. While the inclusion of interest payments in the tax base lessens the increase in the required level of tax rate, the required rate nevertheless rises as interest payments are increased relative to national income. Thus increased tax friction may result.

TABLE 23-5. INTEREST FINANCE AND TAX BURDEN

Budget items	Economy		
	A	B	C
1. Private expenditures....................................	$70	$100	$100
2. Government goods and service expenditures..............	30		
3. Total expenditures or income..........................	100	100	100
4. Government transfers..................................	...	30	43
5. Taxable income (line 3 + line 4)......................	100	130	143
6. Taxes..	30	30	43
7. Disposable income (line 3 + line 4 − line 6 = line 1)......	70	100	100
8. Tax rate (line 6:line 5) in per cent.....................	30	23	30

Let us now consider whether the problem of tax friction is less serious if taxes are used to finance interest payments than if taxes are used to finance goods and service expenditures. Compare economies A and B of Table 23-5. Both have a national income of $100 and government expenditures of $30. In economy A these expenditures are on goods and services, and in economy B they are on interest. Assuming a classical economy where all income is spent, stability of price level requires that the budget be balanced in both cases. In economy A, this involves a tax rate of 30 per cent. In economy B the tax base is larger because interest income is added to earnings; the tax rate is 23 per cent. A comparison between economies A and B suggests that the burden of tax friction is lighter in economy B. This is the case not because the private use of resources is larger in economy B, but because the tax rate is lower. Our conclusion is contingent on the condition that interest payments are taxable; if they are not, the result will be the same in both cases. Putting it differently, the tax rate required with a given level of budget expenditures will be less if these expenditures consist of transfer payments than if they consist of goods and service expenditures. This rule, shown here to hold for the classical system, applies a fortiori in a compensatory setting.[1]

Alternatively, we may compare two economies where the required tax rates are the same. In economy C, government expenditures are again on interest and exceed those of economy A by an amount such as to leave the required rates of tax the same. If tax friction is a function of the rate of tax paid on earned income, the degree of tax friction will be the same in both situations. This is the case even though the ratio of earned income to total income is higher in economy A than in economy C.

The friction aspect of debt burden may be avoided if the debt service itself is loan-financed.[2] In the classical system, loan finance of interest payments involves a further draft on the supply of saving and a corresponding transfer of resources from private investment to consumption. Thus the avoidance of friction is accomplished at a cost only. In the fixed-investment model, interest payments may be financed by borrowing of existing funds or by the creation of new money. As an offset, a somewhat higher level of taxation will be called for to maintain the proper level of aggregate demand. Depending on who receives the interest and who pays the additional taxes, a redistribution of income may result, and a rentier class may come into existence, the disadvantages of which must be measured against the gain of reduced tax friction.

---

[1] We must consider the additional fact that goods and service expenditures are fully spent, while transfer payments are not fully respent. Because of this the required level of tax rate in the transfer case is reduced further.

Beginning with a full-employment income Y and a constant average propensity to consume c, compare the tax rate t_g required to offset the level of goods and service expenditures G, with the tax rate t_u required to offset the level of the interest payments U. Holding private investment I constant, we have

$$t_g = \frac{G(1-c)}{Ic} \quad \text{and} \quad t_u = \frac{U(1-c)}{I}$$

If $U = G$, we obtain $t_u = ct_g$; hence $t_u < t_g$ for $c < 1$.

[2] See A. P. Lerner, "The Burden of the National Debt," in *Income, Employment and Public Policy: Essays in Honor of Alvin H. Hansen*, W. W. Norton & Company, Inc., New York, 1948, pp. 255–275.

[19]

THE BURDEN OF DEBT

Abba P. Lerner

"But look," the Rabbi's wife remonstrated, "when one party to the dispute presented their case to you you said 'you are quite right' and then when the other party presented their case you again said 'you are quite right,' surely they cannot both be right?" To which the Rabbi answered, "My dear, you are quite right!"

MESSRS. Bowen, Davis, and Kopf have shown [1] that the real burden of a project using up resources in the present can be shifted to future generations by internal borrowing, providing one defines "generation" in a particular way. It is just as easy to prove that all politicians are economists or that all economists are dunces, provided one defines "economist" in a particular way. But even if I call the tail of a sheep a leg that will not turn sheep into quintapeds. The issue is of course terminological rather than substantive. It is nevertheless one of the utmost importance because the conclusion reached by Bowen et al., although not incorrect on their own definitions, is bound to be misinterpreted as meaning what it seems to be saying in English and as indeed implying that most politicians understand economics better than the economists — most, if not all, of whom are dunces.

Bowen, Davis, and Kopf are absolutely right when they agree that there is "absolutely nothing" wrong with the standard argument of modern economists that the real burden of a debt can *not* be shifted to future generations if it is defined as "the total amount of private consumption goods given up by the community *at the moment of time the borrowed funds are spent.*" But President Eisenhower "appears convinced that the costs of debt-financed public projects can be passed on to future generations." Like the Rabbi in the story, Bowen et al. want to say that he too is right, but in their enthusiasm they even say that the purpose of their note "is to suggest that in this instance it is the President who is — in at least one highly important sense — right," [2]

thus clearly implying that the economists are wrong.

To make the President appear right, Bowen et al. redefine "present generation" to mean the people who lend the money to finance the project, and they redefine "future generation" to mean the people who pay the taxes that are used to repay the principal and the interest on the loans. The perversity of the redefinitions is obscured by supposing that the lenders ("this generation"), are all 21 years old at the time of the execution of the project when they lend the money and by supposing that they are repaid 44 years later, on their 65th birthday, with funds obtained at that time from 21-year-old taxpayers ("the next generation"). The burden is thereby shifted from "this generation" to "the next generation."

What has been proved, if we obstinately insist in expressing the conclusion in English, is that it is possible to shift the burden from the Lenders to the Taxpayers or, we might say, from the Lowells to the Thomases. The Lowells are better off and the Thomases are worse off than if the Lowells had been taxed to raise the money for the project in the first place.

The "red herring" nature of having the Lowells lend the money now (so that we can call them the present generation) and having the Thomases pay the taxes in the future (so that they can be called the future generation) jumps to the eye if we note that the shifting of the real burden of the project from the Lowells to the Thomases (or indeed of any other burden) could take place just as well at the time of the project (or at any other time) by simply taxing the Thomases instead of the Lowells.

No economist, so far as I am aware, has ever denied the possibility of borrowing or of lending or of taxing some people instead of others, or of any combinations of such oper-

[1] W. G. Bowen, R. G. Davis, and D. H. Kopf, "The Public Debt: A Burden on Future Generations?" *American Economic Review,* L (September 1960), 701–706.

[2] *Ibid.,* 701, where President Eisenhower is quoted as saying, "Personally, I do not feel that any amount can be prop-erly called a surplus as long as the nation is in debt. I prefer to think of such an item as a reduction on our children's inherited mortgage," in his *State of the Union Message,* January 7, 1960.

ations. And if we redefine Mr. Eisenhower's words so that they mean only that such operations are possible, then indeed the words used by the President constitute a true statement. But there is no reason for supposing that the President was trying to use any language other than English, and what the President said is simply wrong (in English), unless indeed all the economists (including Bowen *et al.*, as well as J. M. Buchanan, .who plays similar linguistic tricks [3]) are absolutely wrong.

The real issue, and it is an important one, between the economists and Mr. Eisenhower is not whether it is possible to shift a burden (either in the present or in the future) from some people to other people, but whether it is possible *by internal borrowing* to shift a real burden from the present generation, in the sense of the present economy as a whole, onto a future generation, in the sense of the future economy as a whole. What is important for economists is to teach the President that the latter is impossible because a project that uses up resources needs the resources *at the time that it uses them up*, and not before or after.

This basic proposition is true of all projects that use up resources. The question is traditionally posed in terms of the burden of a *public* project financed by *privately* held internal debt; but the proposition is quite independent of whether the project is public or private as well as of whether the debt is private or public. The proposition holds as long as the project is financed *internally*, so that there are no outsiders to take over the current burden by providing the resources and to hand back the burden in the future by asking for the return of the resources.

It is necessary for economists to keep repeating this basic proposition because one of their main duties is to keep warning people against the fallacy of composition. To anyone who sees only a part of the economy it does seem possible to borrow from the future because he tends to assume that what is true of the part is true of the whole. It *is* possible for the Lowells to borrow from the Thomases, and what this borrowing does is to shift a burden from the Lowells to the Thomases in the pres-

ent, and then to shift an equal burden from the Thomases to the Lowells in the future when the loan is repaid. To the Lowells (and to anyone else who sees only the Lowells) the combination of these two shifts looks like the shifting of a burden from the present into the future or the shifting of resources from the future into the present. To the Thomases, of course, the transactions will look like the opposite, namely, the shifting of a burden from the future into the present or the shifting of resources from the present into the future. But the borrowing and the repayment do not make a Time Machine. There is no shift of resources or of burdens between different points in time. It is possible for a *part* of the economy (the Lowells) to shift *its* burden into the future only as long as *another part* of the present economy (the Thomases) is ready to take it over for the intervening period. It is not possible for *the whole* of the present generation to shift a burden into the future because there are no Thomases left to play the magician's assistant in the illusion.

This is not to say that there is no way at all in which the present generation can shift a burden onto future generations. Our proposition is only that this is not done by internal borrowing. We can impoverish the future by cutting down on our investment in capital resources (or by using up or destroying natural resources) that would have enabled future generations to produce and enjoy higher standards of living. There is even a possible connection between internal debt financing and this way of really impoverishing future generations. If full employment (or some other level of employment) is somehow being maintained, and if the conditions of the borrowing and the kinds of people from whom the borrowing is done are such that they reduce consumption by less than consumption would have been reduced if the money had been raised instead by taxes, then there will be more consumption and there will therefore have to be less investment. The borrowing will then have reduced the real resources inherited by future generations.

But there is no *necessary* connection. It would almost certainly not work this way in the conditions of 1960. Whether the borrow-

[3] In his *Public Principles of Public Debt* (Homewood, Illinois, 1958).

THE BURDEN OF DEBT

ing increases or decreases consumption depends on the nature and on the conditions of the borrowing on the one hand and of the alternative — the taxation — on the other hand. Furthermore, at the present time, when we have considerable unemployment and unused capacity, an increase in consumption is more likely to lead to *more* investment (out of unutilized resources) and therefore to an *increase* in the productive resources inherited by future generations. And it is quite certainly not these complicated considerations that are responsible for the President's belief that internal borrowing increases and repayment reduces "our children's inherited mortgage." In any case even the *possibility* of a genuine impoverishment of future generations by an induced reduction in investment is *explicitly* ruled out by Bowen *et al.* when they say that the resources consumed by the project "*must* entail a contemporaneous reduction in private consumption." [4]

Any genuine impoverishment of future generations must be the result of *not* reducing private consumption by the full amount of the resources used up in the project so that some of these resources must come out of alternative investment (if we rule out the use of unemployed resources). It is only the curtailed alternative investment outside of the project that can tend to impoverish future generations (although this might be more than made up for them by the benefits that these same future generations will derive from the project in question).

We can also impoverish the future by using up in the production of armaments too much of the resources that would have gone into investment; and we can equally impoverish the future by an over-economy in armaments, or by skimping in our contribution to the building of a healthy world, so that we invite aggression or foster resentments and revolutions.

[4] *Ibid.*, 703, my italics.

But both of these possibilities are completely independent of whether we borrow or tax.

Semantic playfulness like that of Bowen *et al.* seriously sabotages economists in their important task in educating the public to the appreciation of an important truth. By their ingenious redefinition of "generations" they have made it more difficult to point out just where the fallacy of composition is perpetrated. It is perpetrated when a part of the economy (as in their definition of this or that generation) is taken for the whole (as in the usual meaning of a generation as *all* the people living at a certain date); and this is exactly what Bowen *et al.* do when they say that President Eisenhower (speaking English) is right.

They have taken a true proposition — i.e., that some people can shift a burden into the future by borrowing from other people — and rewritten it in such a manner that almost everyone will read in it the false proposition that the nation as a whole can filch resources from the future by internal borrowing (public or private), thereby impoverishing future generations. It is unfortunately the false proposition that is implied in the statement by the President, and believed by many people in positions to make vital decisions. The false belief may well contribute to a failure of the free nations to take the steps necessary to maintain and extend freedom in the world. There is even a clear and present danger that because of a baseless fear of impoverishing future generations by leaving them with a larger internal debt (which they will owe to themselves), we may fail to protect them from nuclear war and/or totalitarian domination; the confusion sown by Bowen *et al.* tends to increase that danger. It is to be hoped that these authors will tell the President that they were using a special language of their own and didn't mean what they seemed to be saying when they seemed to be denying a proposition with which, as they themselves declare, there is "absolutely nothing" wrong.

[20]

LONG-RUN IMPLICATIONS OF ALTERNATIVE FISCAL POLICIES AND THE BURDEN OF THE NATIONAL DEBT [1]

I. Introduction

THE time-honoured controversy over the burden of the National Debt has flared up once more. The view, almost unchallenged a few years back, that the National Debt is no burden on the economy and that the real cost of government expenditure, no matter how financed, cannot be shifted to " future generations " has been on the retreat under a powerful counter-attack spearheaded by the contributions of J. M. Buchanan,[2] J. E. Meade [3] and R. A. Musgrave.[4] These authors, while relying to a considerable extent on older arguments, have significantly enriched the analysis by blending the traditional approach with the new insights provided by the Keynesian revolution. But even these most recent contributions have failed, in our view, to provide an altogether adequate framework—a failure resulting at least in part from the Keynesian tendency to emphasise flows while paying inadequate attention to stocks. It is the purpose of this paper to propose a fresh approach to this problem, and to show that, unlike its predecessors, it leads to a consistent and yet straightforward answer to all relevant questions.

Unless otherwise noted, the National Debt will be defined here as consisting of: (1) all claims against the Government held by the private sector of the economy, or by foreigners, whether interest bearing or not (and including therefore bank-held debt and (government currency, if any);

---

[1] A number of colleagues at Massachusetts Institute of Technology and other institutions have greatly helped me with their comments on a preliminary draft of this paper. I wish particularly to acknowledge the many useful suggestions of Ralph Beals, James Buchanan, Sukhamoy Chakravarty, Margaret Hall and Merton Miller.

[2] J. M. Buchanan, *Public Principles of the Public Debt* (Homewood, Illinois: Richard D. Irwin, 1958).

[3] J. E. Meade, " Is the National Debt a Burden? " *Oxford Economic Papers*, Vol. 10. No. 2, June 1958, pp. 163–83, and " Is the National Debt A Burden: A Correction," *ibid.*, Vol. 11, No. 1, February 1959, pp. 109–10.

[4] R. A. Musgrave, *The Theory of Public Finance* (McGraw-Hill, 1959), especially Chapter 23. Other recent contributions include: the reviews of Buchanan's book by A. P. Lerner, *Journal of Political Economy*, Vol. 47, April 1959, pp. 203–6; E. R. Rolph, *American Economic Review*, Vol. 49, March 1959, pp. 183–5, and A. H. Hansen, *Review of Economics and Statistics*, Vol. 41, June 1959, pp. 377–8; also " The Public Debt: A Burden on Future Generations? " by W. G. Bowen, R. G. Davis and D. H. Kopf, *American Economic Review*, Vol. 50, September 1960, pp. 701–6; and the forthcoming note by A. P. Lerner, " The Burden of Debt," *Review of Economics and Statistics*, Vol. 54, No. 2, May 1961.

Since the completion of this paper, three comments on the Bowen, Davis and Kopf communication by W. Vickrey, T. Scitovsky and J. R. Elliott and a reply by the authors have also appeared in the March 1961 issue of the *American Economic Review*, pp. 132–43.

less (2) any claims held by the Government against the private sector and foreigners.[1]

From a methodological point of view, the central contention of our analysis is that to grasp fully the economic effects of alternative fiscal policies and of the National Debt, we must pay proper attention to stocks as well as to the usual flow variables and to the long-run as well as to the impact effects.   Among the substantive implications of this line of approach, the following may be mentioned here by way of a rough summary: (1) Given the government purchase of goods and services, an increase of the (real) National Debt, whether internal or external, is generally advantageous to those present at the time of the increase (or to some subset thereof). (2) Such an increase will generally place a " gross burden " on those living beyond that time through a reduction in the aggregate stock of private capital, which, as long as the (net) marginal productivity of capital is positive, will in turn cause a reduction in the flow of goods and services.   Furthermore, this loss (as well as the gain under (1) above) will tend to occur even when lack of effective private demand would prevent the maintenance of full employment in the absence of the deficit, though the relative size of gain and losses may be quite different in these circumstances.   (3) These conclusions hold in reverse in the case of a reduction in the real National Debt.   That is, such a decline is burdensome on those present at the time of the reduction and tends to generate a gross gain for those living beyond. (4) *If* the rate of interest at which the Government borrows can be taken as a good approximation to the marginal productivity of private capital, then the gross burden (or gain) to " future generations " referred to under (2) and (3) can be *measured* by the interest charges on the National Debt. (5) The gross burden may be offset in part or *in toto*, or may be even more than offset, in so far as the increase in the debt is accompanied by government expenditure which contributes to the real income of future generations, *e.g.*, through productive public capital formation.[2]

This summary is very rough indeed and is subject to numerous qualifications and amendments, many of which will be noted below.   In any event, I should like to emphasise that the stress of this paper is on developing a method of analysis rather than on presenting a body of doctrines.   For this reason I will try to relate my analysis to earlier points of view whenever this seems helpful in clarifying the issues involved.   At the same time I will endeavour to stay clear of many traditional but somewhat sterile controversies, such as whether the analogy between private and public debt is true or false.

---

[1] This definition implies that the National Debt could in principle be negative.   Even in this case we shall refer to it by the same name, although its magnitude will be expressed by a negative number.   Similarly, we refer to an operation that reduces the algebraic value of the National Debt as a " reduction," even if the debt was initially zero or negative.

[2] The difference between the increase in the National Debt in a given interval and the Government expenditure contributing to future income corresponds roughly to the net increase in what Professor Meade has called the " deadweight " debt.   Cf. *op. cit.*

II. A Bird's Eye View of the Classical and Post-Keynesian No-transfer and No-burden Argument

We begin by reviewing the very persuasive arguments supporting the doctrine that the cost of the current government use of resources cannot be transferred to future generations and that the National Debt is no burden on them. Since these arguments have been presented many times in the last couple of centuries and have been extensively restated in recent years, we can afford to recapitulate them very briefly in terms of the three propositions presented below—at the cost of glossing over some of the fine points and of foregoing the pleasure of citing " chapter and verse." [1]

(1) Individuals or sub-groups within an economic system can, by means of borrowing, increase the current flow of goods available to them and pay for this increase out of future output. But they can do so only because their borrowing is " external," *i.e.*, matched by a lender who yields current goods in exchange for later output. But a closed community cannot dispose of more goods and services than it is currently producing. It certainly cannot increase this flow by paying with future output, for there is no way " we can dispose to-day of to-morrow's output." Hence the goods and services acquired by the Government must always be " paid for " by those present at the time in the form of a reduction in the flow of goods available to them for private use, and cannot possibly be paid for by later generations, whether the acquisition is financed by taxes or by internal borrowing. Only through external borrowing is it possible to benefit the current generation and to impose a burden on the future.

(2) Although internal borrowing will leave in its wake an obligation for future tax-payers to pay the interest on the National Debt and, possibly, to repay the principal, this obligation is not a net burden on the community as a whole, because these payments are but transfers of income between future members of the community. The loss of the tax-payers is offset in the aggregate by the gain of the beneficiary of the payment. These transfers may, of course, occur between people of different ages and hence of different " generations," and in this sense internal borrowing may cause " inter-generations transfers," but it will not cause a net loss to society.

The above two arguments, or some reasonable variant thereof, have provided the cornerstone of the no-transfer, no-burden argument over the last two centuries or so. It was left for Keynesian analysis to provide a third argument, removing thereby a potentially troublesome objection to the first two. If the cost of government expenditure always falls on the current generation, no matter how financed, why not forego altogether the painful activity of levying taxes? Yet our common sense rebels at this

---

[1] The reader interested in establishing just who said what will find much useful material in Buchanan, *op. cit.*, especially Chapters 2 and 8, and in B. Griziotti, " La diversa pressione tributaria del prestito e dell'imposta " in *Studi di scienza delle finanze e diritto finanziario* (Milano: Giuffre, 1956), Vol. II, pp. 193–273.

conclusion. A partial answer to this puzzle was provided by recognising that taxes, even when paid back in the form of transfers, generate some " frictional loss," because most if not all feasible methods of raising tax revenue tend to interfere with the optimum allocation of resources.[1] Presumably the ever-increasing level of the National Debt resulting from full deficit financing of current expenditure would require raising through taxes an ever-growing revenue to pay the interest on the debt. Eventually the ratio of such taxes to national income plus transfers would exceed the ratio of government expenditure to national product, giving rise to frictional tax losses which could have been avoided through a balanced budget. While these considerations do provide a *prima facie* case for a balanced-budget policy, the case is not tight, for could not the interest itself be met by further borrowing?

However, we need not follow these fancy possibilities, for the Keynesian analysis has provided a much more cogent argument to support the need for an " appropriate " amount of taxation, although not necessarily for a balanced budget. This argument, which reaches its most elegant formulation in the so-called principle of " functional finance " enunciated by Lerner,[2] can be roughly summarised as follows.

(3) Given the full employment output, say $\bar{X}$, and given the share of this output which it is appropriate to allocate for government use, say $\bar{G}$, there is a maximum amount of output that is left available for the private sector, say $\bar{P} = \bar{X} - \bar{G}$. Now the private sector demand for output, say P, is a function of income and taxes, say $P = \mathscr{P}(X, T)$, with $\frac{\delta P}{\delta T} < 0$. Taxes are then to be set at that level, say $\bar{T}$, which satisfies the equation $\mathscr{P}(X, T) = P$. A higher level of taxes would generate unemployment and a lower level would generate inflation, both evils which it is the task of the Government to avoid. $\bar{T}$ may turn out to be larger than $\bar{G}$, calling for a surplus, or smaller than $\bar{G}$, or even perchance just equal to $\bar{G}$, implying a balanced budget. But in any event, the purpose of taxes is not to make the current members of the community pay for the government use of goods, which they will do in any event, the real reason we need to put up with the unpleasantness of taxes is to prevent the greater social evil of inflation.

III. A BIRD'S EYE VIEW OF THE CLASSICAL AND POST-KEYNESIAN TRANSFER AND BURDEN ARGUMENT

The basic contention of this school of thought, which itself has a long tradition, is that in general—though possibly with some exceptions—a

---

[1] See, *e.g.*, J. E. Meade, " Mr. Lerner on ' The Economics of Control,' " ECONOMIC JOURNAL, Vol. LV, April 1945, pp. 47–70.

[2] See, *e.g.*, " Functional Finance and the Public Debt," *Social Research*, Vol. 10, No. 1, and " The Burden of the National Debt " in *Income Employment and Public Policy* (New York: Norton & Company, 1948).

debt-financed public expenditure will place no burden at all on those present at the very moment in which the expenditure takes place, and will instead place a burden on all tax-payers living thereafter. This burden may fall in part on those present at the time of the expenditure, but only in so far as they are present thereafter. The arguments which support this position have also been repeatedly stated and have been thoroughly reviewed quite recently by Buchanan. It will therefore again be sufficient to summarise them very briefly in the following two propositions:

(1) The cost of a tax-financed expenditure is borne currently, for the resources obtained by the Government come from a forcible reduction in the resources of current tax-payers. But an expenditure financed by debt, whether internal or external, as a rule places no burden on those present at the time of the expenditure in that, and in so far as, the resources acquired by the Government are surrendered in a voluntary exchange by the savers, who thereby acquire government bonds (in lieu of some other asset).

(2) The burden is imposed instead on all future tax-payers, who will have to pay taxes to service the debt. These taxes are *not* a mere transfer of income, but a net burden on society, for, in the absence of the debt-financed expenditure, the taxes would not have been levied, while the investors in bonds would have received the income just the same, directly or indirectly, from the return on the physical assets in which their savings would have been invested. This argument *does not* imply that a debt-financed expenditure will necessarily affect future generations unfavourably. In order to assess the " net outcome," we must subtract from the gross burden represented by the extra taxes benefits, if any, resulting from the expenditure. Thus the net outcome might even be positive if the expenditure undertaken produced greater benefits than the private capital formation which it replaces. But the argument does imply that, through deficit financing, the expenditure of the Government is being " paid for " by future generations.

A careful application of the *reasoning* underlying (1) and (2) will reveal circumstances in which the above conclusions do not hold and the allocation of the burden may be independent of the form of financing used. There are in particular two important cases which are treated at some length by Buchanan and which bring to light the contribution of Keynesian analysis also to this side of the argument. The first is the case of debt-financed expenditure in deep depressions, when private capital formation could not, in any event, provide an adequate offset to full-employment saving. Here, according to Buchanan, not even a gross burden need result to future tax-payers, for the expenditure could in principle be financed by interest-free issuance of currency. The second exception discussed by Buchanan is that of a major war. Unfortunately, the chapter on war financing is one of the least convincing in his book, and what follows may represent more nearly my application of his framework than a faithful summary of his argument. Suppose the war effort is sufficiently severe so that the allocation of resources to various uses, and to capital formation in particular, is completely determined by war necessities. In such a situation the way in which the Government finances its expenditure cannot affect private consumption or capital formation. It would seem therefore that the burden of reduced consumption must be borne by the current generation, even if the reduction is achieved not through taxes but through a combination of rationing and voluntary increases in saving and the unspent disposable income is invested in claims against the Government. Similarly, the burden of the reduction in useful capital formation is borne by those living after the war, again independently of financing. In this case, as well as in the case of depression financing, the taxes levied to pay the interest on the increased debt would indeed seem to result in a pure transfer, for the income associated with the bonds would *not* have come to exist had the Government decided respectively to tax, or to print money, instead of borrowing.

J. E. Meade has also lately associated himself with those maintaining that the National Debt is a burden,[1] but his argument is quite different from the classical one, and bears instead all the marks of post-Keynesian analysis. He is not concerned with the differential effect of deficit versus tax financing, but asserts none the less that government debt in excess of government-owned physical capital—the so-called deadweight debt—is a burden on the economy. Unfortunately his contribution, which is so stimulating in analysing the effects of a major capital levy, is less than convincing in its attempt to establish that the deadweight debt is a burden. For his demonstration seems to rely entirely on the proposition that elimination of the debt would be a blessing for the economy in that it would encourage saving through a " Pigou type " effect, besides reducing the frictional costs of transfers. Now the tax-friction proposition, though valid, is not new,[2] and had already been generally accepted as a second-order amendment to the no-burden argument. On the other hand, the first and central argument is rather unconvincing. For, as Meade himself recognises, a reduction in National Debt, be it through a capital levy, budget surplus or inflation, would spur saving whether or not the debt reduced thereby was " deadweight " debt. In fact, at least the first two means would tend to increase saving, even if they were applied in a situation where the National Debt was zero to begin with, and the outcome would be that of driving the economy into a position of net indebtedness *vis-à-vis* the Government. Finally, Meade's analysis throws no light on whether the increase in saving following the capital levy is a permanent or a purely transitory phenomenon, nor on who, if anyone, bears the burden of a debt reduction. In spite of these apparent shortcomings, I am encouraged to think that Professor Meade's views are fundamentally quite close to those advanced here. I hope this will become gradually apparent, even without much further explicit reference to his argument.

Meade, *op. cit.*

[2] See, *e.g.*, the references in footnote 1, p. 733, above, and in Buchanan, *op. cit.*, p. 14, footnote 8.

IV. Fallacies in the No-transfer No-burden Argument

The classical argument summarised in the last section appears so far rather convincing, and if so we should be able to pinpoint the fallacies in one or more of the three propositions of Section II.

The fallacy in proposition (1) is not difficult to uncover. It is quite true that a closed community cannot increase its current resources by relying on to-morrow's unproduced output. None the less, the way in which we use to-day's resources can affect in three major ways the output that will result to-morrow from to-morrow's labour input: (i) by affecting the natural resources available to the future; (ii) by improving technological knowledge; and (iii) by affecting the stock of man-made means of production, or capital, available to future generations. Hence government expenditure, and the way it is financed, *can* affect the economy in the future if it affects any of the above three items.

The argument in (3) is also seriously inadequate, and the post-war experience has brought this home sharply. For the demand of the private sector consists of consumption C and capital formation I, and at least the latter component depends not only on income and taxes but also on monetary policy. Once we acknowledge this point, the principle of Functional Finance no longer implies a unique level of taxes. To demonstrate this point and its implications, it will be convenient—though it is not essential—to suppose that monetary policy affects P exclusively through the intermediary of the rate of interest r, *i.e.*, that $P = \mathscr{P}(X, T, r)$ with $\dfrac{\delta P}{\delta r} < 0$; and that r in turn depends on X and the quantity of money M. But once we admit that r enters not vacuously in $\mathscr{P}$ we must also recognise that the equation

(1) $$\mathscr{P}(\bar{X}, T, r) = P$$

will be satisfied not by one but by many possible values of T, each value being accompanied by the appropriate value of r, say $r(T)$. Now in most circumstances—that is, except possibly in very deep depression—there will be a range of values of T such that the corresponding $r(T)$ is achievable by an appropriate monetary policy. There is therefore not one but a whole schedule of values of T which are consistent with the maintenance of full employment and price stability, each value of T being accompanied by an appropriate monetary policy. Furthermore, within this range there will tend to be a direct connection between T and the capital formation component of $\bar{P}$. If, starting from a correct combination of T, r and M, we lower taxes we will increase consumption, and to offset this we must reduce capital formation by appropriately tightening monetary policy. Conversely, by increasing taxes we can afford to have a larger capital formation. Thus, given the level of government expenditure, the level of taxes, and

TABLE I

A. *Effects of Government Expenditure and Financing on Private Saving and Capital Formation*

(Full Employment—All variables measured in real terms)

Method of Financing.	Income, Y.	Government Expenditure, G.	Taxes, T.	Disposable Income, Y. $(X - T)$	Consumption, C. $(c_0 + cY)$ $(c = 0 \cdot 6)$	Saving $S = \Delta W$ $(Y - C)$	Deficit, D. $(G - T)$	Private capital formation $I = \Delta K$ $(S - D)$
	(1)	(2)	(3)	(4)	(5)	(6)	(7)	(8)
(a) Initial situation	2,000	300 (G_0)	300	1,700	1,500 (C_0)	200 (S_0)	0	200 (S_0)
(b) Increased expenditure–deficit financed	2,000	400 $(G_0 + dG)$	300	1,700	1,500 (C_0)	200 (S_0)	100 (dG)	100 $(S_0 - dG)$
(c) Increased expenditure—tax financed	2,000	400 $(G_0 + dG)$	400	1,600	1,440 $(C_0 - cdG)$	160 $(S_0 - sdG)$	0	160 $(S_0 - sdG)$

B. *Comparative "Burden" Effects of Alternative Budgetary Policies*

Budgetary policy.	Effect on Private capital formation.	"Burden."
1. Joint effect of increased expenditure *and* deficit financing	$I(b) - I(a)^1 = (S_0 - dG) - S_0 = -dG$	$r^*(dG)$
2. Joint effect of increased expenditure and taxes	$I(c) - I(a) = (S_0 - sdG) - S_0 = -sdG$	$r^*_s(dG)$
3. Differential effect of deficit financing	$I(b) - I(c) = (S_0 - dG) - (S_0 - sdG) = -(1 - s)dG = -cdG$	$r^*_c(dG)$

^{1} $I(a)$ means investment in situation (a), and similarly for $I(b)$ and $I(c)$.

hence of budget deficit, does affect " future generations " through the stock of capital inherited by them.

Having thus brought to light the weaknesses in arguments (1) and (3), it is an easy matter to establish that, at least under certain conditions, the Keynesian framework is perfectly consistent with the classical conclusion stated in Section III.   Suppose we take as a starting-point a given G, and some given combination of T and r consistent with full employment. Suppose further, as is generally assumed in Keynesian analysis, that to a first approximation consumption responds to taxes but not to interest rates. Now let the Government increase its expenditure by dG while keeping taxes constant.   Then the deficit will increase precisely by $dD = dG$.   What will happen to capital formation?   If we are to maintain full employment without inflation we must have

$$dG + dC + dI = 0$$

and since, by assumption, taxes are constant and hence $dC = 0$, we must have

$$dG = dD = -dI$$

i.e., the debt-financed expenditure must be accompanied by an equal reduction in capital formation (with the help of the appropriate monetary policy).

This outcome is illustrated by a numerical example in Table I.   Row (*a*) shows the behaviour of the relevant flows in the initial situation, taken as a standard of comparison: here the budget is assumed to be balanced, although this is of no particular relevance.   In row (*b*) we examine the consequence of an increase of expenditure by 100, with unchanged taxes, and hence consumption.   The amount of resources available for, and hence the level of private capital formation, is cut down precisely by the amount of the deficit-financed expenditure.   It is also apparent that this expenditure puts no burden on the " current " members of the community.   Their (real) disposable income is unchanged by the expenditure, and consequently so is their consumption, as well as the net current addition to their personal wealth or private net worth.   But because capital formation has been cut by the amount of the deficit, the community will thereafter dispose of a stock of private capital curtailed to a corresponding extent.

Thus the deficit-financed expenditure will leave in its wake an overall burden on the economy in the form of a reduced flow of income from the reduced stock of private capital.

V. Interest Charges and the " True " Burden of Debt Financing

The analysis of the last section is seen to agree with the classical conclusion that debt financing transfers the burden of the government expenditure to those living beyond the time of the expenditure.   At the same time it indicates that this burden consists in *the loss of income from capital* and not in *the taxes levied on later members to pay the interest charges*, as the classical argument contends.

In some respects this amendment to the classical burden position may be regarded as rather minor, for it can be argued that, under reasonable assumptions, the interest charges will provide a good *measure* of the true burden.   Indeed, as long as the amount dD is not large in relation to the stock of capital (and the flow of saving), the loss in the future stream of output will be adequately approximated by $r^*(dD)$, where r^* denotes the marginal productivity of capital.   Now if the Government borrows in a competitive market, bidding against other seekers of capital, then the (long-term) interest rate r at which it borrows will also be a reasonable approximation to r^*.   Hence the annual interest charges $r(dD)$ will also be a good approximation to the true social yearly loss, or opportunity cost, $r\ (dD)$ [1]—provided we can also establish that the initial reduction in the stock of capital will not be recouped as long as the debt is not repaid.

One can, however, think of many reasons why the interest bill might not even provide a good *measure* of the true loss.   To begin with, if the government operation is of sizeable proportions it may significantly drive up interest rates, say from r_0 to r_1, since the reduction in private capital will tend to increase its marginal product.   In this case the interest on the debt will overstate the true burden, which will lie somewhere between $r_0(dD)$ and $r_1(dD)$.   More serious are the problems arising from various kinds of imperfections in the commodities as well as in the capital markets.   In particular, the Government may succeed in borrowing at rates well below r^* by forcing banks and other intermediaries to acquire and hold bonds with yields below the market, or, as in war-time, by effectively eliminating the competition of private borrowers.   In the first-mentioned case, *e.g.*, we should add to the interest bill the lost income accruing to the bank depositors (or at least to the bank's stockholders).   There is also the rather nasty problem that, because of uncertainty, the rate of interest may not be a good measure of the productivity of physical capital.   To put it very roughly, r is at best a measure of return net of a risk premium, and the actual return on capital is better thought of as a random variable whose average value is, in general, rather higher than r.[2]

Besides the relation of r to r^* there is another problem that needs to be recognised.   In our discussion so far, and in our table, we have assumed that consumption, and hence private saving, were unaffected because taxes were unchanged.   But once we recognise that the borrowing may increase the interest rate, we must also recognise that it may, through this route, affect consumption even with unchanged taxes.   This problem might well be quickly dismissed under the principle of " *de minimis*."   For, though economists may still argue as to whether an increase in interest rates will

---

[1] This is precisely the position taken by Musgrave, *op. cit.*, p. 577.

[2] Cf. F. Modigliani and M. H. Miller, " The Cost of Capital, Corporation Finance and the Theory of Investment," *American Economic Review*, Vol. 58, No. 3, June 1958, pp. 261–97.   However, Miller has suggested to me that r may be the more relevant measure of return on capital as it deducts an appropriate allowance for the " cost " of risk bearing.

increase or decrease saving, they generally agree that the effect, if any, will be negligible.[1] But even if the rate of saving were to rise from, say, S_0 to $S_0 + e$ and the level of capital formation were accordingly reduced only by $dD - e$, one could still argue that r^*dD and not $r^*(dD - e)$ is the relevant measure of the true loss to society. This is because, as suggested by Bowen *et al.*,[2] the income generated by the extra capital formation e may be quite appropriately regarded as just necessary to offset the extra sacrifice of current consumption undertaken by those who responded to the change in r.

Thus it would appear that the classical-burden position needs to be modified to the extent of recognising that the burden of deficit financing consists not in the increased taxes as such, but rather in the fall in income generated by the reduction in the stock of capital. But this modification would seem rather innocuous, since, admittedly, rdD will generally provide a reasonable approximate *measure* of the true burden. In fact, however, the amendment we have suggested turns out to have rather far-reaching implications as we will show presently.

VI. Shortcomings of the Classical Transfer and Burden Argument: The Differential Effect of Deficit Versus Tax Financing

The classical conclusion that deficit financing of an expenditure places the burden on the future seems to imply that, if the expenditure were financed by taxes, there would be no burden in the future. Interestingly enough, Buchanan's book provides nowhere a systematic treatment of the temporal distribution of the burden from a tax-financed expenditure. Nor is this really surprising, for if the burden were in fact the interest of the debt, then tax financing could generate no burden on the future.[3] But if the relevant criterion is instead the loss of capital formation, then in order to find the true differential effect of debt financing versus tax financing, we must inquire about the effects of tax financing on private saving and capital formation. Only if this effect were nil or negligible would the classical conclusion be strictly valid.

Now, to an economist steeped in the Keynesian tradition, it is at once obvious that raising taxes to finance the government expenditure cannot fail to affect significantly private saving and capital formation. While tax financing will reduce disposable income by the amount of the expenditure, it will reduce consumption only by an amount $cdT = cdG$, where c is the marginal propensity to consume. The rest of the tax will be borne by a reduction in saving by sdT, where $s = 1 - c$ is the marginal propensity to save. Accordingly, if the initial position was one of full employment, as we are assuming, and inflation is to be avoided, private capital formation

---

[1] This is especially true if current consumption is appropriately defined to include the rental value and not the gross purchase of consumers' durables.

[2] Bowen, Davis and Kopf, *op. cit.*, p. 704.

[3] See, however footnote 1, p. 746, for a different explanation of Buchanan's omission.

must itself be reduced by the amount sdG (through the appropriate monetary policy).[1] This outcome is illustrated numerically in row (c) of Table I. By comparing the outcomes (a), (b) and (c) as is done in part B of the table, we find that the differential effect of the deficit versus tax financing is to decrease capital formation by $dG - sdG = cdG$. The balance of the reduction, namely sdG, must be attributed to the expenditure as such, independently of how financed.[2] Hence, even if we are willing to regard the interest rate paid by the Government as a good approximation to r^*, the differential burden of debt financing on the future generations is not rdG but only $rcdG$.

It can readily be seen that the above result is not limited to the case we have explicitly discussed so far, in which the deficit arises from an increase in expenditure. If, for whatever reason, a portion dD of the government expenditure is not financed by taxes but by deficit, capital formation tends to be reduced by approximately $c(dD)$. This conclusion is, however, subject to one important qualification, namely that for $T = \bar{G}$, i.e., with a level of taxation balancing the budget, there exists a monetary policy capable of achieving full employment—or, in terms of our previous notation, of enforcing the required rate of interest $r(\bar{T})$. When this condition is satisfied we shall say that there is a " potentially adequate private demand," or more briefly, an " adequate demand." We shall for the moment concentrate attention on this case, reserving the task of examining the implications of a lack of adequate demand to a later point.

Our result so far, then, is that even with an adequate demand, the net or differential burden placed on the future by debt financing is not nearly as large as suggested by the classical conclusion. But note that the implied error is poor consolation for the no-transfer proponents, for they maintained that the burden is always " paid as you go." The error we have uncovered would seem to lie instead in not recognising that a part of the burden of the expenditure is always shifted to the future. This last conclusion, however, is somewhat puzzling and disquieting. And this uneasiness can be easily increased by asking ourselves the following embarrassing question: roughly how large is the coefficient s which determines the unavoidable burden on the future? This question is embarrassing because recent empirical as well as theoretical research on the consumption function suggests that the answer depends very much on the length of time which is allowed for the adjustment. In the long run, the average propensity to save has remained

---

[1] The need to curtail investment when government expenditure is increased at full employment, even though it is fully tax covered, is the counterpart of the so-called multiplier effect of a balanced budget when starting from less than full utilisation of resources. The tax-financed expenditure *per se* increases the aggregate real demand for goods and services by a dollar per dollar of expenditure. But if we start from full employment, this extra demand could only result in inflation. Hence it must be offset by a fall in investment of s dollars per dollar of expenditure, which, taking into account the multiplier effect, will reduce total demand by $s/s = 1$ dollar per dollar, as required.

[2] This conclusion has also been reached by W. Vickrey, *op. cit.*

pretty constant in the general order of 0·1, meaning that the marginal propensity is of the same order. But the quarterly increase in saving associated with a quarterly increase in income seems to be of a much larger order of magnitude, with estimates ranging as high as 0·5 and even higher.[1] Which is the relevant figure and why? Or does the answer depend on whether we look only at the impact effect of taxation or also at its delayed and ultimate effects? We will argue that this is indeed the case, and that in so far as we are interested in the distribution of the burden over time and between generations, the total effects are paramount.

VII. Impact Versus Total Effects of Deficit and Tax Financing

Let us come back to a comparison of rows (b) and (c) in Table I, but this time let us concentrate on the effect of taxation on the terminal net worth position of the households. We can see that if the expenditure is debt-financed this terminal position is (at least to a first approximation) the same as if the expenditure had not been undertaken. On the other hand, in the case of tax financing, in addition to the concomitant fall in consumption, we find that saving, and hence the increase in net worth, was also cut down from 200 to 160. What effect will this have on later consumption and saving behaviour?

In order to answer this question we need to go beyond the standard Keynesian emphasis on current flows and try to understand why consumers wanted to add 200 to their net worth in the first place and how they will react when this goal has to be scaled down in response to higher taxes. I have elsewhere proposed some answer to these questions by advancing the hypothesis that saving (and dissaving) is not a passive reaction to income but represents instead a purposive endeavour by the households to achieve a desirable allocation of resources to consumption over their lifetime.[2] However, in what follows we do not need to rely, to any significant extent, on that model or any other specific theory of saving behaviour. All that we need to keep before our eyes is the logical proposition that there are, in the final analysis, only two ways in which households can dispose of any addition to their net worth achieved through current saving: namely, either through later consumption or through a bequest to their heirs.

Now let us suppose at first that the bequest motive is small enough to be neglected and that, as a rule and on the average, each household tends to

---

[1] See, *e.g.*, the following two recent and as yet unpublished studies prepared for the Commission on Money and Credit: D. B. Suits, " The Determinants of Consumer Expenditure: a Review of Present Knowledge "; and E. C. Brown, R. M. Solow, A. K. Ando and J. Kareken, " Lags in Fiscal and Monetary Policy," Part II.

[2] F. Modigliani and R. Brumberg, " Utility Analysis and the Consumption Function: An Interpretation of Cross-section Data," in *Post-Keynesian Economics*, K. Kurihara, ed. (Rutgers University Press, 1954).

consume all of its income over its lifetime.   This assumption can be conveniently restated in terms of the notion of the " over-life average propensity to consume " (*oac*), defined as the ratio of (the present value of) life consumption to (the present value of) life resources, and of the " over-life marginal propensity to consume " (*omc*), defined as the ratio of marginal increments in the same two variables.   With this terminology, our current assumption is that both *omc* and *oac* are unity.   It should be noted that, under reasonable hypotheses about the typical individual life cycle of earnings and consumption, an *oac* of unity for each household is consistent with a sizeable stock of aggregate assets, in the order of several times national income.   With a stationary population and unchanged technology—stationary economy—this aggregate stock would tend to be constant in size, implying zero net saving in the aggregate, but it would be undergoing a continuous reshuffling of ownership from dissavers, such as retired persons, to those in the process of accumulating assets for retirement and short-run contingencies.   On the other hand, with a rising population and/or technological progress, there would tend to be positive saving and a rising stock; in fact, the ratio of saving to income and of assets to income would tend to be constant in the long run if the above two forces resulted in an approximately exponential growth trend for aggregate income.[1]

Let us now consider the consequences of a non-repetitive increment in government expenditure *dG*, financed by a deficit, limiting ourselves at first to a stationary economy.   Fig. 1 (*a*) illustrates graphically the effects of this operation on aggregate private net worth *W*, and on the net stock of privately owned capital *K*.   The horizontal dashed line *AA* represents the behaviour of net worth in the absence of *dG*.   It is constant by our assumption of a stationary economy, implying zero net saving, or gross saving and gross investment just sufficient to offset the wear and tear of the capital stock. If we make the further convenient assumption that there is initially no government debt (and ignore non-reproducible tangible wealth), then *W* coincides also with *K*.   The incremental expenditure *dG* is supposed to occur in the interval t_0 to t_1 at the constant rate $dG/(t_1 - t_0)$, and is financed by tapping a portion of the gross saving otherwise devoted to capital maintenance.   As a result, between t_0 and t_1 *K* falls, as shown by the solid curve. But the net worth *W* remains at the same initial level as the fall in *K* is offset in the consumers' balance sheet by the government debt of *dG*.   By t_1 the gap between *W* and *K* amounts to precisely *dG*, and thereafter the curves remain unchanged until and unless some further disturbance occurs. The final outcome is that the debt-financed expenditure, by generating a permanent wedge *dG* = *dD* between *W* and *K*,[2] causes the entire cost of the expenditure to be borne by those living beyond t_1 in the form of a reduction

---

[1] Cf. A. K. Ando and F. Modigliani, " Growth, Fluctuations and Stability," *American Economic Review*, May 1959, pp. 501–24.

[2] Permanent in the sense that it persists as long as the debt remains outstanding.

in the stock of private capital by dG and in disposable income by $r^*(dG)$.[1]
If, in addition, $r^* = r$, then before-tax income will be unaffected and the
fall in disposable income will equal the tax collected to pay the interest, as
claimed by the classical-burden doctrine.[2]

Consider now the effect of full tax financing of dG, illustrated in Fig.
1 (b). The line AA has the same meaning as before. The impact effect of
the tax-financed expenditure—i.e., the effect within the interval $t_0 t_1$—is to
reduce consumption by cdG and saving and private capital formation by
sdG. Hence, as shown by the solid line, by t_1 both W and K have fallen by
sdG. As we had already concluded, this fall in K partly shifts the effect of
the expenditure to those living beyond t_1. However, by following up the
delayed effect of the tax, we can now show that in this case: (a) the shift of
the burden is only temporary, as W, and hence K, will tend to return
gradually to the original pre-expenditure level, and (b) the burden transferred to the period following t_1 is borne, at least to a first approximation,
entirely by those who were taxed between t_0 and t_1.

To establish this result we need only observe that since those taxed have
suffered a loss of over-life (disposable) income amounting to dG as a result of
the tax, they must make a commensurate reduction in over-life consumption.
If the consumption is cut initially only by $c(dG)$ the balance of the tax, or
$s(dG)$, is financed out of a reduction in accumulation—including possibly
borrowing from other households—which at first reduces the net worth at
time t_1 by $s(dG)$, but eventually must be matched by a corresponding
reduction of consumption over the balance of the life span. Let L denote
the length of time until the taxed generations die out. In the interval
t_1 to $t_1 + L$, then, the consumption of this group will be smaller relative
to its income, and hence its rate of saving will be larger, or its rate of
dissaving smaller, than it would have been in the absence of the tax. On
the other hand, over the same interval, the income consumption and saving
of households who have entered the scene after t_1 will be basically unaffected
by the operation. Hence, in the L years following t_1 there will arise some
positive saving which will gradually die down as the taxed generation disappears. The precise path of aggregate saving will depend on the way the
taxed generation chooses to distribute the reduction of consumption over its
life. But, in any event, the cumulated net saving over the entire interval

---

[1] Actually the fall in disposable income consequent upon the fall in K is likely to give rise to a
further fall in W and hence in K, but this indirect effect will tend to be of secondary magnitude.
See on this point footnote 1, p. 750.

[2] If the reduction in K results in a significant rise in r^* and hence r, then, as pointed out by
Vickrey (*op. cit.*, p. 135), there will tend to occur a shift in the distribution of *pre-tax* income. Labour
income will tend to shrink and property income to increase—and, incidentally, this increase will
tend to more than offset the fall in labour's earnings. It does not follow, however, as Vickrey has
concluded, that the "primary burden of diminished future income will be felt by future wage
earners." For the burden consists in the reduction of *disposable* income, and this reduction will
depend on the distribution of the taxes levied to pay the interest as between property and non-
property income.

FIG. 1

Effect of Deficit and Taxes on Net Worth, W, and Capital, K,
(unity over-life propensity to consume)

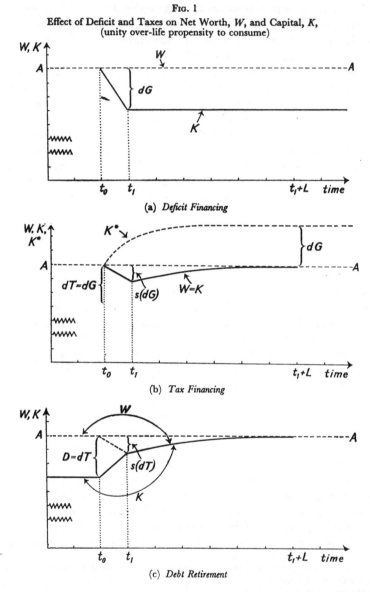

(a) *Deficit Financing*

(b) *Tax Financing*

(c) *Debt Retirement*

t_1 to $t_1 + L$ must come to precisely $s(dG)$, representing the required reduction of consumption relative to income of the taxed generation.[1] This

[1] It may be noted that the cumulated reduction in consumption will tend to be somewhat
larger than $s(dG)$ because the taxed generation will also lose some income as a result of the reduction in their wealth, amounting initially to $s(dG)$. However, the cumulated increase in saving
over the interval is still $s(dG)$ because the additional loss in consumption just matches the reduction
in income from this source. Actually $s(dG)$ measures essentially the *present value* as of t_1 of the
required reduction in consumption.

cumulated saving is just sufficient to make up for the initial fall in the stock of $s(dG)$, so that by $t_1 + L$ the stock of capital (as well as W) has returned to the original level, as shown in Fig. 2 (b), and we are back in the original stationary state.

The above framework can be readily applied to analyse the effects of deficit or surplus generated under different conditions, e.g., by varying taxes, expenditure constant. Fig. 1 (c), for instance, depicts the outcome of an increase in taxes in the interval t_0 to t_1, utilised to retire the debt D outstanding at t_0. Here again the entire burden of the retirement falls on the taxed generation—although it is spread between t_0 and $t_1 + L$—and the gain accrues to those living after t_1 in the form of an increase in the stock of capital by an amount which eventually approaches the amount of debt retired and reflects the elimination of the wedge between W and K.

It is also easy to verify that our results remain valid for a growing economy, the only difference being that the dashed line AA would turn into an upward-sloping curve. With debt financing the graph of K would, from t_1 on, run at a distance dG below this line, while with tax financing the graph of $K = W$ would initially fall below it by $s(dG)$, but would tend to return to it at $t_1 + L$.

In summary, then, under unit oac the cost of an expenditure financed by debt, whether internal or external, tends to fall entirely on those living beyond the time of expenditure, as asserted by the classical-burden position, though it is best measured by $r*dD$ rather than by the incremental tax bill rdD. This burden may be eliminated at a later date by retiring the debt through a budget surplus, but thereby the full cost of the original expenditure is shifted to the later tax-payer, who financed the surplus. On the other hand, the cost of a tax-financed expenditure will tend to be borne by society as a whole, partly at the time and partly for some finite period thereafter. But the burden beyond t_1 still falls primarily on those who initially paid the tax and reflects the spreading of the burden over their lifetime.[1]

In the analysis so far we have concentrated on examining who bears the cost of the expenditure. To complete the picture we must, of course, also reckon the yield, if any, produced by dG beyond t_1. In particular, if dG results in a (permanent) addition to the stock of capital we must distinguish

---

[1] In a stimulating comment to a preliminary draft of this paper, Mr. Buchanan has provided an explanation for his failure to analyse the temporal distribution of the burden of a tax-financed expenditure. He points out that in line with the classic tradition, he defines the burden as the subjective loss of utility suffered by the tax-payer because of the initial loss of resources. The burden in this sense occurs entirely when the tax is levied and the later reduction of consumption cannot be separately counted as burden, as it is merely the embodiment of the original burden. I have serious reservations about the usefulness of this definition. It has, for instance, the peculiar implication that, when as a result of tax financing an heir receives a smaller inheritance or as a result of debt financing he is saddled with a larger tax bill, this cannot be counted as burden on him, as the entire burden is already accounted for in the guise of his father's grief that his heirs will enjoy a smaller net income. It is this peculiar reasoning that underlies Ricardo's famous conclusion that the cost of the government expenditure is always fully borne by those present at the time.

between W, K and K^*, the latter denoting the total stock of private- plus government-owned capital. K^* will exceed K by dG. Thus in the case of a debt-financed capital expenditure, K^* will everywhere tend to coincide with W, the government capital formation simply replacing the private one. For the case of tax financing, the behaviour of K^* is shown by the broken line in Fig. 1 (b). Here the burden on the taxed generation results in a permanent gain for those living beyond t_1, which will gradually approach the yield on dG. In this sense one might well say that the cost of current government services can be paid for not only by the current and future generations but even by past generations.

There remains to consider how far our conclusions need to be modified if the *omc* is less than unity. Since a debt-financed expenditure does not affect the behaviour of net worth, our analysis of this case basically stands, although one can conceive of some rather fancy circumstances in which modifications would be necessary.[1] In the case of tax financing, however, an *omc* of less than one implies that part of the burden of the expenditure will fall on later generations, who will receive a smaller bequest. It can be readily seen that the reduction in $K = W$ available to them will be of the order of $(oms)(dG)$, where *oms* denotes now the over-life marginal propensity to save. The differential burden of debt versus tax financing on society will correspondingly be of the order of $r(omc)(dG)$ instead of rdG.[2] In other words, the propensities to consume and save relevant to the long-run effect are precisely the over-life ones.[3] Unfortunately, these are propensities about which information is currently close to zero, both in terms of order of magnitude and stability, although some attention has begun to be devoted to this question.[4]

Our analysis of the differential burden of tax versus debt financing could stand a great deal of refinement and qualifications to take proper account of the specific nature of the taxes levied to pay for dG or for the interest on the

---

[1] It is conceivable that, *e.g.*, the tax newly imposed to defray the interest cost might reduce the bequests. To this extent an even greater burden is placed on later generations, which will inherit a smaller K for two reasons: because of the smaller W and because of the wedge dG between W and K. An even fancier possibility is that the new tax might spur the initial generation to increase its bequests to help their heirs pay for the new tax. This would, of course, increase the burden on the current generation and decrease that on posterity.

[2] Note that, regardless of the value of *omc*, the current generation must always fare at least as well, and generally better, under debt than under tax financing, even if it capitalised fully the new taxes that must be raised to pay the interest bill on the new debt. For, even in the highly unlikely event that the amount $r(dD)$ per year necessary to pay the interest bill were levied entirely on the initial generations, as long as they lived, this liability is limited by life, and hence represents a finite stream whose present value must be less than the amount dD which would have been taken away in the case of tax financing. See on this point also footnote 1, p. 746.

[3] Even with an *omc* of less than unity it is likely that the impact of the tax on bequests handed down from one generation to the next would gradually disappear so that W and K would eventually be unaffected by the tax-financed expenditure. But this is in the *very* long run indeed.

[4] See, *e.g.*, J. Tobin and H. W. Guthrie, " Intergenerations Transfers of Wealth and The Theory of Saving," Cowles Foundation Discussion Paper No. 98, November 1960.

debt. But it is clear that these refinements can in principle be handled by proper application of the framework set out in this section. We shall therefore make no attempt at working out a long list of specific cases,[1] and will proceed instead to point out the implications of our framework for a somewhat different class of problems, namely where the change in debt occurs without any accompanying change either in government purchases or taxation.

VIII. "Gratuitous" Increases in Debt, Repudiation and Inflation

For analytical convenience we may start out by considering a case which has admittedly rather limited empirical relevance: namely, where the government debt is increased at some date t_0 by an amount dD by a "gratuitous" distribution of a corresponding amount of bonds.[2] Presumably, at least in this case, the proponents of the classical burden argument, if they apply their reasoning consistently, would have to agree with the proponents of the classical non-burden argument that the increment in the National Debt puts *no burden on the economy as a whole*, either at the time of issuance or thereafter, except for frictional transfer costs. For while it is true that from t_0 on, tax-payers are saddled with extra taxes to defray the interest bill, it is also true that the receipt of interest would not have arisen without the creation of extra debt. Note that this conclusion does not rule out the possibility that the operation may result in some transfer between generations, if by a generation we mean the set of members of the economy born at a particular date: thus the interest accruing to those receiving the gift will very likely be paid, at least partly, by a younger generation. But these are still mere income transfers involving no overall burden.

But once we recognise that the overall burden of the National Debt derives from its effects on the private stock of capital, then it becomes clear that, by and large, both classical doctrines agree with the wrong conclusion. This is indeed quite obvious in the case of a unity *oac*, a case illustrated graphically in Fig. 2 (*a*). The solid line *AA* shows as usual the behaviour of $W = K$ in the absence of the gift. For the sake of variety, we deal here with a growing economy with positive saving and rising wealth.[3] If the gift is distributed all in one shot at point t_0, then at that point W will rise by dD, with no change in K. But now between t_0 and $t_0 + L$ the members of the generation that received the gift will gradually dispose of the bonds (or of other assets that they may have exchanged against the bonds) by selling them to current savers and using the proceeds to increase consumption over what it would have been otherwise. As this takes place, the aggregate

---

[1] By so doing we are also deliberately by-passing the other major issue of fiscal policy, that of the distribution of the burden between income classes.

[2] In order to avoid side issues, we will assume that the coupon rate on these bonds is such as to make their market value also equal to dD, and that no change occurs in the government purchase of goods and services, G.

[3] Just for reference, we may note that according to the Modigliani–Brumberg model, if income were growing at approximately exponential rate, W would be growing at the same rate.

rate of saving, and hence the accumulation of net worth and capital, is reduced. The result is that W gradually approaches the base path AA, while K, which is always lower by the wedge dD, falls below it. By $t_0 + L$

FIG. 2

Effect of " Gratuitous " Changes in Debt on Net Worth, W, and Capital, K,
(unity over-life propensity to consume)

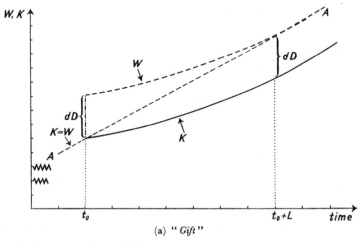

(a) " Gift "

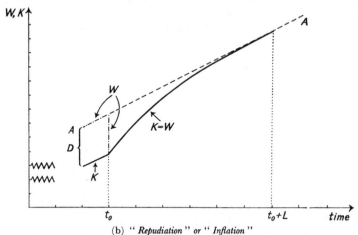

(b) " Repudiation " or " Inflation "

the cumulated rate of saving and physical capital formation will have been reduced by (approximately) dD, so that W will tend to coincide with AA and K to be dD lower, a position that will tend to be maintained thereafter. Thus an increase dD in the National Debt, even if it arises from a free gift, will put a burden on the economy as a whole. Under unity *oac*—after a transient period in which W is increased as a result of the gift—this burden will approach the level $r^*(dD)$, and hence approximately equal the interest on the debt.[1]

If the *omc* is less than unity, then the burden will be smaller, tending to $(omc)(r^*dD)$, because the gift will tend to increase W " permanently " by $(oms)(dD)$ and hence K will tend to fall only by $(omc)(dD)$. As usual, this burden can be removed at any later point by taxation and retirement of the debt, but only at the cost of putting the burden on the taxed generation, which in effect will be paying for the benefits enjoyed by the beneficiaries of the gift.

Our conclusion applies directly, but for an appropriate change of " sign," to the case of a " gratuitous " one-shot reduction in the National Debt, as indicated in Fig. 2 (*b*). Such a reduction might be accomplished by repudiation, total or partial, or by a capital levy, or, much more importantly and frequently, by the simple device of (unanticipated) inflation.

---

[1] This conclusion is strictly valid only in so far as the fall in disposable income brought about by the fall in K is matched by an equal fall in consumption. To the extent, however, that consumption falls somewhat less, cumulated saving may fall somewhat more, pushing W and K to a lower position than in our figure: but this extra adjustment will in any event tend to be of a second order of magnitude. The nature and size of this adjustment can be exhibited explicitly with reference to the Modigliani–Brumberg model of consumption behaviour. As indicated earlier, this model implies that, in the long run, the aggregate net worth of consumers tends to be proportional to their (disposable) income, or (1) $W = gY$, where the proportionality constant is a decreasing function of the rate of growth of income. Suppose initially income is stationary as population and technology are both stationary. We also have the identity (2) $W = K + D$, where D denotes the National Debt. With population and technology given, the effect of capital on income can be stated by a " production function " (3) $Y = f(K)$. We have stated in the text that a gratuitous increase in D, or more generally an increase in D which does not result in government capital formation or otherwise change the production function, will tend to reduce K by dD and Y by r^*dD: *i.e.*, we have asserted $\frac{dK}{dD} \simeq -1$ and $\frac{dY}{dD} \simeq -r^*$, where $r^* = \frac{df}{dK} = f' \simeq r$. By means of equations (1)–(3) we can now evaluate these derivatives exactly. Solving (2) for K and using (1) and (3) we have $K = gf(K) - D$. Hence $\frac{dK}{dD} = gf'\frac{dK}{dD} - 1$ or $\frac{dK}{dD} = \frac{-1}{1-gf'} = \frac{-1}{1-gr^*}$. Similarly, $\frac{dY}{dD} = \frac{-r^*}{1-gr^*}$ and $\frac{dW}{dD} = \frac{-gr^*}{1-gr^*}$. Thus, if $r^* \simeq r = 0 \cdot 05$ and g is in the order of 4, then $\frac{dK}{dD}$ is $-1 \cdot 25$ instead of -1 and $\frac{dY}{dD}$ is $-0 \cdot 625$ instead of $-0 \cdot 05$.

I am indebted to Ralph Beals, presently a graduate student at Massachusetts Institute of Technology, for pointing out that these formulæ are not entirely general, for, within the Modigliani–Brumberg model, the second-order effect is not independent of the nature of taxes employed to defray the interest bill. In fact, the formulæ derived above are strictly valid only if the revenue is raised entirely through an income tax on non-property income. With other kinds of taxes, one obtains somewhat more complicated formulæ. For instance, if the taxes are levied on property income this will depress the net yield of wealth below r, which in turn will, in principle, affect the proportionality constant g of equation (1). However, exploration of several alternative assumptions suggests to me that the outcome is unlikely to be appreciably different from that derived above, at least in the case of direct taxes.

It can also be shown that the above formulæ will tend to hold, at least asymptotically, for an expanding economy in which population grows at an approximately constant rate and/or so does productivity as a result of technological change which is neutral in Harrod's sense (cf. *Toward a Dynamic Economics* (Macmillan, 1949), p. 23). The main features of such a growth model are discussed in Ando and Modigliani, *op. cit.*

Thus a (once and for all) doubling of the price level is entirely equivalent to a repudiation of one-half of the National Debt at the original price level—although it has, of course, all kinds of other widespread economic effects. As far as the National Debt is concerned, this operation puts a burden on the owners of the bonds by reducing the real value of their interest income as well as the real value of the principal.   In so far as the first effect is concerned, we have a mere transfer from the bond-holders to the tax-payers, with no overall effect.   But the reduction in the principal generates an unmatched reduction in consumption, and hence a *transient* higher rate of saving.   The resulting increase in the capital stock will benefit all those living after the inflation—provided, of course, private capital has a positive marginal product and the potentially higher rate of saving is utilised for capital formation rather than being wasted in depressed income and unemployment.

From the content of this section and the previous one it should also be apparent that our analysis basically supports Meade's conclusion concerning the burden of the deadweight debt, although this conclusion is derived by a very different line of reasoning.   The deadweight debt is a burden because: (a) it generates a corresponding gap between aggregate net worth W and the aggregate stock of capital K^*, and (b) we can expect that this gap will result primarily in a fall in K^* rather than in an offsetting rise in W.   Thus, if we conceive two communities A and B identical with respect to natural endowments, technical know-how and habits of private thrift, and which differ only in that A has a deadweight debt D' and B has none, community A will be poorer, roughly, by D' times the marginal productivity of capital plus frictional transfer costs.

IX. Deficit Financing in War and in Depression

In this concluding section we propose to apply our tools to see what light they shed on the two classical and empirically relevant issues: the pre-Keynesian problem of war financing and the post-Keynesian problem of deficit created as part of a counter-cyclical stabilisation policy.

In order to face squarely the core issue of war financing, let us be concerned with the case of a major war effort of the type outlined earlier in Section III, in which the stock of capital in existence at the termination of the war is independent of the methods used to finance it.   It follows immediately that, independently of financing, the war will impose a burden on post-war society as a whole to the extent that the stock of capital in existence at its termination—counting only whatever portion is useful to satisfy the post-war requirements—is less than what would have been there in the absence of war.   In order to examine the residual effects, if any, of methods of financing, we must suppose that, in spite of the war's severity, we have some choice as to the extent of taxation.   Also, to keep separate for the moment the possible role of inflation, we must suppose that untaxed income in excess of the predetermined consumption level is prevented from bidding up the price of goods—whether through voluntary abstention or through a fully successful system of rationing. In these conditions the unspent income must result in an increase in government debt held by the private sector, either directly or through financial intermediaries. Thus the level of taxation versus deficit financing determines essentially the size of the increment in government debt, dD. Now suppose, for the sake of the argument, that the war had been entirely financed by taxes, dD being accordingly zero. It then follows from our earlier analysis that the burden of the war will be borne almost entirely by members of the war generation. For, in addition to the sacrifice of consumption and other amenities *during* the war, they will also bear the brunt of the reduced capital stock, their accumulation of net worth being limited to the permitted privately financed capital formation. Thus the burden falling on society as a whole after the war will fall primarily directly on the members of the war generation (affecting others only to the extent that the reduction in the stock of capital reduces total income by more than the return on capital). They will be forced after the war to maintain a reduced level of consumption over the rest of their life, tending to save heavily in their remaining earning span and to dissave at a greatly reduced rate thereafter. This behaviour in turn will produce, after the war, an abnormally large rate of aggregate saving, gradually declining with the disappearance of the war generation. As a result, by the time the war generation has disappeared, the war-time reduction in capital formation may have been substantially made up—this being more nearly true the closer the *oac* is to unity and the smaller the initial loss of capital.

If, on the other hand, through lower taxes the war generation is permitted to increase its terminal net worth by an additional amount dD, the effect, with respect to the present issue, is essentially the same as though at war's end it had been handed down gratuitously a corresponding amount of government bonds.[1] As usual, this will enable them to maintain a higher post-war consumption, reducing capital formation, by an extent that can range as high as dD, if the *oac* is unity. Thus the debt financing will generate both: (i) a transfer from the post-war to the war generation to the extent of taxes levied on the former to pay interest to the latter, and (ii) a permanent burden on society as a whole to the extent that the stock of capital is permanently reduced by dD—less any increase in W resulting directly from dD.[2] In so far as in the immediate post-war period the

---

[1] If the bonds issued during the war carried an exceptionally low rate of interest because of the monopoly position of the Government in the market the gift in question should be regarded, for present purposes, as represented by the market value of the bonds.

[2] Note that the incremental debt dD could be regarded as a burden on society even if the economy tended to suffer from long-run stagnation, *i.e.*, a chronic tendency for a very low or zero marginal productivity of capital. For while it is true that the larger consumption bestowed on the war generation would help to sustain consumption, and thus full employment, the same result could be achieved by reducing the taxes and expanding the consumption and saving of whoever was present at the appropriate later time.

Government, to speed up the reconstruction, pushes capital formation by raising taxes and creating a surplus, the long-run effect is eliminated. But the burden of debt financing is placed to that extent on those living in the relevant post-war period, which may again consist in part of the very same war generation.

If inflation is permitted to develop in the course of the war or immediately following it our analysis remains valid, provided the increment in the debt is measured in real, rather than money, terms. This net real increment can be expressed as $\dfrac{D_0 + dD}{1 + dP} - D_0$, where D_0 is the pre-war debt and dP is the relative increase in the price level in the course of the war inflation. The above quantity, it will be noted, may even be negative if $dP > \dfrac{dD}{D_0}$, i.e., if the increase in prices exceeds the relative increase in the debt. In this case the war generation will be made to carry even more than the cost of the war (unless its plight is improved by post-war transfers of income); and later generations may conceivably end up by benefiting from the war, at least following the transient period of high saving rates and rapid capital accumulation. Perhaps the picture we have been drawing has some relevance for an understanding of the post-war experience of such countries as Germany, Italy and Japan.

It seems hardly necessary to point out that our analysis in no way implies that in financing a war the use of debt should necessarily be minimised. Quite aside from obvious incentive considerations, there may be perfectly good equity reasons for lightening the burden of the generation that suffered through the war by granting them a more comfortable life after the war, at the expense of later generations.

We come finally to the effects of debt generated as a counter-cyclical measure. In view of the complexity of the problem, we shall have to limit ourselves to a sketchy treatment of a limited class of situations. Our main concern is to show that, even in this case, debt financing, though quite advantageous to the current generation, will generally not be costless to future generations, at least in terms of gross burden.

Consider a situation where, in spite of the easiest possible monetary policy and with the whole structure of interest rates reduced to its lowest feasible level, the demand for private capital formation is inadequate to absorb full-employment saving with a balanced budget. But let us suppose that the situation can be counted upon to be temporary and not to recur for a long time to come. If the Government does not step in there will be a temporary contraction of employment accompanied by a contraction of consumption and of addition to net worth, which is limited to the amount of private capital formation. Suppose, on the other hand, the Government expands its expenditure to the extent needed to fill the deflationary gap, and thereby runs into a deficit dD. Let us also imagine that it succeeds in choosing its action perfectly so as to maintain full employment without inflation. Hence consumption will be kept at the full-employment level and so will the accumulation of net worth; except that this accumulation will now take the form of an addition to the National Debt to the extent dD. Thus the government action involves a current gain to society which can be measured by the income which would have been lost otherwise. What we wish to know is whether this gain places any cost on later generations (and if so, how it can be valued).

Under the assumed conditions the answer would have to be affirmative at least under unity *oac*. In this case, in fact, we can see that the cost which was spared to society would have fallen entirely on the members of the depression generation. They would have been forced over their lifetime to cut their consumption by an amount (whose present value is) equal to the lost income. This reduction would be distributed partly within the depression but partly *after* the recovery, to an extent equal to the loss in accumulation of net worth in the depression. This reduction of consumption would in turn give rise to a somewhat higher rate of capital formation after the recovery, so that by the time the depression generation disappears the stock of capital would tend to be back to where it would have been without depression. In other words, under the assumed conditions failure of the Government to act, though costly to the depression generation, tends to be costless to later generations. On the other hand, if the Government acts, the depression generation does not have to maintain a lower consumption after the recovery, and accordingly, the lost private capital formation during the depression is never made up. The creation of dD introduces again a corresponding wedge between W and K which will tend permanently to reduce the amount of physical capital available to future generations. Hence there is a loss to them to the extent that at later points of time an increment to the stock of capital would make any net positive addition to output. If the debt is never meant to be retired, then at least with well-functioning capital markets, the consol rate, being an average of anticipated future short rates, may provide at least a rough measure of the (appropriate time average) annual loss. And in this sense if the Government borrows long, the interest bill on the incremental debt may provide a rough measure of the average future (gross) burden placed on society as a whole.[1]

Once more, recognising that the government action may involve a gross cost to future society does not imply that the action should not be taken. In the first place, because of multiplier effects the gain in income to those present is likely to be appreciably larger than the lost stock of capital

[1] Of course, under our present assumptions the burden as measured by the opportunity cost will be essentially zero during the period in which the debt is created, regardless of whether it takes the form of long-term debt, short-term debt or currency creation. But in the last two cases the current interest cost will not appropriately reflect the average future burden, unless we also take into account the rate the Government will have to pay on bonds sold at later points of time to re-finance the short-term debt or to reduce the money supply in order to prevent inflation.

which approximates the present value of the sacrificed income stream. In the second place, if the Government spends on projects which produce a yield in the future, then the gross burden will be offset by the gross yield and the net outcome may even be positive. In the third place, the gross burden can be eliminated if at some future point of time the Government runs a surplus and retires the debt. It is true that this will tend to place the burden of the original deficit on those who pay the taxes financing the surplus. But if the surplus follows the deficit in short order these people will be, to a large extent, the very same ones that benefited from the original deficit; thereby the questions of inter-generation equity are minimised. The case for eradicating the deficit with a nearby surplus is, of course, strongest if the government expenditure provides nothing useful for the future, or if the deficit reflects a reduction in the tax bill, expenditure constant, resulting either from built-in flexibility arrangements or from *ad hoc* tax rebates. Thus, our analysis turns out to provide a strong case in favour of what used to be called the cyclically balanced budget.

Although we cannot pursue further here the complex issues raised by the burden aspects of counter-cyclical fiscal operations, we hope to have succeeded in showing how the tools we have developed may provide some insight into the problem. One point should be apparent even from our sketchy treatment: namely, that in so far as counter-cyclical fiscal policy is concerned, our analysis does not require any significant re-evaluation of currently accepted views. Yet, by reminding us that fiscal operations involve considerations of inter-generation equity even when used for stabilisation purposes, it may help to clarify some issues. It does, for example, establish a *prima facie* case, at least with respect to *ad hoc* measures as distinguished from built-in stabilisers, for a course of action that will minimise the " deadweight " deficit and stimulate investment rather than consumption.[1] More generally, considerations of inter-generation equity suggest the desirability of a compromise between the orthodox balanced-budget principle and the principle of functional finance, which might be couched roughly as follows: as a rule, the Government should run a " deadweight " deficit only when full-employment saving exceeds the amount of capital formation consistent with the most favourable feasible monetary policy; and it should run a surplus, in so far as this is consistent with full employment, until it has wiped out previous deficits accumulated in the pursuance of this policy.

Franco Modigliani

Northwestern University,
    Evanston, Illinois.

[1] These considerations, *e.g.*, cast some doubt on the desirability of relying on personal tax cuts explicitly announced to be but temporary. For there is at least some ground for supposing that the temporary nature of the cut will tend to reduce the desirable impact effect on consumption and increase instead short-run saving and the (possibly) undesirable delayed consumption.

[21]

A/ PUBLIC DEBT, COST THEORY, AND THE FISCAL ILLUSION*

BY *James M. Buchanan*

I. Introduction

To what extent does the presence or absence of a "public debt illusion" affect the temporal location of debt burden? This question is important in itself, but in exploring it I hope also to clarify some of the points that remain obscure in the recent literature.[1] Puviani in his unique and highly original work on the fiscal illusion [15] (references on page 162), specifically included public debt as one institution through which such illusions may be generated. In the more recent discussion, Vickrey and others have explicitly made reference to a "public debt illusion," and, at least to some extent, the phenomenon of postponing debt burden through time is held to depend on the presence of some illusion.

Clarification of the term "illusion" is needed at the outset. Fol-

* This paper was written in its original form during the academic year, 1961-62, and it was presented as lectures at both the London School of Economics and at the University of Frankfurt. It has been substantially modified from its original version. In undertaking this revision, in 1963-64, I have benefited from several discussions with my colleagues, James Ferguson and Emilio Giardina.

1. See the references on page 162.

lowing normal usage, illusion will be used here to refer to a phenomenon that appears to be what it is not, at least to some of the persons who encounter it. By implication, errors in behavior may arise because of the presence of illusion, errors that could be avoided by more complete knowledge. Economists are, of course, familiar with the "money illusion," a phenomenon that causes people to interpret money values as real values. Presumably, the introduction of a monetary calculus has the effect of "hiding" or "distorting" the underlying real values of the alternatives that are confronted for choice. Men could be predicted to behave differently from the way they do behave were this illusion not present.

A public debt illusion may be defined similarly. It is, or may be, a phenomenon, inherent in the institution of public credit, that causes some men in the political group to behave differently from the way that they would behave in the absence of any illusion. Two different, but related, forms of an illusion will be discussed; these are considered in Sections II and III. I shall demonstrate that the presence or the absence of an illusion does not modify in any essential respects the elementary proposition that the real cost of public expenditures that are financed through debt tends to be shifted forward in time.

II. Undervaluation of Future Tax Liabilities

Vickrey suggests the most familiar form of a public debt illusion when he says: "if we assume a 'public debt illusion' under which individuals pay no attention to their share in the liability represented by the public debt. . . ."[2] This prompts the question: What is an individual's share in the liability that an issue of interest-bearing public debt represents?

I should specify, first of all, that I am concerned here with the individual as he participates, directly or indirectly, in a collective decision-making process where the creation of public debt is one among several fiscal alternatives. In short, I concentrate on the role of the individual as "voter-taxpayer-beneficiary." I shall assume that public debt, if chosen, will be issued independently of tax payments in subsequent time periods. In such a model, debt is serviced from general governmental revenues that are not earmarked in advance. Under such circumstances, the voter-taxpayer, if he is wholly free of illusion, will recognize that the contractual terms

2. See Vickrey [24], p. 133.

upon which debt is created embody claims upon his income, or that of his heirs, in future accounting periods, claims that the government will implement through some ordinary taxing process. These claims may be discounted and some present value estimated.

If present values, so computed by each individual, are summed over all members of the political group, the aggregate liability so expressed need not be equal to the value of the public debt that is marketed. A divergence may appear between these two magnitudes because of the limited time horizons upon which individual plans are made. Individuals do not expect to live forever, and they may not treat their heirs as linear extensions of themselves for economic decisions. It does not seem appropriate to define as illusory behavior that stems from mere limitations on time horizons. However, I do not want to introduce here the many problems of "rational" behavior that the limitations of human life impose. I shall, therefore, examine the public debt illusion under the simplifying assumption that all persons act "as if" they expect to live forever. Even in this model, the single individual will find it difficult to determine his own particular share in the liability represented by public debt. The distribution of taxes required to service the debt will be independently chosen in each time period, in the absence of tied sources. This political fact requires that the individual consider a probability distribution of outcomes for his own share. Again, however, we assume that he does carry out the necessary calculations, and that each person arrives finally at a certainty equivalent for his own expected tax liability. In this highly rarified model, the sum of the present values separately estimated for all individuals should approximate the value of the debt that is to be issued.

No public debt illusion exists in this model. There is no net undervaluation of the future tax obligations that the debt represents. The question now is one of determining the difference in behavior between this model and one in which an illusion is explicitly assumed to be present. Is it correct, as Vickrey suggests, to say that "elimination of this factor eliminates the shifting to the future entirely. . ."?[3] Is the "burden of public debt" wholly concentrated on the "present generation," in the "here and now" of the initial period, in the absence of an undervaluation illusion?

The answer to each of these questions is, I think, negative. And the failure of economists to recognize this is based, in part, on an

3. Vickrey [24], p. 135.

elemental, but near-universal, confusion in the theory of costs.[4] The presence or absence of an illusion, defined in the sense of some failure to discount properly future tax liabilities, is irrelevant to the question of "shifting" a burden of debt to the future periods. The illusion is important, and relevant, only in its effects on *decisions* made at the moment of the original debt issue or creation. Its presence or absence at this moment determines the individual's estimate of the *subjective cost* that a decision to finance public expenditures with debt issue involves. The illusion has no bearing on the distribution of the *objective cost* of this decision *over time*.

Before elaborating this point, it is useful to clarify the distinction between subjective cost and objective cost in a more general setting unrelated to public debt. Many economists overlook this difference, despite repeated warnings.[5] Subjective cost is the obstacle to decision; it consists in the alternative that is foregone *at the moment of choice*, an alternative which can, because it is rejected, never be attained or realized. This cost is wholly within the "mind" of the individual chooser, and it can never be measured by an external observer. It exists temporally only in the moment preceding an act of choice, if it can be dated at all. It results from the sense of anticipating enjoyments that must be foregone. All subjective cost is anticipatory in this sense; hence, conceptually, there is no distinction between an alternative foregone immediately subsequent to decision and one foregone years afterward. Both are, once and for all, given up once a positive choice is made. For this reason, the subjective cost involved in debt issue, as conceived by the voter-taxpayer who is "choosing," must be concentrated in the moment of decision, despite the fact that this cost arises wholly from some current expectation of *future* tax liabilities. The debt illusion that Vickrey mentions has to do with the individual's estimation of this subjective cost. If illusion exists, there may be some undervaluation of the alternative with which debt issue is compared, and, because of this, errors may be made which would, in the absence of illusion, be avoided.

Subjective cost need not be equal to what is here called objective cost, if equality is meaningful at all between these two magnitudes.

4. In my own earlier writings on public debt, I shared this confusion; hence, my failure to be more explicit concerning the meaning of "burden" in my whole analysis [3, 4].

5. Notably by G. F. Thirlby [21, 22], but also by Hayek [8], Robbins [17], and Wiseman [25].

The fact that, in competitive equilibrium, the ability of the buyer-seller to adjust his behavior to a set of uniform market-determined prices converts subjective costs into an objectively-measurable quantity does not imply that, in nonequilibrium situations of choice, any equality need hold. Objective cost is defined as actual resource services that are "given up" or "paid out" to attain the alternative that is chosen. Conceptually, objective cost can be measured by some person external to the decision maker; a real flow of resource services can be observed. Objective cost is *never* realized until *after* decision. The nature of time itself prevents the simultaneity of choice and consequence that is assumed in so much of economic analysis. For many purposes, of course, this temporal gap between the incurring of subjective cost at the moment of definitive choice and the incurring of objective cost subsequent to choice may be ignored. But the distinction clearly cannot be neglected in any discussion of debt, public or private, since the essence of debt is the postponement of objective cost in time.[6]

It is, of course, the objective cost of the public project that is debt financed which is shifted to the future or postponed. Subjective cost or "burden," that which serves as an obstacle to decision, cannot be shifted, by the fact of decision itself, and it is this cost that is affected by illusion. The resource services that are actually committed upon a decision to borrow, to create debt, that actually must be "paid out" or "given up" in exchange for the benefits of the debt-financed collective services can be dated at the time that resource services are transferred from individuals to the fisc, to the extent that these are drawn from current consumption.[7] This transfer takes place in periods subsequent to debt issue as interest and amortization charges come due. This is as true for private debt as for public debt. There is no conceptual difference between the two other than the greater likelihood that

6. The failure to see that *two* costs are associated with any act of choice, a subjective cost and an objective cost, has plagued much of the recent discussion on public debt, including my own. Note, especially, how the recognition of this point clarifies the ambiguity raised in Footnote 1, page 746, in Modigliani's paper [13]. Among the recent contributors, only Scitovsky [18] seems to note a distinction, but he erroneously labels objective costs as "social" and, because of this, misinterprets its meaning.

7. If the taxes levied for the purpose of servicing the public debt should cause individual taxpayers to draw down capital rather than consumption funds, the objective costs of the collective services are postponed even farther into the future. See the discussion on this point below.

TAXPAYERS' ANTICIPATIONS AND FISCAL ILLUSION   **155**

the illusion herein discussed will be present under public rather than under private debt due to the complex probability calculus that is necessary to determine individual liability. To the extent that the illusion arises in public debt, more mistakes are likely to be made, but no difference in the temporal location of objective cost is generated.

In the complete absence of illusion, the sacrifice of resources may have been fully anticipated when the initial decision to borrow was made. This does not modify the conclusion, however, that, had the project been tax financed and debt not issued, resource services in the amount of current interest-amortization charges could remain in the possession of the individual during those periods when debt service is necessary.

The concepts of national income accounting, when combined with the failure to distinguish properly between subjective and objective cost or "burden," have been largely responsible for the widespread acceptance of the fallacious idea that there is no postponement of cost involved in the creation of internal public debt. If we look at the fiscal operation from an aggregative or "social" point of view, resources are, of course, "given up" during the time period in which the public expenditure project is undertaken. The members of the group who bear this objective cost, who suffer this "burden" in terms of sacrificed potential consumption in the period of debt creation, *are not* the "purchasers" of the public project, the voters-taxpayers-borrowers-beneficiaries. Those who bear this initial-period objective cost are, instead, those members of the group who choose to buy the government securities that are offered for sale in a wholly private, voluntary, noncollective transaction. These persons will also suffer a subjective cost upon their decision to lend current resources to the collectivity. And the objective cost which they bear arises when they "pay out" current purchasing power, current command over resources, to the public treasury in exchange for the bonds. Their exchange is not, however, for the benefits of the project that is being financed through the fiscal process but is, instead, for the future income stream that inheres in the debt instruments, the government securities. The central feature of public credit lies in its facilitation of this dual exchange between the taxpayer-borrower and the bond purchaser-lender. Two decisions are involved, as there must be in any exchange, since two parties to the exchange are present, and each decision has associated with it both a subjective and an objective cost element. The theory of public debt that I have called elsewhere the "new orthodoxy" is based on an oversight of these embarrassingly simple facts.

III. Failure to Distinguish Owned and Non-Owned Assets

Puviani stressed a slightly different, although related, form of public debt illusion from that which has been discussed above. Let us begin with the familiar Ricardian equivalence between a debt obligation, which embodies the levy of an annual tax in perpetuity, and an extraordinary tax, which collects the full capital sum in the initial period. In such an equivalence, any illusion of the Vickrey type is absent, and, also, the model remains at the level of individual decision. To introduce the standard numerical example, the individual is confronted with the choice of paying a tax of $2,000 once and for all, or paying the sum required to service a debt of this amount through an annual levy of $100 in perpetuity, assuming a discount-interest rate of 5 per cent. Puviani suggested that, even here, the individual will not be indifferent between these two alternatives, but that he will tend to choose the annual tax in perpetuity. He will do so, not because he undervalues future tax obligations, but because he will not treat the acknowledged claims as diminution in the value of his owned assets in the same way that he would treat the once-and-for-all current tax alternative. In the first case, argued Puviani, the individual knows that he will continue to administer the same total assets, undiminished in productive power. The fact that the debt, as embodied in the annual tax in perpetuity, alienates a certain share of these assets will not be fully appreciated even though, in strict balance-sheet terms, the tax liability is fully capitalized. In this sense, therefore, a "public debt illusion" may exist.[8]

This argument applies to debt generally; there is no particular difference between public and private debt in this respect. When a decision to borrow is made, alternatives are, as of that moment, foregone. If we assume that loan contracts are enforced, the moment of decision to borrow and spend removes, once and for all, any opportunity that the individual or group may have for utilizing a certain share of income during subsequent time periods. This remains true independently of the rationality of the borrowing-spending decision. As suggested earlier, the subjective cost, which

8. See the citation from Puviani contained in Fasiani [7], p. 131.

exists solely in the anticipation of foregone opportunities, is present only at the moment of choice when, to any external observer, nothing actually "happens." Resources are only "paid out" by the borrower to the lender as interest and amortization charges come due over time. This pay out does have a temporal sequence that may be observed. And this pay out always reduces potential consumption opportunities below what they would be otherwise, but this need not impose any "burden" in the subjective or "felt" sense. Psychologically, however, the alienation that would be required to eliminate all subjective burden here becomes almost impossible to imagine. At the moment of a borrowing decision, it is conceivable that the individual could "chop off" or "earmark" a sufficient portion of his total capital value, produced by discounting his future earnings stream, so that the servicing of the debt could take place "outside" his internal calculus. He could, in this way, simply treat this portion of his "assets" *as if* it were owned by his creditors. Or, in the extreme, he might actually implement a transfer of title. Note, however, that human as well as nonhuman capital must be included in total assets here, and, both institutionally and behaviorally, it is difficult to think of a transfer of ownership of human capital assets.

If such a complete alienation is not made, however, there will appear to be a "burden" of debt, in some genuinely subjective sense. If the borrower retains what we may call psychological or behavioral ownership of assets, even when these are offset by liabilities, he will "receive" income and then "transfer" this to his creditors. He will, as Puviani implies, suffer some "burden" here, a feeling of deprivation, even though he has no alternative open to him. That is to say, he is confronted with no choice; hence, the subjective burden that he suffers here is not analogous to the subjective cost of decision, previously discussed, which arises precisely because he does have alternatives for choice. Indirect evidence of this Puviani-type of asset illusion is to be found in common or ordinary language where reference is universally made to the "burden" of carrying debt, public or private. By contrast, when an individual is observed to have purchased ordinary commodities, we do not find reference to his suffering a "burden of potatoes."

The temporal aspects of life itself make a Puviani-type illusion plausible. The individual who lives in the moment subsequent to choice is not the same person who has chosen, at least in all respects.

The individual who inherits the consequences of past commitments, even those made by himself, in some physical sense of continuity, will always consider "what might have been," and the alternatives as seen retrospectively must look different from those comtemplated at the time of choice.[9] The institution of debt, public or private, makes this attitude especially likely to arise since the indivdual debtor must, in an objectively observable sense, transfer resource services to creditors, resource services that he "might have" retained had not the borrowing commitment been made at some earlier point in time.

Thus, the Puviani hypothesis implies that the individual, when faced with a pure Ricardian choice, will prefer the debt-annual tax alternative, but also that in subsequent periods, despite the full discounting of future taxes that is inherent in the Ricardian equivalence, he will "feel a burden of debt." This should not be taken to suggest that there exists any shifting of the subjective cost of the debt-issue decision to future periods. It is possible that the subjective cost at the time of decision can be accurately estimated (as it is in the Ricardian equivalence), that no Vickrey-type illusion exists at all, and yet there may remain a subjective "burden" during periods of resource transfer. The fallacy to be avoided here is that of assuming that subjective or "felt" burden need add up to any particular sum. "The coward dies a thousand deaths."[10]

A contrast between debt issue and capital consumption illustrates the Puviani illusion. Analytically, an act of borrowing is not different from "using up" or "eating up" capital. In either case, the subjective cost, the negative side of the account that is relevant for decision, the rejected alternative, is represented in the mind of the chooser by some present value of an income stream over subsequent time periods, an income stream which will come into being if a debt creation or capital consumption decision is not made, but which can never come into being at all if a positive option for either debt creation or capital consumption is exercised. The objective cost appears to be different in the two cases, but this ap-

---

9. For an interesting treatment of the intertemporal inconsistency of decision, see the paper by Strotz [20].

10. The analysis developed in this section has much in common with that discussed by James Ferguson, included elsewhere in this volume. Although these treatments were developed independently in the initial stages, I think that there now exists substantial agreement between us on the relevant issues in the controversy.

parent difference is due strictly to the institutional realities that
reflect the presence of the Puviani illusion. The effective transfer
of resource services, in the case of capital consumption as well as
debt, occurs in future periods. By definition, capital, as capital,
embodies potential consumption in future periods. Converting
capital into current consumption potential represents a transfer of
resource services away from potential consumption in the future.
But capital, once consumed, once "eaten up," appears to be consumed. The alienation of assets appears to be made immediately
after decision despite the fact that current consumption is no different here than it would be under borrowing. The individual living in periods after capital is overtly consumed has no sensation of
"owning" assets that have already been destroyed in some "eating
up" process, or of transferring income (potential consumption)
from these nonexistent assets to "creditors." Hence, the presence
of a "felt" burden of past decisions is much less likely to exist under capital consumption than under debt. In any time period, a person's income is, of course, in part the consequence of past decisions
on the accumulation and decumulation of capital, private and public, human and nonhuman. But one does not, normally, feel overburdened by these past decisions. What is done is considered to be
done, and that is that.

This attitude is in evident contrast to that which arises when
debt obligations are outstanding. As suggested, the objective cost
stream is identical in the two cases. Borrowing does not, however,
carry with it the same alienation of claims to assets that capital consumption does. Assets are not really "destroyed" for the individual in the same behavioral sense under these two institutional operations.

In their recent contributions to the debt theory discussion,
Modigliani [13] and Vickrey [24] have stressed the point that
taxation, insofar as it impinges on capital formation, involves a
shifting to the future of the objective cost of the public project
that is financed. Insofar as the taxpayer chooses to meet his current
obligation by drawing down his rate of capital formation instead of
restricting consumption, he is, of course, reducing his income over
future periods. The objective cost of the project is, to this extent,
effectively shifted forward or postponed. Where Modigliani, Vickrey, and, also, Musgrave [14] err is in their suggestion that public debt issue involves such a postponing of objective cost *only* if,

in the aggregate, the rate of capital formation in the economy is less than it would be under the tax alternative. This extension of an argument that is basically correct represents a lapsing back into a sophisticated version of the national accounting fallacy that has distorted the more naïve discussions of public debts. Even if those persons who purchase the bonds should do so wholly out of funds otherwise destined to current consumption, the public debt, as such, still involves a shifting of objective cost to future periods, by the individual members of the political group, considered in their role as "purchasers" of the debt-financed public project, that is, as taxpayers-borrowers. The fact that, in the aggregate, the expanded public utilization of resources on behalf of these persons, or persons acting as taxpayers-borrowers-beneficiaries, is just offset by the reduction in resources devoted to consumption by the lenders-bond purchasers, or persons acting in this capacity, has no relevance for any fiscal decision. It is both meaningless and misleading to talk here in terms of "social" or "global" aggregates. For the individuals, as taxpayer-borrowers, as purchasers of the desired collective goods project, the issue of public debt is a *means of consuming* capital. That is to say, the operation is for them analytically equivalent to the imposition of a capital levy upon themselves to finance the same project, assuming away distributional differences and the Vickrey-type illusion. The capital levy is not normally considered for reason of the Puviani illusion.

As a taxpayer-borrower, the individual's income stream (his potential consumption) in future periods is reduced by the full amount of the debt service charges that are imposed upon him. He could prevent this only if, when the debt is initially created, he should set aside resources and *create capital* sufficient to generate an income equivalent to that necessary to meet future debt service charges. The individual, as taxpayer-borrower, could, in this manner, convert the future objective cost into a current-period objective cost. If, however, the model of political choice is assumed to be a voluntaristic one, the "representative" taxpayer-borrower could accomplish this purpose far more simply by accepting current tax financing rather than debt financing for the public project. Just as capital consumption is the analytical equivalent of debt creation, so capital creation is the analytical equivalent of debt retirement. Hence, capital creation designed to offset the temporal effects of debt creation can occur only if the debt creation is imposed on the individual externally, and not chosen by him.

The point to be emphasized is that whether or not the bond purchaser draws funds from his own consumption or from investment during the initial period is wholly irrelevant to the taxpayer-borrower, except in a remote and indirect way. The aggregate rate of capital formation in an economy is, of course, affected by the source of the funds used to purchase public debt instruments. This rate is a meaningful datum for some purposes. But such an aggregate rate of investment does not directly affect or influence the decisions of individuals as they participate in fiscal decisions made on behalf of the whole collectivity. In this capacity, individuals recognize only that public debt, regardless of the source of funds, will impose an objective cost upon them that is represented by a necessary transfer of resources away from them in future periods. If they do not want to incur this temporal pattern of resource pay-out they will not choose to create debt in the first place.

The fact that the totality of the saving-investing decisions in the whole economy acts to insure that the rate of capital formation shall be such-and-such cannot, directly, modify the essential elements in debt creation as a fiscal operation.

IV. Conclusion

Public debts probably generate fiscal illusions of both the Vickrey and the Puviani sort. Individuals, for many reasons, probably do undervalue the future tax liabilities that an issue of debt embodies, and, even if they do not, they should probably still prefer debt to the current tax alternative. The analysis of this paper has demonstrated, however, that the presence or absence of illusion does not affect the temporal pattern of resource payment which debt issue must involve. The presence of a Vickrey-type illusion may affect the subjective cost estimates involved in making a decision to borrow, and, because of this, it may produce errors in the behavior of individuals as they participate in collective choice processes. Once a decision is made, however, the objective cost of the debt-financed project can be located only in time periods following that in which the debt is created and the funds expended for the provision of collective services.

The Puviani illusion acts to create a behavioral distinction between capital consumption and borrowing, despite the analytical equivalence between these two institutions. This distinction allows us to explain the "felt" burden of debt, even when future tax liabilities have been fully and accurately capitalized in the esti-

162   PUBLIC DEBT AND FUTURE GENERATIONS

mate for subjective cost at the time of decision. A recognition of this analytical equivalence also leads to the conclusion that taxation, insofar as individuals draw down capital funds to meet current tax obligations, can also involve a postponement of objective cost in time. Here, as in the case of debt, the relevant conversion decisions are made by individuals, and serious confusion can result from an undue concentration on "social" aggregates, considered apart from individual choices. Individuals, as taxpayer-borrowers, who are observed to choose public debt as a fiscal alternative, will confront an objective cost in future income periods. This remains true independently of the sources from which the funds that are used to finance the public project are originally drawn.

References

1. Bowen, William G., Richard G. Davis, and David H. Kopf. "The Burden of the Public Debt: Reply," *The American Economic Review*, LI (March, 1961), 141-43.
2. ———. "The Public Debt: A Burden on Future Generations?" *The American Economic Review*, L (September, 1960), 701-6.
3. Buchanan, James M. *Fiscal Theory and Political Economy: Selected Essays*. Chapel Hill: The University of North Carolina Press, 1960, especially pp. 51-59.
4. ———. *Public Principles of Public Debt*, Homewood, Illinois: Richard D. Irwin, Inc., 1958.
5. De Marco De Viti, Antonio. "La pressione tributaria dell'imposta e del prestito," *Giornale degli economisti*, I (1893), 38-67, 216-31.
6. Elliott, James R. "The Burden of the Public Debt: Comment," *The American Economic Review*, LI (March, 1961), 139-41.
7. Fasiani, M. *Principii di scienza delle finanze*. Vol. I, 2nd ed. Torino, 1950, Chapter 3.
8. Hayek, F. A. "Economics and Knowledge," *Economica*, IV (February, 1937), 33-54.
9. Lerner, Abba P. "The Burden of Debt," *The Review of Economics and Statistics*, XLIII (May, 1961), 139-41.
10. Meade, James E. "Is the National Debt a Burden?" *Oxford Economic Papers*, X (June, 1958), 163-83.
11. ———. "Is the National Debt a Burden: A Correction," *Oxford Economic Papers*, XI (June, 1959), 109-11.
12. Miller, H. Lawrence, Jr. "Anticipated and Unanticipated Consequences of Public Debt Creation," *Economica*, XXIX (November, 1962), 410-19.
13. Modigliani, Franco. "Long-Run Implications of Alternative Fiscal Policies and the Burden of the National Debt," *The Economic Journal*, LXXI (December, 1961), 730-55.

14. Musgrave, Richard A. *The Theory of Public Finance.* New York: McGraw-Hill Book Company, Inc., 1959, Chapter 23.
15. Puviani, A. *Teoria dell'illusione finanziaria.* Palermo, 1903.
16. Ricardo, David. *Principles of Political Economy and Taxation, Works and Correspondence.* I, Royal Economic Society, 1951, 244-46.
17. Robbins, L. "Remarks Upon Certain Aspects of the Theory of Costs," *The Economic Journal,* XLIV (March, 1934), 1-18.
18. Scitovsky, Tibor. "The Burden of the Public Debt: Comment," *The American Economic Review,* LI (March, 1961), 137-39.
19. Shoup, Carl S. "Debt Financing and Future Generations," *The Economic Journal,* LXXII (December, 1962), 887-98.
20. Strotz, R. H. "Myopia and Inconsistency in Dynamic Utility Maximization," *The Review of Economic Studies,* XXIII (1956), 165-80.
21. Thirlby, G. F. "Economists' Cost Rules and Equilibrium Theory," *Economica,* XXVII (May, 1960), 148-57.
22. ———. "The Subjective Theory of Value and Accounting 'Cost'," *Economica,* XIII (February, 1946), 32-49.
23. Tullock, Gordon. "Public Debt—Who Bears the Burden?" *Rivista di diritto finanziario e scienza delle finanze,* XXII (June, 1963), 207-13.
24. Vickrey, William. "The Burden of the Public Debt: Comment," *The American Economic Review,* LI (March, 1961), 132-37.
25. Wiseman, J. "Uncertainty, Costs, and Collectivist Economic Planning," *Economica,* XX (May, 1953), 118-28.

[22]

THE BURDEN OF THE PUBLIC DEBT: A REVIEW ARTICLE

James Tobin*

Does debt-financing of public expenditure place a "burden" on future generations? The answer has long been "yes" in conservative financial and political circles, but "no" among academic economists. A lively controversy on the question has raged in economic journals in recent years, provoked mainly by the iconoclastic writings of James Buchanan, who contends that his fellow economists are much farther from the truth than the laymen whom they accuse of primitive error.

Mr. Ferguson has collected twenty-three of the most important and representative contributions to the debate.[1] Three of these, including one previously unpublished paper, are by Buchanan. The anthology is quite different from most of the readings volumes which are pouring from the presses these days to cash in on the growing student market. Although it will be useful to students, Ferguson's volume also serves a definite scholarly and professional purpose. The volume is carefully organized to achieve the unity which a well-defined topic makes possible. The editor has provided the "names and numbers of all the players" in an introduction, a final comment, and a bibliography. His contributions are a useful guide for the reader venturing on to this murky battleground for the first time.

Two ground rules are almost universally respected by the combatants. One is to assume full employment. The other is to assume a fixed program of government expenditure; the "gross" burden in question results from financing a fixed program by issuing debt instead of levying taxes. The debate does not concern the merits of debt-financed government expenditure, which would have to be judged by the "net" burden allowing for benefits. In logic at least, these ground rules deny the political champions of fiscal orthodoxy much of the comfort which the arguments of Buchanan and other discoverers of debt burden might seem to provide. President Eisenhower's strictures, which are much quoted in the book, made no fine distinctions between full employment and unemployment. They were, moreover, directed against increases in public expenditure, without nice calculation whether the benefits to future generations might outweigh the burdens.

No one disputes the fact that in a closed economy with full employment the resources used for government expenditure are drawn from other *current* uses of resources. Given the government program, the reduction in resources available for *current* nongovernment use is independent of the method of financing the government. This reasoning has traditionally led economists to deny that the burden of public expenditure can be shifted forward in time by issuing

* Yale University.
1. *Public Debt & Future Generations*. Edited by James M. Ferguson. University of North Carolina Press, 1964. Pp. 234. $6.75.

679

internal debt rather than taxing. The debt can be no burden, because future payments of interest or principal from taxpayers to bondholders will be transfers involving no aggregate draft on resources. They may involve a redistribution of income. They may even impose a "deadweight loss" because taxes distort incentives. But these recognized qualifications of the traditional view are not what the new heretics have in mind.

They are not all of the same mind. Three views may be distinguished. One is Buchanan's. Stripped of all embellishment, it reduces to the assertion that payment of taxes is *per se* a burden—whether or not the taxes affect incentives and resource allocation. Since debt finance postpones the levy of taxes, it obviously shifts Buchanan's burden to future generations. The justification for this definition is that taxes are compulsory and involuntary. In contrast, market transactions, including the purchase of public debt, are voluntary agreements. Buchanan's view implies that democratic societies "burden" themselves whenever they agree to a social compact binding on all their members. On the other hand, agreements which do not involve governmental coercion evidently burden none of the participants.

The political theory is questionable, and so is the economics. Does Buchanan really mean that government imposes no burden when it acts through the market? It is true that purchasers of government bonds are willing lenders. But is there no burden on would-be private borrowers whom government borrowing displaces from the bond market by raising interest rates? Do excise taxes involve no burden because they are paid only as an incident of voluntary market transactions? Buchanan's simplistic view of burden throws away the whole "incidence and effects" literature of public finance.

The second concept of burden, most forcefully advocated by Modigliani in this volume, is closer to the traditional analysis, of which it is more a refinement than a rejection. The method of financing government expenditure does not alter the size of the draft on current resources. But it may alter the nature of the private uses of resources which are displaced. Modigliani argues that debt finance will displace mainly investment, and tax finance mainly consumption. The burden of debt finance on future generations is that they inherit a smaller capital stock than if tax finance had been used. This is indeed an implication of the widely held view that, while full employment can be maintained by tight money and deficit spending, such a policy mix is unfavorable to capital accumulation and growth. (Modigliani goes further. On the basis of his life-cycle consumption-saving model he contends that each generation will do only so much saving; the more of this which is absorbed by government debt the less will be available for capital formation. Thus even anti-recession deficit finance impairs the inheritance of the next generation.)

Two main comments on the Modigliani view are suggested in or by the debate. First, the crucial matter is the national rate of capital formation, not debts or deficits *per se*. On Modigliani's logic, we impose a burden on future generations whenever we fail to run a surplus, or a bigger surplus, not just when we engage in debt finance. Taxes are not intrinsically virtuous. Some forms of current taxation shift the burden to the future by discouraging current investment; and debt finance keeps the burden in the present to the extent that it discourages consumer borrowing.

More broadly, there are many sins of omission and commission by which the present generation can contrive to bequeath to the future a smaller capital stock than it might. Why single out debt finance to bear the whole burden of guilt? Is it not more to the point, as Mishan argues in his contribution, to ask what is intergenerational equity anyway? If some "burden" of current public expenditure is shifted to the future, so what? Perhaps it should be. The answer cannot be found in any simple budgetary rule. It will depend on the nature of the public expenditure, and it will involve a judgment of the adequacy or over-adequacy of the provisions for the future the current generation is already making through private and public investment.

The second comment questions the consumption-saving behavior assumed in the Modigliani notion of the burden. Is it not based on some asymmetrical illusion? Society fools itself into consuming more, thinking that possession of government paper provides for its future. Why don't those who will have to pay taxes to service the debt—or even those who will be squeezed out of consumer goods markets when the holders of government paper spend it—consider themselves poorer and save more accordingly?

This observation threatens not only Modigliani's concept of debt burden but equally the belief that the government can influence investment and growth by varying the fiscal-monetary mix. Indeed it comes dangerously close to denying that any internal financial and monetary arrangements are of any real consequence. One does not have to assume inconsistent expectations or irrational money illusion to believe that financial intermediation—whether through government or through banks and insurance companies—can by pooling and reallocating risks diminish some of the needs which generate saving. Ultimately this is an empirical question, and the weight of evidence is that, illusion or not, the private income and wealth corresponding to government deficit and debt stimulate consumption.

Bowen, Davis, and Kopf—whose original essay is reprinted here along with several critiques and rejoinders—seem to provide still a third account of how the burden is shifted to future generations. The burden they have in mind seems to be the same as Modigliani's, but in Bowen *et al.* the shift is delayed. They assume that the initial public expenditure, although debt-financed, draws resources from consumption, not from investment. Thus "Generation I" appears to have shouldered the burden squarely, but the authors are at pains to point out how they may later try to unload it on to their heirs. By going on a consumption binge in retirement, financed by selling their government securities, Generation I forces Generation II either to accept a smaller inheritance of real capital or to finance their parents' binge by extra saving. In either case Generation II can play the same game with Generation III. And so on. (Perhaps President Eisenhower would have been less distressed had he known that any burdens we transmit to our grandchildren they can simply pass on to their grandchildren, *ad infinitum.*)

While the authors have provided an interesting account of the possibilities in wars between overlapping generations, it is not clear why government debt should be the central battlefield. Even if Generation I had taxed itself to pay for the government expenditure, they might still have both the desire and the means for compensatory high living in retirement.

Finally, nothing in this volume—unless one accepts Buchanan's identification of burden with tax payments—disturbs economists' customary insistence on the essential difference between internal and foreign debt. This is a distinction which lay critics of debt finance do not respect. For this reason alone, burden finders like Bowen, Davis, and Kopf should never have begun by saying they proposed to prove their fellow economists wrong and President Eisenhower right.

[23]

THE ICONS OF PUBLIC DEBT

James M. Buchanan*

THE THEORY of public debt remains a "murky battleground." My own attempts at clarifying some of the elementary principles, along with those of my supporters-defenders, have failed to convince large numbers of professional economists. Professor James Tobin, in his recent review article[1] of the book edited by James Ferguson, has acutely if indirectly noted the reason for this failure through his reference to my "iconoclastic writings." An iconoclast is defined as a destroyer of religious images or icons. To win the day, the iconoclast must provide more than straightforward logical argument; he must also shatter faith.[2] My notions about debt burden seem to counter images that are more than intellectual constructions, more than scientific paradigms. If this is true, some excuse is provided for repetition and clarification of basic propositions, especially when such a competent economist as James Tobin can seem so fundamentally confused about my own admittedly "simplistic view."

This view, according to Tobin, "throws away the whole 'incidence and effects' literature of public finance." No statement could be more in error. My aim in the whole discussion has been, and remains, that of answering the fundamental question: Who pays, and when, for public expenditures that are financed by debt issue instead of taxation or money creation? This is precisely the incidence question. Who pays the income tax; what is the incidence of the income tax? These are mere short-hand versions of: Who finally pays for the public expenditures that are financed through the income tax? Precisely contrary to Tobin's charge, my efforts can best be interpreted as attempts to bring the theory of public debt back into the incidence framework.

"Stripped of all embellishment, it (Buchanan's view) reduces to the assertion that payment of taxes is *per se* a burden—whether or not the taxes affect incentives and resource allocation. Since debt finance postpones the levy of taxes, it obviously shifts Buchanan's burden to future generations." With this statement I have no quarrel, and, as I have asserted, the point is elementary, obvious, and self-evident. Which makes all the more mysterious the continuing refusal of highly competent economists to acknowledge it. Tobin follows the above with: "The justification for this definition is that taxes are compulsory and involuntary. In contrast, market transactions, including the purchase of public debt, are voluntary agreements." Why does Tobin consider the initial statement to require any justification? There is nothing in my analysis that connects the elementary point with compulsion or coercion of tax payments. In its broadest sense, the underlying political model for my analysis is democratic, and, at some level, individuals can be said to agree to pay taxes in exchange for public goods. Whether the individual,

* University of Virginia.

1. James Tobin, "The Burden of The Public Debt: A Review Article," *The Journal of Finance*, Vol. XX, No. 4 (December 1965), 679-82.

2. Perhaps Nietzsche's statement is relevant here. "Faith means not *wanting* to know what is true." Nietzsche in *Antichrist*, cited by Walter Kaufmann, *The Owl and The Nightingale* (London: Faber and Faber, 1959), p. 173.

in the actual moment of payment, feels himself coerced or whether he feels that he is voluntarily contributing to a worthwhile collective purpose is wholly irrelevant for the validity of my central proposition concerning the temporal location of burden. The fact that *taxes are payments* is, in itself, sufficient. In this sense, taxes are no different from prices paid in market transactions. The payment of prices for ordinary goods and services is also, per se, a burden. This we all accept without the sophistication of economic theory.

Why the confusion here, which Tobin seems to share with other contributors to the debt-burden controversy? As he suggests, the "political theory is questionable," but it is the unstated political theory implicit in the neo-Keynesian debt analysis and not my own. In the latter, individuals, acting as members of a democratically organized collectivity, choose to finance specific public outlays through debt issue, the sale of interest-bearing obligations. In so doing, these same persons, explicitly or implicitly, act to postpone the payment for these outlays through time. In quite a separate, and wholly different, capacity, individuals, domestic or foreign, purchase the interest-bearing bonds. In this, strictly individualistic setting, individuals give up current command over resource services in exchange for future income. The point is that *two*, not one, transactions are involved here. In one the individual acts as a member of the collectivity; in the other he does not. Unless this fact is recognized, debt issue stands in danger of being touted as the fiscal equivalent of the perpetual motion machine which will allow beneficial public programs to be financed without cost on anyone at any time.

There are, of course, secondary effects of debt issue, such as the effects on interest rates, the effects of taxes on allocation, etc., and these may be important. My objective has been, and is, to clarify the primary effects before complicating the analysis with these secondary ones. This comment applies also to the Modigliani-Vickrey analysis of the effects of debt on capital accumulation. This whole aspect of the discussion is not germane to the primary analysis of shifting or postponing the burden of payment through time that debt, public or private, facilitates.

Both Tobin and Musgrave,[3] in their reviews of the Ferguson volume, suggest that the whole analysis is applicable only when full employment is assumed to be present. If this were valid, the analysis would, indeed, be severely limited in scope. The postponement of cost or burden that debt issue facilitates is, however, as valid for unemployment as for full-employment models. Throughout the debate, and through most of the post-Keynesian fiscal policy discussion, there has been a consistent refusal of economists to make the vital distinction between money creation and debt issue. Failing to make this distinction, they have equated deficit creation with debt issue directly. Had they been familiar with the teachings of Henry Simons which, to my knowledge, have not yet been refuted, they would have acknowledged that the issue of interest-bearing debt is never optimal when the aim is to shore up aggregate demand. In the classic Keynesian situation, there are no real costs of employing otherwise idle resources. Money creation is clearly indicated; there are no costs to bear, no burden to be shared, currently or in later periods. If, because of error in analysis or rigidity in institutions, interest-bearing debt is used in such situations, the postponed cost may, indeed, be a small price to pay for the benefits that are secured by the outlay. This fact does not, however, remove the costs on future-period taxpayers, costs which, in this case, are wholly excessive and unnecessary.

3. R. A. Musgrave, "Review" of Ferguson, *Public Debt and Future Generations, American Economic Review*, LV (December 1965), 1226-28.

Tobin concludes by stating that "nothing . . .—unless one accepts Buchanan's identification of burden with tax payments—disturbs economists' customary insistence on the essential difference between internal and foreign debt." With this statement I am in accord, since, presumably, Tobin would allow his orthodoxy to be disturbed if my definition of burden should prevail. The question concerns whether or not burden or cost can be identified with tax payments in the primary sense. If tax payments are not made by individuals in some sort of exchange for public services, in present, past, or future periods, what are they made in exchange for? If we can secure public goods and services without paying taxes (including inflation) then why not private goods without prices? This remains the Tobin mystery upon which we have a right to seek enlightenment. Until I am shown otherwise, I shall continue to hold that many of my fellow economists have been, and remain, wrong in their elementary understanding of public debt.

But, please, fellow iconoclasts, no more references to President Eisenhower! Our task is difficult enough, and the icons will be shattered much more quickly by the opposing procedure. Let us try to invent more complex and abstruse means of stating the simple propositions; only then can we perhaps carry conviction with the majority of modern economists.

[24]

REPLY

JAMES TOBIN*

As I UNDERSTAND IT, the economics of public finance seeks to identify the gains and losses in the utilities of individuals resulting from government transactions. This is the purpose, not always achieved or achievable, of "incidence and effects" analysis. Since utilities are not comparable between individuals, the analysis usually tries to translate changes in utility into equivalent variations of income or consumption and to compare these. Even so, there is by no means any guarantee that the gains and losses to individuals due to a specific government action will sum to zero. There may be a net "dead-weight loss"; or alternatively the action may yield a net gain. For this reason, as well as others, *incidence* is not always well defined; individual "payments" for a government project may total more or less than what is paid for. That is why it is better to look for *effects*.

Other things equal, payment of taxes makes an individual worse off. But a specified government transaction—such as issue of debt followed by a subsequent levy of taxes to retire it—has other effects as well. Market prices, including interest rates and incomes, will generally be different both at the time of debt issue and at the time the taxes are levied. These effects, too, will make some individuals at both dates worse off, and perhaps others better off. Consequently the direct incidence of the taxes on the taxpaying generation is only the beginning of the story.

Buchanan recognizes this in saying that his "objective has been, and is, to clarify the primary effects before complicating the analysis with these secondary ones." By primary analysis he means simple Internal Revenue accounting: who paid taxes when. The secondary effects which he disclaims considering are the indirect repercussions through markets. It is analysis of these that supposedly distinguishes economists from accountants. I think, therefore, that Buchanan has really pleaded guilty to my complaint.

Buchanan's agreement that what he is saying is merely that debt finance postpones the levy of taxes, nothing more, is helpful in clarifying the questions under discussion. I guess I should not have tried to suggest a rationalization (the coercive nature of taxes) for this simplistic definition of burden. Buchanan wants no rationalization. But if tax payments are, in his view, no different from the payment of market prices, his readiness to ignore the market price repercussions of government borrowing and taxation is all the more surprising. If government borrowing raises interest rates and causes me either to pay more for or to forego the purchase of a new car, have not I, a member of the borrowing generation, shouldered some burden?

Finally, absolutely nothing in my review implies that "debt issue [is] the fiscal equivalent of the perpetual motion machine which will allow beneficial public programs to be financed without cost on anyone at any time" or that "we can secure public goods and services without paying taxes." I am as aware as Professor Buchanan that productive resources are scarce. He does not further the discussion by attributing irresponsible views to anyone who finds his concept of burden too simple to be very useful.

* Yale University.

Name Index

The International Library of Critical Writings in Economics

The Economics of Contracts
Lars A. Stole

The Economics of Leisure and
Recreation
Clem Tisdell

Empirical Foundations in Industrial Organization
Michael Waterson

Recent Developments in Evolutionary
Economics
Ulrich Witt